Frommer's®

Seville, Granada & the Best of Andalusia

4th Edition

by Jeremy Head

A John Wiley and Sons, Ltd, Publication

Published by:

WILEY PUBLISHING, INC.

Copyright © 2011 John Wiley & Sons Ltd, The Atrium, Southern Gate, Chichester,
West Sussex PO19 8SQ, UK

Telephone (+44) 1243 779777

Email (for orders and customer service enquiries): cs-books@wiley.co.uk. Visit our Home Page on www.
wiley.com

UK Publisher: Sally Smith
Project Manager: Daniel Mersey
Commissioning Editor: Mark Henshall
Development Editor: Mary Anne Evans
Project Editor: Hannah Clement
Cartography: Elizabeth Puhl
Photo Editor: Jill Emeny
Front cover photo: Seville oranges © CW Images/Alamy.
Back Cover photo: Join in the festivities of the Feria de Sevilla in April © Art Kowalsky/Alamy.

For information on our other products and services or to obtain technical support, please contact our
Customer Care Department within the U.S. at 877/762-2974, outside the U.S. at 317/572-3993 or fax
317/572-4002.

British Library Cataloguing in Publication Data
A catalogue record for this book is available from the British Library
ISBN 978-0-470-97431-5 (pbk)
ISBN 978-1-119-99173-1 (ebk)
ISBN 978-1-119-99445-9 (ebk)
ISBN 978-1-119-97206-8 (ebk)

Typeset by Wiley Indianapolis Composition Services
Printed and bound in the United States of America

5 4 3 2

CONTENTS

LIST OF MAPS

ABOUT THE AUTHOR

Jeremy Head is a travel writer, photographer and broadcaster based in Brighton, UK. Over the past decade or so, his travel writing and photographs have appeared in most of the UK's national newspapers and specialist travel magazines. On TV in the UK he has worked as an undercover reporter for ITV's "Holidays Undercover" and as an expert on Channel 5's "The Hotel Inspector." His obsession with Andalusia began with a weekend break to Seville in 2000 and he has been going back for more ever since. (Maybe it's the wine and sunshine?) As well as writing and completely updating this fourth edition of *Frommer's Seville, Granada & the Best of Andalusia,* he is also the author of *Frommer's Seville Day by Day.* You can find out what he's currently up to by reading his blog: www.travelblather.com.

If you've got comments about this guidebook—good or bad—feel free to email him. He'd be very interested to hear from you: seville@jeremyhead.com

ACKNOWLEDGMENTS

A guidebook is never really written by just one person. The advice, opinions and friendship of many wonderful people have helped make *Frommer's Seville, Granada & the Best of Andalusia* far better than anything I could have achieved alone. Thanks so much to you all.

(Seville) John Harrop, Christine Gesthuysen, David Garcia, David Cox, Luis Salas, Jeff Spielvogel, Eduardo Blanco, Markus Christmann, Francisco Naranjo, Saida Segura, Amanda Corbett, Antony Reid; (Cádiz) Sam Lister; (Granada) Gayle Mackie, Christian Most; (Tarifa) Martina de Rijke, Zoë Ouwehand-Reid; (Vejer de la Frontera) Lee and Amelia Gordon; (Ronda) Christina Piek; (Málaga) Antonio Romero; (Mijas) Alan Roberts; (Marbella) Irene Westerberg, Eva Lindblom, Paul Kockelkorn; (Gibraltar) Tracey Poggio, Gail Francis-Tiron; (elsewhere in Andalusia) Tim and Claire Murray-Walker, Anne Hunt, Anna Carin Nordin, Antonio Pérez Navarro, Pablo Ramón, Guy Hunter-Watts, the excellent staff at the city, provincial and regional tourist offices across the region. (UK) Leah Rosewell at Monarch Airlines, Lauren McNally, Ricardo Moraga Gámez, James Adutt, Paloma Navarro Lizana at the Spanish Tourist Office, Tamsin Hemingray and everyone at iCrossing UK, Mary Johns and the team at Frommer's UK: Scott Totman, Jill Emeny, Mark Henshall.

This book is dedicated to my wife Karen and to baby Joseph Stephen Head who arrived 5 weeks early when your dad was stuck in Málaga doing research for this book—no thanks to French Air Traffic Control, who decided to go on strike that day. I missed your arrival, but I promise I'll be there for the rest of the ride.

HOW TO CONTACT US

In researching this book, we discovered many wonderful places—hotels, restaurants, shops, and more. We're sure you'll find others. Please tell us about them, so we can share the information with your fellow travelers in upcoming editions. If you were disappointed with a recommendation, we'd love to know that, too. Please email frommers@wiley.com or write to:

Frommer's Seville, Granada & the Best of Andalusia, 4th Edition
Wiley Publishing, Inc. • 111 River St. • Hoboken, NJ 07030-5774

AN ADDITIONAL NOTE

Please be advised that travel information is subject to change at any time—and this is especially true of prices. We therefore suggest that you write or call ahead for confirmation when making your travel plans. The authors, editors, and publisher cannot be held responsible for the experiences of readers while traveling. Your safety is important to us, however, so we encourage you to stay alert and be aware of your surroundings. Keep a close eye on cameras, purses, and wallets, all favorite targets of thieves and pickpockets.

FROMMER'S STAR RATINGS, ICONS & ABBREVIATIONS

Every hotel, restaurant, and attraction listing in this guide has been ranked for quality, value, service, amenities, and special features using a **star-rating system.** In country, state, and regional guides, we also rate towns and regions to help you narrow down your choices and budget your time accordingly. Hotels and restaurants are rated on a scale of zero (recommended) to three stars (exceptional). Attractions, shopping, nightlife, towns, and regions are rated according to the following scale: zero stars (recommended), one star (highly recommended), two stars (very highly recommended), and three stars (must-see).

In addition to the star-rating system, we also use **seven feature icons** that point you to the great deals, in-the-know advice, and unique experiences that separate travelers from tourists. Throughout the book, look for:

special finds—those places only insiders know about

fun facts—details that make travelers more informed and their trips more fun

kids—best bets for kids and advice for the whole family

special moments—those experiences that memories are made of

overrated—places or experiences not worth your time or money

insider tips—great ways to save time and money

great values—where to get the best deals

The following abbreviations are used for credit cards:

AE	American Express	DISC	Discover	V	Visa
DC	Diners Club	MC	MasterCard		

TRAVEL RESOURCES AT FROMMERS.COM

Frommer's travel resources don't end with this guide. Frommer's website, **www.frommers.com**, has travel information on more than 4,000 destinations. We update features regularly, giving you access to the most current trip-planning information and the best airfare, lodging, and car-rental bargains. You can also listen to podcasts, connect with other Frommers.com members through our active-reader forums, share your travel photos, read blogs from guidebook editors and fellow travellers, and much more.

THE BEST OF SEVILLE, GRANADA & ANDALUSIA

This once-great stronghold of Muslim Spain is rich in scenery, history, and tradition, and contains some of the country's most celebrated architectural wonders: the world-famous Mezquita in Córdoba, the beautifully ornate Alhambra in Granada, and the great Gothic cathedral in Seville.

Andalusia's smaller towns include historic Ubeda and Baeza, gorge-split Ronda, Jerez de la Frontera, famous for its sherry, laid-back Tarifa and the port city of Cádiz. This dry mountainous region also encompasses the Costa del Sol (Málaga, Marbella, and Torremolinos), a coastal strip for those seeking beach resorts, nightlife, and relaxation.

THE most UNFORGETTABLE TRAVEL EXPERIENCES

- **Getting Lost in the Barrio de Santa Cruz:** In Seville, you can wander at leisure through this old Moorish ghetto of narrow streets. The brilliantly whitewashed little houses festooned with flowering plants and pretty Andalusian courtyards epitomize romantic Seville. Linger over a meal or spend an afternoon at one of the outdoor cafe tables tucked into a tiny, hidden square. Under the Moors, Jews flourished in this ghetto but were chased out by the Christians at the time of the Inquisition. The great artist Murillo also called this barrio (neighborhood) home. See Chapter 6.
- **Drinking Sherry at the Bodegas of Jerez:** Spain's most distinctive fortified wine—"sherry" in English, *jerez* in Spanish—uses this charming little Andalusian town of Jerez de la Frontera as its main production center. Touring the sherry wineries, or *bodegas*, is one of the

province's most evocative undertakings, but nothing is more memorable than an actual tasting. You'll quickly determine your favorite, ranging from *fino* (extra dry) to *dulce* (sweet). It's best to arrive in early September for the annual grape harvest. See Chapter 9.

o **Visiting the Great Alhambra:** People from all over the world flock to Granada to enjoy wandering the Alhambra, Andalusia's finest remaining fortress-palace constructed by the Muslim caliphs, who staged their last stand here against the Catholic monarchs. In 1832, Washington Irving, in his *Tales of the Alhambra,* put it on the tourist map after decades of neglect. Inside its walls is a once-royal city with fountained courtyards, fanciful halls, and miles of intricate plasterwork and precious mosaics, all paying testament to past Muslim glory. See Chapter 8.

o **Touring the Pueblos Blancos:** The delightful old White Villages (*Pueblos Blancos*) that dot the steep hillsides of central Andalusia offer some of the most scenic panoramas in the region. With their warrens of whitewash-housed streets and pretty squares, many feel frozen in time. Spend a few days driving around them; stopping at comfortable boutique hotels en route is the perfect way to experience the Andalusia of old. See Chapter 9.

o **Experiencing a Bullfight:** With origins as old as pagan Andalusia, bullfighting is a pure expression of Spanish temperament and passion. Detractors call the sport cruel, bloody, and savage. Aficionados, however, view bullfighting as a microcosm of death, catharsis, and rebirth. If you strive to understand the bullfight, it can be a powerful, memorable experience, but it's not for animal lovers. Head for the Plaza de Toros (bullring) in any major Andalusian city, but the most spectacular *corridas* (bullfights) are in Seville. See Chapter 6.

o **Feasting on Tapas:** Tapas are reason enough to go to Seville, where the creation of these small plates of food is almost an art form. Locals move from one bar to another, choosing a tapa or two in each. It's social, fun, and very Sevillian. Wash them down with an ice-cold beer or a glass of chilled sherry. Old favorites include cured ham, *gambas* (deep-fried shrimp), and spinach with chickpeas, but these days you'll also find more exotic bites like deep-fried zucchini (courgette) with honey, braised pig's cheek in red wine sauce, and chicken livers on toast with red berry reduction. See Chapter 6.

o **Getting Swept Up in the Passion of Flamenco:** Flamenco, which traces its Spanish roots to Andalusia, is best heard in the old Gypsy taverns of Granada's Albaicín neighborhood or the busy local bars and fragrant patios of Seville's Barrio de Triana and Barrio de Santa Cruz. From the poshest nightclub to the lowest taverna, flamenco's foot stomping, castanet rattling, hand clapping, and sultry Andalusian guitar strains can be heard nightly. Performed by a great *artista,* flamenco's dramatization of inner tension and conflict can tear your heart out with its soulful, passionate singing. See Chapters 6 and 8.

THE best LUXURY HOTELS

o **AC Palacio de Santa Paula** (Granada; ✆ **95-880-57-40;** www.ac-hotels.com): It's not quite as magnificent as the Alhambra, but this post-millennium architectural monument to grandeur harmoniously blends the contemporary and the antique. Many buildings, including a 15th-century medieval cloister and two

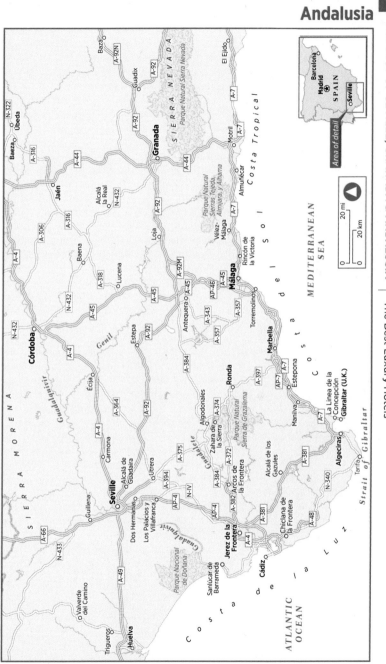

14th-century Arab houses, came together to create this deluxe hotel. Dining in the hotel's restaurant is also a delight. See p. 185.

o **Casa de la Siesta** (Vejer de la Frontera; ✆ 95-623-20-03 /69-961-94-30; www. casalasiesta.com): This tranquil luxury retreat, a 10-minute drive out of Vejer de la Frontera, is the ultimate getaway. There are just seven luxurious guest rooms with sweeping views across the countryside surrounded by fragrant gardens of lavender, citrus trees, and thyme and a spacious salt-water swimming pool. Dine by candlelight in the courtyard. See p. 261.

o **Duques de Medinaceli** (El Puerto de Santa María; ✆ 95-686-07-77; www.jale. com/dmedinaceli): The epitome of style and luxury, this tastefully converted 18th-century palace is one of the most attractive in Andalusia. In beautifully land-scaped gardens, it has the ambience of yesterday with all the modern conveniences of today. Local sherry producers cite this as one of their favorite addresses, for its rooms and its first-rate cuisine. See p. 273.

o **Hacienda de San Rafael** (Las Cabezas de San Juan, between Jerez and Seville; ✆ 95-422-71-16; www.haciendadesanrafael.com): This lovely old olive farm has 11 cloistered duplex rooms surrounding a brilliant white courtyard cascading with bright bougainvillea blooms. But the real find is the three delightful *casitas,* cozy little cottages set apart from the farmhouse amidst fragrant gardens and hidden plunge pools. It's the ultimate getaway retreat. See p. 93.

o **Hospes Palacio Del Bailío** (Córdoba; ✆ 95-749-89-93; www.hospes.es): This stunning palace hotel in the heart of Córdoba blends the historic with cutting-edge designer flourishes with surprisingly harmonious results. Stables, coach houses, lofts, granaries, original paintings, the remains of Roman baths, and a splendid Moorish garden were all incorporated into the new ensemble. The hotel's spa features a swim-through pool right next to the Roman remains. See p. 140.

o **Hotel Alfonso XIII** (Seville; ✆ 800/221-2340 or ✆ 95-491-70-00): This ornate and vast reproduction of a Spanish palace, a fixture in Seville since 1929, is a regal bastion of fine living. From its white marble courtyard to its Moroccan gardens, it is the grandest and most expensive of Andalusia's hotels. See p. 82.

o **Kempinski Hotel Bahía Estepona** (Estepona; ✆ 95-280-95-00; www.kempinski-spain.com): This is modern resort-hotel living at its most luxurious along the Costa del Sol. Not as well known as the Marbella Club, this is, nonetheless, a citadel of luxe living, with airy, spacious bedrooms, first-class service, and some of the best cuisine on the coast. See p. 337.

o **Marbella Club** (Marbella; ✆ 800/448-8355 or ✆ 95-282-22-11; www.marbella club.com): This upmarket, discreet, Costa del Sol resort put Marbella on the board many decades ago. Since 1954 the rich and/or famous have flocked to its plush precincts and they still do so today. Boasting the most lavish hotel gardens along the coast, the club is a hangout for movie stars, fading European aristocracy, and oil-rich sheiks. See p. 344.

o **Parador de Granada** (Granada; ✆ 95-822-14-40; www.parador.es): Within the grounds of the Alhambra itself, the most famous parador in Spain is naturally the most sought after and difficult to get into. With verdant gardens, splashing fountains, and Arab- and Mudéjar-inspired architecture, the parador was converted from a former convent founded by Isabella and Ferdinand. The Catholic monarchs were once buried in its grounds. See p. 188.

ANDALUSIA

- **Parador de Ronda** (Ronda; ✆ **95-287-75-00;** www.parador.es): On a high cliff overlooking the fantastic gorge of Ronda, this parador offers beautifully furnished bedrooms overlooking the torrents of the Guadalevín River. Dramatically perched in this mountain town, it exemplifies good taste and fine living. See p. 235.
- **Vincci Posada del Patio** (Málaga; ✆ **91-490-26-50;** www.vinccihoteles.com): This ultra luxurious hotel is housed in two beautifully renovated 16th-century town houses. Rooms are stylish and contemporary; the two-story suites are remarkable. See p. 374.

THE best MODERATELY PRICED HOTELS

- **Carabeo** (Nerja; ✆ **95-252-54-44;** www.hotelcarabeo.com): There is no more tranquil oasis in Nerja than this little inn—and it's very affordable as well. A boutique hotel of charm and sophistication, Carabeo is in the old sector of town in a typical Andalusian house, but within an easy walk of the center and a 5-minute walk to a good beach. See p. 383.
- **Dar Cilla** (Tarifa; ✆ **65-346-70-25;** www.darcilla.com): You're assured the warmest of welcomes at these atmospheric and friendly apartments ideally located in Tarifa's delightful Old Town. All the rooms are self-catering with simple kitchen facilities ideal for fixing your own breakfasts and cooking simple suppers. There's a delightful roof terrace where you can sip a glass of chilled wine while taking in the lovely views far out across the Strait of Gibraltar to Morocco. See p. 302.
- **Hotel Argantonio** (Cádiz; ✆ **95-621-16-40;** www.hotelargantonio.com): This charming boutique hotel right in the middle of the historic city center is in a restored old town house around a bright patio with a small marble fountain. See p. 291.
- **Hotel Doña María** (Seville; ✆ **95-422-49-90;** www.hdmaria.com): Ideally located just a moment from the cathedral and with one of the most attractive roof terraces in the whole city, the Doña María offers ornate antique-laden interiors and comfortable bedrooms. See p. 88.
- **La Casa del Califa** (Vejer de la Frontera; ✆ **95-644-77-30;** www.lacasadelcalifa. com): Five old town houses that fringe the delightful Plaza de España have been renovated to create this wonderfully atmospheric boutique hotel. The hotel's excellent restaurant is inspired by the flavors of North Africa and the perfect place to sample the cuisine is in the flower-filled patio-garden. See p. 260.
- **Molina Lario** (Málaga; ✆ **95-206-20-02;** www.hotelmolinolario.com): Housed in a six-story town house that has been cleverly renovated with a bright, glass-bedecked atrium at its core, this sophisticated hotel blends the historic and the cutting edge with real style. The trendy bar/restaurant hosts regular jazz sessions, wine tastings, and even poetry readings. See p. 375.
- **NH Amistad Córdoba** (Córdoba; ✆ **95-742-03-35;** www.nh-hoteles.com): This attractive and luxurious renovation of two existing 18th-century mansions is perfectly located for exploring the delightful alleys and squares of Córdoba's Judería barrio. See p. 145.

THE BEST OF SEVILLE, GRANADA & ANDALUSIA

The Best Moderately Priced Hotels

o **Puerta de la Luna** (Baeza; ✆ 95-374-70-19; www.hotelpuertadelaluna.es): In the oldest part of historic Baeza, this gem of a 17th-century palace has been restored with modern comforts but with its Andalusian architectural features intact. The hotel has its own outdoor pool and spa facilities, plus a delightful restaurant and bar serving first-rate cuisine. See p. 171.

o **Taberna del Alabardero** (Seville; ✆ 95-450-27-21): With the city's famous catering academy right next door, the Taberna is the place to stay in Seville for foodies. They've added seven guest rooms to this restored 19th-century mansion, all with antique furniture and whirlpool baths. See p. 90.

o **The Town House** (Marbella; ✆ 95-290-17-91; www.townhouse.nu): Deep in the heart of Marbella's atmospheric Old Town, this former private home has been tastefully converted into the town's most romantic boutique hotel, an oasis of relaxed tranquility. The lovely roof terrace is the perfect place for a sundowner cocktail. See p. 347.

THE best DINING EXPERIENCES

o **Abantal** (Seville; ✆ 95-454-00-00): Michelin-starred chef Julio Fernandez is a modest guy. He lets his immaculate cuisine in his modern, intimate restaurant speak for itself. For serious foodies, the seven-course taster menu paired with regional wines will be the highlight of your visit to Seville. See p. 94.

o **Bodegas Campos** (Córdoba; ✆ 95-749-75-00): Whilst not particularly elegant or grand, this restaurant is stacked with atmosphere and serves the best Spanish and Andalusian food in Córdoba. Going strong since 1908, Bodegas Campos uses market-fresh ingredients for traditional-style dishes with inventive flourishes. See p. 147.

o **Calima** (Marbella; ✆ 95-276-42-52): Marbella native Dani García is Andalusia's most exciting chef, with two Michelin stars to his name. As an example of his inventiveness, he injects liquid nitrogen into olives. When one explodes, he then serves the popcorn-like morsels with fresh lobster salad. See p. 349.

o **Egaña Oriza** (Seville; ✆ 95-422-72-11): In a restored mansion near the Murillo Gardens, Seville's most atmospheric restaurant serves a savory mix of Basque and international specialties. Many of the ingredients, notably the wild game, originate in Andalusia. See p. 95.

o **El Ventorillo del Chato** (Cádiz; ✆ 95-625-00-25): In the ancient port city of Cádiz, this Andalusian restaurant's origins date to 1780. But on the culinary front, it's outpaced the times, turning out a virtual celebration of time-tested regional dishes. For added flavor, flamenco shows are also presented. See p. 292.

o **La Meridiana** (Marbella; ✆ 95-277-61-90): Sophisticated and fashionable, this swanky restaurant in a romantic setting with a garden terrace pleases the most discerning palates of the Costa del Sol. With top-rate service, the chefs turn out the best Italian and international cuisine in Marbella and beyond. See p. 349.

o **Los Santanderinos** (Granada; ✆ 95-812-83-35): In the newer part of Granada, this wonderful dining choice serves a fine mixture of Spanish and Andalusian dishes within the city proper. Chef Jesús Diego Díaz is a media darling of the

Spanish gastronomic press; his tapas are among the tastiest in Granada. See p. 195.

o **Tragabuches** (Ronda; © **95-219-02-91**): It's where Spanish culinary genius Dani García earned his first Michelin star and this impeccably sharp and refined restaurant still turns out modern Spanish and Andalusian cuisine with sublime flavors and inventive, surprising twists. See p. 239.

THE best BEACHES

o **Playa de la Caleta,** Cádiz: Locals call this beach **Baño de la Vina,** after the barrio that abuts it. In the old part of town, the beach forms a half-moon of golden sands to the immediate east of Castillo de Santa Catalina. To the immediate west is another fortification, Castillo de San Sebastián, on an islet reached by causeway. See p. 289.

o **Playa de la Carihuela,** Torremolinos: Even if the beach is not among the world's greatest, you'll have a roaring good time on the beige sands of this wildly popular Costa del Sol resort. An expat population of Germans, Scandinavians, and Brits play volleyball, sun themselves in skimpy swimsuits, or indulge at the bevy of busy bars and restaurants that line the waterfront. See p. 360.

o **Playa Isla Canela,** Ayamonte: The small town of Ayamonte lies 37km (22 miles) east of the provincial capital of Huelva, where Columbus dared to dream "the impossible dream." One of the best beaches along the Costa de la Luz is **Playa Isla Canela,** with tranquil waters protected by huge sandbars 50 to 100m (164–328 ft) offshore. See p. 313.

o **Playa Naguelles and Playa La Fontanilla,** Marbella: Along the beachfront at the Costa del Sol's glossiest resort stretch the sands of these two beaches, both famous and fashionable since the 1960s. Marbella's other beaches closer to the Old Town, the **Playa de la Bajadilla** and the **Playa de Venus** are similarly cool. Both are located between the resort's twin harbors. See Chapter 11.

o **Playa Victoria,** Cádiz: Counted among the best beaches in Spain are the Champagne-colored sands in this historic old port city. The beach stretches for 2km (1¼ miles), making it one of the finest beachfronts in southern Spain. Although built up, the *playa* avoids being tacky. See p. 289.

o **Playa Zahara,** near Tarifa: The little city of Tarifa is the southernmost town in continental Europe. Its reliably windy beaches also make it the wind and kitesurfing capital of Europe. The fishing village of Zahara de los Atunes (p. 301) is home to some of the Costa de la Luz's most beautiful white sandy beaches, and **Playa Zahara** stretches for a total of 8km (5 miles). Nearby **Playa Bolonia** and **Playa de los Alemanes** are also unspoilt, with wonderfully clear water. See p. 301.

THE most CHARMING TOWNS

o **Arcos de la Frontera:** The term *frontera* (frontier) dates from when this town was the boundary between the Muslim territories and the encroaching Catholic lands. Hemmed in on three sides by the Guadalete River, Arcos is one of the most beautiful of the *Pueblos Blancos* (interior Andalusia's White Towns or Villages). See p. 249.

- **Grazalema:** Delightful Grazalema is perhaps the most idyllic of the White Towns. This charming village nestles under the craggy peak of San Cristóbal at 1,525m (5,003 ft). As you wander its sloping, narrow streets, you'll pass white house after white house with window boxes filled with summery flowers. See p. 254.

- **Jerez de la Frontera:** Andalusia's distinctive sherry wines are a prime attraction for any visitor and the town's historic old quarter is a pleasure to wander too. Tour and taste the fortified wine in one of the 100 wineries, or *bodegas*. Since Jerez is the center for the Real Escuela Andaluza del Arte Ecuestre, a rival to Vienna's renowned Spanish Riding School, the "dancing horses" are Jerez's other major attraction. See p. 262.

- **Mijas:** This Pueblo Blanco is the most popular day trip from the Costa del Sol. Though sometimes mobbed with daytrippers, Mijas still retains its original charm, with whitewashed houses perched panoramically on the side of a mountain. On clear days, views across the Mediterranean to the foreboding Rif Mountains of Morocco are stunning. See p. 241.

- **Nerja:** East of Málaga at the mouth of the Río Chillar, this town of whitewashed buildings opens onto the "Balcony of Europe," a marble-paved projection above a headland jutting into the sea. The town, with sandy beaches and fishing boats bobbing at anchor, is the perfect antidote to crowded Torremolinos and Marbella. See p. 381.

- **Tarifa:** The windswept, unspoilt beaches close to little Tarifa have put it on the map for the funky kids of the windsurfing community. As a result, the narrow cobblestone streets of its historic Old Town are abuzz with people spilling out of little bars and cafes all summer long. See p. 297.

- **Ubeda:** The gem of Jaén province, Ubeda contains palaces, churches, mansions, and Plaza Vázquez de Molina, the most architecturally harmonious square in Andalusia. Its Moorish legacy lives on in its *esparto* (grass) weaving and pottery making, but the town mainly evokes 16th-century Spain and the Renaissance. Ubeda is dramatically built over an escarpment overlooking the valley. Nearby **Baeza** is similarly delightful. See p. 172.

THE best ARCHITECTURE

- **Giralda Tower and Cathedral,** Seville: Seville's cathedral is the largest Gothic structure on the planet. "Let us build a cathedral so immense that everyone on beholding it will take us for madmen," the chaplain said when workers were tearing down an ancient mosque to erect this splendid edifice. This cathedral is one of the last to be built in the Gothic style, but it also shows obvious Renaissance motifs. The builders didn't destroy all traces of the mosque, retaining its tower and creating an ornate belfry. Known as the **Giralda,** the cathedral's tower is as much a landmark for Seville as the Eiffel Tower is for Paris. See p. 108.

- **Alcázar,** Seville: Constructed by Pedro the Cruel, this splendid 14th-century Mudéjar palace is the oldest European royal residence still in use. Residents Ferdinand and Isabella, who received Columbus here, greatly influenced its architecture. Remains of the original Alcázar of the Almohads coexist with centuries of ornate pavilions, fountains, pools, patios, and ornamental gardens. Moorish influences join forces with Gothic, Renaissance, and Baroque elements, yet it all melds with harmonious charm. See p. 152.

- **Plaza de España,** Seville: When Seville was chosen to host the great 1929 Spanish-American Exhibition, the Plaza de España was created as the boldest of statements. Designed by Aníbal González, Seville's foremost 20th-century architect, it's a feast of neo-Mudéjar style with curves and towers in a huge crescent shape. The plaza was used as a backdrop to one of the *Star Wars* movies. See p. 113.
- **Alcázar de los Reyes Cristianos,** Córdoba: One of Spain's greatest examples of military architecture was commissioned in 1328 by Alfonso XI. Ferdinand and Isabella lived at this fortress on the Guadalquivir River while they made plans to send their armies to conquer Granada. A vast architectural complex of landscaping, fountains, and pools, the gardens are a tribute to their Moorish origins. See p. 152.
- **Mezquita-Catedral de Córdoba,** Córdoba: This 1,200-year-old masterwork by a succession of caliphs is one of the architectural wonders of Europe. Its interior is a virtual forest of pillars, red-and-white candy-striped Moorish arches, and rows of columns stretching in every direction. In the midst of it all is a florid cathedral in a Gothic and Renaissance architectural motif. See p. 153.
- **Puente Nuevo and El Tajo,** Ronda: The town of Ronda was precariously erected on a rocky geological platform either side of El Tajo, a 100m (328-ft) ravine. The Puente Nuevo bridge, constructed between 1755 and 1793, is a truly spectacular site, a trio of soaring arches on top of a smaller arch, towering 120m (390 ft) above the canyon floor. See p. 233.
- **The Alhambra,** Granada: Set against the snowcapped peaks of the Sierra Nevada, the Alhambra is one of the most fabled landmarks in the world and the single-most visited attraction in all Andalusia. It was the last bastion of luxury living for the Nasrid kings, the last Muslim rulers of Spain, and their harems. The palace-fortress is girded by more than 1.6km (1 mile) of ramparts, enclosing a virtual royal city comprised of three palaces, with courtyards, fountains, fanciful halls, and scalloped windows framing sweeping vistas. See p. 209.

THE best GIFTS & SOUVENIRS

- **Antiques:** Antiques and accessories are a real souvenir-hunter's dream in Andalusia, particularly Seville. A wide range of dealers operate throughout the province, often in some of the smaller villages. Some of the most popular "antiques" are old posters advertising the famous Andalusian fairs or *corridas* (bullfights). See Chapter 6.
- **Ceramics & Tiles:** Throughout the province, stores sell highly distinctive ceramics (many towns have their own style) as well as *azulejos* (hand-painted tiles). Some wall plates are enameled and trimmed in 24-karat gold. Ubeda is a particularly good place for hand-crafted pots and jugs. See Chapter 7.
- **Clothing:** Flamenco and *feria* (fair or festival)-influenced clothing, fills the stores of Granada and Seville in particular. Surprisingly, Seville's boutiques have become centers of high fashion for the 21st century, often tailoring flamboyant creations based on this flamenco heritage. See Chapters 6 and 8.
- **Guitars:** In the land of flamenco, guitars are highly prized by visitors. Artisans in Granada and Seville turn out top-quality, custom-made guitars. Of course, you

can purchase ready-made guitars a lot more cheaply. Along Calle Cuesta de Gomérez in Granada, a narrow and sloping street uphill from the Alhambra, artisans turn out some of the world's finest instruments, many of which end up in the hands of famous musicians. See Chapter 8.

o **Leather Goods:** For centuries, leather products have been associated with Andalusia. Córdoba, in particular, is famed for its embossed leather products, including cigarette boxes, jewel cases, attaché cases, book and folio covers, ottoman covers, and the like. See Chapter 7.

o **Marquetry:** Granada has been famous for its marquetry since the Muslim era. Artisans still make furniture and other items inlaid with ivory and colored woods in the Moorish design. Inlaid boxes are a particularly good item to take home as gifts and souvenirs. See Chapter 8.

THE best OF ANDALUSIA ONLINE

o **Websites about Spain:** Start with the excellent Tourist Office of Spain website: www.spain.info. Also see: All About Spain (www.red2000.com), and CyberSp@in (www.cyberspain.com).

o **Websites about Andalusia:** The content on www.andalucia.com is consistently good and regularly updated.

o **Websites about Seville:** The Seville City Tourist Office website is very good: www.turismosevilla.org. Local accommodation agency, Sevilla5 (www.sevilla5.com) has lots of handy information about visiting the city and accommodation. Jeff Spielvogel, an American living in Seville runs the excellent www.exploreseville.com which is also full of useful information. Run by a Canadian living in Seville, http://azahar-sevilla.com/blog/ is an interesting blog about life in the city and in particular its many great tapas bars.

o **Websites about Málaga:** Málaga City Tourist Office is the best website about Málaga: www.malagaturismo.com. Others include Málaga Travel Guide (www.aboutmalaga.com), Costa del Sol Tourist Board (www.visitcostadelsol.com), and La Costa del Sol (www.costadelsol.net).

o **Websites about Granada:** Granada City Tourist Office: www.granadatur.com is the place to start. Local accommodation agency Granada Info's website is really excellent, with detailed information about visiting the city and region as well as lots of accommodation options: www.granadainfo.com. You can also vist the Granada Travel Guide: www.aboutgranada.com.

o **For English-Language News:** The excellent *Olive Press* has interesting and regularly updated news stories and cultural features specifically for people living in the region. The Spanish regional newspaper *Sur* also has a good English-language website: www.surinenglish.com.

o **For Flamenco Tickets:** A handy resource for booking flamenco tickets online, before you travel to Andalusia, www.flamencotickets.com is run by American Jeff Spielvogel who lives in Seville and knows the region and its flamenco very well.

SOUTHERN SPAIN IN DEPTH

The sea brought the cultures of the East to Andalusia long before civilization had come to other parts of Spain. Empires from the East came and went, none more notable than the Moors, who arrived from North Africa, only 14km (9 miles) to the south.

In a strange reversal of fortune in the centuries to come, after having faced so many conquerors from the East, Spain itself was an eastern empire when it set out to forge a western empire with the "discovery" of the Americas.

SOUTHERN SPAIN TODAY

Home to bullfights and flamenco, Andalusia is sunny, romantic Spain at its best. For some northern Europeans, especially Brits, it's the retirement dream. Its beaches, especially along the Costa de la Luz and the overcrowded Costa del Sol, lure millions of visitors.

Many elderly citizens are still proud that they were some of the last holdouts against the advancing troops of General Franco during the Civil War. Although they are most definitely Spanish, many people of the region still consider themselves "Andalusian," implying a multicultural society, with traces of Roman, Moorish, and Gypsy civilizations.

Once the capital of a Moorish empire, Seville today remains the center of life in Andalusia, and the guardian of its culture.

The region possesses natural wealth, but unemployment remains stubbornly high at around the 20% mark and the European Union rates farm laborers here among the poorest on the Continent. Many Andalusian farmers have chosen to migrate to more industrialized areas such as Madrid, Barcelona, and Bilbao; those who have stayed behind labor at winemaking, olive oil extracting, flour milling, and horse and cattle breeding.

Today, tourism has become the fastest growing segment of the economy. Income from tourism and large influxes of development cash from the European Union have helped to increase standards of living to levels people living here in the 1970s could only have dreamed of.

LOOKING BACK AT SOUTHERN SPAIN

In the Beginning

The Bronze Age Kingdom of Tartessus was founded sometime in the 1st millennium B.C. Establishing itself at the mouth of the Guadalquivir River, bordering Seville and Huelva provinces, Tartessos (its Greek name) flourished for centuries. But siding and trading with the Greeks encouraged the wrath of Carthage. The African kingdom sent fleets across the Mediterranean to destroy the centuries-old Tartessus civilization. Andalusian archaeological museums, particularly those in Seville, display artifacts from Tartessus.

Bloody battles with the Carthaginian forces of Hannibal and his generals ended in the Roman conquest. Rome sent General Publius Cornelius Scipio to Spain in 209 B.C., where he seized Carthaginian bases and either killed the opposition or forced it back to Africa.

After internal fighting, particularly between the forces of Julius Caesar and Pompey, Rome occupied southern Spain, a domination that lasted some 7 centuries. Julius Caesar himself governed Andalusia from 61 B.C. to 60 B.C. The major Roman base was at **Itálica,** the ruins of which you can see outside Seville (p. 135).

Under the Romans, the colony of Andalusia became one of the richest in the Roman Empire. A Golden Age was proclaimed and the economy relied on products like wine, grain, olive oil, and a strong-smelling fish sauce called *garum.*

The Coming of the Barbarians

In time, Rome's control over Andalusia began to decline. Sweeping across the Pyrenees in the 4th century B.C. came the first of the barbarian invasions from the north of Europe. They were not an immediate menace to the south, but by A.D. 409 the Vandals had made inroads. Their rule over Andalusia was weak, their reign marked by much infighting and forced conversions to Christianity, especially among the downtrodden Jews.

Eleven Visigoth kings between 414 and 711 were assassinated. When the invading African Muslims arrived in southern Spain, the Visigothic monarchy was totally unprepared.

With extraordinary speed, Tariq ibn-Ziyad, the governor of Tangier, a far-western outpost of the Caliphate of Damascus, crossed the Straits of Gibraltar in A.D. 711 with only 7,000 Berber warriors. The Moorish conquest of Andalusia had begun in earnest and Tariq ibn-Ziyad established himself at Gibraltar.

The last of the Visigothic kings, Roderick, pulled together an army to confront these African invaders. He disappeared and his fate was lost to history, his armies either killed or fled.

In three decades, Muslim rulers established control of what they called **al-Andalus.** The capital of Islamic Spain became Córdoba, which was to be the leading center of learning and culture in the west.

The Legacy of Al-Andalus

The Moors (Muslims who were an ethnic mixture of Berbers, Hispano-Romans, and Arabs) occupied southern Spain for nearly eight centuries, leaving behind an intellectual and cultural legacy that influences modern life to this day. This was a time of soaring achievement in philosophy, medicine, and music.

Moorish rule brought the importation of the eggplant and the almond, as well as the Arabian steed. It heralded astronomy, a new and different view of Aristotle, Arabic numerals, and algebra. Ibn Muadh of Jaén wrote the first European treatise on trigonometry.

Intellectual giants like the Córdoba-born Jewish philosopher Maimonides emerged. It is said that Columbus evolved his theories about a new route to the East after hours and hours of studying the charts of Idrisi, an Arabian geographer who first sketched a world map in 1154. Arabs relied upon the compass as a navigational aid long before its use among Portuguese explorers.

Córdoba wished to shine more brightly than Baghdad as a center of science and the arts. In time it attracted Abd ar-Rahman II, who introduced the fifth string to the Arab lute, leading to the development of the six-string guitar. He also ordained the way food should be eaten at mealtimes, with courses being served in a regimented order, ending with dessert, fruit, and nuts.

Flamenco claims significant Middle Eastern influences, and Arab poetry may have inspired the first ballads sung by European troubadours; this, in turn, had an enormous impact on later Western literature. Many Spanish words have their origins in the Arabic language, including *alcázar* (fortress), *arroz* (rice), *naranja* (orange), and *limón* (lemon).

The Moors brought an irrigation system to Andalusia, which increased crop production; many of today's systems follow those 1,000-year-old channels. And paper first arrived in Europe through Córdoba.

However, the Moors were not to rule forever. In the 10th century, Abd ar-Rahman III, the Muslim king, proclaimed himself ruler of an independent Western Islamic Empire, breaking with the eastern Caliphate of Baghdad. (Visitors can explore his ruined pleasure palace, **Madinat Al-Zahra,** outside Córdoba, p. 157.) In time, the Muslims began to war among themselves as the Romans had before them. A new invasion arrived from Africa in 1086, the fanatically Islamic **Almoravids,** followed in 1147 by the **Almohads;** the latter left as their legacy the Giralda at Seville.

By 1212, the Reconquista (the Spanish Catholic monarchs' campaign to wrest southern Spain from the Moors) had begun. In that year Alfonso VIII defeated the Muslim armies at the battle of Las Navas de Tolosa in Jaén, a turning point in Spanish history. It was the beginning of the end of al-Andalus, but many more decades would pass before the complete Reconquest had been carried out.

The Reconquista

By 1236 Córdoba had been conquered by King Ferdinand III. But the sultans must have believed they would never lose Andalusia; two years later construction began on the monumental Alhambra in Granada. In all, it would take a final 156 years before the conquest was complete.

In the 13th century, Christian soldiers began to destroy Moorish fortresses and take over their cities. James the Conqueror of Aragón and Fernando III of Castile attacked Baeza and Ubeda in 1233, Córdoba in 1236, Jaén in 1245, and, finally, Seville in 1248.

As the 13th century came to a close, only the Nasrid Kingdom of Granada remained under Muslim rule. One of the reasons the kingdom was to survive for so long was that it made payments to the monarchs of Castile.

Granada's fate was sealed with the marriage of Los Reyes Católicos (the Catholic monarchs), Isabella I of Castile and Ferdinand V of Aragón. Uniting the kingdoms of Aragón and Castile in 1469, they also fired up religious bigotry and in the following year ushered in the dreaded Spanish Inquisition. By 1492 some 400,000 Jews had been forced to flee the country.

The previous year they had set out to reclaim Granada. Boabdil, the last of the Caliphs of Granada, watched in sorrow as his armies fell to 50,000 Christian foot soldiers and cavalrymen.

In the year of the completion of the Reconquista, 1492, a Genoese sailor, Christopher Columbus, sailed from Huelva. Instead of finding the riches of the East as he had hoped, he discovered the West Indies. He laid the foundations for a far-flung empire that brought wealth and power to Spain during the 16th and 17th centuries. Many of those riches from the New World were funneled through Andalusian cities like Cádiz and Seville.

The Habsburgs & the Bourbons

The province as a whole did not benefit from the exploitation of the New World. The crown in Castile grabbed the treasures to fuel foreign wars and other horrors. Except for such ports as Cádiz and Seville, most of Andalusia languished. The people were mired in poverty, and many emigrated to the New World.

Unlike Andalusia, Spain itself had entered its Golden Age, with an empire that extended eventually to the Philippines. But the country squandered much of its resources in religious and secular conflicts. At a great loss to Andalusia, the Jews, then the Muslims, and finally the Catholicized Moors were driven out—and with them much of the country's prosperity.

When a Habsburg, Carlos I (who, five years later, ruled the Holy Roman Empire as Charles V) came to the throne in 1516, little attention was paid to Andalusia. He was more interested in propping up his empire with gold and silver from the New World than in the needs of the people on his southern tier.

When Philip II ascended to the throne in 1556, Spain was at the epicenter of a great empire, not only the New World colonies but the Netherlands, Sicily, and Naples, and even parts of Austria and Germany. But the seeds of destruction had already been planted.

A fanatical Catholic, Philip became the standard-bearer for the Counter-Reformation. He also zealously renewed the Inquisition. He wanted a "final solution" (sound familiar?) to the problems of the Moriscos (Moors) in Las Alpujarras (p. 226), who still clung to their Moorish traditions. He forcibly deported them to other parts of the country. He was followed by Felipe III, who was even harsher in his persecution of the Moriscos of Andalusia.

In April 1587 the forces of Sir Francis Drake attacked the port of Cádiz, which was filled with some 60 vessels. Within 24 hours, the British forces had destroyed or captured almost half of these ships. A year later, Spain launched an Armada against England. The Armada was commanded by Andalusia's premier nobleman, the Duke of Medina Sidonia. The Spaniards were ignominiously defeated. It was a loss that symbolized the decline of Spanish power.

In 1700 Felipe V became king, bringing with him the War of Spanish Succession. His right to the throne was challenged by the Habsburg archduke, Charles of Austria, who was assisted by the British. When the Treaty of Utrecht ended the war in 1713, Spain lost most of its colonies. The British had landed in Gibraltar, conquering it and holding it to this day like a thorn in Spain's side.

At the Battle of Trafalgar off the coast of Cádiz in 1805, the Spanish fleet was defeated by the British. And things went from bad to worse as Spain was then attacked from the north by Napoleon's rampaging French armies. It was only a matter of time before the French took Madrid. King Carlos IV was forced to abdicate in 1808, and Napoleon put his brother, Joseph, on the throne. Most of the artistic heritage of Andalusia was ransacked during this period of French domination. The War of Independence (also called the Peninsular War) saw the arrival of the troops of the Duke of Wellington to the shores of Andalusia. Joseph fled back to France. On another front, the American colonies had begun to assert their independence.

The rest of the century brought little relief to either Spain or Andalusia. The country was at war with itself, as a right-wing monarchy clashed with the aspirations of liberal reformers.

In 1812, the Cortés (Spanish parliament) met in Cádiz and daringly drafted a liberal constitution. It was this constitution that introduced the word "liberal" to describe a political movement. However, when the despotic Fernando VII returned to the throne, he abolished their constitution.

The loss of Spain's colonies was a deathblow to Andalusia's economy, and in the 1870s a phylloxera plague wiped out its vineyards. Despite all these woes, this period in Andalusian history became known as the Romantic Age, as depicted in such operas as *The Barber of Seville* and *Carmen*.

The 19th Century to the Present

In 1876, Spain became a constitutional monarchy. But labor unrest, disputes with the Catholic Church, and war in Morocco combined to create political chaos. Conditions eventually became so bad that the Cortés was dissolved in 1923, and General Miguel Primo de Rivera formed a military directorate. Early in 1930, he resigned, but unrest continued.

On April 14, 1931, a revolution occurred, a republic was proclaimed, and King Alfonso XIII and his family were forced to flee. Initially, the liberal constitutionalists ruled, but they were soon pushed aside by the socialists and anarchists, who adopted a constitution separating church and state, secularizing education, and containing several other radical provisions (for example, agrarian reform and the expulsion of the Jesuits).

The extreme nature of these reforms fostered the growth of the conservative Falange party (*Falange española,* or Spanish Phalanx), modeled after Italy's and Germany's fascist parties. By the 1936 elections, the country was divided equally between left and right, and political violence was common. On July 18, 1936, the army, supported by Mussolini and Hitler, tried to seize power, igniting the Spanish Civil War. General Francisco Franco, coming from Morocco to Spain via Andalusia, led the Nationalist (conservative) forces in three years of fighting that ravaged the country. Towns were bombed and atrocities were committed in abundance. Early in 1939, Franco entered Barcelona and went on to Madrid; thousands of republicans were executed. Franco became chief of state, remaining so until his death in 1975.

Although Franco adopted a neutral position during World War II, his sympathies obviously lay with Germany and Italy. Spain, as a nonbelligerent, assisted the Axis powers, intensifying the diplomatic isolation the country was forced into after the war's end and Spain was excluded from the United Nations until 1955.

Before his death, General Franco selected as his successor Juan Carlos de Borbón y Borbón, son of the pretender to the Spanish throne. After the 1977 elections, a new constitution was approved by the electorate and the king; it guaranteed human and civil rights, free enterprise, and canceled the status of the Roman Catholic Church as the church of Spain. In 1980 Andalusia voted to become an autonomous region of Spain. With a regional government based in Seville, Andalusia assumed control of its destiny for the first time in its history.

In 1981, a group of right-wing military officers seized the Cortés and called upon Juan Carlos to establish a Francoist state. When the king refused and the conspirators were arrested, the fledgling democracy had overcome its first trial. Its second major accomplishment—under the Socialist rule of Prime Minister Felipe González, the country's first liberal government since 1939—was to secure Spain's entry into the European Union in 1986. Spain, and by extension Andalusia, was finally part of the modern world.

Andalusia is immersed in the modern world of vast social change, something unthinkable in the Franco era. In 2006, in one of the most highly publicized weddings in the world, two Spanish air force privates said, "I do" in Seville. In front of family and friends—and the world press—Alberto Linero, 27, and Alberto Sánchez, 24, were married. Same-sex marriages became legal in 2006 in Spain.

Since Spain's entry into the E.U., Andalusia has benefited tremendously from huge influxes of E.U. funds, subsidizing agriculture and the creation of an excellent network of highways which helped contribute to a period of sustained development. The tourism and construction industries were at the forefront of the boom, but this made Andalusia very vulnerable. When the recent world financial crisis hit, Andalusia came off very badly. As tourist numbers have dropped and wealthy northern Europeans have stopped buying property, unemployment has reached record levels of 24%. In some parts of the region, once luxurious resort complexes now lie locked and empty.

SOUTHERN SPAIN'S ART & ARCHITECTURE

Art

In Andalusia the dawn of art actually began 25,000 years ago when prehistoric man decorated caves in the province, painting in charcoal, blood red, and a goldlike ocher. For a look at this prehistoric art, visit **Cueva de la Pileta** near Ronda (p. 241) or **Cueva de Nerja** in Nerja (p. 382).

Andalusia's many museums and churches overflow with treasures dating from Spain's Renaissance and Golden Age of art, a period when Seville stood at the center of an explosion of painting and sculpture.

On October 25, 1881, in the port city of Málaga along Andalusia's southern coast, **Pablo Picasso** was born, becoming the greatest master of 20th-century art.

ROMANESQUE (10TH-13TH C.)

When the Moors subdued Andalusia back in the 8th century, they came to dominate art in the province. As the Koran forbade them to create graven images (human figures, for example), they turned instead to decorative arts. Geometric designs and exaggerated Kufic inscriptions appeared on painted tiles—called *azulejos*—in stucco plasterwork and woodcarvings. Rich and varied artifacts from the Muslim era include wood strap work in geometric designs, weapons, small ivory chests, and brocades.

GOTHIC (13TH-16TH C.)

The schools of Catalonia (Barcelona) and France were the stars of this era in painting. Artists often worked on polyptychs and altarpieces, some reaching a height of 15m (50 ft). Although influenced by the Italian, French, and Flemish schools, Gothic painting in Spain was distinctive in its interpretation. Colors such as deep red and lustrous golds were varied and vivid. Breaking from Romanesque, compositions became more complex. A sense of movement entered painting, as opposed to the more rigid forms of Romanesque art.

The most notable of the Andalusian artists of this period was **Bartolomé Bermejo** (ca. 1440–ca. 1495), who was heavily influenced by van Eyck. The first Spanish painter to use oils, he became the leader of the Italianate Valencian school. He wasn't influenced by the art of his native province at the time—nothing in the art in that period can explain the origin of Bermejo's style or his artistic technique. His paintings are characterized by a profound gravity, evoking Flanders where he once studied. His best work is in Madrid's El Prado.

Pedro Berruguete (1450–1504) straddled the line between Gothic and the Renaissance during a transitional period. Berruguete became the forerunner of the 17th-century Spanish portraitists. At the **Museo Provincial** in Jaén (p. 109), you can see his paintings such as *Christ at the Column.*

THE RENAISSANCE & BAROQUE (16TH-17TH C.)

By the 16th century, the Siglo de Oro (Golden Age) of art finally arrived in Spain. The Renaissance was a long time in coming. When it eventually began to replace Gothic works, the style, which had originated in Florence, had already mutated into the Baroque in Spain. Some of the world's greatest artists emerged from Andalusia during this period. Seville saw the rise of three great artists—Diego Velázquez, El Greco, and Francisco Goya—still hailed as among the greatest who ever lived.

In the Golden Age, **naturalism** came into bloom. A technique called *chiaroscuro,* evocative of that used by Italy's Caravaggio, contrasted light and shadow. Stern realism was often depicted. Portraiture and still life (*bodegón*) flourished.

The late Renaissance and Baroque paintings became more theatrical, colorful, and decorative. Patrons, often with money they'd made from the New World, demanded paintings that were dynamic with realistic figures. No longer was the church, and its draconian dictates, the main patron of art. Rich merchants demanded their own likenesses be captured on canvas, and also flattering images of their families, regardless of what they actually looked like.

The most important painter to emerge from this era was **Diego Velázquez** (1599–1660), the leading artist in the court of King Philip IV. Born in Seville, Velázquez achieved his greatest fame long after his death. In time, his works, such as *Las Meninas,* painted in 1656, would influence Picasso himself and even Salvador Dalí. See examples of his work at the **Hospital de los Venerables** in Seville (p. 117).

While still young, **Francisco Zurbarán** (1598–1662) was sent to study art at the School of Juan de Roelas in Seville. He became the Spanish equivalent of Michelangelo da Caravaggio. He excelled in a forcible, realistic style and painted directly from nature. Most of his paintings focused on ascetic, religious motifs. His color is often bluish to excess. The light seems to come from within the subject of his paintings rather than from an external source. The **Museo Provincial de Bellas Artes de Sevilla** (p. 109) contains several of his works.

Painting tender, intimate, even mystical scenes, **Bartolomé Esteban Murillo** (1617–82), was a leading rival of Zurbarán. The darling of Counter-Reformation art collectors, he is showcased at the **Museo Provincial de Bellas Artes** in Seville (p. 109), and, of course, at El Prado in Madrid. At the age of 26, Murillo went to Madrid, where he studied under Velázquez, but he returned to Seville in 1645. He excelled in the painting of flowers, water, light clouds, drapery, and in the use of color such as in his 1670 work, *The Little Fruit Seller.* Some critics dismiss Murillo as "tenderly sentimental—even saccharine."

The greatest Spanish sculptor of the 17th century, **Juan Martínez Montañés** (1568–1649), was hailed as *el dios de la madera* (the god of wood). For most of his life, he worked in Seville, where the cathedral holds his masterpiece, *Christ of Clemency* (1603–06). In this polychromed wooden statue, he brought a new naturalism to church carving, tempering his "Baroque emotionalism" with a classical sense of dignity. His polychrome wooden sculptures appealed to the Andalusian sense of drama and pathos. Martínez Montañés spread his carving style through a workshop he founded, teaching Cano (see below) among others. Oddly enough, Martínez Montañés is remembered today not for his own work but for a famous painting that Velázquez did of him, now in Madrid's El Prado.

Architect, painter, and sculptor **Alonso Cano** (1601–67) was often called the Spanish Michelangelo because of the diversity of his talents. In spite of his violent temper (he is rumored to have murdered his wife), his paintings for the most part are serene, even sweet. He was commissioned by Philip IV to restore paintings in his royal collection in Madrid. Here, Cano came under the influence of Venetian masters of the 16th century and used many of their techniques in his later works. He is celebrated for designing the facade of the cathedral in Granada (p. 211), one of the grandest and boldest statements in Spanish Baroque architecture. Today the cathedral owns several of Cano's paintings and sculptures, including a polychrome wooden statue of the *Immaculate Conception* from 1655 that is hailed as his masterpiece.

Another painter born in Seville was **Juan de Valdés Leal** (1622–90), who also worked in Córdoba. Along with Murillo, he founded an academy of painting in Seville in 1660. When Murillo died in 1682, Valdés Leal became the leading painter of Seville. Valdés Leal was mostly a religious painter, although he took a radically different approach from Murillo, specializing in the macabre, even the grotesque. With his vivid colors, dramatic light effects, and powerful realism, he sought to challenge "earthly vanities." There are two excellent examples in the chapel in the **Hospital de La Santa Caridad** in Seville (p. 108).

BOURBON ROCOCO & NEOCLASSICAL (18TH–19TH C.)

With the coming of Bourbon rule to Spain, the monarchs set out to attract some of Europe's greatest painters to their court in Madrid. Painting came under the dictates of the Academy of San Fernando, founded in 1752. **Francisco Goya** (1746–1828) dominated this lusty period in Spanish art, but Andalusia had its own homegrown stars.

The singular **Julio Romero de Torres** was born in Córdoba in 1874. The son of a painter, Rafael Romero de Torres, Julio studied art from the age of 10. In time he became famous for his paintings of Andalusian beauties, which were regarded as provocative at the time. His most celebrated work, on display at the **Museo de Julio Romero de Torres** at Córdoba (p. 156) is *Naranjas y Limones* (*Oranges and Lemons*). The dark-haired beauty in the portrait is bare breasted and holding oranges.

20TH CENTURY

After a period of "romantic decline" in the latter 19th century, Spain rose again in the art world at the turn of the 20th century, as Spanish artists helped develop Cubism and Surrealism. A host of Spanish artists—not only Picasso—rose to excite the world. These included the great Surrealist **Joan Miró** (1893–1983); **Juan Gris** (1887–1927), the purest of the cubists; and the outrageous **Salvador Dalí** (1904–89).

Pablo Picasso (1881–1973), of course, is one of the 20th century's greatest modern artists and the most famous founder of Cubism (along with Georges Braque). His body of work changed radically over the years, most famously during his Blue Period when he depicted harlequins, beggars, artists, and prostitutes among others. Although he experienced financial difficulties early in his life, his paintings now sell for millions. *Dora Maar au Chat* (*Dora Maar with Cat*) fetched $95.2 million in 2006. Modern art lovers flock to Málaga, the town of his birth, to see the **Picasso Museum** (p. 372).

After producing some of Spain's greatest artists during the Golden Age, Andalusia became an artistic backwater for most of the 1900s. Nonetheless, **Rafael Zabaleta** (1907–60) rose from obscurity to fame for his bucolic depictions of rural life. Born in Jaén province to a family of rich landowners, he made his Andalusian village of Quesada the subject of most of his work, which is still popular in the art market today.

Architecture

Long before the Muslims crossed the Straits of Gibraltar in 711, Romans controlled Andalusia. Regrettably, not a lot remains of their architecture or monuments. An exception is **Itálica,** the "noble ruins" of a Roman city founded at the end of the 3rd century B.C. by the Roman general, Scipio Africanus. The site is 9km (5½ miles) northwest of Seville near the town of Santiponce.

Itálica (p. 135) was the birthplace of two of the most famous Roman emperors, Hadrian and Trajan. Still impressive, the major achievement here was a colossal amphitheater that held 25,000 spectators screaming for blood. At one time this amphitheater was one of the largest in the Roman Empire. You can still see classic Roman architecture in the foundations of the Hadrianic baths and a well-preserved Roman theater. At the peak of its glory, Itálica was the third largest city in the world, surpassed only by Rome and Alexandria. Over the centuries, seemingly everyone in the area, including the invading Duke of Wellington during the Peninsular Wars, went digging at Itálica for Roman treasures, including statues, rare marbles, and sculpture.

MOORISH ARCHITECTURE (8TH–15TH C.)

After the departure of the Romans and Visigoths, the Muslims subdued Andalusia and began to influence the landscape with their Islamic architecture, including aqueducts, baths, *alcázares* (palaces), and *alcazabas* (fortresses).

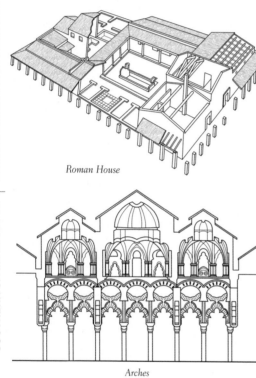

Roman House

Arches

Although there was an earlier "pre-Caliphal period" (notably A.D. 710–929), the true glory of Moorish architecture came under the Cordovan Caliphate (929–1031). Begun in 785, the **Great Mosque of Córdoba** (p. 153) was lavishly and dramatically extended with horseshoe arches and ornate decoration. The most distinguishing feature of the architecture, the **arch,** reached its apogee here in both the decorative multifoil arch and the horseshoe arch—although, the former rulers, the Visigoths, had created the latter. The ornamental use of calligraphy and elaborate stuccowork are other distinctive and important aspects.

Even today many architectural influences are visible at the Great Mosque of Córdoba, in such features as its **Mihrab** (a richly ornamented prayer niche), and its **Puerta del Perdón** (a Mudéjar-style entrance gate that was built during Christian rule). See below for more on Mudéjar, a style reaching its zenith of expression in Andalusia. In the 16th century, a cathedral was built in the heart of the reconsecrated mosque. Part of the Islamic architecture was destroyed to make way for this cathedral with its Italianate dome.

The Caliphal era was replaced by the brief Taifa era (1031–91) which quickly gave way to new rulers, the Almoravid and Almohad dynasties (1091–1248). These austere Islamic fundamentalists brought a purer, less fanciful style of architecture, best seen at **La Giralda** in Seville (p. 109). This minaret, which still graces the skyline, was completed in 1198. At the time of the Reconquista, the Muslim bronze spheres crowning it were replaced by Christian symbols of a bronze portraying Faith.

The Almohads did not eschew adornment completely; their artisans created the *artesonado* ceiling (paneled wood ceilings that were intricately carved and painted), and *azulejos* (glazed tiles beautifully painted with patterns). Although still using the horseshoe arch of the Visigoths, the Almohads introduced the narrow, pointy arch.

The flowering of Muslim architecture in Andalusia occurred during the Nasrid era (1238–1492), the last Moorish rulers before the Reconquista by the Catholic monarchs, Isabella and Ferdinand. These Sultans created one of the most magnificent palaces ever built: the **Alhambra** at Granada (p. 209). *Alhambra* means "the red one," referring to the colored clay used to construct the fortress. In 1238 Muhammad ibn el-Ahmar ordered construction to begin on this impressive fortification. The site was developed over both the 13th and 14th centuries, so it represents a medley of styles. It is a vast complex of palaces, gardens, walls, towers, and residences. Restored after its rediscovery by writers and artists, including Washington Irving, in the 19th century, the palace is filled with architectural wonders, such as the Patio de los Leones. Its arcades are supported by 124 slender marble columns, and at its center a fountain rests on 12 proud marble lions. The salons are stunning achievements, especially Salón de Embajadores, the sumptuous throne room from 1334 to 1354, its ceiling representing the seven heavens of the Muslim cosmos. For the various caliphs of the Nasrid dynasty, this palace represented an earthly paradise, even though modest materials—tile, plaster, and wood—were used.

La Giralda before and after the Reconquista

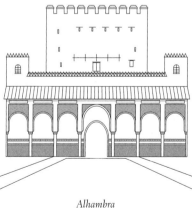

Alhambra

MUDÉJAR OR POST-MOORISH ARCHITECTURE (MID–14TH TO LATE 15TH C.)

After the Muslims were ousted from power, Andalusia continued to construct churches on the sites of former mosques. Original architectural motifs—ornamental brickwork in relief alternating with stone, archways, and even roof tiles—were often incorporated into these Christian churches. Muslims who stayed on after the Reconquista created a new style of architecture called Mudéjar. Since they were better builders, these *mudéjares*—the word literally means "those who were permitted to stay"—were employed to build the new churches and palaces in the reconquered territories.

Their architecture was a hybrid style, one of the best examples being the **Salón de Embajadores** in the Alcázar at Seville (p. 206). This Room of the Ambassadors is part of the palace of King Don Pedro in the Alcázar. It's topped with a wooden dome and flanked with double geminate windows, a stunning achievement. Dozens of Andalusian churches and palaces retain Mudéjar architectural motifs. The Mudéjar tradition lives on in pottery made in Granada and Seville that reflects Moorish design.

Decorative ceramic

As you drive through the **Las Alpujarras region** (p. 226) of Granada province, the final bastion of the *Moriscos* (Muslims who were forced to convert to Christianity), you'll see the flat-roofed houses that evoke the Berber dwellings of the Moroccans living in the Atlas mountains across the Straits of Gibraltar.

Not all Reconquista architecture was Mudéjar. The first major style used by Catholic Andalusia was **Romanesque** (the term had not come into vogue at the time). For its inspiration, this style of architecture drew upon the rounded arches from classical ancient Rome. Romanesque churches were dark and somber with small windows and large piers. There are few remnants of Romanesque architecture in Andalusia.

GOTHIC (13TH–16TH C.)

Somehow the French Gothic style of the **Cathedral of Seville** (p. 108) seems ill suited to the hot plains of Andalusia with its almost desert-like landscape. The rounded arches of Romanesque gave way to pointed arches that could carry far more weight, as in cathedrals. Windows became larger and were filled with stained glass depicting scenes from the Bible, so illiterate peasants could see biblical scenes depicted in the glass panels.

Seville's cathedral also showed the Renaissance influence, characterized by massive column shafts that hold up mammoth arches. Its vaulting is splendid, constructed in the flamboyant Gothic style and rising 56m (184 ft) over the transept crossing. The bulk of this structure was constructed between 1401 and 1507. Styles changed—an altar was added in the late Gothic style (1496–1537) while the Capilla Real (Royal Chapel; 1530–69), was actually Plateresque (see below).

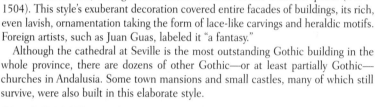
Ayuntamiento

By the end of the 15th century, Spain had developed its own unique style of Gothic architecture, calling it **Isabelline** in honor of the Catholic queen (1474–1504). This style's exuberant decoration covered entire facades of buildings, its rich, even lavish, ornamentation taking the form of lace-like carvings and heraldic motifs. Foreign artists, such as Juan Guas, labeled it "a fantasy."

Although the cathedral at Seville is the most outstanding Gothic building in the whole province, there are dozens of other Gothic—or at least partially Gothic—churches in Andalusia. Some town mansions and small castles, many of which still survive, were also built in this elaborate style.

THE RENAISSANCE (16TH C.)

When the Renaissance finally came to Spain, it changed its name. The very early Renaissance in Spain was termed **Plateresque** because its fine detailing evoked the ornate work of a silversmith, or *platero* in Spanish.

The best example of the Plateresque style preferred by the architect Diego de Riaño is the **Ayuntamiento (town hall)** in Seville (p. 258). Begun in 1527 and completed in 1534, the Plateresque style is best seen on the east side of the town hall opening onto Plaza de San Francisco.

A new style of Renaissance architecture arose in Spain at the end of the 16th century. Called the **Herreran style,** it was named after Juan de Herrera (1530–97), the greatest figure of Spanish classicism. The favorite architect of Philip II, Herrera developed a style of building that was grand but austere as well as geometric in its effect. His greatest achievement was El Escorial, the mammoth royal palace outside Madrid. In Andalusia his work can be seen at the **Archivo de Indias** (p. 106) in Seville. Built between 1584 and 1598, the facade of this structure remains even today one of the most harmonious and classic in all of Seville.

Plateresque gave way to what became known as the **High Renaissance** style, as exemplified by the **Palacio de Carlos V** in Granada (p. 207). Begun in 1526, this palace was incongruously—even scandalously—placed in the heart of the Alhambra. Its elegant and grandiose style evokes the king's power as Holy Roman Emperor. If you can forgive where it was built, the palace is a perfect architectural specimen with pure classical lines. Dignified in appearance, its layout was "a circle within a square." In Andalusia this palace is the crowning achievement of the High Renaissance style.

BAROQUE (17TH–18TH C.)

Baroque suggests flamboyance, but early Spanish Baroque was more austere in the 17th century. A family of architects led by **José de Churriguera** (1665–1725) pioneered the Churriguesque style, a type of architecture noted for its sumptuousness and dense concentrations of ornaments covering entire facades of buildings. This style was later copied by his brothers, other Churriguera family members, and leading architects of the day. The best example of the Churriguesque style in Andalusia is the flamboyant, Baroque sacristy of the **Monasterio de la Cartuja** (p. 212) in Granada.

Andalusia was the one province of Spain where the Baroque blossomed most brilliantly. Seville has more Baroque churches per square kilometer than any other city in the world, notably the delightful little **Iglesia de San José** (p. 116), one of the world's most beautiful examples of a Baroque church.

With the arrival of neoclassicism and modernism, devotees of architecture turned to other parts of Spain, including Bilbao and especially Barcelona, to indulge their passions.

MODERN (20TH C.)

Modern architecture in Andalusia received a boost when Seville hosted Expo '92. Many innovative designs were introduced at this time, notably the **five bridges** spanning the Guadalquivir River. The most exceptional of these are the Puente de Chapina, with a geometrically designed canopy; the Puente del Alamillo, designed by famous Spanish architect Santiago Calatrava (b. 1951) with a single upward arm holding its weight; and the Puente de la Barqueta, a suspension bridge held by one overhead beam.

SOUTHERN SPAIN IN BOOKS, FILM & MUSIC

Books

THE ARTS

The Moors contributed much to Spanish culture, leaving Spain with a distinct legacy that is documented in Titus Burckhardt's *Moorish Culture in Spain.*

Spain's most famous artist was Málaga-born Pablo Picasso. The most controversial book about the late painter is *Picasso, Creator and Destroyer,* by Arianna Stassinopoulos Huffington.

Andalusia, by Eliane Faure and Christian Sappa, is a great picture book on the province, covering major cities such as Seville along with popular customs and old traditions. *Andalusia,* by Brigitte Hintzen-Bohlen, is good for an armchair tour, with architectural drawings along with brief narrative descriptions of the people and places of the province.

ECONOMIC, POLITICAL & SOCIAL HISTORY

Historically, Spain's Golden Age lasted from the late 15th to the early 17th century, a period when the country reached the height of its prestige and influence. This era is well surveyed in J. H. Elliot's *Imperial Spain 1469–1716.*

For more contemporary history, read John Hooper's *The Spaniards.* Hooper provides insight into the events of the post-Franco era, when the country came to grips with democracy after years of fascism.

FICTION & BIOGRAPHY

Denounced by some as superficial, James A. Michener's *Iberia* remains the classic travelogue on Spain.

The latest biography of one of the 20th century's most durable dictators is *Franco: A Concise Biography,* published in 2002. Gabrielle Ashford Hodges documents with great flair the Orwellian repression and widespread corruption that marked the notorious regime of this "deeply flawed" politician.

Probably the most famous Spanish novel of all time is *Don Quixote* by Miguel de Cervantes. Readily available everywhere, it deals with the conflict between the ideal and the real in human nature. Nicholas Wollaston's *Tilting at Don Quixote* takes us on a panoramic tour of Quixote's Spain, unfolding as a backdrop against Wollaston's own personal life journey. The writer has great sympathy for the half-crazed don and his illusions.

Driving Over Lemons: An Optimist in Andalucia, by Chris Stewart, is a charming book, telling the story of an English sheep shearer, Chris Stewart, who buys an isolated farmhouse in the mountains outside Granada.

Film

It might be old, but classic romance *The Loves of Carmen* (1948) is still around, starring Rita Hayworth and Glenn Ford, who achieved screen immortality in their film noir thriller *Gilda.* This is no *Gilda,* but the Technicolor and Rita's Gypsy dance number capture some of the flavor of Andalusia. The chemistry is real between Rita and Glenn, who were lovers off screen.

Belmonte (1995; with English subtitles) is one of the best films ever made about bullfighting in Andalusia, focusing on the famous bullfighter, Belmonte. It starred Achero Manas as Juan Belmonte. Ernest Hemingway once said that he'd met only two geniuses—Einstein and Belmonte. The film is a period piece that faithfully reproduces the backdrop of southern Spain.

The Disappearance of García Lorca (1996) introduced many younger viewers to the work of an artist hailed by some as Spain's greatest poet. Andy Garcia plays Lorca in this tale of a journalist who starts an investigation into the disappearance of famed poet and political agitator García Lorca. He vanished in the early days of the Spanish Civil War in the 1930s. This is definitely Andalusian film noir, and Garcia as Lorca delivers a passionate performance. The shots of the Andalusian countryside are so gorgeous that the film in part is a travelogue in spite of its dark overtones.

Yerma (1998) was director Pilar Távora's attempt to bring this play by Federico García Lorca to life with Aitanas Sánchez-Gijón cast as Yerma. Critics hail Távora as an expert on Andalusian culture and flamenco in particular, and this is definitely a director's picture. *Yerma* provides insights into Andalusian culture as it tells of a woman's "impossible" love for another man. It's filled with violent passions that one critic noted could "come only out of an Andalusian soul."

Oh Marbella! (2003) depicts life along the Costa del Sol as filled with "sun, sea, and sex." Piers Ashworth was both the writer and director of this comedy that even dabbles in goat herding.

Antonio Banderas, who is extremely proud of his home town of Málaga, returned to the city to shoot *El Camino de los Ingleses* (2006—English title *Summer Rain*). This coming-of-age tale charts the first loves, lusts, and obsessions of friends on vacation at the end of the 1970s in Málaga. Banderas also has plans to produce another film in his beloved Andalusian home land. *Malaga en llamas* (Málaga in flames) is his next project. His wife, actress Melanie Griffith, is expected to take the leading role.

Music

Flamenco dancing, with its flash, color, and ritual, is evocative of Spanish culture. The word itself has various translations, meaning everything from "gypsified Andalusian" to "knife," from "blowhard" to "tough guy." Accompanied by stylized guitar music, castanets, and the fervent clapping of the crowd, dancers are filled with tension and emotion.

Experts disagree on the origins of flamenco, but most point to Andalusia as its seat of origin. Although its influences were both Jewish and Islamic, the song and dance of flamenco was perfected by Gypsy artists, who took to flamenco like "rice to paella," in the words of the historian Fernando Quiñones.

The mournful, romantic song of flamenco represents a fatalistic attitude toward life. Marxists said it was a deeply felt protest of the lower classes against their oppressors. Protest or not, rich patrons—often brash young men—liked the sound of flamenco and booked artists to stage *juergas,* or fiestas. Flamenco was linked with pimping, prostitution, and lots and lots of drinking, by both audience and artists. Dancer-prostitutes became the "erotic extras." The style reached its present format by the early 17th century.

By the mid-19th century flamenco had gone legitimate and was prevalent in theaters and *café cantantes,* or "singing cafes." By the 1920s even the pre-Franco Spanish dictator, Primo de Rivera, was singing the flamenco tunes of his native Cádiz. The poet Federico García Lorca and the composer Manuel de Falla preferred a purer form, attacking what they viewed as the degenerate and "ridiculous" burlesque of *flamenquismo,* the jazzed-up, audience-pleasing form of flamenco. The two artists launched a Flamenco Festival in Granada in 1922. In the decades since, their voices have been drowned out, and flamenco is more *flamenquismo* than ever, but that's not to say that you can't experience the rootsier, more authentic style if you look for it.

In his 1995 book *Flamenco Deep Song,* Thomas Mitchell draws a parallel to flamenco's "lowlife roots" and the "orgiastic origins" of jazz. He notes that early jazz, like flamenco, was "associated with despised ethnic groups, gangsters, brothels, free-spending bluebloods, and whoopee hedonism." By disguising their origins, Mitchell notes, both jazz and flamenco have solidly entered the musical mainstream.

EATING & DRINKING IN SOUTHERN SPAIN

The Cuisine

The nearly 8-centuries-old occupation of southern Spain by the Moors left a strong influence on the cuisine of Andalusia. The invasion by the Moors introduced exotic spices and ingredients still in use today, especially almonds, sweet peppers, and saffron.

The Moors also brought courgettes (zucchini), dates, lemons, rice, oranges, aubergines (eggplant), cinnamon, artichokes, and other delights to their capitals at

Granada, Seville, and Córdoba. Ground almonds often replaced flour in cake or pastry making.

The Moors also imported recipes for very sweet pastries. Ziryab, a famous 10th-century Moorish chef, was credited with introducing the custom of beginning a meal with soup and ending with dessert—the standard sequence of dishes that spread across the rest of Europe.

Modern Andalusian cuisine is better than ever, using quality ingredients and skilled preparation. Cooks use very fresh fish and seafood (often deep-fried) as well as extra-virgin olive oils. Parsley and garlic are added to many dishes, and the larder turns up game in the autumn, cured hams, chorizo, and fresh breads often baked in ancient ovens.

The original southern Andalusian recipe for gazpacho now appears on menus around the world. It's a cold soup of ground vegetables, garlic, and bread in freshly picked and pureed tomatoes.

You can make an entire meal of tapas or hors d'oeuvres, going from tavern to tavern on a *tapeo,* the Spanish version of an English pub-crawl, but with food. Cervantes even praised tapas in his masterpiece, *Don Quixote.*

Tapas are said to have originated in Andalusia. Favorites include *calamares fritos,* fried squid or cuttlefish, which first-time visitors sometimes mistake for onion rings. Others include *gambas,* shrimp cooked in olive oil and garlic, or *patatas bravas,* potatoes in spicy sauce. *Salmonetes* (small red mullet) are consumed at bars all along the coast, as are *chancletes* (whitebait cooked in oil and flavored with parsley).

Mushrooms are grilled, as are baby octopi or *chopitos.* Many residents on the coast begin their meal with *sopa de pescado* (fish soup) if not gazpacho. Another cold soup, heralding from Córdoba, is *salmorejo,* a thicker and denser gazpacho. Fresh *sardines,* or sardines, are a favorite in Málaga, though residents of Cádiz prefer *acedias,* or miniature sole filets.

Each city and surrounding region has its specialties. Among meats, Spain's best cured hams come from Huelva, whereas Granada is known for its *morcilla* (blood sausage). From Málaga come Moscatel grapes, *papanduas* (small codfish cakes), and sardines roasted on bamboo spits. Cádiz cooks, in addition to seafood, are known for their cabbage stew and game dishes, along with squid, oysters, sea snails, and shrimp. A specialty is *caldillo de perro* (onion, hake, and tart orange juice). Squid is cooked in its own ink; kidneys cooked in sherry are another favorite.

Huelva cooks are said to make some of the best fish stews along the coast, often of sardines and tuna. *Arroz con almejas* (clams and rice) is another much-favored dish, as is freshly caught swordfish.

The people of Seville feast on *menudo* (tripe) or *cola de toro* (oxtail). *Soldaditos de pavía* are fish sticks, and *pato con aceitunas* (duck with olives) is another specialty. Seville is the place to witness the tapas revolution. Here they're taking tapas to the next level with all sorts of highly original modern interpretations.

The olive-oil based cuisine of Jaén ranges from *alboroinia* (a vegetable stew) to *ajilimojili* (potatoes cooked with red peppers). In Córdoba you can enjoy lamb stew, veal with artichokes, roast pigs' feet, and pigeon with olives.

And don't forget breakfast. Crusty bread soaked in olive oil with ultra-fine slices of serrano ham accompanied by thick milky coffee (*café con leche*) are the order of the day. Or try *chocolate y churros*—a cup of thick hot chocolate served with long thin pieces of donut to dunk into it. Sweet tooths will love it.

Wines

Perhaps introduced into Southern Spain by the Phoenicians, winemaking is a tradition that spans two millennia, and was already a firmly established business by the time of the Roman invasion. During the Moorish invasion that followed, winemaking continued even though the Koran frowned on the consumption of alcohol.

In Andalusia, sherry is the king of wines, its grapes grown in the vineyards surrounding Jerez de la Frontera in the provinces of Cádiz. Ever since Sir Francis Drake ransacked the port of Cádiz in 1587 and sailed back to England with 3,000 barrels of sherry, the British have been the greatest fans of this drink, then called "sack" by the English.

There are various types of sherry, including *fino*, the palest, lightest, most delicate, and generally the driest of sherries. Served chilled, it is one of the best aperitifs, with an earthy aroma of almonds. *Manzanilla*, a *fino* sherry made in Sanlúcar de Barrameda, is very pale and dry with a flavor that is almost salty. Traditionally, the very dry *manzanilla* is the drink of choice among bullfighters and the favored wine in Seville; it does not enjoy much popularity outside Spain.

With the aroma of hazelnuts, an exceptional aperitif is *oloroso*, often consumed with cured ham. This is one of the two basic types of Spanish sherry (as opposed to *fino*). Dark in color, *oloroso* ranges from a dark gold to a deep amber. Most *oloroso* sherry is consumed as an after-dinner wine, and the best examples, or at least the oldest, include Matusalém manufactured by Gonzalez Byass.

Amontillado, produced in the town of Montilla outside Córdoba, is halfway between a *fino* and an *oloroso*. This wine is fairly dry and somewhat pale, but not as dry as a *fino* or *manzanilla*. Its best-known label is Amontillado del Duque, also produced by Gonzalez Byass.

Cream sherry, such as Harvey's Bristol Cream—popular in Great Britain, Germany, and the Netherlands—is *oloroso* that has been sweetened, often with grape concentrate. It is generally served as a dessert wine and is also used in cooking. Another dessert wine is Pedro Ximenez. This very sweet wine when well aged is known as "P.X." Sometimes it's drunk straight as a liqueur.

The sweet wines of Málaga, made from Pedro Ximenez and Moscatel grapes, enjoy favor among the British.

Montilla-Moriles, in the southern tier of Córdoba province, produces a poor cousin of the sherry of Jerez de la Frontera. The region grows the Pedro Ximenez grape, which is often shipped to Jerez to sweeten cream sherries.

That's not to say you can't find local table wine in Andalusia. There's plenty of it too, it's just less well known than the vintages from more popular wine regions of Spain like Rioja. Most villages have home-produced table wine that is eminently drinkable and excellent value.

The most interesting Andalusian wine denomination area right now is Sierras de Málaga. Here they make reds, whites, and rosés using grape varieties like Tempranillo, Cabernet Sauvignon, Chardonnay, and Riesling, plus a few local varieties just to keep things interesting. Ronda, in particular, is a bit of a wine hot-spot at the moment. Wines tend to be classy, but not cheap.

PLANNING YOUR TRIP TO ANDALUSIA

There's a great deal to Andalusia. Far more than you could hope to cover in a single trip, so at the outset, decide on your priorities and plan accordingly. Culture creatures will want to spend most of their time exploring the wonderfully historic cities of Seville, Córdoba, and Granada—all within easy reach of each other. Outdoor enthusiasts could spend several weeks hiking around the wildly beautiful interior. Beach lovers could while away their days on the busy stretches of sand along the Costa del Sol or the wilder, more natural beaches of the Costa de la Luz. Food and wine aficionados will be delighted by the sherry houses in the Sherry Triangle and the delicious seafood at many of the restaurants along the coast. Take a look at some of the suggested itineraries in Chapter 4 as a good starting point for planning your trip.

Visiting this part of the world is generally as straightforward as anywhere else in Europe. But, surprisingly, English is not very widely spoken outside the big cities, so a phrasebook and a basic knowledge of Spanish are useful. And the times of day that locals eat and sleep can be distinctly disorientating. Due to the extreme heat in summer in particular, lunch starts late and goes on a long time, with many people still taking a siesta if they're not at work. Dinner might not get started until 10pm. If you turn up at a restaurant expecting to dine at 7pm anywhere outside the Costa del Sol and Gibraltar, you'll probably find it's not open for at least another hour or two.

Getting into these different local rhythms and adapting to the heat in summer takes a little effort, but it's well worth doing exactly as the locals do.

TOURIST OFFICES A good place to begin your research is Spain's tourist offices:

In the United States   Contact the **Tourist Office of Spain,** 666 Fifth Ave., Fifth Floor, New York, NY 10103 (📞 **212/265-8822**) for sightseeing information, events calendars, train and ferry schedules, and more. Branches of the Tourist Office of Spain are also located at 8383 Wilshire Blvd., Suite 956, Beverly Hills, CA 90211 (📞 **323/658-7188**); 845 N. Michigan Ave., Suite 915E, Chicago, IL 60611 (📞 **312/642-1992**); and 1221 Brickell Ave., Suite 1850, Miami, FL 33131 (📞 **305/358-1992**).

In Canada   Contact the **Tourist Office of Spain,** 102 Bloor St W., Suite 3402, Toronto, Ontario M5S 1M9, Canada (📞 **416/961-3131**).

In Great Britain   Contact the **Spanish National Tourist Office,** 22–23 Manchester Sq., London W1M 5AP (📞 **020/7486-8077**).

WEBSITES   **Tourist Office of Spain** (www.okspain.org), **All About Spain** (www.red2000.com), and **CyberSp@in** (www.cyberspain.com).

For **Seville: Seville City Tourist Office** (www.turismosevilla.org), **Sevilla5** (www.sevilla5.com), **Seville by All About Spain** (www.red2000.com), **Sevilla On Line** (www.sol.com), **Seville Travel Guide** (www.aboutsevilla.com), **Andalucia. com** (www.andalucia.com).

For **Málaga: Málaga City Tourist Office** (www.malagaturismo.com), **Málaga Travel Guide** (www.aboutmalaga.com), **Costa del Sol Tourist Board** (www.visit costadelsol.com), **La Costa del Sol** (www.costadelsol.net).

For **Granada: Granada City Tourist Office** (www.granadatur.com), **Granada Info** (www.granadainfo.com), **Granada Travel Guide** (www.aboutgranada.com).

For **Cádiz: Cádiz Province Tourist Office** (www.cadizturismo.com), **Andalu-cia.com** (www.andalucia.com). See "The Best of Andalusia Online" in Chapter 1 (p. 10) for more information about useful websites.

MAPS   For one of the best overviews of the Iberian Peninsula (Spain and Portugal), get Michelin map no. 990 (folded version) or no. 460 (spiral-bound version). For more detailed maps of Andalusia, Michelin map no. 578 covers the whole region; Michelin map no. 124 Zoom covers the Costa del Sol and surroundings in even more detail.

WHEN TO GO

Climate

Spring and fall/autumn are ideal times to visit Andalusia. May and October are the best months for both weather and crowds. In my view, however, the balmy month of May (with an average temperature of 61°F/16°C) is the choicest time.

In summer it's hot, hot, and hotter in Andalusia, but especially in Seville and Córdoba. Seville has the dubious reputation of being the hottest part of Spain in July and August; the *average* temperature is 93°F (34°C).

August remains Europe's major vacation month. Traffic into the Costa del Sol from France, the Netherlands, Britain, and Germany becomes a veritable migration, and low-cost hotels along the coastal areas are virtually impossible to book. To compound the problem, many restaurants and shops in such inland cities as Seville close for the season.

Andalusia's Average Daily Temperatures and Rainfall

GRANADA	JAN	FEB	MAR	APR	MAY	JUNE	JULY	AUG	SEPT	OCT	NOV	DEC
Temp (°F)	44	46	50	54	63	69	77	77	69	61	50	45
Temp (°C)	7	8	10	12	17	21	25	24	21	16	10	7
Rainfall (in.)	1.30	1.70	2.40	2.00	1.70	.80	.20	.10	1.10	1.90	2.30	1.90
MÁLAGA	JAN	FEB	MAR	APR	MAY	JUNE	JULY	AUG	SEPT	OCT	NOV	DEC
Temp (°F)	54	54	64	70	73	81	84	86	81	73	68	63
Temp (°C)	12	12	18	21	23	27	29	30	27	23	20	17
Rainfall (in.)	2.40	2	2.40	1.80	1	.20	.05	.10	1.20	2.50	2.50	2.40
SEVILLE	JAN	FEB	MAR	APR	MAY	JUNE	JULY	AUG	SEPT	OCT	NOV	DEC
Temp (°F)	59	63	68	75	81	90	97	97	90	79	68	61
Temp (°C)	15	17	20	24	27	32	36	36	32	26	20	16
Rainfall (in.)	2.60	2.40	3.60	2.30	1.60	.30	0	.20	.80	2.80	2.70	3.20

Calendar of Events

Some dates below are approximate, as exact days may not be announced until 6 weeks before the actual festival. Confirm all dates with the Tourist Office of Spain (see "Tourist Offices," above).

JANUARY

Granada Reconquest Festival, Granada. The celebration of the Christians' victory over the Moors in 1492 when the highest tower at the Alhambra opens to the public. Contact the Tourist Office of Granada (© **95-824-82-20;** www.granadatur.com). January 2.

Día de los Reyes (Three Kings' Day), throughout Andalusia. Parades are held all over the province on the eve of the Festival of the Epiphany. Various "kings" dispense candy to kids. January 6.

FEBRUARY

Carnavales de Cádiz, Cádiz. The oldest, best-attended carnival in Spain is full of costumes, parades, strolling troubadours, and drum beating. Information at the Cádiz tourist office © **95-624-10-01;** www. carnavaldecadiz.com. Mid-February.

MARCH

Semana Santa (Holy Week), Seville. Although many of the country's smaller towns stage similar celebrations (especially notable in Málaga), the festivities in Seville are by far the most elaborate. From Palm Sunday until Easter Sunday, a series of processions with hooded penitents moves to the piercing wail of the *saeta,* a love song to the Virgin or Christ. *Pasos* (heavy floats) bear images of the Virgin or Christ. Make hotel reservations way in advance. Details from the Seville Office of Tourism © **95-459-52-88;** www.turismosevilla.org. Usually the last week of March.

APRIL

Bullfights, all over Spain. Holy week traditionally kicks off the season all over Spain, especially in Seville.

Feria de Sevilla (Seville Fair). This is the most celebrated week of revelry in the country, with all-night flamenco dancing, merrymaking in *casetas* (entertainment booths), bullfights, horseback riding, flower-decked coaches, and dancing in the streets. Reserve a hotel early. For general information and festival dates, contact the Office of Tourism in Seville *℡ 95-459-52-88;* www.turismosevilla.org. Second week after Easter.

MAY

Jerez May Horse Fair. Jerez de la Frontera stages this spectacular equestrian event. Many of the greatest riders, and some of the world's finest horses, take part in endurance trials, coach driving, and dressage competitions. Information from the local tourist office *℡ 95-633-88-74;* www.turismojerez.com. First week of May.

Festival de los Patios, Córdoba. At this famous fair, residents decorate their patios with cascades of flowers. Visitors wander from patio to patio. Information from the local tourist office *℡ 90-220-17-74;* www.turismodecordoba.org. First 2 weeks of May.

Festival Internacional de Teatro y Danza, Seville. May heralds the beginning of the month-long Festival Internacional de Teatro y Danza (International Theater and Dance Festival) in Seville, where world-class companies perform in the Teatro de la Maestranza, and at nearby Itálica. More information from the Office of Tourism in Seville *℡ 95-459-52-88;* www.turismosevilla.org.

Romería del Rocío (Pilgrimage of the Virgin of the Dew), El Rocío (Huelva). The most famous pilgrimage in Andalusia attracts a million people. Fifty men carry the statue of the Virgin 15km (9 miles) to Almonte for consecration. See www.andalucia.com/festival/rocio.htm. Third week of May.

JUNE

Corpus Christi, all over Andalusia. A major holiday on the Spanish calendar, this event is marked by big processions, especially in Málaga, Seville, and Granada. Mid-June.

International Music and Dance Festival, Granada. Granada's prestigious program of dance and music attracts international artists who perform at the Alhambra and other venues. It's a major event on Europe's cultural calendar; so reserve well in advance. For the schedule and tickets, contact El Festival Internacional de Música y Danza de Granada (*℡ 95-822-18-44;* www.granadafestival.org). Last week of June to first week of July.

JULY

Fiesta de la Virgen del Carmen. In mid-July, the towns and fishing villages along the southern coast of Spain honor la Virgen del Carmen, the protector of seamen. An effigy of the virgin is paraded through the streets and taken for a sail on one of the gaily adorned boats in the harbor. The best place to see this fiesta is Estepona, but other major events honoring the saint take place in Málaga, Nerja, Torremolinos, Benalmádena, Fuengirola, and Marbella. Check www.andalusia.com. July 16.

AUGUST

Feria de Málaga (Málaga Fair). One of the longest summer fairs in southern Europe (generally lasting 10 days), this celebration kicks off with fireworks and is highlighted by a parade of Arabian horses pulling brightly decorated carriages. Participants are dressed in colorful Andalusian garb. Plazas rattle with castanets, and wine is dispensed by the gallon. Information from the local tourist office *℡ 95-212-20-20;* www.malagaturismo.com. The weekend before August 19.

SEPTEMBER

Feria de Pedro Romero, Ronda. This fair is famous for a bullfight on the first Saturday in September. The matadors dress in "suits of light" from the 18th and 19th centuries. Before they face the bulls, horse-drawn carriages parade through the town to the bullring with participants in what Andalusians call "Goyesque costumes." More information from the local tourist office *℡ 95-218-71-19;* www.turismoderonda.es. First week in September.

Bienal de Arte Flamenco, Seville. This must-visit event for flamenco fans takes place during the last two weeks of September every two years, in even-numbered years in Seville. World-class artists perform to rapturous crowds. See www.bienal-flamenco.org.

Grape Harvest Festival, Jerez de la Frontera. Andalusia's major wine festival honors the famous sherry of Jerez, with 5 days of processions, flamenco dancing, bullfights, livestock on parade, and, of course, sherry drinking. Contact the local tourist office 📞 **95-633-88-74;** www.turismojerez.com for more information. Mid-October (dates vary).

NOVEMBER

All Saints' Day, all over Spain. This public holiday is reverently celebrated with relatives and friends laying flowers on the graves of loved ones. November 1.

Andrés Segovia International Guitar Competition, Almuñecar. The great Segovia, who as a young man fell in love with this part of Spain, created the "Andrés Segovia Award" in recognition of the importance of the Spanish guitar. Talented musicians from all over the world participate. More information from 📞 **95-864-04-25;** www.almunecar.com. 5 days in late November.

DECEMBER

Fiesta Mayor de Verdiales, outside Málaga. *Verdiales* are traditional forms of song and dance in Málaga province. On December 28, there's a competition staged at Venta San Cayetano del Puerto de la Torre on the outskirts of the city, to decide which village troupe can sing and dance the best. The party goes on all night, with music, food stalls, and lots of flowing wine. Check www.andalucia.com. December 28.

For an exhaustive list of events beyond those listed here, check http://events.frommers.com, for a searchable, up-to-the-minute roster of what's happening in cities worldwide.

ENTRY REQUIREMENTS

Passports

A valid **passport** is all that an American, British, Canadian, or New Zealand citizen needs to enter Spain. However, Australians need a visa. For information on how to obtain a passport, go to "Passports" in Chapter 12: Fast Facts, Toll-Free Numbers & Websites (p. 391).

Visas

A valid passport is all that an American, British, Canadian, or New Zealand citizen needs to enter Spain. Australians need a visa, which is issued on arrival.

Customs

WHAT YOU CAN BRING INTO SPAIN

You can bring most personal effects and the following items duty-free: tobacco for personal use, 1 liter each of liquor and wine, a portable radio, a cassette digital recorder, a laptop computer, a bicycle, sports equipment, and fishing gear.

WHAT YOU CAN TAKE HOME FROM SPAIN

U.S. Citizens: For specifics on what you can bring back and the corresponding fees, download the invaluable free pamphlet *Know Before You Go* online at www.cbp.gov. (Click on "Travel," and then click on "Know Before You Go.") Or contact the **U.S. Customs & Border Protection (CBP),** 1300 Pennsylvania Ave., NW, Washington, DC 20229 (📞 **877/287-8667**), and request the pamphlet.

Canadian Citizens: For a clear summary of Canadian rules, write for the booklet *I Declare,* issued by the Canada Border Services Agency (☎ **800/461-9999** in Canada, or ☎ 204/983-3500; **www.cbsa-asfc.gc.ca**).

U.K. Citizens: For information, contact **HM Revenue & Customs** at ☎ **0845/010-9000** (from outside the U.K., ☎ **020/8929-0152**), or consult their website at **www.hmrc.gov.uk**.

Australian Citizens: A helpful brochure from Australian consulates or Customs offices is *Know Before You Go.* For more information, contact the **Australian Customs Service** at ☎ **1300/363-263; www.customs.gov.au**.

New Zealand Citizens: Most questions are answered in a free pamphlet available at New Zealand consulates and Customs offices: *New Zealand Customs Guide for Travellers, Notice no. 4.* For more information, contact **New Zealand Customs,** The Customhouse, 17–21 Whitmore St, Box 2218, Wellington (☎ **04/473-6099** or ☎ 0800/428-786; **www.customs.govt.nz**).

Medical Requirements

Unless you're arriving from an area known to be suffering from an epidemic (particularly cholera or yellow fever), inoculations or vaccinations are not required for entry into Spain.

GETTING THERE & AROUND

Getting To Southern Spain

BY PLANE

FROM NORTH AMERICA   Flights from the U.S. east coast to Spain take 6 to 7 hours.

The easiest air route into southern Spain is with **Delta** (☎ **800/241-4141;** www.delta.com), which runs a direct service to Málaga from New York JFK four times weekly June to September. Delta's Dream Vacation department offers independent fly/drive packages, land packages, and escorted bus tours.

Outside these times of year, the national carrier of Spain, **Iberia Airlines** (☎ **800/772-4642;** www.iberia.com), now combined with British Airways, has more routes into and within Spain than any other airline. It offers almost daily services from most major U.S. cities (New York, Washington, Chicago, Atlanta) to Madrid with good onward connections to Seville, Granada, Málaga, and Jerez. Also available are attractive rates on fly/drive packages within Iberia and Europe which can substantially reduce the cost of air tickets and car rental.

A good money-saver is **Iberia**'s **SpainPass** (*Iberiabono Spain*). Available only to passengers who simultaneously arrange for transatlantic passage on Iberia, the SpainPass has coupons equivalent to a one-way/one-person ticket to destinations on mainland Spain and the Balearic Islands. Travelers must purchase a minimum of two-coupons (120€); extra coupons cost 60€ each.

Iberia's main Spain-based competitor **Air Europa** (☎ **800/238-7672;** www.air-europa.com) has a daily service from JFK and Miami to Madrid, with connecting flights to Málaga. Fares are usually lower than Iberia's.

Travelers from **Canada** have a weekly direct flight by **Transat** (✆ 1-888-TRAN-SAT;** www.airtransat.ca) within Canada, year-round from Montreal with easy connections to Toronto.

FROM THE U.K.   The easiest and cheapest air entry point to southern Spain from the U.K. is Málaga. From the U.K. there are upwards of 10 flights a day arriving at Málaga from airports across the country, including Gatwick, London Stansted, London Heathrow, Manchester, Nottingham East Midlands and Birmingham, Edinburgh, and Glasgow. The best-value deals are usually available from **Monarch Airlines** (✆ 08719-40-50-40 in the U.K., ✆ 800-09-92-60 in Spain; www.monarch.co.uk) from Gatwick, Manchester, and Luton. Other low-cost operators include **easyJet** (✆ 90-229-99-92; www.easyjet.com), from Gatwick, Stansted, Bristol, and Liverpool, and **Ryanair** (✆ 08712-46-00-00 in the U.K., ✆ 807-11-01-62 in Spain; www.ryanair.com) from Stansted. It's worth checking **British Airways** (✆ 08444-93-07-87 in the U.K., ✆ 902-11-13-33 in Spain; www.britishairways.com) running from London Heathrow, though they are usually more expensive.

Direct flights from the U.K. also go to **Seville** with Vueling Airlines (✆ 09067-54-75-41; www.vueling.com) from London Heathrow and with Ryanair (details above) from London Gatwick. You can also fly direct to **Jerez** with Ryanair from London Stansted and direct to **Gibraltar** from London Gatwick with easyJet (details above). Currently no flights go directly to Granada.

FROM AUSTRALIA   From Australia, there are a number of options to fly to Spain. The most popular is **Qantas** (www.qantas.com)/**British Airways** (www.ba.com), which flies daily via Asia and London. Other popular, cheaper options are Qantas/**Lufthansa** (www.lufthansa.com) via Asia and Frankfurt, Qantas/**Air France** (www.airfrance.com) via Asia and Paris, and **Alitalia** (www.alitalia.com) via Bangkok and Rome. The most direct option is on **Singapore Airlines** (www.singaporeair.com), with just one stop in Singapore. Alternatively, flights on **Thai Airways** (www.thaiair.com) go via Bangkok and Rome, but the connections are not always good.

FLYING INTO ANDALUSIA

The major air gateways into Andalusia are Seville (the best gateway to inland Andalusian cities), Málaga (the principal gateway to beach resorts along the Costa del Sol), Granada, and Jerez de la Frontera.

Seville is connected by direct flights from Amsterdam, Brussels, Frankfurt, London, and Paris. But most visitors come from Madrid (45 min.) or Barcelona (55 min.). At least six flights a day fly to Seville from either Barcelona or Madrid.

If **Granada** is your gateway to Andalusia, there are three flights per day from Barcelona (1 hr) and four per day from Madrid (30 min.).

Most passengers fly to Seville and then journey to **Jerez de la Frontera** by car or train. However, Iberia has several flights a day from Madrid and Barcelona, the frequency depending on the time of year.

For Costa del Sol visitors, **Málaga** is an international hub, receiving flights from a huge number of European cities including Amsterdam, Brussels, Dublin, Hamburg, London, Moscow, Oslo, and Paris. Or take one of eight flights daily from Madrid (1 hr) or one of three flights from Barcelona (1½ hr). There are also regular flights from many other Spanish cities such as Valencia.

BY CAR

If you're touring the rest of Europe in a rented car, you might, for an added cost, be able to drop off your vehicle in Málaga or Seville.

Highway approaches to Spain are across France on expressways. The most popular border crossing is near Biarritz, but there are 17 other border stations between Spain and France. To reach southern Spain from the French border you're looking at a journey of over 900km (640 miles), which will take around 10 to 12 hours.

If you're driving from Britain, make sure you have a cross-Channel reservation, as traffic can be very heavy, especially in summer. Also note that Britain drives on the other side of the road to the rest of Europe, so it's not advisable to hire a car in Britain and then drive it on the continent. It's better to drop off your car in England and pick up a new one in France. The journey from Northern France down to the border of Spain takes around 13 hours.

BY TRAIN

If you're already in Europe, you might want to go to Spain by train, especially if you have a **Eurailpass**. Even without a pass, the cost of a train ticket is relatively moderate. Rail passengers from Britain or France should make **reservations** as far in advance as possible, especially in summer.

Europe's high-speed train network (TGV in France and AVE in Spain) is cutting journey times almost yearly, making train travel from elsewhere in Europe a genuine alternative to flying.

To go from London to southern Spain by rail, take an afternoon Eurostar from London to Paris. This high-speed train service goes via the Channel Tunnel and now takes 2 hours 20 minutes, with the cost for a one-way ticket starting at £39. Eurostar services arrive at Paris Gare Du Nord; from here you need to transfer by subway/metro or taxi to Paris Gare d'Austerlitz.

From here take the comfortable Elipsos *trenhotel* (trainhotel) overnight to Madrid, arriving next morning. (See www.elipsos.com for more information.) The trainhotel has cozy bedrooms, a restaurant, and cafe-bar. There's a range of different classes of travel, the most basic is a sleeper chair with typical cost of 148€ one way Paris to Madrid; the most luxurious is Gran Clase. Cabins have a private toilet and shower. A typical one-way fare is 438€.

From Madrid, onward train connections to Córdoba, Seville, and Málaga via Spain's high-speed AVE trains take just 2 to 3 hours. See individual chapters for train travel to your ultimate destination in southern Spain.

The best online resource for timetables is German state railways' website www.bahn.de, which is available in English. For more information see the excellent train website www.seat61.com.

Tickets can be purchased in the United States or Canada at the nearest office of Rail Europe or from any reputable travel agent. Confirmation of your reservation takes about a week.

BY BUS

Bus travel to Spain is possible but not popular—it's quite slow. But coach services do operate regularly from major capitals of western Europe to major hubs in southern Spain, in particular Seville, Granada, Córdoba, and Málaga. The busiest routes are from London, run by **Eurolines Limited,** 52 Grosvenor Gardens, London

SW1W 0AU (☎ **0990/143-219** or ☎ 020/7730-8235; www.nationalexpress. co.uk). The journey from London's Victoria station to Seville takes 35 hours with changes in France and in Spain.

BY BOAT

The ports of Cádiz, Gibraltar, and Málaga are all regularly visited by cruise liners. An interesting option could be to book a cruise that terminates in one of these cities and then hire a car to see more of the region before flying home.

Getting Around

BY PLANE

Andalusia is simply not big enough to merit flight connections between its cities. All are well connected by the high-speed AVE network and good quality road links, so flying within the region is not an option to consider.

BY CAR

To see even just a small amount of the region, you'll need to rent a car. This gives you the greatest flexibility to see as many of the sights as possible; even if you're just doing day trips from Madrid. Don't plan to drive in Seville or Granada for city sightseeing; it's too congested. Rush hour is Monday through Saturday from 8 to 10am, 1 to 2pm, and 4 to 6pm. In reality, it's always busy.

CAR RENTALS   Many of North America's biggest car-rental companies maintain offices throughout Spain. Several Spanish car-rental companies exist, but we've received letters from readers of previous editions telling us they've had hard times resolving billing irregularities and insurance claims, so you might want to stick with the U.S.-based rental firms.

However, one Spanish company I use extensively with no problems is **Auriga Crown** (www.aurigacrown.com). If you're happy with a local company, their rates undercut the big international brands by a significant margin. Two other agencies of note include **Kemwel** (☎ **877/820-0668;** www.kemwel.com) and **Auto Europe** (☎ **800/223-5555;** www.autoeurope.com).

Note that tax on car rentals is a whopping 15%, so don't forget to factor that into your travel budget. Usually, prepaid rates do not include taxes, which will be collected at the rental kiosk itself. Be sure to ask explicitly what's included when you're quoted a rate.

Avis (☎ **800/331-1212;** www.avis.com) has about 100 branches throughout Spain. If you reserve and pay for your rental by telephone at least 2 weeks before your departure from North America, you'll qualify for the company's best rate, with unlimited kilometers included.

You can usually get competitive rates from **Hertz** (☎ **800/654-3131;** www. hertz.com) and **Budget** (☎ **800/472-3325;** www.budget.com); it always pays to comparison shop. Budget doesn't have a drop-off charge if you pick up a car in one Spanish city and return it to another. All three companies require that drivers be at least 21 years of age and, in some cases, not older than 72. To rent a car, you must have a passport and a valid driver's license; you must also have a valid credit card or a prepaid voucher. An international driver's license isn't essential, but present it if you have one; it's available from any North American office of the American Automobile Association (AAA).

Many packages include airfare, accommodations, and a rental car with unlimited mileage. Compare these prices with the cost of booking airline tickets and renting a car separately, to see if these offers are good deals. Internet resources help comparison shopping. **Expedia** (www.expedia.com) and **Travelocity** (www.travelocity.com) compare prices and locate car-rental bargains from companies nationwide. They will even make your reservation for you once you've found the best deal.

Most cars hired in Spain are stick shift, not automatic. Most are air-conditioned and nearly all use unleaded gas.

Usual minimum-age limit for rentals is 21 for compact or intermediate size cars, but some van or larger car rentals require that drivers be 25 years of age (or even older). Upper-age requirements reach 70 to 75 for certain vehicles.

For listings of the major car-rental agencies in Andalusia, please see Chapter 12: Fast Facts, Toll-Free Numbers & Websites (p. 391).

DRIVING RULES   Spaniards drive on the right-hand side of the road. Drivers should pass on the left; local drivers sound their horns when passing another car and flash their lights at you if you're driving slowly (slowly for high-speed Spain) in the left lane. Autos coming from the right have the right of way.

Spain's express highways are known as *autopistas,* which charge a toll, and *autovías,* which don't. To exit in Spain, follow the SALIDA (exit) sign. On most express highways, the speed limit is 120kmph (75 mph). On other roads, speed limits range from 90kmph (56 mph) to 100kmph (62 mph). You will see many drivers far exceeding these limits.

If you must drive through big cities like Seville, Málaga, and Granada, try to avoid morning and evening rush hours. Never park your car facing oncoming traffic—it's against the law. If you are fined by the highway patrol (*Guardia Civil de Tráfico*), you must pay on the spot. Penalties for drinking and driving are very stiff (**breathalyzers** are now being far more strictly used than before).

MAPS   For one of the best overviews of the Iberian Peninsula (Spain and Portugal), get Michelin map no. 990 (folded version) or map no. 460 (spiral-bound version). For more detailed maps of Andalusia, buy Michelin map no. 578 which covers the complete region and Michelin map no. 124 Zoom which covers the Costa del Sol and surroundings in more detail still.

For extensive touring, buy *Mapas de Carreteras—España y Portugal,* published by Almax Editores from most leading bookstores in Spain. This cartographic compendium of Spain provides an overview of the country and includes road and street maps of some of its major cities.

The American Automobile Association (AAA; www.aaa.com) publishes a regional map which is free to members at most AAA offices in the U.S. Incidentally, the AAA is associated with the **Real Automóvil Club de España** (**RACE; ✆ 90-240-45-45;** www.race.es). This organization can supply helpful information about road conditions in Spain, and tourist and travel advice. It will also provide limited road service, in an emergency, if your car breaks down.

BREAKDOWNS   These can be a serious problem. If you're driving a Spanish-made vehicle that needs parts, you'll probably be able to find them. But if you are driving a foreign-made vehicle, you may be stranded. Have the car checked before setting out on a long trek through Spain. On a major motorway you'll find strategically placed emergency phone boxes. On secondary roads, call for help and the

Getting There & Around

PLANNING YOUR TRIP TO ANDALUSIA

Jet lag is a pitfall of traveling across time zones. If you're flying north–south and you feel sluggish when you touch down, it's because of dehydration and the general stress of air travel. When you travel east–west or vice versa, however, your body becomes thoroughly confused about what time it is, and everything from your digestive system to your brain is knocked for a loop. Traveling east, say from Chicago to Málaga, is more difficult on your internal clock than traveling west, say from London to Hawaii, because most people's bodies are more inclined to stay up late than fall asleep early.

○ Here are some tips for combating jet lag:

○ Reset your watch to your destination time before you board the plane.

○ Drink lots of water before, during, and after your flight. Avoid alcohol.

○ Exercise and sleep well for a few days before your trip.

○ If you have trouble sleeping on planes, fly eastward on morning flights.

○ Daylight is the key to resetting your body clock. At the website Outside In (www.bodyclock.com), you can get a customized plan of when to seek and avoid light.

operator for the nearest Guardia Civil, which will put you in touch with a garage that can tow you to a repair shop.

As noted above, the Spanish affiliate of AAA can provide limited assistance in the event of a breakdown.

BY TRAIN

Train is an excellent way to get between the main cities of the region if you're not hiring a car. The high-speed AVE network will whisk you in comfort between Seville and Córdoba in 45 minutes, Córdoba to Málaga in an hour, and Córdoba to Madrid in just under 2 hours. Onward connections from Córdoba to Granada, Málaga down the Costa del Sol, and from Seville to Cádiz and Jerez are also frequent and good value for money. See www.renfe.es for more information.

SPANISH RAIL PASSES   RENFE, the national railway of Spain, offers several discounted rail passes offering a fixed number of days' rail travel within a month at significantly reduced prices. You must buy these passes before leaving your country of departure. For more information, consult a travel agent or **Rail Europe** (✆ **877/272-RAIL** [877/272-7245]; www.raileurope.com in the U.S., or ✆ 08448-48-40-64; www.raileurope.co.uk in the U.K.). In Britain, tickets can also be purchased through European Rail Travel (✆ **020-76-19-10-83**; www.europeanrail.com).

BY BUS

The bus service in southern Spain is extensive, low-priced, and comfortable for short distances.

A bus may be the cheapest mode of transportation, but it's not really the best option for distances of more than 161km (100 miles) if you can take the train instead. On long hauls, buses are often uncomfortable. Another major drawback is the lack of toilet facilities, although rest stops are frequent. It's best for 1-day excursions outside a major tourist center such as Seville. In the rural areas of the country, bus networks are, however, more extensive than the railway system; they go virtually everywhere, connecting every village. In general, a bus ride between two major cities in Spain, such as Córdoba and Seville, is about two-thirds the price of a train ride but it takes considerably longer.

For bus information, contact ALSA (© **90-242-22-42;** www.alsa.es).

MONEY & COSTS

Regrettably, Andalusia is no longer a budget destination. In major cities like Seville or Granada, you can often find hotels charging the same prices as in London or Paris. Taken as a whole, though, Andalusia remains slightly below the cost-of-living index of such countries as England, Italy, Germany, and France.

Prices are generally high, but you get good value for money. Hotels are usually clean and comfortable, and restaurants, for the most part, offer good cuisine, ample portions, and quality ingredients.

In Andalusia, many prices for children—generally defined as ages 6 to 17—are lower than for adults. Children aged 5 and under generally go free.

Foreign money and euros can be brought into Spain without any restrictions. And there is no restriction on taking foreign money out of the country.

For up-to-the-minute conversion rates, check the **Universal Currency Converter** website: **www.xe.com/ucc**.

FOR AMERICAN READERS   At the euro's inception, the U.S. dollar and the euro traded on par (that is, $1 approximately equaled 1€). A few years back the euro gained considerable strength against the dollar, but today (2011) has reached a more favorable figure for U.S. travelers. However, conversion rates fluctuate often, so double-check the exchange rate before you go.

FOR BRITISH READERS   At this writing, £1 equals approximately US$1.60 and trades at 1.23€.

Exchange rates are more favorable at the point of arrival. Nevertheless, it's often helpful to exchange at least some money before going abroad. Currency and traveler's checks (for which you'll receive a better rate than cash), can be changed at all principal airports.

Before leaving, check with your local American Express or Thomas Cook office or major banks. Or order euros in advance from: **American Express** (© **800/221-7282;** www.americanexpress.com), **Thomas Cook** (© **800/223-7373;** www.thomascook.com), or **Capital for Foreign Exchange** (© **888/842-0880**).

When you get to southern Spain, it's best to exchange currency or traveler's checks at a bank, not a *cambio,* hotel, or shop. Note the rates and ask about commission fees; it can sometimes pay to shop around and ask the right questions.

Many hotels don't accept dollar- or pound-denominated checks; those that do will almost certainly charge for the conversion. In some cases, they'll accept countersigned traveler's checks or a credit card, but if you're prepaying a deposit on hotel reservations, it's cheaper and easier to pay with a check drawn on a Spanish bank.

This can be arranged by a large commercial bank or by a specialist such as **Ruesch International,** 700 11th St NW, 4th Floor, Washington, DC 20001-4507 (© **800/424-2923;** www.ruesch.com), which performs a wide variety of conversion-related tasks, usually for only $5 to $15 per transaction.

WHAT THINGS COST IN SEVILLE

	€
Bus from the airport to center	2.30
Public transportation within the city	1.20
Double room at the Alfonso XIII (very expensive)	329.00
Double room at Doña María (moderate)	150.00
Double room at Europa (inexpensive)	64.00
Lunch for one, without wine, at Becerrita (expensive)	18.00
Lunch for one, without wine, at Cafetería Serranito (inexpensive)	14.00
Dinner for one, without wine, at Enrique Becerra (expensive)	25.00
Dinner for one, without wine, at Casa Cuesta (inexpensive)	14.00
Coca-Cola in a restaurant	1.50
Cup of coffee	1.50
Admission to the Alcázar	7.50

Brits can contact **Ruesch International Ltd** at Marble Arch Tower, 14th Floor, 55 Bryanston St, London W14 7AA, England (☏ **0207/563-3300**).

ATMs

The easiest and best way to get cash away from home is from an ATM (automated teller machine), sometimes referred to as a "cash machine" or a "cashpoint." ATMs are widely available throughout Andalusia; even the smaller towns and villages now have them. In Spain, only four-digit PIN numbers are valid, so U.S. travelers should change any five- or six-digit personal identification numbers to four-digit numbers before departing.

The **Cirrus/Mastercard** (☏ 800/424-7787; www.mastercard.com) and **PLUS/VISA** (☏ 800/843-7587; www.visa.com) networks span the globe; look at the back of your bank card to see which network you're on and then call or check online for ATM locations at your destination. Be sure you know your PIN and daily withdrawal limit before you depart. *Note:* Remember that many banks impose a fee every time you use a card at another bank's ATM, and that fee can be higher for international transactions (up to $5 (£3 or more) than for domestic ones (rarely more than $2.50 (£1.50). In addition, the bank from which you withdraw cash may charge its own fee. For international withdrawal fees, ask your bank.

Credit Cards

Credit cards are another safe way to carry money. They also provide a convenient record of all your expenses, and they generally offer relatively good exchange rates. You can withdraw cash advances from your credit cards at banks or ATMs, provided you know your PIN, but it's usually an expensive way to access cash. Keep in mind that you'll pay interest from the moment of your withdrawal, even if you pay your monthly bills on time, and this can add up significantly over the course of a trip. Beware of hidden credit-card fees while traveling too. Check with your credit or

Easy Money

You'll avoid lines at airport ATMs by exchanging at least some money—just enough to cover airport incidentals and transportation to your hotel—before you leave home.

When you change money, ask for some small bills or loose change. Petty cash comes in handy for tipping and public transportation. Keep change separate from your larger bills, so that it's readily accessible and you'll be less of a target for theft.

debit card issuer to see what fees, if any, will be charged for overseas transactions. Recent reform legislation in the U.S., for example, has curbed some exploitative lending practices. But many banks have responded by increasing fees in other areas, including fees for customers who use credit and debit cards while out of the country—even if those charges were made in U.S. dollars. Fees can amount to 3% or more of the purchase price. Check with your bank before departing to avoid any surprise charges on your statement.

Visa and MasterCard credit cards are widely accepted in Spain; American Express and Diners' Club somewhat less. All establishments in Spain now use the Chip and Pin system with a four-digit PIN code, so visitors from the U.S.A. must have a four-digit PIN for their credit cards before traveling.

You usually have to produce photo ID at the time of purchase too. Visitors from the U.K. not used to carrying photo ID should make sure they do so.

Traveler's Checks

Traveler's checks are accepted in Spain at banks, travel agencies, hotels, and some shops, and you can buy them at most banks before you leave.

They are offered in denominations of $20, $50, $100, $500, and sometimes $1,000. Generally, you'll pay a service charge ranging from 1% to 4%.

The most popular traveler's checks are offered by **American Express** (© **800/807-6233** or © **800/221-7282** for cardholders)—this number accepts collect calls, offers service in several foreign languages, and exempts Amex gold and platinum cardholders from the 1% fee; **Visa** (© **800/732-1322**)—AAA members can obtain Visa checks for up to $1,500 at most AAA offices or by calling © **866/339-3378**; and **MasterCard** (© **800/223-9920**).

American Express, Thomas Cook, Visa, and **MasterCard** offer **foreign currency traveler's checks**—useful if you're traveling to one country, or to the Euro zone; they're accepted at locations where dollar checks may not be.

If you carry traveler's checks, keep a record of their serial numbers separate from your checks in case they are stolen or lost. You'll get a refund faster if you know the numbers.

Frommer's lists exact prices in the local currency. However, rates fluctuate, so before departing consult a currency exchange website such as **www.oanda.com/convert/classic** to check up-to-the-minute rates.

STAYING HEALTHY

Andalusia should not pose any major health hazards. The rich cuisine—garlic, olive oil, and wine—may give some travelers mild diarrhea, so take along some anti-diarrhea medicine, moderate your eating habits, and even though the water is generally safe, drink bottled water only. Only eat cooked fish and shellfish from the Mediterranean.

If you're traveling around southern Spain in summer, limit your exposure to the sun, especially during the first few days of your trip, from 11am to 2pm. Use a sunscreen with a high protection factor and apply it liberally.

GENERAL AVAILABILITY OF HEALTHCARE

No shots of any sort are required before traveling to Spain. Once there, medicines for a wide variety of common ailments, from colds to diarrhea, can be obtained over the counter at local pharmacies or *farmacias.* Generic equivalents of common prescription drugs are also usually available in Spain. (However, it does no harm to bring OTC medicines with you to be on the safe side.)

Contact the **International Association for Medical Assistance to Travellers (IAMAT;** ✆ **716/754-4883** or, in Canada, ✆ 416/652-0137; www.iamat.org) for specific tips on travel and health concerns in Spain and for lists of local, English-speaking doctors. The United States **Centers for Disease Control and Prevention** (✆ **800/311-3435;** www.cdc.gov) provides up-to-date information on health hazards by region or country and offers tips on food safety. The website **www.tripprep.com,** sponsored by a consortium of travel medicine practitioners, may also offer helpful advice on traveling abroad. You can find listings of reliable clinics overseas at the **International Society of Travel Medicine** (www.istm.org).

> ### Healthy Travels to You
>
> The following government websites offer up-to-date health-related travel advice.
> - Australia: www.dfat.gov.au/travel
> - Canada: www.hc-sc.gc.ca/index_e.html
> - U.K.: www.nhs.uk/nhsengland/health-careabroad
> - U.S.: www.cdc.gov/travel

What to Do If You Get Sick Away from Home

Spanish medical facilities are among the best in the world. If a medical emergency arises, your hotel staff can usually put you in touch with a reliable doctor. If not, contact your nearest embassy or consulate; each one maintains a list of English-speaking doctors. Medical and hospital services aren't free, so buy appropriate insurance coverage before you travel. For travel abroad, you may have to pay all medical costs upfront and be reimbursed later.

A number of companies offer medical evacuation services anywhere in the world. If you're ever hospitalized more than 150 miles from home, **MedjetAssist** (✆ **800/527-7478;** www.medjetassistance.com) will pick you up and fly you to the hospital of your choice virtually anywhere in the world in a medically equipped and staffed aircraft 24 hours a day, 7 days a week.

U.K. nationals will need a **European Health Insurance Card (EHIC** *℗* **0845/606-2030;** www.ehic.org.uk) to receive free or reduced-cost health benefits during a visit to Spain. For advice, ask at your local post office or see www. dh.gov.uk/travellers.

We list **hospital** and **emergency numbers** under "Fast Facts" in the individual destination chapters.

If you suffer from a chronic illness, consult your doctor before your departure. Pack **prescription medications** in your carry-on luggage, and carry them in their original containers, with pharmacy labels, or they won't make it through airport security. Carry the generic name of prescription medicines in case a local pharmacist is unfamiliar with the brand name.

CRIME & SAFETY

Although most of the estimated one million American and three million British tourists have trouble-free visits to Andalusia each year, the principal tourist areas, Seville and Málaga, in particular, have reported occasional incidents of muggings and attacks, and older tourists and Asian Americans seem to be particularly at risk. Criminals frequent tourist areas and major attractions such as museums, monuments, restaurants, hotels, beach resorts, trains, train stations, airports, subways, and ATMs. Travelers should exercise caution, carry limited cash and credit cards, and leave extra cash, credit cards, passports, and personal documents in a safe location.

Theft from parked cars is also common. So do not leave valuables in parked cars and keep doors locked, windows rolled up, and valuables out of sight when driving. Drivers should be cautious about accepting help from anyone other than a uniformed Spanish police officer or Civil Guard.

To date there is nothing to suggest that Islamic terrorism constitutes a more serious threat in any Spanish city than in any other major world city.

If you lose your passport abroad, report it immediately to the local police and your nearest embassy or consulate.

U.S. citizens may refer to the Department of State's pamphlet, *A Safe Trip Abroad,* for ways to promote a more trouble-free journey. The pamphlet is available by mail from the Superintendent of Documents, U.S. Government Printing Office, 732 North Capitol St NW, Washington, DC 20402; via the Internet at www.gpoaccess. gov/index.html; or via the Bureau of Consular Affairs, home page at http://travel. state.gov.

British citizens can refer to the UK foreign office website for the latest travel advice: www.fco.gov.uk/travel.

SPECIALIZED TRAVEL RESOURCES

Travelers with Disabilities

Most disabilities shouldn't stop anyone from traveling. There are more options and resources out there than ever before.

Because of the endless flights of stairs in most buildings in cities in southern Spain, visitors with disabilities may have difficulty getting around, but conditions are slowly improving. Newer hotels are more sensitive to the needs of people with disabilities, and more expensive restaurants are generally wheelchair-accessible. However, since most places have very limited, if any, facilities for people with disabilities, you might consider taking an organized tour specifically designed to accommodate such travelers.

For names and addresses of these tour operators and other related information, contact the **Society for Accessible Travel and Hospitality (SATH),** 347 Fifth Ave., New York, NY 10016 (© 212/447-7284; www.sath.org). Annual membership dues are $50 for seniors and students. **AirAmbulanceCard.com** is now partnered with SATH and allows you to preselect top-notch hospitals in case of an emergency. Another organization that offers assistance to travelers with disabilities is **Moss Rehab** (www.mossresourcenet.org).

For the blind or visually impaired, the best source is the **American Foundation for the Blind (AFB),** 15 W. 16th St, New York, NY 10011 (© 800/232-5463; www.afb.org). It offers information on travel and various requirements for the transport and border formalities for Seeing Eye dogs. It also issues identification cards to those who are legally blind.

Many travel agencies offer customized tours and itineraries for travelers with disabilities. One of the best organizations serving the needs of people with disabilities (wheelchairs and walkers) is **Flying Wheels Travel,** 143 W. Bridge, P.O. Box 382, Owatonna, MN 55060 (© 800/535-6790 or © 507/451-5005; www.flyingwheels travel.com), which offers various escorted tours and cruises internationally. Others include **Access-Able Travel Source** (© 303/232-2979; www.access-able.com) and **Accessible Journeys** (© 800/846-4537 or © 610/521-0339; www.disability travel.com).

If you're flying around Spain, the airline and ground staff will help you on and off planes and reserve seats for you with sufficient legroom, but you must contact your airline *in advance* to make these arrangements.

Avis Rent a Car has an "Avis Access" program offering such services as a dedicated 24-hour toll-free number (© 888/879-4273) for customers with special travel needs; special car features such as swivel seats, spinner knobs, and hand controls; and an accessible bus service.

Check out the quarterly magazine *Emerging Horizons* (www.emerginghorizons. com), and *Open World* magazine, published by SATH.

FOR BRITISH TRAVELERS WITH DISABILITIES The annual vacation guide *Holidays and Travel Abroad* costs £5 from the **Royal Association for Disability and Rehabilitation (RADAR),** Unit 12, City Forum, 250 City Rd, London EC1V 8AF (© 020/7250-3222; www.radar.org.uk). RADAR provides information packs on such subjects as sports and outdoor vacations, insurance, financial arrangements for people with disabilities, and accommodation in nursing care units for groups or for the elderly. Each of these fact sheets is available for £2. Both the fact sheets and the holiday guides can be mailed outside the United Kingdom for a nominal postage fee.

Another good service is **Holiday Care,** 2nd Floor Imperial Buildings, Victoria Road, Horley, Surrey RH6 7PZ (© 01293/774-535; www.holidaycare.org.uk), a national charity that advises on accessible accommodations for elderly people or those with disabilities. Annual membership costs £25 (U.K. residents) and £40 (abroad). Once you're a member, you receive a newsletter and access to a free reservations network for hotels throughout Britain and, to a lesser degree, Europe and the rest of the world.

For more on organizations that offer resources to travelers with disabilities, go to www.frommers.com/planning.

Gay & Lesbian Travelers

In 1978, Spain legalized homosexuality among consenting adults. In April 1995, the parliament of Spain banned discrimination based on sexual orientation, and marriage between same-sex couples became legal in 2005. In Andalusia the most popular resort for gay and lesbian travelers is Torremolinos, although there are gay bars in all the larger cities such as Seville and Granada. Only problem is, they come and go.

To learn about gay and lesbian travel in Spain, get relevant publications or join data-dispensing organizations before you go. Both lesbians and gay men might want to pick up a copy of *Gay Travel A to Z*, which provides general information as well as listings for bars, hotels, restaurants, and places of interest for gay travelers throughout the world.

The **International Gay & Lesbian Travel Association (IGLTA),** 4331 N. Federal, Suite 304, Ft. Lauderdale, FL 33308 (© **800/448-8550** or © 954/776-2626; www.iglta.com), specializes in connecting travelers with the appropriate gay-friendly service organization or tour specialist. It offers a quarterly newsletter, marketing mailings, and a membership directory updated four times a year. For an online directory of gay- and lesbian-friendly travel businesses, go to their website and click on "Members."

Many agencies offer tours and travel itineraries specifically for gay and lesbian travelers. Among them are **Above and Beyond Tours** (© **800/397-2681;** www. abovebeyondtours.com); **Now, Voyager** (© **800/255-6951;** www.nowvoyager. com); and **Olivia** (© **800/631-6277;** www.olivia.com).

Gay.com Travel (© **800/929-2268** or © 415/644-8044; www.gay.com/travel or www.outandabout.com) provides regularly updated information about gay-owned, gay-oriented, and gay-friendly lodging, dining, sightseeing, nightlife, and shopping establishments in every important destination worldwide.

The following travel guides are available at many bookstores, or order them from any online bookseller: *Spartacus International Gay Guide* (Bruno Gmünder Verlag; www.spartacusworld.com/gayguide); *Odysseus: The International Gay Travel Planner* (Odysseus Enterprises Ltd.); and the *Damron* guides (www. damron.com), with separate, annual books for gay men and lesbians.

For more gay and lesbian travel resources, visit www.frommers.com/planning.

Senior Travel

Many discounts are available for seniors traveling to Andalusia, but often you need to be a member of an association to obtain them.

For information before you go, write for the free booklet, *101 Tips for the Mature Traveler,* available from **Grand Circle Travel,** 347 Congress St, Suite 3A, Boston, MA 02210 (© **800/221-2610** or © 617/350-7500; www.gct.com).

One of the most dynamic travel organizations for seniors is **Elderhostel,** 11 Avenue de Lafayette, Boston, MA 02111 (© **877/426-8056;** www.elderhostel. org). Established in 1975, it operates an array of programs throughout Europe, including Spain. Most programs last around 3 weeks and are good value, since they include airfare, accommodations in student dormitories or modest inns, all meals, and tuition. Courses involve no homework, are not graded, and are often liberal arts oriented. These are not luxury vacations, but they are fun and fulfilling. Participants must be at least 55 years old. A companion must be at least 50 years old; spouses may participate regardless of age. **ElderTreks** (© **800/741-7956;** www.eldertreks. com) offers small-group tours to off-the-beaten-path or adventure-travel locations, restricted again to travelers 50 and older.

In the United States, the best organization to join is the **AARP,** 601 E St NW, Washington, DC 20049 (© **800/424-3410** or © 202/434-AARP [2277]; www. aarp.org). Members get discounts on hotels, airfares, and car rentals. AARP offers members a wide range of benefits, including *AARP: The Magazine* and a monthly newsletter. All over 50 can join.

Recommended publications offering travel resources and discounts for seniors include the quarterly magazine *Travel 50 & Beyond* (www.travel50andbeyond. com); *Travel Unlimited: Uncommon Adventures for the Mature Traveler* (Avalon); *101 Tips for Mature Travelers,* available from Grand Circle Travel (© **800/221-2610** or © 617/350-7500; www.gct.com); and *Unbelievably Good Deals and Great Adventures That You Absolutely Can't Get Unless You're Over 50* (McGraw-Hill) by Joan Rattner Heilman.

For more information and resources on travel for seniors, see www.frommers.com/planning.

Family Travel

Southern Spain is a family-centered culture and children are most welcome in restaurants, shops, and hotels. Car hire agencies can supply car seats for children at additional cost.

To locate hotels, restaurants, and attractions that are particularly kid-friendly, refer to the "Kids" icon throughout this guide.

For more specific information about family travel to this part of the world, get hold of a copy of Frommer's *Mediterranean Spain with Your Family* which can be purchased via www.amazon.com.

Note that children traveling to Spain with companions other than their own parents should have a notarized letter from their parents to this effect. For full entry requirements to Spain, check www.travel.state.gov.

For a list of more family-friendly travel resources, visit www.frommers.com/planning.

Women Travelers

In the cities of southern Spain, women are as emancipated as in any other main European city. If a degree of machismo still exists it is minimal today, and women are increasingly reaching high positions in all walks of life. Women who explore Andalusia on their own should not expect any hassle.

For general advice to female travelers, check out the award-winning website **Journeywoman** (www.journeywoman.com), a women's travel-information network

FROMMERS.COM: THE complete TRAVEL RESOURCE

It should go without saying, but we highly recommend **Frommers.com,** voted Best Travel Site by *PC Magazine.* We think you'll find our expert advice and tips; independent reviews of hotels, restaurants, attractions, and preferred shopping and nightlife venues; vacation giveaways; and an online booking tool indispensable before, during, and after your travels. We publish the complete contents of over 128 travel guides in our **Destinations** section covering nearly 3,600 places worldwide to help you plan your trip. Each weekday, we publish original articles reporting on **Deals and News** via our free **Frommers.com Newsletter**

to help you save time and money and travel smarter. We're betting you'll find our new **Events** listings (http://events. frommers.com) an invaluable resource; it's an up-to-the-minute roster of what's happening in cities everywhere—including concerts, festivals, lectures, and more. We've also added weekly **podcasts, interactive maps,** and hundreds of new images across the site. Check out our **Travel Talk** area featuring **Message Boards** where you can join in conversations with thousands of fellow Frommer's travelers and post your trip report once you return.

where you can sign up for a free e-mail newsletter and get advice on everything from etiquette and dress to safety; or the travel guide *Safety and Security for Women Who Travel* by Sheila Swan and Peter Laufer (Travelers' Tales, Inc.), offering common-sense tips on safe travel.

For general travel resources for women, go to www.frommers.com/planning.

Student Travel

Check out the **International Student Travel Confederation** (**ISTC;** www.istc. org) website for comprehensive travel services information and details on how to get an **International Student Identity Card** (**ISIC),** which qualifies students for substantial savings on rail passes, plane tickets, entrance fees, and more. It also provides students with basic health and life insurance and a 24-hour help line. The card is valid for a maximum of 18 months. You can apply for the card online or in person at **STA Travel** (**©** **800/781-4040** in North America; **©** **132-782** in Australia; **©** **087/1230-0040** in the U.K.; www.statravel.com), which is the biggest student travel agency in the world; check out the website to locate STA Travel offices worldwide. If you're no longer a student but are still under 26, you can get an **International Youth Travel Card** (**IYTC)** from the same people, which entitles you to some discounts. **Travel CUTS** (**©** **800/592-2887;** www.travelcuts.com) offers similar services for both Canadians and U.S. residents. Irish students may prefer to turn to **USIT** (**©** **01/602-1904;** www.usit.ie), an Ireland-based specialist in student, youth, and independent travel.

Single Travelers

On package vacations, single travelers are often hit with a "single supplement" to the base price. To avoid it, you can agree to room with other single travelers or find a compatible roommate before you go, from one of the many roommate-locator agencies.

For more information on traveling single, go to www.frommers.com/planning.

For Vegetarian Visitors

Finding vegetarian food in restaurants in southern Spain remains problematic. If you're munching tapas you'll probably do just fine, although it makes sense to have a phrase book handy and memorize dishes that you know are meat-free. Bigger cities like Málaga, Seville, and Granada now have vegetarian restaurants and, where available, these are included in the relevant chapters of this guide.

RESPONSIBLE TOURISM

If you're arriving from elsewhere in Europe, the best way to be a responsible tourist when visiting southern Spain is to consider catching the **train** rather than flying. High-speed trains now criss-cross much of the continent, making travel by rail a serious alternative to flying. See "Getting There & Around" above.

If you're a golfer, check out the credentials of the courses before you play. With more **golf courses** per square mile than pretty much anywhere else in Europe, the Costa del Sol has long been vulnerable to the accusation of wasting vast amounts of water keeping greens watered, in a region which suffers considerable problems with droughts and water shortages. Does your chosen course use recycled waste water to keep the greens watered is the number one question to ask. More modern resorts are taking these issues seriously and also using solar power to generate much of their electricity needs as well.

For getting around Seville, you can leave the car in the garage and hop aboard one of the *Sevici* **city-bikes**. The urban cycle scheme here has been a big success and it's now available for visitors. See p. 80. There are plans to introduce similar schemes in Córdoba and Granada too.

SPECIAL INTEREST & ESCORTED TRIPS

Special Interest Trips

Andalusia is one of the best destinations in Europe for enjoying the outdoors. Lounging on the beach tops the list of activities for most travelers, but there's a lot more to do. The province's mountains lure thousands of mountaineers and hikers, and fishing and hunting are long-standing Iberian obsessions. Watersports ranging from sailing to kitesurfing are prime summer attractions.

Art Tours

Custom tours of Spain that focus on art and architecture can be arranged, especially by **Heritage Tours** (© **212/206-8400** in New York or © **800/378-4555** outside New York; www.htprivatetravel.com). Founded by an architect, Joel Zack, these tours can be designed to order, and often include guided trips through such art cities as Granada. Without airfares, trips begin at around $4,000 for a 10-day jaunt.

Featuring groups ranging in size from 15 to 25 participants, **ACE Study Tours** (© **01223/835055;** www.acestudytours.co.uk) in Cambridge, England, offers

GENERAL RESOURCES FOR green TRAVEL

In addition to the resources for Andalusia listed above, the following websites provide valuable wide-ranging information on sustainable travel.

o **Responsible Travel** (www.responsibletravel.com) is a great source of sustainable travel ideas; the site is run by a spokesperson for ethical tourism in the travel industry. **Sustainable Travel International** (www.sustainabletravelinternational.org) promotes ethical tourism practices, and manages an extensive directory of sustainable properties and tour operators around the world.

o In the U.K., **Tourism Concern** (www.tourismconcern.org.uk) works to reduce social and environmental problems connected to tourism. The **Association of Independent Tour Operators (AITO)** (www.aito.co.uk) is a group of specialist operators leading the field in making holidays sustainable.

o In Canada, **www.greenlivingonline.com** offers extensive content on how to travel sustainably, including a travel and transport section and profiles of the best green shops and services in Toronto, Vancouver, and Calgary.

o In Australia, the national body which sets guidelines and standards for ecotourism is **Ecotourism Australia** (www.ecotourism.org.au). **The Green Directory** (www.thegreendirectory.com.au), **Green Pages** (www.thegreenpages.com.au), and **Eco Directory** (www.ecodirectory.com.au) offer sustainable travel tips and directories of green businesses.

o **Carbonfund** (www.carbonfund.org), **TerraPass** (www.terrapass.org), and **Cool Climate** (http://coolclimate.berkeley.edu) provide info on "carbon offsetting," or offsetting the greenhouse gas emitted during flights.

o **Greenhotels** (www.greenhotels.com) recommends green-rated member hotels around the world that fulfill the company's stringent environmental requirements. **Environmentally Friendly Hotels** (www.environmentallyfriendlyhotels.com) offers more green accommodation ratings. The **Hotel Association of Canada** (www.hacgreenhotels.com) has a Green Key Eco-Rating Program, which audits the environmental performance of Canadian hotels, motels, and resorts.

o **Sustain Lane** (www.sustainlane.com) lists sustainable eating and drinking choices around the U.S.; also visit **www.eatwellguide.org** for tips on eating sustainably in the U.S. and Canada.

o For information on animal-friendly issues throughout the world, visit **Tread Lightly** (www.treadlightly.org). For information about the ethics of swimming with dolphins, visit the **Whale and Dolphin Conservation Society** (www.wdcs.org).

o **Volunteer International** (www.volunteerinternational.org) has a list of questions to help you determine the intentions and the nature of a volunteer program. For general info on volunteer travel, visit **www.volunteerabroad.org** and **www.idealist.org**.

tours led by an art historian to such highlights of Andalusia as Córdoba, Seville, and Granada. Eight-day trips start at £2,090 and include double occupancy in a hotel, round-trip airfare from London, breakfast and dinner daily.

Biking

The leading U.S.-based outfitter is **Easy Rider Tours,** P.O. Box 228, Newburyport, MA 01950 (© **800/488-8332** or © 978/463-6955; www.easyridertours.com). Their tours average between 48 and 81km (30–50 miles) a day.

In England, the **Cyclists' Touring Club,** Parklands, Railton Road, Guildford, Surrey GU2 9JX (© **0870/873-0060;** www.ctc.org.uk), charges £36 a year for membership; part of the fee covers information and suggested cycling routes through Spain and dozens of other countries.

U.K. operator **Inntravel** (© **01653 61-70-01;** www.intravel.co.uk) has a 6-night self-guided cycle tour around the White Villages of Andalusia from £686 per person with cycle, all gear, accommodations, maps, and most meals.

Birding

The Iberian Peninsula lies directly across migration routes of species that travel with the seasons between Africa and Europe. Some of the most comprehensive studies on these migratory patterns are conducted by Spain's **Centro de Migración de Aves,** SEO/BirdLife, Calle Melquiades Biencinto 34, 28053 Madrid (© **91-434-09-10;** www.seo.org). Based at a rustic outpost near Gibraltar, their summer work camps and field projects appeal to those who want to identify, catalog, and "ring" (mark with an identifying leg band) some of the millions of birds that nest in Spain every year. Participants are expected to pay for their "tuition," room, and board, but can often use the experience toward university credits.

Golf

In recent decades, thousands of British retirees have settled in Spain, and their presence has sparked the development of dozens of new golf courses. More than a third of the country's approximately 160 courses lie within its southern tier, within a short drive of the Costa del Sol. In fact, one of Spain's most talked-about golf courses, **Valderrama,** 11310 Sotogrande, Cádiz (© **95-679-12-00;** www.valderrama.com), is on the western tip of the Costa del Sol, a Robert Trent Jones, Sr-designed course carved out of an oak plantation in the 1980s.

Packages that include guaranteed playing time on some of the country's finest courses, as well as airfare and accommodations, can be arranged through such firms as **Golf International** (© **800/833-1389** or © 212/986-9176 in the U.S.; www.golfinternational.com), and **Comtours** (© **800/248-1331** in the U.S.; www.comtours.com).

Hiking & Walking

To venture into the more rugged countryside of Andalusia, contact **Ramblers Holidays,** Lemsford Mill, Welwyn Garden AL8 7TR, U.K. (© **01707/331-133;** www.ramblersholidays.co.uk). Walking tours include the Sierra de Grazalema and Coto de Doñana Natural Parks.

Horseback Riding

A well-known equestrian center that conducts tours of the Alpujarras highlands is **Cabalgar,** Rutas Alternativas, Bubión, Granada (✆ **95-876-31-35;** www.riding andalucia.com). The farm is best known for its weekend treks through the scrub-covered hills of southern and central Spain, although longer tours are available.

Surfing

The Costa de la Luz has some of the best swells and winds in Europe and is a Mecca for surfers, kitesurfers, and windsurfers who come for the unspoilt beaches as well as the wind and waves. **Tailormade Andalucia** (✆ **95-644-39-22;** www.tailor madeandalucia.com) is run by English surf fanatic Sam Lister and can organize surfing, windsurfing, and kitesurfing lessons and excursions for surf-dudes of all abilities.

Escorted General Interest Tours

Escorted tours are structured and have a group leader. The price usually includes everything from airfare to hotels, meals, tours, admission costs, and local transportation.

There are many escorted tour companies, each offering transportation to and within Spain, prearranged hotels, and such extras as bilingual tour guides and lectures. Many of these include excursions to Morocco or Portugal.

Abercrombie & Kent International (✆ **800/554-7016;** www.abercrombie kent. com) runs some of the most expensive and luxurious tours, like deluxe 9- to 12-day tours of the Iberian Peninsula by train. You stay in top hotels ranging from a late medieval palace to Seville's exquisite Alfonso XIII.

American Express Vacations (✆ **800/297-2977;** www.americanexpress.com) is one of the biggest tour operators in the world. Its escorted tour offerings are comprehensive. Unescorted customized package tours are offered as well. **Trafalgar Tours** (✆ **800/854-0103;** www.trafalgartours.com) is cheaper. One of the most popular tours to Spain is a 16-day trip called "the Best of Spain." This land-only package costs $2,499.

Alternative Travel Group Ltd. (✆ **01865/315-678;** www.atg-oxford.co.uk) is a British firm that organizes walking and cycling vacations, plus wine tours in Spain, Italy, and France. Tours explore the scenic countryside and medieval towns of each country.

Petrabax Tours (✆ **800/634-1188;** www.petrabax.com) attracts those who prefer to see Spain by bus, although fly/drive packages are also offered, featuring stays in *paradores* (inns). A number of city packages are available as well, plus an 8-day trip that tries to capture the essence of Spain, with stops ranging from Madrid to Granada.

Isramworld (✆ **800/223-7460;** www.isram.com) sells both escorted and package tours to Spain. It can book you on bus tours as well as land and air packages. Its grandest offering is "Spanish Splendor," with a private driver and guides. Naturally, only Spain's best hotels are used by this upmarket firm.

Different Spain (✆ **95-598-56-05;** www.differentspain.com) is a Seville-based bespoke concierge and private travel service and it's about as well connected as you can get. It's run by experienced and friendly Andalusia expert Eduardo

ASK before YOU GO

Before you invest in a package deal or an escorted tour:

o Always ask about the **cancellation policy.** Can you get your money back? Is a deposit required?

o Ask about the **accommodations choices and prices** for each. Then look up the hotels' reviews in a Frommer's guide and check their rates online for your specific dates of travel. Also find out what types of rooms are offered.

o For escorted tours only, request a complete **schedule;** ask about the **size** and demographics of the group; and discuss what is included in the **price** (transportation, meals, tips, airport transfers, and such).

o Finally, look for **hidden expenses.** Ask whether airport departure fees and taxes, for example, are included in the total cost—they rarely are.

Blanco. If you're looking for a luxury tour tailored to your individual requirements featuring the very best in accommodation, dining, and cultural experiences in the region, he comes highly recommended.

STAYING CONNECTED

Telephones

To call Spain:

1 Dial the international access code: © **011** from the U.S.; © **00** from the U.K., Ireland, or New Zealand; or © **0011** from Australia.

2 Dial the country code **34.**

3 Dial the nine-digit local number. All telephone numbers in Spain have nine digits.

To make international calls: To make international calls from Spain, first dial © **00** and then the country code (U.S. or Canada © **1,** U.K. © **44,** Ireland © **353,** Australia © **61,** New Zealand © **64**). Next dial the area code and number. So if you want to call the British Embassy in Washington, D.C., dial © **00-1-202-588-7800.**

For directory assistance: Dial © **1003** in Spain.

For operator assistance: If you need operator assistance in making an international call, dial © **025.**

Toll-free numbers: Numbers beginning with © **900** in Spain are toll-free, but calling an © **800** number in the States from Spain is not toll-free. In fact, it costs the same as an overseas call.

The best value way to call home is to use a telephone card purchased from a newsstand or tobacconist. Most offer a toll-free number to dial, followed by a pin number and then the number you're calling. Central post offices in major cities usually have calling booths for making low-cost international calls. Visitors from the U.S.A. and Canada can also dial collect of charge calls to credit cards from newer telephone booths. Using coins at a telephone booth or calling from a hotel room will always be most expensive.

More information is available on the Telefónica website at www.telefonica.es.

When in Spain, the access number for an **AT&T** calling card is ℂ **800/CALL-ATT** (225-5288). The access number for **Sprint** is ℂ **800/888-0013.**

Cellphones/Mobiles

The three letters defining much of the world's **wireless capabilities** are GSM (Global System for Mobiles), a seamless network that makes for easy cross-border cellphone use throughout Europe and dozens of other countries worldwide.

If your cellphone is on a GSM system, and you have a world-capable multiband phone, you can make and receive calls in Spain. Just call your wireless operator and ask for "international roaming" to be activated on your account. Unfortunately, per-minute charges can be high—usually $1 to $1.50 in Western Europe for US customers.

Recent EU legislation restricting the amount that European operators can charge for roaming in Europe means that for visitors from the UK, these costs are now substantially lower. Typical costs are 38 pence per minute to make calls, 15 pence per minute to receive them and 10 pence per SMS message sent.

Data charges for surfing the web on iPhones and other smartphone devices remain however exorbitant, so check with your operator about these costs before leaving.

Many cellphone operators sell "locked" phones that restrict you from using any other removable computer memory phone chip card (called a **SIM card**) other than the ones they supply. Having an "unlocked" phone allows you to install a cheaper local SIM card (found at a local retailer) in your destination country. (Show your phone to the salesperson; not all phones work on all networks.) You'll get a local phone number—and much, much lower calling rates. Getting an already locked phone unlocked can be a complicated process, but it can be done; just call your cellular operator and say you'll be going abroad for several months and want to use the phone with a local provider.

Renting a phone is one option, but expensive. While you can rent a phone from overseas sites, like kiosks at airports and car-rental agencies, I suggest renting the phone before you leave home. Phone rental isn't cheap; it's usually $40 to $60 per week, plus airtime fees of at least $1 a minute. North Americans can rent from **InTouch USA** (ℂ **800/872-7626;** www.intouchglobal.com) or **Roadpost** (ℂ **888/290-1606** or ℂ 905/272-5665; www.roadpost.com). Give them your itinerary, and they'll tell you what wireless products you need. InTouch will advise you, for free, on whether your existing phone will work overseas.

North Americans can rent from **InTouch USA** (ℂ **800/872-7626;** www.intouchglobal.com) or **Roadpost** (ℂ **888/290-1606** or ℂ 905/272-5665; www.roadpost.com). Give them your itinerary, and they'll tell you what wireless products you need. InTouch will advise you, for free, on whether your existing phone will work overseas.

Buying a phone can be economically attractive, as many nations have cheap, no-questions-asked, prepaid phone systems available from El Corte Inglés and FNAC stores everywhere. They start around 50€, but include about a 20€ credit for

Staying Connected | **PLANNING YOUR TRIP TO ANDALUSIA**

calls. Local calls may be as low as 10¢ per minute, and in many countries incoming calls are free. Note that in Spain you must show your passport when you buy a phone and/or phone card.

Voice-over Internet Protocol (VoIP)

If you have Web access while traveling, consider a broadband-based telephone service (in technical terms, **Voice-over Internet protocol,** or **VoIP**) such as Skype (www.skype.com) or Vonage (www.vonage.com), which lets you make free international calls from your laptop or in a cybercafe. Neither service requires the people you're calling to also have that service (though there are fees if they do not). Check the websites for details.

Internet & E-mail
WITH YOUR OWN COMPUTER

More and more hotels, cafes, and retailers offer Wi-Fi "hotspots." Typically you'll pay a fixed fee for a 24-hour period in most hotels, but increasingly access is free. Ask at local tourist offices for locations of city Wi-Fi hotspots.

Wherever you go, make sure to bring the right power and phone adapters, and a spare Ethernet network cable if you don't have Wi-Fi or ask if your hotel supplies them to guests.

In Spain the electricity connection is 220 volts. A two-prong plug is needed.

WITHOUT YOUR OWN COMPUTER

It's hard nowadays to find a city that *doesn't* have a few cybercafes, and major cities in southern Spain are no exception. To find Internet cafes, check **www.cyber captive.com** and **www.cybercafe.com**.

Aside from these formal cybercafes, most **youth hostels** have at least one computer for Internet access. Most **public libraries** across the world also offer Internet access free or for a small charge. Avoid **hotel business centers** unless you're willing to pay exorbitant rates.

Most major airports now have **Internet kiosks** scattered throughout their gates. These kiosks give you basic Web access for a per-minute fee that's usually higher than cybercafe prices. The kiosks' clunkiness and high price mean they're only good for emergencies.

TIPS ON ACCOMMODATIONS

From castles converted into hotels to modern high-rise resorts overlooking the Mediterranean, Spain has some of the most varied hotel accommodations in the world—with equally varied price ranges.

ONE- TO FIVE-STAR HOTELS The Spanish government rates hotels by according them stars. A five-star hotel is truly deluxe, with deluxe prices; a one-star hotel is the most modest accommodation officially recognized as a hotel by the government. A four-star hotel offers first-class accommodation; a three-star hotel is moderately priced; and a one- or two-star hotel is inexpensively priced. The government grants stars based on such amenities as elevators, private bathrooms, and air-conditioning. A hotel classified as a *residencia* serves breakfast (usually) but no other meals.

HOSTALES Not to be confused with a hostel for students, an *hostal* is a modest hotel without services, where you can save money by carrying your own bags and the like. You'll know it's an *hostal* if a small s follows the capital letter H on the blue plaque by the door. *Hostales* with three stars are about the equivalent of hotels with two stars.

PENSIONS These boardinghouses are among the least expensive option, but you must take either full board (three meals) or half board, which is breakfast plus lunch or dinner.

CASAS HUESPEDES & FONDAS These are the cheapest places in Spain and can be recognized by the light-blue plaques at the door displaying CH and F, respectively. They are invariably basic but respectable establishments.

PARADORES The Spanish government runs a series of unique state-owned inns called *paradores,* which now blanket the country. Deserted castles, monasteries, palaces, and other buildings have been converted into hotels. Today there are 86 *paradores* in all, documented in a booklet called *Visiting the Paradores,* available at Spanish tourist offices. (See "Visitor Information," p. 78.)

These establishments are often furnished with antiques or at least good reproductions and decorative objects typical of the country. Meals are also served in these government-owned inns. Usually, typical dishes of the region are featured. *Paradores* are likely to be overcrowded in the summer months, so advance reservations, arranged through any travel agent, are wise.

The central office for *paradores* is **Paradores de España,** Requeña 3, 28013 Madrid (© **90-254-79-79;** www.parador.es). The U.S. representative is **Marketing Ahead,** 381 Park Ave. S., New York, NY 10016 (© **800/223-1356** or © 212/686-9213; www.marketingahead.com).

Renting a House or Apartment

Rent a home or an apartment and you can save money on accommodation and dining and still take daily trips to see the surrounding area.

Apartments in Spain generally fall into two categories: hotel *apartamentos* and *residencia apartamentos.* Hotel apartments have full facilities, with chamber service, equipped kitchenettes, and often restaurants and bars. The cheaper *residencia* apartments, also called *apartamentos turísticos,* are fully furnished with kitchenettes but lack the facilities of the hotel complexes.

International apartment rental company **Home-Away** (www.homeaway.com in the U.S.A., www.homeaway.co.uk in the U.K.) has over 4,000 privately owned properties available for rent in Andalusia, from cheap city center apartments to large luxury villas with private swimming pools.

Locally based apartment rental companies include, in Seville: **Sevilla5** (© **95-438-75-50;** www.sevilla5.com) and **Apartments Sevilla** (© **95-421-69-12;** www.apartmentssevilla.com), and in Granada: **Granadainfo** (www.granadainfo.com).

SUGGESTED ITINERARIES IN ANDALUSIA

There's a great deal to see in Andalusia, so it pays to think carefully about getting the balance right between visiting museums and monuments and just relaxing and enjoying the unique atmosphere and traditions of this wonderful part of the world. It is possible to see the big highlights in one week and I've provided this as the first suggested itinerary. If you've time though, a 10-day visit will offer a far more memorable trip, particularly if you're visiting from the U.S. and dealing with jetlag into the bargain.

Further tours described in this chapter include one that's geared for families; another that's designed for those who want to uncover the less-visited mountainous part of central Andalusia, and another that's all about the most popular stretch of coastline, the Costa del Sol (the Sunshine Coast).

THE REGIONS IN BRIEF

In A.D. 711 Muslim armies swept into Iberia from strongholds in what is now Morocco. Since then, Spain's southernmost district has been enmeshed in the mores, art, and architecture of the Muslim world.

During the 900s, Andalusia blossomed into a sophisticated society—advanced in philosophy, mathematics, and trading—that far outstripped a feudal Europe still trapped in the Dark Ages. Moorish domination ended completely in 1492, when Granada was captured by the armies of Isabella and Ferdinand, but even today the region offers echoes of this Muslim occupation. Andalusia is a dry district that isn't highly prosperous and depends heavily on tourism.

The major cities of Andalusia deserve at least a week, with overnights in **Seville** (hometown of Carmen, Don Giovanni, and the barber); **Córdoba,** site of the Mezquita, one of history's most remarkable religious edifices; and **Jerez de la Frontera,** the most important town in the Sherry Triangle where the world-famous fortified wine is produced.

Perhaps most interesting of all is **Granada,** a town of such impressive artistry that it inspired many of the works by the 20th-century romantic poet Federico García Lorca.

CADIZ & THE COSTA DE LA LUZ   Dotted with churches and monuments, the old port city of Cádiz lies on a limestone rock emerging from the sea at the end of a 9km-long (6-mile) promontory projecting into the Atlantic. This historic core of old Cádiz is linked to Andalusia by a bridge. Walls rising to a height of 15m (50 ft) protect the center from the turbulent waves of the ocean.

Some claim that Cádiz is Europe's oldest city, citing Hercules as its founder. Actually the Phoenicians founded it back in 1100 B.C. Wealth from the Spanish conquistadores arrived here, eventually attracting unwanted attention from Sir Francis Drake, who raided the port in 1587. This was the first of many such attacks from the British fleets. In 1812 Spain's first constitution was declared here.

A day is sufficient to explore the sights in Cádiz, a workaday port whose attractions do not equal those of Granada or Seville. If you have extra time, you can retreat to the city's beaches or those along the **Costa de la Luz,** which extends both east and west of Cádiz. The coast is dotted with unspoilt beaches and fishing villages, many of which make great bases for an away-from-it-all break. In particular, **Tarifa,** the windsurfing capital of Europe, is a bit of an undiscovered gem. On a clear day you can see across the water to Tangier, Morocco from here.

CÓRDOBA   This ancient city, founded by the Carthaginians and later the Roman Baetica, reached its zenith in the 10th century as the capital of the great Caliphate. It was also the greatest spiritual and scientific center of the Western world, with some 300 mosques and one of the world's greatest universities. Whilst those glory days are gone, Córdoba's architecture and atmosphere still make it one of the most appealing cities in Europe.

Today, with a population of some 310,000, Córdoba is visited mainly because of its celebrated cathedral-mosque, La Mezquita. It hasn't been used as a mosque since King Ferdinand and his armies attacked in 1236. After Córdoba fell, the mosque was reconsecrated as a Christian church. As amazing as it sounds, a cathedral was then constructed in 1523 right within the walls of the original mosque and it still stands today—a uniquely strange combination of architectural styles.

You can spend a good couple of days in Córdoba, wandering its old quarter and exploring the *alcázar* (fortress) constructed by Christian kings in 1327.

COSTA DEL SOL   The **Costa del Sol,** Spain's sunshine coast, sprawls across the southernmost edge of Spain between Algeciras to the west—across from the rocky heights of British-controlled Gibraltar—and the rather dull Almería to the east. Think traffic jams, suntan oil, sun-bleached high-rises, and nearly naked flesh. The beaches here are some of the most popular in Europe, but this means they are often overly crowded.

Once known for its scented orange groves and rolling fields of silvery olive trees, much of today's Costa del Sol is an overdeveloped urban sprawl of housing developments, hotels, resorts, tourist complexes, and amusement centers, along with such better attractions as beaches and golf courses.

The tawdry, carnival-like atmosphere of the coast is a turnoff to many visitors who prefer to spend their time exploring the more artistic cities of Andalusia, especially Seville, Córdoba, and Granada.

Unless you travel by car or rail from Madrid, chances are you'll arrive by plane via **Málaga,** the district's most historic city and the capital of the Costa del Sol. Hans Christian Andersen praised it, and Pablo Picasso was born here. Much more staid than Torremolinos, it is more of a workaday city than a sprawling resort and possesses a good handful of interesting monuments including a fortress, cathedral, and bullring, along with the world-class Picasso museum. Málaga also enjoys the best transportation links along the entire coast, both from the air and by rail and bus from other Andalusian cities as well as Madrid and Barcelona.

If you're seeking pockets of posh beach resorts that are still some of the greatest in Spain, anchor at **Marbella,** which in the 1960s was one of the chicest in all Europe. Frank Sinatra, Sophia Loren, and the Duke and Duchess of Windsor were once regulars. Today's star seekers might spot Antonio Banderas.

One modern development that has managed to remain distinctive and upmarket is **Puerto Banús,** a neo-Moorish village that curves around a sheltered marina where the wintering rich dock their yachts.

If **Torremolinos** was ever chic, it was early in the 1960s when two lovers, James Kirkwood (*A Chorus Line*) and James Leo Herlihy (*Midnight Cowboy*), lived here in a romantic little villa. Today the beautiful people are long gone, and Torremolinos gets the low-budget tourists from Britain and other parts of northern Europe. Although some visitors like this urban sprawl of mediocre beaches, "lager life," after-dark diversions, and package tours galore, you should spend time here only if you want to be caught up in the human circus that descends during the summer months. And if you're set on visiting, do so in June before the hordes arrive and it all gets way too busy.

GIBRALTAR   Thrust up from the sea some 200 million years ago, Gibraltar is a tiny peninsula lying between the Spanish town of La Línea de la Concepción on the Costa del Sol and industrial Algeciras. It is just 6.4km (4 miles) long and 2km (1¼ miles) wide.

At 449m (1,476 ft), the Rock of Gibraltar guards the entrance to the Mediterranean. Through its narrow strait, waters from the more turbulent Atlantic pass into the calmer Mediterranean.

This self-governing British colony—"Gib," as locals affectionately call it—has had mixed press over the years. Many visiting journalists consider Gibraltar a tourist trap and border crossings can sometimes be tedious. But there's a vast amount of history packed into this tiny place. Brits and those interested in military history will find sites like the **Great Siege Tunnels,** hewn out of the core of the Rock itself, fascinating. There's easily enough to keep you occupied on a busy day trip.

Often visitors go simply because Gibraltar is there. When you cross the border, you leave Spanish culture behind, but what you find is not quite British either. It's . . . well, it's Gibraltar.

GRANADA   One of the hardest questions a travel writer on Andalusia can be asked is: "If I don't have time for both, should it be Granada or Seville?" Only if forced at gunpoint would I say Granada—and that's because of its **Alhambra,** the resident palace of the Moorish rulers of the Nasrid dynasty, it is one of the world's greatest architectural treasures. The setting, with the snowcapped Sierra Nevada mountains rising up behind, makes it all the more beguiling.

Granada, of course, has much more to offer. Much of its charm derives from a mellow blending of its Eastern and Western architectural influences and customs. Other major attractions include the Gothic **cathedral**; **Capilla Real (Royal Chapel)**, burial place of the Catholic monarchs Ferdinand and Isabella; and the **Albaicín** quarter, a network of tightly packed white houses that was the heart of Muslim Granada. On a hot summer day, there is no cooler place to be than the **Generalife,** the summer palace of the former sultans and their harems, standing on 30 hectares (75 acres) of grounds. Granada's prestigious annual festival of music and dance takes place here.

The capital of eastern Andalusia, Granada lies in the foothills of the Sierra Nevada, with a population of some 300,000. Allow at least 2 to 3 days for a proper visit.

JAÉN   The capital of its own province, the ancient city of Jaén, and the even more interesting historic towns of Ubeda and Baeza, can be visited before you reach Córdoba if you're heading south from Madrid or *en route* from Granada.

Jaén was called *Giyen* when it lay on the ancient caravan route used by the Arabs. At the time of the Christian Reconquest of southern Spain, the armies of Ferdinand and Isabella used it as their gateway to Andalusia. That's not a bad idea for today's visitor, who can spend a half-day exploring Jaén and another day or two visiting the "twin" towns of Ubeda and Baeza.

Jaén is the center of one of the world's largest olive-growing districts, making it a virtual island in a sea of olive trees. Jaén's massive **cathedral** from the 16th century is one of the grandest examples of Spanish Renaissance architecture, and you can wander in its **Old Town,** originally a Moorish settlement.

The town of **Ubeda** is a bit of an undiscovered gem, full of numerous ornate Renaissance buildings. It's a harmonious town filled with churches, monuments, and palaces. Close by, **Baeza,** too, is filled with elegant town houses and noble mansions, many constructed during its heyday in the 16th century. Olive groves and vineyards envelop Baeza. One of the real delights of visiting these two historic old towns is the lack of other tourists.

NERJA   East of Málaga, the town of Nerja—perhaps my favorite along the entire Costa del Sol—opens onto the "Balcony of Europe," a marble-paved promenade jutting out toward the sea. This seaside resort lies at the mouth of the Río Chillar on a site below the Sierra de Mihara.

Although the tourist boom has led to a mass of new buildings on its periphery, its historic core is still charming, with whitewashed houses and narrow streets for rambling at leisure.

Nerja can be easily seen in a day. Its main attraction is the **Cuevas de Nerja,** caves with magnificent stalactites and bizarre rock formations.

RONDA & THE PUEBLOS BLANCOS/SHERRY TRIANGLE   One of the leading attractions of southern Spain, Ronda, at an altitude of 698m (2,300 ft), is a town built on a triangular plateau, with its apex pointing south. It is divided into two towns by the 100m (320-ft) gorge of the Río Guadalevín. At the southern tip of Ronda is **La Ciudad,** or the Old Town, which grew up on the Roman settlement of Arunda. A trio of bridges spanning the gorge links the old and new towns.

Ronda deserves at least 2 days, which will allow you to explore its antique architecture, visit one of the oldest bullrings in Spain, and take in its Moorish and Roman ruins. Those with a car and an extra 2 to 4 days can explore the so-called **Pueblos Blancos (White Villages)** of Andalusia in the hilly hinterland above the Costa del Sol. The houses in these agricultural villages are characterized by whitewashed walls. The higher you climb into the *sierras,* the prettier these villages grow. Favorite destinations are **Vejer de la Frontera, Grazalema,** and **Arcos de la Frontera.** Those with yet another day can do some wine tasting at the sherry-producing wine *bodegas* of **Jerez de la Frontera,** northeast of Cádiz. Jerez is also the equestrian center of Andalusia. Watching a "horse ballet" at a dressage school is one of the highlights of a visit to southern Spain.

SEVILLE Andalusia's grandest city links the heart of the province with its coastal plains and maritime routes. Standing on the Guadalquivir River, it lies 80km (50 miles) north of the Atlantic Ocean with a Mediterranean climate but irregular rainfall, which means the sun shines 2,796 hours per year.

No longer Spain's most populous city, it is still an urban sprawl once you branch out from its historic core. The population numbers more than 800,000 Sevillanos.

Seville reached the zenith of its power in the 15th and 16th centuries when it was the gateway to the New World explored by Columbus. At that time Seville was the fourth-largest city on the globe, the place where treasure ships landed with their cargoes from the Americas.

Allow at least 3 or 4 nights to explore the capital of Andalusia, including such attractions as its world-famous cathedral, **La Giralda,** royal palace, **the Alcázar,** and its wonderful fine arts museum, the **Museo de Bellas Artes,** along with its historic core, **Barrio de Santa Cruz.**

ANDALUSIA IN 1 WEEK

This is Andalusia in a nutshell. It's a whistle-stop tour, but in a week you can visit the highlights, including the major cities of **Córdoba, Seville,** and **Granada,** the land of sherry, **Jerez de la Frontera,** and the ancient port city of **Cádiz.** For those with longer to spend in the region, there's a two-week tour at the end of this chapter.

Most of these tours use Málaga as their starting point. These days, direct flights to Málaga from the U.S.A. (in summer months), Canada, and all parts of the U.K. make it by far the best entry point. If you end up arriving via Madrid, start and finish this tour in Córdoba instead. (It would be wise to drive or take the high-speed train down to Córdoba the night before you begin this tour so you won't have to eat into the 1-week tour time needed.) For more on entry points to Andalusia by plane, see p. 35.

Days 1 & 2: Granada & the Alhambra ★★★

On arrival in Málaga, pick up your hire car and head for **Granada,** home to the Alhambra, one of Europe's most ornate and romantically sited monuments. Take the A-45 north then fork right on to the A-92M and join the A-92 east to Granada. It's a distance of 132 km (82 miles) and takes about 1½ hours.

Once you arrive in Granada, check in to a hotel for one night, but save the main attractions, the Alhambra and the Generalife, for Day 2 so you have some recovery time. If you've not pre-booked tickets for the Alhambra it's essential that you do so straight away. (See p. 205).

Spend Day 1 wandering the atmospheric winding narrow streets and squares of the historic old Arab Quarter, the **Albaicín**, and if you have time visit the **Catedral** (p. 211), dating from the 16th century, with its flamboyant **Capilla Real** (Royal Chapel). In the evening you might want to take in a flamenco show in one of the traditional Gypsy cave houses in the **Sacramonte** district. On the morning of **Day 2,** head up the hill to the **Alhambra** (p. 205) and the **Generalife** (p. 205), Andalusia's greatest attraction and the final seat of the Moors in the West. You'll need at least 3 hours to see everything here.

Mid-to-late afternoon make your way to Córdoba. Heading back the way you came along the A-92 and then north on the A-45, a distance of 204km (127 miles) with a journey time of around 2¼ hours. Check into a hotel for two nights here.

Day 3: Córdoba ★★★

On **Day 3,** head first for the **Mezquita-Catedral de Córdoba** (p. 153), the Great Mosque dating from the 8th century when the Moors ruled over this city. This is one of Andalusia's greatest attractions, second only to the fabled Alhambra at Granada. Give it at least an hour and a half before wandering over to the **Alcázar de los Reyes Cristianos** (p. 152), a grand castle from the 14th century, which once housed King Ferdinand and Queen Isabella. Visits here will take an hour, at which time you'll be ready for lunch. In the afternoon, take about 2 hours wandering through the **Judería** (p. 155), the historic Jewish Quarter, a warren of atmospheric streets. If you've still got some energy left, visit the ancient **Palacio Museo de Viana** (p. 157), with its beautiful gardens and patios, before calling it a day. Start your evening off by hitting some of the tapas bars and then move on to a more contemporary drinking spot for some late-night drinks and maybe some music; coverage begins on p. 159.

Days 4 & 5: Seville ★★★

On the morning of **Day 4,** leave Córdoba and continue on the A-4/E-5 west into Seville, the capital of Andalusia, a distance of 143km (89 miles). Check in to a hotel for 2 nights. Seville's two major attractions, its world-famed **cathedral** and **Giralda tower** (p. 108) and the **Alcázar** (p. 265), will take up the better part of your first day. This Christian cathedral is the largest in Europe. Including a climb up the tower, allow at least 2 hours to tour the complex, and be sure to spend some time relaxing among the orange trees and fountain of the Patio de los Naranjos. Take your time over a typical long Andalusian lunch, then head for the royal residence of the Alcázar, which will occupy most of your afternoon. In the evening go for a stroll through the old, narrow streets of the **Barrio de Santa Cruz** (p. 107). Once the Jewish ghetto, it was restored in the early 20th century. Wander such ancient streets as Calles **Ximénez de Encisco** and **Santa Teresa** and as night falls do as the locals do and visit the busy tapas bars (p. 126).

On **Day 5,** begin the day by taking my **walking tour of the Old City** (coverage begins on p. 113). This will carry you into the lunch hour. After lunch spend a couple of hours admiring the works of the Seville school of painters, including Bartolomé Esteban Murillo, and Juan de Valdés Leal in the **Museo**

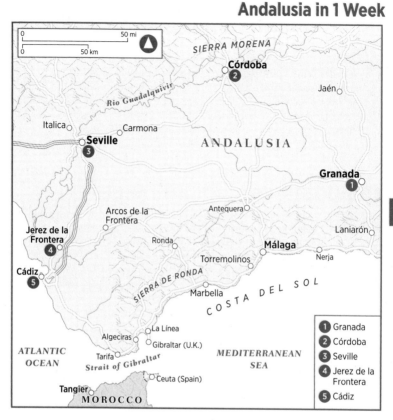

Provincial de Bellas Artes de Sevilla (p. 109). Afterward, take a **horse and carriage ride** around more of the city's landmarks, in particular the remarkable **Plaza de España** (p. 113), in shady Parque de María Luisa. Finally, cap your day by having dinner in a typical Sevillian restaurant or taking in a flamenco show.

Day 6: Jerez de la Frontera ★

On the morning of **Day 6,** head 87km (54 miles) to the south, following the AP-4/E-5 toll road to the turnoff west into Jerez de la Frontera, the land of sherry. Check in to a hotel for the night and set out to explore the *bodegas* (sherry houses). Coverage begins on p. 216. The most famous include **Sandeman, Pedro Domecq,** and **González.** But time your tour of the *bodegas* so that you can see the **Dancing Horses of Jerez** (p. 267). When no performances are scheduled, you can watch the horses as they train. An intriguing curiosity, and only if you have time, is a visit to **Museo de los Relojes** (p. 266), a clock museum with timepieces from the early 17th century. What to do at night? Munch tapas and sip sherry in the busy local tapas bars.

Day 7: Cádiz

If your time is up, head back to Málaga on Day 7, taking the A-381 to Algeciras and then the A-7/E-15 east along the coast back to Málaga. You can take the AP-7 toll road from Estepona which makes the 254km (158-mile) 3-hour journey easier. If you've more time to spare, head south on the AP-4/E-5 for 32km (20 miles) into Cádiz, where you can check in to a hotel for the night. There are no great attractions here, except for the **seaside promenades** (p. 285) around the walls of the Old Town. After lunch, visit the **Catedral de Cádiz** (p. 285) and **El Oratorio de la Santa Cueva** (p. 286), which was constructed in 1789. The rest of the afternoon can be spent exploring the **Old Town** (p. 287).

To return to Málaga take the AP-4/E-5 north to join the A-381 to Algeciras as described above.

THE COSTA DEL SOL IN 1 WEEK

This second 1-week tour is rather more relaxing than the tour above, but offers far less in the way of historic monuments. It's really a tour of resort towns along the Sun Coast of southern Spain where **Marbella** is the most elegant resort, **Nerja** the most charming, **Málaga** the most historic, and **Torremolinos** the most overrun. The one serious bit of history is provided by the uniquely British enclave, the **Rock of Gibraltar.** The tour begins in Málaga. The A-7(AP-7)/E-5 links all the towns along the coast, so as you drive along, you can stop wherever you wish to allow yourself plenty of beach time. For more about the beaches see p. 342.

Day 1: Tarifa ★

On arrival at Málaga, pick up your hire car and drive all the way down the coast to the pretty little town of **Tarifa** where you can check in to a hotel for the night. The short section of road from Algeciras to Tarifa offers wonderful views of the Rock of Gibraltar and the coast of Africa. The best place to admire them is the **Mirador del Estrecho** (p. 300). It's a distance of 168km (104 miles) to Tarifa and it takes just over 2 hours if you use the fast AP-7 toll road.

Tarifa's charm is its narrow cobbled streets and tiny historic squares. If you have time you can also visit its main church, **Iglesia de San Mateo** (p. 300) and the castle **Castillo de Guzmán** (p. 299), built in 960. Tarifa is one of Europe's best bases for kite and windsurfing and in the summer season, **nightlife** here with the surf dudes and girls is great fun. There's a whole host of funky bars and cafes lining the streets of the Old Town (p. 336).

Day 2: The Rock of Gibraltar ★

On **Day 2,** head for Gibraltar. These days, customs formalities rarely delay people for long, so it's relatively easy to drive across the border. Check into a hotel on the Rock for a night.

In one day you can see Gibraltar's major attractions, including the **Upper Rock Nature Reserve** (p. 328) where you'll find **St Michael's Cave** (p. 329), the **Apes' Den** (p. 329), the **Great Siege Tunnels** (p. 330), and the ruins of the old **Moorish Castle** (p. 330). Don't drive up to the Reserve yourself. Either take the **cable car** and walk back down or do a **tourist taxi tour** (p. 327).

The Costa del Sol in 1 Week

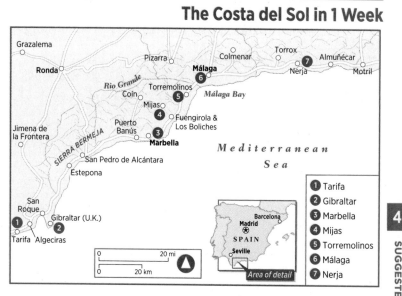

The views from up on top of the Rock are truly spectacular. Cap your afternoon with a panoramic visit to **Europa Point** (p. 331), at the far end of the Rock for more great views across to Africa.

Day 3: Marbella ★

Leave Gibraltar on the morning of **Day 3** and head east to Marbella, queen of the Spanish Riviera, a distance of 60km (37 miles) from Algeciras. Along the way you can stop over at **Estepona,** a town of Roman origin. Unlike the bigger resorts farther along the coast, Estepona is not too developed and has a distinctly Spanish flavor to it. You can spend an hour or so strolling along its **Paseo Marítimo,** with the water on one side, gardens on the other. If you're here in time for lunch, you'll find beach bar cafes for simply cooked fresh seafood.

Next, drive on to Marbella, where you can check into a hotel for the night. Before the day ends, you may want to log some beach time at **Playa de la Baj-adilla** and **Playa de Venus** in front of the Old Town or **Playa Naguelles** and **Playa La Fontanilla** closer to many of the more luxurious hotels. Later take a stroll around the lovely **Old Town,** centering around the colorful **Patio de los Naranjos (Patio of the Orange Trees)** and choose a restaurant for dinner.

Day 4: Mijas ★

For a change of pace, leave the coast on the morning of **Day 4** and head for Mijas, an attractive Andalusian White Village (Pueblo Blanco), a distance of 40km (26 miles) northeast of Marbella. Stay on the AP-7/E-15 as you head east to **Fuengirola,** a distance of 34km (21 miles) from Marbella. The resort of Fuengirola is known for its 8km (5 miles) of beaches, in case you want to take a dip. After leaving Fuengirola, continue east until you reach the signposts pointing north into the mountains for Mijas, just 8km (5 miles) from the coastal road.

Mijas is one of the most famous of the Pueblos Blancos or "White Villages" of Andalusia—a host of brightly whitewashed houses clinging precariously to the mountainside. Welded to the side of a mountain, the town is famous for its location and views. It also has an unusually shaped old bullring which you can visit. Most visitors spend their hours just wandering the narrow streets and going on a shopping expedition for crafts. If you don't want to return to the coast at night, you can check in to a hotel at Mijas.

Day 5: Fun at Torremolinos

Leave Mijas on the morning of **Day 5,** driving south to the coastal road, where you head east into **Torremolinos,** a distance of only 19km (12 miles) but a world apart. Check into a hotel for the night and don't worry about seeing any historical monuments. Torremolinos, the biggest resort along Spain's Mediterranean coast, is strictly for sun, sand, and fun. Try to work in some beach time at one of the town's three main beaches: **El Bajondillo** (aka Playa de Bajondill), **Playa de Playamar,** and **La Carihuela.** At night you can wander around the old streets of the town above, which sits on the cliffs, sampling the food and drink at busy bars. Don't expect anything too sophisticated. Later walk down to the sea to the old **fishing village of La Carihuela** for a seafood dinner to cap off the evening or hang out with trendy Malagueños at the beach bars on **Playa Alamos**. Another good spot for late-night drinking and dancing is **Costa Lago** just off Paseo Marítimo.

Day 6: Málaga ★

Leave Torremolinos on the morning of **Day 6** and head east toward the capital of the Costa del Sol, Málaga, a distance of only 15km (9 miles). Check in to a hotel for the night. Aside from Gibraltar, Málaga is the one place along the coast that has historic and cultural sights, including the remains of the ancient Moorish castle the **Alcazaba** (p. 370) high in the hillside, the vast **cathedral** (p. 372), and the truly excellent Picasso Museum, the **Museo Picasso Málaga** (p. 372). The busy tapas bars off Calle Granada and close to **Plaza Uncibaj** and **Plaza de la Merced** are the ideal spot for some evening tapas bar action.

Day 7: Nerja & the Balcony of Europe ★★

For your final look at the Costa del Sol, leave Málaga on the morning of **Day 7** and head for **Nerja,** a distance of 52km (32 miles) east along the coastal road. Check in to a hotel for the night. The big attraction here is the prehistoric **Cueva de Nerja** (p. 382), with its stalactites and stalagmites. But you'll want to take an hour or so wandering Nerja's narrow streets, strolling along the **Balcony of Europe** (p. 382) and relaxing on one of the sheltered beaches.

You can drive back west to Málaga the following day for transportation connections.

RONDA & THE PUEBLOS BLANCOS IN 1 WEEK

For yet another look at Andalusia, leave the coastline and head inland to the **Pueblos Blancos (White Villages),** so called for their whitewashed houses built closely

Ronda & the Pueblos Blancos in 1 Week

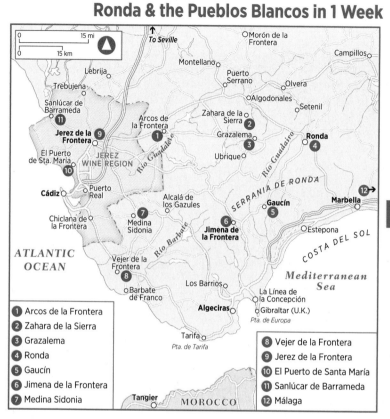

1 Arcos de la Frontera
2 Zahara de la Sierra
3 Grazalema
4 Ronda
5 Gaucín
6 Jimena de la Frontera
7 Medina Sidonia

8 Vejer de la Frontera
9 Jerez de la Frontera
10 El Puerto de Santa María
11 Sanlúcar de Barrameda
12 Málaga

together. So far, we've been treading the beaten touristic path. In these evocative medieval villages, with their Moorish-style alleyways and hidden patios, there are some real opportunities to escape the crowds and become a bit of an adventurer again. The tour also allows time to visit the *bodegas* (wine cellars) at **Jerez de la Frontera,** which forms part of the **Sherry Triangle.**

You can combine some of this tour with the first tour (Andalusia in 1 Week) to get pretty much the ultimate 10-day trip. Do the first tour then add Days 1 to 3 of this before heading back to Málaga from Ronda. For this reason we start this tour in Arcos de la Frontera. Note, too, that there's a more detailed description of this itinerary in Chapter 9. (See p. 233).

Day 1: Arcos de la Frontera ★★

If you're arriving in Andalusia today, drive to Arcos de la Frontera. From Málaga take the AP-7/E-15 all the way down the Costa del Sol then head north on the A-381 towards Jerez de la Frontera, picking up the AP-4/E-5 for one junction before heading to Arcos de la Frontera on the A-382. It's a journey of around 250km (155 miles) and takes about 3 hours.

Along with Ronda, the old Arab town of **Arcos de la Frontera** is one of the highlights of this tour. It's so special it's been declared a National Historic Monument, and once you've checked into your hotel you'll need several hours to wander its narrow atmospheric old streets where ancient Moors once trod. You'll want to spend most of your time exploring the **Medina** (p. 258) or Old Town, and taking in the panoramic lookout point, **Mirador de Abades** (p. 250). If you fancy a spot of **souvenir shopping**, Arcos has a number of nice artists' galleries, in particular **Galería de Arte San Pedro** and **Galería de Arte Arx-Arcis** (p. 250).

Day 2: Arcos de la Frontera ★★ to Ronda ★★★

Leave Arcos after breakfast and return to the A-382 and continue northeast, following the signs to Algodonales. From here head south at the junction with the A-2300 to **Zahara de la Sierra**, one of the most perfect of the province's fortified hilltop *pueblos*, set on the shores of a manmade reservoir. Trip time is about 35 minutes, and the distance is 51km (32 miles). Zahara lies in the heart of the **Natural Park Sierra de Grazalema** (p. 254). You climb a steep path to see a panoramic view and the ruins of a reconstructed castle, where a 10th-century Muslim fortress once stood.

From Zahara, head next for **Grazalema** by taking the tiny CA-9104 (previously called the CA-531) south. It's only 17km (10.5 miles), but don't rush as you'll see some spectacular views en route, especially from the **Puerto de las Palomas,** a mountain pass at 1,157 meters above sea level (3,800 ft).

Delightful **Grazalema** is perhaps the most idyllic of the White Villages, nestling under the craggy peak of San Cristóbal at 1,525m (5,003 ft). As you wander its sloping, narrow streets, you'll pass white house after white house with window boxes filled with summery flowers. You can also visit the **Artesanía Textil de Grazalema** which sells interesting local handicrafts.

From here it's a short half-hour drive to **Ronda** along the A-372 and the A-374. On arrival, check into a hotel for 2 nights to allow a whole day to explore the most famous of the Pueblos Blancos.

Day 3: Ronda ★★★

Spend all of **Day 3** seeing the sights and enjoying the atmosphere of lovely **Ronda,** a town that lies high in the Serranía de Ronda mountains. The highlight is **La Ciudad** (p. 233), the old Moorish town, although **El Mercadillo** (p. 233), the so-called New Town, is also of interest, particularly for the **bullring** which is said to be the oldest in Spain. The bridge that connects the two, the **Puente Nuevo** spanning a ravine in the rock, is truly remarkable. Wander the streets of the Old Town and follow in Hemingway's footsteps by dropping into a series of tapas bars as darkness falls. Overnight in Ronda.

Day 4: Ronda to Vejer de la Frontera ★

On the morning of **Day 4,** take the A-360 southwest to **Gaucín**. Allow about an hour for the 37km (23-mile) trip. At the eastern edge of this pretty little village, you can head up to the **Castillo del Aguila,** the Moorish castle.

Continue next to **Jimena de la Frontera**, the gateway to the **Parque Natural de los Alcornocales.** Take the winding A-369 out of town which becomes the A-405. Wander Jimena's narrow cobblestone streets and explore the impressive ruins of **Castillo-Fortaleza** (p. 257), taking in some of the most panoramic views in the region. You can stop for lunch here too.

From Jimena, take the narrow winding CA-8201 northwest until you come to the junction with the A-2304 heading southwest to the junction with the A-381. Once on the A-381 continue northwest into **Medina Sidonia**. This 86km (54-mile) trip will take 1 to 1½ hours.

You can spend 2 or 3 hours here, taking in Medina Sidonia's central medieval square, **Plaza de España** (p. 113), and paying a visit to **Iglesia Santa María La Coronada** (p. 258), today a church but formerly a mosque. You can also visit the town's Roman sewers.

From here it's a short 86km (54-mile) journey to **Vejer de la Frontera**. Follow the A-396 south to the E-5/N-340 and then take a right and a left following the signs. Check into one of the many delightful boutique hotels in or just outside the town. Spend your evening enjoying the many restaurants and bars here, particularly those around lovely **Plaza de España**.

Day 5: Vejer de la Frontera ★ to Jerez de la Frontera ★

How long you spend exploring the Old Town of Vejer de la Frontera in the morning of **Day 5** depends on whether you plan to see the **Dancing Horses of Jerez** (see p. 267). Shows normally start mid-morning. The journey to Jerez from Vejer takes about 45 minutes. If you've time though, spend a while taking in the sights of the Old Town of Vejer. See if the **Castillo Moro** (p. 260), the Moorish castle, is open, and spend a couple of hours wandering its narrow streets and taking in the views.

From Vejer we leave the Pueblos Blancos and head for **Jerez de la Frontera** at the center of the famous **Sherry Triangle.** To get there, take the A-48/E-5 northwest to reach the A-4, continuing around the Bay of Cádiz. Once in Jerez, check into a hotel for 2 nights.

Spend the rest of the day exploring Jerez. See Day 6 of The Best of Andalusia in 1 Week for more information about visiting the sherry houses and other attractions of this historic city.

Day 6: El Puerto de Santa María and Sanlúcar de Barrameda

On the morning of **Day 6,** leave Jerez and drive south for 12km (7½ miles) to the town of **El Puerto de Santa María,** part of the Sherry Triangle. You can set about exploring the town, enjoying wine tastings at **Terry** (p. 272) and visiting an old mosque, **Castillo de San Marcos** (p. 272) where you can also sample sherry.

After lunch continue to number three of the triangle, **Sanlúcar de Barrameda.** Head northwest from Santa María along the A-2001. At this point, you'll be only 24km (15 miles) west of Jerez. At one of the *bodegas* here, you can enjoy a glass of the distinctive *manzanilla* wine, the driest of all sherries. **Antonio Barbadillo** is one of the most popular. Also consider a 3½-hour river cruise offered by **Real Fernando** (p. 276). On your return, head back to Jerez for your final night.

Day 7: Return to Málaga ★★★

On the morning of **Day 7,** leave Jerez and head back to Málaga, which is likely to be your transportation hub for leaving Spain. To return to Málaga take the AP-4/E-5 south to join the A-381 to Algeciras, then the AP-7/E-15 east along the coast back to Málaga.

ANDALUSIA FOR FAMILIES IN 1 WEEK

Andalusia is sometimes called the playground of Spain, so reckon on amusements here for the entire family to enjoy, in particular the beaches. Your main concern with having children along is likely to be finding the right mix of interesting things to keep them amused and time for relaxation on the beach. I recommend spending 1 day at **Córdoba** but allow 2 days for **Seville,** which has many more attractions. Follow this by a visit south to **Jerez de la Frontera,** fabled for its horses and its sherry. The most scenic journey here will be from Jerez to **Arcos de la Frontera** and on to the dramatic mountain town of **Ronda,** perched over a ravine high in the mountains. Kids will enjoy the final 2 days in Andalusia most of all because they take them to the beach resorts of **Torremolinos** and **Málaga,** the capital of the Costa del Sol.

Day 1: Córdoba ★★★

Assuming you fly into Málaga, on **Day 1,** drive to Córdoba, taking the A-45 north for 163km (101 miles), with a journey time of about 2 hours. Córdoba city isn't as kid-friendly as Seville, but most children will find amusement here. Check in to your hotel and set out to explore, heading first for the **Mezquita-Catedral de Córdoba** (p. 153), the 856 still-standing pillars of which remind kids of giant sticks of red and white candy. Follow up with a walk over the **Puente Romano** river bridge and visit the **Torre de la Calahorra** (p. 158) which has a fun audio tour which older kids will enjoy and nice views from its summit. Spend the rest of the day wandering the ancient narrow cobblestone streets of the **Judería** (p. 86). A visit to the artisan quarter **Zoco** (p. 158), might even offer the chance to see craftsmen at work.

Days 2 & 3: The Ancient City of Seville ★★★

On the morning of **Day 2,** leave Córdoba and drive 129km (80 miles) along the A-4/E-5 west to **Seville,** where you can check into a hotel for 2 nights. For most families, Seville will be one of the highlights of the trip. Launch your tour of Seville by heading for the once-mighty **Alcázar** (p. 104), which will take about 2 hours to visit. With its lavish decorations and ornate rooms, along with its 18th-century gardens, the castle fortress has enough elements to appeal to all ages. Take time for a long lazy Andalusian lunch and then in the afternoon take the family to **Parque María Luisa,** a perfect place for kids to let off steam. There are unusual plants and monuments to explore. You can also hire bicycles and four-person **pedal carts.** The landmark **Plaza de España** (p. 113) here is also worth a visit.

In the morning of Day 3, visit the **Catedral de Sevilla** (p. 108), the largest Gothic structure on Earth. Kids are usually awed by the size of the place. If not, they will be when they get to climb the historic bell tower, **La Giralda**

Andalusia for Families in 1 Week

0 ────── 50 mi	
0 ────── 50 km	

SIERRA MORENA

Córdoba ①

Jaén ○

Rio Guadalquivir

Italica ○ Carmona ○

Seville ②

ANDALUSIA

Granada ○

Arcos de la Frontera ○ ④ Antequera ○

Laniarón ○

Jerez de la Frontera ③ Ronda ○ ⑤ **Málaga** ○ ⑦

Torremolinos ○ ⑥ Nerja ○

Cádiz ○ SIERRA DE RONDA

Marbella ○

COSTA DEL SOL

La Línea ○

Algeciras ○ Gibraltar (U.K.) ○

ATLANTIC OCEAN Tarifa ○ MEDITERRANEAN SEA

Strait of Gibraltar

Ceuta (Spain) ○

Tangier ○
MOROCCO

① Córdoba
② Seville
③ Jerez de la Frontera
④ Arcos de la Frontera
⑤ Ronda
⑥ Torremolinos
⑦ Málaga

(p. 109). Even smaller legs can climb it as there are no steps, just a series of narrow sloping corridors.

But make sure they keep some energy for the afternoon when a visit to the **Isla Mágica** (p. 117) theme park should be a real thrill for them. Built on the site of the 1992 Expo grounds, the park has been turned into a Disney-like playground with themed rollercoaster rides, a log flume, and a Pirates' Cove show. If the kids aren't too tired, spend the evening strolling around the **Barrio de Santa Cruz** (p. 107), having dinner at a restaurant in this ancient barrio.

Day 4: Jerez de la Frontera ★ & Its Dancing Horses

Leave Seville on the morning of **Day 4,** taking the AP-4/E-5 to Jerez, a distance of 87km (54 miles) south of Seville. Check in to a hotel for the night. The big thing here is to tour one of the *bodegas* (wine cellars) (the coverage, "Touring the Bodegas," begins on p. 264). You may have some objections to taking your kids to one of more than 100 *bodegas* in Jerez, but they are fascinating to visitors of all ages. Far more geared to family viewing are the **Dancing Horses of Jerez**

(p. 267). After seeing the remarkable choreography of a performance by these beautiful stallions, you can fill out the afternoon with visits to the the **Museo de los Relojes** (p. 266), the town's clock museum, and the **Alcázar** (p. 105).

Day 5: Arcos de la Frontera ★★ to Ronda ★★★

On the morning of **Day 5,** leave Jerez de la Frontera and head east on the A-382 to **Arcos de la Frontera,** going 32km (20 miles). You'll need about 2 hours to wander its narrow streets where Moors of old once trod. You'll want to spend most of your time exploring the **Medina** (p. 258) or Old Town and taking in the views from the panoramic lookout point, **Mirador de Abades** (p. 250).

After lunch continue on to Ronda, a distance of 86km (54 miles). To reach Ronda you have two options. One is to take the A-382 and head east (it becomes the A-384) to the turning to Ronda at Algondonales, the A-374. But if you have more time, take the slower and far more scenic A-372 which passes through **Grazalema** (p. 254) en route, one of the most unspoilt of the Pueblos Blancos.

Check in to your hotel in Ronda, and spend the rest of the day walking the narrow, cobblestone streets of **La Ciudad** (p. 233), the old Moorish town. Older kids will love a visit to **Museo Lara** which contains over 5,000 unusual exhibits including weapons, antique clocks, knives, musical instruments, and early cameras. Walk across the ancient **Puente Nuevo** (p. 233) with your brood, taking in the panoramic views in all directions and then visit Ronda's historic **bullring**, said to be the oldest in Spain.

Day 6: Summer Fun at Torremolinos

Leave Ronda on the morning of **Day 6** and drive south on the winding A-397 to the coast. Get on the A-7/E-5, heading east to Torremolinos, 80km (50 miles) from Ronda. Check in to a hotel here and set out to have some family fun. The town's three main beaches are **El Bajondillo** (aka Playa de Bajondill), **Playa de Playamar,** and **La Carihuela.**

With its focus on family holidays, it's no surprise that there's a whole host of theme parks and attractions close to Torremolinos. After the beach take the kids to **Aquapark** (p. 362) where they can zoom down huge waterslides and splash to their hearts' content. At Benalmádena, the satellite of Torremolinos, the family can also visit the best aquarium in Andalusia, **Sea Life Benalmádena** (p. 362), and have fun at **Tivoli World** (p. 362), a large amusement park. Cap the day by boarding the *teléferico* (p. 362), a cable car that takes you to the top of Monte Calamorro for a panoramic vista of the Costa del Sol.

Day 7: Málaga ★

On the morning of **Day 7,** it's just a 15km (9-mile) drive east on the coastal road back to Málaga. Check into a hotel here so you'll be close to your flight the following morning.

Ancient Málaga doesn't have the family attractions of Torremolinos, but the Alcazaba (p. 370), a restored Moorish fortress on top of the hill, is fun to explore and the streets of its Old Town are great for a wander. Have lunch at a local tapas bar and then hop aboard one of the city sightseeing buses for an interesting audio tour of the city; ideally take one that does the longer itinerary which includes the **Jardin Botánico-Histórico La Concepción** (p. 372), a huge botanic garden on the outskirts of the city, perfect for kids to run around in.

ANDALUSIA IN 2 WEEKS

A fortnight is the ideal timespan to really explore and enjoy the region, although of course you could easily spend much longer in this beautiful part of the world. This tour follows the same route as Andalusia in 1 Week up to Day 6 at Jerez de La Frontera, see p. 61.

Days 1–6: Granada ★★★, Córdoba ★★★, Seville ★★★, Jerez ★

Follow the first tour in this chapter from Day 1 to Day 6, visiting the major cultural highlights of the region in these great historic cities.

Day 7: Sanlúcar de Barrameda, Cádiz to Vejer de la Frontera ★

From Jerez drive 22km (15 miles) northwest to explore another of the Sherry Triangle towns, **Sanlúcar de Barrameda.** At one of the sherry *bodegas* here, enjoy a glass of the distinctive *manzanilla* wine, the driest of all sherries. **Antonio Barbadillo** is one of the most popular. Also consider a 3½-hour river cruise offered by **Real Fernando** (p. 276).

Next head south on the A-2001 to pick up the N-443 into **Cádiz**, a distance of 53km (37 miles). Here you can visit the Catedral de Cádiz (p. 285) and El Oratorio de la Santa Cueva (p. 286), which was constructed in 1789. If you have time, explore the seaside promenades (p. 285) and more of the atmospheric Old Town.

From Cádiz it's about a half-hour journey of 56km (40 miles) down the A-48 to your stop for the night, the first of the *Pueblos Blancos* (White Villages) on this tour, lovely **Vejer de la Frontera**. Check into one of the nice boutique hotels here and have dinner at one of the restaurants on atmospheric **Plaza de España**.

Day 8: Vejer de la Frontera ★ to Tarifa ★

On **Day 8,** spend a short while taking in the sights of the old town of Vejer. See if the **Castillo Moro** (p. 260), the Moorish castle, is open and spend a couple of hours wandering its narrow streets and taking in the views.

From here, take the E-5/N-340 south to **Tarifa**, a distance of 50km (31 miles). Along the way you might want to stop at some of the wildly beautiful beaches along this stretch of coastline, the Costa de la Luz. **Los Caños de La Meca** close to Barbate, **Playa de Zahara** near the hamlet of **Zahara de los Atunes,** and **Playa Valdevaqueros** shortly before Tarifa are good options (p. 297).

Tarifa's charm is its narrow cobbled streets and tiny historic squares. You can also visit its main church, **Iglesia de San Mateo** (p. 300), and the castle **Castillo de Guzmán** (p. 299), built in 960. Tarifa is one of Europe's best bases for kite and windsurfing and in the summer, **nightlife** here with the surf dudes and girls is great fun. There's a whole host of funky bars and cafes lining the streets of the Old Town (p. 287). Overnight in Tarifa.

Day 9: The Rock of Gibraltar ★

On **Day 9,** head for Gibraltar, one of the most interesting historical visits of the tour. These days customs formalities rarely delay people for long, so it's relatively easy to drive across the border into this tiny British colony. Check into a hotel on the Rock for a night.

In 1 day here you can see Gibraltar's major attractions, including the **Upper Rock Nature Reserve** (p. 328) where you will find **St Michael's Cave** (p. 329), the **Apes' Den** (p. 329), the **Great Siege Tunnels** (p. 330), and the ruins of the old **Moorish Castle** (p. 330). Don't drive up to the Reserve yourself. Either take the **cable car** and walk back down or do a **tourist taxi tour** (p. 327). The views from up on top of the Rock are truly spectacular. Cap your afternoon with a visit to **Europa Point** (p. 331), at the far end of the Rock where there are panoramic views across to Africa.

Day 10: Gibraltar ★ to Arcos de la Frontera ★★

Next we leave the coastline for a while and head into the interior of the region to explore more of the famous White Villages (Pueblos Blancos). Leave Gibraltar after breakfast and head back towards Algeciras along the A-7. Then take the A-381 north to **Medina Sidonia**. It's a distance of 90km (56 miles) and the journey will take about 1½ hours.

You can spend a couple of hours here, taking in Medina Sidonia's central medieval square, **Plaza de España** (p. 113), and paying a visit to **Iglesia Santa María La Coronada** (p. 258), today a church but formerly a mosque. Consider stopping for lunch at **La Vista de Medina,** a restaurant on the square opposite the church. Its terrace has tremendous views of the country-side. You can also visit the town's Roman sewers if you have time.

From Medina Sidonia head north along the A-389 for 33km (20 miles) to **Arcos de la Frontera**, another wonderful White Village. The journey takes about half an hour. Check into a hotel for the night here.

Day 11: Arcos de la Frontera ★★ to Grazalema ★★

Spend a few hours strolling around Arcos de la Frontera after breakfast. You'll want to spend most of your time exploring the **Medina** (p. 258) or Old Town and taking in the panoramic lookout point, **Mirador de Abades** (p. 250). If you fancy a spot of **souvenir shopping,** Arcos has a number of nice artists' galleries, in particular **Galeria de Arte San Pedro** and **Galeria de Arte Arx-Arcis** (p. 250).

From Arcos, head for the A-382 and drive northeast, following the signs to Algodonales. From here head south at the junction with the A-2300 to **Zahara de la Sierra**, one of the most perfect of the province's fortified hilltop *pueblos*, set on the shores of a manmade reservoir. Trip time is about 35 minutes, and the distance is 51km (32 miles). Zahara lies in the heart of the **Natural Park Sierra de Grazalema** (p. 254). You climb a steep path to see a panoramic view and the ruins of a reconstructed castle, where a 10th-century Muslim fortress used to stand. A good lunch stop here is **Al Lago,** which offers some of the best dining in the area and views of the lake too.

From Zahara head next for **Grazalema** by taking the tiny CA-9104 (previously called the CA-531) south. It's only 17km (11 miles), but don't rush as you'll see some spectacular views en route, especially from the **Puerto de las Palomas,** a mountain pass at 1,157 meters above sea level (3,174 ft).

Delightful **Grazalema** is perhaps the most idyllic of the White Villages, nestling under the craggy peak of San Cristóbal at 1,525m (5,003 ft). As you wander its sloping, narrow streets, you'll pass white house after white house with window boxes filled with summery flowers. You can also visit the **Artesanía Textil de Grazalema** which sells interesting local handicrafts. Check into a hotel here for the night. Make sure to reserve well in advance as there is only a handful. If you can't get into a hotel here, drive on to Ronda as it's only half an hour away.

Day 12: Ronda ★★★

From Grazalema it's a short half-hour drive to **Ronda** along the A-372 and the A-374. On arrival, check into a hotel for the night to allow a whole day to explore the most famous of the Pueblos Blancos.

Spend all of **Day 12** seeing the sights and enjoying the atmosphere of lovely **Ronda,** a town that lies high in the Serranía de Ronda mountains. The highlight is **La Ciudad** (p. 233), the old Moorish town, although **El Mercadillo** (p. 233), the so-called New Town, is also of interest, particularly for the **bullring** which is said to be the oldest in Spain. The bridge that connects the two, the **Puente Nuevo** spanning a ravine in the rock, is truly remarkable. Wander the streets of the Old Town and follow in Hemingway's footsteps by dropping into a series of tapas bars as darkness falls. Overnight in Ronda.

Day 13: Ronda ★★★ to Marbella

Next morning leave Ronda and take the twisting turning A-397 south to the A-7 and then drive east to **Marbella**. It's a distance of 55km (34 miles) and will take about an hour to drive.

This stretch of coastline, the **Costa del Sol,** isn't known for its charm or beauty. Much of it has been overdeveloped, but Marbella is genuinely lovely. On arrival check into a hotel.

You can spend the day lazing on the beaches near here: **Playa de la Bajadilla** and **Playa de Venus** in front of the Old Town, or **Playa Naguelles** and **Playa La Fontanilla** closer to many of the more luxurious hotels. Later take a stroll around the lovely Old Town, centering around the colorful **Patio de los Naranjos** (Patio of the Orange Trees) and choose a restaurant near here for dinner.

Day 14: Málaga ★

Leave Marbella on the morning of **Day 14** and head back to Málaga to explore the capital of the Costa del Sol and the last stop on your 2-week tour. It's a distance of 60km (37 miles) and takes about 45 minutes. Check in to a hotel for the night ready to pick up your flight home next morning.

Aside from Gibraltar, **Málaga** is the one place along the Costa del Sol coastline that has historic and cultural sights, including the remains of the ancient Moorish castle, the **Alcazaba** (p. 370) high in the hillside, the vast **cathedral** (p. 372) and the truly excellent Picasso Museum, the **Museo Picasso Málaga** (p. 372).

The busy tapas bars off Calle Granada and close to **Plaza Uncibaj** and **Plaza de la Merced** are the ideal spot for some evening tapas bar action, a perfect location for celebrating the end of what will have been two wonderfully memorable weeks in Andalusia.

SETTLING INTO SEVILLE

Sometimes a city becomes famous simply for its beauty and romantic aura. Seville (*Sevilla* in Spanish), the capital of Andalusia, is such a place. Despite its sultry summer heat, it remains one of Spain's most charming cities. If you're only going to see a few Spanish cities in your lifetime, make one of them Seville.

All the images associated with Andalusia—orange trees, mantillas, love-sick toreros, flower-filled patios, and castanet-rattling Gypsies—come alive in Seville. But this is no mere tourist city; it's also a substantial river port, and it possesses some of the most important artistic works and architectural monuments in Spain.

Unlike many other Spanish cities, Seville fared rather well under most of its conquerors—the Romans, Arabs, and Christians. Rulers from Pedro the Cruel to Ferdinand and Isabella held court here. When Spain entered its 16th-century Golden Age, Seville funneled gold from the New World into the rest of the country, and Columbus docked here after his journey to America. During this time Seville was the richest city in Europe and many of its spectacular buildings date from this era.

ORIENTATION
Getting There

BY PLANE Iberia (© 800/772-4642 in the U.S., or © 90-240-05-00 toll-free in Spain) flies several times a day between Madrid (and elsewhere via Madrid) and Seville's Aeropuerto San Pablo, Calle Almirante Lobo (© 95-444-90-00). Flights from the U.K. are operated by **Ryanair** (© 0871-246-00-00 in the U.K.; www.ryanair.com) daily from London Stansted and London Gatwick and by **Vueling** (© 0911-263-26-32 in the UK; www.vueling.com) daily from London Heathrow.

The airport is about 9.6km (6 miles) from the center of the city, along the A-4 highway leading to Carmona. There's a half-hourly airport bus service (6:15am to 11pm), marked EA on bus maps, which runs to the city center. It costs 2.30€ and takes about 30 minutes. It terminates at the main bus station, Prado de San Sebastián (see "By Bus", below), which is a bit of a walk from most hotels so you'll probably need to jump in a taxi or take the tram to complete your journey. The bus also stops at

Santa Justa, the main rail station (see "By Train", below). A taxi from the airport into town costs about 22€.

BY TRAIN   Trains to Seville arrive at the main Estación Santa Justa, Av. Kansas City s/n (© **90-232-03-20** for information and reservations). Buses C1 and C2 take you from this train station to the bus station at Prado de San Sebastián, and bus EA runs to and from the airport. The high-speed AVE train has reduced travel time from Madrid to Seville to 2½ hours and there are 17 trains a day. Up to 23 trains a day connect Seville and Córdoba; the AVE train takes 45 minutes and a slower TALGO takes 1½ hours. Six trains a day run to Málaga, taking 3 hours; there are also four trains per day to Granada (4 hr).

BY BUS   Most buses arrive and depart from the city's largest bus terminal, on the southeast edge of the Old City, at Prado de San Sebastián, Calle José María Osborne 11 (© **95-441-71-11**). Several different companies make frequent runs to and from Córdoba (2½ hr), Málaga (3½ hr), Granada (4 hr), and Madrid (8 hr). Some long-distance services depart from the newer bus station at Plaza de Armas (© **95-490-80-40**), particularly those going west towards Huelva and Portugal. There are useful timetables at www.andalucia.com/travel/bus/seville.htm.

BY CAR   Seville is 540km (341 miles) southwest of Madrid and 217km (135 miles) northwest of Málaga. Several major highways converge on Seville, connecting it with the rest of Spain and Portugal. During periods of heavy holiday traffic, the A-5/E-90 from Madrid through Extremadura—which, at Mérida, connects with the southbound A-66/E-803—is usually less congested than the A-4/E-5 through eastern Andalusia.

Visitor Information

The excellent main **city tourist office** is at 19 Plaza de San Francisco (© **95-459-52-88;** www.turismosevilla.org). There's also a desk in the arrivals hall at the airport (© **95-444-91-28**). The **Andalusia regional tourist office** is also very helpful, and often not so busy. It's located at 21 Av. de la Constitución (© **95-475-75-78**). If you want to explore more of Seville province, the helpful **tourist office for the province** is at Plaza del Triunfo 1, just after the exit from the Alcázar (© **95-421-00-05**).

City Layout

Seville's **Old Town (Centro Histórico)** was once completely enclosed by walls and it's still fairly compact. The best, and really the only, way to explore it is on foot. In the middle of the Centro Histórico, **Seville Cathedral** and its adjoining **Giralda** tower are an obvious focal point and the ideal place to start exploring. Other major sights like the **Alcázar** palace and **Barrio de Santa Cruz**, the old Jewish Quarter, are just nearby. Running right past the Cathedral is the main street, pedestrianized **Avenida de la Constitución** with the city's modern urban trams running along it. At its north end you'll find Plaza Nueva with the **Town Hall (Ayuntamiento)** and the main **city tourist office**. Just east of the Old Town is the **Arenal** area with the city's famous **Maestranza bullring**, the **Fine Arts Museum (Museo de Bellas Artes),** and opera house on the banks of the Guadalquivir River, which bisects the city. Here, near to Puente de San Telmo, are such sights as the Torre del Oro, the University of Seville, and the Parque de María Luisa. Across on the other side of the river is the **Triana** district, the old Gypsy Quarter of the city with its attractive riverside bars and restaurants.

FINDING AN ADDRESS   Most of Seville's streets run one way, usually toward the Guadalquivir River. Individual buildings are numbered with odd addresses on one side of the street and even numbers on the opposite side, so no. 14 would likely fall opposite nos. 13 and 15. Many addresses are marked s/n, which means the building has no number (*sin número*). When this occurs, be sure to obtain the name of a cross street as a reference point.

MAPS   If you're in Seville for more than a day or two, you might want to invest in a detailed street map. The best are those published by **Euro City,** available at local newsstands and in bookstores. These maps contain not only a detailed street index, but also plot tourist information, places of interest, and even locations of vital services (such as the police station). You can more or less count on getting lost in the intricate maze of the Barrio de Santa Cruz, for which no adequate map exists, but that's half the fun of it.

The Neighborhoods in Brief

Centro Histórico   This is the heart of historic Seville and contains its most imposing sights. Of these, the massive **Seville Cathedral (Catedral de Sevilla)** is the dominant attraction along with the beautiful royal palace, the **Alcázar.** It's the area where you'll want to spend the most time, and it's also where you'll find most of the finest hotels and restaurants.

Barrio de Santa Cruz   This is quintessential Seville, an area of wrought-iron gates, courtyards with Andalusian tiled fountains, art galleries, restaurants, cafes, *tabernas,* flowerpots of geraniums, and winding narrow alleyways. The former ghetto of Seville's Jews, it's today named after a Christian saint and is the single-most colorful part of the city. It can get pretty busy with tourists during the day, but it's genuinely charming.

La Macarena   About a 15-minute walk from the Centro Histórico, this quarter of Seville is far less visited by tourists. If you want to see the city away from the sights, it's full of atmosphere and well worth a visit. Along with some fine churches and convents, you'll find much of the edgier nightlife here, particularly around the

Alameda, a wide tree-lined square fringed with buzzing bars and bistros.

Triana & El Arenal   These two districts were immortalized by Cervantes, Quevedo, and Lope de Vega, the fabled writers of Spain's Golden Age. Either side of the Guadalquivir River, they were the rough-and-tough seafaring quarters when Seville was a thriving port in the 1600s. In El Arenal, the 12-sided **Torre del Oro (Gold Tower),** built by the Almohads in 1220, overlooks the river on Paseo Cristóbal Colón. You can stroll along the riverside esplanade, Marqués de Contadero, which stretches along the banks of the river from the tower. The area's **Museo Provincial de Bellas Artes** houses Spain's best collection of Seville's painters, notably Murillo. Across the river, **Triana** was once the Gypsy Quarter but has now been gentrified.

Parque María Luisa   A welcome escape from the busy city, this large tree-filled expanse of park is ideal for relaxing in the shade or allowing the kids to run around. It's also home to the spectacular crescent-shaped **Plaza de España** and several interesting city museums.

GETTING AROUND

Seville's narrow streets and tiny squares are generally best negotiated on foot and because the main sights are all quite close together, this is usually the best way to get around. You might want to jump on the tram if you're feeling weary or even use one of the Sevici city-bikes to do short hops from one neighborhood to another.

By Bus

Urban bus services operated by the town transport system **Tussam** (www.tussam.es) are frequent but most don't enter the Old City's narrow streets. However the C5 line, often serviced by an electric microbus, does go into the Old City and it's quite handy for getting around, stopping at many of the tourist sights. C1, C2, C3, and C4 also do useful clockwise and anti-clockwise circuits of the perimeter. Single journey tickets costing 1.20€ can be bought on board. Ten-journey multi-tickets (*bónobus*) can be bought from newsstands (*kioscos*). One- and three-day passes are available from the Tussam office at the bus station and Tussam kiosks at Plaza Ponce de Leon and Puerta de Jerez. For general bus information, call ℂ **90-245-99-54.**

By Bicycle

Sevillians are really getting into cycling. Cycle lanes have been laid down on main routes and there are plenty of racks to lock your bike. The recent introduction of the new **Sevici** urban cycle program has been a big success. Visitors can use the Sevici bikes too. Just register with your credit card at one of the many cycle stand booths. You're given a unique user ID and select a PIN code which you input each time you take a bike. The first 30 minutes are completely free, the next hour costs 1€ and subsequent hours 2€. (See www.sevici.es for more info in English.) They are generally well maintained, but check your selected bike is in good order before setting off. During rush hour it's sometimes hard to find a bike or a free parking stand.

By Carriage

They're romantic, the echo of the horses' hooves making an appealing clip-clop on the cobblestones, and the Giralda seems ever-so-evocative from behind a horse's rump. You'll find clusters of such carriages in several locations around the Old Town, most notably on Plaza Virgen de los Reyes right next to the cathedral, and on Plaza del Triunfo next to the Alcázar. There's a standard tour that lasts about an hour and should cost 36.06€ per carriage (43.27€ during Holy Week and 86.54€ during April Fair Week.) Some of the drivers can be a bit brusque and not many speak much

---

📎 Seville: A Driver-Unfriendly City

Be warned that driving here is a nightmare: Seville was planned for the horse and buggy rather than for the car, and the city's one-way system seems to have been designed specifically to frustrate drivers. Locating a hard-to-find restaurant or a hidden little square will require patience and luck. The tourist offices have made great efforts to signpost the location of every hotel however. The signposts respect one-way street routings, and, in most cases, they actually work, even in neighborhoods with streets that are impossibly narrow.

English. Stand your ground if they try to overcharge you. I've had one try to make me pay 50€ for a standard tour.

By Taxi

This is quite a viable means of getting around, especially at night, when it's easy to get lost in the tangle of streets. Local firms include **Tele Taxi** (© **954 622 222, Radio Taxi Giralda** (© **954 675 555,** and **Radio Taxi** (© **954 580 000**/954 571 111. Taxi ranks are well located at Plaza Nueva outside the Hotel Inglaterra, Calle Alemanes right next to Starbucks, and Puerta de Jerez outside Hotel Alfonso XIII. Cabs are metered and charge about .60€ per kilometer at night and .50€ during the day. Meters, even before you get in, start at 3€.

By Street Car/Tram

Seville's first street car line is a modest affair of just four stations, but it's very handy, connecting Prado de San Sebastián, where the airport bus terminates, with the historic center. Line one of Seville's much-awaited subway (underground) is now open, but it's not particularly useful for tourists as it bypasses the historic center.

By Car

Car hire desks are on the ground floor of the airport terminal building as you exit arrivals. The cheapest by far is local company **Auriga/Crown** (© **954 516 808;** en.aurigacrown.com). **Avis** (© **954 449 121**); **Europcar** (© **954 254 298**) and **Hertz** (© **954 514 720**) also have airport hire desks. The downtown location for car hire is the main Santa Justa station on Avenida de Kansas City and all three have offices here too.

[Fast FACTS] SEVILLE

Babysitters If you need a babysitter, ask the concierge or reception desk of your hotel. You will not always get an English-speaker, however.

Bookstore The **Beta Librería,** Calle Sierpes 25. (© **95-429-37-24,** sells books in Spanish and, to a lesser extent, English and French. It's the most centrally located of a large chain of bookstores with other branches throughout the city.

Consulates Most nations only have consulates in Seville, which means passport replacement involves a long trip to the nearest embassy in Madrid or Málaga. Seville contact numbers are: **U.S. consulate** (© **95-421-85-71**; **Canada consulate** (© **95-429-68-19**; **U.K. consulate** (© **95-422-88-74**/95-235-23-00**.

Currency Exchange Many of these offices are scattered within the neighborhood around the cathedral, but some of the biggest and busiest lie immediately adjacent to the post office. As for ATMs, there are dozens around Seville, especially near the cathedral.

Dentists If you have an emergency, check at the reception desk of your hotel. There's also a large dental clinic with extended hours for emergencies. It's the **Centro Dentaire La Macarena,** Rondo Capucinos 8–10 (© **95-441-32-02**).

Emergencies For the police or fire department, call (© **112.** For an ambulance, also call (© **112.**

Hospitals The city's biggest and best equipped is **Virgen del Rocío,** Av. Manuel Siurot s/n (© **95-501-20-00**), about 2km (1¼ miles) from the city center. Your hotel should be able to provide you with the names and addresses of local doctors for minor health emergencies.

Internet Access The **tourist office** on Plaza San Francisco has 10 terminals offering free access, but you often have to wait your turn. Most hotels now offer Wi-Fi, many of them for free.

Newspapers Newsstands in the center of the city as well as many first-class and deluxe hotels have English-language newspapers and magazines available. Two locally edited daily newspapers of note are the somewhat to-the-right-of-center **ABC**, selling at newsstands for around 1€, and the Andalusian edition of **El País,** a centrist to slightly left-of-center publication, selling for 1€.

Pharmacies One of the biggest is the **Farmacia Puerta de la Carne,** Calle Demetrio de los Ríos 3 (☎ **95-441-44-53**). Check any pharmacy window for the name and address of an all-night pharmacy—pharmacies rotate that duty. You can also call **Farmacias de Guardia** at ☎ **90-252-21-11** for the night-duty schedule.

Police The main police station is about a 10-minute walk from the historic center on the Alameda de Hercules (☎ **95-428-95-62**).

Post Office The Central Post Office (**Correos y Telegrafos**) is at Av. de la Constitución 2 (☎ **95-422-47-60**). It's open Monday to Friday 8:30am–8:30pm, Sat 9am–2pm.

Safety Generally Seville is as safe as any other big city, but be vigilant at night around the Alameda and Parque María Luisa districts and avoid leaving cars unguarded with your luggage inside.

Taxis See "Getting Around," above.

Toilets Public toilets (*los servicios*) were once a rarity, but modern, generally well-serviced cubicles (*Aseos*) have appeared around town and cost 20¢ to use. Town center locations include Plaza Nueva and Puerta de Jerez. Locals often just duck into a bar or cafe and use the toilets there, it's not a problem to do so.

WHERE TO STAY

During Holy Week and the Seville Fair (*Féria de Abril*), hotels often double, even triple, their rates. Price increases are often not announced until the last minute. If you're going to be in Seville at these times, arrive with an ironclad reservation and an agreement about the price before checking in.

Very Expensive

Hotel Alfonso XIII ★★ At a corner of the gardens fronting the Alcázar, this is one of Spain's three or four most legendary hotels and considered by many to be Seville's premier address. Built in the Mudéjar/Andalusian revival style as a shelter for patrons of the Ibero-American Exposition of 1929, and named after the then-king of Spain, it reigns as a super-ornate and expensive bastion of glamour. Its rooms and hallways glitter with hand-painted tiles, acres of marble and mahogany, antique furniture embellished with intricately embossed leather, and a spaciousness that's nothing short of majestic. If you're looking for high-end luxury with no expense spared, it's the place to come to, but if you're looking for romantic atmosphere there are several delightful boutique hotels in the Old Town which I think are nicer and offer better value for money. Service here is efficient or a bit cold, depending on your perspective.

San Fernando 2, 41004 Seville. ✆ **800/221-2340** in the U.S. and Canada, or ✆ 95-491-70-00. Fax 95-491-70-99. www.hotel-alfonsoxiii.com. 146 units. 329€–640€ double; from 854€ suite. AE, DC, MC, V. Parking 20€. **Amenities:** 2 restaurants; 3 bars; babysitting; nonsmoking rooms; outdoor pool; room service; tennis courts; Wi-Fi. *In room:* A/C, TV, hair dryer, minibar.

Expensive

Casa Imperial ★★   This building, in the historic center near Casa Pilatos, dates from the 15th century, when it housed the butler to the Marquis of Tarifa. The hotel's modern interior is refined, and there are four Andalusian patios full of exotic plants. The beamed ceilings are original, and sparkling chandeliers hang from the ceilings. The rooms are large—many have small kitchens and ample terraces. Bathrooms are tastefully decorated and feature both showers and luxurious tubs, some of which are antiques. Service is very good here too.

Calle Imperial 29, 41003 Seville. ✆ **95-450-03-00.** Fax 95-450-03-30. 24 units. 185€–214€ double; 220€–449€ suite. AE, DC, MC, V. Limited free parking, otherwise 21€. **Amenities:** Restaurant; bar; babysitting; room service. *In room:* A/C, TV, minibar, hair dryer, Wi-Fi.

Casa Número 7 ★★   This is as close as you can get to staying in an elegant private home in Seville. Next to the Santa Cruz barrio, the little inn is in a beautiful, sensitively restored 19th-century mansion where you live in style, with a butler to serve you breakfast. Small in size, Casa Número 7 portrays itself, with some justification, as a civilized oasis in the midst of a bustling city. The building envelops an old atrium, and is filled with such touches as family photographs, Oriental rugs, a marble fireplace, and floral-print love seats. Rooms are individually decorated in Old Sevillano style, with impeccable taste and an eye to comfort. A favorite is the spacious Yellow Room, with its "Juliet balcony" overlooking the street.

Vírgenes 7, 41004 Seville. ✆ **95-422-15-81.** Fax 95-421-45-27. www.casanumero7.com. 6 units. 177€–280€ double. AE, MC, V. Rates include breakfast. **Amenities:** "Honesty" bar. *In room:* A/C, hair dryer, Wi-Fi.

Corral Del Rey ★★   This lovely, family-run, 17th-century palace house has been stylishly converted into a comfortable boutique hideaway, located moments

---

😊 **FAMILY-**friendly **ACCOMMODATION**

Hotel Bécquer (p. 87)   Well located close to the historic center, this modern, family-run hotel offers a warm welcome to children. Rooms are modern and functional, offering excellent value for money.

Hotel Doña María (p. 88)   Behind the cathedral and the Giralda, this is one of the most gracious hotels in the old quarter of Seville. The garden courtyard and the rooftop pool delight adults and children alike. Rooms contain wide beds and bathrooms with dual sinks, and some rooms are large enough for the entire family.

Hotel Fernando III (p. 88)   This hotel is in the medieval Barrio de Santa Cruz, the old Jewish Quarter. The helpful and polite staff speaks English and is welcoming to families, offering some guest rooms large enough to accommodate children and adults.

Or hire a self-catering apartment so you can come and go as you please. See box **Stay In An Apartment** below.

Where to Stay in Seville

Alcoba de Rey de Sevilla **2**
Amadeus **23**
Bécquer **8**
Casa Imperial **27**
Casa Número 7 **26**
Casa Sacristía Santa Ana **3**
Corral Del Rey **24**
Corregidor Hotel **4**
Gran Meliá Colón **6**
Hotel Alfonso XIII **14**
Hotel Alminar **13**
Hotel Doña María **15**
Hotel Europa **12**
Hotel Fernando III **21**
Hotel Goya **17**
Hotel Inglaterra **10**

Hotel Montecarlo **7**
Hotel Murillo **18**
Hotel Rey Alfonso X **19**
Hotel San Gil Seville **1**
Hotel YH Giralda **16**
Las Casas de la Judería **22**
Las Casas de los Mercaderes **25**
Las Casas del Rey de Baeza **28**
NH Plaza de Armas **5**
Palacio de Villapanés **29**
Taberna del Alabardero **9**
Un Patio en Santa Cruz **20**
Vincci La Rabida **11**

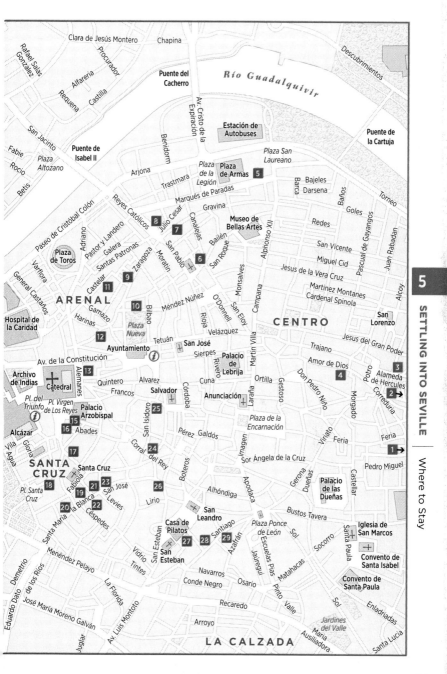

Río Guadalquivir

from the hubbub of Santa Cruz. Rooms and bathrooms are located around a delightful restored Sevillian patio and have all been fitted out to the highest standard, with the latest fixtures and fittings and large comfy beds. There's a nice roof terrace with a plunge pool too. They're in the process of converting the house opposite too, which means there will be more rooms available soon. The Reid family also owns the gorgeous Hacienda de San Rafael just out of town (see "Where To Stay Nearby").

Corral del Rey 12. ⓒ **954 227 116.** www.corraldelrey.com. 6 units. 280€–320€ double; 380€ junior suite. AE, DC, MC, V. **Amenities:** Bar; breakfast lounge; nonsmoking rooms; roof terrace with plunge pool. *In room:* A/C, TV, DVD player, hair dryer, iPod station, minibar, Wi-Fi.

Gran Meliá Colón ★★   The recent makeover of this grand old dame has been a real success. It's still a big hotel, but the rooms are tastefully designed (the top end ones by Spanish designer Agustin Diaz), exquisitely appointed, and genuinely comfortable. All manner of upgrade options are available if budget's not an issue: choose from ten different categories of room from Delux, Panoramic Delux, Premium, and Grand Premium and then keep going to the exclusive "Red Level" area—a boutique hotel within a hotel with its own special lounge area and several penthouses with private roof terraces equipped with Jacuzzis. Common areas have modern flourishes with red and black-themed furniture and modern steel chandeliers. Perhaps the biggest draw though is the El Burladero restaurant where head chef is current Spanish wondercook Dani Garcia.

Canalejas 1, 41001, Seville. ⓒ **95-450-55-99.** Fax 95-422-09-38. www.gran-melia-colon.com. 211 units. 270€–345€ double; 500€–3,500€ suite. AE, DC, MC, V. **Amenities:** Restaurant; bar; lounge; babysitting; gym; massage; room service; spa; nonsmoking rooms; rooms for those w/limited mobility. *In room:* A/C, TV, CD player, hair dryer, minibar, Wi-Fi.

Las Casas de la Judería ★★★   Within easy walking distance of the cathedral and other sights, the building has been a hotel since 1991. It's now one of the best places to stay in Seville, offering excellent value for your euro. Set amidst a luxurious warren of ancient houses and patios connected by underground tunnels, the rooms are all unique, some fantastically opulent; many have four-poster beds and most look out onto tranquil patios. There's an enticing rooftop pool and fantastic spa in the basement, on the site of some old Roman ruins. Service is also excellent.

Plaza Santa María la Blanca, Callejón de Dos Hermanas 7, 41004 Seville. ⓒ **95-441-51-50.** Fax 95-442-21-70. www.casasypalacios.com. 118 units. 140€–265€ double; 385€ junior suite. AE, DC, MC, V. Parking 15€. **Amenities:** Restaurant; bar; babysitting; room service; rooms for those w/limited mobility; Wi-Fi. *In room:* A/C, TV, hair dryer, minibar.

Las Casas del Rey de Baeza ★★   This effortlessly stylish hotel, close to the Casa de Pilatos and well located for the historic center, is part of the boutique Hospes chain which has similarly excellent hotels in Granada and Córdoba too. As is the case with all their properties, this one cleverly blends the historic with the ultra-modern, with stone floors and 19th-century Andalusian architecture coupled with state-of-the-art designer fixtures and fittings. A hotel since 1998, it has an interior patio surrounded by a cozy coterie of rooms and a long Andalusian balcony. Some of the beautifully furnished rooms have living rooms, and the decor is finely honed in marble and wood with comfortable furnishings. Service is excellent here too.

Calle Santiago, Plaza Jesús de la Redención 2, 41003 Seville. ⓒ **95-456-14-96.** Fax 95-456-14-41. www.hospes.es. 41 units. 176€–300€ double; 321€–500€ suite. AE, DC, MC, V. Parking 18€. **Amenities:**

Restaurant; bar; lounge; babysitting; gym; massage; outdoor pool; room service; sauna; nonsmoking rooms; rooms for those w/limited mobility: Internet. *In room:* A/C, TV, hair dryer, minibar.

Palacio de Villapanés ★   In a huge palace house, right opposite the Casas del Rey de Baeza, this Palacio is one of the newest hotels in Seville. Set around a fountain-filled main patio, it has been renovated in luxuriously modern style with lots of dark wood and white upholstery and elaborate chandeliers. The high quality rooms are really spacious, with huge, comfy beds and expansive bathrooms—many with free-standing baths and surprisingly high ceilings. Attractive architectural flourishes like beautifully carved parquet floors and ceiling cornices have been carefully retained. There's a good pool and terrace on the roof with nice views across the Old Town and a fine dining restaurant in the vaulted cellars.

Santiago 31, 41003 Seville. ✆ **95-450-20-63.** Fax **95-450-20-65.** www.almasevilla.com. 55 units. 162€–520€ double. AE, DC, MC, V. **Amenities:** Restaurant; bar; lounge; babysitting; massage; outdoor pool; room service; nonsmoking rooms; rooms for those w/limited mobility. *In room:* A/C, TV, hair dryer, minibar, Wi-Fi.

Moderate

Alcoba de Rey de Sevilla ★ 👬   Located about a 20-minute walk from the historic center in the Macarena district, this small boutique hotel in a little palace dating from the 13th century is inspired by the Seville of al-Andalus in the city's Moorish heyday. Its architectural structure is based on handmade materials used here eight centuries ago. Each midsize bedroom not only has an exotic name—Princess Zaida or Rumaykiyya—but contains a unique decor including horseshoe arches, silk fabrics, carved headboards, king-size beds with canopy, and the scent of cedar furnishings. The stuccoed bathrooms are a special feature with much use made of marble. As a surprise, guests can buy everything they see in the hotel, even the beds and furnishings. There's also a roof terrace with Jacuzzi.

Calle Bécquer, 41009 Seville. ✆ **95-491-58-00.** Fax 95-491-56-75. www.alcobadelrey.com. 15 units. 105€–234€ double; 143€–259€ suite. AE, DC, MC, V. Parking 12€. **Amenities:** Breakfast lounge; cafeteria; room service; nonsmoking rooms; rooms for those w/limited mobility. *In room:* A/C, TV, hair dryer, Wi-Fi.

Bécquer ☺   A short walk from the action of the Seville bullring and only two blocks from the river, Bécquer is on a street full of cafes where you can order tapas and enjoy Andalusian wine. The Museo Provincial de Bellas Artes is also nearby. Built in the 1970s, the hotel has been enlarged and renovated. It occupies the site of a former mansion and is decorated with *objets d'art* rescued before that building was demolished. You register in a modern lobby before being shown to one of the functionally outfitted rooms—good value in a pricey city, as most units are at the lower end of the price scale. There's a new rooftop pool and bar too.

Calle Reyes Católicos 4, 41001 Seville. ✆ **95-422-89-00.** Fax 95-421-44-00. www.hotelbecquer.com. 141 units. 85€–210€ double; 250€–324€ suite. AE, DC, MC, V. Parking 15€. **Amenities:** Restaurant; 2 bars; lounge; babysitting; outdoor rooftop pool; room service; spa. *In room:* A/C, TV, hair dryer; minibar, Internet.

Casa Sacristía Santa Ana ★ 👬   A former 18th-century sacristy has been successfully converted into an attractive boutique hotel right on the busy Alameda plaza, the hub of Seville's cooler nightlife and about a 15-minute walk from the historic center. This country-chic establishment has contemporary gadgetry and plumbing, but still maintains an Andalusian architectural purity. All the romantic,

Stay In An Apartment

If you're planning on spending longer in Seville or you just like doing things yourself, there are lots of good-value, atmospheric apartments available for hire. They can be a really cheap deal if you're a large family or group of friends. Many are located in the up-and-coming Alameda district. Set up by a German and an American who have both made the city their home, **Sevilla 5** (☏ **95-438-75-50;** www.sevilla5.com) has well-managed, well-located apartments to cover most price requirements, particularly good for longer stays. **Apartments Sevilla** (☏ **95-421-69-12;** www.apartments sevilla.com) has several high-standard apartments right in the center with fantastic views of the cathedral. Staff members speak good English at both agencies and are very helpful.

midsize rooms are meticulously decorated and designed for both comfort and style, the ones on the top floor being particularly stylish.

Alameda de Hércules 22, 41022 Seville. ☏ **95-491-57-22.** www.sacristiadesantaana.com. 25 units. 100€–200€ double; 195€–300€ junior suite. MC, V. **Amenities:** Restaurant; bar; room service. *In room:* A/C, TV, minibar, Wi-Fi.

Corregidor Hotel ✒   This is a typical Andalusian hotel with colonial styling such as arches, balconies, tall windows, antiques, lamps, columns, and colorful tiles. In the local style, life revolves around a central patio. The hotel was constructed in 1977 but has been considerably renovated since then. The midsize bedrooms are comfortably and traditionally furnished with tiles and wooden furniture. The English bar is a popular gathering place for guests. The charming atmosphere makes this hotel very good value.

Morgado 17, 41003 Seville. ☏ **95-438-51-11.** Fax 95-438-42-38. www.vimehoteles.com. 76 units. 69€–125€ double; 180€ suite. AE, DC, MC, V. Parking 16€. **Amenities:** Restaurant; bar; babysitting; room service. *In room:* A/C, TV, hair dryer, Internet.

Hotel Doña María ★ ☺   Highlights at this well-situated hotel include the Iberian antiques in the stone lobby and upper hallways and a location a few steps from the cathedral, which allows for dramatic views from the rooftop terrace. An ornate neoclassical entryway is offset with a pure white facade and iron balconies, which hint at the building's origin in the 1840s as a private villa. Amid the flowering plants on the upper floor you'll find garden-style lattices and antique wrought-iron railings. Room sizes range from small to large enough for the entire family, and some have four-poster beds, while others have a handful of antique reproductions. Light sleepers might find the noise of the cathedral's bells jarring. There's a garden courtyard and a rooftop pool.

Don Remondo 19, 41004 Seville. ☏ **95-422-49-90.** Fax 95-421-95-46. www.hdmaria.com. 64 units. 150€–250€ double. AE, DC, MC, V. Parking 20€. **Amenities:** Breakfast room; 2 bars; babysitting; outdoor pool; room service. *In room:* A/C, TV, hair dryer, minibar, Wi-Fi.

Hotel Fernando III ☺   You'll find the Fernando III on a narrow, quiet street at the edge of the Barrio de Santa Cruz, near the northern periphery of the Murillo Gardens. Established in 1969, this hotel is warmer, much bigger, and more obviously "Andalusian" in its decor and presentation than the more modern angularity of its sister hotel, the also-recommended Hotel Alfonso X, just across a narrow alleyway. With sweeping expanses of marble flooring in the lobby, a very plush and posh-looking cocktail bar, a uniformed staff, and a well-manicured and impeccably correct restaurant, it's rather "grand hotel" in its presentation. Many of the rooms—medium in size, comfortably furnished, and well maintained—offer balconies filled with cascading plants. The restaurant features regional Andalusian cuisine.

San José 21, 41001 Seville. ✆ **95-421-77-08.** Fax 95-422-02-46. www.hotelfernandoiii.com. 157 units. 90€–250€ double; 250€–280€ suite. AE, DC, MC, V. Parking 20€. **Amenities:** Restaurant; bar; rooftop pool; room service. *In room:* A/C, TV, minibar, hair dryer, Wi-Fi.

Hotel Inglaterra ★   This is a very comfortable hotel, the historical importance of which has been rather hidden behind contemporary-looking marble sheathing that was added in 1968 as part of a radical modernization. Inaugurated with pomp and circumstance in 1857 and still considered one of the finest hotels in Seville, it has hosted the monarchs of Spain and Belgium (in 1915 and 1921, respectively), Seville-born actress Penelope Cruz, and many Spanish and international luminaries. It occupies one side of a palm-lined plaza (Plaza Nueva) that's home to some of Seville's most upscale shops. Throughout, there's an elegant but unpretentious ambience that's maintained by a top-notch concierge staff. Bedrooms are plush, conservatively modern, and comfortable. On site is a richly decorated Irish pub, the Trinity.

Plaza Nueva 7, 41001 Seville. ✆ **95-422-49-70.** Fax 95-456-13-36. www.hotelinglaterra.es. 86 units. 135€–250€ double; 330€–400€ suite. AE, DC, MC, V. Parking 15€ per day. **Amenities:** Restaurant; bar; babysitting; room service. *In room:* A/C, TV, hair dryer, minibar, radio, Wi-Fi.

Hotel Montecarlo 🔥   The government gives it only a two-star rating, but this stylish 18th-century house is a good choice for those seeking old-fashioned Seville atmosphere. The hotel, with its two main yards, is within walking distance of the historic monuments in the center of Seville. In typically Andalusian manner, there is a fountain-studded central patio filled with plants. Long corridors, columns, colorful tiles, and arches set the architectural style. The bedrooms are midsize to spacious and are comfortably and attractively furnished.

Calle Gravina 51, 41001 Seville. ✆ **95-421-75-01.** Fax 95-421-68-25. www.hotelmontecarlosevilla.com. 49 units. 65€–170€ double. AE, MC, V. **Amenities:** Restaurant; babysitting; room service. *In room:* A/C, TV, hair dryer.

Hotel San Gil Seville ★★ 🎒   This landmark building from 1901, set amongst towering palm trees, captures some of the colonial style of Old Seville. As a guest, you enjoy an aura of old Andalusia while taking advantage of modern amenities. Near the historic Macarena Wall and the Alameda, about a 15-minute walk from the historic center, the hotel has a rooftop swimming pool that opens onto vistas of the surrounding cityscape. Inside, the hotel is richly endowed with old Andalusian styling, including an elaborate use of tiles. Bedrooms are midsize for the most part and decorated in creamy colors with light wooden furnishings, plus tiled bathrooms with tub/shower combos.

Parras 28, 41002 Seville. ✆ **95-490-68-11.** Fax 95-490-69-39. www.sevillahotelsangil.com. 60 units. 75€–211€ double; 100€–233€ junior suite. Rates include continental breakfast. AE, DC, MC, V. Parking 15€. **Amenities:** Restaurant; bar; babysitting; outdoor pool; room service; solarium. *In room:* A/C, TV, hair dryer, kitchenette (in suite), minibar, Wi-Fi.

Las Casas de los Mercaderes Atmospheric and historic, this boutique-style hotel was built in the 18th century (with alterations in the 19th c.) as a patio-centered, three-story private home that's about as Sevillian as you can get. Today, the patio that for many generations remained open to the sky is covered with a Victorian-inspired glass-and-iron canopy, allowing the courtyard to be plushly furnished with kilim carpets and wicker chairs that gracefully show off a ring of delicate granite columns. Bedrooms are cozy and relatively plush, with generous curtains, carpets, hand-carved furniture, and marble floors. The cathedral is just a four-minute walk away and the staff is attentive.

Calle Alvarez Quintero 9–13, 41004 Seville. ☎ **95-422-58-58.** Fax 95-422-98-84. www.casasypalacios. com. 47 units. 112€–128€ double. AE, DC, MC, V. Parking 18€ per day. **Amenities:** 2 bars; coffee bar; babysitting; room service; solarium; Wi-Fi. In room: A/C, TV, hair dryer, minibar.

NH Plaza de Armas Part of the modern NH hotels chain, this glass-and-steel hotel is in direct contrast to the antique *casas* of Seville converted into hotels. Built in 1992, it is the city's most modern-looking structure, in the center close to the Plaza de Armas and about a 10-minute walk from Seville Cathedral. The interior design consists of architectural lines of almost Japanese simplicity intermixed with steel and wood. The rooms are airy and colorful in severe contemporary style, with roomy bathrooms. The rooftop pool has great views across the river.

Av. Marqués de Paradas s/n, 41001 Seville. ☎ **95-490-19-92.** Fax 95-490-12-32. www.nh-hoteles.es. 262 units. 75€–175€ double. AE, DC, MC, V. **Amenities:** Restaurant; bar; babysitting; outdoor swimming pool; room service. In room: A/C, TV, hair dryer, minibar, Wi-Fi.

Taberna del Alabardero ★★ 🎁 With the city's famous catering academy right next door, the Taberna is *the* place to stay for foodies, offering some of Seville's finest dining. The other place to stay for dining delights is the Gran Melia Colón, but the accommodation there is in a different price bracket (see Gran Melia Colón entry above). They've now added seven guest rooms to this restored 19th-century mansion—all with antique furniture and whirlpool baths. The rooms are decorated in specific regional styles such as native Andalusian, Castilian, Extremaduran, or Galician and are reached via a splendid central patio. The attention to detail is so impressive that some guests might feel that they are staying in a museum; others will be delighted with the refined atmosphere this evokes.

Zaragoza 20, 41001 Seville. ☎ **95-450-27-21.** Fax 95-456-36-66. www.tabernadelalabardero. 7 units. 130€–150€ double; 150€–205€ junior suite. Rates include continental breakfast. AE, DC, MC, V. Parking 15€. **Amenities:** Restaurant; bar; lounge; babysitting; room service. In room: A/C, TV, hair dryer, minibar, Wi-Fi.

Vincci La Rabida ★ 🎁 This restored *palacio* in the Barrio del Arenal neighborhood, near the cathedral, was erected in the typical Andalusian style of the 18th century. The hotel is only a short walk from many of the city's major attractions, including its main shopping district. The restored bedrooms are handsomely, even elegantly, furnished. Best are the two suites with large balconies looking out over Seville, offering panoramic views of the cathedral and the Giralda tower. The suites have a separate sitting room and a Jacuzzi. The hotel's restaurant is one of the most romantic in the city with lovely views. The menu features traditional Sevillian cuisine, with such well-prepared dishes as red tuna with soy sauce and honey, Iberian pork tenderloin, and boned bull's tail.

Calle Castelar 24, 41001 Seville. ✆ **95-450-12-80.** Fax 95-421-66-00. www.vinccihoteles.com. 81 units. 86€–390€ double; 190€–506€ suite. AE, DC, MC, V. Parking 15€. **Amenities:** Restaurant; babysitting; room service; sauna; nonsmoking rooms; 1 unit for those w/limited mobility. *In room:* A/C, TV, hair dryer, minibar, Wi-Fi.

Inexpensive

Amadeus ★ 🏨   Seville has long been linked with music, especially opera, and both fans and musicians in town for performances find a perfect romantic retreat at this efficient, family-run hotel dedicated to both music and Mozart. The restored 18th-century town house has an Andalusian patio for the occasional classical concert. Staying here is like lodging in a villa dedicated not only to music but painting and sculpture as well. Bedrooms are soundproof in case any guest wants to take advantage of the music room off the central patio. Ask for one of the dozen or so rooms in the main building as they are more traditional and more comfortable. Additional rooms are in an annex, but it's more fun to stay where the action is. All the rooms are in a traditional Sevillian style. The roof terrace, where breakfast is served, looks out over the Old Town, with views of the Giralda tower in the distance.

Calle Farnesio 6, Barrio de Santa Cruz, 41004 Seville. ✆ **95-450-14-43.** Fax 95-450-00-19. www. hotelamadeussevilla.com. 19 units. 90€–160€ double; 140€–220€ junior suite. AE, DC, MC, V. Parking 17€. **Amenities:** Babysitting; nonsmoking rooms; rooms for those w/limited mobility. *In room:* A/C, TV, hair dryer, minibar, Wi-Fi.

Hotel Alminar ★★   Consistently no.1 on Trip Advisor and rightly so: Francisco and his friendly team are, in my opinion, the most helpful in Seville. Don't be put off by the small reception area; rooms are generally well-sized with hi-fi systems and mod cons. Bathrooms are modern and sparklingly clean. The hotel is perfectly located, just a stone's throw from the cathedral, but what really makes a stay here so memorable is the staff. Nothing is too much trouble for them. Be sure to ask for restaurant recommendations in particular; they really know their stuff.

Álvarez Quintero 52, 41004, Seville. ✆ **95-429-39-13.** www.hotelalminar.com. 13 units. 95€–125€ double. AE, DC, MC, V. **Amenities:** Breakfast room; nonsmoking rooms. *In room:* A/C, TV, minibar, Wi-Fi.

Hotel Europa 🌿   Dating from the 18th century, this hotel is well located just a block or two from the cathedral. It's pretty basic, but offers some of the cheapest room rates in this part of the town. It retains much of its original character, with many traditional Andalusian architectural details still evident—tall windows with iron grilles, wide stairs, marble floors, and wooden screens. Bedrooms for the most part are small, though comfortably furnished with rather dark, heavy wooden pieces and thick curtains. Triple and quad rooms are available for families or larger groups.

Jimios 5, 41001 Seville. ✆ **95-450-04-43.** Fax 95-421-00-16. www.hoteleuropasevilla.com. 25 units. 64€–120€ double. MC, V. Parking 16€. **Amenities:** Babysitting; room service (8am–11pm). *In room:* A/C, TV, hair dryer.

Hotel Goya   Its location, in a narrow-fronted town house in the oldest part of the barrio, is one of the Goya's strongest virtues, but the building's gold-and-white facade, ornate iron railings, and picture-postcard demeanor are all noteworthy. The rooms are cozy and simple. Guests congregate in the marble-floored, ground-level salon, where a skylight floods the couches and comfortable chairs with sunlight. No meals are served. Reserve well in advance. Parking is often available along the street.

Mateus Gago 31, 41004 Seville. ☏ **95-421-11-70.** Fax 95-456-29-88. www.hostalgoyasevilla.com. 19 units. 70€–130€ double. MC, V. **Amenities:** Wi-Fi. *In room:* A/C, TV.

Hotel Murillo ★★ ✒ Tucked away on a narrow street in the very heart of Santa Cruz, the Murillo (named after the artist who used to live in this district) is about as close as you can get to the historic center and I think it offers genuinely great value for money, with amenities more akin to a three-star hotel than the government-rated two stars it currently has. Inside, the lounges have some fine architectural characteristics—particularly an impressive vaulted ceiling and antique reproductions. Behind a grilled screen is a pleasant retreat for drinks. Rooms are bright and modern, some with terraces. All bathrooms have tub/shower combos. The downside to its location is that, like all hotels in the barrio, it's virtually impossible to reach by car. There are also good-value apartments across the way from the hotel, which make a useful base for families.

Calle Lope de Rueda 7–9, 41004 Seville. ☏ **95-421-60-95.** Fax 95-421-96-16. www.hotelmurillo.com. 57 units. 70€–175€ double; 87€–210€ triple. AE, DC, MC, V. Parking 15€ nearby. **Amenities:** Breakfast room; nonsmoking rooms. *In room:* A/C, TV, hair dryer, minibar.

Hotel Rey Alfonso X ★ One of the most arresting hotels in Seville occupies a triangle-shaped plaza just a brisk 7-minute walk—through impossibly narrow alleyways loaded with shops and tapas bars—from the back of the cathedral. In 2002 this former office building was radically gutted and stripped, replaced by an angular and minimalist interior that's entirely sheathed, both in its bedrooms and public areas, with slabs of beige-colored marble, dark-stained hardwoods, and white plaster walls. The best bedrooms directly overlook the lively plaza. Additional bedrooms with less intriguing views overlook courtyards and surrounding buildings.

Ximénez de Enciso 35, 41004 Seville. ☏ **95-421-00-70.** Fax 95-456-42-78. www.reyalfonsox.com. 35 units. 120€–218€ double; 213€–300€ suite. AE, DC, MC, V. Parking 20€. **Amenities:** Bar; access to the rooftop pool at the Hotel Fernando III opposite; room service. *In room:* A/C, TV, minibar.

Hotel YH Giralda ★ ✒ This attractively furnished, comfortable small hotel is well located right in the middle of Barrio de Santa Cruz. Rooms lead off an attractive Sevillian patio and bathrooms are to a high standard. Manageress Pilar and her small team are really friendly and helpful. There's no lift or breakfast room and, like all hotels in the Barrio de Santa Cruz, it's difficult to reach by car, but taxi drivers should find it no problem. There's a suite that sleeps three, and a quad room too.

Abades 30. ☏ **95-422-83-24.** www.yh-hoteles.com. 14 units. 50€–94€ double; 70€–115€ suite. AE, DC, MC, V. **Amenities:** Bar; room service; babysitting; nonsmoking rooms; 1 unit for those w/limited mobility. *In room:* A/C, TV, Wi-Fi.

Un Patio en Santa Cruz ★ ✒ In the historic Old Town, a traditional Sevillian house from the early 19th century has been beautifully restored and made into this modern hotel. Exceptional features are a plant-filled white marble patio and a panoramic terrace with bar opening onto a view of the Giralda. Even though the facade is traditional, the interior is strikingly contemporary, offering reasonably priced bedrooms that are well furnished and cozy with double-glazed windows. The hotel is on a pedestrian street, within walking distance of the cathedral and Alcázar. The rooms on the top floor have direct access to the roof terrace.

Calle Doncellas 15, 41004 Seville. ☏ **95-453-94-13.** Fax 95-453-94-61. www.patiosantacruz.com. 13 units. 70€–128€ double; 78€–138€ triple. AE, DC, MC, V. Parking 15€. **Amenities:** Bar; room service; babysitting; nonsmoking rooms; 1 unit for those w/limited mobility. *In room:* A/C, TV, Wi-Fi.

Where to Stay Nearby

El Palacio de San Benito ★★★ 🎁 The most exclusive B&B in southern Spain, this treasure is in a stunningly converted palace that represents the epitome of luxury living as practiced by Spanish dons in the 14th to 15th centuries. You'll need a car to reach the little Moorish town of Cazalla de la Sierra, a 75km (47-mile) drive north of the center of Seville. Seville's best-known decorator, Manuel Morales de Jódar, is responsible for the restoration of the palace and for its decoration. Various tapestries from Aubusson in France and from Brussels decorate the palace. The library, with its Carrara marble fireplace, evokes the best of 19th-century Victoriana. The bedrooms are sumptuous and beautifully furnished, most often with 17th- and 18th-century pieces.

Cazalla de la Sierra, 41370 Seville. ☎ **95-488-33-36.** Fax 95-488-31-62. www.palaciodesanbenito.com. 9 units. 130€–220€ double with breakfast; 240€–330€ double with full board. AE, DC, DISC, MC, V. Parking 15€. **Amenities:** Restaurant; bar; outdoor pool; room service; 1 room for those w/limited mobility, Wi-Fi. *In room:* A/C, TV, hair dryer, minibar.

Hacienda Benazuza/El Bulli Hotel ★★★ 🎁 On a hillside above the agrarian hamlet of Sanlúcar la Mayor, 19km (12 miles) south of Seville, this legendary manor house is surrounded by 16 hectares (40 acres) of olive groves and farmland. Basque-born entrepreneur Rafael Elejabeitia bought the property and spent millions to transform it into one of Andalusia's most historic hotels. All but a few of the rooms are in the estate's main building, each individually furnished with Andalusian antiques and Moorish trappings. The **kitchen** is run by Ferran Adrià, the famous Catalonian chef who is hailed as one of the top chefs in the world. He's rarely on the premises but his recipes and cooking style are used.

Calle Virgen de las Nieves s/n, 41800 Sanlúcar la Mayor, Seville. ☎ **95-570-33-44.** Fax 95-570-34-10. www.elbullihotel.com. 44 units. 350€–490€ double; 455€–570€ junior suite; 820€–1,440€ suite. AE, DC, MC, V. Free parking. Closed Jan 1–Feb 13. From Seville, follow the signs for Huelva and head south on the A-49 Hwy, taking exit 16. **Amenities:** 3 restaurants; 2 bars; babysitting; Internet; Jacuzzi; outdoor pool; room service; tennis court; rooms for those w/limited mobility. *In room:* A/C, TV, hair dryer, minibar.

Hacienda de San Rafael ★★★ 🎁 Without doubt one of my favorite places to stay in all Andalusia, this lovely, converted old olive farm is located about 50km (31 miles) south of Seville halfway to Jerez. The farmhouse has been made into a huge, high-ceilinged lounge where a fire crackles in the vast open fireplace on cooler evenings, and a cozy, intimate dining room. Eleven cloistered rooms surround a brilliant white courtyard behind the farmhouse cascading with bright bougainvillea blooms. Each room is on two levels, with a huge comfy bed, stylish marble bathrooms with separate shower and tub, heaps of fluffy towels, and vases of freshly plucked herbs from the gardens. The emphasis here is on total relaxation and there are no TVs in the rooms. Set apart from the farmhouse amidst fragrant gardens and hidden plunge pools are three delightful *casitas*—cozy little cottages stuffed with lovely antique furniture, each with its own shady veranda where breakfast is served in the mornings. It's the ultimate getaway retreat. Dinner in the restaurant is also a real delight.

Apartado 28 Carretera N-IV (Km 594) 41730 Las Cabezas de San Juan, Seville. ☎ **95-422-71-16** Fax 95-421-84-14 www.haciendadesanrafael.com. 14 units. 240€ double; 480€ casita. AE, DC, MC, V. Free parking. From Seville, follow the signs for Cádiz and head south on the A-49 Hwy, taking exit 16. **Amenities:** Restaurant; bars; babysitting; massage; 3 outdoor pools; room service; tennis court, Wi-Fi. *In room:* A/C, hair dryer; minibar,

Hotel Palacio Marques de la Gomera ★★ 🏨 This restored *palacio* may be 86km (53 miles) west of Sevilla airport, but it's only a 45-minute trip on the A-92 (Sevilla–Málaga–Granada motorway), in the delightful little town of Osuna. The building itself is a masterpiece of 18th-century Andalusian Baroque, on a street that UNESCO voted the "second-most beautiful in Europe." Behind the facade is an elegant, columned patio with spacious galleries built of wood paneling and hand-crafted bricks. There's even an 18th-century chapel. Most of the furnishings are of the same period, including Baroque mirrors, paintings, bronzes, and sculptures. Bedrooms are tasteful and comfortable, all with luxurious private bathrooms (most with Jacuzzi). The Mediterranean cuisine is an ever-changing array of dishes inspired by the inventive chef who believes in market-fresh, full-flavored dishes.

Calle San Pedro 20, 41640 Osuna (Seville). ✆ **95-481-22-23.** Fax 95-481-02-00. www.hotelpalaciodel marques.com. 20 units. 99€–130€ double; 151€–185€ suite. AE, MC, V. Parking 12€. **Amenities:** Restaurant; cafe/bar; babysitting; 24-hr room service; nonsmoking rooms. *In room:* A/C, TV, hair dryer, minibar, Wi-Fi.

WHERE TO DINE

Expensive

Abades Triana MODERN/CREATIVE Upscale dining in an airy space with fantastic views across the river. Executive chef Oscar Fernandez serves creative cuisine using local produce. Dishes like cod confit with honeyed asparagus don't come cheap, but are worth it for a special occasion. If you're feeling flush, try one of the tempting tasting menus ranging from 30€ to 105€.

Betis 69A ✆ **954 286 459.** www.abadestriana.com. Main courses 24€–28€. AE, MC, V Lunch and dinner daily. Closed Mon and Sun evenings.

Abantal ★★★ MODERN/CREATIVE A graduate of the Seville cookery academy and the only Michelin-starred chef in town, Julio Fernandez lets his immaculate cuisine in this modern, intimate restaurant speak for itself. Dishes are very seasonal and the menu changes regularly, but appetizers might include clams with caviar and cream of cauliflower, or seabass carpaccio with almond broth, tomatoes, and pine nuts, Main courses on the menu when I was there included red tuna with peach jus and grilled figs, young veal sirloin with vegetable couscous and matured cheese, and slow-cooked pork shoulder served with garlic puree and grilled vegetables. For serious foodies, the seven-course taster menu paired with regional wines by the in-house sommelier will be the highlight of your visit to Seville. The restaurant is a little way from the historic center—so book a taxi.

Alcalde Jose de la Bandera 7 ✆ **954 540 000.** www.abantalrestaurante.es. Reservations essential. Main courses 23€–26€. AE, MC, V. Lunch and dinner daily. Closed Mon.

Becerrita ★ 🏨 ANDALUSIAN/SPANISH Frankly, Sevillanos would like to keep this cozy little restaurant to themselves, but word is slowly getting out to the inter-national community. In an elegant setting near Plaza Carmen Benitez, the restaurant is decorated with colorful wallpaper, wooden columns, and a collection of drawings. Locals claim the chefs make the best bull's tail croquettes (*croquetas de cola de toro*) in Seville. Against a backdrop of ceramic walls and linen-covered tables, you can also order tamer fare like young sirloin steak, baked white prawns in garlic sauce with white beans, or cod stuffed with scallops and served in a pastry shell with pine nuts.

Sea bass in a cockle sauce is another delight, as is the asparagus with strips of ham. Also look for the wide array of fresh, tasty tapas such as stuffed calamari. The chef's signature dish is *carrillada de Ibérico estofado* (an Iberian pork stew). If you like fish, ask about the daily fresh catch.

Recaredo 9, Santa Catalina. ✆ **95-441-20-57.** www.becerrita.com. Reservations recommended. Main courses 20€–27€. AE, DC, MC, V. Daily 1–4:30pm; Mon–Sat 8pm–midnight. Closed Aug.

Casa Robles ANDALUSIAN This is one of the most famous restaurants in the city, lauded by locals and major Spanish gourmet writers alike. It began life as an unpretentious bar and *bodega* in 1954 and over the years has evolved into a bustling two-floor restaurant in a building a short walk from the cathedral. In an all-Andalusian decor, you can order such dishes as fish soup in the Andalusian style, *lubina con naranjas* (whitefish with Sevillana oranges), hake baked with strips of serrano ham, and many kinds of fresh fish. The dessert list is long and very tempting.

Calle Alvarez Quintero 58. ✆ **95-421-31-50.** Reservations recommended. Main courses 19€–30€. AE, DC, MC, V. Daily 2–5pm and 9pm–1:30am.

Corral del Agua SEVILLANA In an antique building with a central courtyard, this discovery is charmingly positioned in the old barrio of Santa Cruz. With its marble fountain and plants, it's a cozy, atmospheric choice. Once patronized by Don Juan himself (or so it's claimed), this building was originally a stable. Two recommended starters are the salad of lettuce hearts from Tudela with sauteed garlic and strips of ham, and the salmon pudding with mayonnaise. Among our favorite main courses is sea bass in a dry sherry sauce. Also terrific was a sirloin of veal cooked in the old Sevillana way (garlic, bay leaf, olive oil, vegetables, and lots of black pepper). Aficionados order *cola de toro al estilo de Sevilla* (bull's tail in the style of Seville).

Callejón del Agua 6. ✆ **95-422-48-41.** Reservations recommended. Main courses 17€–23€. AE, DC, MC, V. Mon–Sat noon–4pm and 8pm–midnight. Closed 2 weeks in Jan.

Egaña Oriza ★★★ BASQUE/INTERNATIONAL Seville's most stylish restaurant is within the conservatory of a restored mansion adjacent to the Murillo Gardens. Its reputation stems in large part from a game-heavy menu in a region otherwise devoted to seafood. The restaurant was opened by Basque-born owner/chef José Mari Egaña, who combines his passion for hunting with his flair for cooking. Specialties depend on the season but might include ostrich carpaccio, gazpacho with prawns, steak with foie gras in grape sauce, casserole of wild boar with cherries and raisins, duck *quenelles* (a dumpling made with fish or meat and bound with eggs) in a potato nest with apple puree, and woodcock flamed in Spanish brandy. The wine list provides an ample supply of hearty Spanish reds. Dessert might feature a chocolate tart slathered with freshly whipped cream.

San Fernando 41. ✆ **95-422-72-11.** Reservations required. Main courses 20€–50€. AE, DC, MC, V. Restaurant Mon–Fri 1:30–3:30pm and 9–11:30pm; Sat 9–11:30pm. Closed Aug.

Enrique Becerra ★ 🍴 ANDALUSIAN Near the cathedral and Plaza Nueva, this popular tapas bar and eatery has a cozy, intimate setting that makes you feel instantly welcome. While perusing the menu, you can sip dry Tío Pepe and nibble herb-cured olives with lemon peel. The cookery pleases gourmets and gourmands, with such dishes as grilled cod in a green asparagus sauce, or lamb meatballs flavored with mint. An especially good dessert that is occasionally featured is the yogurt

Where to Dine in Seville

Abades Triana **24**
Abantal **6**
Al Solito Posto **3**
As Sawirah **10**
Az-Zait **1**
Barbiana **2**
Becerrita **5**
Cafetería Serranito **13**
Casa Cuesta **14**
Casa Robles **9**
Cervecería Giralda **19**
Corral del Agua **21**
Egaña Oriza **28**
Enrique Becerra **15**
Flaherty's **17**
Gastromium **31**

La Albahaca **22**
La Habanita **4**
La Isla **18**
La Raza **29**
Maccheroni **16**
Mesón Don Raimundo **7**
Modesto **23**
Porta Coeli **30**
Porta Rossa **11**
Río Grande **25**
Robles Placentines **8**
Salvador Rojo **26**
San Fernando 27 **27**
San Marco Pizzeria **20**
Taberna del
    Alabardero **12**

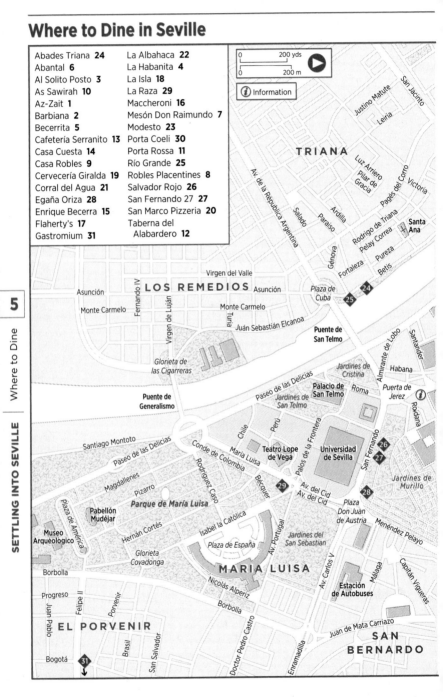

5

SETTLING INTO SEVILLE | Where to Dine

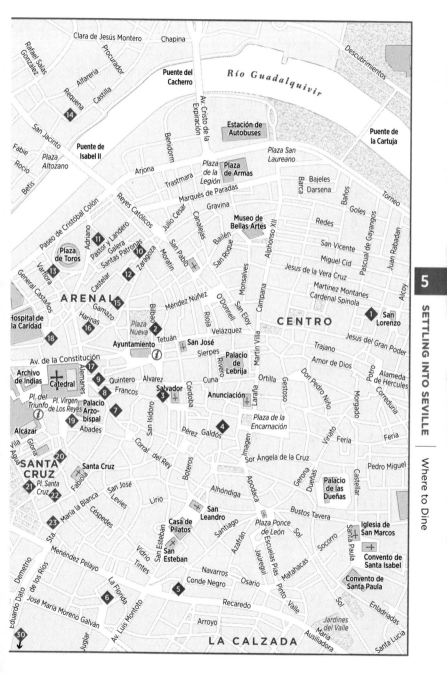

Churros: Fit for a King

Calle Arfe is a short hop from Seville's Alcázar, site of the royal family's residence in Seville. Immediately on the right as you pass through the old Olive Oil Gate (*El Arco del Postigo del Aceite*) you'll find the city's oldest and most famous *churros* stand. This little place has been selling these unsweetened, deep-fried, long thin donut-style pastries for generations. According to local legend, during the royal family's rare residences in Seville, *el Rey* sends someone to buy *churros* for him at this little shop with no name.

mousse with mango and raspberry sauce. The ice cold sangria is great for hot summer days. The wine list is one of Seville's best.

Gamazo 2. ✆ **95-421-30-49.** Reservations recommended. Main courses 14€–22€; fixed-price menus 40€–46€. AE, DC, MC, V. Mon–Sat 1–4:30pm and 8pm–midnight (closed Sat July–Aug).

Gastromium ★★★ CREATIVE   There are two places really setting the pace for fine dining in Seville right now: this place and Abantal (see above). Gastromium is a little more trendy and cool than its competitor; some would say a bit more fussy. Its dark, ultra-modern, designer interior is the perfect setting for adventurous dishes like cod tempura in cider reduction and wild leaf salad, veal cheek glazed in its own juice with beef broth, summer truffle and roasted sweet onions, pigs' trotters with Jerusalem artichoke salad and anise and mashed potatoes. There's a range of set menus, all equally delicious: Genesis 49€, Sibaris 59€, and Gastromium 77€ which runs to 11 courses! If you're not feeling quite so flush, arrive at lunch time and sample many of these dishes as reasonably priced tapas. I bet chef Miguel Diaz gets himself a Michelin star soon.

Ramon Carande 12. ✆ **954 625 555.** www.gastromium.com. Reservations essential. Main courses 20€–30€. AE, MC, V. Lunch and dinner daily. Closed Mon and Sun evenings and Aug.

La Albahaca FRENCH/BASQUE   This elegant restaurant is in the Barrio de Santa Cruz, Seville's most evocative quarter. Juan Talavera, a celebrated architect, constructed this 1920s Andalusian mansion that has attracted visiting celebrities like Charlton Heston. Lovely and graceful, diners move from a high-ceilinged central courtyard into one of several parlor-size dining rooms, each decorated in a smooth, nostalgic style that reflects the tastes and opulence of Spain's Victorian era. High-quality ingredients go into the first-rate cuisine. Intriguing appetizers include a fresh goose liver-and-apple terrine in a pheasant jelly, and baked sea bass with stir-fried plums, raisins, and almonds. Enduring main courses are roasted wild boar with fig marmalade, and a roasted pheasant breast with Iberian bacon. The bitter orange mousse from the dessert menu is one of the best finishes in town.

Plaza Santa Cruz 12. ✆ **95-422-07-14.** Reservations required. Main courses 21€–26€. AE, DC, MC, V. Mon–Sat 1–4pm and 8pm–midnight.

La Isla ★ SEAFOOD/ANDALUSIAN   La Isla consists of two large Andalusian dining rooms (thick plaster walls, tile floors, and bullfighting memorabilia). Always fresh, the seafood is trucked or flown in from either Galicia or Huelva, one of Andalusia's major ports. Menu items include grilled turbot with a marinara sauce and sole filets Cleopatra which come served with shrimp, ham, and fresh mushrooms. Non-fish eaters are catered for with sirloin steak with red peppers and onions, a classic favorite. The restaurant, a short walk from the cathedral, is in a very old building erected, the owners say, on foundations laid by the ancient Romans.

Arfe 25. ✆ **95-421-26-31.** Reservations recommended. Main courses 22€–38€. AE, DC, MC, V. Daily 1:30–5:30pm and 8pm–midnight. Closed Aug.

Taberna del Alabardero ★★★ ANDALUSIAN   One of Seville's most prestigious restaurants occupies a 19th-century town house three blocks from Seville Cathedral. It's attached to the city's culinary academy and, unsurprisingly, the quality of the food here is without equal. It recently hosted the king and queen of Spain, the Spanish president and members of his cabinet. Amid a collection of European antiques and oil paintings, you'll dine in any of two main rooms or three private ones, with a pre-dinner drink or tapas on the flower-filled patio. Tantalizing menu items include spicy peppers stuffed with pulverized thigh of bull, Andalusian fish (*urta*) on a compote of aromatic tomatoes with coriander, cod filet with essence of red peppers, and Iberian beefsteak with foie gras and green peppers.

Calle Zaragoza 20, 41001 Seville. ✆ **95-450-27-21.** Fax 95-456-36-66. Reservations recommended. Main courses 20€–30€. AE, DC, MC, V. Daily 1–4pm and 8pm–midnight. Closed Aug.

Moderate

As Sawirah MOROCCAN   Probably the best North African restaurant in town, this place offers tasty tagines and couscous in an attractive courtyard setting suitably decorated with old lamps and terracotta red walls. I particularly enjoyed the lamb tagine with dates and toasted almonds, which was full of flavor with the very tenderest of lamb. There's also a good-value tasting menu at 19.90€.

Galera 5. ✆ **954 562 268.** Main courses 12€–15€. MC, V. Lunch and dinner daily. Closed Mon and Sun evenings.

Az-Zait ★★ ANDALUSIAN/INTERNATIONAL   Next to the Convent of San Lorenzo, this charming, graceful restaurant has good service and inventive cuisine inspired by the classics. In air-conditioned comfort, you can order dishes often influenced by the Mediterranean. Begin with a refreshing bowl of gazpacho, unusually served with a carpaccio of shrimp. Go on to such main dishes as codfish cooked in the regional style with fresh tomatoes and olives, or the grilled honey-glazed cuttlefish, a preparation preferred by the former Moorish conquerors. Local gastronomes recommend the loin of sea bass in a velvety smooth cream sauce.

Plaza San Lorenzo 1. ✆ **95-490-64-75.** Reservations recommended. Main courses 9€–17€. AE, MC, V. Mon–Sat 1–4pm and 8:30pm–midnight. Closed Aug.

Barbiana ★ ANDALUSIAN/SEAFOOD   Close to the Plaza Nueva in the heart of Seville, this is one of the city's best fish restaurants. Chefs secure the freshest seafood, even though Seville is inland. In classic Andalusian tradition, a tapas bar is up front. In the rear is a cluster of rustically decorated dining rooms. If you go for lunch, you can try the chef's specialty, seafood with rice (not available in the evening). Other dishes of note include *ortiguilla,* a sea anemone quick-fried in oil, and the *tortillitas de camarones,* chickpea fritters with bits of chopped shrimp and fresh scallions (spring onions). If you're going to order shellfish, the specialty here, order it *a la plancha* (fresh from the grill). Fresh fish is also available grilled with a zesty sauce, or deep-fried.

Calle Albaredo 11. ☎ **95-422-44-02.** Reservations recommended. Main courses 10€–20€. AE, DC, MC, V. Mon-Sat noon-4:30pm and 8pm-midnight; Sun 8pm-midnight.

La Raza SPANISH/SEAFOOD   In business for more than half a century, this long-time favorite is on the periphery of the Parque María Luisa. Shaded by palms or rubber trees, sidewalk tables are placed outside in fair weather. This modern restaurant also has a big bar with a patio. Natural flavors and robust spicing characterize the tasty main dishes. A local favorite is *cola de toro* (oxtail); tamer fare includes succulent prawns in garlic butter and flecks of freshly chopped parsley. Sirloin steak is made even more enticing with a flavorful whisky sauce. A cooling bowl of gazpacho is an ideal summer starter.

Av. Isabel la Católica 2, off Plaza de España. ☎ **95-423-20-24.** Reservations recommended. Main courses 15€–25€. AE, MC, V. Daily 9am-2am.

Mesón Don Raimundo ANDALUSIAN/MOORISH   Near the cathedral, this lunch restaurant is tucked away in an alleyway—a bit hard to find—off Calle Argote de Molina. Very cozy, with dark wooden furnishings, it evokes an old convent. Dishes have a real taste of Andalusia, exemplified by the ribs of wild boar baked to perfection over firewood. Sherry from nearby Jerez de la Frontera flavors a sauce for the beef tenderloin. Some of the dishes display a Moorish influence, including the Mozarab-style wild duck braised in sherry. Fish also appears; a favorite is the filet of sea bass with fresh prawns, lots of garlic and olive oil, and pine nuts.

Calle Argote de Molina 26, Santa Cruz. ☎ **95-422-33-55.** Reservations recommended. Main courses 10€–23€. MC, V. Daily 11:30am-4pm and 7:30pm-2am.

Modesto 🍴 SPANISH   Belying its "modest" name, this place fills the ground floors of two old buildings on opposite sides of a cobble-covered square in the Barrio de Santa Cruz. Established around 1900, it more than doubled in size in 2004 by annexing a neighboring building. During good weather, scores of local residents pack into the square to enjoy Modesto's good food and low prices. On warm nights, an army of black-vested, white-shirted waiters dashes about the square, delivering platters of fried fish, grilled meats, olives, salads, and soups. Fish and shellfish soup comes rich with saffron and seafood flavorings. There are platters of Iberian ham, sole, hake (*merluza*), and pork in many different variations, flans, and a wide selection of Andalusian and Spanish wines.

Cano y Cueto 5. ☎ **95-441-68-11.** Main courses 7€–25€. AE, DC, MC, V. Daily 8am-2pm.

Porta Coeli ★★ MEDITERRANEAN   With one of Seville's most sophisticated decors, Porta Coeli offers the finest hotel dining in the city. Even if you're not a hotel guest, consider reserving one of the 15 beautifully laid tables set against a backdrop of tapestry-hung walls. The flavor combinations are contemporary and rely on fresh ingredients. The menu boasts a wide variety of dishes featuring duck with fried white beans and ham. Another savory offering is *ensalada de bacalao con tomate* (salt cod salad with tomatoes) and *arroz marinero con bogavante* (rice with crayfish). Locals rave about the *corazón de solomillo al foie con zetas al vino* (beef heart with liver and mushroom in red-wine sauce), though this might be an acquired taste. For dessert, nothing beats the napoleon, layers of pastry with cream, chocolate, and fresh fruit.

In the Hesperia Sevilla, Eduardo Dato 49. ✆ **95-454-83-00.** Reservations recommended. Main courses 12€–29€. AE, DC, MC, V. Mon–Sat 1:30–4pm and 9pm–midnight. Closed Aug.

Porta Rossa ★★ ITALIAN   This family-run place does truly excellent Italian cuisine—in fact it's a real favorite among my Sevillian friends for its high quality food at very reasonable prices. Paco, who manages the Alminar hotel, raves about the truffle pasta! Other favorites include the rocket salad, mixed cheese and cured meat plates, and a wonderful ravioli stuffed with pine nuts and seta mushrooms served in a cream sauce with nutmeg. The beef tenderloin in a black peppercorn and vodka sauce is also delicious. It's more expensive than budget Italian places, but the quality and experience easily justify the prices.

Arenal 3 ✆ **954 216 139.** Main courses 10€–15€. MC, V. Dinner daily. Closed Sun eve, Mon, Aug.

Río Grande ANDALUSIAN   This classic Sevillian restaurant is named for the Guadalquivir River, which it overlooks from panoramic windows. It sits across from the Torre del Oro on the Triana side of the river, and some diners come here just for the views of the city monuments. Most dishes are priced at the lower end of the scale. A meal might include fish-and-seafood soup seaman's style, salmon, chicken-and-shellfish paella, bull's tail Andalusian-style, or garlic chicken. A selection of fresh shellfish is brought in daily.

Calle Betis s/n. ✆ **95-427-39-56.** Reservations recommended. Main courses 16€–21€. AE, DC, MC, V. Daily 1–4pm and 8pm–midnight.

Robles Placentines ANDALUSIAN   My favorite of the Robles venues, Placentines features a similar modern Andalusian menu to famous and significantly more expensive Casa Robles—one of Seville's finest dining venues—but here you can order tapas-sized portions so it's perfect for a lighter, cheaper bite. Favorites include the bacon-wrapped prawns, grilled assorted wild mushrooms with jamón serrano, and the grilled sirloin in mustard sauce. The jamón serrano is featured on the menu with a description: "the best in the world'" and you know, they might just be right.

Placentines 2. ✆ **954 213 162.** www.casa-robles.com. Main courses 14€–24€. Tapas 4€–8€. AE, DC, MC, V. Lunch and dinner daily.

Salvador Rojo ★★ 🍴 ANDALUSIAN   Just across from the university and a moment away from Seville's most expensive hotel, the Alfonso XIII, this little restaurant is a find. Head chef Salvador trained at the city's famous Alabardero cookery academy and he turns out stylish modern Andalusian dishes with real flair and panache. His *careen de cordero* (slices of lamb with potato puree) was perfect on my last visit. The atmosphere is relaxed and informal and service is attentive and friendly. There's a good wine list too.

San Fernando 23. ✆ **954 229 725**. Main courses 21€–27€. AE, DC, MC, V. Lunch and dinner Mon–Sat. Closed Aug.

San Fernando 27 ★ ANDALUSIAN/CREATIVE   This is a good one for foodies. Virtually next door to the equally excellent Salvador Rojo, this modern, stylish restaurant with big windows and dining rooms flooded with light serves high-end modern Andalusian cuisine with friendly, helpful service to match. Menu items include such delights as red snapper with fresh pasta cooked in squid ink and lobster bisque, cod confit in a white soy sauce with spaghetti, and breast of duck with fruits of the forest sauce with mango leaf and apple salad. There's a range of tasty-looking set menus too in the 40€ range for four courses including wine. The small, intimate terrace is perfect for something a little more romantic.

San Fernando 27. ✆ **954 220 966.** www.sanfernando27.com. Main courses 10€–24€. Lunch and dinner daily. Closed Sun and Aug.

Inexpensive

Al Solito Posto ★ ☺ ITALIAN   This modern, good-value Italian restaurant is rightly popular with locals and an ideal choice for family dining. It's set on the corner of a busy square that's often full of kids and mums with pushchairs in the early evenings. The usual pizza and pasta dishes are well prepared, with thin-crust traditional pizza made with the freshest of ingredients being the specialty. Service is friendly too, but it can be a bit slow during busy periods. They now open for breakfast.

Cuesta del Rosario 15. ✆ **954 220 917.** Main courses 8€–12€. AE, DC, MC, V. 9am–4pm and 8pm–midnight Mon–Sat. Closed Aug.

Cafetería Serranito SPANISH   A cheap, bustling, workaday restaurant where portions are big, service is inscrutable and even gruff (certainly it's monolingual), and cuisine is mass-market but flavorful. Set deliberately near Seville's bullfight ring, this is the more modern (ca. 1980) branch of an older restaurant that dates from 1923. Expect crowds on normal days, and mobs just before and after the fights. Torero memorabilia and at least eight stuffed bull's heads adorn the walls. Dishes include *pijotas* (small fried hake); *cazón en adobo* (seasoned dogfish); *pez espada* (grilled swordfish); a house specialty known as *caldereta de toro* (bull-meat stew); *gambas al ajillo* (prawns fried with garlic); and *serranito de pollo* (cured ham with chicken filets, tomato sauce, and bread).

Antonia Díaz 4. ✆ **95-421-12-43.** Reservations not accepted. Main courses 7€–13€; half-platters 3.60€–6.60€. MC, V. Daily 8am–midnight.

Casa Cuesta ★ 🍴 SPANISH/ANDALUSIAN   This is a fine choice in Triana, the pottery-making district across the river from the medieval core of Old Seville. The venue, which dates from 1880, is warm and old-fashioned. With its geometric tilework, checkerboard-patterned marble floors, high ceilings, and ornate 19th-century bar, Casa Cuesta is a great place for lunch or dinner, or just for drinks and some tapas. The well-prepared Spanish food includes cured Iberian ham, fried meats and fish, *raciones* (servings) of potato salad flavored lightly with olive oil, and a variety of fried meats and fish. A recommended starter is *salmorejo*, a thick Cordovan version of gazpacho. The ambience in Triana is less touristy and a bit more workaday than its counterpart across the river.

Calle Castilla 1, Triana. ✆ **95-433-33-35.** Main courses 10€–21€; tapas 2.20€–3€. MC, V. Daily noon–midnight.

Cervecería Giralda SPANISH/ANDALUSIAN   There are at least a dozen popular tapas bars on the Calle Mateos Gagos, a picturesquely narrow street in the Barrio de Santa Cruz that leads to the plaza beside Seville Cathedral. But this is also one of the most evocative. Established in 1934 on the ruins of a 10th-century Arab bathhouse, it retains the same four central columns and the same elaborate system of domes and vaults as the bath's original construction. Tapas are elaborate and often fish-based, while meals in the restaurant section might include salads, omelets, shellfish, codfish steaks with shellfish sauce, hake stuffed with squid, baked snapper, Iberian ham stuffed with foie gras, and filets of pork with roasted red peppers.

Calle Mateos Gagos 1. ✆ **95-422-74-35.** Reservations recommended for dinner, not for tapas. Tapas 2.50€-3€; main courses in restaurant 13€-18€. AE, DC, MC, V. Daily 9am-midnight.

Flaherty's IRISH/INTERNATIONAL Immediately opposite the Patio de los Naranjos exit from the cathedral, this is the biggest and busiest Irish pub in Seville. With massive ceiling beams and very thick walls, its antique labyrinthine space includes a vine-covered open-air patio, one end of which is devoted to the busy toilets, the other to an open grill for burgers, sausages, and steaks. Big-screen TVs show sporting events, and there are at least four kinds of beer on tap. The menu features sandwiches, burgers, and chicken burgers, plus charbroiled chicken, lamb cutlets, steaks, and Caribbean-style jerk ribs. You'll have no problem ordering in English here.

Calle Alemanes 7. ✆ **95-421-04-51.** Tapas and *raciones* 2.50€-7€; salads, sandwiches, and platters 5€-16€. AE, DC, MC, V. Daily 11am-2am.

La Habanita ★ VEGETARIAN/CUBAN It can be hard to find tucked down a side street off busy Calle Pérez Galdós in the Alfalfa area just behind San Salvador, but it's worth the effort. Don't expect haute cuisine, but veggies in particular will love dishes like the deep-fried banana balls in tomato sauce. Meat eaters will be happy too; the lamb *empanadas* (small pastry parcels) were a real hit for me. There's a distinctly Cuban edge to some of the dishes, with favorites like ropa vieja and a host of original drinks being an extra reason to visit. There's a menu in English; service is friendly and prices are very reasonable. Gluten-free and vegan dishes are also available.

Golfo 3. ✆ **954 220 202.** Main courses 3€-7€. MC, V. Lunch and dinner daily. Lunch Sun.

Maccheroni ITALIAN On a side street behind Plaza Nueva, this bright, modern Italian place is run by a family from central Italy and they pride themselves on their tiramisu. Lasagna, pizza, and pasta are also good.

Harinas 13. ✆ **954 501 015.** Main courses 7€-10€. MC, V. Lunch and dinner daily. Closed Mon eve, Tues and last 2 weeks Aug.

San Marco Pizzeria ITALIAN Possibly the best of the San Marco group's settings, this one serves slightly less expensive—but very tasty—pizza and pasta dishes in an old Arab bathhouse. The mixed antipasti is a great starter for two.

Mesón del Moro 6. ✆ **954 564 390.** Pizza 6€-10€. AE, DC, MC, V. Lunch and dinner daily.

WHAT TO SEE & DO IN SEVILLE

With one of the richest cultural heritages of any city in Europe, Seville deserves at least 3 days of your time. Most of your time will be spent in the city's historic core which can be covered on foot.

Top sights to try and include in a 3-day stay include the Cathedral, the Royal Palace (the Alcázar), the Fine Arts Museum (Museo Provincial de Bellas Artes), the Casa de Pilatos, and the bullring. When it comes to eating and entertainment, tapas in Seville are some of the best in Spain, so make sure to try some, and the flamenco shows here are very good too.

If you've got some more time, add the Torre de Oro, the Flamenco museum, and the Parque María Luisa with the remarkable Plaza de España to your list.

SEEING THE SIGHTS

The only way to explore Seville is on foot, with a good map in hand. You might want to hop aboard a horse-drawn carriage too and clip-clop around the Old Town for an hour or so.

The Top Attractions

Alcázar ★★★   Pedro I, king of Castile who built the magnificent royal palace in the 14th century, was known as Pedro the Cruel, but he must have had a softer side. His complex of courtyards and patios is graced with the deftest of carvings and a fragrant shady garden. Pedro used Moorish craftsmen from Granada to create this ultimate homage to Moorish architecture, at a time when Seville had long been reconquered by the Christians. The result is an exquisite blend of Moorish and Christian influences—known as the *Mudéjar* style. On visits to Seville, King Juan Carlos and Queen Sofía still stay here.

Allow at least 2 hours to go through the palace complex and visit the gardens with their fountains and pavilions. You'll enter through the Puerta de León (Lion's Door), which is flanked by two towers. Continue straight ahead into the Patio de la Montería, where the court once

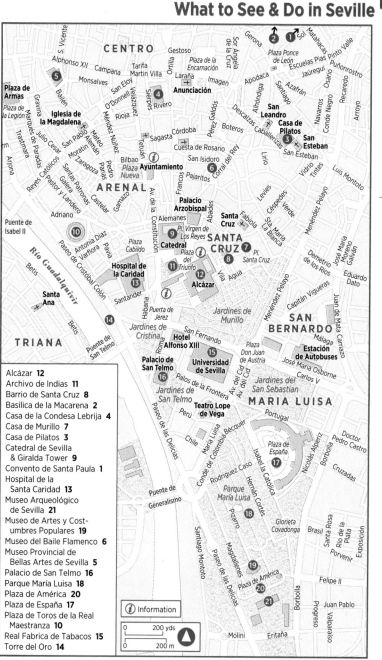

Alcázar **12**
Archivo de Indias **11**
Barrio de Santa Cruz **8**
Basilica de la Macarena **2**
Casa de la Condesa Lebrija **4**
Casa de Murillo **7**
Casa de Pilatos **3**
Catedral de Sevilla
& Giralda Tower **9**
Convento de Santa Paula **1**
Hospital de la
Santa Caridad **13**
Museo Arqueológico
de Sevilla **21**
Museo de Artes y Cost-
umbres Populares **19**
Museo del Baile Flamenco **6**
Museo Provincial de
Bellas Artes de Sevilla **5**
Palacio de San Telmo **16**
Parque María Luisa **18**
Plaza de América **20**
Plaza de España **17**
Plaza de Toros de la Real
Maestranza **10**
Real Fabrica de Tabacos **15**
Torre del Oro **14**

(i) Information

0   200 yds
0   200 m

assembled. From this courtyard the facade of the **Palacio Pedro** ★ confronts you. In the audience chamber just to the right, you can see a replica of the *Santa María,* the ship that Christopher Columbus sailed in to discover the Americas, and an impressive altarpiece, ***Virgin of the Navigators*** ★, painted by Alejo Fernández in 1531.

Walk back out to the Patio de la Montería and into the Palacio Pedro to reach the delightful **Patio de las Doncellas (Court of the Maidens)** ★★★, decorated by the skilled Moorish architects from Granada. An upper story was added to this exquisite patio in the 1500s.

Other landmarks in this remarkable palace include the Salón de Embajadores (Ambassadors' Hall), constructed in 1427 and dominated by an impressive cedar-wood **cupola** ★★ that is often described as a "half orange." This hall also has a trio of symmetrically arranged and ornate arches, each one with three horseshoe arches.

The Salón del Techo is notable for its coffered ceiling, and the **Patio de las Muñecas (Dolls' Court)** ★★ is small, but splendidly and delicately ornamented; it was also designed by the Alhambra's craftsmen.

The **Salones de Carlos V** ★, built on the site of an older Gothic palace and extensively rebuilt during the Renaissance period by King Charles V of Spain, lie to the immediate right. They face Pedro's palace and present an interesting counterpoint. These rooms are decorated with beautiful 16th-century *azulejos* (tiles) and contain a stunning collection of 16th-century **tapestries** ★★ from Brussels that depict the life of the emperor and his conquest of Tunis in 1535.

Save time for the **gardens** ★, a wonderful oasis from the heat of a summer day. The Jardín Inglés, modeled on 18th-century English gardens, dates from 1909, and the Jardín de los Poetas (Poets' Garden) features two ponds evocative of those once designed by the Arabs.

Plaza del Triunfo s/n. ✆ **95-450-23-23**. www.patronato-alcazarsevilla.es. Admission 7.50€, children under 12 free. Oct–Mar daily 9:30am–5pm. Apr–Sept daily 9:30am–7pm. Audio tour recommended 3€.

Cathedral Alert

Shorts and T-shirts are not allowed in the cathedral. Remember to dress appropriately, so you're not turned away.

Archivo de Indias ★   Built between 1584 and 1598, the Archivo was originally a traders' market where New World deals were sealed and wares sold. In 1785, Carlos III, with remarkable foresight, had all documents relating to the Spanish Indies colonies collected here. The result is an archive of more than 80 million documents, including letters exchanged between patron Queen Isabella and explorer Columbus (he detailing his discoveries and impressions). You can enter a small section of the Archivo. There are temporary exhibitions on the ground floor, and up a vast red marble staircase you'll find displays of documents and portraits of Columbus. The first is opposite the top of the staircase and shows Columbus with his hand on a globe, the words in Latin *Non Sufficit Orbis* ("the world is not enough") written around it. It's highly inaccurate: Columbus is wearing clothes that were fashionable when the portrait was painted, more than 100 years after his death. There's a simpler portrait on the wall to the right between two of the windows. Here he is in a sober black smock. In fact, no one knows what Columbus looked like; even this likeness is painted from descriptions given to the painter by his son.

Av. de la Constitución 3. (✆ **95-421-12-34.** Free admission. Mon–Sat 10am–4pm; Sun 10am–2pm.

Barrio de Santa Cruz ★★★ What was once a ghetto for Spanish Jews, who were forced out of Spain in the late 15th century in the wake of the Inquisition, is today Seville's most colorful district. Near the old walls of the Alcázar, winding medieval streets with names like *Vida* (Life) and *Muerte* (Death) open onto pocket-sized plazas. Flower-filled balconies with draping bougainvillea and potted geraniums jut over this labyrinth, shading you from the hot Andalusian summer sun. Feel free to look through numerous wrought-iron gates into patios filled with fountains and plants. In the evening it's common to see Sevillanos sitting outside drinking cold beer and munching tapas under the glow of lanterns.

To enter the Barrio de Santa Cruz, turn right after leaving the Patio de Banderas exit of the Alcázar. Turn right again at the Plaza de la Alianza, going down Calle Rodrigo Caro to the Plaza de Doña Elvira.

Casa de Pilatos ★★ Still inhabited by the Dukes of Medinaceli, this is one of Seville's finest palaces and one of my favorites. The name "Pilate's House" probably refers to the fact that one of its owners—the first Marquis of Tarifa—made a pilgrimage to the Holy Land in 1518. He came back from his trip so enthused by the Greek and Roman-inspired "classical" architecture of Renaissance Italy that he set about creating a new interior for his palace, inspired by the Roman governor Pontius Pilate's house in Jerusalem. The result is a harmonious mixture of styles—Mudéjar, Renaissance, and Gothic. The main patio has a fountain imported from Genoa and Roman and Greek marble busts in each corner, Mudéjar-style tiles and arches at ground level, and Gothic balustrades and arches above. Rooms leading off the patio are similarly ornate, in particular the Salon de Pretorio and Gabinete de Pilatos—both with intricate coffered ceilings and Mudéjar tiles and walls. The gardens are a tranquil series of fragrant bushes, vast trees, and a fountain. The upper level, which contains family portraits, antique furniture, and more vaulted ceilings, is reached by climbing a tiled staircase with a golden dome above; this part can only be visited on

---

DNA Enters the Debate over Columbus's Bones

DNA samples from 500-year-old bone slivers could contradict the Dominican Republic's competing claim that Columbus was laid to rest in Santo Domingo, and not in Seville. Scientists in 2006 confirmed that "at least some of the explorer's remains" were buried in Seville. But the debate still rages. It is entirely possible that some of Columbus's remains could have been buried in the Dominican Republic; his body was moved several times after his death. A forensic team compared DNA from the bones buried in Seville with that of the remains known to be from Columbus's brother Diego. "There was an absolute match-up," geneticists said.

These claims were refuted by Juan Bautista Mieses, the director of the Columbus Lighthouse in Santo Domingo, where the explorer's alleged remains rest. He has, however, turned down requests to take DNA samples, stating that "Christians believe that one does not bother the dead."

a half-hourly guided tour. The palace is about a 15-minute walk northeast of the cathedral on the northern edge of Barrio de Santa Cruz, amid a warren of labyrinthine streets.

Plaza de Pilatos 1. ✆ **95-422-52-98.** Ground floor: Mar–Sept 9am–7pm daily (6pm Oct–Feb); upper floor: 10am–2pm, 4–5:30pm. Admission: Ground floor and gardens 5€, upper floor as well 8€.

Catedral de Sevilla & Giralda Tower ★★★ The largest Gothic building in the world and the third-largest church in Europe (after St Peter's in Rome and St Paul's in London), the Catedral de Sevilla was designed by builders whose stated goal was that "those who come after us will take us for madmen." Construction began in the late 1400s on the site of an ancient mosque and took centuries to complete. The cathedral claims to contain the remains of Columbus; his tomb held aloft by figures of four knights representing the Spanish kingdoms of Castile, Aragón, Navarra, and Léon. Works of art abound, many of them architectural, such as the 15th-century stained-glass windows, the iron screens (*rejas*) closing off the chapels, the elaborate 15th-century choir stalls, and the **golden central altarpiece ★** which is the world's largest, containing over 2,000 statues illustrating 45 scenes from the Bible. In the Chapel of Saint Anthony you'll find paintings by two of the city's most famous painters. A section from *The Vision of Saint Anthony* by Murillo (1617–82) was stolen in 1874 and subsequently recovered and stitched back—you can just see the join towards the bottom right of the canvas. *Saints Justa and Rufina* by Zurbarán (1598–1664) shows the city's patron saints protecting the Giralda tower. The remarkable ceiling decoration in the oval Chapter House is also by Murillo.

Hospital de la Santa Caridad ★ This charity hospital still cares for the elderly and infirm as it did when founded in 1674. It has a colorful history. It was built on land which belonged to the brotherhood of Santa Caridad, who dedicated themselves to burying abandoned corpses washed up on the riverside. A new hospital and

---

DISCOVERING MURILLO: THE great PAINTER OF SENTIMENT

Why did Seville-born **Bartolomé Estéban Murillo** (1618–82) become so popular in the latter part of the 1800s? Partly because he painted the most beautiful and sentimental Madonnas of his era. But the very reason behind his success caused him to fall out of favor with critics during most of the 20th century. Today some art historians are taking another look at Murillo, and his reputation is making a sort of comeback. If you'd like to form your own opinion of Murillo, there's a fabulous display of some of his most important works in

a room devoted to him at the **Museo Provincial de Bellas Artes**.

Other places where you'll come upon his paintings include the **Cathedral** and the less-visited, delightful little church at the **Hospital de la Santa Caridad**.

The true devotee can also visit **Casa de Murillo,** Calle Santa Teresa 8. The house where Murillo lived is being turned into a museum. At the time of writing you could wander into the courtyard and poke about on the lower floor. Ask at the tourist office for the latest news.

church were commissioned in 1661 by Miguel de Mañara, the playboy son of a wealthy landowner. It's often said that the character of Don Juan was based upon him, but at the age of 34 he had a vision of his own death and gave up his philandering ways and joined the brotherhood. It's rarely visited, but the church here contains some of Seville's most sumptuous Baroque sculpture and painting, worthy of any museum. Mañara commissioned his friend Murillo (see box "Discovering Murillo"), one of Seville's most famous painters, to paint 11 canvases on the theme of Mercy. Seven survive today. He also commissioned works by Juan de Valdés Leal, whose two morbidly fascinating paintings, *The End of the World's Glories* and *In The Blink of an Eye*, above and opposite the entrance, are considered his finest. The altarpiece features an incredibly life-like carving of the burial of Christ by another celebrity craftsman of the day, Pedro Roldan.

Calle Temprado 3. ☏ **95-422-32-32.** Admission 5€ adults, free for children 11 and under. Audio guide included. Mon–Sat 9am–1:30pm and 3:30–7:30pm; Sun 9am–12:30pm.

La Giralda ★ The tower next to the cathedral is the city's most recognizable monument. You enter it on the right just before the exit from the cathedral. Erected as a minaret in the 12th century, its later additions include 16th-century bells and a weathervane known as El Giraldillo (hence the name Giralda). Despite being 91 meters (298 ft) high it's an easy climb—there are no steps, just gentle ramps, built so that the *muezzin* could ride his horse to the top when it was time for him to make the call to prayer. The views of the city and the cathedral's remarkably complex buttresses are tremendous. Seville's foremost landmark is often depicted protected by the city's patron saints, Justa and Rufina.

After admiring the views from the Giralda, you exit the cathedal and emerge into the sunlight of the Patio of Orange Trees, with its fresh citrus scents and chirping birds. **Note:** Shorts and T-shirts are not allowed in the cathedral. Remember to dress appropriately before you set out so you're not turned away.

Av. de la Constitución s/n. ☏ **95-421-49-71.** www.catedraldesevilla.es. Cathedral and Giralda 8€ adults, free for children 12 and under; free for all Sun. Mon–Sat 11am–5pm; Sun 2:30–6pm (July–Aug Mon–Sat 9:30am–4pm; Sun 2:30–6pm).

Museo del Baile Flamenco ★ This ranks among my top recommended museums in Seville—that's assuming you like hi-tech displays using video and touch screens. Spain's most celebrated flamenco dancer, Cristina Hoyos, is artistic director. Five rooms of audiovisual displays in six different languages (including English) chart the history and development of the dance and its connection with the soul of Andalusia. Particularly informative are the demonstrations of the different styles of dance in room two, showing the unique colors and emotions of each technique. Dance classes take place here too; even complete beginners can participate. There are also nightly flamenco shows. The museum is housed in an old town house with a patio for relaxing.

Calle Manuel Rojas Marcos 3. ☏ **95-434-03-11.** www.museoflamenco.com. Admission 10€ adults, 6€ children. Reductions for groups and families available. Daily 9am–7pm.

Museo Provincial de Bellas Artes de Sevilla ★★ This lovely old convent off Calle de Alfonso XII houses one of the most important collections of Spanish art in the country. The Renaissance collection includes an almost frighteningly life-like sculpture of *San Jerónimo Penitente* by Italian Florentine Torrigiano (1472–1578), a

Seville on the Cheap

If you're looking to save money, be selective about which days you visit places and, if you hold an E.U. passport or ID card, remember to carry it with you.

Free to all: Museo Histórico Militar; Costurero de la Reina Museum; Castillo de San Jorge Museum; Archivo de Indias; Convento de Santa Clara; Torre del Oro (Tuesdays only); Hospital de Los Venerables (4–8pm Sundays only); Casa de la Condesa Lebrija (10:30am–12:30pm Wednesdays only).

Free to E.U. passport holders: Museo Provincial de Bellas Artes, Museo Arqueológico, Museo de Artes y Costumbres Populares; Casa de Pilatos (Tuesdays 1–5pm only); Monasterio de la Cartuja and Centro Andaluz de Arte Contemporáneo (Tuesdays only).
And to get from one place to another, use the Sevici city bikes for no more than half an hour and they are free too!

graphic painting of the *Day of Judgement* by Martin de Vos, and an anatomically gruesome sculpture of the *Head of John the Baptist* by Gaspar Núñez Delgado, who worked in Seville between 1576 and 1606. The spectacularly domed space of Room V ★ is the perfect backdrop for the collection of vast canvases by Seville's most famous painter, Bartolomé Estéban Murillo. *Saints Justa and Rufina* holding the Giralda is among his best-known works. There's a whole series of works by his contemporaries from the Seville School, Juan de Valdés Leal in Room VIII and Zurbarán in Room X. Rooms in upper galleries contain more recent works including eight interesting views of Seville by Domingo Martínez (1699–1749), and a large intimate portrait of the *cigarreras*, the girls who rolled cigars in the tobacco factory, by Gonzalo Bilbao Martínez (d. 1938). Room XIII has vivid portraits of bullfighters and flamenco dancers by José García Ramos (d. 1921).

Plaza del Museo 9. ✆ **95-478-65-00.** Admission 1.50€, free to E.U. passport holders.Tues 3–8pm; Wed–Sat 9am–8pm, Sun 9am–2pm. Closed Mon. Buses C3 and C4.

Plaza de Toros de la Real Maestranza ★★
Seville is often referred to as the birthplace of modern bullfighting and its 14,000-seater bullring is a beauty. Whilst it isn't the country's biggest, aficionados claim it's the most atmospheric. Even if you don't much like the idea of bullfights, you may like to take a guided tour of the arena and museum (in Spanish or English). It traces the origins of the sport from bull-less jousting competitions to today's complex theatrical spectacle, with displays of costumes, paintings, and stuffed bulls' heads. The first thing that hits you when you walk into the arena is its intimacy. Apparently its incredible acoustics mean that during a bullfight you can even hear the shallowest snort of a bull's breath. The structure was built between 1761 and 1881 by the Royal Order of Chivalry of Seville. Seville's bullfighting season runs from Easter through to October, with bullfights taking place most Sundays and on Thursday evenings during July and August. There are daily bullfights during the festivities of the *Feria de Abril* in April. For information about buying tickets, see "Spectator Sports" on p. 120.

Paseo de Colón 18, ✆ **95-422-45-77.** Admission 6€. No credit cards. 9:30am–7pm daily by guided tour only every 20 min.

Torre del Oro   Built in 1220 by the Moors as part of the city wall constructed to protect Seville against Christian invaders, the "tower of gold" is one of Seville's most iconic landmarks. Its 12 sides—one for each of the different winds that the Moors gave names to—make it unique. The turret on top is more recent, added in 1760. Originally another tower was sited across the river and a huge chain was stretched between them to stop ships sailing upriver. It sounded like a good idea, but it didn't work. The Christian fleet easily broke the chain during the reconquest of the city in 1248. Today, it houses a small naval museum with two floors of maps and curios, including a model of the *Santa María,* the ship in which Columbus sailed to America. Climb to the top and you see what a great vantage point it is—handy today for taking photos of the city skyline.

Paseo de Cristóbal Colón. ✆ **95-422-24-19.** Admission 2€. Free on Tues. Mon–Fri 10am–2pm; Sat–Sun 11am–2pm. Closed Aug.

More to See & Do

Basilica de la Macarena   The *Virgin de la Esperanza Macarena*, the much-adored 17th-century statue of the Virgin Mary which gives this district its name, sits above the main altar in this church, surrounded by a cascade of gold and silver. During the pulsating festivities of *Semana Santa,* the Virgin is paraded through the streets. You can see her unbelievably ornate processional platforms laden with Baroque cherubs and dripping with gold and silver in the museum to the left of the church. There are also interesting descriptions of the history of the processions in English. The scale of their extravagance is simply incredible. There's also a small shop selling rather tacky Virgin mementos and a handy Seville tourist board information desk.

Too far to walk from the historic center, the church is best approached by taxi or buses C1 and C3 going along the outer ring from Colón to Torneo to Resolano Andueza.

Puerta de la Macarena, La Macarena. ✆ **95-490-18-00.** Church 9am–2pm, 5–9pm daily. Free admission. Museum 9:30am–1:30pm, 5–8:30pm daily (closed Sun afternoons), admission 5€. No credit cards.

Casa de la Condesa Lebrija ★   Off the tourist trail, this house gets far fewer visitors than it should. The Countess of Lebrija was an enlightened lady antiquarian who traveled the world—something single women didn't generally do in the 19th century. Her home is testament to her life. She remodeled this 15th-century house adding artifacts discovered at the Roman ruins in nearby Itálica together with curios from her travels. The relocated Roman marble floors are some of the most complete in Europe. The main patio's exceptionally well-preserved mosaic, found in an olive grove in 1914, features Cyclops in the center with four female heads depicting the seasons at the corners. Look for the portrait of the Countess in the first room on the right off the main patio. She's in fancy dress, wearing an Egyptian costume. The main staircase to the upper level is an extravagant combination of Mudéjar tilework and coffered ceilings. The upper level can be visited on a half-hourly guided tour—the guide speaks English—which includes the book-lined library, the Arabic-style tea room, and the dining room with its 240-piece dining set made by the English pottery firm Spode.

Cuna 8. ✆ **95-422-78-02.** www.palaciodelebrija.com. Admission 4€ ground floor, 8€ includes upper floor tour. Mon–Fri 10:30am–7:30pm (July–Aug 9am–3pm), Sat–Sun 10am–2pm. (July–Aug closed Sun.)

Convento de Santa Paula   There are 17 cloistered women's convents still functioning (in some cases, flourishing) in Seville today. Some are very small, some are in steep decline, and some are so obscure that their doors are almost always closed to casual visitors. But if a peek into this medieval lifestyle intrigues you, the most interesting (and most accessible) cloistered convent is **Santa Paula**. The convent dates from 1475 and is still home to around 40 nuns. Enter through the door marked number 11 on Calle Santa Paula. You'll probably have to knock. Steps lead into two galleries crammed with religious artifacts. The windows of the second look onto the nuns' cloister. The nuns make jams and marmalades, which you can buy in a room near the exit. Ring the bell by the brick doorway to the left of no. 11 to visit the convent church, reached through a garden. The church is a blend of Gothic, Mudéjar, and Renaissance features, the nave has an elaborate carved roof, and there are statues of St John the Evangelist and St John the Baptist.

Santa Paula. ✆ **95-453-63-30.** Admission 3€. Tues–Sun 10:30am–1pm.

Parque María Luisa & Palacio de San Telmo ★★ Parque María Luisa, named for and dedicated to the sister of Isabella II, was once the grounds of the **Palacio de San Telmo**. The palace, the Baroque facade of which is crowned with statues of famous Sevillians, is visible just behind the deluxe Alfonso XIII Hotel. Originally conceived as the Universidad de Mareantes (University for Sailors), the palace was named for St Elmo, patron saint of navigation. A lavish celebration of the Baroque style, it is largely the work of architect Leonardo de Figueroa and was constructed between 1682 and 1796. In time it became the mansion of the Dukes of Montpensier of the Bourbon dynasty. Today the palace is the seat of the Andalusian government. Its most outstanding feature is its elaborately ornate **Churriguesque-style main portal ★★**, dating from 1734. There are plans to create a permanent exhibition about the building's history here. Ask at the tourist office for the latest information.

The former private royal park is now open to the public. In 1929, when Seville was host to the Spanish American Exhibition, many pavilions from around the world were erected here. The Depression put a damper on the exhibition, but the pavilions still stand. Running south along the Guadalquivir River, the park is an attractive respite from the heat of the city. You can walk along flower-bordered paths, relax in the shade, go for a jog, or go bicycling. The most romantic way to traverse it is by rented horse and carriage. See the "Getting Around" section in Chapter 5 for more information.

Plaza de América Set within the Parque María Luisa, this is a landmark Sevillian square. Here you can walk through gardens planted with roses, enjoying the lily ponds and fountains. The trio of elaborate buildings is left over from the Spanish American Exhibition. Two of them now house museums.

The **Museo Arqueológico de Sevilla,** Plaza de América s/n (✆ **95-478-64-74;** www.museosdeandalucia.es), contains many artifacts from prehistoric times and the days of the Romans, Visigoths, and Moors. The Roman collection is particularly impressive with several superbly preserved mosaics, most notably the *Triumph of Bacchus* depicting the god of wine being pulled in a chariot by two tigers in room 13. It's open Tuesday to Saturday 9am to 8:30pm, Sunday and holidays 9am to 2:30pm. Admission is 1.50€ and it's free for E.U. passport holders.

Right opposite is the **Museo de Artes y Costumbres Populares,** Plaza de América 3 (✆ **95-471-23-91**), Seville's museum of folklore artifacts. Displays include workshop scenes showing local crafts such as leatherwork and ironmongery and ceramics through the ages—such as finely painted vases from nearby Cartuja. The upper floor was being renovated at the time of writing. The displays generally feel a little dated and disorganized, but kids who like exploring will enjoy it. Descriptions are in Spanish, but there's a free brochure in English. It has the same opening hours and admission fees as the Museo Arqueológico.

Plaza de España ★   The park was the perfect place to host the 1929 Spanish American Exhibition and Seville's pavilion needed to be star of the show, so the Plaza de España was created as the boldest of statements. Designed by Aníbal González, Seville's foremost 20th-century architect, it's a feast of Mudéjar-style curves and towers. The plaza was used as a backdrop to one of the *Star Wars* movies. Each region of Spain is depicted with a tiled panel along the walls. González insisted on supervising the works to make sure they conformed to his specifications. The result is spectacular. Be wary of the sun here; there's little shade and on bright days it's easy to get burnt.

Real Fabrica de Tabacos   When Carmen waltzed out of the tobacco factory in the first act of Bizet's opera, she made its 18th-century inspiration world famous. This old tobacco factory was constructed between 1750 and 1766, and 100 years later it employed 10,000 *cigarreras,* of which Carmen was one in the opera. (She rolled cigars on her thighs.) In the 19th century, these tobacco women made up the largest female workforce in Spain. Many visitors arriving today, in fact, ask guides to take them to "Carmen's tobacco factory." The building, on Calle San Fernando near the city's landmark luxury hotel, the Alfonso XIII, is now part of the Universidad de Sevilla. Look for signs of its former role, however, in the bas-reliefs of tobacco plants and Native Americans over the main entrances. You'll also see bas-reliefs of Columbus and Cortés. Then you can wander through the grounds for a look at Sevillian-style student life.

WALKING TOUR: **THE OLD CITY**

START:	**At the Giralda by the cathedral.**
FINISH:	**At the Hospital de los Venerables in the Barrio de Santa Cruz.**
TIME:	**4 hours, including rapid visits to some interiors.**
BEST TIMES:	**Morning (8–midday) and late afternoon (3–7pm).**
WORST TIMES:	**After dark or during the heat of midday.**

Seville is loaded with architectural and artistic treasures and this brisk overview of the central zone doesn't begin to do justice to its cultural wealth. But it does serve as a good introduction to some of the city's most obvious (and spectacular) monuments, such as the Giralda and the Alcázar, the city's most desirable shopping district, and the labyrinthine alleyways of the Barrio de Santa Cruz.

Begin with a visit to the:

1 Cathedral & Giralda

This Gothic structure is so enormous that even its builders recognized the folly and fanaticism of their dreams. Its crowning summit, the Giralda, one of

Europe's most famous towers, was begun in the late 1100s by the Moors and was raised even higher by the Catholic monarchs in 1568.

After your visit, walk to the cathedral compound's northeastern corner for a visit to the:

2 Palacio Arzobispal (Archbishop's Palace)

This 16th-century building rests on 13th-century foundations, with a 17th-century Baroque facade of great beauty. Although designed to house the overseer of the nearby cathedral, it was sometimes pressed into service for secular visitors. One of these was Napoleon's representative, Maréchal Soult, after he conquered Seville in the name of the Bonaparte family and France early in the 19th century.

From here, walk across Plaza Virgen de los Reyes, into Plaza del Triunfo and onwards to the entrance of one of the most exotic palaces in Europe, the:

3 Reales Alcázar (Royal Alcázar)

The oldest royal seat in Spain was originally built for the Moorish caliphs in A.D. 712 as a fortress, then enlarged and embellished over the next thousand years by successive generations of Moors and, beginning in 1248, Christian rulers. Its superimposed combination of Arab and Christian Gothic architecture makes for one of the most interesting monuments in Iberia. Lavish gardens, as exotic as you'd expect from the Old Testament, sprawl in an easterly direction at the back. More than any other monument on this tour, with the exception of the cathedral, the Alcázar deserves a second visit.

Exit from the Alcázar back onto Plaza del Triunfo. At the plaza's southwestern edge rises the imposing bulk of the:

4 Archivo de Indias (Archive of the Indies)

Built as a commodities exchange, it was abandoned for a site in Cádiz when that port replaced Seville as the most convenient debarkation point for ships coming from the New World. In 1758 it was reconfigured as the repository for the financial records and political and cultural archives of anything concerning the development of the Western Hemisphere. Its closets and storerooms contain more than four million dossiers.

From here, walk a half-block north along Avenida de la Constitución bypassing the western facade of the already visited cathedral. The avenida will end within two blocks at the ornate bulk of Seville's:

5 Ayuntamiento (Town Hall)

Begun in 1527, and enlarged during the 19th century, this is the city's political showcase. To see its most interesting (*Plateresque*) facade, turn right (east) when you reach it; then flank the building's eastern edge for a view of the medallions and allegorical figures that kept teams of stonemasons busy for generations.

6 Robles Laredo 🍴

On the corner right next to the Town Hall at the bottom of Calle Sierpes, Robles Laredo, Sierpes 90 (📞 95-429-32-32) is one of Seville's most delectable coffee and cake shops. Try the sweet chocolatey Stracciatela with cherries soaked in a local liquor called Miura.

After your visit take a wander along Seville's most famous shopping street:

Walking Tour: The Old City

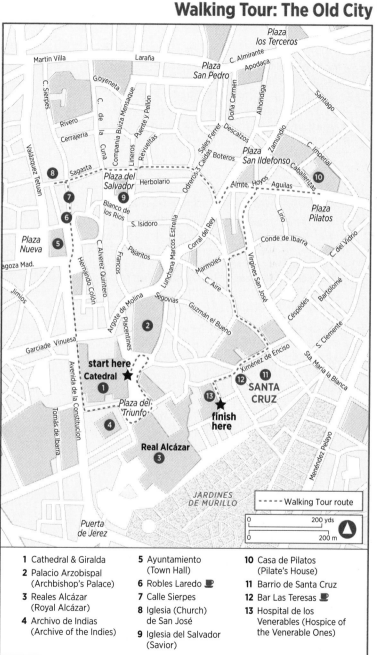

1 Cathedral & Giralda

2 Palacio Arzobispal
   (Archbishop's Palace)

3 Reales Alcázar
   (Royal Alcázar)

4 Archivo de Indias
   (Archive of the Indies)

5 Ayuntamiento
   (Town Hall)

6 Robles Laredo ☕

7 Calle Sierpes

8 Iglesia (Church)
   de San José

9 Iglesia del Salvador
   (Savior)

10 Casa de Pilatos
    (Pilate's House)

11 Barrio de Santa Cruz

12 Bar Las Teresas ☕

13 Hospital de los
    Venerables (Hospice of
    the Venerable Ones)

7 Calle Sierpes

This street stretches north from the Town Hall. Its southern terminus, where you're standing, was once the site of a debtors' prison where Miguel de Cervantes languished for several years.

Walk along the western edge of this famous street, turning left (west) after two blocks onto Calle Jovellanos for a view of the:

8 Iglesia (Church) de San José

Named in honor of a famous carpenter (St Joseph, husband of the Virgin), this gorgeous little Baroque chapel has a fabulously decorated altarpiece—all gold leaf swirls and ornate statues. The church functioned as the seat of the carpenters' guild after its completion in 1747.

Retrace your steps along Calle Jovellanos to Calle Sierpes, traverse the busy street and continue walking due east along Calle Sagasta. Within a block, Calle Sagasta will deposit you in Plaza del Salvador, in front of the elaborate facade of the:

9 Iglesia del Salvador (Savior)

One of the grandest churches of Seville, now beautifully restored, this is preferred by many visitors to the rather chilly pomposity of the cathedral. The enormous building was begun in 1674 on the site of one of the Muslim world's holiest sites, the mosque of Ibn Addabas. Beneath the Catholic iconography you can still make out the base of the Moorish minaret (converted long ago into a Christian belfry) and the Moorish layout of the building's courtyard.

Walk around the back of the cathedral and head east along narrow Calle Alcaiceria. Continue in the same direction across Plaza Alfalfa. Bear right at Bar Alfalfa at the top of the square and then turn left down Calle Alguilas. Walk a couple of blocks to reach Plaza de Pilatos and the:

10 Casa de Pilatos (Pilate's House)

One of the city's most frequently visited museums, Pilate's House was built in 1521 by the Marquis de Tarifa after his trip to the Holy Land where, according to legend, he was inspired by the ruined house in Jerusalem from which Pontius Pilate is said to have governed. The main entrance, modeled after an ancient Roman triumphal arch, is fashioned from bronze, jasper, and Carrara marble, and the overall effect is one of imperial Roman grandeur.

From Plaza de Pilatos retrace your steps along Calle Aguilas for two blocks and turn left onto Calle Virgenes. Continue along this road for about 5 minutes: the road becomes Calle San Jose and then Calle Santa Maria La Blanca. Turn left down Calle Ximénez de Enciso to reach one of Seville's most colorful antique neighborhoods, the narrow and labyrinthine alleyways of the:

11 Barrio de Santa Cruz

Before 1492, when the Jews were driven from Spain by the repressive edicts of Ferdinand and Isabella, this was the Jewish ghetto of Seville. Today it's highly desirable real estate—thick-walled houses, window boxes full of flowers, and severe exteriors opening onto private patios that ooze Andalusian charm.

12 Bar Las Teresas 🍺

Located on the corner of Calle Ximenez de Ensico and Calle Santa Teresa in the busiest part of Barrio de Santa Cruz, Bar Las Teresas, Santa Teresa 2 (© 95-421-30-69) is fantastically atmospheric with its long bar with huge hams hung from the ceilings. Tapas and wines are excellent.

Wander at will through the neighborhood, and don't be surprised if you quickly get lost in the maze of twisting streets. Know that your final destination is uphill (to the southwest) at a point near the cathedral (discreet signs indicate its direction). At the barrio's southwestern edge, beside Plaza de los Venerables, you'll want to visit one of the barrio's greatest monuments, the:

13 Hospital de los Venerables (Hospice of the Venerable Ones)

It was founded in 1675 as a retirement home for aged priests and it's now been restored as a cultural center. Its tree-lined patio with sunken fountain is one of Seville's most unusual. Its church is a feast of Baroque painting and sculpture. A room off the patio contains a permanent exhibition of works by the great Sevillian painter Diego Velázquez (1599–1660).

ESPECIALLY FOR KIDS

The greatest thrill for kids in Seville is climbing **La Giralda,** the former minaret of the Great Mosque that once stood here. The view from this 20-story bell tower is certainly worth it, but most kids delight in the journey up. With inclined ramps rather than steps, the climb was originally designed to be ridden up on horseback. Little gargoyle-framed windows along the way allow you to preview the skyline of Seville.

With your family in tow, head for **Parque María Luisa.** Seville's largest park is a shady respite from the heat of the sun and perfect for kids to let off steam. It's far more than an open patch of grass. There are unusual trees and plants from all over the world and monuments and enclosures to explore. In the center there's a lake with a gazebo (the Isleta de los Patos) and nearby there's Monte Gurugu, a mini-mountain with a waterfall. You can climb up to the top or walk through the tunnel underneath. You can also hire bicycles and four-person **pedal carts** (© 66-381-10-43; www.cyclotouristic.com) at the entrance next to the Plaza de España and in the Plaza de América. They're great fun and cost from 7€ for 30 minutes.

Older kids will also enjoy renting *pedalos* (pedal boats) for trips along the **Guadalquivir River,** or renting bikes for rides along the riverbank and around the park. See "Staying Active" below for more information.

Isla Mágica, Pabellón de España, Isla de la Cartuja (© 90-216-17-16; www.islamagica.es), is on the island of La Cartuja, across the river from the city's historic core. It's installed on the site of the 1992 World Expo grounds. Today the site has been transformed into a Disneyesque playground. The whole park has a 16th-century motif in honor of the fact that Seville was the departure point for many of the great discoveries of that century. The seven different adventure zones include Sevilla, Port of the Indies, where you can boat on the lake or take a 70-meter plunge and then come to a stomach-churningly abrupt halt; Quetzal, World of the Maya, which has a vertiginous spinning slide ride; the Gateway to America, with its big dipper and log flume; and Amazonia, which features a hanging rollercoaster, like riding a chairlift only much, much faster. Little ones are catered for with small boat ponds and radio-controlled boats, and there's often live entertainment in the cafes and restaurants. There's also a show spectacular two or three times daily (depending on the season) based around the galleon, with roaring cannons, flashing cutlasses, pirate queens, and ships boarded from the rigging. It's open daily from 11am to 11pm (summer), to 10pm (spring), and to 9pm (fall). Admission costs from 25€ to 28€ for adults and from 18€ to 20€ for children for a full day depending on the time of year. Children under 4 go free. Family and half-day tickets are also available. To get there, take a taxi or buses C1 and C2.

To cap a family trip to Seville, take one of the **horse-and-buggy rides** that leave from Plaza Virgen de los Reyes on Adolfo Rodríguez Jurado, or from the Parque de María Luisa at Plaza de España.

ORGANIZED TOURS

There are two companies that conduct double-decker **bus tours** of Seville, each with a recorded commentary about the sights you're passing, and each with a choice of at least six different languages, including English. Participation in one of these tours is hardly essential. The Old Town's streets are too narrow for the buses so they are restricted to itineraries that skirt the Old City walls, cross the river to Cartuja— stopping at Isla Mágica (see "Especially for Kids" above) and back along the river bank. They also offer add-on tours through the Triana neighborhood across the river. The commentary is fairly superficial, but the cost of 16€ for adults and 7€ for children aged 5 to 15 is reasonable (free for children aged 4 and under), and you'll see some parts of the town that would be hard to cover completely on your own. Itineraries for both companies are virtually identical, as are ticket prices: Sevillatour (✆ **90-210-10-81;** www.sevillatour.com) and Sevirama ✆ **95-456-06-93** *Tip:* The upper deck of each of the buses offers unobstructed views, but if you plan this during the heat of midday, bring a sun hat and sunglasses.

If you're looking for really interesting **walking tours** to less-discovered parts of the Old Town, David Cox and Luis Salas's **Really Discover tours** are highly recommended (✆ **64-535-07-50**/95-511-39-12; www.reallydiscover.com). Luis is, in my opinion, the best guide in Seville and he knows the city inside out. Along with their daily walking tour of the sights, which in itself takes you quite a way off the tourist trail, they have a number of more unusual itineraries aimed at helping you get to know Seville like a local. These include an evening tapas tour, a flamenco tour, a ham and olive tasting tour, and a new craft and artisans tour. Prices are usually 20€ to 30€ per person depending on the tour. They also offer tours in, and day trips to, **Granada** and **Córdoba**.

Andalusian Excursions

In addition to being loaded with monuments of consuming historical and cultural interest, Seville is a good base for exploring Andalusia.

For bespoke day trips tailored to your specific requirements, **Tailormade Andalucia** (✆ **95-644-39-22**; www.tailormadeandalucia.com) offers a range of options which include sherry tasting in Jerez, visits to bull farms, excursions to the White Villages, and watersports on the Costa de la Luz.

If you're looking for regular organized tours, **Visitours**, Calle Torricelli 32, Isla de la Cartuja (© **95-446-09-85;** www.visitours.es) offers interesting cultural day trips. Their buses, which hold between 8 and 48 passengers, always have the option of picking up and dropping off clients at their hotels. Reservations a day in advance are strongly recommended. Three of the company's most popular tours depart several times each week. A tour of **Granada** leaves Seville at 6:30am, explores all that city's major monuments and neighborhoods, and returns to Seville around 7pm. The price is 120€. A tour of **Córdoba** departs Seville between 8 and 9am, returns around 7pm, and costs 95€ per person. A tour to **Jerez de la Frontera** and **Cádiz** departs around 8:15am and returns around 6:30pm and costs 105€ per person.

The river cruise company **Cruceros Turísticos Torre del Oro** (see "Staying Active" below) also offers a nice cruise excursion at weekends. You take the boat all the way down river to the sea to the pretty sherry town of **Sanlúcar de Barrameda** (see p. 275) and then return by bus after you've had time to explore the town, sample a glass or two of the local *manzanilla* sherry and dine in one of its many excellent seafood restaurants. Departures are every Saturday and Sunday from May to October at 9am. The cruise down to Sanlúcar takes 4 to 5 hours. The cost is 35€ for adults and 20€ for children under 14. Reservations are recommended.

STAYING ACTIVE

Boating

Seville is hardly on the beach, but the Guadalquivir River is used for cruises, canoeing, and paddle boating. Seville, perhaps, looks its most scenic from the river. Near Torre del Oro, you can get information and details, including prices, about boating. Check with **Cruceros Turísticos Torre del Oro,** Paseo Marqués de Contadero, Arenal (© **95-421-13-96;** www.crucerostorredeloro.com) about river cruises. Costing 16€ per person, these run every 30 to 60 minutes daily from 11am to 7pm November to February and 11am to 11pm March to October. If you want to take to the water yourself, you can hire pedalos and canoes just along from where the cruise boats depart, from the Pedalquivir floating bar. The cost is 10€ per hour for a two-person pedalo and hire is available from 11:30am to 9pm.

Cycling

Seville is embracing the bicycle in a big way. There's a well organized network of cycle paths and a city-wide bicycle loan program, *Sevici,* which tourists can use too (see Chapter 5 "Getting Around," "By Bicycle" for more info). Hopping into the saddle for a pedal is a great way to see more of Parque María Luisa and to enjoy the riverbank with its imposing bridges, the Cartuja monastery, and the pavilions (*pabellones*) built for the 1992 Exhibition.

If you want to do guided tours by bike of the city or farther afield, **Rentabikesevilla** (© **61-946-14-91;** www.rentabikesevilla.com) is recommended and can deliver to your hotel. Folding bikes cost 12€ per day, 9€ for each subsequent day, and 50€ per week. Mountain bikes are also available.

Swimming

A hotel above three government stars without a swimming pool is rare in Seville. The largest, most state-of-the-art, and most comprehensive of the city's public pools is **Aquopolis**, Poligono del Aeropuerto, Av. del Deporte (☎ **95-440-66-22**; www. aquopolis.es). Popular with families and children alike, this sprawling water park is set in the Barrio de las Delicias to the east of the center and has slides, gardens, splashing fountains, and cafeterias. There are quieter pools for younger water babes too. Rates are 19.95€ adults, 14.95€ children aged 3 to 10 years. It's open May to September noon to 7pm daily. (Open to 8pm July/August.) Take bus L22, L55.

SPECTATOR SPORTS

Bullfighting

From Easter until late October, some of the best bullfighters in Spain appear at the **Plaza de Toros Real Maestranza** on Paseo de Colón 12 (☎ **95-422-45-77**). One of the leading bullrings in Spain, the stadium attracts matadors whose fights often receive TV and newspaper coverage throughout Iberia. Unless there's a special festival going on, bullfights (*corridas*) occur on Sunday. The best are staged during the April Fair celebrations.

Tickets should be purchased in advance at the Ticket Office (*despacho de entradas*) on Calle Adriano (☎ **95-450-13-82**), beside the stadium. If you speak Spanish you can buy online at www.plazadetorosdelamaestranza.com. You'll also find many unofficial kiosks selling tickets placed strategically around town, in particular along the main shopping street, Calle Sierpes. However, they charge a 20% commission for their tickets—a lot more if they think they can get it. The prices vary, often beginning at 11€ for a nosebleed seat (*grado del sol*), which means you'll be at a hard-to-see elevation in the fierce sun. For a front-row seat in the shade at a major bullfight—*barrera de sombra*—expect to pay as much as 120€.

The major bullfights are called *corridas de toros* and feature more experienced matadors. For apprentice bullfighters with younger bulls, the bullfights are advertised as *novilladas*. Because of the excessive heat in July and August, *corridas* most often occur on Thursday nights at 9pm or Sunday afternoons at 5:30pm. Posters around town advertise the various bullfights.

Soccer/Football

Like any Spanish city, Seville has a fanatically loyal following for its two football teams. Soccer matches in Spain are usually played September to May on Sunday afternoons. The more successful of the two teams is **Sevilla FC** (Estadio Sanchez Pizjuán, Av. Eduardo Dato ☎ **90-250-19-01**; www.sevillafc.es). Currently in the top league, watching a game against Real Madrid or FC Barcelona ranks as one of Spain's biggest sporting highlights. The stadium is in the Nervion district, a short taxi or bus ride (buses C1, C2, 5, 22, 23, 32) from the historic center. **Real Betis Balompie** (Estadio Ruiz de Lopera, Av. de Heliopolis. ☎ **95-461-03-40**; www. realbetisbalompie.es) is the city's second team and as underdogs they enjoy fiercely loyal support. Their stadium is a little farther out of town but still easy enough to reach by taxi or buses 6 and 34. You can sometimes watch reserve games for free here on Sunday mornings. Whichever team you decide to watch, it's advisable to buy tickets in advance.

SHOPPING

The pedestrian strip of **Calle Sierpes** is the principal shopping street of Seville. Store after store stand side by side along this monument to 19th-century architecture. Other great places for both window and actual shopping are the side streets branching off from Sierpes, especially **Calle Tetuán**. **Calle Cuna** is the third major shopping street. Calle Sierpes tends to attract the most dedicated local consumers, and its stores rarely include real cutting-edge or high-fashion shops. These tend to cluster near or at the edge of **Plaza Nueva.**

If you're seeking Andalusian handicrafts, head for the narrow streets of **Barrio de Santa Cruz.** For specific shopping streets in Santa Cruz, seek out **Rodrigo Caro** and **Mateos Gago.** You could fill many a mansion with the trinkets and antiques for sale here. Other antiques and handicraft shops are found in the sector west of the cathedral, including **El Arenal.** Major stores are open Monday to Saturday from 9:30am to 8pm; smaller establishments, however, often take a siesta, doing business from 9:30 or 10am to 1:30 or 2pm and again from 4:30 or 5 to 8pm. Exceptions to this are listed below.

Shopping A to Z
ANTIQUES
Félix In the center of Seville, in front of the cathedral, this shop is the best outlet in Seville for antique Andalusian posters. Most popular are scenes, some in the Art Deco style, from the Feria de Abril (April Fair), from one of the *corridas* at the bullring, or from Semana Santa. Locals call these posters "propaganda" of major events. Open Monday to Friday 10am to 2pm and 5 to 8pm, Saturday 10am to 2pm. Av. de la Constitución 26. ✆ **95-421-80-26.**

Morales Ortega Right in the heart of Barrio de Santa Cruz, this place is full of diverse artifacts: ancient ceramics, old paintings, Arabic coffee pots, pewter, and postcards are just some of the curiosities on show. Jamerdana 2. ✆ **95-422-36-06.**

Popularte This is another treasure trove of pots, signs, door knockers and more in a U-shaped little shop in Santa Cruz that could require a prolonged browsing session. It's a personal favorite of mine. Pasaje de Vila 4. ✆ **95-422-94-44.**

ART GALLERIES
Isabel Ignacio A small, one-room gallery, close to the bullring, which hosts contemporary art exhibitions from up-and-coming artists—painting, sculpture installations, video. Works are for sale. Open Monday 6–9pm, Tuesday to Friday 11am to 1:30pm and 6 to 9pm, Saturdays 11am–2pm (closed on Saturdays June to August). Velarde 9. ✆ **95-456-25-55.** www.galeriaisabelignacio.com.

Rafael Ortiz ★ This is one of Seville's most respected art galleries, specializing in contemporary paintings, usually by Iberian artists. Exhibitions change frequently and inventories sell out quickly. Marmoles 12. ✆ **95-421-48-74.**

121

BOOKS

Beta This is the best of Beta's eight branches. It's housed in an old theater reached through a short passageway that doesn't hint at the remarkable two-floor auditorium inside, stacked with books, including a couple of shelves of English stock. Calle Sierpes 25. ✆ **95-429-37-24.**

FNAC This cool modern French chain right next to the cathedral sells books in English (top floor), CDs, software and more on four floors. It also has a good range of iPod, camera, and PC accessories if you've lost or broken any of your essential gear. Av. de la Constitución 8. ✆ **95-459-65-17.**

CERAMICS

El Postigo Set in the town center near the cathedral, this arts and crafts gallery contains one of the biggest selections of Andalusian ceramics in town. Some of the pieces are much, much too big to fit into your suitcase; others, especially the hand-painted tiles, make charming souvenirs that can easily be transported. Open Monday to Saturday 10am to 2pm, Monday to Friday 5 to 8:30pm. Arfe s/n. ✆ **95-456-00-13.**

La Cartuja de Sevilla ★ Delicate chinaware of the highest quality is sold here from the famous Cartuja china factory, originally set up by Englishman Charles Pickman in 1839. If you're looking for high quality, beautifully worked pieces, this is the place to come to. Av. de la Constitución 16. ✆ **95-421-41-55.** www.lacartujadesevilla.es.

Martian On one of the city's main shopping streets, this outfit sells a wide array of painted tiles and ceramics. The inventory includes vases, plates, cups, serving dishes, and statues, all made in or near Seville. Many of the pieces exhibit ancient geometric patterns of Andalusia. Other floral motifs are rooted in Spanish traditions of the 18th century. Open Monday to Saturday 10am to 1:30pm, Monday to Friday 5 to 8pm. Calle Sierpes 74. ✆ **95-421-34-13.**

DEPARTMENT STORES

El Corte Inglés This is the best of the several department stores clustered in Seville's commercial center. A well-accessorized branch of a nationwide chain, it features multilingual translators and rack after rack of every conceivable kind of merchandise for the well-stocked home, kitchen, and closet. If you're in the market for the brightly colored *feria* costumes worn by young girls during Seville's holidays, there's an impressive selection of the memorable folkloric Andalusian accessories. Open Monday to Saturday 10am to 10pm. Plaza Duque 8. ✆ **95-459-70-00.** www.elcorteingles.es.

FASHION

Bimba & Lola Cool, funky, and unique, B&L's range of elegant designer clothes, bags, and shoes is just perfect for a young sassy lady looking for something a little different with some serious Andalusian style. Rioja 58. ✆ **95-421-93-75.** www.bimbaylola.com.

Carolina Herrera Standing on Seville's stylish Plaza Nueva, this boutique sells high-priced scarves, shoes, belts, wallets, handbags, and luxury goods. It's supremely luxurious and surprisingly macho, outfitted in tones of dark leather and dark woods, and permeated with rock music. Open Monday to Saturday from 10am to 8:30pm; in August, Monday to Saturday from 10:30am to 1:30pm and 5 to 8:30pm. Plaza Nueva 8. ✆ **95-450-04-18.**

Market Forces

Seville's markets make a very cultural shopping alternative. The main **food market** is on Pastor Y Landero but those at Triana (Plaza del Altozano) and Macarena (halfway along Feria) are both good, with fresh fruit, fish, cheese and more: all of these are open from 8am to 1pm daily except Sundays. One of my favorite places for browsing is the street **flea market** on Calle Feria in the Macarena district on Thursday mornings. On Sunday mornings there's a great **art market** featuring paintings by local artists outside the Museo Provincial de Bellas Artes (Plaza del Museo) and a small **coin and stamp market** in Plaza del Cabildo.

Loewe ★ This is the Sevillian branch of the oldest (established in 1856) and most famous purveyor of fine leather goods in Spain. You'll enter a big-windowed and sun-flooded store where top-notch leather goods are artfully displayed. Check out the new line of scarves, as designed by Oscar Marine, one of the graphic artists associated with Pedro Almodovar's films. Discerning women make a beeline for shoes they can really strut their stuff in, and the briefcases. Open Monday to Friday 10am to 8:30pm, Saturday 10am to 2pm. Plaza Nueva 12. ✆ **95-422-52-53.** www.loewe.com.

MaxMara There are only two branches of this hip and upscale store in all of Andalusia (the other one is in Marbella). MaxMara stocks both sportswear and elegant evening wear for busy, urban women. Lately, according to a spokesperson, the wives of many of the region's most visible politicians have been cropping up in MaxMara after pantsuits and business suits. Open Monday to Saturday from 10am to 8:30pm; in August, Monday to Saturday from 10am to 2pm, Monday to Friday from 6 to 9pm. Plaza Nueva 3. ✆ **95-421-48-25.** www.maxmara.com.

Padilla Crespo Owner Manolo's grandfather started this lovely sombrero shop many decades ago and he continues its fine tradition of handmade hat making. These typically Sevillian hats are all made on the premises and each one of them is unique. Tom Cruise is one of the many satisfied customers. Manolo speaks good English too. Adriano 18B. ✆ **95-456-44-14.**

Pilar Burgos Pilar is another local designer with a bit of a following. He specializes in brightly colored, seriously sexy heels for women. He's a huge hit with the Sevillians who love to dress flamboyantly, but will any of his colorful creations go with your wardrobe? There's of course only one way to find out! Tetuán 16. ✆ **95-456-21-17.** www.pilarburgos.com.

Victorio & Lucchino ★★ This is the commercial headquarters of the most famous designers in Seville. Their names are known to virtually everybody in town, because of the hot press coverage they've generated and because of the cachet they've brought to the Sevillano's self-image. Even Penelope Cruz was one of their models before she went to Hollywood. Fortunately, you don't have to be shaped like Penelope to wear these cutting-edge fashions. They stock garments up to size 46 (roughly an American size 14 and U.K. size 16) and have expanded their line to include both children's clothing and menswear. The few clothes on display are riveting. Some have hints of leather, some evoke an updated version of *feria* modish, and some focus

Bitter Orange

Seville has more than 20,000 bitter orange trees, the fruits of which are often exported to England to make into marmalade. The local name for these trees is **Azahar**, a word that translates directly from the Arabic as "white flower." For 2 weeks in early April, the city is permeated with the scent of the Azahar, an intoxicating smell that everyone in Seville delights in.

exclusively on colors like magenta. At Plaza Nueva 10: Monday to Saturday 10am to 8pm; in July and August Monday to Friday 10am to 9pm and Saturday 10am to 2pm. At Sierpes 87: Monday to Saturday 10am to 2pm and 5 to 8:30pm; July and August Monday to Saturday 10am to 2pm, Monday to Friday 5 to 8:30pm. Plaza Nueva 10. ✆ **95-450-26-60.** Calle Sierpes 87. ✆ **95-422-79-51.** www.victorioylucchino.com.

FOOD

El Reloj ★   Brothers Antonio and Francisco run this most delightful old provisions store (*ultramarinos* in Spanish) with an antique facade and shelves and counters stacked with cheeses, hams, and canned produce. The shop is a bit of an icon now having featured in a local American Express press advert, but Antonio and Francisco seem totally unfazed by the attention. Arfe 18. ✆ **95-422-24-60.**

La Alacena Tienda   This is *the* place to find top quality local hams, cheeses, and wines. They're all beautifully laid out in this immaculate shop. A full leg of serrano ham can set you back hundreds of euros, but there's produce in all price ranges. And before you buy, you can sample some of the produce in their stylish wine bar next door. San Eloy 31. ✆ **95-421-55-80.**

Las Delicias del Barrio   Tucked away in a cubbyhole space on a street that's otherwise devoted to tapas bars, this stylish boutique specializes in upscale food products of Andalusia. On display are a variety of olives, wines, cheeses, honey, and most important of all, a diverse array of olive oils that show off the fertility and rich culinary traditions of southern Spain. Open daily from 11am to 9pm. Calle Mateos Gagos 15. ✆ **95-421-06-29.**

GIFTS

For another prestigious gift shop, see **Sevillarte** under "Porcelain," below.

Coco Sevilla   There's a selection of the usual Moorish-style souvenirs like bowls and light shades here. The proprietor is a friendly Frenchman and his shop is easy to find, on the main street in Barrio de Santa Cruz. Ximénez de Enciso 28. ✆ **954 214 532.** www.cocosevilla.com.

El Azulejo   Bigger than most of its competitors within this crowded neighborhood near the cathedral, as well as classier and less claustrophobic, this shop sells upscale pottery, jewelry, and some of the most beautiful fans I've seen in Seville. Priced from 18€ to 160€, they shimmer with hand-painted flowers or architectural renderings of actual sites in Seville. Open Monday to Saturday 9am to 7:30pm. Calle Mateos Gagos 10. ✆ **95-422-00-85.**

Las Moradas   In a little patio, Alicia San Martin's tasteful shop sells Andalusian handicrafts a notch up from much of the tourist tat on sale elsewhere in Santa Cruz.

Lots of Moorish elements, like bowls, fans, jewelry, and light shades too. Rodrigo Caro 20. ✆ **95-456-39-17.**

JEWELRY

El Cronómetro   All the top brands are here at this distinguished family watch-makers with its eye-catching old shop front with clocks showing time in London, Paris, and elsewhere. Along with the Rolexes and Tags look out for Spanish brand Cuervo y Sobrinos. Calle Sierpes 19-21. ✆ **95-422-50-28.** www.elcronometro.com.

Tous   This outlet celebrates "jewelry full of life" (in the owner's words) and displays some of the most innovative gems in Andalusia. Many of the designs are created by some of southern Spain's best artisans. Although there may be slight seasonal varia-tions, regular hours are Monday to Friday 10am to 2pm and 5 to 8:30pm, Saturday 10am to 8pm. Calle Sagasta 8. ✆ **95-456-35-36.**

LEATHER

El Caballo   Possibly Seville's best leatherware shop, Caballo sells classic hand-bags, suitcases, belts, wallets, and shoes. The leather used is of the highest quality, soft, beautifully cut and stitched. There's another branch on Plaza Nueva. Antonia Díaz 7. ✆ **95-422-95-39.**

MUSIC & MUSICAL INSTRUMENTS

Compás Sur ★   If you've seen some flamenco and want to take a piece of the music home as a souvenir, this independent music shop is the place to visit. It spe-cializes in flamenco and Andalusian music, selling CDs, instruments, and sheet music. Owner Rafael really knows his stuff and he speaks some English too. Cuesta del Rosario 7-F. ✆ **95-421-56-62.** www.compas-sur.com.

Guitarras de Artesanía   Or if you don't mind paying the excess baggage charge, how about buying one of the flamenco guitars? One of Seville's best traditional fla-menco guitar shops is, surprisingly, right in the middle of the tourist district; you can sometimes see the proprietors making them. Mesón del Moro 12. ✆ **95-422-78-98.**

PASTRIES

Confitería la Campana   This is one of the oldest and most respected pastry shops in Seville, with a pedigree going back to 1885, a sense of Victorian propriety,

---

🎁 A Fine Song & Dance

Tucked away on a side street off Calle Santa María La Blanca at the north end of Barrio de Santa Cruz is **La Carbon-ería**, Calle Levíes 18 (✆ **95-421-44-60**), which is unique in Seville. A former charcoal factory has been converted into a concert hall with an array of bars and stage areas leading off it. Here you'll find a friendly, quite boisterous crowd of locals and tourists being entertained by a series of Andalusian-style concerts and flamenco shows from around 10:30pm. You often sit on chairs placed at small wooden tables under low ceilings. In the rear is a large, plant-filled courtyard and in warmer months the shows take place here. It's noisy, often pretty disorganized, and lots of fun. Entrance is free and a beer or a glass of regional wine costs from 1.50€ and up. It's open daily from 8pm to 3am.

and a location near the beginning of an all-pedestrian street that's been considered a shopping Mecca for years. They often provide the pastries at very grand and elegant diplomatic receptions. You'll select your calorific goodies beneath a splendid ceiling of white plaster and gilt. There's a cafe on the premises and take-away service as well. Open daily 8am to 10pm. Calle Sierpes 1-3. © **95-422-35-70.**

PORCELAIN

Sevillarte   This is a glisteningly upscale gift shop that's the only officially authorized outlet for the full line of Lladróporcelain statues. Also in stock is an impressive array of silk "Manila" shawls—the kind of richly embroidered, jewel-toned shoulder wraps that no dignified Sevillana could live without. There's also a worthy display of porcelain, elaborately decorated fans (the kind that could transform virtually anyone into a hopeless flirt), and jewelry. Open Monday to Friday 10am to 7pm, Saturday 10am to 6pm, and Sunday 10am to 2pm. Calle Vida 17. © **95-450-00-04.**

SCENTS

Agua de Seville ★★   No scent emanating from Seville has elicited as much poetry as the blossoms from the city's 20,000 orange trees. In 1992, in honor of the Seville Expo, a team of designers came up with the world's ultimate orange-blossom-scented cologne, Agua de Seville, which today is a household name throughout Andalusia. The bottle that contains it, shaped like the barrel of one of Napoleon's cannons, was inspired by the chimneys jutting skyward from the kilns of the Cartuja monastery on the site of Seville Expo. Both the men's and the women's version of the cologne is rich with the scents of jasmine and orange blossom, although the men's version has a stronger dose of sandalwood. Also on display are some carefully chosen gift items, housewares, and fashion accessories. Open Monday to Friday 10am to 2pm and 5 to 9pm, Saturday 10am to 2pm. Plaza Nueva 9. © **95-421-31-45.**

SEVILLE AFTER DARK

Everyone from Lord Byron to Jacqueline Onassis has appreciated the unique blend of heat, rhythm, and sensuality that make up nightlife in Seville. If you're looking for a theme to define your nightlife wanderings, let it be food and dancing. Things get going late here and go on even later—often 'til dawn and beyond. It's perfectly normal to start your evening as late as 9pm or even 10 with some fine-flavored tapas and an ice cold beer or sherry. Locals tend to stop off at several different places, sampling their favorite tapas at each. Indeed, the Spanish verb *tapeo* means just that—to go on a tapas bar crawl. After several drinks and tapas, you might venture to a club where the focus revolves around the uniquely Andalusian blend of dance and song that is flamenco—surely one of the world's most captivating and beguiling spectacles. And when you've finished with that, and if you're not wilted from the heat and the chaos, there's always the possibility of heading on to a late night dance club or bar and keeping going until dawn.

To keep abreast of what's happening in the arts and after dark in Seville, pick up a copy of the free monthly magazine *El Giraldillo*, or the monthly *ABC Sevilla*. Another good source of information is the main city tourist office at 19 Plaza de San Francisco where there are regularly updated events listings posted on a board.

Keep an eye out for classical concerts that are sometimes presented in the cathedral of Seville, the church of San Salvador, and the Conservatorio Superior de Música

A More Cultured Flamenco

Whilst many of the flamenco clubs in Seville are geared to tourists, if you'd like to see a more formal and academic presentation of this art form, there are two options, both in the Barrio de Santa Cruz and both consistently excellent. At **Casa de la Memoria**, Calle Ximénez de Enciso 28 (© **95-456-06-70**; www.casadelamemoria.es), young up-and-coming artists perform in an intimate Andalusian patio with room for just 30 or so spectators. The price is only 15€ for adults and, depending on the time of year, there are one or two shows each night. Reservations are essential. Similar in style in an intimate patio setting, **Museo del Baile Flamenco**, Manuel Rojas Marcos 3, (© **95-434-03-11**; www.museoflamenco.com), Seville's excellent flamenco museum, has shows on Fridays and Saturdays usually starting at 7:30pm. Tickets cost 25€ for adults.

at Jesús del Gran Poder. Variety productions, including some plays for the kids, are presented at **Teatro Alameda,** Calle Crédito (© **95-438-83-12**), and comedy and alternative theater are staged at the excellent **Sala La Imperdible,** Plaza del Duque s/n. (© **95-490-54-58**; www.imperdible.org), but both only stage performances in Spanish. (Note that Sala La Imperdible is set to move to new premises, so check with the tourist office.) The venerable **Teatro Lope de Vega,** Avenida María Luisa (© **95-459-08-53**), is the setting for ballet performances and classical concerts, among other events. Near Parque María Luisa, this is Seville's leading stage.

Opera

Teatro de la Maestranza ★★★ It wasn't until the 1990s that Seville got its own opera house, but it quickly became one of the world's premier venues for operatic performances. Naturally, the focus is on works inspired by Seville itself, including Verdi's *La Forza del Destino* and Mozart's *Marriage of Figaro*. Jazz, classical music, and even the quintessentially Spanish *zarzuelas* (operettas) are also performed. The opera house can't be visited except during performances. Tickets (which vary in price, depending on the event staged) can be purchased daily 10am to 2pm and 6 to 9pm at the box office in front of the theater. Paseo de Colón 22. © **95-422-33-44.** www.teatromaestranza.com.

Flamenco

Flamenco in Seville comes in all sorts of guises, from full-on Broadway-show style productions with dinner included to impromptu bursts of song and dance in tiny corner bars. Purists will argue the spontaneous stuff is more authentic, but even the big shows allow you to sample the beguiling blend of passionate rhythm and song that is uniquely flamenco.

Casa Anselma ★ 👯 If you're bored with touristy flamenco shows, seek out this little hideaway deep in the heart of Triana on the western bank of the river. The building, which is completely covered in decorative tiles called *azulejos,* is hard to miss. Inside it's wildly decorated with a lot of Spanish memorabilia, including bullfighting paraphernalia. The owner, Anselma, is the most celebrated flamenco performer in Seville, a secret the locals who flock here would like to keep to themselves. Flamenco performances are unrehearsed and spontaneous. Sometimes the joint jumps with communal singalongs or dancing, with guitarists striking up their instruments. The club keeps no set hours, but it's usually packed and the action begins at midnight, Monday to Saturday. Instead of a cover, you're charged for what you have to drink. It's best reached by taxi and is four blocks back from Calle Betis. Pagès del Corro 49, corner of Calle Antillano Campos. No phone.

El Arenal ★ 🎁 The singers clap, the guitars strum, the tension builds, and the room fills with the ancient and mysterious magic of the flamenco. In the rear of a 17th-century structure, two shows are performed nightly at 10pm. Drinks and food are served at minuscule tables in a sweltering back room that evokes Old Andalusia. The location is between Varflora and Dos de Mayo in the vicinity of the Paseo Colón and the bullring. Cover 36€ including first drink, or 60€ for a fixed-price dinner. Calle Rodó 7. ✆ **95-421-64-92.**

El Palacio Andaluz Lights, luxury, and a big venue: this is one of the most upscale *tablaos* in Seville where you can choose dinner with the show or just a drink. It's more of a razzle-dazzle musical than a flamenco show, but good entertainment nonetheless. Tickets cost from 36€ to 74€. María Auxiliadora 18. ✆ **95-453-47-20.** www.elpalacioandaluz.com.

El Patio Sevillano In central Seville on the Guadalquivir riverbank between two historic bridges, El Patio Sevillano is another of the big showcases for Spanish folk song and dance, performed by exotically costumed dancers. The presentation includes a wide variety of Andalusian flamenco and songs, as well as classical pieces by such composers as de Falla, Albéniz, Granados, and Chueca. There are two shows nightly, at 7:30 and 10pm. The cover of 35€ includes the first drink. Paseo de Cristóbal Colón 11. ✆ **95-421-41-20.**

Tablao Los Gallos ★ Negotiating the labyrinth of narrow streets of the Barrio de Santa Cruz somehow contributes to the authenticity of this small, high-energy flamenco club. It's one of the more authentic spaces offering more intimate *flamenco puro* performance than the Palacio or the Patio. The location is two blocks south of Ximénez de Enciso along Santa Teresa. No food is served during the shows, which begin every night at around 8 and 10:30pm. Cover 30€ including first drink. Plaza de Santa Cruz 11. ✆ **95-421-69-81.** www.tablaolosgallos.com.

Clubs & Dance Bars

In Seville, some of these dance clubs have the life span of sickly butterflies. Check locally to see what's open at the time of your visit. Cover charges can vary depending on the night, but count on spending at least 6€ to get in, plus drinks.

Antique Teatro If you're into celeb-spotting, this is the place: actors and soccer players are sometimes seen here. It's been completely renovated and is fit to please the most avid disco-goer. You need to dress to impress to get in. Hours are Thursday to Saturday 11pm to 7am. In summer a terrace with torchlights opens up. Matemáticos Rey Pastor y Castor s/n, Pabellón Olímpico de Expo 92. ✆ **95-446-22-07.**

Boss Boss has four bars on different levels and a very large, stadium-type dance area. It's a favorite of many for the late-night scene but the door policy is pretty

Waiter!

You might think you've done the hard part finding a table, but it's sometimes really difficult to get the attention of busy tapas bar waiting staff. Locals seem to glide in, order almost as they sit down, and get served whilst you sit trying desperately to catch the waiter's eye. There's not much of a sense of waiting your turn in Seville, so wave a hand and call out as the waiter passes, no matter how stressed they look. A great alternative is to stand or perch at the bar. Here you're close to the bar staff so service is never a problem and you're right in the thick of the action, which is always great fun.

arrogant. Dress well and go in small groups but be prepared to be turned away if you're not cool enough. Betis 67. ℂ **95-499-01-04.**

Disco Catedral Playing the latest euro-dance tunes, Disco Catedral opens Wednesday to Saturday at 11pm and usually shuts down at sunrise. It's popular with the younger crowd and a bit teeny at times. Cuesta del Rosario 12. ℂ **95-456-28-26.**

Elefunk ★ An older, less glam crowd gathers here for the relaxed vibe. No snooty doormen or beautiful people, just a genuinely friendly place with eclectic sounds from funk to hip hop to electronica. Adriano 10. ℂ **95-422-25-81.**

El Jackson Funk and soul are the order of the day in this converted house on a side street just off the end of the Alameda. Laid back and friendly, as you'd expect for the Alameda district. Free entry and good-value drinks too. Relator 21. No phone.

Groucho One of central Seville's coolest bars, Groucho is full of gorgeous Sevillians, drinking long drinks and letting their hair down. Live flamenco and disco at weekends. There's a very strict door policy, so dress up smart. Federico Sánchez Bedoya 30. No phone. www.grouchobar.com.

Malandar Funk, rock, pop, jazz, flamenco: there's all kinds of interesting stuff going on here. Definitely one of the most progressive live music places in Seville, but you need to stay up late. Most nights don't start 'til past midnight. See website for more info. Av. Torneo 43. ℂ **954 221 417.** www.malandar.net.

Sala Obbio ★ Wear what you want and be what you want. Indie, soul, and funk with a friendly crowd make this one of my favorite late-night spots. Art house movies are shown Monday thru Wednesday. Club nights are Fridays and Saturdays. Trastamara 29. No phone. www.myspace.com/salaobbio.

Tapas & Drinks

Bar Alfalfa There's an Italian twist to the tapas in this atmospheric corner bar, with tasty bruschettas being my personal favorite; a nice change to the more standard offerings elsewhere. It has to be one of the smallest places in town—the mens' room is literally in a cupboard! Candilejo 1. ℂ **65-480-92-97.**

Bar Las Teresas A busy tapas bar in the Barrio de Santa Cruz district, this, for me, is one of the area's most authentic places. Along with tourists there are usually lots of locals in here, which is always a good sign. Cheeses and house wines are very good, as is the excellent ham. Santa Teresa 2. ℂ **95-421-30-69.**

Casablanca ★   The King of Spain often tries the tapas here when he's in town. This corner bar just on Avenida de la Constitución is slightly upmarket and a tad pricey, but absolutely worth it for the great flavors. The daily specials are always good. Adolfo Rodríguez Jurado 12. ℂ **95-422-41-14.**

Casa Morales ★★   Just across Avenida de la Constitución, this is an "Abaceria" (corner shop and bar) dating from 1850 and decorated in a traditional Andalusian style with rustic wooden furniture and huge old wine vats upright against the wall. It serves some of the best tapas in Seville and it's just stacked with atmosphere. The cook's specialties are sausages, including spicy chorizo. García de Vinuesa 11. ℂ **95-422-12-42.**

Casa Román   Tapas are said to have originated in Andalusia, and this old-fashioned bar looks as if it has been dishing them up since day one (actually since 1934). It's one of the less touristy places in Barrio de Santa Cruz and the tapas aren't bad either, but they're a bit pricier than you'd pay farther off the tourist track. Plaza de los Venerables. ℂ **95-422-84-83.**

El Rinconcillo ★   El Rinconcillo is the oldest and one of the most famous bars in Seville, with a history that dates from 1670. Legend has it that tapas were created here. The friendly bartender will mark your tab in chalk on a well-worn wooden countertop. Tapas are a tad predictable, but you have to go at least once for the experience. El Rinconcillo is at the northern edge of the Barrio de Santa Cruz, near the Santa Catalina Church. Gerona 40. ℂ **95-422-31-83.**

Estrella   A seriously authentic tapas bar and small restaurant tucked down a side street, this place is always popular with the locals. The tapas menu is available in English and includes traditional favorites and a few more exotic dishes. Try the avocado stuffed with large prawns, which is delicious. House wines are good too. Estrella 3. ℂ **95-456-14-26.**

Europa ★★   My friend Luis raves about the tapas here. And rightly so, they are simply delicious, a really good example of the way some of the more creative places in town are now taking tapas to the next level. There's a menu available in English too. My favorite is the deep-fried langoustine—with just a hint of lime in the batter and the aroma of fresh mint in the aioli, but to be honest, everything here is good. Siete Revueltas 35. ℂ **95-421-79-08.**

La Bodega   The best *montaditos* in town in my opinion. These are small sandwiches with delicious fillings like pork marinated in sherry. They're easy to buy too—just point to what you like the look of from the huge selection stacked under the glass bar top. Plaza de Alfalfa 4. ℂ **95-421-42-52.**

Las Columnas ★   This classic traditional tapas bar manages to retain its authenticity despite being right in the midst of the tourist district. With people spilling out onto the pavement and friendly staff, it's loads of fun. It's one of my wife's favorites too. You're best off trying to get a spot at the bar to get your order in as it's always busy. Deep-fried eggplant with honey is one we always order. Rodrigo Caro 1. ℂ **95-421-32-46.**

La Tasca de El Burladero ★   Overseen by two Michelin-starred Dani Garcia, this famous eaterie has had a makeover to create a stylish gastrobar serving haute cuisine tapas and raciones. Cheap eats these aren't—but memorable dining is assured. Tapas cost 9€–12€. Canalejas 1. ℂ **95-450-78-62.**

Bars, Live Music & Pubs

Antiguedades Just down a side street from the cathedral, Antiguedades would make a good place for Halloween considering the weird stuff hanging from the ceiling: bodies, faces, and other creepy things. It's good fun and attracts a mixed crowd of locals and tourists, getting genuinely crazy later on at night. They do a mean rum and coke here too. Argote de Molina 40. No phone.

Bar Entrecalles No matter how late it is, this place within the narrow and claustrophobic alleyways in Barrio de Santa Cruz is always busy. It's my favorite bar in the tourist district with its relaxed vibe with a mixture of American and Moroccan bits and pieces on the walls and the odd parrot hanging from the ceiling. The guys behind the bar speak some English and are really friendly. Its name ("between streets") derives from doors inside that open onto both Calle Ximénez de Enciso and an even narrower street, the Lope de Rueda, in back. Calle Ximénez de Enciso 14. ✆ **61-786-77-52.**

Cafe Naima With so much focus on home-grown flamenco music, you struggle to find much in the way of jazz in Seville, but this relaxed, small bar on a street corner just off Plaza Alameda, does feature live jazz from time to time. It's named after the first wife of John Coltrane and has walls full of pictures of jazz legends. Trajano 47. ✆ **95-438-24-85.** www.naimacafejazz.com.

Central One of the most popular places on buzzing Plaza Alameda, this young busy bar has lots of space outside and gets full-on noisy and chaotic later on. Great atmosphere and good beer are a winning combination all the way to 3am. Alameda de Hércules 62. ✆ **95-437-09-99.**

El Garlochi ★ Possibly the quirkiest bar in Seville, this dim drinking den is dripping with religious memorabilia, statues, artwork, pictures, and paintings. It ought to be kitsch but there's so much authenticity to the icons and statues it really does feel like a church. The barman's a quirky chap and can be a bit grumpy, probably because his bar is now firmly on the tourist map and I think he'd probably prefer it if it wasn't. Boteros 26. No phone.

El Perro Andaluz This smoky little bar is a real creative hub, located towards the Macarena district. Rock, blues, flamenco, country-rock, reggae—they do a little of everything here. Local actors and artists are often among the clientele. Open from 11pm. Bustos Tavera 11. No phone.

Etnia Espacio Universal 📖 Take the elevator in the rather unpromising lobby of the Espacio Azahar hotel and you'll be amazed as you step out onto a cool rooftop conservatory with hot tub, lounging chairs, and twinkling candles. Definitely one of the coolest venues in town, often with a DJ spinning ambient groovy tunes in the background. Jesús del Gran Poder 28. ✆ **95-438-41-09.**

Fundición You'll feel like you've walked into a college bar in the U.S. here. Pool tables, Budweiser, beer pong on a Tuesday night, and *Sweet Home Chicago* on the sound system. Friendly atmosphere, but few locals would set foot in the place. Pureza 105. No phone.

Sopa de Ganso Offering tapas as well as drinks, this bar gets louder as the night goes on. Music varies but they play more rock and Spanish pop than anything else.

Being a *bar de copas*, the beverages of choice are mixed drinks, but there's beer here too. Pérez Galdós. 8. ✆ **95-421-25-26.**

Trinity Irish Pub   Seville has several highly visible Irish pubs, but this one is the classiest, most elegant, and in some ways, most evocative of good times and the literary wealth of Ireland. Open daily from 10:30am to 1:30am. In the Hotel Inglaterra, Plaza Nueva. ✆ **95-422-49-70.**

Gay & Lesbian Nightlife

Being the region's biggest city, Seville has a large gay and lesbian population, much of it composed of foreigners and of Andalusians who fled here for a better life, escaping smaller, less tolerant towns and villages. The funky, slightly grungy Alameda district is the center of gay nightlife, with a good range of bars and clubs from full-on gay nightclubs to gay-friendly mixed bars and pubs.

Café Ciudad Condal   This funky, gay-friendly bar right on the Alameda has a terrace space under the shady trees and it's open all day and long into the night. Alameda de Hércules, 94. ✆ **95-490-36-20.**

El Hombre y el Oso   Founded in 1999 near the Alameda de Hércules, this place is a bit passe for those in the know these days, but it remains the most popular and most frequently visited bear bar in Andalusia, with a decor that's loaded with depictions of bears of all shapes and sizes. Open nightly from around 10:30pm. Amor de Dios 32. ✆ **95-456-30-29.**

Emporio   Almost anything goes at this glam, funky mixed club. Regular *Planeta Coneja* nights (usually on Sundays) attract a rainbow crowd in all sorts of finery. Dress code—as outrageous as you dare. Music—Techno. Av. Marie Curie. ✆ **95-443-31-69;** www.myspace.com/emporiosevilla.

Poseidon   Seville's grand old dame of the gay scene is back after several years of absence and it's just as fab. It caters to a glam mixed crowd these days. Drag acts and general late-night craziness are all but guaranteed. From 11pm nightly. Marqués de Paradas 30. No phone.

República   Another of Alameda's gay-friendly spots. This cool cafe bar is a notch up from the usual Alameda drinking haunts, all white walls and dark furniture. There are great cakes on offer too, plus free Wi-Fi and friendly staff who speak good English. Alameda de Hércules 27. ✆ **95-490-94-35.**

SIDE TRIPS FROM SEVILLE

Carmona ★

34km (21 miles) E of Seville

If you're driving to Carmona, exit from Seville's eastern periphery onto the N-V superhighway, following the signs to the airport and then to Carmona on the road to Madrid. The Carmona turnoff is clearly marked.

An easy hour-long bus trip from the main terminal at Prado de San Sebastián in Seville, Carmona is an ancient city dating from Neolithic times. It grew in power and prestige under the Moors, establishing ties with Castile in 1252. Surrounded by

Seville Environs

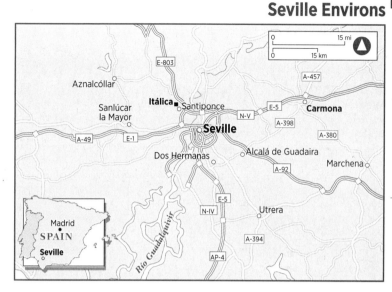

fortified walls, today it's a prosperous, refined place. Inside its old walls you'll find a dense concentration of mansions, churches, cobbled streets, and palaces.

The top attraction is **Alcázar de la Puerta de Sevilla.** The city's most prominent sight is this solid old fortified fortress and gateway into the Old Town. It now houses the helpful tourist information office and you can visit many of the rooms, some of which house exhibits. You can also climb up into the battlements crossing above the two huge gateways where you see the shoots down which boiling liquids were poured to repel invaders. Farther up there's an elevated patio, and on up the tower there are views in all directions.

Plaza San Fernando is the most important square, with many elegant 17th-century houses and several pleasant tapas bars. The most important church is dedicated to **Santa María** and is on the Calle Martín López. You enter a Moorish patio before exploring the interior with its 15th-century white vaulting.

Carmona's city museum, **Museo de la Ciudad**, although small, deserves a visit. Housed on two floors of an attractive Baroque town house, it traces the history of the city through the ages. Arrowheads, tools, and ceramics from the Carthaginian, Roman, and Moorish eras are on display, along with the Saltillo Collection—several virtually complete Tartessian earthenware pots from around the 6th century B.C., decorated with oriental scenes.

Note, too, the **Puerta de Córdoba** on Calle Santa María de Gracia, the second surviving gate from the Roman era. Carmona architect José de Echamorro gave the gate its romantic Renaissance facade between 1786 and 1800.

A little way out of the Old Town and only really accessible if you have a car are the **Roman amphitheater** and a **Roman necropolis** at Calle Emmedio. The necropolis is particularly interesting, containing the remains of 1,000 families that lived in and around Carmona 2,000 years ago. Of the two important tombs, the **Elephant Vault** consists of three dining rooms and a kitchen. The other, the **Servilia Tomb,** was the size of a nobleman's villa.

Carmona can be visited relatively easily on a day trip from Seville, but because it has some of the most romantic and evocative hotels in the area, many visitors try to schedule an overnight visit.

WHERE TO STAY

Alcázar de La Reina ★★   After the parador, this is the second-most important hotel in town, superior to the also-recommended Casa de Carmona. Known for its elegance, the hotel is stylish with an interior inspired by Mudéjar architecture. With a sleek but inviting decor, it offers a warm welcome and friendly service. The decoration is very personalized; no two rooms are the same. All the midsize to spacious bedrooms have flair, often with canopied or four-poster beds. Each comes with a luxurious marble-clad bathroom with a tub and shower. The suites are exceptional, especially El Mirador, which features a Jacuzzi and opens onto a panoramic view over the Vega de Carmona landscape. Even if you're just passing through Carmona for the day, consider eating at the first-class restaurant, which is warmly decorated and serves a market-fresh cuisine, with meals costing from 25€ to 35€.

Calle Hermana Concepción Oriana 2, 41410 Carmona. © **95-419-62-00.** Fax 95-414-01-13. www. alcazar-reina.es. 68 units. 100€–175€ double; 200€–295€ suite. Rates include breakfast. AE, DC, MC, V. **Amenities:** Restaurant; bar; Irish pub; babysitting; outdoor pool; room service; rooms for those w/limited mobility, Wi-Fi. *In room:* A/C, TV, hair dryer, minibar.

Casa de Carmona ★ 🏨   One of the most elegant and intimate hotels in Andalusia, this plushly furnished hideaway was originally built as the home of the Lasso family during the 1500s. Several years ago, a team of entrepreneurs added the many features needed in a luxury hotel while retaining the marble columns, massive masonry, and graceful proportions of the building's original construction. Each bedroom is a cozy enclave of opulent furnishings, with distinct decor inspired by ancient Rome, medieval Andalusia, or Renaissance Spain. Set at the edge of the village, the hotel also has a flowery terrace and an inner courtyard covered against the midsummer heat with canvas awnings.

Plaza de Lasso 1, 41410 Carmona. © **95-419-10-00.** Fax 95-419-01-89. www.casadecarmona.com. 32 units. 110€–250€ double; 600€–1,100€ suite. Add about 30% for Feria de Sevilla and Easter (Semana Santa). AE, DC, MC, V. Free parking. **Amenities:** Restaurant; bar; babysitting; library; outdoor pool; room service. *In room:* A/C, TV, hair dryer, minibar.

Parador de Carmona ★★★   This looks more like a fortress than a parador, with windows opening on wide vistas of the River Corbones plains. In fact, it's one of the best paradors in Andalusia, offering plenty of charm and atmosphere, beautiful landscaping, a grand swimming pool, an Andalusian patio with a Mudéjar fountain, and terraces with panoramic views. The foundations of the hotel date from the 14th century. Bedrooms are bright, spacious, and furnished in a classical style, with Sevillano tiles and luxury bathrooms with tub/shower combos. The former refectory has been turned into an elegant dining room, serving local specialties such as *caruja de perdiz* (partridge), codfish pies, and a rich buffet of desserts. The parador hires the finest chefs in town, with meals costing from 30€.

Alcázar s/n, 41410 Carmona. ✆ **95-414-10-10.** Fax 95-414-17-12. www.parador.es. 63 units. 150€–175€ double. AE, DC. Free parking. **Amenities:** Restaurant; bar; babysitting; outdoor pool; room service; 1 room for those w/limited mobility. *In room:* A/C, TV, hair dryer, minibar.

WHERE TO DINE

San Fernando INTERNATIONAL/ANDALUSIAN   Outside of the luxury dining rooms of the hotels, this is the best restaurant in town. Dating from the 1700s, it is decorated with fabrics and wooden furnishings. Entered from a side street, the old-fashioned restaurant is on the second floor of an antique building, its windows opening onto the landmark square, Plaza de San Fernando, from which it takes its name. This is good local cooking, the type that's been served in the region for years. Classic soups include gazpacho and *ajo blanco*, a garlic soup flavored with almonds. Although it's an inland town, fresh fish reaches Carmona daily. Both cod and hake (*merluza*) appear perfectly grilled and spiced.

Calle Sacramento 3. ✆ **95-414-35-56.** Reservations recommended. Main courses 15€–19€. AE, DC, MC, V. Tues-Sun 1:30-4pm; Tues-Sat 9-11pm. Closed Aug.

Itálica

9km (5½ miles) NW of Seville

Lovers of Roman history will flock to **Conjunto Arqueológico Itálica,** Av. De Extremadura 2 (✆ **95-562-22-66;** www.museosdeandalucia.es), the remarkable ruins of this ancient Roman city northwest of Seville in a small town today known as **Santiponce**.

If you're driving, exit from the northwest periphery of Seville, following the signs for highway E-803 in the direction of Zafra and Lisbon. A bus marked M-172 also goes to Santiponce. Departures are from the Estación de Autobuses at Plaza de Armas. Buses depart several times an hour for the 30-minute trip.

After the battle of Ilipa, Publius Cornelius Scipio Africanus founded Itálica in 206 B.C. Two of the most famous Roman emperors, Trajan and Hadrian, were born here, and indeed, master builder Hadrian had a major influence on his hometown. During his reign, the **amphitheater** was among the largest in the Roman Empire and it's the central focus of the ruins today. You can wander its tiered seating galleries and the underground pits where animals and gladiators waited before entering the arena. It's a hugely evocative walk around the tunnels on the ground floor too. There are also remains of villas with mosaics, in particular in the **House of Neptune** and **House of the Birds**, where a mosaic depicts 30 bird species in surprising detail. There's another fine mosaic of the seven deities of days of the week in the **House of the Planetarium**. Admission costs 1.50€ and it's free for E.U. passport holders. The site is open April to September, Tuesday to Saturday 8:30am to 8:30pm and Sunday 9am to 3pm. From October to March, it's open Tuesday to Saturday 9am to 5:30pm and Sunday 10am to 4pm. It's closed all day Mondays.

Itálica is best visited on a day trip; you can see the sights in about 2½ hours.

CÓRDOBA

7

Ten centuries ago Córdoba was the capital of Muslim Spain with a population of 900,000, as opposed to today's population of 320,000. It was Europe's largest cultural and intellectual center.

Much has changed since those days, but Córdoba still retains many wonderfully atmospheric reminders of its Moorish legacy. Chief among them is the world-famous Mezquita. One of Europe's most remarkable historic buildings, today it's the city's cathedral, but its Moorish origins are what make it so spectacular. The old Arab and Jewish Quarters are also famous for their narrow streets full of whitewashed houses with flower-filled patios and balconies. Córdoba has recently joined the ranks of UNESCO's World Heritage Sites, so you'll want to spend at least 2 days here.

From the 8th to the 11th centuries, the Umayyad caliphs brought an opulent lifestyle and great learning and culture to Córdoba while most of the rest of Europe languished in the Dark Ages. In those days, Córdoba was the biggest city in Western Europe. In its heyday, a pilgrimage to the Great Mezquita in Córdoba by a Muslim was said to have equaled a journey to Mecca.

Prior to the arrival of the Arabs, Córdoba had prospered in Roman times. Seneca the Elder (4 B.C.–A.D. 65), one of the greatest philosophers of the ancient world, lived here.

After the fall of the Romans, the city declined when it was taken over by the Visigoths, who in turn gave way to the more cultured Arabs. The invaders brought in scientists, scholars, and philosophers, while at the same time generating great prosperity from trade.

Córdoba became known for its pleasure palaces, mosques, and luxurious baths. It also boasted a library with 400,000 hand-copied books. The city was host to the first university in Europe, and Córdovan silverwork and tooled leathers became famous around the world.

Infighting among the Muslims led to the collapse of Córdoba in 1031, at which time Seville replaced the city as the capital of Moorish Iberia.

Even in this period of decline, Córdoba saw the birth of Moisés Maimonides (1135–1204), the fabled Jewish philosopher and Talmudist. In time he was driven from the city by the Almohads and sought refuge in the Ayyubid court in Egypt.

The Reconquista, the recapturing of Muslim Andalusia by the Christians, occurred in 1236 long before Ferdinand and Isabella took back Granada in 1492. Under various Catholic monarchs, Córdoba went into a decline that lasted for centuries.

Córdoba today is a modern city with broad, tree-lined boulevards and an up-to-date business community, but you can still glimpse its former glory. Stroll the cobblestone streets of the Judería (Jewish Quarter), wander through Queen Isabella's garden in the Alcázar, visit Renaissance churches and palaces, explore some of Andalusia's finest museums, and visit the excavations of Madinat Al-Zahra, a country palace and royal city built by a 10th-century caliph.

ORIENTATION
Getting There

BY TRAIN   This is the most convenient and popular means of transport to Córdoba, as the city is a rail junction for routes to the rest of Andalusia. The most popular line is the **AVE high-speed train** between Madrid and Córdoba or Córdoba and Seville. These days travel time between Seville and Córdoba is just 25 minutes, making Córdoba an easy day trip from Seville for travelers with a tight schedule. The AVE train between Madrid in the north and Córdoba in the south now takes 1¾ hours.

Over 20 trains arrive per day from Madrid, costing 67€ one way. A one-way ticket between Córdoba and Seville sells for 32€. The AVE network now extends to Málaga too if you're on the Costa del Sol and want to reach Córdoba in under an hour. Upwards of 12 trains per day make the journey and it costs 45€ for a one-way ticket.

The main train station at Córdoba is on the northern periphery of the Old Town, at Glorieta de las Tres Culturas, off Avenida de América. Bus no. 3 runs between the rail station and the historic core of the city. For rail information, call ✆ **90-224-02-02;** for AVE schedules or information call ✆ **90-232-03-20.** To reach the heart of the Old Town from the station on foot, head south on Avenida de Cervantes or Avenida del Gran Capitán. It's about a 15-minute walk. Taxis are available from the station too, or call **Radio Taxis** ✆ **957-76-44-44**.

BY PLANE   Air travel is not an option for reaching Córdoba. It does have a municipal airport that is 9km (5½ miles) from town, but it's mainly for private planes. Most visitors arriving by air fly to Seville or Málaga (capital of the Costa del Sol) and then travel by rail or car to reach Córdoba.

BY BUS   Córdoba is an important link in the Andalusian bus network. Most major bus routes into Córdoba are operated by **Alsina Graells** (✆ **913-27-05-40;** www.alsa.es) Ticket offices are in Córdoba's bus station, behind the railway station, on Glorieta de las Tres Culturas. You can also purchase online from the website above. Eight buses a day connect Seville and Córdoba, taking 2¼ hours and costing 10€ one way, four a day arrive from Málaga, taking 3½ hours and costing 13€ one way, and eight from Granada, taking 2 hours 40 minutes and costing 13€ one way. Buses between Córdoba and Madrid take just under 5 hours and are operated by **Secorbus** (✆ **90-222-92-92;** www.socibus.es). A one-way ticket costs 16€.

BY CAR   Córdoba is also well connected for driving. Córdoba is 105km (65 miles) west of Jaén and 419km (260 miles) southwest of Madrid. It is also 166km (103 miles) northwest of Granada and 129km (80 miles) east of Seville. From Seville the journey takes around 90 minutes on the fast A-4/E-5. From Madrid it's about a 3-hour drive also on the A-4/E-5.

Visitor Information

The **Córdoba City Tourist Office** (© **90-220-17-74;** www.turismodecordoba. org) has three outlets. There's one at the rail station open daily 9:30am to 2pm and 5 to 8pm, another right opposite the Alcázar at Calle Campo Santo de los Mártires right in the historic center, open Monday to Saturday 9:30am to 2pm and 4:30 to 7:30pm, Sundays 9am to 2pm and 4:30 to 7pm, and a third at Plaza de las Tendillas, convenient for some of the main hotels, open daily 9:30am to 2pm and 5:30 to 8:30pm.

The **Andalusia Regional Tourist Office** also hands out maps and lists of accommodation at Calle Torrijos 10 (© **95-735-51-79;** www.andalucia.org), right next to the Mezquita—the town's most famous monument. It's open Monday to Friday 9am to 7:30pm, Saturday 10am to 2pm and 5 to 7pm, and Sunday and holidays from 10am to 2pm.

City Layout

Córdoba is roughly divided into two sectors, the historic Old Town consisting of the **Judería (Jewish Quarter)** and the area around the **Mezquita,** plus the newer commercial section with broad, tree-lined boulevards and busy shopping streets. The commercial sector extends from the railway station on Avenida de América/ Plaza de las Tres Culturas down to the Plaza de las Tendillas (more often called Plaza Tendillas), which is the heart of contemporary Córdoba.

Most of your time will be spent in the historic center, which borders the Río Guadalquivir, the river that flows through Córdoba. From Plaza Tendillas, a maze of narrow streets extends downhill towards the banks of the river and the city's highlight attraction, the **Mezquita**.

Immediately south of the Mezquita is **Puente Romano,** the restored Roman bridge spanning the Guadalquivir and linking the "right bank" of Córdoba with the "left bank." To the immediate west of the Mezquita, you reach **Plaza Campo Santo de los Mártires** where several other important sights are located, including the **Alcázar de los Reyes Cristianos,** the adjacent **Jardines del Alcázar,** and the **Baños Califales.** North of the Plaza Campo de los Mártires is the pretty old Medieval Quarter, the **Barrio de la Judería**—a warren of narrow whitewash-housed streets where Arabs and Jews once lived in harmony. A section of restored old city wall runs beside a moat and gardens along Calle Cairuán at the barrio's western edge. At the northern end of the wall you'll see a bronze statue of a former resident, the philosopher Seneca, standing beside the **Puerta de Almodóvar,** a gate that once protected the old quarter and that is even today the principal western entrance to the Judería.

From Puente Romano, you can walk along Ronda de Isasa, which becomes Paseo de la Rivera. This will take you to another cluster of attractions, including **Iglesia de San Francisco, Museo de Bellas Artes, Posada del Potro,** and **Museo Julio Romero de Torres.** These attractions center on another landmark square, **Plaza del Potro.**

Getting Around

BY FOOT The historic core of Córdoba is relatively small, and the best way to get around it is to walk. Many of its labyrinthine and cobblestone streets such as those around the Mezquita and in the Judería (the old Jewish Quarter) are pedestrian-only.

BY BUS You can cover the relatively compact historic district on foot, but if you want to branch out to bordering areas, take a city bus. If you're staying on the outskirts, three main buses run into the historic core: bus nos. 3, 4, and 16. For bus information, call ✆ **95-776-46-76** or see www.aucorsa.es.

BY TAXI A typical fare—say from the Mezquita to the train station—can range from 4€ to 5€ depending on traffic. **Radio Taxi** (✆ **95-776-44-44**) has taxi stands at most busy intersections, including Avenida del Gran Capitán, Plaza Colón, Plaza Tendillas, Calle Cañero, Calle Ciudad Jardín, Calle Arcos de la Frontera, and Calle Agustín Moreno.

BY CAR The complicated maze of one-way streets in the Old Town is not particularly easy to navigate with a car. Many of the hotels have private car parks, so call ahead for detailed descriptions of how to reach them. There are handy public car parks on Avenida del Aeropuerto, Avenida de America, and Paseo de La Victoria.

If you plan to tour the countryside around Córdoba, a car is the best (and most expensive) option. Major car-rental companies in Córdoba include **Avis**, at the railway station on Glorieta de las Tres Culturas (✆ **95-740-14-45;** www.avis.es) and **Hertz** at the bus station, Glorieta de las Tres Culturas (✆ **95-740-20-61;** www. hertz.com).

BY HORSE & CARRIAGE *Coches de caballo* are for rent around the Mezquita and the Plaza de Alcázar, and this is the most romantic and old-fashioned way to see Córdoba. You'll find carriages waiting in line at Calle Torrijos adjoining the Mezquita and Campo Santo de los Mártires next to the Alcázar. Prices may vary but a typical cost for the standard tour of the main sites, which lasts between an hour and 90 minutes, is 45€. Don't be afraid to negotiate a better price.

[FastFACTS] CÓRDOBA

Currency Exchange ATMs are easily available, with several in the commercial sector off Plaza Tendillas and along Avenida del Gran Capitán. **Banco Santander,** Av. del Gran Capitán 8 (✆ **95-722-28-44**) is open Monday to Friday 8:30am to 2pm.

Emergency For medical assistance, dial ✆ **061.** For a police emergency, phone ✆ **091.**

Hospital The most central is the **Cruz Roja**

Española Hospital, Paseo de la Victoria (✆ **95-742-06-66**). Other hospitals include **Hospital Reina Sofía** at Av. Menéndez Pidal s/n (✆ **95-721-70-00**) and **Hospital Los Morales,** Sierra de Córdoba s/n (✆ **95-727-56-50**).

Internet Access If you're looking for free Internet access, head for the library at Calle Amador de dos Rios, the street that connects the Mezquita with the Alcázar, open Monday to Friday 9am to

9pm, Saturday 9am to 2pm.

Maps The best free map is provided by the **Andalusia Tourist Office** at Calle Torrijos 10 (see above). If you need more detailed maps, go to the book department of **El Corte Inglés,** Ronda de los Tejares 30 (✆ **95-722-28-81;** www.elcorteingles.es), the city's leading department store. Store hours are Monday to Saturday 10am to 10pm.

Pharmacy Farmacía Jesus Beltrami, Calle Conde De Gondomar 2 (📞 95-747-26-20) is well located right on the corner of Plaza Tendillas. It's open Monday to Friday 8:30am to 10pm and Saturday 10am to 1:30pm. Outside these hours city pharmacies open on a rota basis

and details should be displayed in the window here.

Police The main station is at Campo Madre Dios 11 (📞 **95-743-76-19**).

Post Office The main post office is at Calle Cruz Conde 15 (📞 **95-749-63-42**). It's open Monday to Friday from 8:30am to

8:30pm, Saturday from 9:30am to 2pm.

Toilets There are automatic toilet booths in several of the main tourist zones now, in particular Plaza de las Tendillas and Campo Santo de los Mártires. Insert 30¢ to use them. Otherwise duck into a cafe or bar and ask to use the toilets.

WHERE TO STAY

At the peak of its summer season, Córdoba has too few good hotels to meet the demand, so reserve as far in advance as possible.

Expensive

Hespería Córdoba ★   Personally I prefer places with a bit of history and atmosphere, but if you're looking for modern amenities and high quality modern accommodation, this first-class member of a chain is well located just across the Guadalquivir River from the historic center. Impressive architecturally, its rooms open onto attractive cityscape vistas. Its most alluring feature, especially in summer, is a swimming pool in an Andalusian courtyard. Midsize bedrooms are attractively furnished in a mix of Andalusian traditional and contemporary, with much use of blue tiles and wooden furnishings. If you're staying in for the night, the on-site restaurant, **Al Punto,** serves a first-class medley of Spanish and international specialties, and the garden bar is idyllic for a drink before or after dinner.

Av. Fray Albino 1, 14009 Córdoba. 📞 **95-742-10-42.** Fax 95-729-99-97. www.hesperia-cordoba.com. 108 units. 60€–208€ double; 210€–251€ suite. Rates include breakfast. AE, DC, MC, V. Parking 16€. **Amenities:** Restaurant; bar/cafeteria; outdoor pool; room service; nonsmoking wing; rooms for those w/limited mobility. *In room:* A/C, TV, minibar, hair dryer, Wi-Fi.

Hospes Palacio Del Bailío ★★★ 🏨   Without question the best hotel in town, this luxurious palace hotel opened in the heart of Córdoba in 2007 after 18 months of careful renovation. Like the other Andalusian hotels in the Hospes group in Granada and Seville, the building manages to blend the historic with cutting-edge designer flourishes with surprisingly harmonious results. The rooms are a wonderful merger of luxurious contemporary furnishings with the original 16th-century palace. Stables, coach houses, lofts, granaries, original paintings, the remains of Roman baths, and a splendid Moorish-style garden were all incorporated into the new ensemble. Each bedroom is unique, with pure materials such as natural-colored velvet and leather; some offer a view of the hotel's patios from private balconies. The Gran Capitan suite, with its original mural paintings from the 18th and 19th centuries, is remarkable. The hotel's restaurant has a glass floor revealing the foundations of original Roman buildings beneath, and the spa features a swim-through pool next to the Roman remains, a truly extraordinary feature.

Ramírez de las Casas Deza 10–12, 14010 Córdoba. ✆ **95-749-89-93.** Fax 95-749-89-94. www.hospes. es. 53 units. 171€–315€ double; 299€–358€ junior suite; 428€–674€ suite. AE, DC, MC, V. Parking 18€. **Amenities:** Restaurant; bar; babysitting; barber/salon; indoor heated pool; room service; spa; nonsmoking rooms; rooms for those w/limited mobility. *In room:* A/C, TV, hair dryer, minibar, Wi-Fi.

Las Casas de la Judería   If the sister hotel in Seville is anything to go by, this super-luxury conversion of a series of historic houses in the Judería barrio of the town could give the Hospes (see above) a run for its money once it's fully open. No expense has been spared, with a rooftop terrace and a swimming pool, attractive courtyards and patios. As you'd expect in a building created from antique houses, rooms are not very spacious, but the standard of fixtures and fittings is very luxurious, with Jacuzzi baths in the bathrooms. At the time of writing the hotel was open, but the spa remained under construction and service was taking a while to get properly organized.

Calle Tomas Conde 10, 14004 Córdoba. ✆ **95-720-20-95.** Fax 95-729-35-03. www.casasypalacios. com. 29 units. 170€–270€ double. AE, MC, V. **Amenities:** Restaurant; bar; room service; 1 room for those w/limited mobility. *In room:* A/C, TV, hair dryer, Wi-Fi.

Macia Alfaros ★   About a 10-minute walk from the Mezquita, this modern hotel with a mock-Moorish look is a government-rated four-star palace, five floors high near the ruins of a Roman temple. The entrance through a garage area is not an attractive debut, but the hotel improves inside. Small bedrooms are recently refurbished in contemporary style with built-in furnishings and shower/tub combos in the good-sized bathrooms. A cool swimming pool is in a courtyard that architects spruced up with references to old Andalusia. Buffet breakfast in the hotel restaurant is also pretty good.

Alfaros 18, 14001 Córdoba. ✆ **95-749-19-20.** Fax 95-749-22-10. www.maciahoteles.com. 131 units. 155€–175€ double. AE, DC, MC, V. **Amenities:** Restaurant; bar; babysitting; fitness center; outdoor pool; room service. *In room:* A/C, TV, hair dryer, minibar, Wi-Fi.

Parador de Córdoba ★★ 🐾   Found inconveniently 4km (2½ miles) outside of town in a suburb called El Brillante, this parador offers the conveniences and facilities of a luxurious resort hotel at reasonable rates. Don't expect a historic structure however—whilst it occupies the site of a former Caliphate palace, it's a modern, rather odd-looking building. But it does have wonderful views and attractive landscaped gardens with a swimming pool. The spacious guest rooms have fine dark-wood pieces, and some have balconies. For what it is, it offers decent value for money, but its location means it's not very useful for visiting the historic sights.

Av. de la Arruzafa 33, 14012 Córdoba. ✆ **95-727-59-00.** Fax 95-728-04-09. www.parador.es. 94 units. 142€–177€ double; 227€–246€ suite. AE, DC, MC, V. Free parking. **Amenities:** Restaurant; bar; babysitting; fitness center; outdoor pool; room service; sauna; tennis court; nonsmoking rooms; rooms for those w/limited mobility. *In room:* A/C, TV, hair dryer, minibar, Wi-Fi.

Moderate

Casa de los Azulejos ★ 🏨   In the heart of Córdoba and with an authentic Andalusian flavor, this attractive town house has been converted into a charming small boutique hotel. A 17th-century colonial-style house is now a little government-rated two-star inn with modern comforts, such as private bathrooms. Surprisingly,

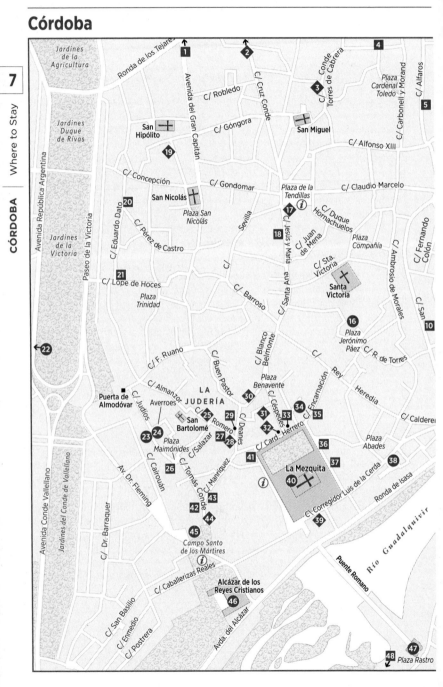

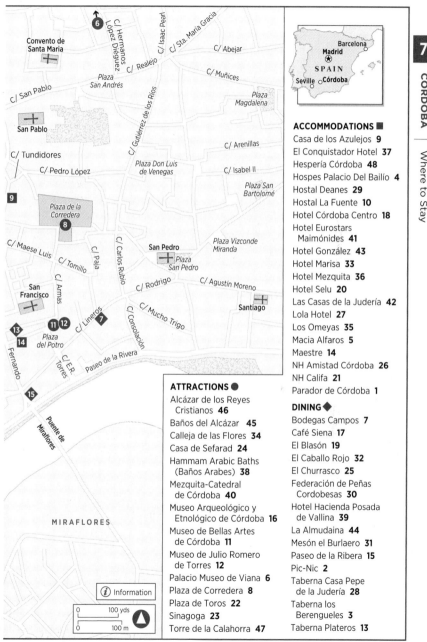

Convento de
Santa Maria

C/ Hermanos
López Diéguez

C/ Isaac Pearl

C/ Sta. Maria Gracia

C/ Abejar

C/ Realejo

C/ Muñices

Plaza
San Andrés

C/ San Pablo

C/ Gutiérrez de los Ríos

Plaza
Magdalena

San Pablo

C/ Arenillas

C/ Tundidores

Plaza Don Luis
de Venegas

C/ Isabel II

C/ Pedro López

Plaza San
Bartolomé

9

Plaza de la
Corredera

8

C/ Maese Luis

C/ Tomillo

C/ Paja

C/ Carlos Rubio

Plaza Vizconde
Miranda

San Pedro

Plaza
San Pedro

San
Francisco

C/ Armas

C/ Rodrigo

C/ Agustín Moreno

C/ Lineros

7

C/ Mucho Trigo

Santiago

13

C/ Consolación

11 12

14

Plaza
del Potro

C/ E.R.
Torres

Fernando

Paseo de la Rivera

15

Puente de
Miraflores

MIRAFLORES

ⓘ Information

0   100 yds
0   100 m

ACCOMMODATIONS ■

Casa de los Azulejos **9**
El Conquistador Hotel **37**
Hesperia Córdoba **48**
Hospes Palacio Del Bailío **4**
Hostal Deanes **29**
Hostal La Fuente **10**
Hotel Córdoba Centro **18**
Hotel Eurostars
   Maimónides **41**
Hotel González **43**
Hotel Marisa **33**
Hotel Mezquita **36**
Hotel Selu **20**
Las Casas de la Judería **42**
Lola Hotel **27**
Los Omeyas **35**
Macia Alfaros **5**
Maestre **14**
NH Amistad Córdoba **26**
NH Califa **21**
Parador de Córdoba **1**

DINING ◆

Bodegas Campos **7**
Café Siena **17**
El Blasón **19**
El Caballo Rojo **32**
El Churrasco **25**
Federación de Peñas
   Cordobesas **30**
Hotel Hacienda Posada
   de Vallina **39**
La Almudaina **44**
Mesón el Burlaero **31**
Paseo de la Ribera **15**
Pic-Nic **2**
Taberna Casa Pepe
   de la Judería **28**
Taberna los
   Berengueles **3**
Taberna Plateros **13**

ATTRACTIONS ●

Alcázar de los Reyes
   Cristianos **46**
Baños del Alcázar **45**
Calleja de las Flores **34**
Casa de Sefarad **24**
Hammam Arabic Baths
   (Baños Arabes) **38**
Mezquita-Catedral
   de Córdoba **40**
Museo Arqueológico y
   Etnológico de Córdoba **16**
Museo de Bellas Artes
   de Córdoba **11**
Museo de Julio Romero
   de Torres **12**
Palacio Museo de Viana **6**
Plaza de Corredera **8**
Plaza de Toros **22**
Sinagoga **23**
Torre de la Calahorra **47**

the house still has its original subterranean rooms with vaulted ceilings. On the main floors, there's a central courtyard decorated with beautiful tiles—hence, the name *"azulejos,"* or tiles. The bedrooms, midsize to spacious, are brightly and comfortably decorated, often with antiques, each opening onto the central courtyard. Among the Latin American and Mexican touches is the cantina serving south-of-the-border specialties.

Calle Fernando Colón 5, 14002 Córdoba. ✆ **95-747-00-00.** Fax 95-747-54-96. www.casadelos azulejos.com. 8 units. 108€–130€ double; 140€–170€ suite. Rates include continental breakfast. AE, MC, V. Parking 14€. **Amenities:** Restaurant; bar; room service; 1 room for those w/limited mobility. *In room:* A/C, TV, hair dryer, Wi-Fi.

El Conquistador Hotel   Built centuries ago as a private villa, this hotel has been tastefully renovated with triple rows of stone-trimmed windows and ornate iron balustrades. It's about as close to the Mezquita as you could get—across the street from the eastern wall. The marble-and-granite lobby opens onto an interior courtyard filled with seasonal flowers, a pair of splashing fountains, and a symmetrical stone arcade. The quality and comfort of the rooms—each with a black-and-white marble floor and a private bathroom—are pretty impressive, but they are a little on the small side.

González Francés 15, 14003 Córdoba. ✆ **95-748-11-02.** Fax 95-747-46-77. www.hotelconquistador cordoba.com. 132 units. 109€–168€ double. AE, MC, V. Parking 15€. **Amenities:** Restaurant; bar; lounge; babysitting; room service; nonsmoking rooms; rooms for those w/limited mobility. *In room:* A/C, TV, minibar, hair dryer, Wi-Fi.

Hotel Córdoba Centro   This is a well-conceived but somewhat staid modern building using beige and white polished marble. Rooms are clean, streamlined, quiet, comfortable, and unpretentious, with very modern tiled bathrooms, angular furniture, but, in almost every case, without particularly noteworthy views. The entrance is tricky to find, at the end of a long passageway leading from a mostly pedestrian shopping street. (Phone in advance for directions to the nearest garage.) The landmark Plaza Tendillas is a few steps away, and there's a coffee shop and cafe.

Calle Jesús y María 8, 14003 Córdoba. ✆ **95-749-78-50.** Fax 95-749-78-51. www.hotel-cordobacentro. es. 27 units. 100€–135€ double. MC, V. Parking 12€ per day. **Amenities:** Cafe; TV lounge; room service. *In room:* A/C, TV, minibar, Wi-Fi.

Hotel Eurostars Maimónides ★   A few steps from the entrance to the Mezquita, this is one of the best government-rated three-star hotels. The result of the radical overhaul of an antique building, it's a lovely enclave of Andalusian tilework set out in geometrical patterns, a splashing fountain, friendly, hardworking staff, and an appealing mix of old-fashioned Mudéjar-inspired touches and modern comforts. Bedrooms are streamlined, sunny, and comfortable, each with a writing table, medium-to-large-size bathroom, and lots of glossily polished stone and marble. As you might expect, a marble portrait bust of the hotel's namesake, the Jewish philosopher and mathematician Maimonides (1135–1204), stands in a corner of the lobby.

Calle Torrijos 4, 14003 Córdoba. ✆ **95-747-15-00.** Fax 95-748-38-03. www.eurostarshotels.com. 82 units. 60€–200€ double; 120€–260€ suite. AE, DC, MC, V. **Amenities:** Restaurant; bar; babysitting. *In room:* A/C, TV, hair dryer, minibar, Wi-Fi.

Lola Hotel ★   If you're looking for a small and intimate boutique hotel in the shadow of the Mezquita, this is a pretty good option. Lola Hotel is set behind the thick masonry walls of what was originally built as a private home in 1888. You register, relax, socialize with your fellow guests, eat breakfast, and order drinks from the bar all in the same cramped but convivial area: a small but cozy open-air courtyard ringed with stone columns. Bedrooms are larger and more plush than you might expect, with good quality bathrooms, some with gorgeous tilework. Each guest room bears a name popular for 19th-century Muslim women: Aixa, Aida, Alzára, Jasmina, and Suleima.

Calle Romero 3, 14001 Córdoba. ✆ **95-720-03-05.** Fax 95-720-02-18. www.hotelconencantolola.com. 8 units. 84€–121€ double. Rates include breakfast. AE, DC, MC, V. No parking. **Amenities:** Open-air rooftop terrace w/view. *In room:* A/C, TV, minibar.

NH Amistad Córdoba ★★   If you want to be in the heart of the Judería (old Jewish Quarter) this hotel is one of the best options. It's an attractive and luxurious renovation of two existing 18th-century mansions facing each other and linked by a small patio of beautiful Andalusian arches and colorful Spanish tiles. The careful renovation has restored the interior Mudéjar-style courtyard, the neoclassical facade and the ornate woodwork ceilings to their original grandeur. The spacious rooms come with neat bathrooms containing tub/shower combos, and excellent beds, and the design is a tasteful combination of wood and fabric. A more modern wing features rooms that are equivalent in comfort, but lacking a little in charm.

Plaza de Maimónides 3, 14004 Córdoba. ✆ **95-742-03-35.** Fax 95-742-03-65. www.nh-hoteles.com. 84 units. 85€–155€ double. AE, DC, MC, V. Parking 18€. **Amenities:** Restaurant; bar; room service; babysitting; nonsmoking rooms. *In room:* A/C, TV, hair dryer, minibar, Wi-Fi.

NH Califa ✦   Part of the same NH hotel chain as the Amistad, the Califa, just a 10-minute walk from the Mezquita, offers similar good quality modern and contemporary rooms in a more impersonal building. It's austere, but good value. It has russet-colored marble floors, velour wall coverings, a spacious lounge, and a TV that seems to broadcast soccer matches nonstop. Midsize rooms are reasonably comfortable and furnished in a functional modern style. Parking is available along the street.

Lope de Hoces 14, 14003 Córdoba. ✆ **95-729-94-00.** Fax 95-729-57-16. www.nh-hoteles.es. 65 units. 60€–137€ double; 70€–160€ suite. AE, DC, MC, V. Parking 18€. **Amenities:** Bar; lounge; babysitting; room service; nonsmoking rooms; rooms for those w/limited mobility; Wi-Fi. *In room:* A/C, TV, hair dryer, minibar.

Inexpensive

Hostal Deanes ✦   A traditional Moorish house, only 50m (164 ft) from the Mezquita, this former 16th-century private home was turned into a little inn in 1997. If you're seeking old-fashioned Andalusian charm, you'll be happy here. The bedrooms surround a busy patio cafe open Tuesday to Saturday from 9am to 10:30pm, Sunday noon to 4pm, and Monday 10am to 4pm. In an adjoining bar you can see photographs of the well-known bullfighters who have stayed or eaten here. Bedrooms are small but bathrooms (with shower) are spacious. This is one of Córdoba's true bargains.

Calle Deanes 6, Judería, 14003 Córdoba. ✆ **95-729-37-44.** Fax 95-742-17-23. 5 units. 45€ double. MC, V. Parking 11€ nearby. Bus: 3. **Amenities:** Tapas bar. *In room:* No phone.

Hostal La Fuente   This is not a high-end hotel—fellow guests are likely to be students who like to stay out late and the staff seems to revel in the fact that they speak not a solitary word of anything except local dialect. But the setting on two floors of a once-palatial, mid-19th-century private home, around a tile-clad, plant-filled courtyard, is charming. Simple rooms are not overly large, but are comfortable and clean, and renovated with angular, earth-toned enclaves. But there are tables in the courtyard, enough plants to evoke the Amazon rainforest, and a feeling of old-fashioned Andalusia at good-value prices. A terrace overlooks Iglesia de San Francisco.

Calle San Fernando 51, 14003 Córdoba. ✆ **95-748-78-27** or ✆ 748-14-78. Fax 95-748-78-27. www.hostallafuente.com. 40 units. 45€–55€ double. AE, MC, V. **Amenities:** Restaurant; cafe next door; Wi-Fi. *In room:* A/C, TV.

Hotel González ✎ In the heart of the Judería, only 40m (131 ft) from the Mezquita, this small town palace dates from the 16th century. In the mid-1980s it was successfully converted into a little hotel. All the bedrooms overlook either Plaza Judá Leví, one of the Jewish Quarter's most charming squares, or the inner Andalusian courtyard. The central hall and corridors are decorated with original artwork. Bedrooms are small and furnished in a bland, functional way with light wooden furnishings, but they are well maintained and comfortable. If there is no room at this inn, try the owners' other bargain hotel, Hotel Mezquita (see below).

Calle Manríquez 3, 14003 Córdoba. ✆ **95-747-98-19.** Fax 95-748-61-87. www.hotel-gonzalez.com. 16 units. 45€–76€ double. AE, DC, MC, V. Parking 13€. **Amenities:** Breakfast room; Wi-Fi. *In room:* A/C, TV.

Hotel Marisa ✎ In front of the Mezquita, this modest hotel is one of the most central in Córdoba—not to mention one of the city's best-value options. It was built in the early 1970s, but ongoing renovations keep it in good order. The rooms are small but cozily comfortable—request one with a balcony overlooking the statue of the Virgin of Rosales or the Patio de los Naranjos. The architecture and furnishings are in a vaguely Andalusian style.

Cardenal Herrero 6, 14003 Córdoba. ✆ **95-747-31-42.** Fax 95-747-41-44. www.hotelmarisacordoba.com. 28 units. 50€–68€ double. AE, DC, MC, V. Parking 12€. **Amenities:** Cafeteria; room service; rooms for those w/limited mobility. *In room:* A/C.

Hotel Mezquita ✎ This is another hotel very close to the Mezquita, facing its east side. It was constructed on the site of two old houses that are now connected by a patio. The decor includes tastefully arranged antiques throughout. The architecture is typically Andalusian—arches, interior patios, and hand-painted tiles, along with old mirrors and chandeliers. The small but comfortable rooms are painted in pastels to contrast with the dark oak furnishings. Bathrooms have tub/shower combos. Naturally, the rooms overlooking the Mezquita are the first to be booked.

Plaza Santa Catalina 1, 14003 Córdoba. ✆ **95-747-55-85.** Fax 95-747-62-19. www.hotelmezquita.com. 31 units. 52€–108€ double. DC, MC, V. Parking nearby 15€. **Amenities:** Breakfast room; rooms for those w/limited mobility. *In room:* A/C, TV.

Hotel Selu ✎ In a commercial part of town near the Judería, the Mezquita, and the town center, this well-run and very professional hotel is ideal for bargain hunters who plan to spend most of their time sightseeing and need a hotel only for sleep and rest. It is well maintained, its midsize guest rooms modern and comfortable, with a few Andalusian decorations sprinkled in.

Eduardo Dato 7, 14003 Córdoba. ✆ **95-747-65-00.** Fax 95-747-83-76. www.sercotelhoteles.com. 99 units. 60€–90€ double. AE, DC, MC, V. **Amenities:** Bar; breakfast room; cafeteria; room service. *In room:* A/C, TV, hair dryer, minibar, Wi-Fi.

Los Omeyas ★ If you want to stay in the very heart of Córdoba, you can't find a better location than this hotel in the Jewish Quarter. The name comes from the Umayyad dynasty that ruled the Muslim empire of al-Andalús (the Arab tradition is still clearly visible in white marble and latticework). The hotel is lit naturally through a central colonnaded patio furnished with tables. Although in no way grand, rooms are very comfortable and tasteful; bathrooms have tub/shower combos. Top-floor rooms look out on the ancient tower of the mosque, which is literally around the corner.

Calle Encarnación 17, 14003 Córdoba. ☎ **95-749-22-67.** Fax 95-749-16-59. www.hotel-losomeyas.com. 33 units. 55€–75€ double; 68€–88€ triple; 81€–101€ quad. AE, DC, MC, V. Parking 12€. **Amenities:** Hotel restaurant nearby; cafeteria; bar; lounge. *In room:* A/C, TV, Wi-Fi.

Maestre 🍴 On busy Calle San Fernando, this old house with traditional Moorish architecture has an interior courtyard with arches, white walls, red tiles, columns, and corridors. The location is convenient—a 10-minute stroll from the Judería and the Mezquita. Dating from 1992, the small to midsize bedrooms are hardly exciting but are simply, yet comfortably, furnished with wooden furniture and carpeted floors. Each comes with a small bathroom with shower stall. Management also operates the even less expensive and much less plush **Hostal Maestre** nearby, where doubles are a mere 38€ to 42€.

Romero Barros 4-6, San Pedro, 14003 Córdoba. ☎ **95-747-24-10.** Fax 95-747-53-95. www.hotel-maestre.com. 26 units. 42€–62€ double. AE, MC, V. **Amenities:** Breakfast lounge; rooms for those w/ limited mobility. *In room:* A/C, TV.

WHERE TO DINE
Expensive

Bodegas Campos ★★★ SPANISH/ANDALUSIAN This place is one of the best restaurants in Córdoba, located on a narrow cobblestone street 10 minutes from the Mezquita. In front is one of Córdoba's most crowded tapas bars. Bodegas Campos has a welcoming rustic atmosphere and has been going strong since 1908 as both a wine cellar (*bodega*) and a tavern. The well-chosen menu, using fresh ingredients, offers local fare like salt cod salad with orange dressing, *frituritas de la casa con salmorejo* (tiny fried fish served with thick Andalusian gazpacho), and *escabeche de perdiz* (pickled pieces of partridge). Other specialties are *merluza rellena con verduritas* (hake stuffed with julienne vegetables) and an Iberian pig's cheek casserole.

Calle de los Lineros 32. ☎ **95-749-75-00.** www.bodegascampos.com. Reservations recommended. Main courses 17€–28€; gastronomic menu 49€. MC, V. Mon–Sat 11am–midnight; Sun 11am–5pm. Closed Dec 25 and 31.

La Almudaina ★★★ SPANISH The owners of this historic restaurant near the Alcázar deserve as much credit for their renovations of a decrepit 15th-century palace as they do for their excellent cuisine. Fronting the river in the old Jewish Quarter, La Almudaina is one of the most attractive eateries in Córdoba; you can dine in one of the lace-curtained salons or on a glass-roofed central courtyard. Nearly all the chef's dishes are based on fresh produce purchased daily at local markets. Start with local favorites like a tasty *salmorejo* (soup made with bread, tomato, fresh garlic, Iberian ham, and virgin olive oil). Anglerfish filets with a frothy seafood-brandy sauce taste ultrafresh and a tenderloin of pork is cooked to perfection and served with a delicate wine sauce. A favorite dessert is Córdovan quince pastry prepared according to a 19th-century recipe.

Plaza Campos de los Santos Mártires 1. ✆ **95-747-43-42.** www.restaurantealmudaina.com. Reservations required. Main courses 16€–18€. AE, MC, V. Mon–Sat 12:30–4pm and 8:30pm–midnight; Sun 12:30–4pm. Closed Sun June 15–Aug 30.

Mesón el Burlaero ★ MEDITERRANEAN/ANDALUSIAN   In a 16th-century house that belonged to the first bishops of Córdoba, this restaurant in the Jewish Quarter is in the center of the tourist area. The *mesón* has seven dining areas, along with balconies and a central patio with antique-style murals. The whole place has been lovingly restored and tastefully decorated. The most lavish way to dine here is to order the *menú gastronómico de degustación,* a selection of various house specialties. From the a la carte menu, begin with *salmorejo* (thick Andalusian gazpacho), and then follow with *rabo de toro en salsa* (bull's tail in savory tomato sauce) or *dorada a la sal* (gilthead sea bream that has been baked in a salt crust to retain its juices).

Calle de la Hoguera 5. ✆ **95-747-27-19.** www.restauranteelburlaero.com Reservations recommended. Main courses 12€–18€; set menus 13€–30€. AE, DC; MC, V. Daily 11am–4pm and 7:30pm–midnight.

Pic-Nic ★ CONTINENTAL   Walking a little way north of the historic center into the commercial neighborhood will convince visitors there's a lot more to Córdoba than medieval barrios. The restaurant occupies the most distant corner of a long, narrow, and slightly battered square. It was created as part of the courtyard that fronts a residential apartment complex, whose entranceway opens onto the busy traffic of the Avenida de los Tejares. In late 1970s style, it's behind a *moderno* entrance of varnished pine. Popular with Córdoba's business community, the superb cuisine here makes it one of the finest restaurants in the city. Impeccably sharp and precise cooking produces the likes of filets of pork in sherry sauce, a divine foie gras of goose, and an extraordinary magret of duckling flavored with port. For dessert, try the *tarta de chocolate y naranja* (an orange-flavored chocolate tart).

Av. de los Tejares 16. ✆ **95-748-22-33.** Reservations required. Main courses 17€–25€. AE, MC, V. Mon–Sat 1:30–4pm; Tues–Sat 9pm–midnight.

Moderate

El Blasón ✦ ANDALUSIAN/MOORISH   The tab, with wine, rarely exceeds 30€ at El Blasón, a restaurant in a relatively modern building near the Gran Teatro. You'll dine in any of four separate rooms, each evoking the mid-19th century with crystal chandeliers and antiques. Especially appealing is an enclosed patio where ivy creeps up walls and the noises from the city are muffled. The cuisine is well prepared and in some cases described in terms that verge on the poetic. Try salmon with oranges from the mosque, and goose thigh in fruited wine. Braised oxtail is always a good bet, as are any of the roasted lamb dishes, redolent with the scent of olive oil and herbs.

José Zorrilla 11. ✆ **95-748-06-25.** Reservations recommended. Main courses 11€–24€. AE, DC, MC, V. Sun–Thurs 11am–11:30pm; Fri–Sat 11am–12:30am. Closed Dec 24.

El Caballo Rojo ★★ SPANISH   Within walking distance of the Mezquita in the Old Town, this restaurant is one of the best in Córdoba. The place has a noise level no other restaurant matches, but the skilled waiters manage to cope with all demands. Stop in the restaurant's popular bar for a pre-dinner drink, then take the iron-railed stairs to the dining room for a typical meal of gazpacho, a main dish of chicken, then ice cream (often homemade pistachio), and sangria. A good variation on the typical gazpacho is an almond-flavored broth with apple. In addition to Andalusian dishes, the chef offers both Sephardic and Mozarabic specialties, like monkfish with pine nuts, currants, carrots, and cream. A local favorite is *rabo de toro* (bull's tail stew).

Cardinal Herrero 28, Plaza de la Hoguera. (📞) **95-747-53-75.** www.elcaballorojo.com Reservations required. Main courses 12€–27€. AE, DC, MC, V. Daily 1–4:30pm and 8pm–midnight.

El Churrasco ★★ ANDALUSIAN   In an antique stone-fronted building in the Jewish Quarter northwest of the Mezquita, El Churrasco is another of Córdoba's top restaurants serving elegant meals in five dining rooms at very reasonable prices. You'll pass a bar and an open grill before reaching a ground-floor dining room that resembles a Moorish courtyard with rounded arches and a fountain. Upstairs, more formal rooms display the owner's collection of paintings. On offer are such specialties as grilled filet of beef with whisky sauce, succulent roast lamb, grilled salmon, and monkfish in pine nut sauce. The signature dish is the charcoal-grilled pork loin. Service is very good.

Romero 16. (📞) **95-729-08-19.** www.elchurrasco.com Reservations required. Main courses 13€–25€. AE, DC, MC, V. Daily 1–4pm and 8pm–midnight. Closed Aug.

Federación de Peñas Cordobesas ANDALUSIAN   In a historic house built in 1900, this restaurant nestles in the old Judería, midway between the Mezquita and the landmark Plaza Tendillas. In fair weather tables are placed outside around an old fountain in a courtyard. Inside, the traditional Andalusian atmosphere is cozy. In business for 2 decades, the restaurant serves reliable regional favorites with a *carte* of affordable regional wines. A favorite dish is the *zarzuela de pescado* (an assorted kettle of fresh fish cooked in their own juices). The sirloin *a la serrana,* another favorite, is stuffed with serrano ham and served with a white sauce, mushrooms, and fresh asparagus. Homemade desserts are prepared daily.

Conde y Luque 8, Judería. (📞) **95-747-54-27.** Main courses 12€–18€.. AE, DC, MC, V. Thurs–Tues 12:30–4pm and 7:30–11pm.

Taberna Casa Pepe de la Judería ★ CORDOVAN   Around the corner from the mosque and on the route to the Judería, this is one of the best-located restaurants in Córdoba. A series of little rooms, decorated in typical Andalusian style, are spread over three floors. From May to October, tables are placed on the rooftop, where meats such as chicken and pork are barbecued, and an Andalusian guitarist entertains. The hearty, regional fare includes dishes like cod cooked with raisins, pine nuts, and mussels that may date back to recipes from the days when the Arabs controlled Córdoba. The chef prepares excellent soups such as a typical Andalusian gazpacho or one made with fresh fish and shellfish. *Merluza* (hake), prepared Cordobesa-style with sweet peppers, garlic, and onions is a particular favorite, as is the baked lamb, another specialty.

Calle Romero 1 (📞) **95-720-07-44.** Reservations recommended. Fixed-price menu 26€. AE, DC, MC, V. Sun–Thurs 1–4pm and 8:30–11:30pm; Fri–Sat 1–4pm and 8:30pm–12:30am.

Taberna los Berengueles SPANISH/SEAFOOD   The dignified and elegant 19th-century building housing this seafood restaurant might be like many others in this quiet residential neighborhood north of the Mezquita, but it's right across the street from the birthplace of Spain's most famous bullfighter, Manolete (Manuel Rodríguez Sancho, born here July 4, 1917). Inside, you'll find some spectacular Mudéjar-style tilework, a series of cozy dining rooms, and a plant-filled patio. The best dishes on the regular menu include *salmorejo,* the thick tomato soup of Andalusia; broad beans with strips of cured Iberian ham; pork chops braised over charcoal; succulent veal steaks; pasta with codfish; and a savory hake and shellfish stew. A separate fish menu features the array of seafood hauled in daily from the fishing port of Almuñécar.

Calle Conde de Torres Cabrera 7. (©) **95-747-28-28.** Reservations recommended. Main courses 12€–23€. AE, MC, V. Set menus 45€–55€. Daily 1:30–4pm; Tues–Sat 8:30–11:30pm.

Inexpensive

Café Siena 🍴 SPANISH   The layout of Córdoba makes it far too easy to get enmeshed in the medieval neighborhood around the Mezquita and not venture anywhere else. This big, angular, and *moderno* cafe is the most appealing of those that ring the centerpiece of Córdoba's 19th- and early-20th-century commercial core, the Plaza Tendillas. In good weather, opt for a table on the square. As day turns to evening, the clientele morphs from shoppers and local office workers to night owls. The food is fairly standard, a litany of the country's favorite dishes, but the ingredients are fresh and the atmosphere convivial. The daily menu features ingredients from the market.

Plaza de las Tendillas s/n. (©) **95-747-30-05.** Tapas 3€–9€; main courses 9€–15€; *menú del día* 12€. AE, DC, MC, V. Mon–Sat 9am–2am.

Hotel Hacienda Posada de Vallina 🍴 ANDALUSIAN/CORDOVAN   Facing the south wall of the Mezquita, this restaurant is built on some of the foundations in Córdoba, with a history going back 16 centuries. From a much later date are remnants of Roman columns and an old wall. The restaurant itself is in the inner courtyard of a little hotel below the balconies and gallery of the second floor. The chef proudly calls his food *la cocina córdobesa,* and so it is. Delicious treats appear on the menu, like *salmorejo* (cold tomato soup) or artichokes vinaigrette. The freshly baked hake served in a sauce made with clams and shrimp and the savory oxtail are also well worth trying. Desserts are homemade. Most main courses are priced at the lower end of the scale.

Corregidor Luis de la Cerda 83, Judería. (©) **95-749-87-50.** Reservations recommended. Main courses 6€–20€. AE, DC, MC. Tues 1–4pm and 8–11pm; Sun 1–4pm.

Paseo de la Ribera ☺ ANDALUSIAN/MEDITERRANEAN   Established in 1999, this popular choice is known for affordable, traditional food and a reasonably priced wine list. For fish lovers there's hearty rice with baby squid and perfectly prepared swordfish with prawn sauce. Carnivores might go for beef ribs, pork tenderloin with three sauces, or a well-seasoned grilled steak. The grotto-like decor, with plastered walls and chairs and tables on wooden floors, is evocative of a Roman cave. There are plenty of pizza and pasta dishes on the menu too, ideal for children.

Plaza Cruz del Rastro 3. (©) **95-747-15-30.** Main courses 6€–16€. AE, MC, V. Mon–Fri 11am–12:30am; Sat–Sun 9am–12:30am.

Taberna Plateros ★ ANDALUSIAN   Dating from 1872—though previous owners claimed its origins might go as far back as the 1600s—this is one of the oldest

A Moroccan Teahouse Salon

Salon de Thé, Calle Buon Pastor 13 (☏ **95-748-79-84;** daily 11am–11pm), is an idyllic spot. On a hot summer day you might not immediately think of drinking tea, but the cool, Moroccan-style setting here and the way it presents tea as refreshment for the senses might tempt you. The setting, in a labyrinth of narrow alleys near the Mezquita in the Judería, is a small-scale arcaded courtyard of a once-private home that was originally built in the 14th century, with low-slung (and somewhat uncomfortable) divans covered with Moroccan carpets, over-stuffed cushions, and low tables. The menu lists more than 30 kinds of tea, as well as coffee and fruited drinks made, Moroccan-style, from condensed syrups mixed with crushed ice and water. A small fountain splashes fitfully in the courtyard's center, and the background music is rooted in the early Arabic roots of old Córdoba. The place, as you might expect, is busiest every day between 4 and 7pm.

establishments in Córdoba. Choose from tables in a spacious courtyard or one of the dining rooms. The traditional marble bar is a rendezvous point for locals, who gather when the nearby stores close for the evening. Pictures of the famous hometown bullfighter, Manolete, line the walls, and the decor is Andalusian tiles and red brick. Dishes have authentic flavor, as one businessman described it to me "The cooking is just what my grandmother fed me when I was a boy." The appetizers are very large, some big enough to satisfy a small appetite. Frequently changing main dishes might feature grilled swordfish, grilled cuttlefish, or variations of *bacalao* (dried codfish).

San Francisco 6, San Pedro. ☏ **95-747-00-42.** Reservations recommended on weekends. Main courses 7€–11€. AE, DC, MC, V. Tues–Sun 8am–4:30pm and 8pm–midnight.

SEEING THE SIGHTS

The city's main historic attractions could take the best part of a day to see. Get to the **Mezquita** early to avoid the daytrippers who usually arrive late morning. Along with this, the absolute must-see sights here are the nearby **Alcázar de los Reyes Cristianos** and **Baños del Alcázar.** The historic warren of ancient streets known as the **Judería** also gets busy with tourists, but it's a delight to wander nonetheless and good for shopping too. If you're interested in the Jewish history of this area, visits to the **Synagogue** and the **Casa de Sefarad** are recommended. Other museums of note in Córdoba include the **Museo Arqueológico** and **Museo de Bellas Artes,** both to the east of the Mezquita.

It's also well worth taking a stroll across the **Puente Romano (Roman bridge),** dating from Augustus and crossing the Guadalquivir River. There's not a huge amount to see on this side of the river but the views back to the city are impressive. The bridge itself is not Roman—not one of its 16 supporting arches is original. The sculptor Bernabé Gómez del Río erected a statue of St Raphael on the bridge in 1651.

One of the city's most impressive squares is the **Plaza de Corredera.** This fine Castilian-style, arcaded 17th-century square was originally the setting for bullfights and other public events. It has an air of gentle dilapidation nowadays, with a jumble

Get the Latest Opening Hours

It was when the girl in the tourist office told me she sometimes turns up for work at the wrong time because she gets confused about opening hours that I realized just how complicated it can be working out when places are open here. (The city has three tourist offices and they keep different opening hours. Goodness knows why.)

It's more complicated still for many of the monuments. There are typically three or even four sets of opening hours depending on the time of year. And they can change from one year to the next as well. I've gone with the most up-to-date details I could get hold of at the time of writing, but I recommend you step into one of the city tourist offices and pick up the latest opening hours list. Alternatively, visit the website at www.turismodecordoba.org and you'll find them available as a PDF file.

of antiques shops and cafes housed in the cloisters. In the evenings it's a pleasant place for a leisurely drink away from the touristy chaos of the historic center.

The **Plaza de Toros,** on Gran Vía del Parque, stages its major bullfights in May, although fights are also presented at other times of the year. Watch for local announcements. Most hotels will arrange tickets for you, ranging in price (in general) from 25€ to 115€. Call ✆ **95-723-25-07** for information.

Alcázar de los Reyes Cristianos ★   Commissioned in 1328 by Alfonso XI, the Alcázar (fortress) of the Christian monarchs is a fine example of military architecture. Ferdinand and Isabella governed from this fortress on the Guadalquivir River as they prepared to reconquer Granada, the last Moorish stronghold in Spain. Columbus journeyed here to fill Isabella's ears with his plans for discovery. And it was at the Alcázar that Ferdinand and Isabella bade Columbus farewell as he set out to chart unknown territory and discover what (for Europeans) was a new world.

On a less happy note, the Alcázar was the headquarters of the dreaded Spanish Inquisition for 3 centuries. A former Arab bathhouse in the basement was turned into a Counter-Reformation interrogation center.

Originally, the Alcázar was the abode of the Umayyad caliphs. Of their former palace, little remains except ruins. You can see some Moorish courtyards with ornamental basins and some cooling pools and baths. Also on view in what was once the Inquisition chapel are some impressive **Roman mosaics ★** from the time of the Emperor Augustus. One of them has alternating geometrical motifs, and yet another depicts Polyphemus and Galatea. A **Roman sarcophagus ★** is representational of 2nd- and 3rd-century funereal art.

The centerpiece of the fortress, the **Patio Morisco (Court of the Moors)** is a lovely spot, with twin pools, an ivy-covered grotto, and a pavement decorated with the coats of arms of León and Castile.

The **Gardens of the Alcázar ★★** display their Arabic origins, complete with terraces, pools, and cooling fountains, and they offer respite from the heat of the city in summer. You can wander amidst fragrant flower beds to the tinkle of water fountains and admire the towering cypresses and palms.

Caballerizas Reales. ✆ **95-742-01-51.** Admission 4€ adults (2€ for gardens), free for children aged 14 and under with parent. May–June Tues–Sat 10am–2pm and 5:30–7:30pm, Sun 9:30am–2:30pm; Oct–

Apr Tues-Sat 10am-2pm and 4:30-6:30pm, Sun 9:30am-2:30pm; July-Sept Tues-Sat 8:30am-2:30pm. Gardens illuminated July-Sept 10pm-midnight.

Baños del Alcázar ★ The Moorish Caliph's private baths featured marble-decked rooms and heated pools. They've been well excavated and there are interesting descriptions in English too. This civilization was advanced, using furnaces to heat the water and pipe it to the different bathing chambers. Caliph Rahman V was assassinated in the hot room here in 1024. Most noticeable though is the situation—several meters below modern-day ground level. The introductory film is available in English too—ask at reception if need be.

Campo Santo de los Martires. No phone. Same opening hours as the Alcázar above. 2€ adults, 1€ concessions. Free Wednesdays.

Casa de Sefarad ★★ Whilst the Synagogue (see below) doesn't offer much detail about Córdoba's remarkable Jewish history, this vibrant little museum just across the way from it fills the gap very well. Spanish Jews were known as the Sephardim—hence the name of this restored 14th-century house which contains five rooms with collections of clothing and jewelry from Jewish families of that era with detailed descriptions in English. New rooms being added will provide information about famous Sephardic scholars of the time—in particular the hugely influential physician and philosopher Maimonides. Jaime, who runs the museum, is a real authority on the city's Jewish history and passionate about preserving what's left of it.

Corner Calle Judios and Calle Averroes. ✆ **97-542-14-04**. www.casadesefarad.com. Mon-Sat 10am-6pm; Sun 11am-2pm. 4€ adults; 3€ concessions.

Mezquita-Catedral de Córdoba ★★★ In the 8th century, this Mezquita (Great Mosque) became the crowning glory of Muslim architecture in the West. With its fantastic labyrinth of red-and-white striped Moorish horseshoe arches, it remains one of the grandest attractions in Europe.

The Caliph of Córdoba, Abd el-Rahman I, began the construction of this remarkable place of worship in 785. To do so, he razed an earlier Visigothic basilica, which itself had replaced a Roman temple. Initially, the Great Mosque covered 23,400 sq. m (251,000 sq. ft). Unusually it was oriented towards Damascus—the caliph's home city—rather than Mecca. The Mezquita was built in various stages, following an overall plan of a crenellated square perimeter enclosing **El Patio de los Naranjos (Court of Orange Trees)** ★★, which is one of the principal entrances to the mosque. This courtyard was redesigned following the Reconquista. Still visible are the irrigation channels dug by the Muslims. **Puerta del Perdón (Gate of Forgiveness),** on the north wall, is the former entrance into the mosque.

Before the Catholic takeover, the mosque had a total of 900 pillars. Remarkably, **856 pillars** ★★★ are still standing. Their red-and-white peppermint stripes are formed in large part by white stone and red-brick *voussoirs* (arch stone). The pillars are also built of onyx, granite, marble, and jasper, filling a total of 19 aisles. A second row of arches set above the first almost doubles the height of the ceiling. Some of the most interesting pillars came from the ancient Visigothic basilica. You can pick these out by the impressive carvings on their capitals. Since some of the pillars brought in were taller than others, they had to be sunk into the floor of the mosque. The oldest known pillar came from Egypt and dates from the reign of Amenophis IV.

Visiting the Mezquita

If you're on a budget, visit between the hours of 8:30am and 10am Monday to Saturday. Entry at these times is **free**. Conversely, if budget is no issue, consider doing one of the **night visits** which include a sound and light show and are wonderfully atmospheric. They have to be booked in advance at the ticket booth and they sell out fast. The cost is 18€ per person. If you speak Spanish you can also book on-line at the website below. Audio guides, giving elaborate, somewhat disorganised commentary about the Mezquita in any of a half-dozen different languages, are available from a separate kiosk next to the ticket booth at the mosque's main entrance. They rent for 3.50€ each and require a cash deposit of 20€, or some valid credit card or document left as insurance that you'll return the equipment. Photographs are allowed, but not if you use a tripod. And there are strict security regulations (no big bags or suitcases allowed) at the entrance. For further information, call ✆ **95-747-05-12** or see www.catedraldecordoba.es.

On the south wall of the Mezquita is the **Maksura ★★★**, the enclosure reserved for the caliph and his entourage. It's roofed with a trio of beautiful domes resting on interweaving multifoil arches and it features golden mosaics, arabesques, carvings, cupolas, palm-leaf motifs framed by Sufic script, and marble panels. The **Byzantine mosaics,** which have hundreds of pieces of tiny gold, glass, and ceramic tiles, were a gift of the 10th-century Emperor of Constantinople.

Set within the Maksura, the **Mihrab ★★★** (the prayer niche) is bordered by wonderfully ornate Koranic sculptures and with carved stucco adorning its upper walls. Traditionally the Mihrab was orientated towards Mecca, but unusually, here in Cordoba it faces Damascus, the home city of Emir Abd al Rahman I who began the mosque's construction. The **frieze** in gold and blue that runs all the way around the Mihrab lists the 99 names of Allah. Its **interior** is covered by a scallop-shaped dome, which is richly decorated with beautiful colored mosaics and gilded tiles.

In later years the addition of Christian chapels destroyed the architectural harmony of the Mezquita. The **Capilla Villaviciosa ★**, which was completed in 1371, features a stalactite ceiling and stunning plaster lacework. Also added was the **Chapel Royal ★**, decorated in the 1200s with Mudéjar stucco.

Although the people of Córdoba rallied against the idea, Emperor Carlos V allowed himself to be persuaded by his Bishop Alonso Manrique that part of the mosque should be torn down to make way for the **Catedral ★★**, which was to be built right in the midst of the mosque. Later the Emperor regretted his decision, saying to his architects, "What you are building here can be found anywhere, but what you have destroyed exists nowhere." Construction began in 1523 in the Gothic style, although later additions were in the Plateresque and Baroque styles, and even the Renaissance shows up in decorative figures in the medallions in the apsidal vaulting in 1560.

The greatest achievement is the Baroque **choir stalls ★★★** by Pedro Duque Cornejo, the Andalusian sculptor, created around 1750. On either side of the stalls he depicted the Ascension and scenes from the lives of Jesus and the Virgin Mary in life-like detail. Almost equally stunning are two **pulpits ★★** in marble, mahogany, and jasper. One of the pulpits rests on a pink marble ox.

In the Sacristy, next to the Mihrab, is the **Treasury,** displaying beautiful examples of Córdovan silver and gold artistry.

Calles Torrijos and Cardenal Herrero s/n (south of the train station, just north of the Roman bridge). ℓ **95-822-52-45.** www.catedraldecordoba.es. Admission 8€ adults, 4€ children aged 13 and under. Mar–Oct Mon–Sat 10am–7pm, Sun and hols 8:30–10am and 2–7pm; Nov–Feb Mon–Sat 10am–6pm, Sun and hols 8:30–10am and 2–6pm. Free admission Mon–Sat 8:30–10am. Ticket office closes 30 minutes before closing time.

Judería (Jewish Quarter)

North and west of the Mezquita, the city's old Jewish Quarter is one of the highlights of a visit to Córdoba, despite being rather overrun with tourists in summer. Two of the world's greatest thinkers, the Jewish philosopher Maimonides and the Arab philosopher and mathematician Averroès, once called the **Judería ★★★** home.

The restored neighborhood makes for a very pleasant and atmospheric stroll. You can spend at least 2 hours here wandering about—and be prepared to get lost. Many upper-middle-class locals now occupy these old whitewashed houses and have restored them. The rest are souvenir shops, restaurants, and small hotels. If you are approaching from the Mezquita, walk up Calle Judería at the top of Calle Torrijos. There are several other entrances to the barrio including the Puerta de Almódovar and the Puerta del Sol, ancient archways in what remains of the old city walls at the western frontier.

The Jewish and Muslim communities existed in great harmony during much of the Moorish era and the Judería reached the zenith of its prosperity during the Caliphate (929–1031). A great Talmudic school was founded here in this era of tolerance. The only physical evidence left of its former Jewish population now is the small **synagogue** (p. 157) and close by, the recently opened **Casa de Sefarad**.

The Judería is also filled with delightful little squares that you'll stumble into after wandering down a dark alleyway into the bright sunshine of Andalusia. There's also a small arcade of interesting craft galleries called **Zoco** selling ceramics, glass, and leatherware which is ideal for picking up some more authentic souvenirs. (See "Shopping" p. 158.)

◯ Reviving Moorish Customs: Baños Arabes

A popular Moorish custom survives at **Hammam Arabic Baths (Baños Arabes),** Corregidor Luís de la Cerda 51 (ℓ **95-748-47-46;** www.hammamspain.com/cordoba), a short walk east from the Mezquita. Wallowing in hot water baths, sweating in the hot room, and having a massage are probably as close as you'll come to experiencing life as the ancient sultans lived it. Whilst little of the fabric of the building is original, it's delightfully atmospheric with red-and-white striped arches like those in the Mezquita in the bathing area, Arabic music strumming quietly in the background, and fountains tinkling gently in the anterooms. You need to bring a swimsuit and you cannot wear shoes or sandals inside. Each bathing session lasts 1½ hours and includes a massage and Moroccan tea for 36€. Hours are daily from 10am to 10pm; make a reservation and be sure to show up on time.

If there is one street you should seek out, it's **Calleja de las Flores** ★★, "little street of flowers." Actually, it's a narrow deadend alleyway off Calle Victor Bosco. The window boxes of the houses here are filled with bright geraniums. Turn around and look back and you get a great view of the tower of the Mezquita fringed by bright flowers, terracotta-tiled roofs, and whitewashed walls. It's the perfect photo opportunity. You'll also find the excellent leather workshop of Meyran on this little street where you can see artists at work making the uniquely colorful painted leather creations that Córdoba is famous for. Some of the larger pictures and chests are truly spectacular. (See "Shopping" p. 158 for more details.)

Museo Arqueológico y Etnológico de Córdoba ★ Córdoba's archaeological museum, two blocks northeast of the Mezquita, is one of the most important in Spain. Housed in a palace dating from 1505, it displays artifacts left behind by the various peoples and conquerors that swept through the province. There are Paleolithic and Neolithic items, Iberian hand weapons and ceramics, and Roman sculptures, bronzes, ceramics, inscriptions, and mosaics. Especially interesting are the Visigothic artifacts. The most outstanding collection, however, is devoted to Arabic art and spans the entire Muslim occupation. There are delightful patios with fountains and ponds. Right next door you can view the ruins of a Roman theater, which was discovered only in 2000.

Plaza Jerónimo Páez 7, Judería. ⓒ **95-735-55-17.** www.museosdeandalucia.es. Admission 1.50€,. free to E.U. passport holders. Tues 2:30–8:30pm; Wed–Sat 9am–8:30pm; Sun and public hols 9am–2:30pm.

Museo de Bellas Artes de Córdoba As you cross the Plaza del Potro to reach this fine-arts museum, notice the fountain in the square here. Built in 1557, it shows a young stallion, with forelegs raised, holding the shield of Córdoba. Housed in an old charity hospital on the plaza, the museum contains medieval Andalusian paintings, examples of Spanish Baroque art, and works by many of Spain's important 19th- and 20th-century painters, including Goya, Sorolla, Zurbarán, Murillo, and Valdés Leal. Of particular interest on the ground floor are sculptures by the Spanish artists Juan de Mesa and Mateo Inurria. Ferdinand and Isabella themselves founded this former Hospital de la Caridad, and twice they received Columbus here. The museum is east of the Mezquita, about a block south of the Church of San Francisco.

Plaza del Potro 1. ⓒ **95-735-55-50.** www.museosdeandalucia.es. Admission 1.60€ adults, free to E.U. passport holders. Tues 2:30–8:30pm; Wed–Sat 9am–8:30pm; Sun and public hols 9am–2:30pm.

Museo de Julio Romero de Torres ★ Across the patio from the Museo de Bellas Artes, this museum honors Julio Romero de Torres (1874–1930), Córdoba's most famous 20th-century artist. He was particularly known for his sensual portraits of women. He caused the greatest scandal with his "hyper-realistic nudes," and in 1906 the National Exhibition of Fine Arts banned his *Vivadoras del Amor.* On display here is his celebrated *Oranges and Lemons,* and other notable works such as *The Little Girl Who Sells Fuel, Sin,* and *A Dedication to the Art of the Bullfight.* A corner of Romero's Madrid studio has been reproduced in one of the rooms, displaying the paintings left unfinished at his death. The large canvas entitled *Look How Lovely She Was* (1895) on the ground floor features a deathbed scene with the artist himself among the mourners. **Note:** At the time of writing the museum was closed for renovations. Ask at the tourist office for the latest information about opening hours.

Plaza del Potro 1. ℗ **95-749-19-09.** www.museojulioromero.com. Admission 3€. Oct-Apr Tues-Sat 10am-2pm and 4:30-6:30pm, Sun 9:30am-2:30pm; May-June and Sept Tues-Sat 10am-2pm and 5:30-7:30pm, Sun 9:30am-2:30pm; July-Aug Tues-Sat 8:30am-2:30pm, Sun 9:30am-2:30pm.

Palacio Museo de Viana ★★   Few of Córdoba's palaces have been open to the public in the past, but that's changed with the opening of this museum. You can wander at leisure through the **garden and patios ★★**. These patios, 14 in all, are particularly stunning. You can also do a guided tour of the **interior ★** which lasts about an hour. The guides aren't up to much, but the rooms themselves are splendid. Ask for the short pamphlet in English too. You see upwards of 30 rooms, in rather whirlwind fashion; all of them ornately decorated and filled with antiques. Stand-out rooms include the Marchioness' Study and Main Dining Room which both feature wonderful carved ceilings and the Gobelans Room which has four huge tapestries on its walls, each depicting wild animals from far-flung shores. The palace is about a 15-minute walk from the historic center, four blocks southeast of the Plaza de Colón.

Plaza de Don Gome 2. ℗ **95-749-67-41.** Palace admission 6€; patios 3€. June-Sept Tues-Sat 9am-3pm; Oct-May Tues-Fri 10am-1pm and 4-6pm, Sat 10am-1pm. Closed June 1-15.

Sinagoga In Córdoba you'll find one of Spain's three remaining pre-Inquisition synagogues, built in 1315 in the Barrio de la Judería (Jewish Quarter). The synagogue is noted for its stuccowork; the east wall contains a large orifice where the Tabernacle was once placed with the scrolls of the Pentateuch inside. Note the various adornments of *mozárabe* patterns and Hebrew inscriptions. You can still see

A STATELY pleasure DOME: THE MOORISH VERSAILLES

The **Conjunto Arqueológico Madinat Al-Zahra,** a kind of Moorish Versailles just outside Córdoba, was constructed in the 10th century by the first Caliph of al-Andalús, Abd ar-Rahman III. Thousands of workers and animals slaved to build this mammoth pleasure palace, said to have contained 300 baths and 400 houses. The Berbers sacked the place in 1013.

Over the years the site has been plundered for building materials. Some of these, it's said, went to build the Alcázar in Seville. The **Royal House,** today a rendezvous point for the ministers, has been reconstructed. The principal salon remains in fragments, so you have to imagine it in its majesty. Just beyond the Royal House are the ruins of a **mosque** constructed to face Mecca.

It's at Carretera Palma de Río Km 8 (℗ **95-735-28-74;** www.museosde andalucia.es). Admission is 1.50€, but it's free to E.U. passport holders. Hours are May 1 to September 15, Tuesday to Saturday 10am to 8:30pm, Sunday 10am to 2pm; September 16 to April 30, Tuesday to Saturday 10am to 6:30pm. The tourist office runs a daily bus service to the site. It leaves Córdoba at 10:30am and picks up at two stops at either end of Paseo de la Victoria. The bus returns to Córdoba three hours after it arrives in Madinat al-Zahra. In the summer season there's a second bus departure at 5pm for evening visits to the site when it's cooler. Ask at the tourist office for more information or call ℗ **90-220-17-74.**

the balcony where women were sequestered during worship. After the Jews were expelled from Spain, the synagogue was turned into a hospital, until it became a Catholic chapel in 1588.

Calle de los Judíos 20. ✆ **95-720-29-28.** Admission .30€. Free to E.U. passport holders. Tues–Sat 9:30am–2pm and 3:30–5:30pm; Sun 9:30am–1:30pm. Closed May.

Torre de la Calahorra The Tower of Calahorra is across the river from the Mezquita at the southern end of the Roman bridge. Commissioned by Henry II of Trastamara in 1369 to protect him from his brother, Peter I, it now houses a town museum, Museo Vivo de al-Andalús. Take a headset for a self-guided tour. One room holds wax figures of Córdoba's famous philosophers, including Maimonides. Other rooms exhibit a miniature model of the Alhambra at Granada, complete with water fountains, a miniature Mezquita, and Arab musical instruments. From the top of the tower there are panoramic views of the Roman bridge, the river, and the cathedral/mosque.

Av. de la Confederación, Puente Romano. ✆ **95-729-39-29.** www.torrecalahorra.com. Admission to museum 4.50€ adults, 3€ students and children aged 7 and under. May–Sept daily 10am–2pm and 4:30–8:30pm; Oct–Apr daily 10am–6pm.

SHOPPING

In Moorish times Córdoba's leather workers were legendary. Highly valued in 15th-century Europe, their leather was studded with gold and silver ornaments, and then painted with embossed designs (*guadamec*). Large panels often took the place of tapestries. Although the industry has fallen into decline and the market is filled mostly with cheap imitations, you can still find excellently crafted embossed leather products at **Taller Meryan** (see below).

Córdoba has a branch of Spain's major department store, **El Corte Inglés,** at Ronda de los Tejares 30 (✆ **95-722-28-81;** www.elcorteingles.es). Some of the staff speaks English. It's open Monday to Saturday from 10am to 10pm.

The other shops listed below are open Monday to Saturday from 10am to 7pm; smaller establishments, however, often take a siesta, doing business from 9:30 or 10am to 1:30 or 2pm and again from 4:30 or 5 to 8pm. Exceptions are listed below.

Aldefa Campos This gift and souvenir shop is trendier, glossier, and a bit more urban in its selection of porcelain and gift items than many of the more folklore-oriented shops that surround it. It's especially strong on housewares. Open daily from 10am to 9pm. Velásquez Bosco 8. ✆ **95-748-24-52.**

Andalusi This lovely old-fashioned deli is just before the north entrance of the Plaza Corredera, about a 10-minute walk from the Mezquita. Here you'll find olive oils, cheeses, cured meats, and all manner of local foodie attractions. Rodriguez Marin 22. ✆ **95-748-89-61.**

Arte Zoco This is the largest association of craftspeople in Córdoba, established in the Jewish Quarter in the mid-1980s. Here you'll find about a dozen artisans whose media include leather, wood, silver, crystal, terracotta, and iron. About a half-dozen of the artisans maintain their studios on the premises, so you can visit and check out the techniques and tools they use. You'll find everything from new, iconoclastic, and avant-garde designs to pieces that honor centuries-old traditions. Of special interest is the revival of the Califar pottery first introduced to Córdoba during the regimes of the Muslim caliphs. The shop is open in winter Monday to Friday 9:30am to 8pm, Saturday and Sunday 9:30am to 2pm, and in summer daily 10am to 8pm. The workshops and studios of the various artisans open and close according to the occupants' whims but are usually open Monday to Friday 10am to 2pm and 5:30 to 8pm. Calle de los Judíos s/n. ✆ **95-720-40-33.**

Galerías Turísticas, S.L. Set very close to the main entrance of the Mezquita, this is the biggest and most upscale of the gift, jewelry, and souvenir shops in Córdoba's Medieval Quarter. In a sprawling stone-and-masonry-sheathed environment that might remind you of the ground floor of a large department store, you'll find lots of sales clerks plus glass display cases containing Majorcan pearls, *feria* dolls from Cádiz, castanets, inlaid marquetry boxes from Morocco, jewelry, hand-painted fans, Lladro porcelain, and some very tasteful and upscale gift items. Open daily 9am to 7pm. Calle Torrijos 8. ✆ **95-748-56-02.**

Joyería Manuel J. Regalos Large, expensively outfitted, and elegant, with many of its more upscale gift items showcased in glass-fronted display cases, this store has a particularly appealing collection of Mantones de Manila (Manila shawls), many of them lavishly embroidered, and *feria* accessories. No self-respecting Andalusian woman would do without these shawls to ward off an evening chill. There are also faux tortoiseshell hair combs, some imperious enough to transform a Carmen wannabe into a Carmen clone in just a few passes of a hairbrush. Open Monday to Saturday 10am to 9pm and Sunday 10am to 8pm. Cardenal Herrero 30-32. ✆ **95-748-41-97.**

Taller Meryan ★ Alejandro and Carlos López Obrero operate out of this 250-year-old building. The street it's on is so enchanting you might want to come here even if you don't want to shop (check the information on Calleja de las Flores in "Seeing the Sights," for details). This is the best store in Córdoba for embossed leather products. You can see artisans plying their trades; although most items must be custom-ordered, some ready-made pieces are for sale, including cigarette boxes, jewel cases, attaché cases, book and folio covers, and ottoman covers. It's open Monday to Friday 9am to 8pm and Saturday 9am to 2pm. Calleja de las Flores 2. ✆ **95-747-59-02.**

CÓRDOBA AFTER DARK

Tapas & Wine

You can begin your tapas crawl at the previously recommended **Bodegas Campos** (p. 147), which has some of the classiest tapas in town. But there are many other options, particularly if you're wandering the streets of the Judería, which is particularly colorful in the evening. A couple of more upscale places to try here are **Taberna Casa Pepe de la Judería** (p. 149), and **El Caballo Rojo** (p. 148). As well as having first-class restaurants, both offer a good supply of tapas.

There's another nice clutch of tapas places just through the **Puerta de Almódovar** in the Jewish Quarter. Also try the wonderful Castilian-style, arcaded 17th-century square **Plaza Corredera** which is abuzz with busy terrace bars in the evenings, perfect for a tapa or two and some people-watching.

Some of my favorite tapas bars include those listed below.

Bar Círculo Taurino A real local corner bar, this place is where aficionados meet to debate—often loudly—the relative merits (or lack thereof) of Andalusian bullfighters. In between a lot of wine or beer, Andalusian olives, and hunks of cheese are consumed, among other tapas. The bar is small, cramped, and loaded with bullfighting memorabilia. It's located about a 15-minute walk north of the Mezquita in the vicinity of the Plaza Colón. Open daily 1 to 4pm and 8:30 to 11:30pm. Calle Manuel María Arjona 1. (2) **95-747-19-53**.

Casa Bar Santos   This busy little bar right next to the Mezquita, has a big reputation for its huge tortillas. Not to be confused with the Mexican cornflour snack, Spanish tortilla is a thick potato omelet and none come thicker than Francisco Santos's, made using nothing more than extra virgin olive oil, potatoes, and the freshest eggs. A slice costs just 1.50€ and a cold beer is the perfect accompaniment. Magistral González Francés, 3 (2) **95-747-93-60**.

Casa Miguel/El Pisto ★   This is apparently the oldest *bodega* in Córdoba—some say it dates from 1812, some 1880. It is certainly one of the most authentic of all the tabernas. Each of the small rooms has a different theme. *Azulejos* (earthenware tiles) form a large part of the decor, as do wine barrels, photographs of bullfighters, and even guitars and lanterns. Cooks prepare a series of some of the best and freshest tapas in town. Open Monday to Saturday 1 to 4pm and 8pm to midnight. Closed August. Plaza San Miguel 1. (2) **95-747-83-28**.

Casa Pepe   In the Judería, close to the Mezquita, this is an atmospheric old hideaway in an antique building where many generations have lifted glasses of wine. Try a glass of *montilla* (a regional version of dry sherry) along with some serrano ham. Open Sunday to Thursday 1 to 4pm and 8:30 to 11:30pm, Friday and Saturday 1 to 4pm and 8:30pm to midnight. Calle Romano 1. (2) **95-720-07-44**.

Casa Rubio   A busy local bar with Mezquita-style arches and a small interior courtyard, Casa Rubio is one of several atmospheric, friendly places just inside the Puerta de Almódovar. Tapas are good value and I particularly like the *salmorejo*—a thick local style of cold tomato soup with garlic and small pieces of ham. Open daily 1 to 4pm and 8:30 to 11:30pm. Puerta de Almódovar 5. (2) **95-742-08-53**.

El Juramento   Tucked away behind Plaza Corredera, this tapas bar is old-fashioned enough to be cozy and crowded enough to be convivial. It attracts a wide-ranging age group, and there are 18 tables for patrons who actually want to sit. The cooks whip up everything from a *rabo de toro* (bull's tail simmered in tomato sauce) to fried slices of hake. Open Wednesday to Monday 1:15 to 4pm and 9:15pm to midnight. Calle Juramento 6. (2) **95-748-54-77**.

El Sotano   Located on one of the city's most striking squares, Plaza Corredera, this funky little terrace bar, just inside the northwest entrance to the square, attracts a young crowd with its good-value beer and tapas and noisy atmosphere. A perfect spot for a little people-watching and a cold beer or glass of wine. Open daily 9am to 5pm and 8pm to 2am. If the tables here are all full, La Paloma right next door is also good. Plaza de la Corredera 1. (2) **95-748-45-70**.

Taberna Casa Salinas ★   This is another atmospheric old dive just inside the Puerta de Almódovar, offering glasses of sherry and plates of freshly made tapas along with spicy Andalusian sausages and buckets of olives. Pepe Salinas is now in his 4th decade of running this crowded bar and old-fashioned dining room. In fair weather the action spills onto the street. Open Monday to Saturday 11:30am to 4:30pm and 8:30pm to midnight (closes at 5:30pm Sun). Puerta de Almódovar s/n. (2) **95-729-08-46**.

Hanging Out With the Cool Crowd

Most of the old tapas bars are in the historic center of Córdoba, but 20- and 30-somethings have migrated a little way north to a strip of cool dance bars on Avenida de la Liberdade close to the main rail station. **MOMA,** Avenida de la Liberdade, at the corner of Miguel Gila (𝓒 **95-727-19-12**), is probably my favorite. It's all about sleek design and decor with lots of glass and steel and the crowd here is smooth and sophisticated. Unless there's a live concert scheduled, music on conventional bar nights focuses on pop, rock 'n' roll, and international hits from the '70s, '80s, and '90s. Cover charges apply only when there's live music. Otherwise, entrance is free. Cocktails begin at around 7€ each. Sunday to Thursday 9am to 3am, Friday to Saturday 10am to 4am. Other bars along this strip that are also well worth a visit include **Bambuddha,** one block left of MOMA on the corner of Avenida del Gran Capitán, and **Blue Café,** one block right on the corner of Calle Francisco Rabal.

Flamenco Clubs & More

Tablao Cardenal, Calle Torrijos 10 (𝓒 **95-748-33-20**), is Córdoba's most popular and dynamic flamenco club just across from the Mezquita and featuring international and award-winning flamenco artists. Some of the purest styles of Andalusian flamenco—*soleá, bulerías,* and *alegrías*—are showcased here. Shows are presented Monday to Saturday at 10:30pm, with a cover of 20€ that includes your first drink.

For a more authentic flamenco venue, head to **Mesón Flamenco La Bulería,** Pedro López 3 (𝓒 **95-748-38-39**), close to the Plaza de la Corredera on the outskirts of the old part of town. This is one of the most reasonably priced flamenco shows in Andalusia, considering the class of its talent. The cover of 12€ includes your first drink. Most shows start nightly around 10:30pm. The club is generally closed from December to February.

For more formal entertainment, check out the listings at the city's theatrical *grande dame,* the early 20th-century **Gran Teatro de Córdoba,** Av. del Gran Capitán 3 (𝓒 **95-748-02-37;** www.teatrocordoba.com), site of most of the ballet, opera, chamber music, and symphony performances in town.

Dance Bars & Nightclubs

Jazz Café   Don't even think of coming here until very late; most of the jazz acts begin around midnight, and the doors only open (reluctantly) at around 11pm. You have to ring a bell to gain entrance to this club, which sits on a steeply sloping street behind fortress-like iron gates. Inside, tiny marble tables and spinning ceiling fans evoke colonial Havana. In addition to regularly scheduled music featuring local and visiting musicians, management encourages anyone with musical talent to participate in the frequent jam sessions. Cover charges range from 4€ to 8€ depending on the night of the week. Open Tuesday to Saturday 11pm to 4am. Calle Rodríguez Marín s/n, corner of Calle Tundidores. 𝓒 **95-748-58-54.**

La Comuna   Lots of students on the make show up here hoping to score. High energy and a hot DJ keep the place electric. Pop and funk dominate. Open Thursday to Saturday 7pm to 4am. Calle del Caño 1. 𝓒 **95-742-16-73.** No cover.

ON THE WAY TO GRANADA: JAÉN, BAEZA & UBEDA

Many visitors whiz through the province of Jaén on the way south to the more famous attractions in Granada, Córdoba, and Seville. But if you have a day or two to spare, provincial capital Jaén and in particular the historic little towns of Baeza and Ubeda offer ornate and beautiful architecture and several attractive hotels and restaurants too. Unlike the more popular tourist cities, they're wonderfully free of other visitors. If you have time for only one stop, make it ancient Baeza, which has the most charm and the nicest hotels.

If you're en route from Córdoba to Granada, the quickest route is to head east along the A-4/E-5 to the turnoff town of Bailén and head south on the A-44/E-902. An alternative is to take the slower N-432 across country and stop on the way to explore the undiscovered area around Priego de Córdoba. (See box "The Next Undiscovered Frontier" below.)

Back at Bailén, if you want to visit Ubeda and Baeza (or both), get onto the N-322 and head east, following the signs to either Ubeda or Baeza. Ubeda is on the main route, N-322. Baeza, however, is a short drive southwest of Ubeda and is reached by taking a secondary route, the N-316.

Jaén

97km (60 miles) E of Córdoba

In the center of Spain's major olive-growing district, **Jaén** is sandwiched between Córdoba and Granada and has always been a gateway between Castile and Andalusia. This city is east of Córdoba and can be reached from that city in less than an hour. It's also possible to drive down from Madrid, visiting Jaén (and subsequently

---

🔘 The Next Undiscovered Frontier

If you're looking for a part of Andalusia that's totally undiscovered, take the direct route to Granada, the N-432. It's a slower road, but you'll see few other tourists. It takes you through the beautiful Sierras Subbéticas—an area of natural park and wide olive groves fringed with mountain peaks and dotted with old towns. This area was once the frontier of Moorish al-Andalus, which explains the medieval watchtowers dotted about the countryside; they once served as lookout posts. The little town of **Priego de Córdoba** is particularly attractive with lovely Baroque churches, the ruins of an old castle, and a maze of pretty whitewash-housed streets.

If you want to stay a while, base yourself at new eco-friendly guesthouse **Casa Olea** (📞 **69-674-82-09**; www.casa olea.com). This 150-year-old farmhouse has been restored by British couple Tim and Claire Murray-Walker. It boasts solar panels and a biomass boiler that runs on waste olive pellets and has six simple white guest rooms with comfortable beds and wonderful views across the olive groves. There's a solar-heated swimming pool too. It's a nice place to unwind and both Granada and Córdoba are within easy day trip distance.

Jaén

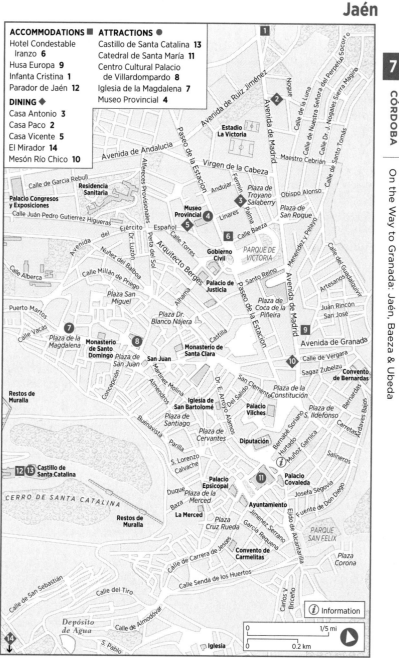

ACCOMMODATIONS ■
Hotel Condestable
  Iranzo **6**
Husa Europa **9**
Infanta Cristina **1**
Parador de Jaén **12**

DINING ◆
Casa Antonio **3**
Casa Paco **2**
Casa Vicente **5**
El Mirador **14**
Mesón Río Chico **10**

ATTRACTIONS ●
Castillo de Santa Catalina **13**
Catedral de Santa María **11**
Centro Cultural Palacio
  de Villardompardo **8**
Iglesia de la Magdalena **7**
Museo Provincial **4**

Ubeda or Baeza) before visiting either Granada or Córdoba. The drive south via the A-4/E-5 to Jaén is 338km (210 miles) from Madrid.

Jaén's bustling modern section is of little interest to visitors, but the **Moorish Old Town,** where narrow cobblestone streets hug the mountainside, is reason enough to visit. A hilltop castle, now a parador hotel, dominates the city. On clear days you can see the snow-covered peaks of the Sierra Nevada from here.

The city of Jaén is the center of a large province of 13,491 sq. km (5,189 sq. miles) framed by mountains: the Sierra Morena to the north, the Segura and Cazorla ranges to the east, and those of Huelma, Noalejo, and Valdepeñas to the south. To the west, plains widen into the fertile Guadalquivir Valley. Jaén province comprises three well-defined districts: the Sierra de Cazorla, a land of wild scenery; the plains of Bailén, Ajona, and Arjonilla, filled with wheat fields, vineyards, and old olive trees; and the valleys of the tributaries of the Guadalquivir River.

Life in Jaén revolves around the landmark **Plaza de la Constitución.** From here, take Calle Bernabé Soriano uphill to the **cathedral** and the **Old Town.**

ESSENTIALS

GETTING THERE   If you're **driving,** see routing details above. You can also drive north from Granada along the A-44/E-902, a distance of 93km (58 miles).

If you're taking the **train** from Córdoba in the west, it takes just over 1½ hours to reach Jaén. There are three trains per day and it costs 11.60€ for a one-way ticket. There are two trains per day from Madrid, taking 4 to 5 hours and costing 25€ for a one-way ticket. Trains arrive in Jaén at the RENFE station on Paseo de la Estación (✆ **90-232-03-20;** www.renfe.es), north of the center of town. The new city street-car/tram line now connects the rail station with the Plaza de la Constitución.

If you are coming north from Granada, **Alsina Graells** (✆ **90-242-22-42;** www.alsa.es) runs **buses** from Granada every hour during the day, taking 1½ hours and costing 7€ for a one-way ticket. Buses arrive in Jaén at the Estación de Auto-buses (✆ **95-323-23-00;** www.epassa.es) just off the Avenida de Madrid, a block south of Parque de la Victoria.

VISITOR INFORMATION   The combined city and regional tourist office is handily located right behind the cathedral at Calle Ramón y Cajal s/n (✆ **95-319-32-81** and **95-331-32-81**; www.turjaen.org). It's open Monday to Friday from 9am to 7:30pm, Saturday and Sunday from 10am to 3pm. Staff here are really helpful.

EXPLORING JAÉN

Castillo de Santa Catalina ★   On a rocky crag 5km (3 miles) from the center of Jaén, this restored castle dominates the city. Today it is the site of the Parador de Jaén, reason enough for many visitors to stop over here. Originally the Moors constructed the fortress, although it is said that Hannibal's men built the first watchtower here. The Nasrid caliph, Alhamar, builder of the Alcázar at Granada, ordered construction of the castle. Later King Ferdinand III captured it and took the Castillo in 1246 in time to celebrate the Feast Day of patron saint Santa Catalina (St Catherine). Of course, you can stay or dine at the parador, but the reason many sightseers trek up here is to enjoy the finest and most panoramic view in the province. At the time of writing the Castillo was closed for renovations. Ask at the tourist office for the latest information.

Castillo de Santa Catalina. ✆ **95-312-07-33.** Admission 3.50€. June–Sept Tues–Sun 10am–2pm and 5–9pm; Oct–May Tues–Sun 10am–2pm and 3:30–7:30pm.

Catedral de Santa María   The formality and grandeur of Jaén's cathedral bears witness to the city's past importance. Begun in 1555 on the site of a former mosque and completed in 1802, it's a honey-colored blend of Gothic, Baroque, and Renaissance styles, with an emphasis on the latter. The original architect was Andrés de Vandelvira (1509–75), who designed many buildings at Baeza and Ubeda. A huge dome dominates the interior with its richly carved choir stalls. The **cathedral museum** ★ contains an important collection of historical objects in two underground chambers, including paintings by **Jusepe de Ribera,** the Baroque painter. Its most celebrated relic is the Santo Rostro (Holy Face) cloth, which, according to legend, was used by Veronica to wipe Jesus's face on his way to Calvary. Evocative of Italy's Shroud of Turin, the image of Christ is said to have imprinted on the fabric. The cathedral is southwest of the Plaza de la Constitución.

Plaza de Santa María. *℗* **95-323-42-33**, www.catedraldejaen.org**.** Admission 5€. Mon–Thurs 10am–2pm and 4-6pm; Fri and Sat 10am-6pm.

Centro Cultural Palacio de Villardompardo   This is a three-in-one attraction, including some former Arab baths (known as *hamman*) and two museums, the Museo de Artes y Costumbres Populares and the Museo Internacional de Arte Naif.

Underneath the palace, near Calle San Juan and the Chapel of Saint Andrew (San Andrés), are the former **Arab baths.** They represent some of the most important Moorish architecture from the 11th century ever discovered in Spain. You can visit a warm room, a hot room, and a cold room—the last with a barrel vault and 12 star-shaped chandeliers.

The **Museo de Artes y Costumbres Populares** houses a collection of primarily 19th-century folkloric artifacts, including costumes, dolls, ceramics, and even photographs from Andalusia's past. The **Museo Internacional de Arte Naif** features a changing art exhibit featuring the work of artists from around the globe who have created professional, skilled paintings without any formal art instruction.

The Most Extra Virgin Oil

If you drive around the province of Jaén, the landscape before you will often be rows of olive trees stretching as far as you can see. Jaén province is the world's biggest producer of this liquid gold and 77% of its farmed land is given over to the humble olive tree. Unsurprisingly there are several places where you can sample some of the finest extra virgin olive oils, as sought after by connoisseurs as the finest of wines. Many of the olive mills are owned by local cooperatives. The closest to the city center is **Sociedad Cooperativa Andaluza de Campo San Juan,** Calle Frailes s/n

(*℗* **95-308-14-00**; www.acetesanjuan. com), located on the Los Olivares industrial estate on the northern outskirts. Visitor hours are November to February daily 9am to 1pm and 4 to 7pm. Don't expect old-fashioned millstones though, this is high-tech stainless steel and high-speed bottling.

If you'd just like to try and buy some, head for **Panaceite**—a smart shop and bar at Calle Bernabé Soriano 1 (*℗* **95-310-01-47**), just round the corner from the tourist office, behind the cathedral.

Plaza de Santa Luisa de Marillac s/n. ✆ **95-324-80-68.** Free admission. Winter Tues–Sat 9am–8:30pm, Sun 9am–2:45pm; summer Tues–Sat 9am–9:30pm, Sun 9:30am–2:45pm. You must go on foot: in the Old Quarter of Jaén, follow signs indicating either Baños Arabes or Barrio de la Magdalena.

Iglesia de la Magdalena   Of the many churches worth visiting in Jaén, La Magdalena is the oldest and most interesting. This Gothic church was once an Arab mosque. The minaret of the former mosque is now the bell tower of the church. If you wander to the back of the church, you can see a courtyard that was used by Arab worshippers for ritualized ablutions. In the cloisters are several tombstones from the era of the Roman occupation of Andalusia.

Plaza de la Magdalena. ✆ **95-319-03-09/**95-319-00-31. Free admission. Tues–Thurs and Sat 10am–1pm and 5–8pm (7–9pm July and Aug). Closed Fri mornings. Sun 9am–1pm.

Museo Provincial ★   In this dusty, offbeat, and little-visited museum, one of the finest Spanish collections of pre-Roman artifacts is found, along with other treasures. The collection, housed in a 1547 mansion, includes Roman mosaics, a Mudéjar arch, and many ceramics from the early Iberian, Greek, and Roman periods. On the upper floor is an exhibit of Pedro Berruguete paintings, including *Christ at the Column.* Look for a paleo-Christian sarcophagus from Martos. In the most modern section stand nearly a dozen life-size Iberian sculptures that were unearthed in 1975 near the village of Porcuna. The museum is between the bus and train stations.

Paseo de la Estación 27. ✆ **95-331-33-39.** Admission 1.50€. Tues 2:30–8:30pm; Wed–Sat 9am–8pm; Sun 9am–2:30pm.

WHERE TO STAY

Hotel Condestable Iranzo ⚔   There's no old-fashioned Andalusian charm here. This eight-floor hotel occupying an entire corner of one of the town's main squares is no beauty, but it is well located, has a good view of the castle and the mountains, and offers a wide range of facilities. The midsize rooms are functional and comfortable, all with bathrooms containing tub/shower combos. The on-site restaurant serves good, inexpensive Andalusian food.

Paseo de la Estación 32, 23008 Jaén. ✆ **95-322-28-00.** Fax 95-326-38-07. 159 units. 80€–115€ double. AE, MC, V. Parking 14€. **Amenities:** Restaurant; bar; room service. *In room:* A/C, TV, hair dryer, Wi-Fi.

Husa Europa ⚔   In the commercial and historical center of Jaén, this little hotel is cozy and contemporary at the same time. It was closed for renovation work at the time of writing, so should continue to offer good value for money when it reopens.

Plaza de Belén 1, 23001 Jaén. ✆ **95-322-27-00.** Fax 95-322-26-92. www.husa.es. 37 units. 70€ double; 83€ triple. Rates may include continental breakfast. AE, DC, MC, V. Parking 9€. **Amenities:** Cafeteria; bar; bicycles; nonsmoking rooms; rooms for those w/limited mobility. *In room:* A/C, TV, hair dryer, Wi-Fi.

Infanta Cristina   After the Parador de Jaén, this hotel is the best place to stay in town, as long as your expectations aren't too high. Instead of a dramatic mountaintop perch like the parador, Infanta Cristina is in the modern part of the city near the train station. The corner hotel is serviceable and well run; spacious bedrooms have modern wooden furniture and views. The on-site restaurant, Az-zait, attracts non-residents for its regional specialties. A complete meal costs 35€ to 40€.

Av. de Madrid, 23009 Jaén. ✆ **95-326-30-40.** Fax 95-327-42-96. www.hotelinfantacristina.com. 83 units. 64€–130€ double. AE, DC, MC, V. Parking 8€. **Amenities:** Restaurant; cafeteria; babysitting; gym; outdoor pool (summer only); room service; rooms for those w/limited mobility. *In room:* A/C, TV, hair dryer, minibar, Wi-Fi.

Parador de Jaén ★ Five kilometers (3 miles) to the east on the hill overlooking the city, this castle is one of the government's showplace *paradores*. In the 10th century, the castle was a Muslim fortress surrounded by high protective walls and approached only by a steep winding road. The castle is still reached by the same road; you enter through a three-story-high baronial hallway. Rooms are midsized with canopied beds and good-sized tile bathrooms equipped with tub/shower combos. The most impressive feature of the bedrooms is the panoramic views of mountains. It's without doubt still the best place to stay in Jaén, but whilst the location is exceptional, it does at times feel a little as if it's trading on its reputation.

Castillo de Santa Catalina, 23001 Jaén. © **95-323-00-00.** Fax 95-323-09-30. www.parador.es. 45 units. 151€–199€ double. AE, DC, MC, V. Free parking. **Amenities:** Restaurant; bar; seasonal outdoor pool; room service; nonsmoking rooms. *In room:* A/C, TV, hair dryer, minibar.

WHERE TO DINE

Casa Antonio ★★ ANDALUSIAN Some of the best Andalusian food in the province is served here in a traditional setting of tiny dining rooms decorated with contemporary paintings and dark-wood paneling. Recommended items include mushrooms in a cream sauce served with prawns and black olives, scallops with mashed potatoes, and tender roast suckling pig baked with potatoes, Castilian style.

Calle Fermín Palma 3. © **95-327-02-62.** Reservations recommended. Main courses 12€–40€. AE, DC, MC, V. Tues–Sat 1:30–4:15pm and 9–11:30pm. Closed Aug.

Casa Paco 𝄞 ANDALUSIAN In the center of Jaén, this is a simple place with wood panels and a few tables favored by blue-collar workers with big appetites and small budgets. The food isn't haute, but in the words of the chef, "it's honest and true food, even noble." Try his oven-baked hake (*merluza*) or a particularly delightful trout grilled with lemon grass Thai-style. A well-flavored tenderloin of beef is also featured, as are omelets, a favorite being one made with fresh mushrooms, ham, and prawns.

Flores 4. © **95-325-54-41.** Reservations required. Main courses 10€–16€. AE, DC, MC, V. Mon–Tues 7am–6pm; Wed–Sun 7am–11pm. Closed Aug.

Casa Vicente ★ ANDALUSIAN This modern restaurant is praised locally for the quality of its tapas and its wine. The area surrounding the town is known for its vegetables, which are showcased in such dishes as *espinaca esparragada* (spinach with vegetable sauce) and *alcachofa natural* (artichokes in garlic). For a main dish, try the *lomo de orsa mozárabe* (lamb in sweet-and-sour sauce) or *bacalao encebollado* (salt cod sautéed with onions and sweet peppers). Two local desserts are rice pudding and *manjarblanco mozárabe* (Moorish-style fudge).

Calle Cristo Rey 3. © **95-323-22-22.** Reservations recommended. Main courses 16€–20€; set menu 40€. MC, V. Tues–Sun 1:30–4pm and 8–11:30pm. Closed Aug.

El Mirador INTERNATIONAL/ANDALUSIAN Decorated like a Swiss chalet, this local favorite serves the best barbecue in town. Patrons opt for a seat on its big terrace to enjoy the specialties of the evening in big portions at affordable prices. For starters, there are two versions of the cold tomato soups that are famous in Andalusia: gazpacho and *salmorejo*. Or begin with fresh anchovies marinated with onion and green pepper or a homemade pâté of partridge. Move onto one of the barbecued meats as a main course—roast suckling pig is particularly popular. The place has lots of character, and when there's a full house, it feels like a party.

Carretera Los Villares Km 5. ✆ **95-323-51-31.** Reservations recommended. Main courses 8€–16€. AE, DC, MC, V. Tues–Sun 1:30–4pm and 9–11pm. Closed 2 weeks in Aug.

Mesón Río Chico 🍴 ANDALUSIAN   Serving authentic regional cuisine, this informal restaurant has been around since 1962 in a simple modern building in the heart of Jaén. Menu items include strongly flavored versions of hake, beefsteak, roasted pork, and chicken. Because there's room for only 45 diners at a time, it's important to reserve in advance. Many locals call this their favorite restaurant in town, even though many recipes and dishes haven't changed since the 1960s.

Calle Nueva 12. ✆ **95-324-08-02.** Reservations recommended. Main courses 8€–17€. MC, V. Tues–Sat 2–4pm and 9–11pm; Sun noon–3:30pm.

JAÉN AFTER DARK

If you fancy some **tapas and *copas*** (glasses of wine) try heading for the clutch of narrow alleys just to the west of the cathedral. Head up Calle Maestra and take the first tiny turn right. You'll find yourself in Calle Francisco Martin Mora which leads onto **Calle Arco del Consuelo**—a narrow dogleg street with several busy and very authentic tapas bars along it. My favorite is the slightly more modern **Café del Consuelo,** Arco del Consuelo 6, (✆ **95-323-89-03**). **Café Moka** at the far end at number 11 (✆ **95-323-10-45**) is also quite fun and good for coffee and people-watching earlier in the day too. Tapas are mostly served free of charge in Jaén, just buy a drink and, as if by magic, a snack will appear beside it.

For a night of Andalusian flamenco, head on up Calle Maestra to **Peña Flamenca Jaén,** Calle Maestra 11 (✆ **95-323-17-10** or ✆ 64-620-26-56; flamenco jaen@terra.es). Some rising flamenco artists strut their stuff here. Artists perform on a wooden stage that's overly adorned with regional artifacts, and there's a wooden bar. Hours are Monday to Friday from 8pm to 1am, Sunday from noon to 11am. There is no cover, and tapas range from 1.50€ to 6€.

A hip bar, **Moët,** Avenida de Andalucía (✆ **95-327-30-94**), near the train station, attracts a young crowd, especially students, with its DJ-spun Iberian pop. At the weekend it's a disco. There's no cover but mixed drinks cost 4.25€ and up. Beer is only 2€. Tapas cost from 2€ to 6€. Open Monday to Wednesday 4pm to 4:30am, Thursday to Saturday 4pm until "we have to toss out the last drunk," as the waiter put it.

Baeza ★★

45km (28 miles) NE of Jaén

Historic Baeza (known to the Romans as *Vilvatia*), with its Gothic and Plateresque buildings and cobblestone streets, is one of the best-preserved old towns in Spain. At twilight, when lanterns hanging from walls of plastered stone light the narrow streets, you might feel you've stumbled back into the 15th century. The town's heyday was in the 16th and 17th centuries. Even if you don't go inside many monuments—and, indeed, many of the most charming buildings aren't open to the public—you can still enjoy the architecture and atmosphere by strolling through the Barrio Monumental and admiring the old buildings.

ESSENTIALS

GETTING THERE   The nearest important rail junction, receiving **trains** from Madrid and most of Andalusia, is the **Estación Linares-Baeza** (✆ 90-232-03-20; www.renfe.es), 14km (8½ miles) west of Baeza's center. There is one train per day from Córdoba which leaves at 10am and takes 1½ hours, and four per day from Madrid taking 3½ hours. There are three daily trains from Jaén with a journey time of 40 minutes. **Alsina Graells** (✆ 90-242-22-42; www.alsa.es) runs a bus service connecting the station with Baeza but with only three to four departures a day, you're best off just catching a taxi to complete your journey.

Around 20 daily **buses** arrive in Baeza from Ubeda; the ride is 15 minutes long. From Jaén, there are 15 buses per day with a trip time of around 45 minutes, arriving at the bus station at Avenida Puche Pardo (✆ 95-374-24-53). The bus station is around a 15-minute walk from the historic center.

To reach Baeza by car from Jaén (see earlier), follow Route A-316 northeast for 45km (28 miles). The town is 308km (191 miles) south of Madrid.

VISITOR INFORMATION   The **tourist office,** at the Plaza del Pópulo s/n 23440 (✆ 95-377-99-82; www.andalucia.org), is open Monday to Friday 9am to 7:30pm and 9:30am to 3pm at weekends.

EXPLORING BAEZA

Baeza's main square, the **Plaza del Pópulo ★**, is a two-story open colonnade. The buildings here date in part from the 16th century, and the tourist office, where you can get a town map, is housed in one of the most interesting. Look for the fountain containing four half-effaced lions, the **Fuente de los Leones,** which may have been brought here from the Roman town of Cantulo.

Head south and uphill along the Cuesta de San Gil then take a left at little Plaza Cruz Verde down narrow Calle Commendadores to the Gothic and Renaissance **Santa Iglesia Catedral ★**, Plaza de la Fuente de Santa María (✆ 95-374-04-44), built in the 16th century on the foundations of an earlier mosque. In the interior, remodeled by Andrés de Vandelvira (architect of Jaén's cathedral) and his pupils, the carved wood and the brilliant painted *rejas* (iron screens) are particularly impressive, as is the **Gold Chapel.** The edifice possesses one of the most important Corpus Christi icons in Spain, *La Custodia de Baeza.* You can climb the clock tower for a panoramic view of town. The cathedral is open October to May Monday to Friday daily 10:30am to 2pm and 4 to 6pm (June to September open later until 7pm). At weekends it's open 10:30am to 7pm (closing an hour earlier at 6pm on Sunday). Admission is 4€.

After leaving the cathedral, walk around into lovely Plaza de la Fuente de Santa María with its old and ornate fountain in the center. And take a look, too, at the ornate north doorway of the cathedral the **Puerta de la Luna (Moon Door).**

Opposite the cathedral across the plaza on the other side of the fountain is the **Seminario Concilar de San Felipe Neri** (✆ 95-374-27-75). The ornate two-story patio is worth a look. You can duck inside it by walking down Calle San Felipe Neri to the right. Just past this entrance to the Seminario you come to the **Palacio de Jabalquinto ★** (✆ 95-374-27-75), a beautiful example of civil architecture in the flamboyant Gothic style, built by Juan Alfonso de Benavides, a relative of King Ferdinand. Its facade is filled with interesting decorative elements, and there's a simple Renaissance-style courtyard with marble columns. Inside, two lions guard the ornate Baroque stairway. Visiting hours are Monday to Friday 9am to 2pm. Admission is free.

Right opposite the Palacio de Jabalquinto across Plaza Santa Cruz is tiny **Iglesia de Santa Cruz.** Built sometime in the 1200s, this is the town's oldest church and one of the few Romanesque buildings still standing in Andalusia. Inside you can see frescoes of the Virgin Mary, San Sebastián, and St Catherine. Admission is free and hours are usually Monday to Saturday 11am to 1pm and 4 to 6pm, and Sunday noon to 2pm.

Next door, a small **museum** displays florid icons, ornately gilded carriages, and regional artifacts. Its most interesting exhibits are bizarre costumes worn in the annual procession of the religious brotherhood of Santa Vera Cruz at the *Semana Santa.* Don't make a special point of visiting the museum, but if the doors are open, you might pop in for a look. Admission is free and it is usually open Monday to Saturday 11am to 1pm and 4 to 7pm, and Sunday noon to 2pm. But don't count on those hours being honored.

Completing this cluster of historic buildings, the **Antigua Universidad** (⏱ **95-374-04-44**), the town's university, is just down Calle Beato Juan de Avila to the right of the Palacio de Jabalquinto. Founded in 1595, it's one of the oldest in the area. The poet Antonio Machado taught French here from 1912 to 1919; ask for a key to visit his classroom. Open daily 10am to 2pm and 4 to 7pm. Admission is free.

Before leaving Baeza, you might take in the facades of two more buildings. The **Ayuntamiento** (the old town hall) is at Plaza Cardenal Benavides, northwest of the landmark Plaza del Pópulo, across the Plaza de la Constitución. It was designed by the same Andrés de Vandelvira who worked on the cathedral and the facade is a stellar example of the Plateresque style. Between the balconies note the coat of arms of Philip II, among others. Sometimes a custodian will let you in for a look at the Salón de Plenos, the primary hall of the building, noted for its carved and painted woodwork.

Just a short stroll west of the Ayuntamiento is the **Convento de San Francisco,** Calle de San Francisco, another of Vandelvira's architectural masterpieces, dating from the 16th century. In the 1800s an earthquake struck the building, partially destroying it; it was further damaged when the French army came through. Although it's been partially restored, wander around to the rear of the building and you'll see the remains of an ornate facade now surrounded by a supporting steel framework.

To cap your visit to Baeza, head for the park on top of the old city wall. To reach it, stroll back through the historic core to reach Paseo de las Murallas. From here there's a **panoramic view ★** of the Guadalquivir Valley, studded with olive trees.

WHERE TO STAY

Hospedería Fuentenueva ★ ⛊ Within walking distance of the town's major monuments, this cozy boutique hotel occupies a renovated 19th-century home. The antique trappings of the building itself are in direct contrast to the post-*movida*, ultra-*moderno* bedrooms, often with minimalist furniture and cramped but contemporary bathrooms that in some cases retain the building's original stonemasonry. A walled-in garden in back has a terrace and a tiny swimming pool, all of it designed in a style cool enough for Madrid or Barcelona.

Calle Carmen 15, 23440 Baeza. ⏱ **95-374-31-00.** Fax 95-374-32-00. www.fuentenueva.com. 12 units. 78€–88€ double. AE, MC, V. Free parking. **Amenities:** Cafeteria; library; outdoor pool; room service; nonsmoking rooms; Wi-Fi. *In room:* A/C, TV, hair dryer.

Hotel TRH Baeza In the 16th century, this building was a convent for the Clarisas order. Today it's a government-rated three-star hotel on a large square in the heart of the Old Town. The traditionally furnished midsize bedrooms are comfortable, each with a private tiled bathroom; antiques are scattered throughout. The hotel also operates a restaurant specializing in regional food and international specialties, as well as a snack bar. There are some great deals online if you book early.

Calle Concepción 3, 23440 Baeza. ⓒ **95-374-81-52** or ⓒ 95-374-81-30. Fax 95-374-25-19. www. trhhoteles.es. 84 units. 55€–115€ double; 70€–160€ suite. AE, DC, MC, V. Parking 11€. **Amenities:** Restaurant; bar; babysitting; rooms for those w/limited mobility. *In room:* A/C, TV, hair dryer, minibar, Wi-Fi.

La Casona del Arco ★★ 🎁 Puerta de la Luna (see below) probably just beats this lovely boutique hotel into second place, but there's little to choose between them. La Casona is housed in a lovely renovation of two town houses in the town's historic core. Rooms are midsized with wooden floors, wood-beamed ceilings, and antique furniture. Bright bathrooms combine ancient stonework and hand-painted tiles with modern fixtures and fittings. The bathrooms of the four junior suites are equipped with hydromassage baths. There's a cool terrace with an inviting swimming pool tucked away at the back of the hotel too, and a small spa with Jacuzzi and a massage menu.

Calle Sacramento 3, 23440 Baeza. ⓒ **95-374-72-08.** Fax 95-374-72-09. www.lacasonadelarco.com. 18 units. 75€–107€ double; 112€–139€ junior suite. MC, V. **Amenities:** Bar. *In room:* A/C, TV, Wi-Fi.

La Loma 🌿 This small, traditional Andalusian house is generally conceded to be the town's best bang for the buck, considering its comfort and its low prices. Unfortunately its location is not good for sightseeing as it's right on the outskirts of town on the road to Ubeda, so you must have a car. Modern rooms are exceedingly comfortable and pleasant enough, and the hospitable owners are friendly. Bedrooms are a bit small with wooden furniture and tiled floors. More tiles are used in the well-maintained and tidy little bathrooms. Many bedrooms open onto beautiful views of the Guadalquivir River, and the location is 1km (½ mile) east of the historic core.

Carretera de Ubeda, 23440 Baeza. ⓒ **95-374-33-02.** Fax 95-374-82-66. 10 units. 45€ double. MC, V. Free parking. **Amenities:** Restaurant. *In room:* A/C, TV.

Palacete Santa Ana ★ 🌿 A 5-minute walk from the historic center near the town hall, this restored 16th-century mansion is one of the best places in town to stay and it offers great value for money too. It's Andalusian in character with a strong Moorish influence in the blue tiles and stones, and an interior patio with a bubbling fountain. Attractively decorated and comfortably furnished bedrooms are midsize. In 2005 Palacete Santa Ana added 13 units in three houses that were built in the 16th century and, like the mansion, were restored. Each room is distinctively decorated according to one of many styles present in Andalusia since the 16th century.

Santa Ana Vieja 9, 23440 Baeza. ⓒ **95-374-16-57.** Fax 95-374-16-57. www.palacetesantana.com. 26 units. 50€–80€ double. AE, MC, V. **Amenities:** Laundry service. *In room:* A/C, TV, hair dryer, minibar (in some).

Puerta de la Luna ★★ 🎁 In the oldest part of the historic zone, a stone's throw from the cathedral, this gem of a 17th-century palace has been restored with modern comforts but with its Andalusian architectural features intact. A massive restoration effort went into this place using a decorator with an obvious sense of style. Every comfortable room has a different decor and a unique personality. It is housed in three buildings, each linked by a courtyard. In Baeza, the palace comes as a surprise as it has its own outdoor pool and spa facilities, plus the delightful restaurant and bar, **La Pintada** (see below), serving a first-rate cuisine with many regional dishes.

Calle Canónigo Melgares Raya 7, 23440 Baeza. © **95-374-70-19.** Fax 95-374-70-95. www.hotelpuert-adelaluna.es. 44 units. 77€–165€ double; 135€–255€ suite. AE, DC, MC, V. Parking 15€. **Amenities:** Restaurant; bar; babysitting; fitness center; outdoor pool; room service; sauna and spa; nonsmoking rooms; rooms for those w/limited mobility. *In room:* A/C, TV, hair dryer, minibar, Wi-Fi.

WHERE TO DINE

Casa Juanito ★ 👔 ANDALUSIAN   This restaurant is a drive away from the historic center on the outskirts of town on the road to Ubeda, but for foodies it's worth the journey. Owner Juan Luis Pedro Salcedo is a devotee of the lost art of Jaén cookery, and revives ancient recipes in his frequently changing specials. He runs a small olive oil outlet and meals are made with only his own produce. Game is served in season, and many vegetable dishes incorporate ham. Among the savory and well-prepared menu items are *habas* (beans), filet of beef with tomatoes and peppers, partridge in pastry crust, house-style cod, and venison.

In the Hotel Juanito, Plaza del Arca del Agua s/n. © **95-374-00-40.** www.juanitobaeza.com. Reservations required on weekends. Main courses 15€–35€. MC, V. Sun–Mon 1:30–3:30pm; Tues–Sat 1:30–3:30pm and 8–10:30pm. Closed 1st 2 weeks of July.

La Gondola ANDALUSIAN   In the very heart of the Renaissance town, this is one of the most convenient places to dine when you're exploring the town's monuments. The decor is in a traditional regional style, warm and inviting. The staff is cordial and helpful in guiding you through the menu of regional dishes. The fresh fish dishes, especially the salmon with a Champagne-like wine sauce and the grilled hake (*merluza*) with fresh, locally grown vegetables, are particularly good. Main dishes such as pork cutlets and barbecued entrecôte of veal with green peppers are also satisfying. Desserts are made fresh daily.

Portales Carbonería 13. © **95-374-29-84.** www.asadorlagondola.com. Reservations recommended. Main courses 10€–17€; fixed-price menus 15€–35€. AE, DC, MC, V. Daily 8am–4:30pm and 8pm–midnight.

La Pintada ★★ ANDALUSIAN/MODERN   The best hotel in town also has one of the best restaurants. On the ground floor of the Hotel Puerta de la Luna (see above) with a bright airy dining room and tables on the romantic terrace, chef Xavi Xufré and his team turn out modern, stylish dishes using the best locally sourced ingredients. You might start with warm duck salad with Roquefort cheese and raspberry vinaigrette, then move on to cod filet baked with garlic and spinach mousseline or entrecôte of veal with green peppers and finish with the house special tiramisu.

Calle Canónigo Melgares Raya 7 © **95-374-70-19**. www.hotelpuertadelaluna.es Reservations recommended. Main courses 14€–20€. AE, MC, V. Tues–Sat 8pm–midnight.

Ubeda ★★

57km (35 miles) NE of Jaén

A former stronghold of the Arabs, and today often called the "Florence of Andalusia," Ubeda is a Spanish National Landmark filled with ornate golden-brown Renaissance palaces and tile-roofed, whitewashed houses. The best way to discover its charm is to wander the cobblestone streets and squares of the **Casco Antiguo (Old**

Ubeda

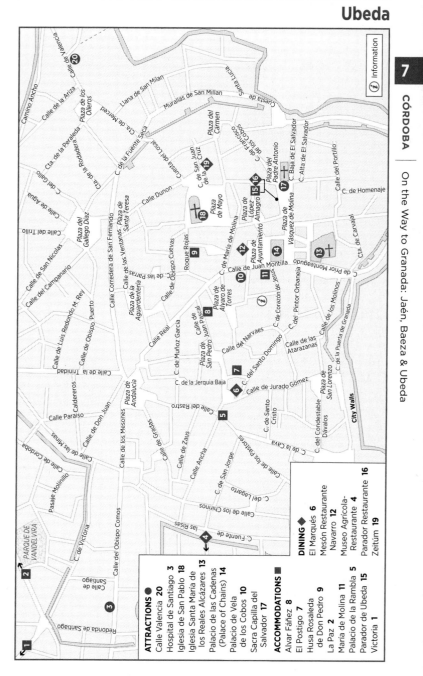

(i) Information

ATTRACTIONS ●
Calle Valencia **20**
Hospital de Santiago **3**
Iglesia de San Pablo **18**
Iglesia Santa Maria de los Reales Alcázares **13**
Palacio de las Cadenas (Palace of Chains) **14**
Palacio de Vela de los Cobos **10**
Sacra Capilla del Salvador **17**

ACCOMMODATIONS ■
Alvar Fáñez **8**
El Postigo **7**
Husa Rosaleda de Don Pedro **9**
La Paz **2**
Maria de Molina **11**
Palacio de la Rambla **5**
Parador de Ubeda **15**
Victoria **1**

DINING ◆
El Marqués **6**
Mesón Restaurante Navarro **12**
Museo Agricola-Restaurante **4**
Parador Restaurante **16**
Zeitúm **19**

Town) ★★★. There's also a delightful parador here in a renovated ducal palace where you might stop in for lunch. Allow time, too, for a stroll through Ubeda's shops, specializing in crafts like esparto grass carpets and pottery.

ESSENTIALS

GETTING THERE For information on **trains** serving the area, see "Getting There" under "Baeza," earlier in this chapter.

There are 10 **buses** daily to Baeza, less than 10km (6¼ miles) away, and a similar number to Jaén. Seven buses per day go to the railway station at Linares-Baeza, where a train can take you virtually anywhere in Spain. Bus services to and from Córdoba (4 times daily), Seville (4 times daily), and Granada (8 times daily) are also available. **Alsina Graells** (© 90-242-22-42; www.alsa.es) runs most of these services. Ubeda's bus station is in the modern town, on Calle San José (© 95-375-21-57). It's about a 15-minute walk to the historic center.

To **drive,** turn off the Madrid–Córdoba road, head east for Linares, and then move on to Ubeda, a detour of 42km (26 miles). The turnoff is at the junction with the A-32/N-322. From Jaén, the capital of the province, take the A-316 northeast for 57km (35 miles).

VISITOR INFORMATION The **tourist office,** Calle Baja del Marques 4 (© 95-377-92-04; www.andalucia.com), is open Monday to Friday from 8:30am to 3:30pm, Saturday and Sunday from 10am to 2pm. When I visited they were planning to extend opening hours to 7:30pm daily depending on staffing.

EXPLORING UBEDA

The highlight of a visit to Ubeda is its trio of central squares flanked by wonderfully ornate Renaissance buildings and churches.

Start your tour at **Plaza del Ayuntamiento** at the center. The famous Spanish architect Andrés de Vandelvira designed many of the most impressive mansions of old Ubeda. The architect's crowning achievement is the privately owned **Palacio de Vela de los Cobos,** which is just off the top of the Plaza del Ayuntamiento along Calle Juan Montilla. It was designed in the mid-1500s for Francisco de Vela de los Cobos, the town's magistrate. Its impressive facade has an arcaded gallery and the L-shaped architecture of the building is most unusual. At the south end of the plaza is the town hall—also known as the **Palacio de las Cadenas (Palace of Chains).** It takes its name from the decorative iron chains once fixed to the columns of its main portal. The interior patio of slender arches was also designed by Andrés de Vandelvira. You can enter it from Plaza del Ayuntamiento and walk across it to exit onto Plaza Vázquez de Molina behind.

Plaza Vázquez de Molina ★★ behind the town hall is perhaps the most harmonious square in Andalusia. Opposite the town hall is the **Iglesia Santa María de los Reales Alcázares.** It dates mainly from the 17th century, although its cloisters predate the building by at least a century. Inside you see a series of beautiful **chapels ★** protected by stunning **wrought-iron grilles ★**, most of them created by Master Bartolomé. *Note:* The church was closed for renovation work at the time of updating.

To the east of the town hall, still on Plaza Vázquez de Molina, you come to the town's **parador,** one of the best places to stay and dine and worth a look inside if you're passing. And right next to it at the east end of the plaza there's the wonderful **Sacra Capilla del Salvador** ★★. See below for a more detailed description.

Before the completion of Plaza Vázquez de Molina, the third of these delightful squares, **Plaza Primero de Mayo,** was the heart of the Old Town. Today it's the scene of an outdoor market. So-called heretics were burned here during the Inquisition. You'll also find the interesting **Iglesia de San Pablo** ★ here. (See below.)

Finally return to Plaza Vázquez de Molina and wander down any of the streets heading south until you reach the old town walls. From here there are expansive **views** ★ across the olive-groved countryside to the hillsides behind.

Hospital de Santiago   On the western edge of town off Calle del Obispo Coros, the Hospital of Santiago, built by Andrés de Vandelvira, completed in 1575, is still in use. Over the main entrance is a carving of St James "the Moorslayer" in a traditional pose on horseback. The chapel has some marvelous woodcarvings. Today the hospital is a cultural venue, hosting concerts and containing a minor modern art museum.

Av. Cristo Rey. © **95-375-08-42.** Free admission. Mon-Fri 8am-2:30pm and 3:30-10pm; Sat-Sun 10am-2:30pm and 4-9:30pm.

Iglesia de San Pablo ★   This Gothic church in the center of the Old Town is almost as fascinating as the Sacra Capilla del Salvador (see below). The Gothic San Pablo is famous for its 1511 **south portal** ★ in the florid Isabelline style opening onto Plaza 1 de Mayo, and for its **chapels** ★ decorated with beautiful wrought-iron grilles. Vandelvira himself designed the "Heads of the Dead Chapel," which is the most stunning. Also see the richly carved Chapel of Las Mercedes in the Isabelline style.

Plaza 1 de Mayo. © **95-375-06-37.** Free admission. Mon-Sat 11am-midday and 5-7:30pm (closed Mon evening); Sun 12:15-1:30pm (and 7-9pm in summer).

Sacra Capilla del Salvador ★★   One of the grandest examples of Spanish Renaissance architecture, this church was designed in 1536 by Diego de Siloé as a family chapel and mausoleum for Francisco de los Cobos, secretary of the Holy Roman Emperor Charles V. The richly embellished exterior portal is mere window dressing for the wealth of **decoration inside** ★ the church, including the truly fabulous **sacristy** ★★ designed by Andrés de Vandelvira with medallions, caryatids, *atlantes*, and coffered decorations and ornamentations. The many sculptures and altarpieces and the spectacular rose windows are also of special interest.

Plaza Vázquez de Molina s/n. © **95-375-81-50.** Admission 3€ adults, 1€ children. Mon-Sat 10am-2pm and 5-7:30pm; Sun 11:15am-2pm and 5-8pm.

SHOPPING

Ubeda is hailed as "the crafts capital of Andalusia" and many visitors come here just to shop. Walk its ancient streets, particularly those just off the Plaza del Ayuntamiento and you'll come upon a good number of interesting shops where artisans sell stained glass, stone carvings, woven baskets, wrought iron, and more.

Pottery is king, however. The town's legendary potter was Pablo Tito, whose works are highly valued collectors' items today. He left his trade secrets to his offspring, who still carry on in his tradition. Friendly, outgoing **Juan Tito** is behind the potter's wheel in his workshop and showroom on Plaza del Ayuntamiento at no. 12. It's usually open daily from 9am to 2pm and 4 to 8pm (© **95-375-13-02**). The highly decorated blue and green jugs and plates are all made by hand.

Before potters were sufficiently famous and wealthy to open workshops on the main square, **Calle Valencia,** just outside the old town walls about a 15-minute walk to the northeast, was "pottery row" and it remains so today. Another of Pablo's offspring, **Paco Tito** (📞 **95-375-14-96**), has an attractive workshop and showroom at Calle Valencia 22, which is usually open daily from 9am to 2pm and 4 to 8pm. His specialty is making clay sculptures based on characters from *Don Quixote.* Yet a third potter drawing upon the Tito legend is **Melchor Tito,** whose studio is open daily from 9am to 2pm and 4 to 8pm at Calle Valencia 44 (📞 **95-375-36-92**). He was actually the son-in-law of the fabulous Pablo and specializes in a stunning green glaze pottery. Another specialist in the green glaze pottery identified with Ubeda is **Antonio Almazara,** Calle Valencia 34 (📞 **95-375-12-00**). He's available daily from 9am to 2pm and 4 to 9pm.

WHERE TO STAY
Expensive
Palacio de la Rambla ★★ 🎒   To really sample the atmosphere of one of the many old palace houses that line the streets and squares of Ubeda, why not stay in one? Don't expect high-tech luxury here, but do expect a truly memorable stay. The front entrance of this old house is fortress-like, with colored tiles in the Mudéjar style. Inside, the cloistered courtyard has Plateresque and Renaissance-style carvings, granite columns, and forests of ivy. There are eight rooms. The spacious manorial rooms boast many of their original furnishings, but large bathrooms and air conditioning have been installed. Each is individually furnished, often with antiques, tapestries, *objets d'art,* and other remnants of old Spain's aristocratic life. It all feels frozen in time. You can still visit two incredibly formal salons, seemingly waiting for a visit from Philip II.

Plaza del Marqués 1, 23400 Ubeda. 📞 **95-375-01-96.** Fax 95-375-02-67. www.palaciodelarambla.com. 8 units. 120€ double; 140€ suite. Rates include buffet breakfast. AE, MC, V. Parking 10€. Closed Jan 7–30 and July 13–Aug 8. **Amenities:** Wi-Fi. *In room:* A/C, TV, hair dryer, minibar.

Parador de Ubeda ★★★   On the town's central square, this 16th-century palace-turned-parador shares an old paved plaza with the Sacra Capilla del Salvador and its dazzling facade. The formal entrance to this Renaissance palace leads to an enclosed patio, encircled by two levels of Moorish arches, where palms and potted plants sit on the tiled floors. The rooms are nearly two stories high, with beamed ceilings, tall windows, antiques, and reproductions. If you fancy splashing out, go for the Ducal room. The largest, most welcoming, elegant and comfortable of the rooms features the original palace flooring, coffered ceiling, and cornice. It also houses a pretty decorative fireplace where the only painting in the palace of the "Constable" himself hangs. A king-size bed and Jacuzzi in the bathroom complete the package.

Plaza Vázquez de Molina 1, 23400 Ubeda. 📞 **95-375-03-45.** Fax 95-375-12-59. www.parador.es. 36 units. 160€–175€ double; 240€–280€ suite. AE, DC, MC, V. **Amenities:** Restaurant; bar; babysitting; room service; sauna; nonsmoking rooms. *In room:* A/C, TV, hair dryer, minibar.

Moderate
Alvar Fáñez ★ 🎒   This well-designed hotel resulted from the radical overhaul of a 16th-century building in the late 1990s. There's a cozy cafe and bar at street level, and a restaurant where the tables spill into the hotel's glass-covered courtyard. The upper floors of the arcades around the courtyard have mirador-style glass windows

around the perimeter, making the place intimate, weather-tight, and very charming. Check out the covered veranda on the building's third (top) floor, where cane and rattan chairs provide deep seating amid flickering candles set on marble-topped tables. Bedrooms have comfortable, contemporary furniture; simple bathrooms have tubs and showers.

Calle Juan Pasquau 5, 23400 Ubeda. (C) **95-379-60-43.** Fax 95-375-71-97. www.alvarfanez.com. 14 units. 72€–119€ double. AE, DC, MC, V. **Amenities:** Restaurant; bar. *In room:* A/C, TV, minibar.

El Postigo ★ This bright modern addition to the hotel scene in Ubeda is a good mid-priced option within the historic center. Bedrooms are decorated in contemporary style with parquet wooden flooring and brown and red hues to the drapes and bed covers. Bathrooms are modern and stylish with good quality showers. Some rooms also have bathtubs. Outside at the rear of the hotel there's a small, but very pleasant, sun terrace and swimming pool, perfect for cooling off in the heat of the day. The hotel's restaurant is run by the same team that run Zeitúm (see below), so well worth a visit.

Calle Postigo 5, 23400 Ubeda. (C) **95-375-00-00.** Fax 95-375-53-09. www.hotelpostigo.com. 25 units. 70€–100€ double; 110€–140€ suite. MC, V. **Amenities:** Restaurant; bar. *In room:* A/C, TV, Wi-Fi.

Husa Rosaleda de Don Pedro 🍴 In the *zona monumental,* the attraction-rich center of town, this former family mansion has been virtually rebuilt and turned into a three-story hotel with a facade covered with balconies. Government-rated three stars, it is part of the Husa chain now and one of the better and more agreeable mid-bracket hotels in town. Bedrooms are a bit small but tastefully and comfortably furnished, each with a bathroom, also small, that is tiled and well laid out. Given its location, it offers good value for money.

Obispo Toral 2, 23400 Ubeda. (C) **95-379-61-11.** Fax 95-379-51-49. www.husa.es. 45 units. 55€–110€ double. AE, DC, MC, V. Parking 10€. **Amenities:** Restaurant; bar; outdoor pool; room service; rooms for those w/limited mobility, Wi-Fi. *In room:* A/C, TV, hair dryer, minibar (in some).

María de Molina ★ 🏨 The parador (above) is the number-one place to stay in Ubeda, but this hotel gives it serious competition, particularly on price. In a beautifully restored, once-decaying palace, the three-story hotel is in the center of the historic district. Much of the past, including stone-vaulted ceilings downstairs, hand-carved wooden doors, and marble arches over stairwells, was retained by the modern architects. The hotel opens onto a marble-columned atrium with chairs in the center and a skylight overhead. In contrast, the bedrooms are thoroughly modernized, ranging from rather cramped to spacious suites. I prefer the rooms with terraces or balconies, which you must book well in advance. Each room has a small bathroom with Andalusian tiles and equipped with tub and shower. Try to eat in the restaurant, it serves good Andalusian cuisine and is particularly inviting at night.

Plaza del Ayuntamiento, 23400 Ubeda. (C) **95-379-53-56.** Fax 95-379-36-94. www.hotel-maria-de-molina.com. 27 units. Sun–Thurs 83€–105€ double; 105€–134€ suite. AE, DC, MC, V. **Amenities:** Cafeteria; lap pool; room service; rooms for those w/limited mobility; Wi-Fi. *In room:* A/C, TV, minibar.

Inexpensive

La Paz 🍴 This hotel is so reasonably priced and agreeable that it's often filled with a diverse collection of value seekers. In the heart of the commercial district opposite the statue of a military hero, the architecture is Andalusian. Bedrooms are midsize and decorated in a simple Iberian fashion with wooden furniture and papered walls. Each comes with a small, tiled bathroom with a tub/shower combo. The traditional dark-wood furnishings contrast with the stark white walls. It's fairly well located given the price, being about a 10-minute walk from the historic center. But you may secure a cheaper rate at the Husa if you book well ahead. (See above.)

Calle Andalucía 1, 23400 Ubeda. ☎/fax **95-375-21-40.** www.hotel-lapaz.com. 40 units. 70€ double. AE, DC, MC, V. Parking 10€. **Amenities:** Bar; Internet. *In room:* A/C, TV, hair dryer.

Victoria 🍴 Near Plaza de Toros this is the town's rock-bottom bargain. The rooms are adequately comfortable, each with a little en-suite tiled bathroom with shower, but it's not a hotel to hang out in. For an affordable room for the night, it's fine. All rooms come with a small balcony, but there are no real hotel amenities to speak of. It's within a 10-minute walk of the historic center.

Alaminos 5, 23400 Ubeda. ☎ **95-375-29-52.** 15 units. 38€–40€ double. MC, V. *In room:* A/C, TV.

WHERE TO DINE

El Marqués 🍴 SPANISH   At the edge of a small, charming square a few steps from the also recommended Hotel Palacio de la Rambla, this is one of the best-managed and most highly recommended restaurants in town. In a setting of immaculate napery and bright lighting, uniformed waiters bring you tempting platters of Iberian cured ham, salads, grilled steaks or fish, soups, and desserts such as ice creams and flans. Especially memorable are the salmon in wine sauce and veal stew.

Plaza Marqués de la Rambla s/n. ☎ **95-375-72-55.** Main courses 10€–20€; fixed-price menu 18€. MC, V. June–Sept daily 1:30–4pm, Mon–Sat 8:30–11:30pm.

Mesón Restaurante Navarro ANDALUSIAN   On the north edge of lovely Plaza del Ayuntamiento, this amicable, lively restaurant does a thriving business selling beer and tapas every evening 'til about midnight. There are a handful of dining tables on the square outside and more in a back room, which seems like an afterthought to the heavy bar trade that packs in locals throughout the evening. Hearty, flavorful fare includes roast goat with tomatoes, hake medallions, and grilled swordfish.

Plaza del Ayuntamiento 2. ☎ **95-379-06-38.** Main courses 9€–18€; tapas 1.50€–6€. AE, DC, MC, V. Daily 11am–4pm and 8pm–2am.

Museo Agrícola-Restaurante ANDALUSIAN   This restaurant has an extraordinary decor and serves good, hearty food. The walls are hung with a museum's worth of agricultural tools and other regional artifacts. The chef is known locally for his succulent barbecued meat roasted over olive branches or almond tree leaves. Try the signature dish of oven-baked baby goat or a platter of the king prawns in white sauce, and start with the traditional local soup, *ajo blanco* (white garlic).

Calle San Cristóbal 17. ☎ **95-379-04-73.** Reservations recommended. Main courses 11€–20€. MC, V. Daily 10:30am–6pm and 8pm–midnight. Closed last 2 weeks in July.

Parador Restaurante ★ SPANISH/ANDALUSIAN   Ubeda's parador is the best place to dine for miles around. The cuisine isn't particularly creative, but it uses market-fresh ingredients prepared from decades-old recipes. From the wide-ranging menu, start with the typical regional cold soup with almonds or stuffed green peppers with partridge, stewed partridge with plums, or a salad with marinated partridge. The best fish dishes are the grilled monkfish in saffron sauce and the grilled sole with garlic-and-apple vinegar sauce. Meat eaters might go for oxtail in red wine sauce or stewed kid with pine nuts. The three-course *menú del parador* is a good bet.

Plaza Vázquez de Molina 1. ✆ **95-375-03-45.** Reservations recommended. Main courses 10€–22€; *menú del parador* 31€. AE, MC, V. Daily 1:30–4pm and 8:30–11pm.

Zeitúm ★ ANDALUSIAN/MODERN   If the rather heavy traditional approach to dining taken by the parador isn't to your liking, this new addition to the restaurant scene in Ubeda could be just the ticket. In an atmospheric, restored 17th-century house in the center of the historic zone, the three intimate dining rooms are the perfect setting for a memorable meal. Head chef Anselma Juarez Viedma's cuisine makes special use of the Jaén region's world-famous olive oil. Dishes are unfussy and interesting, like zuchini risotto with Parmesan shavings for starters, sirloin with deep fried onion and pine nuts, or salmon in raisin and sherry sauce.

Calle San Juan de la Cruz 10. ✆ **95-375-58-00.** Reservations recommended. Main courses 11€–20€. MC, V. Tues–Sun 1–4pm and 8:30–11:30pm.

GRANADA

About 660m (2,200 ft) above sea level in the foot-hills of the Sierra Nevada, Granada sprawls over two main hills, the Alhambra and the Albaicín, and is crossed by two rivers, the Genil and the Darro. This former stronghold of Moorish Spain is full of romance and folklore.

Granada's Alhambra, the hilltop fortress palace of the Nasrid kings, the last Muslim rulers of Spain, is one of the world's fabled landmarks. This monumental edifice is arguably Spain's greatest attraction. (Castilians claim that the Prado in Madrid is *número uno*.)

Washington Irving (*Tales of the Alhambra*) used the symbol of the city, the pomegranate (*granada*), to conjure a spirit of romance. In fact, the name probably derives from the Moorish word *karnattah*. Some historians have suggested that it comes from *Garnatha Alyehud*, the name of an old Jewish ghetto.

In Spain the city is known for its ties to another writer: Federico García Lorca. Born in 1898, this Spanish poet/dramatist was shot by soldiers in 1936 in the first months of the Spanish Civil War. During Franco's rule, García Lorca's works were banned in Spain, but he's once again honored in Granada, where he grew up, and worldwide.

Granada came to prominence in the 1200s at the peak of Muslim power. Even after Seville and Córdoba had fallen to the Catholic monarchs, Granada stood as the last surviving Islamic capital in Spain. It's where the sultans took their final stand against the Catholic invaders.

Fleeing Seville and Córdoba to the west, thousands of Moors flocked to this last stronghold. Many of them were artisans, and the Alhambra and other buildings testify to their skills.

On January 2, 1492, Granada fell to the Catholics when Boabdil, the last of the Moorish kings, turned his beloved city over to Ferdinand and Isabella. Isabella immediately began to "Christianize" Granada, ordering the construction of a cathedral and its adjoining royal chapel. She also ordered that Muslim mosques be repurposed for Christian use. Although some great architectural monuments were destroyed in the process, the Moorish district of the Albaicín fortunately remains more or less intact, allowing a glimpse at the architecture and atmosphere that existed during the Middle Ages.

Under subsequent Catholic monarchs, Granada prospered until the 1500s when it fell into a decline that lasted many years.

Today Granada is back, with an economy fueled by tourism, light industry, and the University of Granada.

Budget at least 2 days—preferably 3—to see this city of the pomegranate.

ORIENTATION

Getting There

BY PLANE   **Iberia** flies to Granada from Barcelona and Madrid, and several times a week from Palma de Majorca. Two planes a day land from Barcelona (trip time: 1 hr and 20 min.); four planes fly in from Madrid, taking 1 hour. Granada's **Federico García Lorca Granada-Jaén Airport** is 16km (10 miles) west of the center of town on Carretera Málaga; ✆ **90-240-47-04** or see www.aena.es for information. Other than a minor tourist information booth and an ATM, there are few services.

The airport bus run by **Autocares J. Gonzalez** (✆ **95-849-01 64;** 68-743-95-47; www.autocaresjosegonzalez.com) departs from the airport after each flight arrival, and costs 3€ one way. It has seven drop-off points across the city. The most central is no. 3 at Gran Vía de Colón. Trip time is 45 minutes. It returns to the airport hourly from 5:20am until 8pm every day. The tourist offices (see "Visitor Information" below) have timetables and further details. Taxis line up outside the terminals at the airport and charge about 17€ to the city's center.

BY TRAIN   The train station is **Estación de RENFE de Granada,** Av. Andaluces s/n (✆ **90-232-03-20;** www.renfe.es).

Granada is well linked with the most important Spanish cities, especially those of Andalusia. Four trains per day arrive from Seville, taking 3 hours, depending on the train, and costing 24€ for a one-way ticket. From Madrid, two daily trains arrive in Granada, taking 4 to 5 hours and costing 67€ per one-way ticket.

BY BUS   Granada is served by many more buses than trains. It has links to virtually all the major towns and cities in Andalusia, even to Madrid. The main bus terminal is **Estación de Autobuses de Granada,** Carretera de Jaén s/n (✆ **95-818-54-80**). One of the most heavily used bus routes is the one between Seville and Granada. Seven to ten buses run per day, costing 19€ for a one-way ticket. The trip takes 3 hours. You can also reach Granada in 3 hours on a bus from Córdoba, which costs 12€ for a one-way ticket with between seven and ten buses per day. If you're on the Costa del Sol, the run is just 2 hours, costing 9.20€ per one-way ticket. This is a very popular routing with 19 buses going back and forth between Granada and the coast per day. For bus information, call **Alsina Graells** (✆ **90-242-22-42;** www.alsa.es).

BY CAR   Granada is connected by superhighway to Madrid, Málaga, and Seville. Many sightseers prefer to make the drive from Madrid to Granada in 2 days rather than 1. If that is your plan, Jaén, Ubeda, and Baeza make good stopovers. See Chapter 7.

From Seville in the west, head east along the A-92, a good fast road which takes you all the way. Many visitors head to Granada from Málaga, capital of the Costa del Sol. Take the A-45 north from Málaga, cutting northeast onto the A-92M just before Antequera and joining the A-92 for its final run into Granada. From Madrid, head south on the A-4 (also called the E-5) until you reach the town of Bailén. Once here, continue south onto the A-44 (E-902) toward Jaén and on to Granada.

Granada is 415km (258 miles) south of Madrid, 122km (76 miles) northeast of Málaga, 261km (162 miles) east of Córdoba, and 250km (155 miles) east of Seville.

Visitor Information

Three tourist offices in the city center are run by a different branch of local bureaucracy. All offer maps, lists of hotels, and English staff, so just choose the closest. The **Provincial Tourist Office,** Plaza de Marian Pineda 10 bajo (© **95-824-71-46;** www.turgranada.es), is open Monday to Friday from 9am to 8pm, Saturday from 10am to 7pm, and Sunday from 10am to 3pm. The **Town Hall Tourist Office**, Ayuntamiento, Plaza del Carmen (© **95-824-82-20**) is open Monday to Saturday from 10am to 7pm and Sundays and holidays from 10am to 2pm. The **Andalucía Tourist Information Office,** Calle Santa Ana 4 (© **95-857-52-02** or © 822-59-90; www.andalucia.org), is open Monday to Friday from 9am to 7:30pm, Saturday, Sunday, and holidays from 9:30am to 3pm. This one has the best city maps, but the least helpful staff.

City Layout

There are free maps aplenty in Granada. The ones in hotel receptions aren't too bad, but those provided by the tourist offices are better. My favorite is the one from the Andalucía Tourist Office in Calle Santa Ana.

Essentially Granada is divided into **upper and lower towns.** Crowning the city is the **Alhambra district,** dominated by the graceful towers and ancient walls of the fortress palace of the Alhambra. The upper city is composed of two hills facing each other across the narrow gorge of the Río Darro. On the southern hill stands the Alhambra itself and the nearby summer palace of the **Generalife,** also once the gardens of the Nasrid kings.

The old Arab Quarter occupies the second, or northern, hill, the **Albaicín,** a former ghetto that's now a rapidly gentrifying district with many friendly restaurants and attractive boutique hotels. Expect tiny alleyways and peaceful little squares with fountains tinkling at their center. From higher up the Albaicín, the views across the valley to the Alhambra palace with the snowcapped peaks of the Sierra Nevada rising behind are truly spectacular. Ancient Arab baths and the remains of the old Moorish walls can still be seen here too.

Another satellite hill leads off from the Albaicín, wandering into the **Sacromonte district,** long a haven for Granada's famous Gypsies. A warren of little whitewashed homes trails out to a rocky mountainside riddled with caves.

Cuesta de Gomérez is one of the most important streets in the lower town, often called the **Cathedral district.** This is **centro Granada,** or "downtown," as Americans call it. Congested and compact, it is relatively easy to navigate. This is Granada's business center, home to most of its restaurants, shops, and hotels. It climbs uphill from the Plaza Nueva, the center of the modern city, to the Alhambra. At the Plaza Nueva, the east–west artery, **Calle de los Reyes Católicos,** goes to the heart of the 19th-century city and the towers of the cathedral. Granada's principal north–south artery is the **Gran Vía de Colón.**

Calle de los Reyes Católicos and the Gran Vía de Colón meet at the circular **Plaza de Isabel la Católica,** graced by a bronze statue of the Queen offering Columbus the Santa Fe agreement, which granted the rights to the epochal voyage to the New

World. Going west, Calle de los Reyes Católicos passes near the cathedral and other major sights in the downtown section of Granada. The street runs to **Puerta Real,** Granada's commercial hub, with many stores, hotels, cafes, and restaurants.

GETTING AROUND

Granada is extremely congested and also compact. Once you're in the district of your choice, you can walk to most points of interest. Don't even attempt to drive here.

By Bus

Buses in Granada are small enough and narrow enough to navigate some of the little streets leading from the town's commercial center to the Alhambra.

For short-term visitors, bus **no. 32** is the best choice, since it makes frequent runs from Old Granada to the Alhambra. Another good one is **no. 30,** or "Destination Alhambra," running from Plaza Nueva to the Alhambra. Two other handy routes are **no. 31,** which also leaves from Plaza Nueva and runs to the old Arabic Quarter, the Albaicín, and **no. 34** which takes the same route and then turns off up the winding hill to the Sacramonte district, location of the Gypsy caves and their flamenco shows. To hit the major boulevards, which are good for shopping, the **no. 3** bus runs from the bus terminal to Avenida de la Constitución, Gran Vía, and Plaza Isabel la Católica.

A single ride costs 1.20€. If you plan to use the buses even a little, it's cheaper and more convenient to purchase a *BonoBus* smart card from the driver. Cards come in 5€ and 10€ denominations and you pay an additional 2€ refundable deposit for the card itself. You can recharge the card with more cash as often as you need to. Using the card typically reduces the cost of a single journey to as little as 60 cents. A number of free bus rides are also included with a **Bono Turístico sightseeing pass** (see box "Buy A Bargain Pass" on p. 204).

For information about public transportation, pick up a map from one of the tourist offices or contact the local bus service provider: ✆ **90-071-09-00;** www.transportesrober.com.

By Taxi

Most trips in the city cost around 8€ to 12€. Taxis can be hailed in the streets; a green dome light indicates the vehicle is free. Taxis often line up outside first-class hotels, in the vicinity of the Alhambra, and at the landmark Plaza Nueva. To summon a cab, call **Radio Taxi** at ✆ **95-828-06-54.** Not all drivers speak English, so it's a good idea to have your destination written on a piece of paper if your Spanish isn't too good.

By Car

It's pretty nerve-wracking trying to get around Granada by driving. The one-way system is confusing and many of the old streets are very narrow. A rented car is best left for exploring the surrounding Sierra Nevada. Rental prices vary greatly, depending on the time of the year and the agency, but count on shelling out around 300€ per week, including unlimited mileage and insurance. For most rentals, you must be 21 or older and have had a valid national driver's license for at least a year.

Major car-rental agencies include: **Avis,** railway station, Av. de Andaluces s/n (☎ **95-825-23-58;** www.avis.com); and **Europcar,** Av. Andaluces s/n (☎ **95-829-50-65;** www.europcar.com). Europcar, Hertz, and Avis also maintain kiosks at the airport. Local car hire company **Auriga Crown,** Paseo de Violon, Palacio de Congreso Bajo no.3 (☎ **95-881-41-64;** en.aurigacrown.com) often works out cheapest.

By Bicycle

If you want to get around the old center more quickly and you're happy negotiating the traffic, hiring a bike for a day or half-day is a handy option. **Ecoway,** Plaza Cuchilleros (☎ **95-805-06-91** or ☎ 63-034-15-83; www.ecowayrental.com) offers bikes from 10€ for a half-day and 15€ for a full day. The office is open 10am to 6pm daily. It's on a side street off Plaza Nueva so it's very convenient. They speak English too.

By Foot

As the center of Granada is pretty compact, you'll spend much of your time walking. The hilly Albaicín and Alhambra districts particularly are best tackled on foot.

[FastFACTS] GRANADA

Bookstore The best English-language outlet is **Metro,** Calle Gracia 31 (☎ **95-826-15-65**), which has a large section, including travel guides and maps, in its English-language department. Open Monday to Friday from 10am to 2pm and 5 to 8:30pm, Saturday 11am to 2pm.

Consulates The nearest are in Seville. See Chapter 5.

Currency Exchange The best and most central office is the **Banco Santander,** Gran Vía 3 (☎ **95-821-73-00;** www.santander.com), open May to September Monday to Friday 9am to 2pm; October to April Monday to Saturday 8:30am to 2:30pm. Any of the main counters should be able to exchange money for you. Americans might want to use the branch of **Citibank**

a little farther along on the same side of Gran Vía. You'll find several 24-hour ATMs here on Gran Vía too and at Puerta Real and Plaza de Isabel la Católica.

Emergencies For emergencies that necessitate the police, the fire department, or an ambulance, dial ☎ **112.**

Hospital One of the town's biggest is the **Hospital Clínico Universitario San Cecilio,** Av. Doctor Oloriz, 16 ☎ **95-802-32-59.**

Internet Cafe With many cafes and hotels offering free Wi-Fi these days, the Internet cafe is becoming a rarer creature in Granada. One that's still in business and well located is **Azahara Cyber,** Calle Colcha 4 (☎ **95-821-58-32**). It's on a small side street off Reyes Catolicos

just down from Plaza Nueva.

Newspapers Daily newspapers edited and published in Granada include the right-of-center *Ideal* and the slightly left-of-center *Granada Hoy.* For listings of the cultural events presented in and around Granada, pick up a copy of *Guía de Granada del Ocio.*

Pharmacy A large 24-hour pharmacy just down from Plaza Nueva is **Farmacia Martin Valarde,** Reyes Catolicos 5 (☎ **95-826-26-64**). A slightly smaller option is **Farmacia Oeste,** Doctor Olorez 1 (☎ **95-828-75-75**).

Post Office Called **Correos Granada,** the main post office is at Puerta Real 2 (☎ **95-822-11-38**). It's open Monday to Friday

8:30am to 8:30pm and Saturday 9:30am to 2pm.

Telephones Pay phones are scattered throughout Granada. They are easy to use with detailed explanation in English and a button that allows you to select prompts in English too. To find out in advance how much a call will cost, dial ✆ **03** and follow the instructions. Many pay phones also accept credit cards which is really convenient, but not particularly good value. U.S. and Canadian visitors can also call collect by dialing ✆ **90-095-75-55**. If you plan to call home, the cheapest option is to buy a phone card, available at local tobacco stands and news kiosks in increments of 6€, 12€, and 21€. For directory assistance for phone numbers within Spain, call ✆ **11818** or ✆ **11888**.

Toilets You'll find an automatic public toilet booth in many of the main squares in Granada. Insert .30€ to open the door. There are booths at Plaza Nueva, Plaza Isabella Catolicos and Plaza de Mariana Pineda. Otherwise, duck into the nearest bar or cafe to buy a coffee as part of the process.

WHERE TO STAY

Expensive

AC Palacio de Santa Paula ★★★ If you're looking for luxury and style, and you've got the money to spend, this is one of the best options in the city. Behind the very large, sienna-colored facade of what was once a 19th-century convent, you'll find one of the most imaginative combinations of modern and antique architecture in Spain. The hotel is a brilliantly schizophrenic integration of buildings with a 15th-century medieval cloister, two 14th-century Arab houses, a deconsecrated Baroque chapel, and high-ceilinged vestiges of Granada's Catholic Reconquista. All of these structures are interlinked with a sophisticated ultra-modern shell of glass, steel, aluminum, and polished stone. Even the simplest rooms are soothingly comfortable and well designed, with soundproof windows protecting sleepers from the traffic of the Gran Vía de Colón. Bigger, more upscale rooms and suites occupy the site of the Moorish houses and the cloister. Scattered throughout the premises are a half-dozen imaginative suites. There's also an excellent restaurant here, **El Claustro**. (See "Where to Dine".)

Gran Vía de Colón 31, 18001 Granada. ✆ **95-880-57-40.** Fax 95-880-57-41. www.ac-hotels.com. 75 units. 150€–327€ double; from 233€ suite. AE, DC, MC, V. Parking 15€ per day. **Amenities:** Restaurant; babysitting; gym; room service; sauna; nonsmoking rooms; Wi-Fi. *In room:* A/C, TV, minibar.

Andalucía Center This is one of Granada's most modern hotels, but it's located near the convention center, a good 25-minute walk from the historic core of the city. It has a rooftop pool and sun terrace, something you won't find in many of the hotels closer to the center. So if you're more into relaxing in stylish surroundings with a quick flip into the city by taxi to visit the cultural monuments, it's a good option. It's modern and cool in its own restrained and tasteful way—a pretty luxurious choice, with vast expanses of glistening beige stone, lots of dark hardwoods, and theatrical lighting fixtures. A first-class restaurant and a stylish and macho-looking bar—the kind that makes you want to linger—are on the lobby level. A generous breakfast buffet completes the package. Bedrooms, scattered over five floors, are large and comfortable, adjoining first-class bathrooms with tub and shower.

Where to Stay & Dine in Granada

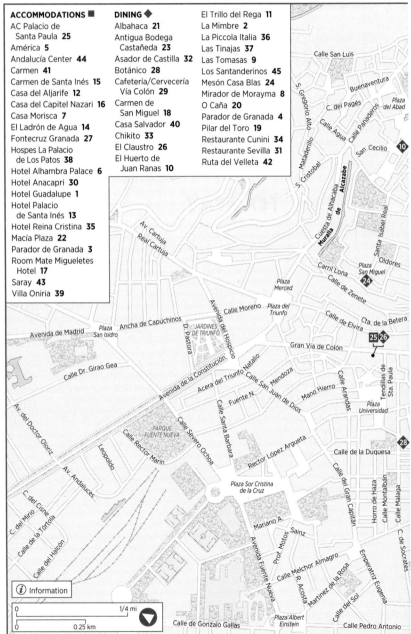

ACCOMMODATIONS ■
AC Palacio de
  Santa Paula **25**
América **5**
Andalucía Center **44**
Carmen **41**
Carmen de Santa Inés **15**
Casa del Aljarife **12**
Casa del Capitel Nazari **16**
Casa Morisca **7**
El Ladrón de Agua **14**
Fontecruz Granada **27**
Hospes La Palacio
  de Los Patos **38**
Hotel Alhambra Palace **6**
Hotel Anacapri **30**
Hotel Guadalupe **1**
Hotel Palacio
  de Santa Inés **13**
Hotel Reina Cristina **35**
Macía Plaza **22**
Parador de Granada **3**
Room Mate Migueletes
  Hotel **17**
Saray **43**
Villa Oniria **39**

DINING ◆
Albahaca **21**
Antigua Bodega
  Castañeda **23**
Asador de Castilla **32**
Botánico **28**
Cafetería/Cervecería
  Vía Colón **29**
Carmen de
  San Miguel **18**
Casa Salvador **40**
Chikito **33**
El Claustro **26**
El Huerto de
  Juan Ranas **10**

El Trillo del Rega **11**
La Mimbre **2**
La Piccola Italia **36**
Las Tinajas **37**
Las Tomasas **9**
Los Santanderinos **45**
Mesón Casa Blas **24**
Mirador de Morayma **8**
O Caña **20**
Parador de Granada **4**
Pilar del Toro **19**
Restaurante Cunini **34**
Restaurante Sevilla **31**
Ruta del Velleta **42**

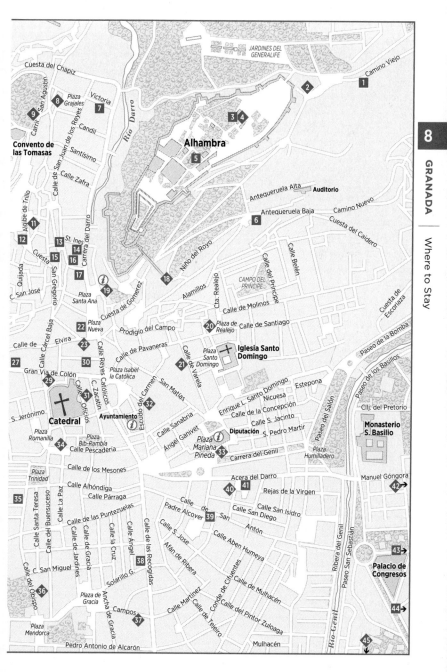

JARDINES DEL GENERALIFE

Cuesta del Chapiz

Camino Viejo

1

2

Victoria

Plaza Grajales

7

8

9

Carril de San Agustín

Candil

Calle de San Juan de los Reyes

3 **4**

Santísimo

Alhambra

Calle Zafra

Convento de las Tomasas

5

Río Darro

Antequeruela Alta   **Auditorio**

Aljibe de Trillo

Antequeruela Baja

Camino Nuevo

6

Cuesta del Caldero

11

12

Cuesta

St. Ines

13 **14**

15 **16**

Carrera del Darro

C. Quijada

San Gregorio

C. San José

17

Niño del Royo

Alamillos

Calle del Príncipe

Calle Belén

Cuesta de Escoriaza

Plaza Santa Ana

19

18

Cta. Realejo

CAMPO DEL PRÍNCIPE

Cuesta de Gomerez

Calle de Molinos

Plaza Nueva

22

Prodigio del Campo

Plaza de Realejo

Calle de Santiago

20

Paseo de la Bomba

Calle de   Elvira

23

Calle de Pavaneras

Calle Cárcel Baja

Plaza Santo Domingo

Iglesia Santo Domingo

Paseo de los Basilios

27

30

Gran Vía de Colón

29

Plaza Isabel la Católica

Calle Reyes Católicos

San Matías

21

Calle de Varela

Enrique L. Santo Domingo

Estepona

Nicuesa

Paseo del Salón

Cllj. del Pretorio

S. Jerónimo

Catedral

31

C. Zacatín

Calle Oficios

Ayuntamiento

32

Escudo del Carmen

Calle Sanabria

Calle de la Concepción

Calle S. Jacinto

Monasterio S. Basilio

Plaza Romanilla

34

Plaza Bib-Rambla

Calle Pescadería

Ángel Ganivet

Plaza Mariana Pineda

Diputación

33

S. Pedro Martir

Carrera del Genil

Plaza Humilladero

Plaza Trinidad

Calle de los Mesones

Acera del Darro

Manuel Góngora

42 →

35

Calle Santa Teresa

Calle Alhóndiga

Calle Párraga

41

40

Rejas de la Virgen

Calle del Buensuceso

Calle La Paz

Calle de las Puntezuelas

Calle   de

Padre Alcover

39

Calle San Diego

Calle San Isidro

San   Antón

Ribera del Genil

Calle de Gracia

Calle de Jardines

Calle Ángel

Calle S. Jose

Afán de Ribera

Calle Aben Humeya

Calle la Cruz

Calle de las Recogidas

43 →

Palacio de Congresos

C. San Miguel

36

38

Solarillo G.

Conde de Cifuentes

Calle de Mulhacén

Calle del Obispo

Plaza de Gracia

Ancha de Gracia

Campos

37

Calle Martínez

Calle de Tejeiro

Calle del Pintor Zuloaga

Paseo San Sebastián

44 →

Plaza Mendorca

Pedro Antonio de Alcarón

Mulhacén

Río Genil

45 ↓

Av. de América 3, 18006 Granada. ✆ **95-818-15-00.** Fax 95-812-94-84. www.andaluciacenterhotel. com. 115 units. 60€–260€ double; 228€–400€ junior suite. AE, DC, MC, V. Parking 13€. **Amenities:** Restaurant; bar; pool; room service; solarium. *In room:* A/C, TV, hair dryer, minibar, Wi-Fi.

Hospes La Palacio de Los Patos ★★★ 🎒   In a vast, beautifully restored old palace house and located close to the historic center, the Palacio offers the very best in designer-style luxury with friendly, unobtrusive service too. Outside there's a large leafy terrace with an avenue of sleek glass-bottomed pools with modern fountains. And beneath them at basement level with the shimmering sunlight dancing through the waters above, you'll find a small, but stylishly designed and very comfortable, spa with all kinds of relaxing treatments. Choose from the ultra-modern extension to the side of the hotel or the historic converted rooms in the palacio itself. All the very spacious rooms are furnished with cutting-edge designer furnishings which should feel a little out of place in such an old building—but they don't. Choose from six different levels of luxury from Dreamer's Double to the ornate Presidential Suite.

Solarillo de Gracia 1, 18002 Granada. ✆ **95-853-57-90.** Fax 95-853-69-68. www.hospes.com. 42 units. 199€–225€ double; 250€–750€ suite. AE, DC, MC, V. Parking 20€. **Amenities:** Restaurant; terrace bar; babysitting; room service; spa; nonsmoking rooms; rooms for those w/limited mobility. *In room:* A/C, TV, DVD, hair dryer; minibar, Wi-Fi.

Hotel Alhambra Palace ★   Like a Moorish fortress complete with a crenellated roofline, a rather gaudy crowning dome, geometric tile work, and the suggestion of a minaret, this legendary hotel was built by Duke San Pedro de Galatino in 1910 in a secluded spot just a 10-minute walk from the Alhambra. But up here on the hillside, it's not particularly well located for exploring the rest of the city. The ornately deco-rated interior is genuinely impressive, but the rooms, whilst spacious and comfort-able, don't quite live up to the dramatic public areas. What really makes this place are the views though. It's perched high above the city with expansive vistas far out across the valley. Try for a room with a balcony opening onto Granada, but avoid the court rooms, the windows of which lack double-glazing. If you don't stay here, drop in for a coffee or beer on the terrace just for a sight of that view. It's spectacular.

Plaza Arquitecto García de Paredes 1, 18009 Granada. ✆ **95-822-14-68.** Fax 95-822-64-04. www. h-alhambrapalace.es. 126 units. 190€ double; 275€ suite. AE, DC, MC, V. Free parking. **Amenities:** Res-taurant; bar; babysitting; room service; Internet. *In room:* A/C, TV, hair dryer; minibar.

Parador de Granada ★★★   This most famous parador in Spain—and the hard-est to get into—is in the grounds of the Alhambra. It's like an extension of the palace itself, rich with Mudéjar- and Arab-inspired architectural touches, including splash-ing fountains, wraparound loggias, gardens laden with wisteria, and aromatic herbs. Unfortunately, it's consistently booked, so reserve as far as possible in advance. The Andalusian decor is tasteful and evokes the past. From the shady terrace you have views of the Generalife gardens and the Sacromonte caves. The guest rooms are roomy and comfortable. Ask for one in the older section, furnished with antiques; rooms in the more modern wing are less inspired. Like the Alhambra Palace, here up on the hill, it's a steep walk down to the rest of the historic center.

Real de la Alhambra s/n, 18009 Granada. ✆ **95-822-14-40.** Fax 95-822-22-64. www.parador.es. 36 units. 310€–347€ double; 481€–598€ suite. AE, DC, MC, V. Free parking. **Amenities:** Restaurant; bar; room service; rooms for those w/limited mobility. *In room:* A/C, TV, hair dryer, minibar, Wi-Fi.

ROYAL burials, ROYAL IRONIES

Even if you're not staying at the **Parador de Granada** (see above), try to make a detour into its gardens. During its role in the 16th century as a Franciscan monastery, it adapted an existing Muslim structure as the temporary burial chamber of the ardently Catholic Queen Isabella (1451–1504), whose body rested here for 17 years. A few years later when Ferdinand (1452–1516) died, he, too, was buried here temporarily. Eventually, both Isabella and Ferdinand were disinterred and moved to more luxurious digs in the Capilla Real, now an annex of Granada's enormous cathedral. The Capilla Real was originally envisioned as a royal mausoleum for the descendants of the Catholic kings, but it had not been completed at the time of Ferdinand and Isabella's deaths.

Today in the parador's gardens, birds sing and flowers bloom. A simple plaque denotes the former burial site of the Catholic monarchs. Ironically, the surrounding motifs were developed by their hated enemies, the Muslims, and some of the lavish calligraphy that covers the walls of the burial chamber refers to Allah. One wonders if Isabella—who generally tended to shun excess luxury of any type—ever realized this. If she had, would her spirit have rested peacefully?

Room Mate Migueletes Hotel ★★ 👔 Room Mate hotels tend to be about good-value accommodation with trendy designer flourishes, but this is far superior. It's one of the best furnished of the atmospheric boutique hotels that have sprung up in medieval houses in the Albaicín. The structure was built in 1642 and used by the local police force (known as Los Migueletes for the weapons they carried) for most of the 1800s. Although it carries a three-star government rating, the hotel has extras you'd associate with four-stars. Some rooms, especially the spectacular suite, feel baronial, thanks to high ceilings, majestic proportions, superior mattresses, and flagstone- or tile-covered floors. All bedrooms are different in size and layout, some opening onto the interior courtyard, others with a view of the Alhambra. Public areas are graceful—a fountain splashes in the courtyard, wraparound verandas above the stone-floored patio are supported by delicate granite columns, and breakfast is served in a vaulted white-brick cellar. Note: The elevator grants access to only about 80% of the rooms.

Calle Benelua 11, 18010 Granada. ✆ **95-821-07-00.** Fax 95-821-07-02. www.room-matehotels.com. 25 units. 129€–199€ double; 170€–229€ junior suite; 279€–375€ suite. AE, DC, MC, V. Parking 20€ per night. **Amenities:** Breakfast room; nonsmoking rooms; Internet. *In room:* A/C, TV, hair dryer, minibar.

Saray ★★ This modern, five-star hotel is one of the most comfortable and best-run in town, and in terms of room size, amenities, and luxuries it's right up there with the best. But, a good 20-minute walk from the historic center, it's not very well located. In honor of Granada's former conquerors, postmodern Arabesque overtones include a Moorish garden, mosaics, plaster fretwork, and fountains. Fine furnishings and the odd rare antique add graceful notes to public lounges. Plenty of mirrors, wooden furniture, overstuffed armchairs, and elegant fabrics add luxe touches throughout. Bedrooms are midsize to spacious with stylish comfort and plenty of amenities from bedside controls to mirrored closets, double-glazed windows to tiled bathrooms. The alcove rooms are bigger and have charming love seats.

Paseo de Enrique Tierno Galván, 18006 Granada. ✆ **95-813-00-09.** Fax 95-812-91-61. www.h-santos. es. 213 units. 90€–200€ double; from 300€–600€ suite. Rates include breakfast. AE, DC, MC, V. **Amenities:** Restaurant; cafeteria; bar; outdoor pool; room service; nonsmoking rooms; rooms for those w/ limited mobility. *In room:* A/C, TV, hair dryer, minibar, Wi-Fi.

Villa Oniria ★★★ 🎁 This brand new conversion of a stately 19th-century palace house, well situated in the city center, oozes charm and sophistication and is one of my favorites. Restoration has been achieved sensitively and with real attention to detail. There's a hint of 1920s Havana about the common areas, with comfy sofas, a piano, and dark hardwood chairs and tables. There's a large leafy terrace with pool and fountain and a book-filled library too. The 31 rooms are comfortably furnished in a modern style with big beds—many of them four posters—and comfy sofas. Try for a room with a balcony overlooking the patio. An intimate restaurant and candlelit spa in the basement complete the package.

San Anton 28, 18005, Granada. ✆ **95-853-53-58**. Fax 95-853-55-17. www.villaoniria.com. 31 units. 120€– 250€ double; 350€–600€ suite. AE, DC, MC, V. Parking 18€. **Amenities:** Restaurant; bar; room service; spa; nonsmoking rooms; rooms for those w/limited mobility. *In room:* A/C, TV, hair dryer, minibar, Wi-Fi.

Moderate

América ★★ 🌿 This is one of only two hotels on the actual grounds of the Alhambra, the other being the much more expensive (and better-furnished) Parador de Granada (see above). Hotel América was built in the mid-19th century as a private home, then transformed in 1928 into this intimate, small-scale Victorian-era hotel, full of antiques, curios, and photos of past literati guests. The shady rear courtyard is festooned with grapevines and dotted with blue-and-white ceramic tiles. Small rooms are comfortably and decently furnished and well maintained. As for the Parador and the Alhambra Palace (see above) if your reason for visiting is to spend most of your time exploring the Alhambra, this is a good option. But be aware that there are only a handful of restaurants in the vicinity and it's a steep walk down the hill into town. (And an even steeper one back up!)

Real de la Alhambra 53, 18009 Granada. ✆ **95-822-74-71.** Fax 95-822-74-70. www.hotelamerica-granada.com. 17 units. 120€ double; 150€ suite. MC, V. Parking nearby 15€. **Amenities:** Restaurant (breakfast and lunch only); outdoor patio and bar; rooms for those w/limited mobility; Wi-Fi. *In room:* A/C, hair dryer.

Carmen There's nothing particularly special about this hotel, but it's well located and well run. It's under constant renovations to keep it up to date and the owners have done much to imbue the place with some grace and Andalusian style. Midsize to spacious bedrooms are attractively furnished with first-class bathrooms. The hotel is now beginning its 4th decade and enjoys the most repeat visitors of any establishment in Granada, so it must be doing something right. Usually only doubles open onto terraces; here six singles have this luxury.

Acera del Darro 62, 18005 Granada. ✆ **95-825-83-00.** Fax 95-825-64-62. www.hotelcarmen.com. 283 units. 177€ double; 400€ suite. AE, DC, MC, V. Parking 17€. **Amenities:** 2 restaurants; 2 bars; babysitting; outdoor pool; room service; nonsmoking rooms; rooms for those w/limited mobility. *In room:* A/C, TV, hair dryer, minibar, Wi-Fi.

Moorish-style Relaxation

Along with Córdoba and Seville, Granada has modern-day **hammams** (bathhouses) modeled on the old Arabic style with intricately decorated tile work, horseshoe-shaped arches, star-shaped windows and hot and cold pools for bathing. A trip to the baths is a great way to relax and unwind after a long day of sightseeing. There are two hammams to choose from. **Hammams de Al Andalus** are situated just off Plaza Nueva at Calle Santa Ana 16 (© **95-822-99-78;** www.hammam.es) and tend to get quite busy, but the decor and style are very atmospheric. Quieter and so more relaxing are the **Baños Arabes Aljibe de San Miguel** at San Miguel Alta 41 (© **95-852-28-67;** www.aljibesan miguel.es.) Both offer similar types of package of baths plus a short massage for around 30€ per person.

Carmen de Santa Inés ★ 🍴 Graciously restored, Carmen de Santa Inés will house you stylishly, comfortably, and affordably. In the historical Albaicín area, this old Moorish house on a quiet street has kept much of its past, including original wooden beams, a patio, Arab fountains, a marble staircase and columns. Small comfortable bedrooms are full of character. If you've got a few extra euros to spare, book "El Mirador," with its balcony terrace opening onto panoramic views of the Alhambra and the city (250€) There's no elevator, and breakfast only is served.

Placeta de Porras 7, 18018 Granada. © **95-822-63-80.** Fax 95-822-44-04. www.carmendesantaines. com. 9 units. 90€–120€ double; 250€ suite. AE, DC, MC, V. **Amenities:** Breakfast room. *In room:* A/C, TV, hair dryer, minibar.

Casa Morisca ★★ 📖 I thought the charms of the two Ineses: Carmen de Santa Inés and Palacio de Santa Inés (see above and below, respectively) were pretty hard to beat. Then I found Casa Morisca. In the historic lower district of Albaicín, this house dates from the end of the 15th century. On the patio you can still see the remains of a Moorish pool and galleries supported by pilasters and columns. The interior was kept and restored, although the facade was given a 17th-century overlay. Bedrooms are individually decorated in traditional style but with all modern comforts. The only minor downside (if you're really looking for one) is the location—about 5 or 10 minutes farther up Paseo de los Tristes from Plaza Nueva than the other boutique places, so a slightly longer walk back from the bars and restaurants.

Cuesta de la Victoria 9, 18010 Granada. © **95-822-11-00.** Fax 95-821-57-96. www.hotelcasamorisca. com. 14 units. 114€–144€ double; 196€ suite. AE, DC, MC, V. Free parking. **Amenities:** Breakfast room; room service; nonsmoking rooms; rooms for those w/limited mobility. *In room:* A/C, TV, hair dryer, minibar, Wi-Fi.

El Ladrón de Agua ★ Behind a frescoed 16th-century Italianate facade on one of Granada's narrow streets, this is one of the newest of the historic boutique hotels of the Albaicín. It's simpler, more stripped down, and more modern in style than its competitors. The name, El Ladrón de Agua (the Water Thief), refers to a collection of poems by Nobel Prize-winning Andalusian poet Juan Ramón Jiménez. Some of his verses are stenciled or highlighted in metallic cutouts, or projected with laser beams onto the stark white walls of the hotel's artfully minimalist interior. You'll also find high-tech lighting and fountains from which—in a nod to the hotel's name—water dribbles out to be "stolen" away into hidden drains. Bedrooms are comfortable and tasteful, with high ceilings, tiled bathrooms, and a mix of modern and antique design, and eight have views over the Alhambra, on the opposite side of the river. Each room is named after a poem, or a snippet of a poem, by either Jiménez or his hosts during his sojourns in Granada—Federico García Lorca or Manuel de Falla.

Carrera del Darro 13, 18010 Granada. ✆ **95-821-50-40.** Fax 95-822-43-45. www.ladrondeagua.com. 15 units. 110€–175€ double; 218€–237€ suite. AE, DC, MC, V. **Amenities:** Breakfast room. *In room:* A/C, TV, minibar, Wi-Fi.

Fontecruz Granada ★ 🍴   One of a new small chain of modern, elegant, design-led hotels in six locations across Spain and Portugal, the Fontecruz is located on busy Gran Vía de Colón in a restored Baroque apartment building. Public areas are bright and airy with stylish white furnishings; bedrooms have large beds, hi-tech bathrooms, and the mod cons you expect from a luxury hotel. Rooms that look onto the Gran Vía have nice views over the cathedral, but there is the slight background drone of traffic. There's a cozy roof terrace restaurant with expansive views right across the city and the regular jazz nights here make for an atmospheric evening. There's a small well-equipped spa in the basement too.

Calle Gran Vía de Colón 20, 18001 Granada. ✆ **95-821-78-10.** www.fontecruzhoteles.com. 39 units. 81€–150€ double. AE, DC, MC, V. **Amenities:** Restaurant; bar; laundry service; nonsmoking rooms; spa. *In room:* A/C, TV, hair dryer, minibar.

Hotel Palacio de Santa Inés ★★   This *antigua casa*, consisting of two small Mudéjar buildings constructed in the first third of the 16th century, is one of the most enchanting places to stay in Granada. It's in the colorful Albaicín district, just a 5-minute walk from Plaza Nueva. The painstakingly restored little palace was in complete ruins until the mid-1990s. Today it's a lovely, graceful inn with a 16th-century courtyard, old wooden beamed ceilings, and silver chandeliers. The rooms are medium-size; some have small sitting rooms, and several open onto views of Granada. Much of the furniture is antique.

Cuesta de Santa Inés 9, 18010 Granada. ✆ **95-822-23-62.** Fax 95-822-24-65. www.palaciosantaines. com. 35 units. 75€–160€ double; 150€–260€ suite. AE, DC, MC, V. Parking 17€. **Amenities:** Breakfast room; babysitting; nonsmoking rooms. *In room:* A/C, TV, hair dryer, minibar.

Hotel Reina Cristina   In the center of the city, a 3-minute walk from the cathedral in a renovated 19th-century *casa granadina* (mansion), this hotel had a role in a dark moment of Granada's history. Here, the right-wing forces of Generalísimo Franco abducted one of the nation's greatest writers and Granada's favorite son, the poet/playwright Federico García Lorca. He was taken 3km (2 miles) away and executed. The family-operated hotel now exudes grace, charm, and tranquility, and the service is helpful. Much of the original furnishing remains in the renovated rooms.

Calle Tablas 4, 18002 Granada. ✆ **95-825-32-11.** Fax 95-825-57-28. www.hotelreinacristina.com. 58 units. 85€ per person double; 160€ per person triple. Rates include breakfast. AE, DC, MC, V. Parking 15€. **Amenities:** Restaurant; bar; room service; rooms for those w/limited mobility; Internet. *In room:* A/C, TV, hair dryer, minibar.

Stay in An Apartment

If you're planning on spending longer in Granada, or you just like doing things yourself, there are lots of good-value, atmospheric apartments available to rent. They can be a really cheap deal if you're a large family or group of friends. Many are located in the little houses of the Albaicín barrio and have terraces with views across to the Alhambra. Efficient local accommodation agency **Granadainfo** (www.granadainfo.com) features lots of them. Two-person studio apartments start at around 80€ per night but there are more expensive luxury apartments as well.

Inexpensive

Casa del Aljarife ★★ 🏨   In the Albaicín district four blocks from the Plaza Santa Ana, this friendly little boutique hotel tucked away up a side street is relatively unknown. In a recently renovated 17th-century structure, it has an intimate patio with trees and a Moorish fountain. Owner Christian Most is a perfect host and there's a really welcoming atmosphere to the place. Be sure to ask him for restaurant recommendations as he's lived in the city over 30 years and knows every nook and cranny. There are just four different sized rooms. Room 1 has views of the Alhambra and a cozy separate sitting room that can sleep two more adults. Room 4, at the top of the house, has a bath tub (other rooms only have shower stalls) and whilst it's quite small, it offers lovely views of the Alhambra too.

Placeta de la Cruz Verde 2, 18010 Granada. ✆/fax **95-822-24-25.** www.casadelaljarife.com. 4 units. 91€ double; 116€ triple; 134€ junior suite; 168€ suite. MC, V. Parking nearby 15€. **Amenities:** Breakfast room; TV salon. *In room:* A/C.

Casa del Capitel Nazari ★ 🍴   This is another of the clutch of atmospheric boutique hotels in the cramped but evocative medieval neighborhood, the Albaicín, a few steps uphill from the Plaza Nueva. In a private, patio-centered home built at least 400 years ago, it's been extensively renovated so it's a cozy, appealing mixture of antique and modern. The well-furnished and rather small bedrooms are full of antique features, including old Spanish-style wooden beams. Rooms are spread over three floors, accessed from the main courtyard. Service is efficient and friendly.

Cuesta Aceituneros 6, 18010 Granada. ✆ **95-821-52-60.** Fax 95-821-58-06. www.hotelcasacapitel.com. 17 units. 85€–110€ double. DC, MC, V. Parking 19€ per day. **Amenities:** Breakfast room; all rooms non-smoking; Internet. *In room:* A/C, TV, hair dryer, minibar.

Hotel Anacapri   In the center of Granada next to the cathedral, the unpretentious Anacapri is a two-minute walk from Plaza Nueva. The small rooms are comfortable, but have a mix of nice old furniture with modern touches. The best rooms have antique windows, jutting beams, and terraces overlooking the street. Bathrooms are equipped with showers and tubs. Relax in the Salón Social, look at the 18th-century patio with a central fountain, or check your e-mails using the free Wi-Fi.

Calle Joaquín Costa 7, 18010 Granada. ✆ **95-822-74-77.** Fax 95-822-89-09. www.hotelanacapri.com. 49 units. 70€–110€ double. AE, DC, MC, V. Parking 16€. **Amenities:** Bar; laundry service; Wi-Fi. *In room:* A/C, TV.

Hotel Guadalupe On five floors on a road leading up to the Alhambra, Hotel Guadalupe uses marble and stonework to add architectural character. Built in 1969, the three-star government-rated hotel is unfortunately an oasis for the tour-bus set. Nonetheless, it remains one of the better choices in this price range, with rustic arches, a beamed lobby, marble floors, and a fireplace. The better units are in the hotel's main core, while the less-desirable ones are in an annex a few yards away.

Paseo de la Sabica s/n, 18009 Granada. © **95-822-34-23.** Fax 95-822-37-98. www.hotelguadalupe.es. 58 units. 65€–111€ double. AE, DC, MC, V. Parking 15€. **Amenities:** Restaurant; bar; babysitting; room service. *In room:* A/C, TV, hair dryer, minibar, Wi-Fi.

Macía Plaza 🏆 This attractive 1970s hotel at the bottom of the hill leading up to the Alhambra is a bargain for a government-rated two-star and it's been recently renovated too. In the center of the tourist district on busy Plaza Nueva, it's ideal if you want to be in the eye of the storm. All the small guest rooms are functionally but comfortably furnished with good beds and tiled bathrooms. Standard wooden furniture is used throughout the three-story building, the balconies and wide windows of which make it look like an antique house. Service here is friendly and helpful too.

Plaza Nueva 5, 18010 Granada. © **95-822-75-36.** Fax 95-822-75-33. www.maciahoteles.com. 44 units. 50€–120€ double. AE, DC, MC, V. Parking 15€. **Amenities:** Breakfast lounge; nonsmoking rooms; rooms for those w/limited mobility. *In room:* A/C, TV.

WHERE TO DINE

Expensive

Asador de Castilla CASTILIAN In the cathedral district, this long-time favorite is on a small square near the old town hall (Ayuntamiento). An authentic Castilian *asador* (barbecue) restaurant favored by many of the city's leading politicians, journalists, and Andalusian families celebrating rites of passage, it has a solid stone facade, medieval coats of arms, and stone carvings. The chefs are famous locally for their roast lamb with herbs, and top quality Argentinian steaks cooked on the barbecue. They also turn out impressive local dishes like casseroled beans with Iberian ham and homemade stews. Fish and seafood dishes are also good and there's an impressive wine list.

Calle Escudo del Carmen 17. © **95-822-29-10.** Reservations recommended. Main courses 18€–33€. AE, DC, MC, V. Wed–Mon 1–4pm and 9pm–midnight. Closed Aug.

Carmen de San Miguel ANDALUSIAN On the hill leading up to the Alhambra, this likable restaurant offers spectacular views over the city center from a glassed-in dining room and terrace, full of banks of flowers. Specialties include grilled hake, a pate of partridge with a vinaigrette sauce, Iberian ham with Manchego cheese, and a casserole of monkfish and fresh clams. The food, although good, doesn't quite match the view. The wines are from all over Spain, with a strong selection of Riojas.

Plaza de Torres Bermejas 3. © **95-822-67-23.** Reservations recommended. Main courses 17€–23€; 4-course *menú degustación* 55€. AE, DC, MC, V. Mon–Sat 1:30–4pm and 8:30–11:30pm; winter Sun 1:30–4pm.

El Claustro ★★ SPANISH/CONTINENTAL The in-house restaurant at the ultra-cool AC Palacio de Santa Paula hotel offers some of the most inventive fine dining in the city. The location is also pretty perfect, set in what was originally built in 1540 as a cloister for nuns. The room's heavily beamed ceiling exudes Renaissance artistry, and windows overlook a graceful arcaded courtyard where diners can enjoy an *alfresco* summer meal. Head chef Juan Andres Morilla is a rising local star and his seasonal menus are well conceived and imaginative. Last time I visited, starters included butterfish ravioli filled with tartar of sturgeon and avocado cream, red shrimp with pancetta and paprika jus, and a Granada-style salad of cod with oranges. Main courses change several times a year, and include such delights as oxtail stuffed with truffles and grilled foie gras, sea bass with squash, and succulent roast suckling pig.

In the AC Palacio de Santa Paula, Gran Vía de Colón 31, 18001 Granada. © **95-880-57-40.** Reservations recommended. Main courses 16€-26€. AE, DC, MC, V. Daily 1:30-4pm and 8:30-11:30pm.

El Huerto de Juan Ranas ★★★ 🎒 HISPANO/ISLAMIC   Immediately below the San Nicolas *mirador* (viewpoint) right at the top of the Albaicín barrio, the Huerto's vine-clad terraces command spectacular views of the floodlit Alhambra at night, making it perfect for a truly romantic evening. Converted from an antique private home, the Mudéjar-inspired tilework and streams of water create a Hispano-Moorish environment of enormous charm. Members of King Fahd of Saudi Arabia's family are said to have abandoned their vacation home in Marbella occasionally for meals here. Dine on the terrace, with that tremendous view or descend, like the local gastronomes, into the dining room. Dishes incorporate Spanish and Arab traditions, and might include Iberian steak with caramelized onions, a Moroccan version of *pastela* (meat cakes with eggplant), rack of lamb with crackling herbs, eggplant (aubergine) with honey sauce, and scrambled eggs with fresh salmon. Unless you know the area, you might want to take a taxi.

Calle de Atarazana 8 (Mirador de San Nicolás). © **95-828-69-25.** Reservations recommended for the restaurant. Main courses 19€-35€. AE, DC, MC, V. Daily 8-11:30pm.

Las Tomasas ★★ ANDALUSIAN/INTERNATIONAL   This is another place in the Albaicín area with a great terrace and gardens offering lovely views of the Alhambra. It's a favorite of my friend Christian (who runs the Casa del Aljarife hotel nearby). Serving top quality food since 1989, this friendly restaurant is perfect for a special meal or a real treat. Dishes are seriously tasty and inventive. The menu is seasonal, but the best dishes when I visited were filet of beef with homemade pate and warm apple compote and cinnamon candied seabass with caviar and lentils. For the more adventurous, how about pan-fried ostrich breast with pistachio crust and mousseline? Warm chocolate souffle for dessert rounded off the meal very well. There's a good wine list too, with some interesting Spanish vintages.

C Carril De San Agustín, 10. © **95-822-41-08.** Reservations recommended. Main courses 12€-30€. AE, MC, V. Jun-Oct Tues-Sat 8:30pm-midnight; July-Sept Wed-Sun 2-4pm and 8:30-11:30pm. Closed 1st 2 weeks of Nov and Jan.

Los Santanderinos ★★ SPANISH/ANDALUSIAN   In the new part of town, just across the river between the Parque de Las Ciencias and the Palacio de Congresos, this is arguably the best restaurant in Granada. It's a genuinely wonderful dining choice—don't be disappointed by its location in a modern-day apartment complex. There's a small tapas bar near the entrance, an immaculate, rather formal dining room packed with members of the local bourgeoisie and business community, and an attentive staff. Chef Jesús Diego Díaz prepares dishes that include green asparagus "in the style of Santanderinos," with Iberian ham, shavings of cheese, and ingredients we couldn't even guess at. Tasty main courses include stuffed squid covered with a squid-ink-based black sauce, beef, lamb, and other fish dishes. Come for the food and a look at modern-day, nontouristic Granada. Note that some maps misname the street as Rey Abu Said; it's actually a continuation of Calle Albahaca.

Albahaca 1 (Urbanización Jardín de la Reina). ℭ **95-812-83-35.** Main courses 14€–24€. MC, V. Mon–Sat 1-3:30pm; Tues–Sat 8-11:30pm.

Ruta del Velleta ★★ ANDALUSIAN/INTERNATIONAL   Despite its 1976 origins as an unpretentious roadhouse restaurant, this place rapidly evolved into what's often described as the best restaurant in or around Granada. In Cenés de la Vega, about 6km (3½ miles) northwest of Granada's center, it has six different sized dining rooms, each with a mix of English and Andalusian furniture and accessories. The owners, Granada-born brothers, Miguel and José Pedraza, direct the impeccable service. Menu items change seasonally but might include roast suckling pig; roasted game birds like pheasant and partridge, often served with Rioja wine sauce; fish and shellfish, including monkfish with Andalusian herbs and strips of serrano ham; and a dessert specialty of frozen rice pudding on a bed of warm chocolate sauce. The wine list is one of the region's most comprehensive.

Carretera Vieja de la Sierra Nevada Km 5.5, Cenés de la Vega. ℭ **95-848-61-34.** www.rutadelveleta. com. Reservations recommended. Main courses 12€–30€; fixed-price menus 45€–120€ without wine. AE, DC, MC, V. Daily 1-4pm; Mon–Sat 8pm–midnight.

Moderate

Albahaca ★ 🖬 ANDALUSIAN/SPANISH   Calle Varela is a bit up-and-coming at the moment, with several great value and good fun bars and restaurants. One of my favorites, Albahaca, is a little *mesón* (inn) on a street corner in a century-old building. Owner Javier Jiménez seats 28 diners at eight tables in an old-fashioned restaurant decorated in a rustic style with bare white walls. His unpretentious traditional dishes are tasty, especially the *salmorejo* (creamy tomato gazpacho) and *ensalada de dos salsas* (green salad with two dressings). The stuffed salmon is marvelous, as is the pork sirloin with Roquefort sauce. For dessert, I recommend the velvety yogurt mousse.

Calle Varela 17. ℭ **95-822-49-23.** Reservations recommended on weekends. Main courses 9€–12€; *menú del día* 12€. MC, V. Tues–Sat 1:30-3:30pm and 8:30-10:30pm; Sun 1-4pm. Closed Aug.

La Mimbre ANDALUSIAN/GRANADINO   If you fancy a lazy lunch or evening meal after you've explored the Alhambra, there is no more conveniently located dining spot than this little eatery tucked right into the walls of the sultan's palace itself, a minute or so's walk down on the right from the main entrance. Over the years it's been a popular place for the poets and artists who have flocked to Granada. The late 19th-century building has a traditional decor; a garden with an old Andalusian fountain makes for romantic summer dining. The menu is backed by a good and affordable selection of regional wines. Oxtail is one of the chef's specialties. He also features oven-baked cod with a rich tomato sauce, *choto al ajillo* (braised kid studded with garlic) and a lighter salad of string beans and slices of serrano ham.

Granadinos are rediscovering their Islamic roots in laid-back *teterias,* lounges that serve mint tea, traditional Arab pastries, and tapas accompanied by wafts from pungently scented traditional waterpipes. V-shaped **Calle Caldereía,** which is crammed with them, leads up the hill from busy Calle Elvira and then abruptly turns right and goes back down to it. You'd be forgiven for thinking you were in Marrakech. My two favorites are **Al-Andalús,** Calle Calderería Vieja 34 (© **95-822-46-41**) and **Kasbah** Calle Calderería Vieja 4 (© **95-822-79-36**). They're on different sides of the V—so whichever side you walk up, you'll find one of them. The best time to visit is late afternoon or early evening. Both are open daily from around 11:30am to 2am.

If you want to sample more traditionally Spanish cafe culture try **López Mezquita Café Pastelería,** Calle de los Reyes Católicos 39–41 (© **95-822-12-05**), a short walk down from Plaza Nueva. It's a classic Andalusían coffee and cake shop with mounds of tempting pastries lined up behind gleaming glass counters. You can enjoy various cheeses from the province of Granada, along with spicy chorizo sausage pies. Pastry specialties, costing from 2€, include *pastela monunos,* which can be filled with different ingredients—meat, chicken, prunes, dried grapes, nuts, and more. Or try a *cuajado de carnaval,* a mousselike concoction made with seasonal fruit. Hours are Monday to Saturday 9am to noon and 5 to 11pm.

Locals also like to indulge in *chocolate con churros* (doughnut sticks dipped in hot chocolate). You'll see people dunking and chewing them mid-morning as a late breakfast snack or when it's cold as a winter-warmer treat. Although this may be an acquired taste, chocoholics will love it. Many little cafes around the cathedral serve this treat, but you can enjoy it at virtually any cafe within the city limits.

8

GRANADA | Where to Dine

Av. del Generalife, Alhambra. © **95-822-22-76.** Main courses 14€–21€. AE, MC, V. Oct-Apr daily noon-4pm; May-Sept daily 8-11:30pm. Closed part of Jan.

La Piccola Italia ITALIAN This elegantly decorated and inviting restaurant several blocks south of Plaza de la Trinidad and the cathedral is one of Granada's best Italian restaurants offering a change from Spanish food. Tables are set with beautiful linens, drawings adorn the walls, and there is much use of glass and wooden furniture. Local families come here for pizzas straight from the ovens, and the pasta dishes, especially the ravioli filled with fresh spinach and a regional cheese. The chefs are also adept at such dishes as fried chicken cutlet or salmon in a creamy white sauce. Desserts are homemade and luscious. The ice cream is particularly good.

Obispo Hurtado 3. © **95-825-96-78.** Reservations required. Main courses 16€–29€. AE, MC, V. Daily 1:30-4:30pm and 8:30pm-midnight. Bus: 2, 7, or 11.

Las Tinajas ★★ ANDALUSIAN This restaurant, a short walk from the cathedral, is named for the huge amphorae depicted on its facade. For over 30 years it's been the culinary showcase of José Alvarez and is still a local favorite. The decor is classical Andalusian, with wooden walls adorned with ceramic tiles and pictures of Old Granada. Antique ornaments are mixed with modern elements and fixtures. There's a convivial, crowded bar where locals and visitors order Andalusian wines and a wide range of delicious tapas. Or try the chef's direct cooking style using fresh ingredients and local recipes like sirloin steak with mushrooms and Jabugo ham in sherry sauce, loin of lamb stuffed with nuts and mint, or sea bass stuffed with prawns.

Martínez Campos 17. © **95-825-43-93.** Reservations recommended. Main courses 16€–23€. Gourmet set menus at 40€, 43€, and 46€. AE, DC, MC, V. Daily noon–5pm and 8pm–midnight. Closed July 15–Aug 15.

Parador de Granada ★★ ANDALUSIAN/SPANISH   Even if you can't afford to stay at this luxurious parador (see "Where to Stay," in this chapter), the most famous in Spain, consider the restaurant for a quiet retreat after the tourist hordes in the Alhambra itself. The dining room is spacious, service is polite, and there's a view of the rose gardens and a distant view of the Generalife. Lunch is the best time to dine here, as the terrace overlooking the palace is open. Order sandwiches and salads if you're not up for heavy Spanish food in the heat of the day. The cuisine is competent in every way, although not rising to any culinary heights. When in doubt, order the Andalusian specialties rather than the Spanish national dishes, as most of the chefs are Andalusian.

Real de la Alhambra. © **95-822-14-40.** Main courses 12€–30€; fixed-price menu 33€. AE, DC, MC, V. Daily 1–4pm and 8:30–11pm.

Restaurante Cunini ★★ SEAFOOD/SPANISH   Given its location on Plaza de la Pescadería (fishmarket square), it's not surprising that this place specializes in seafood. The array of fishy dishes, perhaps 100 in all, starts with tapas at the long, stand-up bar where you can have a drink before moving into the paneled ground-floor restaurant. Meals often begin with soup—perhaps *sopa sevillana* (with ham, shrimp, and whitefish) or a deep fry of small fish called a *fritura Cunini*. Other specialties include rice with seafood, *zarzuela* (seafood stew), smoked salmon, and grilled shrimp.

Plaza de la Pescadería 14. © **95-826-75-87.** Reservations recommended. Main courses 13€–34€; fixed-price menu 25€. AE, DC, MC, V. Tues–Sat noon–4pm and 8pm–midnight; Sun noon–4pm.

Inexpensive

Of course the cheapest way to dine in Granada is to munch tapas whilst you sip chilled beer or sherry. See the "Granada After Dark" section for recommendations.

Antigua Bodega Castañeda ★ 📖 ANDALUSIAN   If you're looking for somewhere on busy Calle Elvira that still retains a vibe and isn't too overrun with guidebook-clutching tourists, try this typical old *bodega*. It's been here for over a century and is the oldest of its type around here, run by the same family for generations. This convivial spot is usually full of locals here for the tasty but unpretentious food at low, low prices and the excellent selection of wines. Winning high praise is the wide range of tapas. Other meals include a variety of thick stews served in traditional clay bowls, ideal on a cold day. You can order a *surtido,* a selection of small dishes featuring cheese, ham, crab, shrimp, and venison.

Calle Elvira 5. © **95-822-63-62.** Main courses 9€–15€. Tapas from 2.90€. AE, MC, V. Daily 12:30–5pm and 8pm–1am.

Botánico ★ VEGETARIAN/ANDALUSIAN In front of the Botanical Gardens of the University of Granada and popular with university students, this bright airy cafe and restaurant is known for vegetarian dishes influenced by the cooking of Asia and North Africa. Chefs are known for their creative salads featuring different flavors and combinations, including mushrooms and sweet red peppers; and every day there are about three vegetarian casserole offerings, like meatless lasagna. Among the more challenging selections is a Moorish-inspired cake-like dish filled with chicken, meat, and cinnamon. The signature dish here is oven-baked duck with couscous. There's a limited but good selection of homemade desserts as well.

Málaga 3. ⓒ **95-827-15-98.** Reservations recommended. Main courses 8€–20€. MC, V. Daily 1pm–2am.

Cafetería/Cervecería Vía Colón ☺ SPANISH This is one of the best spots behind the cathedral for fast but traditional Spanish food. Although less than a decade old, the restaurant looks much older, thanks to marble countertops, faux Baroque decorations, and elaborate ceiling moldings. In summertime, outdoor tables are set up in the shadow of the cathedral's foundations. Perhaps best of all, the salads, burgers, omelets, crepes, and sandwiches available at this bustling place can give you a break from heavy Spanish food. There are good vegetarian options and *platos combinados* (pork steaks with rice and vegetables, fish with trimmings), good value at 10€ each. Don't come here for a leisurely meal; the setting isn't conducive to lingering.

Gran Vía de Colón 13. ⓒ **95-822-07-52.** Reservations not accepted. Sandwiches, salads, crepes from 3.50€; main courses 9.50€–17€. AE, MC, V. Daily 8am–1am.

Casa Salvador GRANADINO A third-generation family restaurant, this friendly tavern has been feeding locals since it opened in 1947. Traditional in decor, locals flock here for *platos típicos de Granada*. The chefs specialize in choice cuts of meat and fresh fish. Main courses include fried swordfish in a shrimp sauce and a platter of savory barbecued meats. For a perennial favorite, try the oxtail.

Duende 6. ⓒ **95-826-19-55.** Reservations recommended. Main courses 10€–17€. DC, MC, V. Mon–Sun 1–4pm; Tues–Sat 8–11:30pm. Closed mid-July to mid-Aug.

Chikito SPANISH Chikito is across from the famous tree-shaded square where García Lorca met with other members of El Rinconcillo (the Little Corner), a group of young men who brought a brief but dazzling cultural renaissance to their hometown in the 1920s. The cafe where they met has now changed its name, and today is a friendly tapas bar and restaurant. In fair weather, you can enjoy drinks and snacks on tables in the square; in winter, retreat inside to the tapas bar. Specialties include *sopa sevillana*, shrimp cocktail, Basque hake, baked tuna, oxtail, *zarzuela*, and grilled swordfish.

Plaza del Campilio 9. ⓒ **95-822-33-64.** Reservations recommended. Main courses 14€–20€; *menu del dia* 23€. AE, DC, MC, V. Daily noon–4pm and 7:30–11:30pm. Closed Wed.

El Trillo del Rega ★★ ☺ 🍴 BASQUE In a typical *carmen,* near Placeta de Carvajales in the Albaicín area, this little hideaway is treasured by locals for its intimate, homey atmosphere and tasty great value dishes. And it has a shady terrace with tinkling water fountain and views of the Alhambra. El Trillo is a family favorite, and, if asked, the chef will prepare plates for children—perhaps spaghetti or chicken. Service is relaxed and friendly. Dishes are Basque in style, hearty, and full of flavor. I tried an oven-cooked rice dish with wild boar and mushrooms, followed by sauteed broad beans with ham and squid. Cream of figs with ham shavings and potatoes with paprika sausage and quail's egg are two other house specialties. Vegetarians might go for a pastry filled with leek and cheese with a quiche-like consistency.

Callejón del Aljibe de Trillo 3. ✆ **95-822-51-82.** Reservations recommended. Main courses 12€–19€. DC, MC, V. Mon-Sat noon–4pm and 8pm–midnight. No lunch July-Aug. Bus: 1, 5, or 12.

Mesón Casa Blas ANDALUSIAN   This old restaurant is set on one of the nicest squares of the Albaicín, perfect for a lazy lunch in the shade watching the world go by. Inside it's staunchly traditional, in a former private home, with dark wooden furniture and tiled floors. With the snow falling and the fireplace lit, it's warm and cozy. In summer, the roof terrace offers views across to the floodlit Alhambra. The chef turns out delicious garlic-studded lamb or leg of pork from a wood-burning stove. Another intriguing platter is *antología de salmón y gulash* (a goulash of salmon au gratin). That classic local dish *rabo de toro* (oxtail) also appears. Staff members are friendly and helpful too.

Plaza San Miguel Bajo 15, Albaicín. ✆ **95-827-31-11.** Reservations recommended. Main courses 11€–18€. MC, V. Tues-Sun noon–5pm; Tues-Sat 8pm–midnight. Closed 2 weeks at Christmas.

Mirador de Morayma ★ ANDALUSIAN/SPANISH   Facing the Alhambra in an antique Renaissance-era house in the Albaicín, this large, rambling restaurant has a half-dozen dining rooms and three romantic outdoor terraces. Don't expect subtlety or big-city sophistication—what you'll get are generous portions of good cooking and a deep pride in the region's rural traditions. According to tradition, Morayma, the wife of Boabdil, last of the Muslim kings, was born here. The hardworking staff prepare dishes like gazpacho, *Granadine ajo blanco* (similar to gazpacho but with almonds and garlic), roasted goat in wine sauce, and oven-cooked cod filet with almonds.

Calle Pianista García Carrillo 2. ✆ **95-822-82-90.** Reservations recommended. Main courses 16€–23€. AE, MC, V. Mon-Sat 1:30–3:30pm and 8:30–11:30pm; Sun 1:30–3:30pm.

O Caña 🍴 SPANISH   Behind a mosaic-sheathed facade in an antique building in Granada's Jewish Quarter, this typical neighborhood bar with small dining room behind offers generous portions of well-flavored Andalusian food at very reasonable prices. Since it opened in 1905, it has turned out endless versions of its no-nonsense specialties (oxtail, grilled *solomillo* of beefsteak, Spanish sausages, grilled duck breast, and endless amounts of suckling pig and roasted lamb). Generations of loyal families come en masse to dine together, especially on Sundays. Last time I visited there was a huge pan of paella simmering on the stove. It was just delicious.

Plaza de Realejo 1. ✆ **95-825-64-70.** Main courses 5€–12€; *menu del dia* 15€. AE, DC, MC, V. Daily 7am–midnight.

Pilar del Toro SPANISH/ANDALUSIAN   Pilar del Toro is a multipurpose drinking-and-dining venue whose charms and diversity only become visible if you take a tour through the labyrinth of its upper dining rooms. It's housed in a private home dating from 1879. The typical Andalusian interior patio with fountain at its center is, with comfy chairs and sofas, perfect for a drink. Above you'll find three

Strolling Andalusia's Most Romantic Street

The most-walked street in Granada is **Carrera del Darro,** running north along the Darro River. It was discovered by the Romantic artists of the 19th century; many of their etchings (subsequently engraved) of scenes along this street were widely circulated, doing much to spread the fame of Granada throughout Europe. You can still find some of these engravings in musty antiques shops. Carrera del Darro ends at Paseo de los Tristes (Avenue of the Sad Ones), named for the funeral corteges that once passed by en route to the cemetery.

snug dining areas, including a sheltered garden with dining tables and two romantic and intimate candlelit dining rooms. Enjoy dishes like puff pastry filled with spinach and ham, codfish with a mousseline of avocado, roasted striped bass with mushroom sauce, and sliced or roasted lamb with fig sauce.

Hospital de Santa Ana 12. © **95-822-54-70.** Reservations recommended for the restaurant, not for the tapas bar. Main courses 10€–18€. AE, DC, MC, V. Daily 1–4pm and 8:30–11pm.

Restaurante Sevilla SPANISH/ANDALUSIAN   Attracting a mixed crowd of all ages, the Sevilla is definitely *típico*. It's lost some of its atmosphere since they've chosen to hive off the front portion of the bar into a souvenir shop. You now enter just off Calle Oficios down Calle Estribo. In the past it was a hang out for the rich and famous—the "great broads" and "fabulous studs" of the '50s and '60s like Ava Gardner, Marlon Brando, Salvador Dalí, André Segovia, Gene Kelly, and Ingrid Bergman, whose photos are pinned above the bar. The place was first discovered by García Lorca, a patron in the 1930s, and Manuel de Falla. Most dishes are at the lower end of the price scale. The gazpacho, Andalusian veal with fresh vegetables, flan, crusty homemade bread, and the wine of Valdepeñas are among the most popular items. For a main course, the *cordero a la pastoril* is always good (lamb with herbs and paprika served with couscous).

Calle Oficios 12. © **95-822-12-23.** Reservations recommended. Main courses 12€–24€. AE, DC, MC, V. Mon–Sat 1–4:30pm and 8–11:30pm.

EXPLORING GRANADA

It's worth noting that most sites and monuments—apart from the Alhambra—close for a long lunch break from about 1:30 to 3:30pm. Many also close on Mondays.

Try to spend some time walking around Old Granada, just soaking up the atmosphere. The best times of day to do this in summer are early morning or evening, when it's a little cooler. About 3 hours will allow you to see the most interesting sights. If you want some commentary along the way, hire an audio tour player and map from the **This.Is:Granada** tourist booth in Plaza Nueva (© **95-821-02-39;** www.thisis.ws). There are several themed walks with numbered commentary stops along the way. Included are commentaries for visiting the cathedral and the Alhambra, so you won't need to hire an audio guide at those attractions.

Puerta de Elvira is the gate through which Ferdinand and Isabella made their triumphant entry into Granada in 1492. It was once a grisly place, with the rotting

What to See & Do in Granada

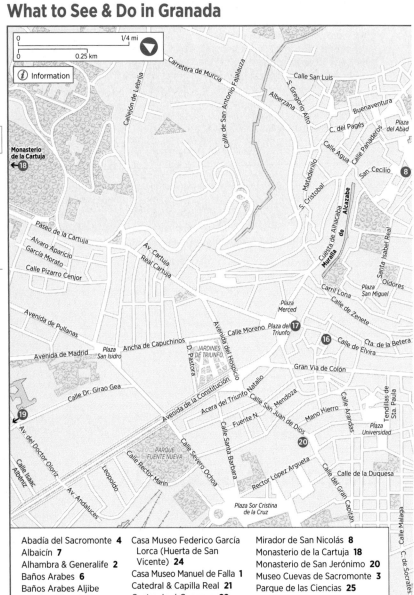

Abadía del Sacromonte **4**
Albaicín **7**
Alhambra & Generalife **2**
Baños Arabes **6**
Baños Arabes Aljibe
de San Miguel **23**
Calle Calderería **15**
Casa de Castril (Museo
Arqueológico) **5**
Casa de los Tiros **14**

Casa Museo Federico García
Lorca (Huerta de San
Vicente) **24**
Casa Museo Manuel de Falla **1**
Catedral & Capilla Real **21**
Centro José Guerrero **22**
Hammams de Al Andalus **10**
Iglesia de San Andrés **16**
Iglesia de Santa Ana **9**
Iglesia de Santiago **13**

Mirador de San Nicolás **8**
Monasterio de la Cartuja **18**
Monasterio de San Jerónimo **20**
Museo Cuevas de Sacromonte **3**
Parque de las Ciencias **25**
Plaza de Toros **19**
Plaza Nueva **12**
Puerta de Elvira **17**
This.Is.Granada tourist booth **11**

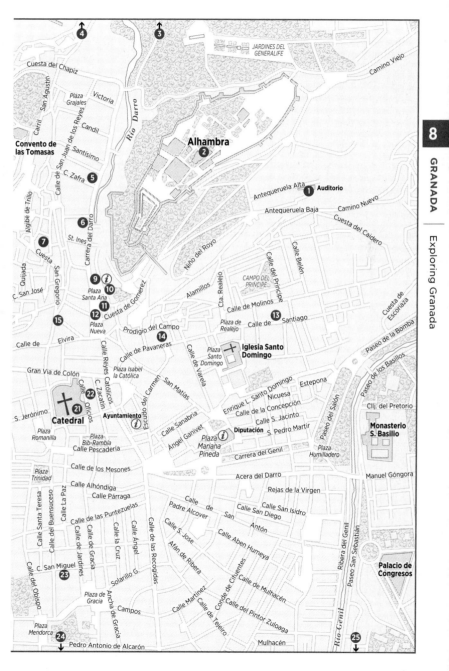

JARDINES DEL GENERALIFE

Cuesta del Chapiz

Camino Viejo

Plaza Grajales
Victoria
Candil
San Agustín
Carril
Río Darro

Convento de las Tomasas

Calle de San Juan de los Reyes
Santísimo
Calle de C. Zafra

Alhambra

Antequeruela Alta **Auditorio**

Antequeruela Baja
Camino Nuevo
Cuesta del Caidero

Algibe de Trillo
Carrera del Darro
St. Inés

Cuesta
San Gregorio
C. Quijada
C. San José

Niño del Royo

Calle de Belén

CAMPO DEL PRINCIPE

Cta. Realejo
Alamillos
Calle del Príncipe

Cuesta de Escoriaza

Plaza Santa Ana
Cuesta de Gomérez
Plaza Nueva
Prodigio del Campo

Calle de Molinos

Plaza de Realejo
Calle de Santiago

Paseo de la Bomba

Calle de
Elvira
Calle de Pavaneras
Calle de Varela

Plaza Santo Domingo
Iglesia Santo Domingo

Paseo de los Basilios

Gran Vía de Colón

Plaza Isabel la Católica
Calle Reyes Católicos
C. Zacatín
Calle Oficios

San Matías
Escudo del Carmen

Enrique L. Santo Domingo
Nicuesa
Estepona

Paseo del Salón

Clj. del Pretorio

S. Jerónimo
Catedral
Ayuntamiento

Calle Sanabria
Ángel Ganivet

Calle de la Concepción
Calle S. Jacinto
Plaza Mariana Pineda
Diputación S. Pedro Martir

Monasterio S. Basilio

Plaza Romanilla
Plaza Bib-Rambla
Calle Pescadería

Carrera del Genil
Plaza Humilladero

Plaza Trinidad
Calle de los Mesones
Acera del Darro

Manuel Góngora

Calle Alhóndiga
Calle Párraga

Rejas de la Virgen

Calle Santa Teresa
Calle del Buensuceso
Calle La Paz

Calle de las Puntezuelas
Calle de Gracia
Calle de Jardines
Calle la Cruz
Calle Ángel
Calle de las Recogidas

Calle de Padre Alcover
Calle S. José
Afán de Ribera

Calle de San Diego
Calle San Isidro
Antón
Calle Aben Humeya

Ribera del Genil

Paseo San Sebastián

C. San Miguel

Solarillo G.

Conde de Cifuentes
Calle de Mulhacén
Calle del Pintor Zuloaga

Palacio de Congresos

Plaza de Gracia
Ancha de Gracia
Campos

Calle Martínez
Calle de Tejeiro

Río Genil

Plaza Mendorca
Pedro Antonio de Alcarón

Mulhacén

Buy A Bargain Pass

If you plan on seeing most of the city's main tourist sights, consider buying a **Bono Turístico Pass.** Valid for 3 or 5 days they cost 25€ and 30€ respectively (9€ for children for either pass). The monuments included are the Cathedral and Capilla Real, the Alhambra and the Generalife, the Monasterio Cartuja, the Monasterio de San Jerónimo, and the Parque de las Ciencas. The 3-day pass also includes 5 free city bus rides and the 5-day pass includes nine free bus rides and a 24-hour pass for the Granadatour City-sightseeing bus. They can be purchased at the This.Is:Granada ticket booth in Plaza Nueva (📞 95-821 02-39) and the **Caja Granada bank** (Plaza Isabel la Catolica 6, 📞 95-872 100 51). The bank charges a small additional booking fee. You need to specify a day and time for visiting the Alhambra when you buy your pass. (See p. 205). For more information, see www.turgranada.es/bono-turistico/bono-turistico.php.

heads of executed criminals hanging from its portals. The quarter surrounding the gate was the Arab section (*morería*) until all the Arabs were driven out of the city after the Reconquista.

One of the most fascinating streets is **Calle de Elvira;** west of it the Albaicín (old Arab Quarter) rises on a hill. In the 17th and 18th centuries, artisans occupied the shops and ateliers along here and in the surrounding streets. On Calle de Elvira is the **Iglesia de San Andrés,** begun in 1528, with a Mudéjar bell tower. Much of the church was destroyed in the early 19th century, but several interesting paintings and sculptures remain. Another old church in this area is the **Iglesia de Santiago,** constructed in 1501 and dedicated to St James, patron saint of Spain. Built on the site of an Arab mosque, it was damaged in an 1884 earthquake. The church contains the tomb of architect Diego de Siloé (1495–1563), who did much to change the face of the city.

Despite its name, the oldest square is the **Plaza Nueva,** which, under the Muslims, was the site of the bridge of the woodcutters. The river Darro was covered over here, but its waters still flow underneath the square (which in Franco's time was named the Plaza del General Franco). On the east side of the Plaza Nueva is the 16th-century **Iglesia de Santa Ana,** built by Siloé. Inside its five-nave interior you can see a Churriguesque reredos and coffered ceiling.

The *corrida* isn't very popular here, but if you want to check out a bullfight anyway, they're usually limited to the week of the Fiesta de Corpus Christi from May 29 to June 6, or the Día de la Cruz (Day of the Cross) observed on May 3. There's also a fight on the last Sunday in September. **Plaza de Toros,** the bullring, is on Avenida de Doctor Olóriz, close to the soccer stadium. For more information, call 📞 **95-827-24-51.**

Abadía del Sacromonte   Crowning the Sacromonte (Sacred Hill) is this once-dilapidated abbey, now much restored. Originally, this was a Benedictine monastery, and the ashes of San Cecilio, the patron saint of Granada, are stored inside. It's a bit of a trek to get to, but if you make the journey you'll be well rewarded. Inside you'll find an impressive collection of religious art and treasures surrounded by Baroque

The Alhambra

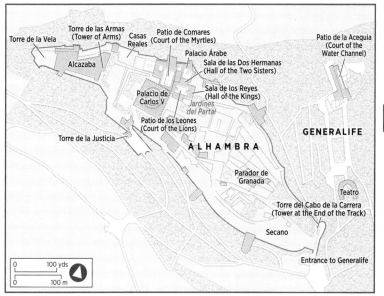

flourishes and columns. It's said that the local specialty *tortilla de sacromonte*, a thick Spanish omelet made with sheeps' brains, was concocted by the monks here.

Camino del Sacromonte, Sacromonte. Ⓒ **95-822-14-45.** Admission 3€ adults, 2€ children aged 17 and under. Tues–Sat 10am–1pm and 4–6pm; Sun 11am–1pm and 4–6pm. Guided tours every 30 min.

Albaicín ★★ This old Arab Quarter on one of Granada's two main hills doesn't belong to the city of 19th-century buildings and wide boulevards. It, and the surrounding Gypsy caves of Sacromonte, are holdovers from an older past. The Albaicín once flourished as the residential section of the Moors, but fell into decline when the Christians drove them out. This narrow labyrinth of crooked streets escaped the fate that befell much of Granada, torn down in the name of progress. Preserved are its alleyways, cisterns, fountains, plazas, whitewashed houses, villas, and the decaying remnants of the old city gate. Here and there you can catch a glimpse of a private patio filled with fountains and plants, a traditional, elegant way of life that continues.

Alhambra and Generalife ★★★ The stunningly beautiful and celebrated **Calat Alhambra (Red Castle)** is perhaps the most remarkable fortress ever constructed and without doubt Andalusia's most beautiful. Muslim architecture in Spain reached its apogee at this pleasure palace once occupied by Nasrid princes and their harems. Although later Moorish occupants turned the Alhambra into a lavish palace, it was originally constructed for defensive purposes on a rocky hilltop outcropping above the Darro River. The modern city of Granada was built across the river from the Alhambra, about .8km (½ mile) from its western foundations.

When you first see the Alhambra, its somewhat somber exterior may surprise you. The true delights of this Moorish palace are within. You pick up your ticket, which you need to have **booked in advance** (see p. 204) at the Entrada del Generalife y de la Alhambra. There's an informative audio guide available here at the entrada for 4€. Allow at least 3 hours for your visit—there's a great deal to see.

The tour begins in the **Mexuar,** also known as Palacio Nazaríes (Palace of the Nasrids), the first of the trio of palaces that compose the Alhambra. This was the main council chamber where the sultan's chief ministers met. The largest of these chambers, the Hall of the Mexuar, was converted to a Catholic chapel in the 1600s. From this chapel a panoramic view spreads over the rooftops of the Albaicín.

Pass through another chamber of the sultan's ministers, the Cuarto Dorado (Golden Room), and you'll find yourself in the small but beautiful **Patio del Mexuar.** Constructed in 1365, this is where the sultan sat on giant cushions and listened to the petitions of his subjects or met privately with his chief ministers. The windows here are surrounded by panels and richly decorated with tiles and stucco.

The Palace of the Nasrids, Mexuar was constructed around two courtyards, the **Patio de los Arrayanes (Court of the Myrtles)** and the **Patio de los Leonares (Court of the Lions) ★★★**. The latter was the royal residence.

The Court of the Myrtles has a narrow reflecting pool banked by myrtle trees. Note the decorative and rare tiles, arguably the finest in the Alhambra. Behind it is the **Sala de Comares,** also called the **Salón de Embajadores (Hall of the Ambassadors)**, with an elaborately carved throne room built between 1334 and 1354. The crowning cedar wood dome of this salon evokes the seven heavens of the Muslim cosmos.

An opening off the Court of the Myrtles leads to the greatest architectural achievement of the Alhambra, the **Patio de los Leonares (Court of Lions) ★★★** built by Muhammad V. At its center is Andalusia's finest fountain, which rests on 12 marble lions. These marble lions represent the hours of the day, the months of the year, and the signs of the zodiac. Legend claims that water flowed from the mouth of a different lion each hour of the day. The courtyard is lined with arcades supported by 124 (count them) slender marble columns. This was the heart of the palace, the most private section where the sultan enjoyed his harem of both male and female beauties.

At the back of the Leonares courtyard is the **Sala de los Abencerrajes ★**, named for a noble family who were rivals of the last emir, Boabdil. This hall has a richly adorned honeycombed ceiling. To get rid of his rivals, Boabdil invited them to a banquet. In the middle of the banquet, his guards entered and massacred his guests.

Opening onto the Court of Lions are other salons of intrigue, notably the **Hall of the Two Sisters (Sala de las Dos Hermanas),** where the sultan kept his "favorite" of the moment. The Hall of the Two Sisters takes its name from the two large identical white marble slabs in the pavement. Boabdil's stern, unforgiving mother, Ayesha, once lived in the Hall of the Two Sisters. This salon has a honeycomb dome and is celebrated as the finest example of Spanish Islamic architecture in the world.

The nearby **Sala de los Reyes (Hall of Kings)** was the great banqueting hall of the Alhambra, site of parties, orgies, and feasts. Its ceiling paintings are on leather and date from the 1300s. Eunuchs guarded the harem but not always well. According to legend, one sultan beheaded 36 Moorish princes here because one of them was suspected of being intimate with his favorite.

A gallery leads to the **Patio de la Reja (Court of the Window Grille).** This is where Washington Irving lived in furnished rooms and where he began to write his famous book *Tales of the Alhambra.* The best-known tale is the legend of Zayda, Zorayda, and Zorahayda, the three beautiful princesses who fell in love with three captured Spanish soldiers outside the Torre de las Infantas. Irving credits the French with saving the Alhambra for posterity, but in fact they were responsible for blowing up seven of the towers in 1812, and it was a Spanish soldier who cut the fuse before more damage could be done. When the Duke of Wellington arrived a few years later, he chased out the chickens, the Gypsies, and the transient beggars who were using the Alhambra as a tenement and set up house here himself.

Before going on to the Emperor Charles V's palace, see the other gems around the Court of Lions, including the **Baños Reales (Royal Baths),** with their lavish multi-colored decorations. Light enters through star-shaped apertures in the ceilings. To the immediate east of the baths is the **Daraxa Garden,** and to its immediate south the lovely **Mirador de Daraxa,** the sultana's private balcony onto Granada.

To the immediate southeast of these attractions are the **Jardines del Partal ★★** and their perimeter towers. The beautiful gardens occupy a space that once was the kitchen garden, filled with servants preparing the sultan's banquets. The gardens are dominated by the **Torre de Las Damas (Ladies' Tower).** This tower and its pavilion, with its five-arched portico, are all that is left of the once-famous Palacio del Partal, the oldest palace at the Alhambra. Of less interest are the perimeter towers, including the Mihrab Tower, a former Nasrid oratory; the Torre de las Infantas (Tower of the Princesses), and Torre de la Cautiva (Tower of the Captive). Like the Damas tower, these were also once sumptuously decorated inside; today only some decoration remains.

Finally, move to the immediate southwest to visit **Emperor Charles V's Palace (Palacio de Carlos V) ★**, where the Holy Roman emperor lived. Charles may have been horrified when he saw a cathedral placed in the middle of the great mosque at Córdoba, but he's also responsible for some serious architectural confusion in Granada. He literally built a Renaissance palace in the middle of this Moorish stronghold. It's quite beautiful, but distinctly out of place in such a setting—Charles V did not consider the Nasrid palaces grand enough. In 1526 he ordered Pedro Machuca,

---

 Walking to and from the Alhambra

Many visitors opt for a taxi or the bus (nos. 31 and 32) to the Alhambra, but if you're feeling fit, you can walk up. The most direct route is to take **Cuesta de Gomérez** from Plaza Nueva. It's a steep but very pleasant half-hour walk. Pass under the Puerta de las Granadas at the top of the street and just follow the wide, steep tree-fringed pathway on up the hill. You'll come to the Puerta de la Justicia which was previously the entrance to the Alhambra. Nowadays you need to continue for another 10 minutes on around the walls of the Alhambra until you reach the main entrance. Another, slightly shorter, route, the **Cuesta de los Chinos** leads from the top end of Paseo de los Tristes. Personally I take the bus up and then choose one of these two routes to walk down. Cuesta de los Chinos is my favorite. To pick it up, take a right out of the main entrance as you leave, follow the pavement a short distance and take a right at the La Mimbre restaurant. The path continues on under a large archway.

a student of Michelangelo, to design him a fitting royal residence and financed the palace by levying a tax on the Muslims. In spite of its incongruous location, the final result is one of the purest examples of classical Renaissance in Spain.

The square exterior opens to reveal a magnificent circular, two-story courtyard that is open to the sky. Inside the palace are two museums. The first, **Museo de la Alhambra** (© 95-802-79-00), is a museum of Hispano-Muslim Art, its salons opening onto the Myrtle and Mexuar Courts. They display artifacts retrieved from the Alcázar, including fragments of sculpture, but also unusual braziers and even perfume burners used in the harems. The most outstanding exhibit is a **blue amphora ★** that is 132 centimeters (52 in.) high. This precious object stood for years in the Hall of the Two Sisters. Also look for an ablutions basin dating from the 10th century and adorned with lions chasing stags and an ibex. The museum is open Tuesday to Saturday from 9am to 7:15pm and Sunday from 9am to 5:45pm.

The palace also houses the **Museo Bellas Artes en la Alhambra** (© 95-822-48-43), open Tuesday 2:30pm to 8pm, Wednesday to Saturday from 9am to 8pm, and Sunday from 9am to 2:30pm. The first public museum in Spain, it's strong on religious paintings and sculpture from the 16th to the 18th centuries, particularly those by Granada's most famous artist, Alonso Cano.

Before leaving the Alhambra precincts, try to see the **Alcazaba,** which dates from the 9th century and is the oldest part of the complex. This rugged Middle Ages fortress was built for defensive purposes. For a spectacular **view ★★**, climb the **Torre de la Vela (Watchtower).** You look into the lower town onto Plaza Nueva, and also see the snowcapped Sierra Nevada in the distance. From here you can also view the Generalife (see below) and the "Gypsy hill" of Sacromonte.

Return the way you came until you reach the gardens of the summer palace, where a left turn onto the Paseo de los Cipreses leads you to the main building of the **Generalife ★★**, built in the 13th century to overlook the Alhambra and set in 30 lush hectares (75 acres). The sultans used to spend their summers in this palace (pronounced "heh-neh-rah-*lee*-feh"), safely locked away with their harems. The palace is mainly noted for its beautiful courtyards, including **Patio de Polo,** where the visitors of old arrived on horseback. The highlight is its **gardens ★★★**, begun in the 13th century but much modified over the years. Originally, they contained orchards and pastures for domestic animals. An enclosed Oriental garden, **Patio de la Acequía,** was constructed around a long pool, with rows of water jets making graceful arches above it. The **Patio de la Sultana** (also called the Patio de los Cipreses) was the secret rendezvous point for Zoraxda, wife of Sultan Abu Hasan, and her lover, the chief of the Abencerrajes. The **Escalera del Agua (the Water Staircase)** with water flowing gently down the handrails, not only sounds soothing, but is also a clever form of early air conditioning. The cool air from the water wafts around you as you climb.

Palacio de Carlos V. © **90-244-12-21.** www.alhambra-patronato.es. Comprehensive ticket, including Alhambra and Generalife, 12€; Museo Bellas Artes 1.50€, E.U. citizens free on production of ID card or passport; Garden visits 6€; illuminated visits 12€. Mar–Oct daily 8:30am–8pm, floodlit visits Tues–Sat 10pm–midnight; Nov–Feb daily 8:30am–6pm, floodlit visits Fri–Sat 8–10pm.

Baños Arabes Remarkably, these "baths of the walnut tree," as they were known by the Moors, escaped destruction during the reign of the Reyes Católicos (Ferdinand

The Alhambra is the most-visited monument in Spain, receiving 3.2 million visitors a year, more than the Prado in Madrid. Only 7,700 tickets are sold per day and the actual number of tickets available on any particular day depends on how many of the quota have already been sold in advance. You can queue up at the entrance and hope to get tickets which cost 12€ when the ticket offices open at 8am, but it can be a long wait and you are not guaranteed a ticket. Often the day's quota is exhausted by 1pm, forcing gatekeepers to turn many hopefuls away, especially during peak season in spring and summer. After the day's allotment of tickets has been sold, the curators will sell tickets just to the gardens and the fortress which cost 6€. These are not particularly attractive, and some visitors feel they've been ripped off. The gardens to which visitors have access are relatively small and creations of the late 19th and early 20th centuries. And the fortress, a ruin that survives without many changes from the Arab era, is big, sprawling, and austere, without the joy and architectural verve of the palace, which is the most photographed, most charming, and most evocative part of the Alhambra.

However, you can **avoid the long lines** entirely by purchasing **advance tickets** and I strongly advise that you do. You can do this by calling ✆ **90-288-80-01; www.alhambra-tickets.es.**

(From outside Spain call ✆ **00-34-93-492-37-50.**) You pay a 1€ service charge but it's most certainly worth it. You can also purchase advance tickets from any Caixa Bank ATM throughout Spain.

Each ticket indicates the 30-minute block of time during which you're granted access to the Nasrid Palace at the heart of the complex and it's essential you **arrive in good time**. Pick up your tickets at ticket booths at the entrance with your reservation number and the credit card you used to make the booking. It's then a good 15- to 20-minute walk through some of the gardens to reach the palace. You may also want to rent an audio guide which costs 4€ and requires you to leave some ID (credit card or passport) as a security deposit. E.U. citizens should leave a credit card and keep hold of their passport as you need your passport to gain free entry to the Museo de Bellas Artes which is also in the complex.

Another way to avoid standing in line to buy tickets is to take a **guided tour.** Most of the travel agencies in Granada charge between 38€ and 45€ per person for a 3- to 4-hour visit. Ask at the tourist information offices for details.

Experts recommend spending at least 3 hours for even the briefest visit to the Alhambra. If you're driving there, you'll find plenty of **free parking** spaces at the main entrance.

and Isabella). Among the oldest buildings still standing in Granada, and among the best-preserved Muslim baths in Spain, they predate the Alhambra. Visigothic and Roman building materials are supposed to have gone into their construction.

Carrera del Darro 31. ✆ **95-802-78-00.** Free admission. Tues–Sat 10am–2pm.

Casa de Castril (Museo Arqueológico)   This building has always been one of the most handsome Renaissance palaces in Granada. The Plateresque facade of

1539 has been attributed to Diego de Siloé. In 1869, it was converted into a museum with a collection of minor artifacts found in the area. The most outstanding exhibit here is a collection of Egyptian alabaster vases that were dug up in a necropolis in Almuñécar. Look especially for the figure of a bull from Arjona. There is also a selection of decorative Moorish art that the Arabs left behind as they retreated from Granada.

Museo Arqueológico, Carrera del Darro 41-43. ✆ **95-857-54-08.** www.museosdeandalucia.es. Admission 1.50€. Free to E.U. passport holders. Tues 2:30-8pm; Wed-Sat 9am-8:30pm; Sun 9am-2:30pm.

Casa de los Tiros   The "House of Shots" is a fortress-like palace that is Renaissance in its architecture, dating from the 1500s. Its name comes from the musket barrels protruding from its facade. Once it was owned by a noble family who were given the Generalife after the Reconquest of Granada. Their proudest possession was the sword of Boabdil, the last Muslim king. A carving of that sword can be seen in the facade of the building along with statues of Mercury, Theseus, Hercules, Hector, and Jason.

Inside you'll find intriguing portraits of Catholic monarchs, including Ferdinand, Isabella, and even Philip IV. Each royal looks rather dour. The major feature of the house is the **Cuadra Dorada (Hall of Gold),** which is decorated with gold lettering and more royal portraits. Various photos, engravings, and centuries-old lithographs depict Granada in the 19th and early 20th centuries.

Plaza Padres Suárez, Calle Pavaneras 19, Realejo. ✆ **95-822-10-72.** www.museosdeandalucia.es. Admission 1.50€. Free to E.U. passport holders. Tues 2:30-8:30pm; Wed-Sat 9am-8:30pm; Sun 9am-2:30pm.

Casa Museo Federico García Lorca (Huerta de San Vicente) ★ 🎁   Poet/dramatist Federico García Lorca, author of *Blood Wedding, The House of Bernarda Alba,* and *A Poet in New York,* spent many happy summers with his family here at their vacation home. He moved to Granada in 1909, a dreamy-eyed schoolboy, and was endlessly fascinated with its life, including the Alhambra and the Gypsies, whom he later described compassionately in his *Gypsy Ballads.* The house is decorated with green trim and grillwork and filled with family memorabilia like furniture and portraits. You can look out at the Alhambra from one of its balconies. You can inspect the poet's upstairs bedroom and see his oak desk stained with ink. Look for the white stool that he carried to the terrace to watch the sun set over Granada. The house is set in the middle of Parque Federico García Lorca amidst leafy trees filled with twittering birds. Unfortunately the peace is somewhat shattered by the roar of traffic from the nearby roads. If you're a serious Lorca fan you can also make the journey to Fuente Vaqueros about a half-hour drive out of town to visit his birthplace. See p. 222.

Calle de la Virgen Blanca s/n, Parque Federico García Lorca. ✆ **95-825-84-66.** www.huertadesanvicente.com. Admission 3€. Apr 1-June 30 and Sept Tues-Sun 10am-12:30pm and 5-7:30pm; July-Aug Tues-Sun 10am-2:30pm; Oct-Mar Tues-Sun 10am-12:30pm and 4-6:30pm.

Casa Museo Manuel de Falla   The composer Manuel de Falla (1876–1946) lived in this charming whitewashed house on the Alhambra hill. His villa—called a carmen—is pretty much as he left it and is filled with memorabilia. You can see his piano and his original furniture, plus photographs, manuscripts, and other mementos. The garden is awash with roses, and you can stand at the same spot the composer did to enjoy the panoramic view. The location is across from the Alhambra Palace Hotel.

Calle Antequerela Alta 11. © **95-822-21-89.** www.manueldefalla.org. Admission 3.50€. Tues–Fri 10am–1:30pm.

Catedral and Capilla Real ★★★ This richly ornate Renaissance cathedral with its spectacular altar is one of the country's architectural highlights, acclaimed for its beautiful facade and gold-and-white interior. Begun in 1521, it was completed in 1714.

Enrique de Egas created the original Gothic-style plans, but it was Renaissance maestro Diego de Siloé who designed the facade and the chief attraction inside the cathedral, the **Capilla Mayor ★★**, a rotunda circled by an ambulatory. The Capilla Mayor is surmounted by a 45m (150 ft) dome. The graceful rotunda has two architectural layers, the upper one adorned by art by Alonso Cano depicting the life of the Madonna along with stunning stained glass that dates from the 1500s. At the entrance to the rotunda is a pair of panels, one depicting Ferdinand and Isabella in prayer, the other by Alonso Cano depicting Adam and Eve.

Several glittering side chapels also decorate the cathedral, and one is especially extravagant, the carved and gilded Capilla de Nuestra Señora de la Antigua, also known as the Capilla Dorada, on the north wall. Before leaving the area, and once outside, note the Puerta del Perdón, a notably elaborate side entrance facing north on Calle de la Cárcel.

Behind the cathedral is the flamboyant Gothic and Plateresque **Royal Chapel.** Visitors enter through the Lonja (Exchange House), which is an adjoining structure on Calle de los Oficios, a narrow pedestrian street that runs alongside the cathedral. Here you'll find the remains of Queen Isabella and her husband Ferdinand. It was their wish to be buried in recaptured Granada, not Castile or Aragón. Work was begun by Enrique de Egas in 1506 but completed in 1521 when Charles V reigned as emperor. Nonetheless, the chapel still has a unity of architectural style. Inside, the chapel is a virtual celebration of the Isabelline style, with its ribbed vaulting along with walls emblazoned with the arms of Isabella and Ferdinand, the conquerors of Granada.

A highlight is a visit to the chancel, enclosed by a **screen ★** by Master Bartolomé. This adornment contains the **mausoleums ★★** of Ferdinand and Isabella on the right. You may be surprised by how short they were. Occupying much larger tombs are the remains of their daughter, Joanna the Mad, and her husband, Philip the Handsome. Domenico Fancelli of Florence sculpted the recumbent Carrera marble figures of the Catholic monarchs in 1517 and Bartolomé Ordóñez the figures of Juana la Loca and Felipe el Hermoso, the parents of Charles V, in 1520.

Look for the stairs at the royal feet of the sculptures. These lead to a crypt that contains a quartet of lead caskets where the royal ashes actually lie, including a very small casket for one royal grandchild. Of special interest is the **high altar *retablo* ★** dating from 1520. This was one of the first *retablos* in Spain to show no Gothic influence. If you head for the north transept, you will encounter the most celebrated triptych in Granada (much reproduced on postcards), the *Triptych of the Passion* by the Flemish artist Thierry Bouts.

The sacristy displays Isabella's personal **art collection ★★**, including many works by Flemish masters and various Spanish and Italian artists, like Rogier Van der

Weyden and Botticelli. Some of the most outstanding pieces of art are by Memling, Bartolomé, and Bermejo. A glass case contains Ferdinand of Aragón's sword and Isabella's scepter and crown, a reliquary, and a missal. You can also see the queen's ornate jewel chest. Church vestments are on display in the sacristy. Above the chapel's exit doorway is a copy of the famous painting of Boabdil's surrender to Isabella. She is depicted wearing her filigree crown—which you've just seen.

The cathedral is in the center of Granada off two prominent streets, Gran Vía de Colón and Calle de San Jerónimo. The Capilla Real abuts the cathedral's eastern edge.

Plaza de la Lonja, Gran Vía de Colón 5. ✆ **95-822-29-59.** Cathedral 3.50€; chapel 3.50€. Mon–Sat 10:30am–1:30pm and 3:30–6:30pm (4–8pm in summer). Sun afternoon hours only.

Centro José Guerrero   The artist José Guerrero was born in Granada in 1914. By the time of his death in 1991, his paintings were owned by some of the most important Spanish museums of contemporary art. The collection at this center covers the entire scope of his life, with a representation of his key works and milestones in his artistic production. This museum displays some of his best works.

Calle Oficios 8. ✆ **95-822-51-85.** www.centroguerrero.org. Free admission. Tues–Sun 11am–2pm; Tues–Sat 5–9pm.

Monasterio de la Cartuja ★   This 16th-century monastery, off the Albaicín on the outskirts of Granada, is sometimes called the Christian answer to the Alhambra because of its ornate stucco and marble and the Baroque Churriguesque fantasy in the sacristy. Its most notable paintings are by Bocanegra, its outstanding sculpture by Mora. The church of this Carthusian monastery was decorated with Baroque stucco in the 17th century, and its 18th-century sacristy is an excellent example of latter-day Baroque style. Napoleon's armies killed St Bruno here. Sometimes one of the Carthusian monks will take you on a guided tour.

Paseo de Cartujar s/n. ✆ **95-816-19-32.** Admission 3.50€. Daily 10am–1pm and 4–8pm (closes at 6pm in winter).

Monasterio de San Jerónimo ★   Following the Reconquest of Granada by Ferdinand and Isabella, this was the first monastery to be founded. Dating from the 16th century, the restored monastery-church is one of the grandest buildings designed by Diego de Siloé. Its public cloister represents a magnificent use of space, with double tiers of arcaded ambulatories enveloping an orange grove. The monastery was severely damaged by Napoleon's troops.

Calle Rector López Argüeta. ✆ **95-827-93-37.** Admission 3.50€. Winter Mon–Sun 10am–2pm and 3–6:30pm, Sun and hols 11am–1:30pm; summer Mon–Fri 10am–1:30pm and 4–7:30pm, weekends and hols 10am–2:30pm and 4–7:30pm.

Museo Cuevas de Sacromonte   For decades under Franco's rule, Gypsies were scorned—along with the architecture on their hill, Sacromonte—and even persecuted. Times have changed, and today their flamenco music is taken seriously, regarded as an art form, and approached with a high degree of scholarship.

This living, breathing museum of a formerly vital but now-dying way of life combines 10 separate caves, each a former residence or crafts studio, along with common exposition areas and a botanical garden. Many tools are displayed, including a formidable-looking loom. There's also a carpenter's studio, a kiosk selling flamenco recordings and

Marquetry the Old-Fashioned Way

Connoisseurs of the fine art of marquetry (the craft in which tiny pieces of bone and colored hardwoods are arranged into geometric patterns and glued into wooden frames) may be interested in the demonstration of this art form. You'll find the shop inside the Alhambra complex, just before the entrances to the palaces. **Laguna Taracea,** Real de la Alhambra 30 (© **95-822-70-46; www.laguna-taracea.com).**

The company was established by the ancestors of today's owner, Miguel Laguna, in 1877. Know before you buy that prices vary with the percentage of real bone in the raw materials. Marquetry work that's crafted from authentic hardwoods and bone sells for up to three times as much as clones made from colored plastic. After a few moments under the tutelage of this place, you'll recognize the difference.

For sale in the shop are elaborately patterned, and very beautiful, trays, boxes, chess sets, picture frames, and more, as well as large, heirloom-quality chests of drawers, each emulating a different 17th-century Iberian design and each selling for several thousand euros.

gift items, plus a staff who works to produce an ongoing series of cultural and ecological events that change on a rotating basis.

To get there, take bus no. 34 from Plaza Nueva or any of the stops along Carrera del Darro and alight at stop Sacramonte 2. Don't consider walking—it's a really long way. Barranco de los Negros s/n. © **95-821-51-20.** www.sacromontegranada.com. Admission 5€. Winter Mon–Sun 10am–2pm and 4–7pm; summer Mon–Sun 10am–2pm and 5–9pm.

Parque de las Ciencias ★ ☺   Across from the convention center of Granada, this science park is a vast array of attractions, embracing everything from a Biosphere Room to a Planetarium, from the Explora Room to a Butterfly Park. Dominating the park is an observation tower, soaring 50m (165 ft) with panoramic views over Granada. The on-site museum has interactive exhibits and conducts scientific experiments. To reach it from the old center, jump aboard bus 1 or 5. Av. del Mediterráneo, Zaidín. © **95-813-19-00.** www.parqueciencias.com. Park 6€; planetarium 2.50€. Tues–Sat 10am–7pm; Sun 10am–3pm.

SHOPPING

Alcaicería ★★, once the Moorish silk market, is next to the cathedral in the lower city just at the bottom of Calle Oficios. The narrow streets of this rebuilt village of shops are filled with vendors selling the arts and crafts of Granada province. For the souvenir hunter, the Alcaicería offers one of the most splendid assortments in Spain of tiles, castanets, and wire figures of Don Quixote chasing windmills. Lots of Spanish jewelry can be found here, on a par with the finest Toledan work.

Handicraft stores virtually line the main shopping arteries, especially those centered on **Puerta Real,** including **Gran Vía de Colón, Reyes Católicos,** and **Angel Ganivet.** For the best selection of antiques stores, mainly selling furnishings of Andalusia, browse the shops along **Cuesta de Elvira.**

SHOPPING FOR spanish GUITARS

Granada and the art of guitar making have always been intricately intertwined. Even if you don't want to haul a guitar back from Andalusia, you might want to check out the neighborhood where they're manufactured.

Calle Cuesta de Gomérez, a narrow and steeply sloping street that runs uphill to the Alhambra from a point near the Plaza Nueva in Old Granada, is the centerpiece of the city's guitar-making trade. Today there are at least five guitar-making studios—usually small shops with no more than two, and usually only one, artisan per cubbyhole. Prices for the most basic instruments might, at a pinch, begin at 325€. Costs for some of the most resonant guitars can easily exceed 3,500€.

The oldest studio, **Casa Ferrer,** Calle Cuesta de Gomérez 26 (☎ **95-822-18-32**),

was established in 1875. A competitor is **José López Bellido,** at no. 36 (☎ **95-822-27-41**). At least one additional craft shop, **Germán Pérez Barranco,** still maintains a presence at Calle Cuesta de Gomérez 10 (☎ **95-822-70-33;** www. guitarreria.com). Most business is conducted from premises at Reyes Católicos 47; the cubbyhole on Calle Cuesta de Gomérez is maintained primarily as a prestigious and highly visible link to the company's origins.

In most places along Calle Cuesta de Gomérez, expect gruff but courteous responses to your questions. Settings are unpretentious, usually in a working crafts studio littered with gluepots and tools for fine woodworking.

Fashion

Adolfo Dominguez ★ One of the newer names on the European fashion scene, Adolfo Dominguez dresses women and, to a lesser degree, men, children, and homes in a rich, ultra-stylish look that is popular throughout Europe. This branch in Granada is one of about a dozen in Spain. Prices and levels of chic are both relatively high. Alhóndiga 5. ☎ **95-852-31-32.**

Bimba Y Lola Cool, funky, and unique, B&L's range of elegant designer clothes, bags, and shoes is perfect for young sassy ladies looking for something a little different with serious Andalusian style. Av. Reyes Católicos 16. ☎ **95-822-97-02.**

El Caballo Possibly Granada's best leatherware shop, Caballo sells classic handbags, suitcases, belts, wallets, and shoes. The leather used is of the highest quality, soft, and beautifully cut and stitched. Av. Reyes Católicos 45. ☎ **95-822-22-54.**

Loewe ★ In business since 1846 and supplying the royal household since 1905, Loewe is the byword for luxurious Spanish leatherware. Come here for utterly elegant, easy-to-wear bags that age beautifully. Fashion editors favor the house's signature "oro" mustard-gold shade of leather. Calle Ángel Ganivet 6 ☎ **95-822-62-22.**

Oxia If you happen to have teenage children of your own, the merchandise in this shop might remind you of exactly what you *don't* want them to wear. The place defines itself as a repository for "urban fashion." Calle Gracia 21. ☎ **95-825-84-49.**

Gifts

El Zoco Nazari This small but choice shop is packed, cheek-by-jowl, against junkier-looking competitors on either side. Much of what it sells is carefully chosen and attractive, but of particular interest are Art Deco era (1930s) replicas of posters advertising the glories of flamenco in Andalusia; Moroccan mirror frames set with bone; porcelain, sometimes with silver appliqués that emulate the *La Loza Dorada* motifs of the 10th-century Nazari dynasty; and some very fine leather goods. Reyes Católicos 50. ✆ **95-822-59-77.**

Local Specialties

La Alacena de Andalucia Andalusia is famous throughout the world for its fine, delicately flavored olive oils and this little shop run by a New Zealander called Kris is the place to come to try some, learn about how olives are harvested and the oil produced, and of course purchase some too. Calle San Jeronimo 3. ✆ **95-820-88-00.**

Moroccan Crafts

Bazar Abdel You can't leave this shop without a distinct sense of Granada's Moorish antecedents, and the vivid tradition of craftsmanship that flourishes in Morocco, just across the Straits of Gibraltar. Come here for inlaid boxes, chastened copper and brassware, porcelain in the jewel tones of the sub-Sahara, and for some genuinely intriguing mirror frames crafted from hammered silver and mosaics of exotic hardwoods and bone. Carrera del Darro 49. ✆ **95-822-23-29.**

Tienda "Morocco" On display in this store are mirror frames crafted from bone, copper, and silver together with parchment lamps, porcelain, marquetry-inlaid boxes, and gift items. Carrera del Darro 15. ✆ **95-822-13-71.**

Silver

Rafael Moreno Orfebre This is one of the most important silversmiths in Granada. Look for chandeliers, religious votive objects, boxes, tableware, and sculptures. Reyes Católicos 28A. ✆ **95-822-99-16.**

GRANADA AFTER DARK

In addition to its vast array of tapas bars, flamenco shows, and dance clubs, Granada is also a major center of Andalusian culture. Ask at the tourist office for a current list of cultural presentations, including dance, concert, and theater performances.

A Shopping Secret

There is a street in Granada that every local shopper of artifacts and cheap clothing knows about: **Calle Calderería Nueva.** Too narrow for cars, and evoking an Arab souk, it slopes abruptly from the Albaicín into the more modern neighborhoods of the town close to Plaza Nueva. Either side is thickly populated with stores of all degrees of junkiness. Some of the crafts stores, especially those selling Moroccan handicrafts, are a little more upscale.

Tapas Bar-Hopping

Here's the remarkable thing about tapas in Granada. They're free! Order a drink and, presto! a free snack gets plonked down beside it. Sometimes there's even a short menu of free tapas for you to choose from. Locals—particularly students and young people—often don't bother ordering dinner, they just hop from bar to bar grazing on tapas along the way. (Prices I quote here are for more substantial plates of food called *raciones*.)

Good streets for a tapas bar crawl include **Calle Navas** which starts at the town hall (Ayuntamiento), **Calle Rosario** and **Plazeta del Agua** which follow on from Navas, and **Calle Elvira**—though quality varies here as it's rather touristy.

Another good place for a tapas crawl is along **Campo del Príncipe,** where at least seven old-fashioned tapas bars do a rollicking business during the cool of the evening.

If you'd like someone to take you on a tapas tour to some of the lesser-visited, seriously good and atmospheric tapas bars, then contact my friend Gayle Mackie at **Granada Tapas Tours** (© **61-944-49-84; www.granadatapas tours.com**). What Gayle doesn't know about tapas in Granada isn't worth knowing. She's even written a book about them. Tours cost 65€ for two people and usually last 2 to 3 hours. (Drinks aren't included in the price.)

The Best Tapas Bars

Bar Pilar del Toro ★ Near the cathedral and the central Plaza Nueva, this tapas bar is attached to an even more famous restaurant. The lovely covered patio with its fountain and rattan sofas is perfect for a chilled glass of sherry and a tapa or two. The building itself is from the 1600s and the restaurant is upstairs. There's also a tearoom in the courtyard in the afternoon. Open daily from 9am to 2am. Entrance on Plaza Santa Ana 12. © **95-822-54-70.**

Bodegas Espadafor ★ This bar has been dishing up tapas since 1910 and with that kind of pedigree, you can be sure they're good. Big sherry-filled barrels line the bar and the walls are decorated with beautiful tiled pictures. The prawn tapa here is particularly tasty. Calle Gran Vía de Colón 59. © **95-820-21-38.**

Casa de Vinos La Brujidera ★ A great variety of regional wine and special tapas are served at this *típico* tavern between Plaza Isabel la Católica and Plaza Nueva in the center of the lower town. Most of the clients are locals and they flock here for one of the best choices of affordable wine from all over Spain. The best tapas are particularly choice cuts of cold meats. In fair weather, umbrella-shaded chairs are placed outside. In the background you'll usually hear jazz playing. Hours are daily from 12:30 to 4pm and 8pm to 2am. Monjas del Carmen 2. © **95-822-25-95.**

Casa Enrique ★★ Near Puerta Real in the center of town, this is arguably Granada's most famous *tasca* (wine bar). It's an old-fashioned masonry-sided hole in the wall—and very cramped. For decor, it relies on antique barrels of wine and sherry. It's known for its *vino costa*, a smooth little wine that goes well with any of the tapas served here. A specialty is thin-sliced serrano ham, and heaped platters of steamed mussels flavored with fresh herbs and white wine. Also try the goat's cheese with fresh anchovies. *Raciones* range from 6€ to 18€. Open from noon to 4pm and 8pm to midnight Monday to Saturday. Calle Accero de Darro 8. ⓒ **95-812-35-08.**

Corrada del Carbón ★   A cozy, convivial place, the interior of which resembles the slightly cluttered patio of a prosperous farmhouse deep in the Iberian countryside, this tapas bar is one of the town center's busiest. Meaty tapas are particularly good. You can hang your coat from one of the branches of the tree in the bar! Open daily 1 to 4pm; Monday–Saturday 8:30pm to midnight. Mariana Pineda 8. ⓒ **95-822-38-10.**

El Agua   This well-maintained, popular bar hidden away in the heart of the Albaicín has an adjoining restaurant in a small garden. The lure is the small *raciones* of cheeses, pâtés, and salads, ranging from 7€ to 10€. Unusual for Andalusia, fondue is also a specialty, as is smoked fish and even caviar. Some of the food is "cooked on the stone," on a hot stone brought to your table. Open Monday to Saturday 8pm to midnight, Sunday 1 to 5pm. Calle Algibe de Trillo 7. ⓒ **95-822-43-56.**

Jamoneria La Musa   Jamoneria kind of gives the game away—it specializes in ham, ham, and ham. You'll see huge legs of it hanging from the ceiling and you'll get to sample some of this melt-in-the-mouth loveliness when you order a glass of wine or a beer. You can sit at the tables here inside on the terrace and still just munch free tapas. No need to order anything more substantial. Calle Alhamar s/n. ⓒ **95-843-44-37.**

La Gran Taverna   In the very center of Granada, on the corner of Cuesta de Gomerez opposite the busy terrace bars of Plaza Neuva, this modern and popular tapas bar attracts both coffee drinkers and wine tasters, as well as lovers of sliced serrano ham, fondues, and liqueurs. Rich and dark, the wooden bar was installed in the building back in the 19th century. Their *montaditos*—slices of bread with tasty toppings like pork steak and tomatoes, or serrano ham and cheese—are a real highlight. Open daily from 9:15am to 2am. Plaza Nueva 2. ⓒ **95-822-88-46.**

Reca   Run by the same team that dish up really tasty food at El Trillo de Reca (see "Where to Dine") this modern, friendly bar right on busy Plaza de la Trinidad is perfect for people-watching. Grab a stool at one of the tables, order a glass of their excellent house wine, and wait and see what the tapa of the day will be. When I was there it was really nice couscous and lamb. Plaza de la Trinidad s/n. ⓒ **63-689-11-89.**

Nightclubs

Most nightclubs begin slowly revving their engines at 11pm but don't really wake up until around midnight. They really get percolating around 2am, continuing on until at least 4am or even sunrise. If you're a nightlife fanatic, consider going out to any of the coffee bars of the city for omelets and breakfast fare beginning around 6:30am.

Camborio   A 20-minute walk uphill from Plaza Nueva, this is a particularly popular address with students. Many of these young people stand on the rooftop terraces for a panoramic view of the Alhambra at sunrise, one of the most striking vistas in all of Andalusia. Each of the four bars plays different music. There's a cover charge

THE GYPSY caves OF SACROMONTE

These inhabited Gypsy caves near the Albaicín are the subject of much controversy. Admittedly, they're a bit of a tourist trap, but they can be a potent enough attraction if you follow some rules.

Once, thousands of Gypsies lived on **Sacromonte (Holy Mountain),** named for several Christians martyred here. However, many of the caves were heavily damaged by rain in 1962, forcing hundreds of occupants to seek shelter elsewhere. Nearly all the Gypsies remaining are involved in one way or another with tourism. (Some don't even live here—they commute from modern apartments in the city.)

When evening settles over Granada, loads of visitors descend on these caves. From each one, you'll hear the rattle of castanets and the strumming of guitars, while everybody in the Gypsy family struts their stuff. Popularly known as the **zambra,** this is intriguing entertainment only if you have an appreciation for the grotesque. Whenever a Gypsy boy or girl comes along with genuine talent, he or she is often grabbed up and hustled off to the more expensive clubs. Those left at home can be rather pathetic in their attempts to entertain.

One of the main reasons for going is to see the caves themselves. If you're expecting primitive living, you may be in for a surprise—many are quite comfortable, with conveniences like telephones and electricity. Often they're decorated with copper and ceramic items—and the inhabitants need no encouragement to sell them to you.

If you want to see the caves, you can walk up the hill or better still take bus number 34 as it's quite a long way. Attempts will be made to lure you inside one or another of the caves—and to get money from you in return for visiting. Alternatively, you can book an organized tour arranged by one of the travel agencies in Granada. Even at the end of one of these group outings—with all expenses theoretically paid in advance—there's likely to be an attempt by the cave dwellers to extract more money from you. As soon as the *zambra* ends, hurry out of the cave as quickly as possible. **Be warned:** Many of our readers have been critical of these tours.

A visit to the caves is almost always included as part of the morning and (more frequently) afternoon city tours offered every day by such companies as **Visitar Granada** (✆ **90-233-00-02;** www. visitargranada.com). The cost is typically 49€ per person. They can also organize transport and tickets to see flamenco at Cueva María La Canastera (see below).

You can, of course, visit the *cuevas* on your own. The clubs below offer a package deal including transportation to and from your hotel and your first drink. Most of these caves are along **Camino del Sacromonte.** The best of these *zambras* include **Cueva La Rocío,** Camino del Sacromonte 70 (✆ **95-822-71-29**), with shows at 10 and 11pm. Entrance, including bus and drink, is 25€. Other Sacromonte clubs include **Cueva María La Canastera (Cueva Museo)** at Camino del Sacromonte 89 (✆ **95-812-11-83**), with an admission of 25€. Shows are at 10:30pm. **Venta El Gallo,** Barranco de los Negroes 5 (✆ **95-822-84-76;** www. ventaelgallo.com), offers shows at 9 and 11pm nightly, including the bus and a first drink for 28€. If you want dinner, too, the total cost is 58€. I've had mixed reviews of this place though. Finally, **Cueva Los Tarantos,** Camino del Sacromonte 9 (✆ **95-822-45-25;** www.cuevaslostarantos.com), features shows at 9:30 and 11pm. Bus fare is included in the cover of 26€, which includes your first drink, or 22€ without transportation.

of between 6€ and 8€ on some nights. Open Thursday to Saturday from 11pm to 7am. Camino del Sacromonte 47. ⓒ **95-822-12-15.**

Copas La Fontana This is one of the biggest and hippest of the *bodegas* lining the edge of the Carrera del Darro, a street that's legendary for its nightlife and its sense of medieval history. The interior is a sprawling labyrinth of ocher-colored rooms, each with lots of wood trim, terracotta floors, and ongoing surges of recently released music from Madrid, Los Angeles, New York, London, and Havana. The paintings decorating the walls include some interesting portraits—and they're all for sale. Amid the permissive madness, you'll see age-old artisans' tools artfully displayed on the thick masonry walls. Cocktails cost 5€. Open Sunday to Thursday from 2pm to 3am, Friday and Saturday from 2pm to 4am. Carrera del Darro 19. ⓒ **95-822-77-59.**

El Príncipe Stylish and well-dressed patrons arrive very late at this disco which only really gets going around 2am. The setting is beneath the high timbered ceiling of an old grain warehouse. The sound system is sophisticated and up to date, sending waves of house and garage music reverberating down to the dance floor from the ceiling above. If you get hungry with all this dance, dance, dance, consider any of the selection of tapas sold until the early hours. El Campo del Príncipe. ⓒ **95-822-80-88.**

Granada 10 Beginning around 2am, the club, close to the Gran Vía and the cathedral, is abuzz with the dance moves of hip 30-somethings and Spanish soap-opera stars. The dress code is a bit posh—hopefuls in sweat suits have been turned away. The sometime-movie theater that houses this place has a cruciform-shaped floor plan, and you'll probably be sandwiched into areas that aren't otherwise devoted to movie seats. A cover charge of 10€ includes a first drink. Open Monday to Friday from 12:30 to 5am, Saturday and Sunday from 12:30 to 7am. Carcel Baja 10. ⓒ **95-822-40-01.**

Kasbah This is like a candlelit cafe you might come across in the sub-Sahara, with silk-embroidered, overstuffed pillows, cozy nooks, and a huge selection of Moroccan teas from 2.80€ to 3€. Hours are daily noon to 2:30am. If you're feeling a little more 21st century, they have Wi-Fi too. Calle Calderería Nueva 4. ⓒ **95-822-79-36.**

Paprika This is a happening place, beginning with an extensive wine and cocktail list. It's also host to monthly art exhibitions and wine tastings. Close to the cathedral, it presents small jazz concerts, even occasional flamenco shows. There's no cover; you pay just for the drinks consumed. You can also dine here from a tasty menu, a fixed-price meal costs 15€ to 30€. A fusion cuisine is offered ranging from Thai curries to Greek moussaka to Italian gnocchi. Open daily 1:30 to 4pm and 8:30pm to 2am. Cuesta del Abarqueros 3. ⓒ **95-880-47-85.**

Planta Baja Live bands from Spain and all over Europe regularly play at this techno dance club. In a central lower-town location, the club is heavily patronized by university students. Look for the listing of bands and their performance times in the front window. There's live music from 10pm. After midnight a DJ takes over. The 6€ cover includes a first drink. Open Thursday to Saturday from 10pm to 6am; closed in July and August. Calle Horno de Abad 11. ⓒ **95-825-35-09.**

Salsero Major   If Latin rhythms are your thing, this is the place to come to. Girls and boys dancing to a South American beat swing and move on the dancefloor. It's not at all pretentious and great fun. Come prepared to dance, particularly if you're female! You can also take dancing classes here during the day. Calle La Paz 20. (No phone.)

Gay & Lesbian Bars

Granada has the largest and most concentrated gay scene in inland Andalusia after Seville. For coastal gay life, head for Torremolinos (see Chapter 11).

El Rincón de San Pedro   This used to be the best gay-friendly bar in Granada but it's fallen out of favor a bit these days. It occupies a 400-year-old building on Carrera del Darro. You enter a room full of flickering candles in candelabras, near an illuminated polychrome copy of a medieval statue devoted to San Pedro. Add lots of shimmering gilt and enough brushed aluminum and industrial-looking hardware to appeal to the butch crowd, and you have El Rincón de San Pedro. In midsummer, arrive before midnight, when the staff closes the French doors looking over the Alhambra. Beer costs from 2.50€. The club is usually open Thursday to Saturday from 5pm to 4am. Carrera del Darro 12. (No phone.)

Infrarojo ★★   A few blocks back from the cathedral, this is probably the coolest, most happening gay and lesbian bar in town at the moment. It's in Plaza de los Lobos, which is a good spot for gay nightlife generally. It's a tapas bar and a funky club for cool, fashionable people in their 20s and 30s relaxing and having fun. There are drag shows and other entertainments several nights of the week too. Music, when it gets going, is a real mixture of Indie, Latin, and House. Plaza de los Lobos 9, (No phone.)

Pub Fondo Reservado   Woodsy-looking and battered, this is the leading gay and lesbian pub in the Albaicín area, with a strict policy of not even opening its doors 'til around midnight. Once you're inside, you'll find yourself among a group of people who seem to have known a lot about one another for years. Nonetheless, the ambience is laid-back, and the clientele can direct you to more current, and trendier, gay venues in other parts of the Albaicín. There's a drag show Friday and Saturday nights. Open Tuesday to Sunday from 11pm to 4am. Cuesta de Santa Inés. ✆ **95-822-10-24.** www.fondoreservado.es.

Six Colours ★   Located just off Gran Vía de Colón a couple of blocks from the cathedral, this cool, funky bar with faux-Baroque leanings—think swirls of odd-patterned wallpaper, the occasional statue of a cherub, and marble pillars—attracts a young, fun, up-for it, fashionable crowd. The music, when it gets going, is House in style. There's a room for girls who like girls here too. It's open Tuesday to Sunday from 4:30pm. C. Tendillas de Santa Paula 6. ✆ **95-820-39-95.** www.sixcolours.com.

Zoo ★   This straight-friendly gay disco in the center of Granada is fun, informal, and great if you're a mixed crowd. It's mainly chilled out with people in their 20s and 30s up for a good dance, a few drinks, and some fun. It's usually busiest in the early morning soon after the bars have closed. It's open Thursday to Sunday from midnight to 3 or 4am. Entrance is usually free before 3am. Calle Moras 2. ✆ **65-976-03-91.**

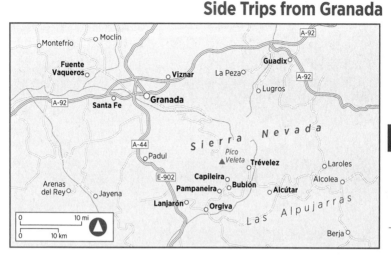

SIDE TRIPS FROM GRANADA

The snowcapped peaks of the **Sierra Nevada** surround the city of Granada, and a number of intriguing excursions exist in several directions. From the top of the highest peak, you can see the African coast and, on the clearest of days, even Castilla la Mancha in the central part of eastern Spain. The mountain range is also the home of the Spanish ibex. For those who like to go on trekking jaunts, the Sierra Nevada is the most rewarding territory in all of Andalusia.

The province of Granada is filled with other attractions. You can visit **Guadix,** known for its cave dwellers, and **Las Alpujarras,** one of the most remote—and most fascinating—parts of Andalusia. But first, here are a couple of trips closer to Granada.

Santa Fe: The "Cradle of America"

If you head southwest of Granada along the A-92, you come to the little town of Santa Fe, 8km (5 miles) from the city. This unimpressive-looking town looms large in history: it was here in the winter of 1491 that Isabella and Ferdinand summoned some 150,000 Spanish troops to besiege Granada, the last territory in Spain under Muslim control.

After the Moorish armies were defeated, it was at Santa Fe that a document of surrender was signed between the Catholic monarchs and the last sultan, Boabdil. These terms of surrender were known as "the Capitulation of Santa Fe," the final act of the Reconquista. When Isabella learned that the Turks had closed the Gibraltar Straits, denying Spain access to the silk route, an alternative route had to be found to the East. In an appendix to the capitulation document, the monarchs agreed to a "wild dream" proposed by an explorer from Genoa and sent Cristóbal Colón

(Christopher Columbus) on a journey to the so-called New World. That's why the little town of Santa Fe today is known as the "Cradle of America."

Santa Fe has long spread beyond its original cross-shaped boundaries. At each of the four ends of the "cross" was a gate, emblazoned with the initials of the Catholic monarchs. The gates remain and you can explore or photograph them. In the center of the Old Town is a church. Opening hours are erratic, so you'll just have to see when you get there. You can reach Santa Fe by bus from Granada too. The same bus continues to Fuente Vaqueros. See below for full details.

Fuente Vaqueros

Fans of the famous Spanish playwright and poet, Federico García Lorca (1898–1936) can journey 17km (11 miles) northwest of Granada to visit the house where he was born on June 5, 1898. The **Casa-Museo Federico García Lorca,** García Lorca 4 (𝄢 **95-851-64-53;** www.museogarcialorca.org), features rooms on the ground floor virtually untouched from the period when he lived here with his parents until the age of 6, and many of the original family furnishings are still in place. His mother was a teacher at the village school, which accounts for the fact that he is in the center of formal class photos from his school on the wall in the bedroom (both the one of the boys and the one of the girls!). Upstairs and in the converted former stables behind the house there are exhibition spaces with photographs of the artist, posters of his plays, and costumes that bring back his spirit. A short video at the end of a visit shows Lorca in action and on tour with the Teatro Barraca.

The museum was opened in 1986 in honor of the 50th anniversary of the assassination of the artist by Franco's troops during the Spanish Civil War. These fascist assassins cited homosexuality as the reason for Lorca's death, but the real reason for his death was his outspoken defense of the Republic and his criticisms of monarchism, Catholicism, and fascism.

Today Spain has restored Lorca to his rightful place in Spanish letters. A highly revered poet and dramatist, he is viewed by scholars as one of the two greatest poets Spain produced in the 20th century, and is certainly one of the country's greatest dramatists since the Golden Age.

You have to visit as part of a guided tour (Spanish language only), which lasts about 45 minutes. Buy tickets at 1.80€ from the Lorca Foundation Office in Calle Manuel de Falla, at the rear of the house complex. The house is open October to March, Tuesday to Sunday with tours at 10am, 11am, midday, 1pm, 4pm, and 5pm; April to June and September, the same morning tours and afternoon tours at 5pm and 6pm; July and August tours at 10am, 11am, midday, 1pm, and 2pm. Closed Mondays and Sundays.

Bus no. 242 runs hourly from 9am to 10pm from the main bus station (Av. de Andalucía), with a journey time of 20 minutes. The bus stops at Santa Fe on the way. If you're driving, head out of Granada on the A-92 towards Seville and take exit 227.

True Lorca fans can also visit the village of **Viznar,** 9km (5½ miles) northeast of Granada. Head out along the A-92 towards Guadix and follow the signs for the turnoff to Viznar. It was here that the fascists brought Lorca to be beaten and shot in 1936 when they took over Granada. Friends had urged him to flee Spain and escape to France or even America, but he refused.

Outside the village, up the hill on the main road to Alfacar is the **Federico García Lorca Memorial Park,** 3km (2 miles) from Viznar. A marker pinpoints the spot where the poet was assassinated. Lorca's body was never recovered, so there is no grave for pilgrims to seek out.

Guadix

If you continue east of Granada along the A-92 for 58km (36 miles), you'll reach the old mining town of Guadix, a land of cave communities perched on a 304m (1,000-ft) plateau. The town is one of the oldest in Spain and has been inhabited for centuries. Amazingly, half of its estimated population of 21,000 souls inhabit troglodyte cave houses, known as *casas cueva* in Spanish.

In Guadix, there is a **tourist office** with very friendly staff on Avenida Mariana Pineda (© **95-869-95-74;** www.andalucia.org), open Monday to Friday from 9am to 1:30pm and 4 to 6pm. At the time of writing there were plans to move the location to the main town hall building on Plaza de la Constitución in the Old Town's center.

Begin your tour in the center of town in Plaza de la Constitución. This was formerly where the Moorish souk (market) was located. It's now a stately two-story square fringed with 16th-century noblemen's houses. The town hall (*ayuntamiento*) at the east end is particularly impressive.

Directly through the archway out of the west end of the Plaza de la Constitución you come upon the stately and ornate **cathedral** (© **95-866-51-08**), which dominates the Old Town. Built between 1594 and 1706, it was designed by Diego de Siloé, the architect who helped change the face of Granada. It's open Monday to Saturday from 10:30am to 1pm and 4 to 6pm in winter, 5 to 7pm in summer. Admission is free Monday and Tuesday afternoons and 3.50€ the rest of the time. Entry includes a free audio guide available in English.

The other town landmark is the nearby **Alcazaba Arabe,** an 11th-century Muslim fort opening onto panoramic views of the Ermita Nueva. Facing the cathedral, head up any of the slanting side streets to the left to reach the hilltop fortress with its series of turrets. Recent excavations here have uncovered several important new finds and at the time of writing it was closed whilst the archeologists continued to dig. Check with the tourist office for the latest information.

Guadix is also famous for its pottery and ceramics. You can find out about the history of the craft at the **Cueva-Museo de Alfarería,** Calle San Miguel 46 (© **95-866-47-67**). On display is a collection of domestic and decorative ceramics, many of them antique. The museum also contains a water well dating from the mid-17th century. Open Monday to Friday from 10am to 1:30pm and 4 to 7pm, 5 to 8:30pm in summer; Saturday and Sunday from 11am to 2pm. Admission is 2€. You can buy pots, dishes, decorated tiles, and more here. To see a potter at work and buy beautifully detailed pots and ceramics, visit **Ceramica Alfareria Gabarrón,** Calle San Miguel 54 (© **95-866-47-67**) opposite the museum. It's open Monday to Friday 9am to 2pm and 4 to 8pm and Saturdays 9am to 2pm.

If you're feeling tired go by car, but otherwise, it's another 20-minute walk uphill from the Cueva-Museo de Alfarería, following the signs, along Calle Cañada de las Perales. This will take you through part of the **Barriada de Cuevas ★★**, site of some of the 2,000 cave dwellings that were carved out of the soft sandstone mountains and have existed for half a millennium. Most of these *cuevas* are still occupied by families. From the street, about all you'll see is a whitewashed front door. Almost every cave, however, has a TV antenna. Amazingly these caves are often comfortably furnished and have pleasant year-round temperatures despite the scalding heat that descends in July and August. A few also operate as boardinghouses and will rent you a room.

At the top of the hill you'll come finally to Plaza Ermita Nueva—site of a pretty church, the **Iglesia de las Cuevas** and, opposite, the **Cueva-Museo de Costumbres Populares,** Plaza de la Ermita Nueva s/n (© **95-866-55-69;** www.cueva-museoguadix.com). Inside there's a completely preserved cave house that's furnished with artifacts; it's easy to imagine living here. Open Monday to Friday from 10am to 1:30pm and 4 to 7pm, 5 to 8:30pm in summer; weekends from 11am to 2pm. Admission is 2.50€.

Alsina Graells buses (© **90-242-22-42;** www.alsa.es) depart from Granada to Guadix at the rate of 11 per day Monday to Saturday. On Sunday only six buses make the run. It costs 4.70€ for a one-way ticket. You can also catch the train. There are four trains a day and the journey offers great countryside views. The train from Granada costs 6.10€ one-way. Either trip takes an hour.

WHERE TO STAY & DINE

Hotel Abentofail ★ 👗 In a tiny back street near the cathedral, this brand new boutique hotel makes staying in Guadix a real pleasure. The building is a converted old palace house, with a cool, leafy patio—a tinkling fountain burbling at its center. The lovely original wooden beams and ceilings have been retained, but the 16 comfortable, quite small rooms on two floors are stylish. Recycled hardwood floors and furniture come from Indonesia; bedding is the best and whitest of cottons. Bathrooms have shower/tub combos or just shower. Some rooms offer great views to the mountains. The hotel's airy, modern restaurant Buho, one of the best in town, specializes in adventurous interpretations of traditional local dishes, costing 16€ to 23€.

Calle Abentofail s/n, 18500 Guadix. © **95-866-92-81.** www.hotelabentofail.com. 26 units. 71€–121€ double; 152€ suite. AE, MC, V. **Amenities:** Restaurant; patio; rooms for those w/limited mobility. *In room:* A/C, TV, Wi-Fi.

Hotel Comercio A couple of streets east of the Plaza de La Constitución, this is a decent second choice if the Abentofail is full. Built a century ago, the family-run, friendly hotel has been frequently renovated. Once a private home, the two-story hotel contains an internal patio with beautiful stairs, corridors, and arches. Bedrooms are small to midsize and filled with dark-wood furnishings and marble floors. In the public area there's a music concert room along with a small art gallery.

Calle Mira de Amezcua 3, 18500 Guadix. © **95-866-05-00.** Fax 95-866-50-72. www.hotelcomercio. com. 42 units. 65€ double; 185€–285€ suite. AE, DC, MC, V. Parking 7€. **Amenities:** Restaurant; bar; gym; Jacuzzi; rooms for those w/limited mobility. *In room:* A/C, TV, minibar, Wi-Fi.

Cuevas Pedro Antonio de Alarcón It's back to being a cave dweller here, although conditions are far from prehistoric. At this *aparthotel,* you're not in the main *cueva* district but in a cave right outside town. Each sleeps anywhere from two to five guests and comes with kitchenette. There's even a suite with a whirlpool bathtub. There are furnishings, but this ain't the Ritz. The decor relies on crafts and hand-woven rugs and Alpujarras tapestries which may serve as doors between rooms. White walls, wooden furniture, bricks, and ceramic tiles provide the backdrop. Most rooms are spacious and come complete with a tidy bathroom. You can enjoy Andalusian specialties in the subterranean restaurant. The caves are near the train station, about 1km (⅔ mile) from Guadix's historic core, entered on N-342 between the town and the motorway.

Barriada San Torcuato, 18500 Guadix. ⓒ **95-866-49-86.** Fax 95-866-17-21. www.cuevaspedroantonio. es. 23 units. 64€–78€ double; various other apartment sizes available. MC, V. **Amenities:** Restaurant; outdoor pool; tennis court. *In room:* TV, hair dryer, minibar.

Sierra Nevada ★★★

A summer hiking center and a vast winter ski resort, the snowcapped Sierra Nevada mountain range is where locals go to play any season of the year. In 1986, UNESCO declared the Sierra Nevada a biosphere reserve. Because of the mountain range's proximity to the Mediterranean, there is a great diversity of flora and fauna. There are more than 2,100 cataloged flora species, 175 native to Iberia and 65 native to the Sierra Nevada. In spring you can see birds like the common chaffinch and the firecrest, and in fall, the ring ouzel. The rare golden eagle is also found here.

Only an hour's drive from Granada, its dramatic centerpiece, **Mulhacén,** is the highest peak in Spain, rising 3,478m (11,410 ft). Many other peaks reach a height of 3,000m (9,842 ft) or more. This vast mountain range extends some 75km (47 miles) west to east. Most of the 1,710 sq. km (660 sq. miles) of wilderness are part of the **Parque Nacional.**

Pradollano is the country's southernmost ski resort and the largest and busiest in Andalusia, a province not normally associated with **snow.** The resort has 45 downhill runs, for a total of 61km (38 miles), plus 19 lifts. The ski season begins in December and normally lasts until April, although in some years it's been known to last into early June. In winter **Autocares Tocina/Bonal** (ⓒ **95-846-50-22;** www. grupotocina.com) operates buses from the main bus station in Granada to Pradollano, leaving Monday to Friday at 8am, 10am, and 5pm with an extra 3pm departure at weekends. Buses return at 9am, 4pm, and 6:30pm with an additional departure at 1pm at weekends.

Exploring the Sierra Nevada isn't limited to winter. In **summer** you can drive or take the bus to Pradollano. Two of the main chairlifts operate from late June to the end of August, giving direct access to **Pico de Veleta,** the third-highest mountain in Spain at 3,390m (11,125 ft) and the top of the ski resort. The view from its **summit ★★** is one of the most panoramic in all of Spain, sweeping over the vast range of Las Alpujarras (the southern slopes of the Sierra Nevada) and all the way to the sea. On a clear day you can even see the coast of North Africa.

Walking trails of varying degrees of difficulty span out from the summit, all offering spectacular views. The easiest trail is simply back down the mountain to the base of the chairlift station, taking about an hour. You can walk to the top of Mulhacén, but it's a 6-hour hike one way so is only recommended for serious hikers. Even on the hottest day in August, it's cold at the top—bring a coat and sweater, and decent walking shoes. And don't forget sunscreen too, as the sun's rays are particularly fierce at this altitude.

If you prefer not to use the chairlift, microbuses run quite close to the summit from just above Pradollano along the highest road in Europe. Reservations are essential for this service. It's a great day out with older kids here as there's a downhill toboggan-kart run and an ice rink at the Miro Blanco center, just above the chairlift station.

For more information on trails at the summit of Pico de Veleta and to book places on the microbus, get in touch with the **Sierra Nevada Tourist Office** (© **90-270-80-90;** www.sierranevada.es) or ask at the Provincial Tourist Office in Granada, Plaza de Marian Pineda 10 bajo (© **95-824-71-46**). In summer, bus departures to Pradollano are once daily at 9am, with a return at 5pm. A round-trip ticket costs 8.50€.

To reach Pradollano by car, 33km (21 miles) southeast of Granada, take the A-395. It's well signposted from the main A-44/E-902 that skirts the city. For information about road and snow conditions in winter, contact the Tourist Office at Pradollano on © **95-824-91-00.**

WHERE TO STAY & DINE

El Lodge   This is the finest hotel in the Sierra Nevada, and in peak season you must reserve far in advance. (It's only open for the winter season.) In a three-story wooden building, the ski lodge is at El Balcón de Pradollano, a height of 2,100m (6,889 ft). It has an alpine feel and an intimate, cozy atmosphere. Rooms tend to be very small, however—almost ship-cabin size. Completely encased in wood, they come with equally small bathrooms, with a tub and shower. The on-site restaurant serves regional specialties. If you want to stay in summer months, ask at the tourist offices in Granada or Sierra Nevada (contact details above) for hotels that are open. Opening schedules change from year to year.

Maribel 8 Sierra Nevada, 18196 Monachil. © **95-848-06-00.** Fax 95-848-13-14. www.ellodge.com. 21 units. 212€–295€ double; 360€–490€ suite. AE, DC, MC, V. Parking 20€. Closed May–Oct. **Amenities:** Restaurant; bar; babysitting; Jacuzzi; room service; spa. *In room:* A/C, TV, hair dryer.

Las Alpujarras ★

The southern flank of the Sierra Nevada, where deep ravines split arid hillsides, was, for centuries, one of Spain's most remote and isolated corners. A journey here is like a journey back in time. Muslim shepherds and farmers lived here until being replaced by Christian settlers in the 1500s.

In the wake of the Reconquista in Seville in 1248 and Granada in 1492, Moors fled to the area to start out a new life. Ill-fated Boabdil, last emir of Granada, fled here with his mother when Isabella and Ferdinand defeated his armies.

Isolated for centuries from the rest of the world, most of the Alpujarreños still cling to their old rural way of life. You'll see, for example, communal laundry troughs where, until recently, women gathered to wash the family clothing. Writers like Richard Ford and Washington Irving were attracted by the rural idyll of this district.

Las Alpujarras is like a piece of the Orient in the western extreme of Europe. Whitewashed cubic houses, terrace farming, towns hugging the contours of mountains, and incredible scenery await you at every turn. The scenery is dotted with the remains of fortresses and towers, most erected during the period of Islamic domination.

The donkey is still used as a beast of burden and a means of transport. In the high range live the mountain goat and other species such as the fox, wild boar, and genet. Wildcats still call Las Alpujarras home, as does the jeweled lizard.

By the mid-20th century, struggling artists, writers, poets, and hippies settled in the area, along with various expats. Islamic influences have remained strong in the area, particularly in the Berber-style villages and the terraced and irrigated landscape. Much of the architecture of Las Alpujarras still shows a marked Moorish influence, especially in the clay roofs with chimneys. In little villages, narrow streets wind between houses built one above the other. Most houses are of local materials such as stone, mud, slate, gray clay (launa), and chestnut roof beams. Houses are almost always whitewashed, and are cubic in shape with few exterior openings.

Alpujarras handicrafts, once in danger of extinction, have been revived and some visitors tour the region merely to shop. Embroidery, esparto work, jewelry making, basket weaving, wrought iron, pottery, leather goods, and highly coveted Alpujarra blankets are just part of the wide range of crafts for sale from village to village.

GETTING THERE & EXPLORING

To explore the area, you can drive from Granada on the A-44/E-902 then the A-348 to the town of **Lanjarón,** 46km (29 miles) southeast of Granada. This spa town is known for its mineral waters. Continue from here to **Orgiva,** the gateway to the Western Alpujarras. Orgiva is the largest town of the region. It's known for its Baroque church on the main street and a lively Thursday morning market. Orgiva can also be reached from the coastal motorway by taking the A-44 towards Granada then the A-346.

From Orgiva you can take the A-4132, following the signs to the village of **Pampaneira** along a road that winds in serpentine curves. At 1,059m (3,474 ft), this village overlooks the Poqueira Gorge, a mammoth ravine carved by the Poqueira River. The town's craft looms are well known, as are its fountains, springs, and tiny squares. Pampaneira is 14km (8½ miles) northeast of Orgiva.

From Pampaneira, you can climb to two of the best-known villages. It takes about ten minutes to reach **Bubión** and a further five minutes to reach **Capileira**. The latter is at 1,436m (4,711 ft) and also overlooks the Poqueira Gorge. Explore the winding lanes until you reach a little museum with an excellent display of Alpujarras handicrafts. It's open Tuesday to Sunday from 11:30am to 2pm. Bubión, on the other hand, is best for its village charm and Berber architecture. Both villages have many artisan shops, *teterias* (tea shops), bars, and restaurants.

Drive back down to the main road to leave the Poqueira Gorge and turn left into the equally spectacular but less visited **Trevélez Gorge.** You'll be driving along one of the highest roads in Europe (see "Sierra Nevada" above). En route take time to explore the area known as **La Taha** where tiny, unspoilt traditional hamlets like **Ferreirola** and **Fondales,** surrounded by almond groves and terraced meadows, give a glimpse of life in Moorish times. After about 45 minutes you'll reach the village of **Trevélez**. Known for its *jamón serrano* (serrano ham), this is Spain's second-highest community, at 1,476m (4,842 ft). It's on the slopes of Mulhacén, and many hikers use it as their base for climbing the mountain. After finishing your tour in Trevélez, work your way back to Orgiva and Lanjarón (the original gateway), connecting to the E-902 that will take you north back to Granada.

It's best to explore Las Alpujarras by car, although buses run by **Alsina Graells** (𝒞 **90-242-22-42;** www.alsa.es) leave Granada daily at noon and 4:30pm for the most scenic of the villages. Buses return to Granada from Alcutar, the farthest town out, at 5:15am and 5pm. The journey all the way to Alcutar takes just under 4 hours and costs 14.88€. Ask at the tourist offices for the most recent schedule.

WHERE TO STAY & DINE

Casa Ana ★★ 🎁 This is the ultimate, away-from-it-all experience. Casa Ana is a delightfully intimate and relaxing B&B in the pretty little village of Ferreirola. The accommodations around a secluded courtyard include the house, stables, and outbuildings which Anne, the present owner, has beautifully renovated. Throughout you'll see original chestnut beams, old doors, and thick stone walls. All the floors have natural terracotta tiles scattered with rugs. Modern comforts such as underfloor heating and new bathrooms with rain showers have been sensitively incorporated. Outside there are lovely garden terraces on different levels and a secluded walled garden, all with seating areas and flower beds and spectacular views of the mountains and the Trevélez River gorge. There's an excellent restaurant a few minutes from the house and lovely walking trails right on the doorstep. Self-catering options are also available.

Calle Artesa, Ferreirola, 18414 La Taha, Granada. 𝒞 **95-876-62-70.** Cellphone/mobile 𝒞 **67-829-84-97.** www.casa-ana.com. 4 units. 68€ double; 70€ suite. Packed lunches can also be arranged.

Hotel de Mecina Only 200m (656 ft) from the center of Mecina Fondales, this hotel's traditional-style Alpujarras architecture blends into this tiny hamlet. Bedrooms are small with whitewashed walls, comfortable furnishings, and a little bathroom. Some rooms have a private balcony or terrace. The nearby restaurant, L'Atelier, Calle Alverca 21 (𝒞 **95-885-75-01**), serves vegetarian and Mediterranean specialties. Main courses cost from 9€ to 17€, and it makes a good lunch stop if you're touring the area. Hours are daily 8 to 11am, 1 to 4pm, and 8 to 11pm.

Calle La Fuente s/n, Mecina Fondales 18416. 𝒞 **95-876-62-41.** Fax 95-876-62-55. www.hoteldemecina. com.es. 21 units. 88€ double. AE, DC, MC, V. Free parking. **Amenities:** Restaurant; babysitting; outdoor pool; rooms for those w/limited mobility. In room: A/C, TV.

Hotel Taray ★ 🍴 An ideal base for exploring Las Alpujarras, this hotel is in Orgiva, the largest town in the region. The hotel, looking older than its 10 years, is very cozy, with wooden furnishings, regional ornaments and crafts, hand-woven bedspreads and curtains. The best rooms are the three opening onto rooftop terraces with views of the hotel gardens. All guests share a terrace with panoramic views. This is one of the better places for dining in the area, even if you aren't a hotel guest. The Taray uses ingredients like lamb, trout, berries, and oranges from its own farm.

Carretera Tablate-Albuñol Km 18, Orgiva 18400. 𝒞 **95-878-45-25.** Fax 95-878-45-31. www.hoteltaray. com. 15 units. 77€–107€ double. AE, DC, MC, V. Free parking. **Amenities:** Restaurant; bar; babysitting; pool; room service; rooms for those w/limited mobility. In room: A/C, TV, minibar.

La Fragua In a characteristic village home near the town hall, this two-story house, built in 1991 of stone with whitewashed walls, is in the village of Trevélez high in the mountains. Rooms are slightly better, though more expensive, in an adjoining annex. Most are midsize, each tastefully and comfortably furnished. There's a comfortable lounge in each of the hotel's two buildings. Guests head for the rooftop terrace for its panoramic views. A family-run enterprise, the hotel generates more business for its cafe/bar/restaurant than it does for its rooms. The restaurant serves regional specialties and affordable wines and has great mountain views.

San Antonio 4, Barrio Medio, 18417 Trevélez. © **95-885-86-26.** Fax 95-885-86-14. www.hotellafragua. com. 14 units. 40€–50€ double. MC, V. Free parking. **Amenities:** Restaurant; rooms for those w/limited mobility. *In room:* A/C, TV.

RONDA & THE PUEBLOS BLANCOS/ SHERRY TRIANGLE

Although not in the league of Granada, Seville, and Córdoba, the tiny inland city of Ronda enjoys an incomparable setting, perched high above the Tajo Gorge, where political prisoners were once thrown to their deaths. Ronda also has beautiful and historic art and architecture, with one of the oldest bullrings in the country and plenty of Roman and Moorish ruins.

Ronda is the best known of Spain's *Pueblos Blancos* (White Villages), so called for their whitewashed houses built closely together. Visitors with more time can visit the other Pueblos Blancos in and around Ronda. Below I've provided a driving tour that will take you to my favorite (and the most beautiful) of these towns. This is one of Spain's most scenic routes and has plenty of fascinating stops along the way. You could do it in a couple of days at a real push, but three or four is far preferable.

Another wonderful series of towns are those that make up the famous "Sherry Triangle": Jerez de la Frontera, El Puerto de Santa María, and the port of Sanlúcar de Barrameda. As the name suggests, these towns are known for their sherry (*jerez* in Spanish). Indulging in a wine-tasting tour in their sweet-smelling old cellars (*bodegas*) is one of the best ways to experience these towns. If you have time for only one, make it Jerez de la Frontera, with the best *bodegas* and the world headquarters of the sherry industry. In Jerez you can also see the dancing horses of Andalusia.

Ronda

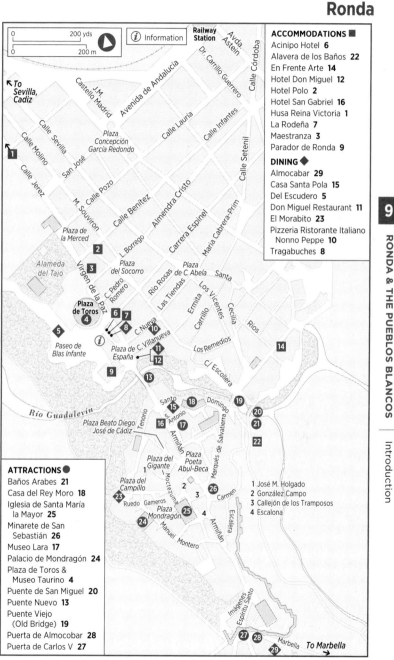

1 José M. Holgado
2 González Campo
3 Callejón de los Tramposos
4 Escalona

9

RONDA & THE PUEBLOS BLANCOS

Introduction

RONDA ★★

102km (63 miles) NE of Algeciras, 97km (60 miles) W of Málaga, 147km (91 miles) SE of Seville, 591km (367 miles) S of Madrid

This little town high in the Serranía de Ronda Mountains (698m/2,300 ft above sea level) is one of the oldest and most aristocratic places in Spain. Ronda's near-impregnable position kept the reconquering Catholic troops at bay until 1485. The main attraction is a deep gorge, spanned by three bridges over the Guadalevín River. On both sides of this hole in the earth are houses clinging to the cliff that look as though they might plunge into the chasm at the slightest push.

Ronda is an incredible sight. The town and the surrounding mountains were legendary hide-outs for bandits and smugglers. The gorge divides the town into an older part, the Moorish and aristocratic quarter, and the newer section south of the gorge, built principally after the Reconquista. The old quarter is by far the more fascinating; it contains narrow, rough streets and buildings with a marked Moorish influence. It gets its fair share of tourists these days, so it can feel a bit mobbed in summer, but it's still one of the region's most remarkable and attractive towns.

Essentials

GETTING THERE   Most visitors take a **train** to the main station at Avenida Andalucía (✆ **95-287-16-73** or ✆ 90-232-03-20; www.renfe.es). Three trains arrive from Granada per day. The trip takes 2½ hours and costs 13.60€ one way. It's a really scenic ride and worth doing just for the journey. You can also visit Ronda from the Costa del Sol, where one daily train makes the 2-hour trip from Málaga to Ronda, costing 9.90€ one way. Two trains daily connect Ronda and Madrid. The trip takes just under 3 hours and costs 60€ one way.

The main **bus** station is at Plaza Concepción García Redondo s/n, Los Amarillos (✆ **95-218-70-61;** www.losamarillos.es). Five buses a day run from Seville, taking 2 hours and costing 11€ one way. There is also a service from Málaga, provided by **CTSA Portillo** (✆ **90-245-05-50;** www.ctsa-portillo.com), taking 2¾ hours and costing 11€ one way. It also runs five buses a day from Marbella, taking 1 hour and costing 6€ one way. **TGComes** (✆ **90-219-92-08;** www.tgcomes.es) runs buses from Jerez to Ronda, taking just over 2 hours and costing 11€ one way.

Reaching Ronda by **road** involves driving some steep, winding secondary roads. From Seville, the quickest route is to take toll highway A-4/E-5 south to Jerez and then cut across along the A-382 to Arcos, then the A-384 and the A-374. If you're in Granada, take the A-92 west to Antequera and then the A-384 and A-374. If you're on the Costa del Sol, you can reach Ronda from Málaga traveling northwest via the scenic A-397 from junction 172 on the AP-7/E-15 tollroad.

VISITOR INFORMATION   The **Officina Municipal de Turismo**, Paseo Blas Infante s/n (✆ **95-218-71-19;** www.turismoderonda.es) is open Monday to Friday 10am to 7pm, Saturday 10am to 2pm and 3 to 5pm, and Sunday 10am to 2:30pm. It's easy to find, right opposite the historic bullring.

GETTING AROUND   The town is small, so you can walk to most places of inter-est. If you have to go farther afield, taxis are usually found in front of the Plaza Carmen Abela, the bullring, and the station. A typical fare—say from the train sta-tion to Plaza de España—costs 5€.

[FastFACTS] RONDA

Currency Exchange
The most central bank, with ATMs, is **Banco Santander,** Av. de Málaga 11 (📞 **95-287-99-85**). It's open Monday to Friday from 8:30am to 2pm and Saturday from 8:30am to 1pm.

Emergencies Dial 📞 **092** or 📞 061.

Hospital The main hospital is **Hospital General**

Básico, Carretera El Burgo (📞 **95-106-50-01**).

Internet Access The tourist office can provide a handy map of Internet cafes. The nearest to the main tourist area is **Rondatelecom,** Calle Jerez 4-Bajo, open Monday to Saturday 10am to 3pm and 4:30 to 11:30pm, and Sunday 3 to11pm.

Pharmacy The most central is **Santos Zafra,** Plaza de España 5 (📞 **95-287-15-80**), open Monday to Friday 9:30am to 2pm and 5 to 8:30pm.

Post Office Calle Virgen de la Paz 20 (📞 **95-287-25-57**) is opposite the bullring. It's open Monday to Friday 8:30am to 8:30pm and Saturday 9:30am to 1pm.

Exploring Ronda

You can scoot around the main sights of Ronda in half a day, but if you have more time, spend a full day or even two wandering the narrow streets of the walled Old Town and exploring the museums, churches, and palaces. The best time to visit is in the spring when the weather is cooler and the orange trees in bloom.

Ronda was precariously erected at the edge of the mountain range of the Serranía de Ronda on a rocky geological **platform site ★★** that was cut by the Guadalevín River in prehistoric times. **El Tajo,** a 100m (328 ft) ravine, divides Ronda into two distinct parts, including **La Ciudad ★★★**, the Moorish Old Town with a labyrinth of streets and alleyways, flanked by whitewashed houses with wrought-iron balconies. La Ciudad is on the south side of El Tajo ("the ravine" in English).

The newer town, **El Mercadillo ★**, is to the north. This town sprang up after the Christian Reconquest and is filled with a number of attractions, including the Plaza de Toros (bullring; see below).

Three bridges cross the gorge, the main one being **Puente Nuevo ★**, from which you can enjoy a panoramic view of Ronda and its countryside. This is Ronda's most famous bridge and was an architectural marvel when it was constructed between 1755 and 1793. A lantern-lit parapet graces the bridge. Over the years many people have fallen to their deaths from here—even the original architect did so during an inspection. During the bitter Spanish Civil War, it was a place of execution for Franco's troops or the rebels, depending on which group was controlling Ronda at the time. Ernest Hemingway in *For Whom the Bell Tolls* recorded how prisoners were thrown alive into this deep gorge.

Ronda's two other bridges are both north of Puente Nuevo: **Puente Viejo (Old Bridge),** dating from 1616, and the single-span Moorish bridge, **Puente de San Miguel.** Ronda is still entered by two ancient gates, the 13th-century **Puerta de Almocobar** and the 16th-century **Puerta de Carlos V.**

In the center of La Ciudad, the old Moorish Quarter, is **Iglesia de Santa María la Mayor,** Plaza Duquesa de Parcent s/n (📞 **95-287-40-48**), a collegiate church that acts as a cathedral. The landmark square it occupies is Ronda's most beautiful, with a tree-lined center and burbling fountain. Like many churches in Andalusia, Santa María is constructed on a former mosque, in this case the Great Mosque of Ronda. As a result, both the interior and exterior are a mix of architectural styles. Outside you see Moorish, Gothic, and Renaissance influences, with a belfry constructed on top of the old Moorish minaret. Inside you'll find naves in the late Gothic style, a main altar heavy with Baroque gold leaf, a Plateresque chancel, and an arch still covered with Arabic calligraphy. You can see an old Muslim *mihrab* (prayer niche) in front of the current street door. The two-tiered balcony on the facade was a gallery where notables could watch special events staged on the square below. Admission is 4€. The church is open daily May to October 10am to 8pm (daily 10am–6pm in the off season).

East of the church if you follow Callejón de los Tramposos, you can see a Moorish tower, **Minarete de San Sebastián,** part of the original Great Mosque of Ronda dating from the 14th century.

The nearby **Palacio de Mondragón,** Plaza de Mondragón (© **95-287-08-18**), was once the 14th-century private home of the Moorish King Abomelic. But after the Reconquista, it was renovated to receive King Ferdinand and Queen Isabella, who stayed here. Inside you can see a trio of courtyards and a collection of Moorish mosaics and a beautiful carved wooden ceiling. A small museum houses artifacts devoted to regional archaeology. Better than the museum is the restored Mudéjar courtyard where you take in a panoramic view of El Tajo with the Serranía de Ronda looming in the background. Flanked by two Mudéjar towers, the building now has a Baroque facade. It's open Monday to Friday 10am to 7pm, Saturday and Sunday 10am to 3pm; admission is 3€ for adults and free for children aged 13 and under.

Museo Lara, Calle Armiñan 29 (© **95-287-12-63;** www.museolara.org), contains the private art collection of a well-known local, Juan Antonio Lara. He started collecting "things" when he was a young boy, and this extensive museum is filled with what he accumulated in his lifetime—some 5,000 artifacts in all. These are divided into seven different compartments—galleries devoted to bullfighting, archaeology, weapons, antique clocks, knives, musical instruments, and early cameras and cinematographic equipment. Admission is 4€ for adults and 2€ for students, children, and seniors. Hours are daily 11am to 8pm.

Casa del Rey Moro, Calle Santo Domingo 17 (© **95-218-72-00**), is misnamed, as this House of the Moorish King was actually built in 1709. However, it's believed to have been constructed over Moorish foundations. The interior is closed, but from the garden you can take a steep stairway cut into the rockface, called La Mina, which leads you to the river, a distance of 365 steps. Christian slaves cut these steps in the 14th century to guarantee a steady water supply in case Ronda came under siege. At the time of writing there were plans to turn the Casa into a luxury hotel, so check with the tourist office for opening hours and prices.

The still-functioning **Baños Arabes** ★ are located in Calle San Miguel (© **65-695-09-37**) just to the north of the Old Town and are best reached by a pleasant stroll down Calle Santo Domingo, where you'll find the old city gate, the Puerta de Felipe V, and the two other bridges that span the Tajo gorge. Dating from the 13th century, the baths, the finest examples of Moorish baths in Spain, have glass roof-windows and hump-shaped cupolas. The star-shaped vents in the roof

On a hot day—and summers are very hot in Ronda—you can retreat to the town's loveliest spot, the gardens of **Alameda del Tojo ★**, beyond the Plaza de Toros in El Mercadillo, the New Town. This park dates from the heyday of the British invasion in the 19th century. The city fathers at the time raised money to create the gardens by heavily fining citizens who used obscene language in public. Apparently, there was a lot of cussing going on because the park is truly beautiful. If you walk to the end of the gardens, a panoramic balcony emerges from the face of the cliff. If you don't have vertigo, take in a vast sweep of countryside beyond and the views of Serranía de Ronda in the distance. A cliff-top walk leads to the Hotel Reina Victoria.

were modeled after the ceiling of the more famous bathhouse at the Alhambra in Granada. Note the beautiful octagonal brick columns supporting horseshoe arches. A channel from the nearby river carried water into the complex, once surrounded by landscaped Moorish gardens. Admission is 3€ Monday to Saturday and free on Sunday. The baths are open Monday to Friday 10am to 7pm, Saturday and Sunday 10am to 3pm.

Across the bridge in the New Town, El Mercadillo, you'll find Ronda's exquisite bullring, said to be the oldest in Spain. Built in 1785, the **Plaza de Toros ★★** is the setting for the yearly *Corrida Goyesca* in honor of Ronda's native son, Pedro Romero, one of the greatest bullfighters of all time. The bullring is a work of architectural beauty, built of limestone with double arches and 136 Tuscan-like columns. If you want to know more about Ronda's bullfighting heritage, visit the **Museo Taurino,** inside the bullring at Calle Virgen de la Paz 15 (📞 **95-287-41-32;** www.rmcr.org). It's open daily March to October 10am to 8pm and November to February 10am to 7pm. Admission is 6€. Exhibits document the exploits of the noted Romero family. Francesco invented the killing sword and the *muleta,* and his grandson, Pedro (1754–1839), killed 5,600 bulls during his 30-year career. Pedro was the inspiration for Goya's famous *Tauromaquia* series of paintings. There are also exhibits devoted to Cayetano Ordóñez, the matador immortalized by Hemingway in *The Sun Also Rises.*

Where to Stay
EXPENSIVE
Parador de Ronda ★★★   This parador is the grandest hotel in the area and has a spectacular location. It sits on a high cliff overlooking the fantastic gorge that cuts a swathe more than 150m (492 ft) deep and 90m (295 ft) wide through the center of this mountain town. Stretching along the edge of the gorge to a bridge, the Puente Nuevo, the parador is circled by a footpath with scenic views of the gorge and the Guadalevín River below. The good-size rooms are beautifully furnished; many open onto balconies with views of the peaks surrounding Ronda.

Plaza de España s/n, 29400 Ronda. 📞 **95-287-75-00.** Fax 95-287-81-88. www.parador.es. 78 units. 160€–171€ double; 256€–274€ suite. AE, DC, MC, V. Parking 10€. **Amenities:** Restaurant; bar; outdoor pool; room service; Wi-Fi. *In room:* A/C, TV, hair dryer, minibar,

MODERATE

Acinipo Hotel ★ 🏷 Close to the bullring, this modern hotel was created from two buildings—one a restored antique, the other completely contemporary. The older structure was the home of two celebrated artists, Téllez Loriguillo and Miki Haruta of Japan. Small to spacious bedrooms open onto views of the ravine and the distant mountains. The plumbing, lighting, and furnishings are ultra contemporary, in tasteful, comfortable surroundings. The best bedrooms have a hydromassage tub and a living room. The on-site restaurant specializes in regional cuisine and Mediterranean dishes. Particularly good are desserts like delectable chestnuts with brandy cream.

Paseo Blas Infante s/n, 29400 Ronda. ✆/fax **95-216-10-02.** www.hotelacinipo.com. 16 units. 97€–120€ double; 150€ junior suite. AE, DC, MC, V. **Amenities:** Restaurant; bar/cafeteria; babysitting; room service; nonsmoking rooms; rooms for those w/limited mobility. *In room:* A/C, TV, hair dryer, minibar.

En Frente Arte ★ 🏷 On Ronda's oldest paved street and surrounded by historic buildings, this little inn faces the natural park, Sierra de las Nieves. The mansion, parts of which date from the 13th century, has been beautifully decorated and handsomely restored, with whitewashed walls and a roof of red tiles. Bedrooms ranging from small to spacious have different decorative themes, from Arabic to Spanish to French. The dramatic tower room has the best views. Above the intimate bar and informal restaurant there's a recreation room with pool table, TV, library, and computer with free Internet access. A subtropical garden has exotic plants, and the courtyards and terraces open onto views of the Old Town and the countryside.

Calle Real 40, 29400 Ronda. ✆ **95-287-90-88.** Fax 95-287-72-17. www.enfrentearte.com. 14 units. 78€–107€ double. Rates include drinks and brunch. MC, V. Free parking. **Amenities:** Restaurant; bar; babysitting; outdoor pool; room service; sauna. *In room:* A/C, TV, hair dryer, minibar.

Husa Reina Victoria ★ On the eastern periphery of town, this country-style hotel was built in 1906 by an Englishman in honor of Queen Victoria. It's near the bullring and has terraces that hang over a 147m (490 ft) precipice. Hemingway frequently visited, but the Reina Victoria is known best as the place where poet Rainer Maria Rilke wrote *The Spanish Trilogy.* His third-floor room is now a museum with first editions, manuscripts, photographs, and even a framed copy of his hotel bill. The hotel, with its Victorian architecture, gardens, and terraces, has an enduring appeal. Rooms are big and airy, some with living rooms and many with private terraces.

Paseo Doctor Fleming 25, 29400 Ronda. ✆ **95-287-12-40.** Fax 95-287-10-75. www.husa.es. 89 units. 120€–150€ double; 165€–190€ suite. AE, DC, MC, V. Free parking. **Amenities:** Restaurant; bar; babysitting; outdoor pool; room service; nonsmoking rooms; rooms for those w/limited mobility; Wi-Fi. *In room:* A/C, TV, hair dryer, minibar.

INEXPENSIVE

Alavera de los Baños ★ 🎁 In the San Miguel quarter of the Old Town, this hotel near the Baños Arabes (Arab baths) dates from the 17th century. It's an atmospheric place with great character, low ceilings, and wooden beams. The inn was featured as a backdrop in the classic movie *Carmen.* Bedrooms have panoramic views of the Serranía de Ronda and the city walls. There's a garden and a pool. Bedrooms are small but comfortably and tastefully furnished with little shower-only bathrooms.

Hoyo San Miguel, 29400 Ronda. ✆ **95-287-91-43.** Fax 95-287-91-43. www.alaveradelosbanos.com. 9 units. 85€–100€ double. Rates include breakfast. AE, DC, MC, V. Free parking. **Amenities:** Outdoor pool. *In room:* no phone, Wi-Fi.

Hotel Don Miguel ★ 🥄 A few steps east of the Plaza de España, this hotel of several interconnected houses offers a vine-strewn patio above the river, a modernized interior with exposed brick and varnished pine, and simple but comfortable small rooms. Overflow guests are housed in a building (no. 13) across the street. Rooms here have the same dramatic views and are similar to those in the main building.

Calle Villanueva 4, 29400 Ronda. ✆ **95-287-77-22.** Fax 95-287-83-77. www.dmiguel.com. 30 units. 85€ double. Rates include breakfast. AE, DC, MC, V. Parking 9€. **Amenities:** Restaurant; lounge; rooms for those w/limited mobility. *In room:* A/C, TV.

Hotel Polo 🥄 The hotel in its present incarnation dates from 1973, but the building itself has been housing frugal travelers for over a century. Today the Puya brothers are in charge of this family business, running a well-maintained and decent four-story corner building right in the center within walking distance of the Puente Nuevo. Bedrooms are small with white walls and carpeting, along with tiled bathrooms. The hotel is especially popular with young people.

Maríano Soubiron 8, 29400 Ronda. ✆ **95-287-24-47.** Fax 95-287-24-49. www.hotelpolo.net. 36 units. 87€–96€ double. Rates include breakfast. AE, DC, MC, V. Parking 15€. **Amenities:** Restaurant; bar; Wi-Fi. *In room:* A/C, TV, hair dryer.

Hotel San Gabriel ★★ 📋 This charming 1736 mansion is in the historic core of the city, a 5-minute walk from the gorge. The building was painstakingly renovated by the owner and his family, who give guests Ronda's warmest welcome. Everything is stylish and homelike, with antiques, stained-glass windows, a Spanish-style billiard table, a *cine* salon (with seats taken from the city's old theater), and even an old library. Each room is spacious and well appointed, all with exterior views and individual decoration. Try for no. 15, a cozy top-floor nest on two levels.

Marqués de Moctezuma 19 (just off Calle Armiñán), 29400 Ronda. ✆ **95-219-03-92.** Fax 95-219-01-17. www.hotelsangabriel.com. 16 units. 82€–124€ double; 103€–183€ suite. AE, MC, V. **Amenities:** Breakfast room; bar; game room; Wi-Fi. *In room:* A/C, TV, hair dryer, minibar.

La Rodeña 🥄 A two-minute walk from the gorge and next to the bullring, this two-story family-style house attracts bargain hunters. Small bedrooms, with full bathrooms, are relatively simple, albeit comfortable, but without dramatic views of the gorge. Rooms do, however, open onto the landscaped grounds and the Sierras in the distance. The public areas are decorated in Andalusian style. The on-site restaurant serves typical dishes from the mountains of Ronda. Eat at tables on a covered terrace and listen to live music from the town.

José Aparicio 3, 29400 Ronda. ✆ **95-287-34-88.** Fax 95-287-99-03. www.hotelrondena.com. 16 units. 80€–128€ double. Rates include continental breakfast. AE, DC, MC, V. **Amenities:** Restaurant; bar. *In room:* A/C, TV, hair dryer; Wi-Fi.

Maestranza ★ 🥄 This modern hotel is on the site of a villa, now disappeared, once inhabited by legendary bullfighter Pedro Romero. In the center of town, facing the oldest bullring in the world, the hotel is one of the best and most contemporary in Ronda. The bedrooms are small to midsize, but are designed for comfort, with modern furnishings, carpets, and draperies. The public rooms are tastefully furnished, and the helpful staff provides excellent service. Guests can use the facilities of a nearby private country club, with a swimming pool and tennis courts.

Calle Virgen de la Paz 24, 29400 Ronda. ☏ **95-218-70-72.** Fax 95-219-01-70. www.hotelmaestranza. com. 54 units. 94€–115€ double; 131€–147€ suite. AE, DC, MC, V. Parking 10€. **Amenities:** Restaurant; bar; babysitting; room service; nonsmoking rooms; rooms for those w/limited mobility; Wi-Fi. *In room:* A/C, TV, hair dryer, minibar.

ON THE OUTSKIRTS

El Molino del Santo ★ 🎁   This place is a real discovery. The landscaped inn beside a rushing stream outside Benaoján is an easy 10km (7-mile) drive west of Ronda. It's a great place for escapists—particularly in summer when Ronda is overcrowded. Converted from an old olive-and-flour watermill, it's set in the mountains in the Natural Park of Grazalema. Once a private home, it opened as a British-managed hotel in 1987. Guests relax in the gardens near the solar-heated pool, under shady willow or fig trees. Or they can wander through the flower-filled terrace, with outside dining from May to September. Good-size bedrooms are comfortably and tastefully furnished, some large enough for extra beds for families. Most have terraces with views. The main lounge has a log fireplace for chilly winter nights; upstairs there's a well-stocked library. The chefs specialize in regional dishes, and the menu varies according to the seasons. Breakfast is buffet style.

Estación de Benaoján, 29370 Benaoján. ☏ **95-216-71-51.** Fax 95-216-73-27. www.molinodelsanto.com. 18 units. 90€–120€ double; 100€–190€ junior suite. Rates include breakfast. AE, DC, MC, V. Closed mid-Nov to mid-Dec. **Amenities:** Restaurant; bar; pool. *In room:* A/C, hair dryer, minibar.

La Fuente de la Higuera ★★★ 🎁   A 10-minute drive from cosmopolitan Ronda but with all the country-house comforts to tempt you to siesta by the pool, this is one of my favorite hotels in all of Andalusia. This renovated rural olive oil mill is pretty perfect, marrying up traditional Andalusian charm with understated stylish design. Huge rooms have whitewashed walls, painted wooden floorboards, interesting antique furniture, and designer lamp lights. In the airy central patio there's a log burner that looks like an aircraft engine and interesting art on the walls. There's an open-house atmosphere to the place with an honesty bar and fridge with ice creams as well as drinks. Dinner on the terrace overlooking the pool by candlelight is a treat, and the food dished up by owner Tina's son, who is head chef, is delicious. I had fabulous pancetta-wrapped cod with mushroom and mango sauce. Service was impeccable too. A self-contained lodge just down the road is perfect for large families or groups of friends.

Partido de los Frontones, 29400 Ronda. ☏ **95-211-43-55.** Fax 95-211-43-56. www.hotellafuente.com and www.thelodgeronda.com. 12 units. 148€ double; 179€–280€ suite. Rates include breakfast. Dinner from around 42€. AE, MC, V. **Amenities:** Restaurant; bar; pool, Wi-Fi. *In room:* A/C.

Where to Dine
EXPENSIVE

Casa Santa Pola INTERNATIONAL/ANDALUSIAN   Constructed in the 19th century but altered and rebuilt over the years, this building opens onto expansive views of the gorge. On three levels built onto the mountainside, access is through the third floor. The interior is a mix of Moorish, Rococo, and contemporary, decorated with antique ornaments, wooden floors, archways, and terracotta walls. Many dishes are cooked in a traditional brick oven. Dine off *cochinillo* (roast suckling pig), *lomo asado* (grilled filet beefsteak), or the savory *rabo de toro* (roast oxtail). Desserts are homemade, traditional, and regional. Expect odd closings (often Monday or Tuesday).

Cuesta Santo Domingo 3. ✆ **95-287-92-08.** Main courses 18€–26€; set menu 35€–60€. AE, DC, MC, V. Daily 11:30am–5pm and 7:30–11pm.

Del Escudero ★ ANDALUSIAN   The second best restaurant in town occupies a baronial-looking 19th-century villa that was originally a private house, just across from the bullring. Inside, three white-walled dining rooms look out through huge windows to the jagged mountains nearby. There's a dining terrace in good weather. Dishes are upscale Andalusian—a homemade gooseliver pate sweetened with the local Pedro Ximénez; filets of freshwater trout served with almond sauce and strips of Iberian ham; and slices of chocolate tart served with mango-flavored sherbet. Former clients include Michelle Obama with the children on their summer holiday.

Paseo Blas Infante 1. ✆ **95-287-13-67.** Reservations recommended. Main courses 8€–24€. AE, DC, MC, V. Daily noon–5pm; Mon–Sat 7–10pm.

Tragabuches ★★★ MODERN SPANISH/ANDALUSIAN   This restaurant serves the finest and most creative cuisine in Ronda. The two dining rooms are stylish and contemporary, with white walls and tables decked out with pastel cloths and seat covers. The inventive menu might feature well-crafted dishes like *cochinillo asado* (grilled suckling pig) or *rape en salsa de vinagreta, pulpo y verdura* (monkfish in a vinaigrette sauce with octopus and fresh vegetables). Begin, perhaps, with a cheese taco or the tasty liver pate. It's not cheap, but you are guaranteed a memorable meal.

José Aparicio 1 (btw. Plaza de España and Plaza de Toros). ✆ **95-219-02-91.** Reservations recommended on weekends. Main courses 21€–32€; set menu 74€. AE, DC, MC, V. Sun 1:30–3:30pm; Tues–Sat 1:30–3:30pm and 8:30–10:30pm. Closed Mon.

MODERATE
Almocabar ★★ ANDALUSIAN   In the quieter and more authentic San Francisco barrio just outside the old town gates at the bottom of Cuesta las Imagenes, this nice local restaurant serves up tasty tapas in the bar out front and interesting Andalusian dishes with Moorish flourishes in its cozy restaurant. Meat cooked on hot stones is particularly good, as is the exceptional roast lamb accompanied by some great value local wines. Well worth walking down the hill for.

Plaza Ruedo Alameda 5. ✆ **95-287-59-77.** Main courses 11€–18€. MC, V. Mon and Wed–Sun 1–5pm and 7–11:30pm.

Don Miguel Restaurant ★ ANDALUSIAN   At the end of the bridge facing the river, and with views of the upper gorge, the outside tables on two levels can seat 300 people. There's a pleasant bar for drinks and tapas and friendly staff who speak some English. The food is good. Try a seafood selection or the house specialty, stewed oxtail. The Hotel Don Miguel (see "Where to Stay," above) runs the restaurant.

Calle Villanueva 3. ✆ **95-287-10-90.** Main courses 12€–18€. AE, DC, MC, V. Daily 12:30–4pm and 7:30–10:30pm.

El Morabito ★★ ANDALUSIAN   Husband-and-wife team Che-Che and Begona run this delightful little restaurant in the Old Town. Located right on the cliff edge, it has stunning views across the plains. Service takes a while as it's literally just the two of them, but the food is totally worth waiting for. Stand out dishes include a paella full of fishy flavor and a lemon tart that's absolutely to die for. And with views like that, you won't want to leave in a hurry anyway.

Plaza Maria Auxiliadora 4. ☎ **95-287-59-12.** Main courses 9€–17€. MC, V. Daily 8–11:30pm.

INEXPENSIVE

Pizzeria Ristorante Italiano Nonno Peppe ☺ PIZZA/ITALIAN   In front of Plaza Nueva, this joint makes the best pizzas in town as well as homemade pasta—at affordable prices. A young crowd and families patronize the place, which has a friendly spirit of camaraderie. Many of the ingredients are imported from Italy. The lasagna is excellent, and there's pizza for vegetarians. Salads are fresh and crisp with tantalizing dressings; freshly made Italian desserts include a very good tiramisu.

Calle Nueva 18. ☎ **95-287-28-50.** Reservations recommended. Pizzas 3.50€–8€; pasta 3.50€–7.50€; main courses 6€–12€. MC, V. Daily noon–4:30pm and 8pm–1am.

Shopping

Crafts, antiques, and some gift items are available, but save your serious shopping for Granada or Seville. **Muñoz Soto,** San Juan de Dios de Córdoba 34 (☎ **95-287-14-51**), has a range of decorative accessories, antiques, drawings of local scenes, and various souvenirs. It's open Monday to Saturday from 10am to 2pm and 4 to 7:30pm. Another good address for shoppers is **El Pensamiento Ronda,** Calle Espinel 16 (☎ **95-287-21-93;** www.elpensamiento.com), in a small shopping center. It has a wide range of merchandise from antiques to china, from paintings to pottery to glass and gift items. It's open Monday to Saturday 10am to 2:30pm and 5 to 8:30pm.

Ronda after Dark

Dropping into a few local tapas bars is a good way to spend the early part of the evening. Plaza del Socorro—a block north of the bullring—is the natural focus for touristy tapas bars and it's very atmospheric, full of buzz and chatter. The tapas here tend to be rather average and overpriced however. If you're after something more properly local and don't mind a bit of a walk, head for Plaza Ruedo Alameda in the San Francisco barrio at the foot of the hill just outside the Old Town. Just cross the bridge into the Old Town and keep walking for about 10 minutes. **Bodega San Fransisco,** Calle Ruedo Alameda 32 (☎ **95-287-81-62**) is the best of the bunch down here, serving up deliciously fresh deep-fried prawns in particular. Next door, **Casa Maria** at Calle Ruedo Alameda 27 (☎ **95-287-62-12**) is a good second bet, though service can be slow.

For something a little smarter, **Café de Ronda,** Calle Tenorio 1 (☎ **95-287-40-91**), just across the Puente Nuevo in the Old Town, occupies the first floor of a large mansion. Its main feature is a plant-filled courtyard with lots of outdoor seating. Try one of the specialty coffees or interesting sandwiches. It's open Monday to Thursday 9am to 9pm and Friday to Sunday 9am to midnight.

Later at night there are various *discotecas* that come and go with the seasons. Along with a collection of routine pubs, they are found along **Calle Jerez** and

Prehistoric Cave Paintings

Near Benaoján, the **Cueva de la Pileta** ★ (© **95-216-73-43;** www.cuevadelapileta. org), 25km (16 miles) southwest of Ronda, plus a 2km (1¼-mile) hard climb, has been compared to the Caves of Altamira in northern Spain, where prehistoric paintings were discovered toward the end of the 19th century. In a wild area known as the Serranía de Ronda, José Bullón Lobato, grandfather of the present owners, discovered this cave in 1905. More than a mile in length and filled with oddly and beautifully shaped stalagmites and stalactites, the cave also contained five fossilized human skeletons and two animal skeletons.

In the darkness, **prehistoric paintings** depict animals in yellow, red, black, and ocher, as well as mysterious symbols. One of the highlights of the tour is a trip to the chamber of the fish, containing a wall painting of a great, black, seal-like creature about 1m (3 ft) long. This chamber, the innermost heart of the cave, ends in a precipice that drops vertically nearly 75m (250 ft). Plan to spend at least an hour here. Visits by guided tour only are given daily from 10am to 1pm and 4 to 6pm (Nov to mid-Apr 10am–1pm and 4–5pm). Admission, including the hour-long tour, is 8€ for adults, 5€ for children aged 10 to 13.

around **Plaza de Abela.** The streets across from **Plaza de España** and **Plaza de Toros** are also busy but more touristy. Favorites in this area include **Huskies Sport Bar,** Calle Molino 1 (no phone). Open Monday at 8:30pm and Tuesday to Sunday from 5:30pm. Closing time depends on business and can get very late during the busy summer months. Another bar favored by young locals is **Bar Antonio,** Calle San José 4 (no phone), with some of the cheapest beer and tapas in town. It's open Monday to Friday 7am to 11pm, Saturday 9am to 4pm.

MIJAS ★

30km (19 miles) W of Málaga, 18km (11 miles) W of Torremolinos, 585km (363 miles) S of Madrid

Just 8km (5 miles) north of coastal road N-340/E-15, the pretty town of **Mijas** is at the foot of a mountain range near the turnoff to Fuengirola, and from its lofty height—450m (1,476 ft) above sea level—you get beautiful panoramic views out across the coastline and the Mediterranean.

Celts, Phoenicians, and Moors preceded today's tourists to Mijas. The main attractions are the setting and the town itself, with its narrow streets, whitewashed houses draped in bougainvillea and jasmine, and panoramic views. Because it's so close to the Costa del Sol, Mijas attracts a significant number of tour groups, which means that at the wrong time of day it can feel a bit inundated. It's got the inevitable souvenir and craft shops, and waiters will try and talk you into their restaurants, but despite this, Mijas retains its Andalusian village atmosphere surprisingly well. Visit outside the mid-morning to mid-afternoon tourist time and you'll find a charming little place with plenty to keep your interest for a few hours or even overnight.

Essentials

GETTING THERE   From the Costa del Sol (the usual approach to Mijas), buses leave the terminal at Fuengirola every 30 minutes during the day for the 8km (5-mile) trip north. Motorists in Fuengirola on the coast can follow the signs north into the hills, leading directly to Mijas. The twisting, turning drive takes only 20 minutes. There are similarly frequent buses from Torremolinos, which take 50 minutes, and four buses a day from Málaga, taking 1 hour 45 minutes.

VISITOR INFORMATION   The helpful local **tourist office** (**✆ 95-258-90-34;** www.mijas.es) is located in the town's central square, **Plaza Virgen de la Peña,** a 2-minute walk from the bus stop, past the town hall. Hours are Monday to Friday 9am to 7pm (8pm in summer months), Saturday 9am to 2pm. There's a handy leaflet available outlining scenic walks in the surrounding hills. Most take a couple of hours and are at varying levels of difficulty—none especially hard.

Exploring Mijas

The town's **location ★★** alone is what continues to draw visitors; its pretty whitewashed houses are set against the mountain, which is heavy with pine trees. From many places in Mijas, there are lookout points. On a clear day you can see across the Mediterranean to the Rif Mountains in Morocco.

There's not a huge amount to see in Mijas and you're best off wandering the tiny streets or sitting at a terrace cafe watching the world go by or admiring the views. From the tourist office, head left and stroll up Avenida del Compás. Kids and the curious might want to visit the slightly tacky museum of curiosities, **Carromato de Max,** Avenida del Compás (no phone; daily 11:30am–12:30pm and 5–8pm; admission 3€). Inside, you can gaze upon Leonardo's *The Last Supper* painted on a grain of rice, Abraham Lincoln painted on a pinhead, the shrunken head of a white man retrieved from South American Indians, and even fleas wearing clothes.

Just past the curiosities museum, take a right down Calle de los Caños if you want to souvenir shop or continue on to pretty **Plaza de la Constitución** where there are several nice pavement cafes and more shops selling a good range of Moroccan leatherware. If you exit the plaza on the far side and walk up Calle Cuesta de la Villa you'll find the town's bullring. Many Costa del Sol visitors come here to watch the *corridas* at the **Plaza de Toros** (**✆ 95-248-52-48**), particularly because they take place year-round rather than during a set season. It's a tiny arena compared to the bullrings in places like Ronda and Málaga and unusual because it's oval-shaped. Bullfights take place on Sunday at 5:30pm (or 7pm in hot summer months), with seats selling for between 50€ and 95€ each. If you just want to check out the bullring itself, you can visit its premises every day 10am to 10pm for a fee of 3€.

Right next to the bullring you'll find the town's pretty main church, the **Iglesia Parroquial de la Inmaculada Concepción (Church of the Immaculate Conception).** The church itself is not rich in treasures, but its setting is. At the crest of a small hill, it has a beautiful terrace and gardens, from which you can enjoy the best panoramic views in the town.

Where to Stay

La Cala Resort ★★   Golfers go to Mijas just for this stylishly contemporary inland resort. The two golf courses at La Cala are its main attraction. Both La Cala

North (par 73) and La Cala South (par 72) were designed by the noted golf architect Cabell B. Robinson, who cited the Costa del Sol terrain as his most challenging project. Even if you're not a golfer, this is one of the finest hotels in the area, unless you prefer to be right on the sea rather than 7km (4⅓ miles) away. Bedrooms are midsize to spacious, attractively furnished in a contemporary mode, with superb bathrooms with tub and shower. Every unit opens onto a large balcony overlooking the fairways and greens and the Mijas hills beyond. The food here, a mix of Spanish and Continental dishes, is first rate and uses quality ingredients.

La Cala de Mijas, 29649 Mijas. ✆ **95-266-90-16.** Fax 95-266-90-13. www.lacala.com. 107 units. 99€–235€ double; 230€–270€ junior suite. AE, DC, MC, V. **Amenities:** 2 restaurants; bar; babysitting; fitness center; Jacuzzi; 2 heated pools (1 indoor); room service; sauna; spa; squash; 2 tennis courts; nonsmoking rooms; rooms for those w/limited mobility; Wi-Fi. *In room:* A/C, TV, hair dryer, minibar.

Hotel Mijas ★★   The only decent place to stay in town, this is one of the most inviting hotels on the Costa del Sol. Built in 1970, it's an Andalusian-inspired block of white walls and flowering terraces which is sun-filled and comfortable. Views sweep to the Mediterranean from most of the public areas and the quite small but comfortable rooms. There's an attractive outdoor pool with more of those stunning views, tennis court, sauna, and gym. The in-house restaurant is pretty good and the staff is tactful and hardworking too. Triple rooms are handy for families.

Calle Tamisa 2, 29650 Mijas. ✆ **95-248-58-00.** Fax 95-248-58-25. www.trhhoteles.es. 204 units. 86€–142€ double; 163€–253€ suite. DC, MC, V. Free parking. **Amenities:** Restaurant; bar; babysitting; health club; Jacuzzi; outdoor pool; sauna; room service; nonsmoking rooms; rooms for those w/limited mobility. *In room:* A/C, TV, hair dryer.

Where to Dine

El Capricho ★ SPANISH/ANDALUSIAN/INTERNATIONAL   In the old part of the city, the restaurant is in a centuries-old house, the age of which even the owners don't know. It's in typical Andalusian style with a wooden roof and interior whitewashed walls decorated with regional ceramics and drawings. In good weather the terrace is the place to be. Prices tend to be high as the restaurant caters to tourists. The cooks make the best shellfish paella in town, and the sauteed prawns zestily flavored with fresh parsley and pepper are also winners. Desserts are homemade and very good.

Los Caños 5. ✆ **95-248-51-11.** Reservations recommended. Main courses 12€–21€. AE, MC, V. Mon–Sat noon–4pm and 7–11pm.

El Olivar INTERNATIONAL/SPANISH   Next to the town hall in the very center of town, this tavern serves some of Mijas's best tapas. Dishes may not be unusual, but they're delicious, prepared fresh daily, and offered along with an affordable selection of regional Andalusian wines. The chefs prepare a tantalizing array of recently harvested *mariscos* (shellfish) from the coast, plus a perfectly grilled filet of sole. The decor is rustic with whitewashed walls, handcrafted local furniture, and, best of all, a terrace.

Av. Virgen de la Peña, Edificio El Rosario. ✆ **95-248-61-96.** Reservations recommended. Main courses 16€–28€. AE, DC, MC, V. Sun–Fri 1–4pm and 7–11pm. Closed Feb.

Mirlo Blanco ★ BASQUE   In the center of town, this 150-year-old, rustically decorated former house is one of the better restaurants in Mijas with Basque-style cooking. The Basques are known for their *merluza* (hake) dishes, so try the version here with pepper, paprika, bay leaf, and cream sauce. Other recommendations are the aromatic honey-flavored lamb, and perfectly grilled tenderloin with peppercorns.

Plaza Constitución 2. ⓒ **95-248-57-00.** Reservations recommended. Main courses 12€–25€. AE, MC, V. Daily 1–3:30pm and 8–11:30pm. Closed Jan 10–30.

ANTEQUERA ★

48km (29 miles) N of Málaga, 99km (61 miles) E of Granada, 164km (101 miles) SE of Seville

Celebrated for its Moorish castle and its dozens of antique churches, Antequera is one of Andalusia's most historic, yet undiscovered, towns. Recent excavations indicate that it was populated as early as the 1st century A.D. Christian settlers who moved in after the Reconquista left a legacy of two dozen historic churches.

This market town and industrial city with a population of 40,000 straddles two hills in the valley of the Guadalhorce River. Antequera is on the main rail route to Granada and at the junction of three arteries leading to the most important cities of Andalusia: Seville, Granada, and Córdoba. It's also a convenient day trip from Málaga.

Allow at least a half-day to see the highlights of Antequera; set aside more time if you wish to explore the rugged, mountainous country to its south and east.

Essentials

GETTING THERE   Antequera's rail station is rather inconveniently located 1.5km (0.9 miles) north of the city center at Plaza de la Estación s/n (ⓒ **95-284-32-26**). Up to eight **trains** per day arrive from Granada, taking 1½ hours and costing 7.50€ one way; up to 10 trains pull in from Seville, also taking 1½ hours and costing from 14.50€ one way. There is also a service from Ronda, with four trains a day making the 1-hour trip, costing 6.50€ one way. Call ⓒ **90-232-03-20** or visit www.renfe.es for more information.

There is a second Antequera rail station. **Antequera Santa Ana** is 16 km (10 miles) outside the city. High-speed AVE trains from Madrid and Málaga call here. Four trains daily arrive from Madrid, taking 2½ hours, and up to seven from Málaga, taking around 20 minutes. There are six daily bus connections from Antequera Santa Ana to the Antequera's main bus station (see below) and the journey takes 30 minutes.

The main **bus** station is at Paseo Garcí de Olmo s/n. **Alsina Graells** (ⓒ **90-242-22-42;** www.alsa.es) has three **buses** a day making the run from Málaga. The trip takes 45 minutes and costs 4€ one way. Two buses a day run from Córdoba, taking 2 hours and costing 9.15€ one way; five run each day from Granada, taking 2 hours and costing 7.50€ one way; and five a day run from Seville, taking 2½ hours and costing 12€ one way.

GETTING AROUND   You can walk around the center of Antequera, but there are currently no bus services from the main station, which is some way out of town, into the center. **Taxi Radio Antequera** (ⓒ **95-284-55-30**) services the area, with most fares averaging 5€. Taxis meet all arriving trains and buses.

VISITOR INFORMATION   For information, go to the **tourist office,** Plaza de San Sebastián 7 (ⓒ **95-270-25-05;** www.antequera.es). From June 16 to September 30, the office is open Monday to Saturday 10:30am to 2pm and 5 to 8pm,

Sunday 10am to 2pm. In off season, hours are Monday to Saturday 10am to 1:30pm and 4 to 7pm, Sunday 10am to 2pm.

[FastFACTS] ANTEQUERA

Currency Exchange
For an ATM, head to
Banco Santander Central Hispano, Calle Infante Don Fernando 51 (📞 **90-224-24-24**). It's open Monday to Friday from 8:30am to 2pm, Saturday from 8:30am to 1pm.

Emergencies Dial
📞 **112.** In a **medical** emergency, call 📞 **95-106-11-50.**

Hospital The local **Hospital Comarcal** is at Polígono de la Azucarera s/n (📞 **95-284-62-63**) on the Málaga road out of town.

Pharmacy Farmacia Cortes (📞 **95-284-13-84**) is at Calle Infante Don Fernando, just off Plaza San Sebastián where the tourist office is located. It's open Monday to Friday from 9:30am to 1:30pm

and 5 to 8:30pm (4:40pm to 8pm in winter), Saturday from 10:30am to 1:30pm.

Police The station is on Avenida de la Legión (📞 **95-270-01-03**).

Post Office The main branch is on Calle Nájera (📞 **95-284-20-83**). It's open Monday to Friday 8:30am to 8:30pm, Saturday 9:30am to 1pm.

Exploring Antequera

The core of the white-walled town was made for walking. As you stroll, you can explore ancient churches and cobblestone alleyways and see windows pierced with the characteristic wrought-iron grilles of Andalusia.

At the top of the hill, a steep stroll up from Plaza San Sebastián, you'll find the town's most impressive monument—the **Alcazaba (Fortress).** Recently renovated, this is where the Moors staged their last defense before being conquered by Catholic troops in 1410. The fortress then became a military base for the Reconquest of Granada. It's open Tuesday to Friday 10:30am to 2pm and 7 to 9pm, Saturdays 10:30am to 2pm, and Sundays 11:30am to 2pm. Admission is free.

From the main tower, **Torre del Homenaje,** you can take in a **panoramic view ★** of the town; note the unusual roofs with their colored tiles. The view goes beyond the town to the surrounding plains and **Peña de los Enamorados (Lover's Rock),** from which two lovers—one a Christian, the other a Muslim—are said to have committed suicide when their parents forbade them to marry. The Alcazaba gardens are always open, although it's best to go during the day so that you can take in the views.

The town is full of churches, but one is more notable than the rest. Right next to the Alcazaba, go through the 16th-century **Arco de los Gigantes (Arch of the Giants)** at the far end of Plaza Alta to the **Real Colegiata de Santa María** at Plaza Santa María (📞 **95-284-61-43**). Dating from 1514, this church has a facade with geometric motifs, which is said to have been the first example of Renaissance-style architecture in the province. In fact the monument betrays several architectural influences, including Mudéjar, Plateresque, and Gothic styles. The church is open Tuesdays 10:30am to 2pm and 7 to 9pm, Wednesdays to Fridays 10:30am to

2pm and 9 to 11pm. Saturdays 10:30am to 2pm and Sundays 11.30am to 2pm. Admission is free.

Facing the church, on the left you can see the ruins of **Las Termas de Santa María,** a Roman thermal bath excavated in 1988. All that remains are mosaic tiles and ruins.

Another attraction is the **Museo Municipal,** Calle Nájera (**©** 95-270-40-21), housed in the 18th-century Palacio de Nájera. At the time of writing it was closed for renovation. Roman artifacts unearthed in the area are its chief attraction. The major exhibit is the **Efebo de Antequera ★★**, a Roman statue about 1.4m (5 ft) high. Discovered outside of town in the 1970s, it's a stunning Roman bronze statue of a boy. Another notable sculpture is an eerily life-like woodcarving by Pedro de Mena, a well-known 17th-century Andalusian sculptor, of **St Francis of Assisi.** Unusually, the museum exhibits the avant-garde 1970s art of native son Cristóbal Toral. Before closing for renovation the museum opening hours were Tuesday to Friday 10am to 1:30pm and 4:30 to 6:30pm, Saturday 10am to 1:30pm, and Sunday 11am to 1:30pm. It's believed they will be the same when it reopens, but check with the tourist office.

One final notable church is **Iglesia del Carmen (Church of Our Lady of Carmen)** (no phone), east of the Postigo de la Estrella, approached by heading up Cuesta de los Rojas or down from the Alcazaba. This is a rare 17th-century Mudéjar church. Behind a plain facade is a lavish interior with a coffered ceiling from the 18th century. Its greatest treasure—found at the main altar—is a *retablo* (altar) **★★**. This is one of the finest of its kind in the whole province, a masterpiece of late Baroque extravaganza. In the center, carvers Diego Márquez and Antonio Primo created a Madonna flanked by several polychromed saints and angels. Visiting hours are Tuesday to Sunday 11am to 1:30pm. Admission is 2€.

ON THE OUTSKIRTS

Only 1km (½ mile) east of Antequera, on the northern outskirts of town, are some of the most important prehistoric discoveries in Europe: **Viera, Romeral,** and **Menga** are funerary chambers (dolmens) dating from 2500 to 1800 B.C. and known for their Cyclopean size. The chambers were carved out of massive slabs of stone, including a 180-ton monolith.

The **Dolmens of Antequera Archeological site**, Ctra de Málaga 5 (**©** 95-271-22-06), houses Menga and Viera in a new visitor center complex where you can watch a short explanatory film before visiting the chambers. Menga is the best preserved and it's also the oldest and largest of the trio. At one time these chambers were filled with great riches, but, of course, this treasure has long since been looted. Viera starts out with a narrow passageway that leads deep into the bowels of the earth. It's an eerie and strangely evocative prehistoric site. From the center of Antequera, follow signs out of town toward Granada and Málaga. Once past a gas station, watch for a sign directing you to **Los Dólmenes.** The visitor center is on the left.

The Romeral dolmen site consists of a long corridor leading to two round chambers. Small flat stones are laid out to produce a trapezoidal section in the corridor. To reach it, continue past the Menga and Viera site across three small roundabouts then follow the signs left, then left again. It's located down an unsurfaced track in a small industrial estate. Both sites are open Tuesday to Saturday from 9am to 6pm and Sunday from 9:30am to 2:30pm. Admission is free. Last admission is 15 minutes before closing time.

The best day trip in the area is to **El Torcal ★★**, a natural park consisting of a strangely shaped series of limestone rocks. Some visitors compare its surface to the landscape of an otherworldly planet. Towering over the park is a 1,370m (4,494 ft) peak. Several trails circle this dramatic summit; others cross the entire park, stretching out for 12km (7¼ miles). Take the path marked with a green arrow on your own for 1.5km (just under a mile). El Torcal is 16km (10 miles) south of Antequera. Take the A-343 south from the center and then turn left on to the A-7075 towards Villanueva de la Concepción. Admission is free. There's a small visitor center (© **95-203-13-89**) with toilets and an information desk. You can watch a short introductory film to the park and its unique geology.

Where to Stay

Antequera Golf Hotel ★★   The best hotel in town, with all the latest hotel gadgetry, is only a 15-minute walk from the city center. Golfers come for the deluxe 18-hole course surrounded by the scenic El Torcal de Antequera Nature Reserve. Spacious, stylish bedrooms have tasteful, comfortable furnishings, and most open onto views of the town or the hotel's well-manicured gardens. In lieu of any hotshot local eateries, dine here on dishes using the best regional produce. Choose from a formal restaurant serving Andalusian and international specialties or a buffet restaurant. From its heated indoor swimming pool to its mud-therapy center, the hotel is the best equipped in the area, even offering makeover treatments in its beauty center.

Urbanización Santa Catalina s/n, 29200 Antequera. © **95-270-45-31.** Fax 95-284-52-32. www.hotel antequera.com. 180 units. 105€ double; 200€ suite. AE, DC, MC, V. Parking 7€ in indoor garage. **Amenities:** 2 restaurants; cafeteria; bar; aerobics and weight room; disco; golf course; gym; mud-therapy center; 2 pools (indoor and outdoor); room service; sauna; Turkish bath; 24-hr. medical service; Wi-Fi. *In room:* A/C, TV, hair dryer, minibar, Jacuzzi in suites.

Hotel Coso Viejo 🔥   This new renovation of an 18th-century town house is ideally located for sightseeing, a couple of blocks from the tourist office with El Angelote restaurant (reviewed below) opposite. An attractive restored central patio has marble columns and floor. Rooms are simply furnished, but clean and comfortable. Service is friendly and with prices like this, the whole package is pretty attractive.

Calle Encarnación 9, 29200 Antequera. © **95-270-50-45.** Fax 95-270-48-42. www.hotelcosoviejo. com. 21 units. 63€–83€ double. AE, MC, V. Closed Jan. **Amenities:** Restaurant; bar; room service; non-smoking rooms. *In room:* A/C, TV, Internet.

Where to Dine

El Angelote   SPANISH/ANDALUSIAN   Across the square from the Museo Municipal, this nice local restaurant is decorated in rustic *bodega* style. The two wooden-beamed dining rooms were originally part of a 17th-century private house. Chefs are big on flavor, and portions are hearty, using local produce when available. Start with a creamy gazpacho and follow (on a hot day) with such dishes as codfish salad flavored with onions and dressed with virgin olive oil. Local foodies swear by the oxtail and the partridge with almonds and white wine. The signature dessert is *bienmesabe,* a sponge cake with almonds and a sugar and cinnamon "dusting."

Plaza Coso Viejo. Ⓒ **95-270-34-65.** Reservations recommended. Main courses 11€–25€. DC, MC, V. Tues–Sat 8–11:30am; Tues–Sun noon–5pm. Closed 15 days in Aug (dates vary).

A DRIVING TOUR OF THE PUEBLOS BLANCOS

The brilliantly whitewashed villages and towns of inland Andalusia are known as the Pueblos Blancos, archetypal towns and villages that dot the steep slopes of the mountains north of Gibraltar, spread out across the provinces of Cádiz and Málaga, east of Seville, which is often the gateway for tours of this landscape.

Many towns have "de la Frontera" as part of their name, an ancient reference to the frontier towns that formed a boundary between Christian-held territories and Muslim towns and villages during the Middle Ages. Although the Catholic troops eventually triumphed, it is often the Moorish influence that makes these towns architecturally interesting, with their labyrinths of narrow, cobblestone streets, their fortress-like walls, and their little whitewashed houses clinging precariously to the steep sides of the hills.

If you take the drive outlined below, you'll pass some of the great scenic landscapes of southern Spain too, various thickly wooded areas that are often the home to some rare botanical species, including the Spanish fir, *Abies pinsap,* which only grows in four locations at more than 1,000m (3,281 ft). As you drive along you'll approach limestone slopes that might rise as high as 1,640m (5,000 ft). Castle ruins and old church bell towers also form part of the landscape.

The ideal time to drive through the Pueblos Blancos is spring, when all the wild flowers in the valleys burst into bloom. Fall/autumn is another good time. Allow at least a day for Ronda, covered in detail at the beginning of this chapter. You can pass through the other villages, admiring the life and the architecture and then moving on if you're in a hurry. However, part of the delight of this tour is taking your time and enjoying the laid-back yesteryear ambiance of these little places and the views of the surrounding countryside. There are an increasing number of delightful rural hotels and guesthouses dotted among the Pueblos Blancos too, so if you have time, plan overnight stops at places like Arcos de la Frontera, Ronda, Grazalema, and Vejer de la Frontera.

The first part of the tour from Arcos to Ronda can be done in one day, with an overnight in Ronda. I'd recommend spending two nights in Ronda and giving yourself a complete day to explore this, the most famous of the Pueblos Blancos. Then hit the road for day three and the second part of the tour, from Ronda to Jerez de la Frontera in the west, which can also be done in a day. Those with more time can easily extend this tour to four or five days. There's a suggested summary itinerary for doing this as part of a longer tour along with the Sherry Triangle towns on p. 66.

The villages are all fairly close together, so driving times, as indicated below, are fairly short. From Seville, you can begin your tour by heading to the Pueblos Blancos along the AP-4/E-5 toll road to junction 78 at Jerez. Here, take a left along the A-382 and then take the A-372 to Arcos de la Frontera, first stop on the tour.

A Driving Tour of the Pueblos Blancos

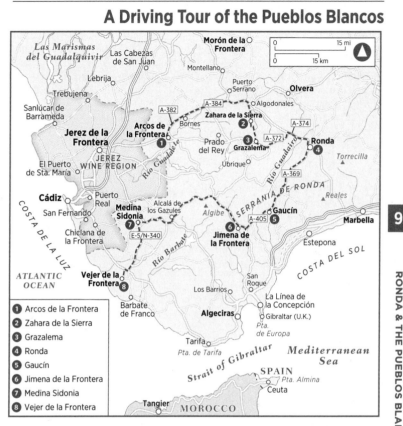

1 Arcos de la Frontera
2 Zahara de la Sierra
3 Grazalema
4 Ronda
5 Gaucín
6 Jimena de la Frontera
7 Medina Sidonia
8 Vejer de la Frontera

Arcos de la Frontera ★★

Along with Ronda, this old Arab town is one of the highlights of the Pueblos Blancos. Now a National Historic Monument, Arcos de la Frontera was built in the form of an amphitheater. The major attraction here is the village itself. Wander at leisure and don't worry about skipping a particular monument.

Once under the control of the Caliphate of Córdoba, Arcos's period of glory ended when the kingdom collapsed in the 11th century. By 1264, the Catholic troops had moved in, signaling the end of Muslim rule forever. Nearly all that interests the casual visitor will be found in the elevated **Medina (Old Town) ★★**, towering over the flatlands. The Old Town is huddled against the crenellated castle walls.

Negotiating the Old Town's narrow one-way system is not for the faint-hearted. I recommend you park your car below in the car park at the Plaza de España. Pick up a map at the handy **tourist information booth** here (no phone), open Monday to Friday 10am to 1:30pm. Unfortunately maps currently cost (.50€ small map, 1€ large) but I was told that they plan to make them free from 2011.

From here it's a 10-minute walk up Calle Corredera to pretty **Plaza del Cabildo,** the focus of the Old Town. The main t**ourist office** (© **95-670-22-64;** www. ayuntamientoarcos.org), is here with a bigger selection of brochures and helpful staff. Hours are May to October, Monday to Friday 10am to 2:30pm and 5 to 8pm, Saturday 10am to 1:30pm and 5 to 7pm, and Sunday 10am to 1:30pm; off season Monday to Friday 10am to 2:30pm and 4 to 7pm, Saturday 10am to 1:30pm and 4 to 6pm, and Sunday 10am to 1:30pm. There's an interesting **guided tour** available departing daily at 11am and costing 6€ per person.

Arcos's main attraction is its location perched high above the plains; the view ★★ from the **Balcon de Arcos,** a rectangular esplanade overhanging a deep river cleft, is truly breathtaking. Also here, on Plaza del Cabildo, are the restored remains of a Moorish castle, but it's privately owned and not open to the public. The town's main church, **Iglesia de Santa María,** is, however, open to view. It costs 2€ and is open Monday to Friday 10am to 1pm and 3:30 to 6pm (4 to 7pm in summer) and Sundays 10am to 2pm. Built in 1732, the exterior is an interesting blend of Renaissance, Gothic, and Baroque styles. Its **western facade ★**, in the Plateresque style, is its most stunning achievement. The interior is a similar mix—Plateresque, Gothic, Mudéjar, and Baroque. Look for the beautiful star-vaulting and a late Renaissance altarpiece.

Turn right out of the top of Plaza del Cabildo and continue through the maze of tiny streets to **Iglesia de San Pedro,** with its Baroque bell tower. It's open Monday to Friday 9:30am to 2pm and 4 to 6:30pm (4 to 7pm in summer) and Sundays 9:30am to 2pm. Entry is free, but a donation is suggested. Paintings inside include *Dolorosa* by Pacheco, the tutor of the great Velázquez, and works by Ribera and students of the school of Zurbarán. Continue in the same direction around the back of Iglesia de San Pedro to another excellent panoramic lookout point, the **Mirador de Abades ★**, at the end of Calle Abades.

If you fancy a spot of **souvenir shopping,** Arcos has a number of nice artists' galleries. They are a bit touristy but the quality of workmanship is pretty good none-theless. My favorites are **Galeria de Arte San Pedro** at Calle San Pedro 7 (© **95-670-18-00**), just next to the Iglesia de San Pedro, where you can buy nice paintings, colorful tiles, and ceramics, and **Galeria de Arte Arx-Arcis,** a little war-ren of rooms at Calle Marques de Torresoto 11 (© 9**5-670-39-51**).

WHERE TO STAY

Cortijo Fain ★ 🍴   A real discovery, this 17th-century farmhouse has been turned into a hacienda hotel 3km (2 miles) southeast of Arcos near the hamlet of Algar (reached via the CA-52). It's part of a top-end golf complex surrounded by land-scaped gardens and an 18-hole golf course. Draped with purple bougainvillea, the house is warm and inviting with arches, white walls, and Andalusian courtyards. The inn offers large, comfortably and rather charmingly furnished bedrooms, each with a tub/shower combo. The inn is in a vast olive grove, and has a swimming pool and a library. Rates have been significantly reduced, probably due to the economic down-turn, so it's really good value. The inn can arrange horseback rides to explore the countryside. The restaurant is very good, see below.

Carretera Arcos-Algar Km 3, 11630 Arcos de la Frontera. © **95-670-41-31.** Fax 95-671-79-32. www. arcosgardens.com. 9 units. 93€–121€ double. AE, DC, MC, V. **Amenities:** Restaurant; outdoor pool; 18-hole golf course; room service. *In room:* A/C, TV, hair dryer, minibar, Wi-Fi.

El Convento 🍴 Nicely located just off Plaza del Cabildo, this building was originally the Convento Las Mercedarías, but was turned into an inn in 1987. The hotel is reached via a tiny cobblestone alleyway at the back of the Parador Casa del Corregidor (see below). In classic style, with a red-tile roof and wrought-iron grilles, the hotel is a snug nest. It's furnished with rustic wooden pieces and beautifully maintained. Inviting, midsize bedrooms are comfortable enough to make you want to linger, particularly at such prices. Many have terraces with that fantastic view too.

Maldonado 2, 11630 Arcos de la Frontera. ✆ **95-670-23-33.** Fax 95-670-41-28. www.hotelelconvento. es. 11 units. 55€–88€ double. AE, DC, MC, V. Parking 4€ nearby. **Amenities:** Bar; room service; sun terrace. *In room:* A/C, TV, hair dryer, Wi-Fi (in some).

La Casa Grande ★ Of the several nice hotels in the Old Town with views across the plains, this is probably my favorite, just beating El Convento by a short hop. It's not top-end luxury by any means, but it's big on atmosphere, feeling more like a slightly eclectic private house than a hotel. The house was first built in 1729 and was once the home of famous dancer Antonio Ruiz Soler. Its current owners have created a comfortable intimate little hotel with just six rooms—four doubles and two suites—around a small central patio. The roof terrace is perfect for an evening drink. Moorish touches include old lanterns and decorative tiles. The attractive lounge has books and a log-burning stove for cold winter days.

Maldonado 10, 11630 Arcos de la Frontera. ✆ **95-670-39-30.** Fax 95-670-39-30. www.lacasagrande. net. 6 units. 59€–110€ double; 81€–159€ suite. AE, MC, V. Parking 4€ nearby. **Amenities:** Library; sun terrace. *In room:* A/C, TV, hair dryer, CD player, Wi-Fi. Closed Jan.

Los Olivos This former private home, with its whitewashed walls, yellowish tile roofs, and attractive internal courtyard, is built in traditional Andalusian style with balconies and wide windows. It's a dependable choice, the rather small bedrooms simply furnished with wooden beds and tile floors, wicker chairs, long curtains, and drawings. Whilst it doesn't have the cliff-top location of many other Arcos hotels, bedrooms at the front of the hotel still have nice views of the countryside.

Paseo de Boliches 30, 11630 Arcos de la Frontera. ✆ **95-670-08-11.** Fax 95-670-20-18. www.hotel-losolivos.es. 19 units. 60€–75€ double. AE, DC, MC, V. Parking 8€. **Amenities:** Bar; Wi-Fi. *In room:* A/C, TV, hair dryer, minibar.

Marqués de Torresoto ☺ At the center of Arcos, just behind Plaza del Cabildo, this converted palace dates from the 17th century and still has its original chapel. It was a private family home built by a local nobleman, Marqués de Torresoto. Turned into a hotel in 1994, it has interior patios, corridors, columns, and arches in the typical Andalusian style. Rooms are a bit minimalist, evocative of a monastery, with white walls and wooden furniture, each room with a tiled bathroom with a tub/shower combo. A triple and a quad room make this hotel a good choice for families.

Marqués de Torresoto 4, 11630 Arcos de la Frontera. ✆ **95-670-07-17.** Fax 95-670-42-05. www.hotel marquestorresoto.com. 15 units. 50€ double; 65€ triple; 80€ quad. AE, DC, MC, V. Parking 6€ nearby. **Amenities:** Restaurant; bar; babysitting; room service; Wi-Fi. *In room:* A/C, TV, hair dryer, minibar.

Parador Casa del Corregidor ★★ Perfectly located for the Old Town right on Plaza del Cabildo, Arcos's parador was originally the house of the *corregidor* (king's magistrate). It dates from the late 14th century and from its balconies and terraces there are panoramic views of the Guadalete River and the plains and farms beyond. Midsize bedrooms are traditionally and comfortably furnished, matching the style of the house. Many open onto views, and each comes with a small, tiled bathroom. The on-site restaurant is the best bet in the Old Town, serving typical Sierra region dishes (that oxtail again), but also other dishes like pork in red wine and trout in almond sauce.

Plaza del Cabildo s/n, 11630 Arcos de la Frontera. ✆ **95-670-05-00.** Fax 95-670-11-16. www.parador. es. 24 units. 143€–155€ double. AE, DC, MC, V. Limited free parking nearby. **Amenities:** Restaurant; bar; room service; rooms for those w/limited mobility; Wi-Fi. *In room:* A/C, TV, hair dryer, minibar.

WHERE TO DINE

Perhaps because it gets so many tourists visiting it, Arcos is pretty awful for dining. I can safely say I ate the worst tapas I've tasted in Andalusia here. Aside from the parador's dependable restaurant (see above) there is a small glimmer of hope, but it takes a little finding.

Cortijo Fain Restaurant ★ ANDALUSIAN   The dining room at this impressive resort hotel (see above) is one of the best culinary spots around Arcos. Elegant and antique looking, the decor is that of an upscale but rustic tavern. In summer, grilled partridge from the local countryside is a specialty, as is aromatically spiced leg of lamb with fresh herbs and plenty of garlic. Whenever possible, the chef uses locally grown and market-fresh ingredients.

Carretera Arcos-Algar Km 3. ✆ **95-670-41-31.** Reservations not needed. Main courses 15€–25€ fixed-price menus 20€–32€. AE, DC, MC, V. Daily 8–10:30pm.

La Taberna de Boabdil TAPAS   La Taberna de Boabdil is reached down a narrow set of stairs about a third of the way up Calle Corredera from the Plaza de España. Look out for the signpost. The place is high on atmosphere, but it's rustic and quirky. Don't expect fine dining. The tapas on a good day though are a genuinely remarkable mix of Moorish, Andalusian, and even Sephardic (traditional Spanish–Jewish) recipes and there's a nice selection for veggies too. I've had reports that the owner tries to get people to take a tasting menu at 25€ per head; some have loved this and others felt a bit ripped off. Either go for the big feed or ask for the tapas menu.

Paseo de los Boliches 35. ✆ **95-670-51-91.** Tapas 3€–5€; tasting menu 25€. MC, V. Daily 10am–midnight.

Zahara de la Sierra ★

From Arcos de la Frontera, return to the A-382 and continue northeast, following the signs to Algodonales (the road becomes the A-384 at Villamartin about halfway). Once you reach Algodonales, head south at the junction with the A-2300 to Zahara de la Sierra, one of the most perfect of the province's fortified hilltop *pueblos,* set on the shores of a manmade reservoir. Trip time from Arcos is about 35 minutes, and the distance is 51km (32 miles).

The White Village of Zahara itself zigzags up the foot of a rock topped by a reconstructed *castillo.* Houses covered in characteristic red tiles huddle up to the ruined castle. Count on a 15- to 20-minute climb to reach what was once a 10th-century Muslim fortress constructed on Roman foundations 511m (1,676 ft) above sea level. Zahara was, in fact, so prized by the Moors that the ruler, Abu al'Hasan of Granada, recaptured it in 1481 from the Catholic troops. But with the fall of Granada at the Reconquista, Zahara once again fell into the hands of the Catholic monarchs.

The **Tourist Information Office** (📞 95-612-31-14; www.zaharadelasierra.es) is at Plaza del Rey 3, at the eastern end of the main street, Calle San Juan. In theory, hours are daily from 9am to 2pm, however it was closed when I visited and local contacts tell me it often is. From Plaza del Rey there are wonderful views out across the lake and you can walk down towards it along a recently constructed walkway that winds through attractive gardens. Also located here is **Iglesia San Juan,** one of the town's most important churches. If you walk a short way up the pretty cobbled main street, Calle San Juan, you'll reach **Iglesia Santa María de la Mesa.** This 18th-century Baroque church is worth a look inside if it's open. It has an impressive retable with a 16th-century image of the Madonna.

The best time to be here is in June for the Corpus Christi celebration (annual dates vary). Streets and walls seem to disappear under a mass of flowers and greenery.

WHERE TO STAY & DINE

Al Lago ★★ 🏨   This delightful boutique hotel and restaurant is the best place to stay and to dine in Zahara. Chef Stefan Crites trained in the U.S.A. for 12 years in New York then moved to southern Spain with his wife Mona to open a boutique hotel and restaurant. Mona, a textile designer, has decorated Al Lago with imaginative flair using local materials to create simple interiors of understated luxury with large comfortable beds, crisp linens, polished natural plaster walls, and soothing earth tones. Wrought-iron French doors open onto balconies with views over the lake. The modern, contemporary bathrooms, finished in local Ronda stone, have walk-in wet room-style showers. Stefan uses the very freshest locally sourced ingredients to cook seriously tasty dishes that make a lunch stop a great idea even if you're not staying. You might start with char-grilled vegetables with toasted local goat's cheese, then move on to slow roasted leg of lamb with couscous and almonds or baby lamb chops with homemade mint chutney. Homemade desserts include summer berry sundae with vanilla ice cream and New York-style vanilla cheesecake. Main courses cost 10€ to 24€ and there's a good selection of dishes for vegetarians too.

Calle Felix Rodriguez de la Fuente 11, 11688 Zahara de la Sierra. 📞 **95-612-30-32**/66-205-25-53. Fax 95-612-32-44. www.al-lago.es. 4 units. 75€–100€ double. Rates includes breakfast. MC, V. Free parking. **Amenities:** Restaurant, Wi-Fi. *In room:* A/C, TV. Closed mid-Nov to mid-Jan.

Arco de la Villa   In business since 1998, this rural inn is a rustic stone house with a low roof and set near a promontory in front of the castle, a short walk from Plaza del Rey. It's modern and minimally decorated with whitewashed walls and light wooden furnishings. Bedrooms are small and simply but comfortably furnished, with little tile bathrooms. A reasonably good meal costing 18€ is served in the on-site restaurant if you're just passing through Zahara and need lunch.

Paseo Nazari s/n, 11688 Zahara de la Sierra. 📞 **95-612-32-30.** Fax 95-612-32-44. www.tugasa.com. 17 units. 59€ double. MC, V. Free parking. **Amenities:** Restaurant; bar; room service; rooms for those w/ limited mobility. *In room:* A/C, TV.

Los Tadeos   This rural inn is a family-run business in a two-story structure outside town near the municipal swimming pool. Its restaurant is more popular than its hotel rooms. At tables placed on the terrace, order typically Andalusian and budget-priced dishes that change daily. Simple, small bedrooms are comfortable with a little tiled bathroom with tub and shower. The best open onto private balconies with views.

Paseo de la Fuente, 11688 Zahara de la Sierra. ⓒ /fax **95-612-30-86.** 10 units. 50€ double. MC, V. Free parking. **Amenities:** Restaurant; bar. *In room:* A/C, TV, no phone.

Marqués de Zahara This small hotel on the town's pretty main street, Calle San Juan, is housed in a 17th-century former private house now converted to receive guests on its three floors. The location is central, and the decoration is very rustic, with heavy curtains and dark colors. Furnishings are rather flea-markety, but comfortable for a night. The most expensive doubles have private balconies. The handsomest feature is an attractive courtyard and delightful bar and dining room, where nonguests can enjoy regional meals, usually costing under 18€.

Calle San Juan 3, 11688 Zahara de la Sierra. ⓒ **95-612-30-61.** Fax 95-612-32-68. www.marquesde zahara.com. 11 units. 50€ double. MC, V. Free parking. **Amenities:** Restaurant; bar; Wi-Fi. *In room:* A/C, TV.

Grazalema ★★

After visiting Zahara, head to the village of Grazalema by taking the tiny CA-9104 (previously called the CA-531) south. It's a distance of just 17km (10.5 miles), but don't rush the journey as you'll see some of the most spectacular views along the way as the road winds its way up the steep hillside round hairpin bend after hairpin bend. At the top you reach the **Puerto de las Palomas,** a mountain pass at 1,157m (3,800 ft) above see level. There's a *mirador* (viewpoint) ★★ with spectacular views back down the valley. (In winter check the snow situation before attempting the drive.)

Delightful Grazalema is perhaps the most idyllic of the White Villages. This charming village nestles under the craggy peak of San Cristóbal at 1,525m (5,003 ft). As you wander its sloping, narrow streets, you'll pass white house after white house with window boxes filled with summery flowers.

Grazalema's **tourist office** at Plaza Asomaderas 3, (ⓒ **95-613-20-52;** www. grazalemaguide.com) is one of the best in the region, offering lots of advice and a handy pamphlet for 3€ with a host of interesting things to do in and around the town and detailed descriptions of walking and driving tours. You can rent bikes and hook up to free Wi-Fi here too. You can also get information and permits which cost 2€ for exploring the **Natural Park Sierra de Grazalema ★★**, a 50,590-hectare (125,000-acre) park. An important reserve for Eurasian griffon vultures, among other creatures, the park is studded with pine trees and oak forests and criss-crossed by walking trails. In spring, some 30 different species of orchids flower here. Four routes inside the park are self-guided, except in July and August when risk of forest fire means an accompanying guide. You can also rock climb, canoe, paraglide, and horse trek here.

The town has two beautiful old churches, **Iglesia de la Aurora** on Plaza de España and the nearby **Iglesia de la Encarnación.** Both date from the 17th century. Unfortunately they are rarely open for tourist visits. Pretty tree-lined Plaza de España ★ is one of the most delightful squares in the region.

Towering limestone crags overlook the town. For the best view, climb the marked trail which starts just a short way back down the road to Zahara to the **Mirador El**

Santo where a statue of Christ is set on top of a brick tower. Close by are the remains of the tiny El Calvario hermitage.

Grazalema is also known for its local products, especially pure wool blankets and rugs and leatherware. Lots of small shops selling artisanal products are dotted around the narrow streets leading off Plaza de España. The best place to buy blankets is **Artesanía Textil de Grazalema,** Carretera de Ronda (© **95-613-20-08**), a 5-minute walk from Plaza de España. It also sells souvenirs, handicrafts, and traditional gifts. At this small factory you can buy blankets and ponchos made from local wool using hand-operated looms and antique machinery. It's open Monday to Thursday 8am to 2pm and 3 to 6:30pm, Friday 8am to 2pm. Closed weekends and holidays.

WHERE TO STAY

Casa de las Piedras ⚑   The building housing this inn dates from the 19th century. On one of the oldest streets of the little town, 50m (164 ft) from the central square, it's a traditional Andalusian house on two floors. The bedrooms themselves are small and simple. The hotel's dining room is one of the best in town (see below). Helpful staff members speak a little English. There are also fully equipped apartments.

Las Piedras 32, 11610 Grazalema. © **95-613-20-14.** Fax 95-613-20-14. www.casadelaspiedras.org. 32 units, 16 without bathrooms. 48€ double; 40€ double without bathroom. DC, MC, V. **Amenities:** Restaurant; Wi-Fi. *In room:* A/C.

La Mejorana ★   This friendly rural guesthouse is tucked away up a couple of winding streets off the Plaza de España. The old house has been attractively renovated to create six comfortable, welcoming rooms with traditional furniture and interesting antiques. Several have lovely views across the valley. The pretty, tranquil garden is filled with olive trees, shrubs, and flowers and has a nice swimming pool, perfect after a day walking in the nearby Natural Park.

Calle Santa Clara 6, 11610 Grazalema. © **95-613-23-27**/64-961-32-72. www.lamejorana.net. 6 units. 58€ double. Rate includes breakfast. MC, V. **Amenities:** Outdoor swimming pool; Wi-Fi.

WHERE TO STAY NEARBY

Hotel El Horcajo ★ ☺   Set on a working estate in the Natural Park, this is a traditional Spanish colonial-style 19th-century farmhouse with whitewashed walls and iron grilles at the windows. The bedrooms are in the former stables. The main country house, still with its original character, vaulted arches, and wood-beamed ceilings, feels like a family home. Sober but cozy bedrooms are furnished with tiles and light wooden pieces. Near the main building, 10 family units in traditional style have a large double bed plus two single beds upstairs. Many rooms open onto a private terrace. Rooms are decorated with locally crafted materials, and there's a comfortable lounge. Typical local food is served, including some produce grown on the estate. The hotel is located on the main road connecting Ronda with Algodonales (A-374).

Carretera de Ronda Km 149, 29400 Ronda. © **95-218-40-80.** Fax 95-218-41-71. www.elhorcajo.com. 26 units. 66€–82€ double; 97€ suite. AE, MC, V. **Amenities:** Restaurant; pool; room service; nonsmoking rooms; rooms for those w/limited mobility. *In room:* A/C, TV, hair dryer.

WHERE TO DINE

Cádiz El Chico ANDALUSIAN   The best restaurant in town is right on the main square. In an antique building, it's typically decorated, even using blankets made in town. The simplified classic cuisine is inexpensive and good, such as shoulder of lamb studded with garlic and cooked over firewood. Oven-baked deer is another signature dish, as is wild boar with almond and raspberry jus. Of course, you'll also find that Andalusian favorite, oxtail. Desserts are simple.

Plaza de España 8. ✆ **95-613-20-67.** Reservations recommended. Main courses 10€–14€. AE, MC, V. Tues–Sun 1–4pm; Tues–Sat 8–11pm.

Casa de las Piedras ANDALUSIAN   In this hotel (see above), near the central square, authentic, full-flavored regional dishes are presented in a 19th-century house decorated in (what else?) Andalusian regional style with wooden tables and chairs. Perhaps begin with gazpacho (tomato) soup followed by shredded veal with vegetables. A signature dish is the oven-baked wild boar with spices. Prices are extremely reasonable considering the quality of the food and the generous portions.

Las Piedras 32. ✆ **95-613-20-14.** Reservations recommended. Main courses 8€–13€. MC, V. Tues–Sun 1:30–3:30pm and 7:30–10pm. Open Mon in peak season.

Continuing on to Ronda

To reach Ronda, the capital of the White Villages, take the A-372 until you reach the main A-374 road. Turn right here and continue to Ronda. It's a distance of just 33 km (20.5 miles) and takes about 30 minutes. For more on Ronda, see p. 232. Spend at least 1 night in Ronda, ideally 2, before continuing the driving tour.

Gaucín

From Ronda take the A-369 southwest to Gaucín. Allow about an hour for the 37km (23-mile) trip.

This pretty whitewashed mountain town is perched on a ridge below a former Muslim fortress, which opens onto a panoramic vista of the countryside. Many expats, Brits in particular, live or own holiday apartments here. There's not much to see, but the town's pretty narrow streets make for a very pleasant wander.

At the eastern edge of the village, head up to the **Castillo del Aguila,** the Moorish castle. From its battlements, look out over the countryside—on a clear day you can see all the way to the Rock of Gibraltar. It's open Wednesday to Sunday and holidays 10:30am to 1:30pm and 4 to 6pm (8pm June to September). Admission is free.

WHERE TO STAY & DINE

La Fructuosa ★ 🎁   In the center of Gaucín, this lovely guesthouse has been carefully renovated with style. Bedrooms are simply but comfortably furnished, nicely balancing old and new furnishings and rugs from Tunisia and Afghanistan. Bathrooms have handmade tiles and hydromassage baths. Views from most of the rooms and the hotel terrace are spectacular, across the hills and on to Gibraltar. The restaurant is open Friday and Saturday evenings. Mediterranean dishes include specialties like fresh goat's cheese grilled with local honey, and fresh tuna fish with onion, fresh tomato, and mint.

Convento 67, 29480 Gaucín. ✆ **95-215-10-72**/61-769-27-84; fax 95-215-15-80. www.lafructuosa.com. 5 units. 88€–98€ double. Rate includes breakfast. MC, V. **Amenities:** Restaurant; Wi-Fi. *In room:* TV.

Jimena de la Frontera

To reach this White Village from Gaucín, take the winding A-369 out of town, which becomes the A-405, traveling southwest for some 30 minutes, a distance of 23km (14 miles). Enveloped by Los Alcornocales Natural Park, Jimena was built 200m (656 ft) above sea level. It is so close to San Roque on the Costa del Sol and its string of beaches that it gets a lot of visitors on day trips, especially from the exclusive golf and polo coastal belt. Chic Sotorgrande, an upmarket resort, is a short drive to the south.

You enter Jimena through a gateway of three arches. Over the years the town has had many rulers, from the Phoenicians and Romans to the Moors and ultimately the Christian armies. There's not a huge amount to see here, but several of the restored steep and narrow cobblestone streets are a real delight. It takes about 15 minutes to walk to the highest point, the castle-fortress built on Roman ruins. Today the **Castillo-Fortaleza** is in ruins but still impressive. Inside the castle enclosure, you can take in one of the most panoramic **views** ★ of the Costa del Sol, including the Rock of Gibraltar and the port of Algeciras. It's open daily and entry is free.

Visitors with more time will find that Jimena is the gateway to the **Parque Natural de los Alcornocales** ★★, stretching south to the Mediterranean and north to one of the White Villages, El Bosque. The park is named for its cork oaks (*alcornocales*), which are among the largest in the world, but is also home to the gall and the holm oak as well as wild olive trees. Creatures such as the Egyptian mongoose, the Spanish Imperial eagle, eagle owls, and the roebuck also inhabit the park. The park is one of the most heavily forested in Spain and gives you a sense of what Iberia used to look like before much of its forest was uprooted to plant olive groves. There's an **information center** at the top of the hill just below the castle at Calle Misericordia s/n ✆ **95-664-05-69**. Unfortunately opening hours are erratic to say the least. In theory they are 10am to 2pm and 4 to 8pm Monday to Friday and 10am to 2pm weekends.

WHERE TO STAY

Casa Grande ☺ If you want to overnight in Jimena, this little guesthouse is a good bet and among the most affordable along the trail of Pueblos Blancos. Run by English expatriates, residents come and go as they like in between frequent excursions for hill-climbing, bird-watching, and in some cases, mushroom-hunting. It's set in an old two-storied Andalusian house in the traditional architectural style, with an internal courtyard. Bedrooms are small and very basic, with wooden furniture. Families can book an apartment here with kitchen. Ask for a room with private bath.

Calle Fuente Nueva 42, 11330 Jimena de la Frontera. ✆ **95-664-11-20.** Fax 95-640-13-94. www. posadalacasagrande.es. 7 units. 35€ double without bathroom; 40€ double with bathroom. MC, V. Free parking. **Amenities:** Bar; library; nonsmoking rooms; solarium. *In room:* A/C, TV, no phone.

WHERE TO STAY & DINE

Hostal El Anon ★ Hostal el Anon is owned by Suzana Odell, an American by birth who traveled extensively before settling in Jimena in 1977. Her knowledge of the area is extensive for walking, bird-watching, botany, and interesting excursions by car or train. Her friendly small hotel was converted from several adjoining houses and stables. There is an inviting Andalusian courtyard, a comfortable restaurant, and even a rooftop pool. The style is rustic with wooden furniture, antique ceramics, and copper ornaments. Some of the simple, comfortable rooms have balconies onto inner courtyards. A couple of quad rooms are handy for families. Food in the restaurant is fresh and tasty. Begin with kidney pate and follow with the freshly caught catch of the day from the Costa del Sol, grilled as you order. Local chicken comes with grapes, and a tender sirloin of beef with a blue cheese sauce. Main courses cost 10€ to 15€.

Calle Consuelo 36, 11330, Jimena de la Frontera ✆ **95-664-01-13.** Fax 95-664-11-10. www.hostalanon. com. 12 units. 60€ double; 117€ quad. MC, V. **Amenities**: Restaurant; bar; outdoor pool; Wi-Fi. *In room*: A/C, no phone. Closed 2 weeks in late June and 2 weeks in mid-Nov.

Medina Sidonia ★

From Jimena, take the CA-8201 (formerly the CA-3331) northwest until you come to the junction with the A-2304 (formerly the A-375) heading southwest to the junction with the A-381. Once on the A-381 continue northwest into Medina Sidonia. This trip takes you across 86km (54 miles) and the first section in particular is slow going along the narrow winding roads through olive groves and moorland. Allow 1 to 1½ hours.

The ancient hilltop Muslim fortress of Medina Sidonia fell to Catholic troops in 1264 under King Alfonso X. In the Middle Ages it became a famous seat of the Duke de Medina Sidonia, a title bestowed on the heirs of Guzmán El Bueno who helped recapture the town from the Moors. The title today is held by the Duquesa de Medina Sidonia, known as *la duquesa roja* (the red duchess) for her left-wing political views. A champion of the poor and downtrodden, her politics have even landed her in jail.

The village today is one of the most unspoilt of the Pueblos Blancos. It retains a real local feel and is a little more rough round the edges, which I think adds to its charm. Start at the central square, **Plaza de España.** The most impressive architecture here is the Renaissance facade of the 17th-century **Ayuntamiento (town hall).** Just up Calle San Juan at the opposite end of the plaza you'll find the town's attractive, recently renovated traditional market, dating back to 1871. It houses the **tourist office** (✆ **95-641-24-04;** www.medinasidon ia.com), usually open daily 10am to 2pm and 4 to 8pm.

From here, turn right up the hill onto Calle Victoria and bear right until you reach one of the old town gates, the **Arco de Belen.** Pass through this and up the hill to reach the town's second-most beautiful square, **Plaza Iglesia Mayor,** and visit **Iglesia Santa María La Coronada,** open daily from 10:30am to 2pm and 5 to 8pm; admission 2.50€. Built on the foundations of a former mosque, it is known for its stunning *retablo* ★★, standing 15m (49 ft) high. The *retablo* depicts scenes from the life of Jesus and is a master work in polychrome wood painted by the artisans of the Middle Ages. Walk up round behind the church to see the ruins of a former castle and for great views far out across the surrounding countryside.

From here, walk west down the narrow streets to Calle Cervantes and through another attractive old town gate, the **Arco de la Pastoria,** which has a very Moorish horseshoe shape to it. Then visit the **Roman Sewers** at the Conjunto Arqueológico Romano, Calle Ortega 10. They're open daily from 10am to 2pm and 4 to

8pm, and admission is 4.30€. The sewers date from the 1st century A.D. With the same ticket, you can also see the ruins of a well-preserved **Roman road** nearby.

If you're driving on from Medina and fancy some lunch, try **Venta La Duquesa** (⌀ **95-641-08-36**), along the A-393 3km (1¼ miles) to the southeast. The food is good and well prepared, without rising to any spectacular heights. You'll find a well-spiced and tasty loin of pork, or a more local dish of partridge baked with onions and mushrooms. The restaurant is on Carretera de Jerez A-393, and main courses cost 11€ to 17€. Open Wednesday to Monday noon to 4pm and Friday and Saturday 7:30 to 11:30pm.

WHERE TO STAY & DINE

La Vista de Medina ★ 🏠   Run by British couple Gary and Kirsty Biston, La Vista de Medina is named after the exceptional views from many of its terraces and flower-filled gardens. The outdoor pool is a natural focal point on hot summer days. Five self-catering suites have crisp cotton sheets, plump feather pillows, and comfy living-dining areas with an attractive kitchenette for rustling up tasty meals—perfect for summer living. This imaginatively finished rambling property offers unparalleled views over a patchwork of undulating tiled roofs and church spires to the rural splendor of rolling hills fringed by the Atlantic Ocean. The restaurant also enjoys fabulous views across the countryside and serves local specialties with a Mediterranean flourish at dinner. Main courses cost 9€ to 18€. Gary and Kirsty also own Casa de Medina—a stylish self-catering town house with pool close by.

Plaza de la Iglesia Mayor, 11170, Medina Sidonia ⌀ **95-641-00-69.** Fax 95-641-00-69. www.lavistademedina.com. 6 units. 60€–100€ suite. MC, V. **Amenities:** Restaurant; bar; outdoor pool; Wi-Fi. *In room:* A/C, hair dryer, kitchen.

Vejer de la Frontera ★

From Medina Sidonia, follow the A-396 south to the E-5/N-340 and then take a right and a left following the signs to Vejer de la Frontera. The 26km (17-mile) journey usually takes 20 minutes. This is one of the more dazzling Pueblos Blancos. It's also quite popular with expatriate Brits, and several have set up charming boutique hotels here. Like most of the other towns, this Pueblo Blanco also reflects its Moorish history.

Vejer, still partially walled, is perched high on a clifftop on the road between Tarifa (southernmost point in Spain) and the port of Cádiz, 10km (6¼ miles) inland.

For orientation, head to the **tourist office** at Avenida de los Remedios (⌀ **95-645-17-36;** www.vejerdelafrontera.es) on the main road into town. Hours are June to August, Monday to Friday 10am to 2pm and 6 to 8pm. In August it's also open on Saturday from 10:30am to 2pm. In other months, it keeps no set hours. Park in the car park and walk from here, as the Old Town's narrow streets are hard to negotiate in a car.

There's just a handful of monuments to see in Vejer; the real pleasure of the place is in walking its winding streets, enjoying the fabulous **views ★**—particularly along Calle Corredera—and sipping a coffee or chilled glass of wine watching the world go by in the town's delightful main square, the palm-fringed **Plaza de España ★**.

The **Iglesia del Divino Salvador,** the town's main church, sits on the top of the hill, on Calle Nostra Señora de la Oliva. It was built on the remains of the town's mosque from the Moorish era. It's a mix of styles, including Romanesque, Mudéjar, and Gothic. It's usually open daily 11am to 2pm and 5 to 8pm.

Castillo Moro, or the **Moorish castle,** is reached by heading down Calle Ramón y Cajal from the church. Over the years it's been altered drastically, but as of 1000 B.C. it is known to have been some sort of fortress, standing watch over the fishing grounds and factories along the coast for the approach of an enemy vessel by sea. The site was also used by the Phoenicians and Carthaginians long before the coming of the Romans. The castle keeps such erratic opening hours it's best to inquire at the tourist office. In theory, it's open 10am to 2pm and 5:30 to 8:30pm daily in July and August only.

WHERE TO STAY & DINE

Casa Cinco ★   This is a lovely Vejer-style boutique B&B. The interiors have a more modern contemporary vibe than those at Escondrijo (see below). Owners Collette and Glen have done a great job marrying original doors and lintels with up-to-date colors and modern fixtures and fittings. All are individually furnished and designed, reflecting the Riad-style house layout with its open inner courtyard. Rooms have open-plan shower/bathrooms and come with CD players, heating, and ceiling fans. Star of the show here is the lovely roof terrace where guests meet and chat with a sundowner drink taking in the vast views of the surrounding countryside.

Calle Sancho IV El Bravo 5, 11150 Vejer de la Frontera. ℓ **95-645-50-29**/62-648-13-01. Fax: 95-645-11-25. www.hotelcasacinco.com. 5 units. 75€–119€ suite. Rates include breakfast. MC, V. **Amenities:** Bar; roof terrace. *In room:* Hi-Fi.

El Cobijo de Vejer   This much-restored Moorish-style house with an Andalusian courtyard is 250 years old. Its flower-filled patio is a delight, and it has individually decorated bedrooms that are midsize and vary in quality. The best open onto vistas of the town and countryside. Each comes with a tiled bathroom. Some of the rooms also come with small kitchen units and private sitting rooms.

Calle San Filmo 7, 11150 Vejer de la Frontera. ℓ **95-645-50-23.** Fax 95-645-17-20. www.elcobijo.com. 7 units. 75€–116€ double. Rates include continental breakfast. AE, DC, MC, V. Free parking. **Amenities:** Breakfast lounge. *In room:* A/C, TV, fridge, Wi-Fi.

Escondrijo ★   This is B&B boutique style: a beautifully renovated house, originally built from the remains of the Vera Cruz Chapel but ruined in the 18th century. In a quiet pedestrian lane at the heart of the Old Town, it's just a short stroll from Vejer's excellent restaurants and bars. The house retains its big lofty rooms and generous common spaces, including the original galleried internal courtyard. As well as a large shared terrace, the two rooms have their own private terraces. Both offer big, comfortable, and well-dressed beds and great showers plus fridges and facilities for your own drinks or snacks. The view from the house's main roof terrace is truly spectacular.

Callejon Oscuro 3, 11150 Vejer de la Frontera. ℓ **95-644-74-38**/66-995-03-05. www.escondrijo.com. 2 units. 120€–140€ suite. Rates include breakfast. MC, V. **Amenities:** Bar; roof terrace. *In room:* A/C, TV, fridge, Hi-Fi, Wi-Fi.

La Casa del Califa ★★   Five old town houses on the delightful Plaza de España have been carefully renovated to create this wonderfully atmospheric boutique hotel.

Bedrooms are all different shapes and sizes, many with views across the rooftops. Some are quite small, but all are attractively decorated with Moorish touches and antique furniture. Most have tub/shower combos in well-equipped bathrooms. Best is the Africa Suite, a large, loft-style, double-fronted room with views to the sea and across the plaza. The bathroom has a Jacuzzi bath and separate walk-in shower. The hotel's excellent restaurant is inspired by North Africa; the perfect place for a meal is in the flower-filled patio garden. There's a small free-form outdoor swimming pool.

Plaza de España 16, 11150 Vejer de la Frontera. © **95-644-77-30.** Fax 95-645-16-25. www.lacasa delcalifa.com. 19 units. 69€–125€ double ; 126€–142€ suite. Rates include breakfast. AE, MC, V. **Amenities:** Restaurant; bar; outdoor pool. *In room:* A/C, TV, hair dryer.

ON THE OUTSKIRTS

Casa de la Siesta ★★★ If you're looking for the ultimate getaway for total relaxation and delicious food, this is the place. A 10-minute drive out of Vejer down a small country lane, this tranquil luxury retreat is a notch up on places in Vejer itself. You enter through the vast lounge with wooden beams, antique furnishings, and a huge fireplace. Step out into the fragrant gardens, full of lavender, citrus trees, and thyme, and relax. There's a large salt-water swimming pool. The seven double guest rooms have sweeping views of the surrounding countryside. Each has its own private terrace and a unique decorative style. Large comfortable beds have fine Egyptian cotton. In the bathrooms, there are rain showers and grooming products by REN, and some suites have gorgeous free-standing baths. Dining here is a real pleasure. Freshly prepared creative dishes using local ingredients, many from the hotel's own gardens, are complemented by a great selection of wines. It's particularly delightful in the cool of a summer evening with candles on the terrace. Owners Lee and Amelia are wonderful hosts and can organize day trips and recommend restaurants.

Los Parralejos 11150 Vejer de la Frontera. © **95-623-20-03** or © 69-961-94-30. Fax: 95-645-11-25. www.casalasiesta.com. 7 units. 170€ double; 200€ suite; 230€ superior suite. Rates include breakfast. Lunch 18€; dinner 35€. MC, V. **Amenities:** Outdoor pool; free use of bicycles. *In room:* A/C, Wi-Fi.

Continuing on to the Sherry Triangle

After your tour of Vejer, you can take the A-48/E-5 northwest. At the junction with the A-4, continue northeast around the Bay of Cádiz and on to Jerez de la Frontera. The distance from Vejer to Jerez is 62km (39 miles) and it takes 45 minutes. Once in Jerez, you'll be in the center of the sherry-producing district of Andalusia, the Sherry Triangle.

Three cities make up this region: **Jerez de la Frontera** and the port cities of **El Puerto de Santa María** and **Sanlúcar de Barrameda.** If you have time to visit only one, make it Jerez: it has the best *bodegas* to see how sherry is produced and taste samples.

Jerez also gets the nod because it is a great equestrian center, known for its Carthusian horses, and it is also one of the best places to hear authentic flamenco.

Visitors flock to Sanlúcar de Barrameda for its fine fish restaurants, its beaches, and also for its sherry *bodegas*. Those arriving at Puerto de Santa María find a dilapidated but intriguing little fishing port with lovely beaches nearby. Columbus once lived here. It deserves at least a half-day to visit its sherry and brandy *bodegas* and sample its *marisco* (shellfish) bars along the water.

JEREZ DE LA FRONTERA ★

87km (54 miles) S of Seville, 593km (368 miles) SW of Madrid, 34km (21 miles) NE of Cádiz

Over the centuries, the charming little Andalusian town of Jerez de la Frontera has shipped thousands of casks of golden sherry around the world. Dating back nearly 3,000 years, Jerez is today a modern, progressive town with wide boulevards and an interesting old quarter. Busloads of visitors pour in every year to sample the famous sherry wines at one of the many *bodegas* where they're aged and bottled.

The name of the town is pronounced "Heh-*res*" or "Heh-*reth*," in Andalusian or Castilian, respectively. The French and the Moors called it various names, including Heres and Scheris, which the English corrupted to sherry.

Essentials

GETTING THERE   Iberia offers **flights** to Jerez daily from Barcelona and three times daily from Madrid. Ryanair has a daily flight from London Stansted. You can also fly to Jerez from Frankfurt and Munich in Germany. The airport at **Carretera Jerez-Sevilla** is about 11km (7 miles) northeast of the city center (follow the signs to Seville). Call ✆ **95-615-00-00** or visit www.aena.es for information.

There are frequent **buses** (✆ **90-245-05-50;** www.cmtbc.es) from the airport into the city center running about every 90 minutes. The journey takes 25 minutes and costs 1€. A number of these buses then continue on to Cádiz.

Train connections are fast and convenient with up to 14 **trains** per day arriving from Seville, taking just over an hour and costing 8.90€ one way. A similar number of trains from Cádiz take around 45 minutes and cost 4.90€. Trains from Madrid arrive three times daily. A ticket from Madrid to Jerez costs 68€, and the trip takes 3½ hours. The railway station in Jerez is at the Plaza de la Estación s/n (✆ **90-224-02-02**) at the eastern end of Calle Medina.

Bus connections are frequent too. The location of the bus terminal is also Plaza de la Estación (✆ **95-614-99-90**). About 12 buses arrive daily from Cádiz (✆ **90-245-05-50;** www.cmtbc.es) taking about 1 hour. Four buses per day travel from Ronda (2½ hr) operated by **TG Comes** (✆ **90-219-92-08;** www.tgcomes.es). There are seven buses a day from Seville (1¼ hr) operated by **Linesur** (✆ **95-498-82-22;** www.linesur.com).

Jerez is on the highway (E-5) connecting Seville with Cádiz, Algeciras, and the ferryboat landing for Tangier, Morocco. There's also an overland road connecting Jerez with Antequera and Granada.

VISITOR INFORMATION   The **tourist office** is at Alameda Cristina s/n (✆ **95-633-88-74;** www.turismojerez.com). Open Monday to Friday 9:30am to 3pm and 4:30 to 6:30pm (5 to 7pm from June to September), Saturday and Sunday 9:30am to 2:30pm (8am to 4pm in August and September). The English speaking staff can provide maps, transportation suggestions, and open hours for any *bodega* you might want to visit. You'll also be given a map pinpointing the location of various *bodegas*.

Jerez de la Frontera

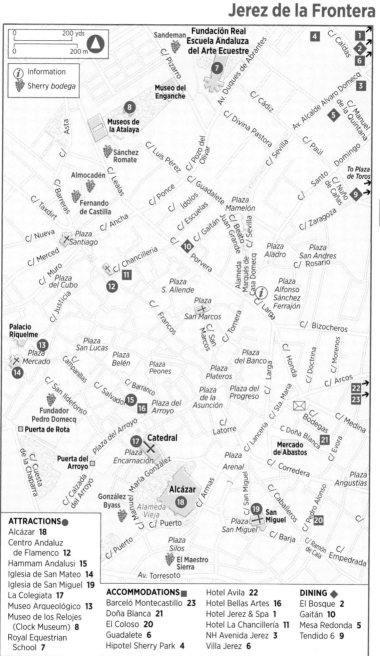

ATTRACTIONS ●
Alcázar **18**
Centro Andaluz
  de Flamenco **12**
Hammam Andalusi **15**
Iglesia de San Mateo **14**
Iglesia de San Miguel **19**
La Colegiata **17**
Museo Arqueológico **13**
Museo de los Relojes
  (Clock Museum) **8**
Royal Equestrian
  School **7**

ACCOMMODATIONS ■
Barceló Montecastillo **23**
Doña Blanca **21**
El Coloso **20**
Guadalete **6**
Hipotel Sherry Park **4**

Hotel Avila **22**
Hotel Bellas Artes **16**
Hotel Jerez & Spa **1**
Hotel La Chancillería **11**
NH Avenida Jerez **3**
Villa Jerez **6**

DINING ◆
El Bosque **2**
Gaitán **10**
Mesa Redonda **5**
Tendido 6 **9**

[FastFACTS] JEREZ DE LA FRONTERA

Currency Exchange
The most convenient location to **exchange money** is **Banco Santander,** Plaza del Arenal 5 (© **95-635-65-27**), where you'll find ATMs. It's open Monday to Friday from 8:30am to 2:30pm.

Emergencies In case of an **emergency,** dial © **061;** for the **police,** call © **091.**

Hospital If you need a **hospital,** head to **Hospital Juan Grande,** Felix Rodriguez de la Fuenta s/n (© **95-635-73-00**).

Pharmacy There's a helpful 24-hour pharmacy at Calle Porvera 32 ((© **95-634-23-23;** www.farmaciaporvera.com).

Post Office The main branch is at Calle Cerrón 2 ((© **95-632-67-33**). It's open Monday to Friday 8:30am to 8:30pm, Saturday 9:30am to 2pm.

Exploring the Area

TOURING THE BODEGAS ★★

Jerez is not surrounded by vineyards as you might expect. Instead, the vineyards are to the north and west in the "Sherry Triangle" marked by Jerez, Sanlúcar de Barrameda, and El Puerto de Santa María (the latter two towns are on the coast).

In and around Jerez there are upwards of 20 *bodegas* where you can see how sherry is made, bottled, and aged and also sample some. Among the most famous producers are **Sandeman, Pedro Domecq,** and **González Byass,** the maker of Tío Pepe. On a typical visit, you'll be taken through several buildings in which sherry and brandy are manufactured. In one you'll see grapes being pressed and sorted; in another, the bottling process; in a third, thousands of large oak casks. Then it's on to an attractive bar to sample the sherries—amber, dark gold, cream, red, sweet, and velvety. Be aware that the alcohol content in sherry is considerably higher than standard table wine, so sip slowly. (See box "Ma Sherry Amour" for more information.)

Of the dozens of *bodegas* you can visit, the most popular are listed below. Some charge an admission fee and prefer a reservation, although in practice if you show up unannounced at the appropriate time, they are unlikely to turn you away.

A favorite among British visitors is **Harveys of Bristol,** Calle Pintor Muñoz Cebrián s/n (© **95-615-15-00;** www.bodegasharveys.com), home of the world's most popular sherry brand, Harveys Bristol Cream. An English-speaking guide leads a 2-hour tour. Tours are Monday to Friday at noon and cost 8€. Another famous name is **González Byass,** Manuel María González 12 (© **95-635-70-16;** www.bodegastiopepe.com); admission is 8€ and reservations are required. Tours in English depart at midday, 1pm, and 2pm daily and additionally at 5pm and 6:30pm on weekdays. Equally famous is **Domecq,** Calle San Ildefonso 3 (© **95-615-15-00**). Reservations are required and admission is 8€. Tours usually start at 10 and 11am, noon, and 2pm Monday to Friday (Saturday tours May–Sept at noon and 2pm). And then there's **Sandeman,** Calle Pizarro 10 (© **95-615-17-00;** www.sandeman.es), another of the big sherry brands in Jerez where no reservations are required Monday, Wednesday, and Friday at 11:30am, 12:30pm, and 1:30pm, Tuesday and Thursday at 10:30am, midday, 1pm, and 2pm. There are tours on Saturdays too, at 11am, 1pm, and 2pm when booking is advised. Entry costs either 6.50€ for three standard sherry tastings, or 12€ if you want to sample older, rarer sherries.

All these large sherry houses offer similar, well-organized tours which give you a good introduction to sherry and allow you to sample some. If you're looking for something a little more serious and less touristy, the smaller, more intimate family-run sherry house **Bodegas Tradición,** ★★ Plaza Cordobeses 3 (© **95-616-86-28;** www.bodegastradicion.com) is highly recommended. This is top-end boutique-style sherry hand-blended using only the best vintage sherries. The 15€ entry fee includes tastings, but you can organize more in-depth tasting sessions too. Just for good measure, the *bodega* contains an exceptional private art collection. The **Colección Joaquin Rivero** literally took my breath away: fabulous canvases by Zurbarán, Goya, Velázquez and more, right there in two well-lit, climate-controlled rooms in the *bodega*. The *bodega* is open Monday to Friday from 9am to 3pm and from 4:30 to 6:30pm. It's best to call ahead, particularly to sample the really top-end sherries.

OTHER ATTRACTIONS

Aside from the *bodegas,* the chief historic attraction is the **Alcázar,** Alameda Vieja s/n (© **95-614-99-55**), the former residence of the Caliph of Seville, complete with an octagonal mosque and ancient baths. The complex was taken by Christian knights in the Reconquista in 1255. The walls of the old Moorish fortress are now surrounded by gardens through which you can stroll, south of Plaza del Arenal. The planting here has been modeled as closely as possible on the original gardens. Inside you can view a well-preserved mosque with a *mihrab.* The baths were constructed by the Almohads and based on Roman designs. In the complex is the 18th-century **Palacio de Villavicencio,** constructed on the site of the original Muslim castle. Inside, the *cámara obscura,* a lens-and-mirrors device, projects views of the major landmarks of Jerez onto a large indoor screen. Views of the sherry vineyards and the sea beyond are also projected. Admission is 3€, 5.40€ including *cámara obscura.* It's open May to mid-September daily 10am to 8pm; mid-September to April daily 10am to 6pm.

If you've not found it already, the **Plaza del Arenal** just around the corner from the Alcázar is a natural focus for the Old Town. There's a host of pretty terrace bars and restaurants here, ideal for a chilled glass of wine (sherry of course) and a people-watch. Just to the south of the plaza you'll find one of the oldest churches in Andalusia, the **Iglesia de San Miguel,** Plaza de San Miguel (© **95-634-33-47**). Its original Gothic structure dates from the 15th century, but much of its ornate facade was added three centuries later. The bell tower is decorated with blue-and-white Andalusian tiles and the interior is a medley of Gothic architecture over different periods. Note the magnificent stained-glass windows. It's open Tuesday to Saturday 10am to 1pm and from 7 to 8pm. The entrance fee is 2.50€.

La Colegiata, or Cathedral of San Salvador, Plaza de Arroyo, is primarily an 18th-century Baroque structure with five aisles and both Renaissance and Baroque adornments. Some of the building, however, dates from the 16th and 17th centuries. Inside you can see such treasures as Zurbarán's *The Sleeping Girl* in the sacristy. The transept crossing is covered by a dome. The cathedral is at the top of a wide Baroque flight of stairs. The first grapes of the harvest are pressed here on the steps each year in early September. Set slightly apart is a 15th-century Mudéjar belfry. Admission is free. The cathedral is open Monday to Friday 11am to 1pm and 6 to 8pm, Saturday 11am to 2pm and 6 to 8pm, and Sunday 11am to 2pm and 5:30 to 8pm. Call ✆ **95-634-84-82** for more information.

If you visit the **Royal Equestrian School ★★** (see box "The Dancing Horses of Jerez"), you might want to stop by the **Museo de los Relojes (Clock Museum) ★** in the Palacio de Atalaya, Cervantes 3 (✆ **90-218-21-00;** www.elmisteriodejerez. org), which is just across the way. This treasure-trove of 300 British and French timepieces includes many dating from the 1600s. They come in all shapes and sizes, as well as designs, their chimes ringing out in "concert" at noon. Outside, peacocks walk the grounds. It's open Tuesday to Sunday 10am to 3pm and 6 to 8pm March to October. Admission is 6€. There's also **El Misterio de Jerez (the Story of Sherry)** exhibition in this complex. If you've done a *bodega* tour, you will know plenty about the history and manufacture of sherry, but otherwise this high-tech audio-visual exhibition does a pretty good job. The opening hours are the same as the clock museum. Admission is 5€. To see both museums, buy a combined ticket for 9€.

If you still have time for a stroll, head for the old quarter, **Barrio de Santiago ★**, which stretches uphill from the cathedral. Wander its slightly down-at-heel, labyrinthine maze of narrow lanes and alleyways. If you're interested in flamenco, visit the **Centro Andaluz de Flamenco,** Palacio Pemartín 1, Plaza San Juan (✆ **95-634-92-65**). Housed in a traditional Andalusian patio house, it's Spain's main flamenco archive, containing over 3,000 books, 800 music scores, and 900 videos. There's not a great deal to see here unless you speak Spanish and are seriously into flamenco, but it does put on daily films showcasing great classical dancers and singers through the ages. Admission is free, and it's open Monday to Friday from 9am to 2pm.

From here it's a five-minute walk to Plaza del Mercado, a slightly run-down, tree-lined square with a fountain at its center. Here you'll find the town's **Museo Arqueológico** (✆ **95-635-01-33**), housed in an 18th-century mansion. At the time of writing it was closed for renovation. A local contact told me that the renovation works are quite stunning and completely finished, but that issues with paying staff salaries to run the place have kept the doors closed. If it's open when you visit, you should see such treasures as a 7th-century-B.C. Greek helmet found in the Guadalete River. Other pieces include a ram's head from the 3rd century B.C., artifacts unearthed at the ancient town of Hasta Regia, and a collection of Muslim and medieval artifacts, including Moorish ceramics and a Caliphal bottle vase with Kufic script from the 10th century.

Finally, exit Plaza del Mercado on the side opposite the museum to reach Plaza San Mateo and its church, the **Iglesia de San Mateo,** noted for its Mudéjar chapels. It's only open for visits on Mondays (5 to 9pm) and Saturdays (7 to 9:30pm). If you can get inside, look for its impressive retable and the beautiful vaulting over its chapels.

If the sightseeing is taking its toll, just across the way from the cathedral, the Moorish-themed **Hammam Andalusi,** Calle Salvador 6 (✆ **95-634-90-66;** www. hammamandalusi.com), offers the ideal way to relax and rejuvenate. Here you can wallow in different temperature pools, relax in the sauna, and indulge in various sumptuous massages and treatments like Aloe Vera baths and chocolate scrubs.

The Dancing Horses of Jerez

A rival of sorts to Vienna's famous Spanish Riding School is the **Escuela Andaluza del Arte Ecuestre (Andalusian School of Equestrian Art)**, Av. Duque de Abrantes s/n (① **95-631-96-35**; www.realescuela.org). In fact, the long, hard schooling that brings horse and rider into perfect harmony originated in this province. The Viennese school was started with Hispano-Arab horses sent from this region, the same breeds you can see today. The highlight of a visit is the **Dancing Horses of Jerez ★★**, a performance that's often referred to as equestrian ballet. Riders and horses perform complex choreography in perfect symmetry to traditional Spanish music. The arena has a capacity of 1,600 people and you're quite a way from the horses, so I recommend you pay the extra euros to sit in rows 1 and 2 (called the preference rows), which cost 24€; rows 3 to 7 cost 18€. You should book seats as early as possible. Most hotels can do this for you. Performances are every Thursday and most Tuesdays at midday, with additional performances on Fridays in August and on a number of Saturdays. When performances aren't scheduled, you can visit the stables and tack room and watch the horses being trained. Hours are Mondays and Wednesdays (along with Tuesdays and Fridays when there's no performance scheduled) from 11am to 2pm and entry costs 10€. You can also visit **Museo del Enganche**, the harness museum in the school's grounds, which displays antique carriages. Entrance is 4€. Bus no. 18 goes here.

Prices start at 32€ for use of the baths and a 15-minute massage. Reservations essential.

Where to Stay

There are a lot of hotels in Jerez and competition, particularly outside the high season, is fierce. Room rates here tend to be very reasonable so shop around if you're on a budget or consider upgrading to a higher standard of room for less than you'd pay elsewhere. The expensive hotels are all a bit of a walk from the center, so if you want to be really close to the history, consider one of the smaller, moderate-priced ones.

EXPENSIVE

Barceló Montecastillo ★★   This deluxe country club in the rolling hills of the sherry *campiña* (wine country) is a real delight. The area's most tranquil retreat, it has rooms with balconies overlooking the plush, scenic landscape and the resort's Jack Nicklaus-designed 18-hole golf course. There's plenty here for non-golfers too, with an on-site spa, tennis courts, and swimming pools. Spacious rooms are decorated in provincial French style with elegant fabrics, beautiful linens, and large beds and there's a choice of suites and even self-contained villas for groups or families. The hotel is a 10-minute ride from Jerez. At certain times, there's a minimum stay of two nights.

Carretera de Arcos, 11406 Jerez de la Frontera. ① **95-615-12-00.** Fax 95-615-12-09. www.barcelo montecastillo.com. 208 units. 75€–199€ double; 140€–300€ suite. AE, DC, MC, V. Free parking. **Amenities:** 3 restaurants; breakfast room; bar; babysitting; golf course; health spa; Jacuzzi; 3 pools (2 outdoor, 1 heated indoor); sauna; tennis court. *In room:* A/C, TV, hair dryer, minibar, Wi-Fi.

Guadalete ★   In a tranquil, exclusive area north of Jerez, this modern, first-class hotel is a 20-minute walk from the historic core. It may not be quite as good or well located as the Hipotel Sherry Park, but it's still one of the town's leading hotels, favored by business travelers dealing with the sherry industry. A marble-floored lobby, spacious and contemporary public rooms, and palm-tree gardens give this place a resort aura. The rooms are midsize to spacious, with state-of-the-art bathrooms with tub/shower combos. The hotel is decorated with original watercolors and lithographs painted by local artists in the 1970s.

Av. Duque de Abrantes 50, 11407 Jerez de la Frontera. ✆ **95-618-22-88.** Fax 95-618-22-93. www. hotelguadalete.com. 137 units. 75€–199€ double; 160€–299€ suite. Rates include breakfast. AE, MC, V. Free parking. **Amenities:** Restaurant; bar; babysitting; Jacuzzi; outdoor pool; room service; sauna; rooms for those w/limited mobility. In room: A/C, TV, hair dryer, minibar, Wi-Fi.

Hipotel Sherry Park ★   Especially noted for its setting in a palm-fringed garden, the tiled borders of which attract many sun-loving guests, this is one of the best modern hotels in Jerez. Completely renovated in 2008, the Hipotel is well located on a wide boulevard about a 10-minute walk north of the historic center of town. It has a marble-floored lobby, modern public rooms, and fairly standard but comfortable guest rooms. The uniformed staff lays out a copious breakfast buffet and serves drinks at several hideaways, both indoors and in the garden.

Av. Alcalde Alvaro Domecq 11 bis, 11405 Jerez de la Frontera. ✆ **95-631-76-14.** Fax 95-631-13-00. www. hipotels.com. 174 units. 126€–250€ double; 287€ suite. AE, DC, MC, V. Free parking. **Amenities:** 3 restaurants; bar; babysitting; health club; 2 pools (1 indoor); room service; sauna. In room: A/C, TV, hair dryer, minibar, Wi-Fi.

Hotel Jerez & Spa ★★   This place is the preferred address of the sherry-bottling crowd. Bedrooms are warmly decorated, stylish, and well-equipped and all have good views. Slightly dated bathrooms come with Jacuzzi tubs and shower massages. There's a choice of standard or deluxe doubles, and superior suites overlooking the pool and gardens from private balconies. There's a spa on site and the dining is deluxe, with luxurious ingredients used in the top-rated cuisine. Sample a glass of sherry by the pool or on a patio surrounded by fragrant orange trees. But it's a good 20-minute walk or a cab ride from the Old Town.

Av. Alcalde Alvaro Domecq 35, 11405 Jerez de la Frontera. ✆ **95-630-06-00.** Fax 95-630-50-01. www. jerezhotel.com. 131 units. 75€–295€ double; 125€–535€ suite. AE, DC, MC, V. Free parking. **Amenities:** Restaurant; bar; babysitting; barber and salon; bike rentals; gym; 2 pools (1 indoor); room service; 2 tennis courts; nonsmoking rooms; rooms for those w/limited mobility. In room: A/C, TV, minibar, Wi-Fi.

Villa Jerez ★★★   The best of the bunch of hotels along or off Avenida Alcalde Alvaro Domecq, this little gem is a pocket of posh for luxurious living and it offers top-rate regional and international cuisine in **Las Yucas.** The 18 rooms are individually decorated like rooms in a Spanish mansion; all open onto views of the pool or lush gardens where well-heeled guests sip sherry. Bedrooms are spacious and tastefully furnished, with luxe tiled bathrooms that have hydromassage tubs. It's a short walk from the Royal Equestrian School and about a 15-minute walk from the historic center.

Av. de la Cruz Roja 7, 11407 Jerez de la Frontera. ✆ **95-615-31-00.** Fax 95-630-04-30. www.villajerez. com. 18 units. 120€–180€ double; 220€–500€ suite. AE, DC, MC, V. Free parking. **Amenities:** Restaurant; bar; babysitting; gym; outdoor pool; room service; sauna; nonsmoking rooms; rooms for those w/limited mobility. In room: A/C, TV, hair dryer, minibar, Wi-Fi.

MODERATE

Doña Blanca   A serviceable, adequately comfortable hotel, this middle-bracket choice has been in business since 1994 and was last renovated in 2006. It is in the very center of Jerez, within walking distance of both the Alcázar and cathedral. The structure is typical Andalusian style. The staff is welcoming and the midsize bedrooms are furnished simply but comfortably with hardwood floors and minimal decorations.

Calle Bodegas 11, 11402 Jerez de la Frontera. ✆ **95-634-87-61.** Fax 95-634-85-86. www.hotel-donablanca.com. 30 units. 77€–152€ double. AE, DC, MC, V. Parking 11€. **Amenities:** Breakfast room; bar; babysitting; nonsmoking rooms. *In room:* A/C, TV, hair dryer.

Hotel Bellas Artes ★★ 🏠   This attractive boutique hotel is ideally located for the historic center, almost opposite the cathedral. It's housed in a tastefully renovated 18th-century mansion house. Original features like the main marble staircase and fine stucco moldings have been retained, whilst the rooms have a contemporary warm blend of hues like blue and terracotta. Antiques and restored furniture in the lounge complete the package. The views from the roof terrace of the cathedral are splendid.

Plaza del Arroyo 45, 11403 Jerez de la Frontera. ✆ **95-634-84-30.** Fax 95-616-96-33. www.hotel-bellasartes.com. 19 units. 50€–140€ double; 105€–190€ suite. AE, MC, V. **Amenities:** Breakfast room. *In room:* A/C, TV, hair dryer, minibar, Wi-Fi.

Hotel La Chancillería ★★ 🏠   A welcome addition to the historic center hotel list, this inviting boutique hotel has been carefully created from two 19th-century houses, close to the old city wall. The renovation has full eco-credentials with solar power providing much of the hot water and heating. Most bedrooms face onto the tranquil interior garden, a real treat given the hotel's central location. Rooms are well proportioned, light, and airy with contemporary furniture and bright bathrooms. The on-site restaurant **Sabores** serves up excellent local cuisine with a contemporary twist. There's a roof terrace with lovely views across the Old Town.

Calle Chancillería 21, 11403 Jerez de la Frontera. ✆ **95-630-10-38.** Fax 95-630-10-38. www.hotel-chancilleria.com. 14 units. 60€–70€ single; 80€–100€ double. Rates include breakfast. MC, V. **Amenities:** Restaurant; breakfast room; rooms for those w/limited mobility. *In room:* A/C, TV, hair dryer, minibar, Wi-Fi.

INEXPENSIVE

El Coloso 🍴   A few steps from the Plaza de las Angustias in the historic center, this is one of the best bargains in town, modest but well recommended. The hotel opened in 1969 and its rooms have been renovated and are well maintained. Once past the slightly dated-looking foyer, the decor is in the conventional local style with whitewashed walls and three peaceful Andalusian-style patios. Some of the well-equipped and spotlessly clean rooms have balconies. Four self-contained apartments have small kitchens and good-sized bathrooms. Breakfast is the only meal served.

Calle Pedro Alonso 13, 11402 Jerez de la Frontera. ✆/fax **95-634-90-08.** www.elcolosohotel.com. 26 units. 55€–95€ double. AE, MC, V. Parking 7€. *In room:* A/C, TV, hair dryer.

Hotel Avila   If you've not managed to get yourself a good-value deal elsewhere, this is a good budget-priced option. The Avila is a modern building erected in 1968 and renovated in 1987. It's near the post office and the Plaza del Arenal in the commercial center of town. Its rooms are clean and well maintained, although not special in any way. The beds are comfortable and bathrooms are equipped with shower stalls.

Calle Avila 3, 11401 Jerez de la Frontera. ✆ **95-633-48-08.** Fax 95-633-68-07. www.hotelavila.com. 33 units. 57€–118€ double. DC, MC, V. Parking 8€ nearby. **Amenities:** Bar; cafeteria; lounge. *In room:* A/C, TV, hair dryer.

NH Avenida Jerez   As part of the NH hotel chain, this place offers modern, stylish, good-value accommodation about a 10-minute walk from the historic heart of Jerez. The hotel occupies a modern balconied structure and inside, cool polished stone floors, leather armchairs, and potted plants create a restful haven. The good-size rooms are discreetly contemporary and decorated in neutral colors, with big windows and comfortable beds.

Av. Alcalde Alvaro Domecq 10, 11405 Jerez de la Frontera. ✆ **95-634-74-11.** Fax 95-633-72-96. www. nh-hoteles.es. 95 units. 45€–95€ double. AE, DC, MC, V. Parking 14€. **Amenities:** Restaurant; bar; babysitting; room service. *In room:* A/C, TV, hair dryer, minibar, Wi-Fi.

Where to Dine

El Bosque ★ SPANISH/INTERNATIONAL   If you're staying at one of the hotels along Alcalde Alvaro Domecq, this place is a short step from your hotel. About a mile outside the historic center, El Bosque opened after World War II and is still the city's most elegant restaurant. A favorite of the sherry-producing aristocracy, its bullfighting memorabilia makes up most of the decor. Dine like a native on the excellent *rabo de toro* (oxtail stew). Begin with gazpacho, then try one of the fried fish dishes, like hake prepared Seville-style. The pistachio ice cream is especially good.

Av. Alcalde Alvaro Domecq 26. ✆ **95-630-70-30.** Reservations required. Main courses 18€–25€; *menú del día* 36€. AE, DC, MC, V. Mon–Sat 1:30–5pm and 8:30pm–midnight.

Gaitán ★ ANDALUSIAN   Owner Juan Hurtado continues to win acclaim for the food served here at his small restaurant near the Puerta Santa María. Surrounded by celebrity photographs, enjoy such Andalusian dishes as garlic soup, various stews, duck *a la Sevillana,* and fried seafood. One special dish is lamb cooked with honey, based on a recipe that dates from the Muslim occupation of Spain. For dessert, the almond tart is a favorite.

Calle Gaitán 3. ✆ **95-634-58-59.** Reservations recommended. Main courses 12€–16€; fixed-price menu 19€. AE, DC, MC, V. Daily 1–4:30pm and 8:30–11:30pm.

Mesa Redonda ★★ 🍴 TRADITIONAL SPANISH   This restaurant is a rare treat, but it's difficult to find as it's hidden away at the base of an apartment building reached through a gate on Calle Alcalde Alvaro Domecq just after the right turn into Manuel de la Quintana coming out of town. Owner/chef José Antonio Romero and his wife, Margarita, have sought out traditional recipes once served in the homes of the aristocratic sherry dons of Jerez. They serve them in what feels like a private residence, complete with a library filled with old recipe books and literature about food and wine. The 10 tables fill quickly. The menu is ever changing; try the *albondiguillas marineras* (fish meatballs in shellfish sauce) and *hojaldre de rape y gambas* (a pastry filled with monkfish and prawns). Finish with lemon-and-almond cake.

Manuel de la Quintana 3. ✆ **95-634-00-69.** Reservations required. Main courses 12€–16€. AE, MC, V. Mon–Sat 1:30–4pm and 9–11:30pm. Closed last week in July and 1st 3 weeks in Aug.

Tendido 6 ★ ANDALUSIAN/INTERNATIONAL Situated right next to the bullring, this well-run local restaurant has been serving good, affordable, traditional Andalusian food since 1960, when it started as a small wine shop serving olives and chicken with garlic. A bar with an open-air terrace was added, and soon it was a fully fledged restaurant. The tapas and regional wines are among the best in Jerez, served in a typically Andalusian setting, with tiled walls, wood-beamed ceilings, and, of course, a bull's head on the wall. Since Jerez is near the sea, the fresh catch of the day is worth ordering, perhaps anglerfish in a savory green sauce, or swordfish cooked over firewood. Also recommended are grilled sirloin with pepper sauce, and artichoke with clams and wild-asparagus croquettes.

Calle Circo 10. ✆ **95-634-48-35.** www.tendido6.com. Reservations recommended. Main courses 8€–15€. AE, DC, MC, V. Mon–Sat 1–4pm and 8–11:30pm.

Jerez de la Frontera after Dark

A great way to start your evening is with local sherry and some of the best tapas in town at **Bar Juanito** ★, Calle Pescaderia Vieja 8 (✆ **95-633-48-38;** www.bar-juanito.com). Tucked down a busy alleyway off Plaza del Arenal, this traditional tapas bar and restaurant dates back to 1943. It offers a delectable display of food, including Spanish *tortillas* (thick omelets with layers of potato), cured hams, regional cheese, mushrooms, and shrimp or bull meat marinated in sherry. Plates (*raciones*) cost from 5€ to 8€, tapas start at 1.75€. It's open 1 to 5pm and 8:30pm to 11:30am.

Only a short hop across Plaza del Arenal and down a tiny backstreet, **Tabanco San Pablo** ★★, Calle San Pablo 12 (✆ 95-633-84-36) is just fabulous. *Tabancos* are traditional old sherry stores where locals would sample the wines and indulge in some singing and dancing. There aren't many left these days, so this place is a real find with huge sherry barrels behind its long bar and a tiny flamenco stage at the far end. Stand at the bar, order a sherry, and just take in the atmosphere. If you're in luck, you'll catch some impromptu flamenco into the bargain.

Jerez is known for its flamenco and there are a number of venues that offer good quality, untouristy shows. My two favorites are both in the Barrio de Santiago, close to the Museo Arqueológico. At **El Lagá de Tío Parrilla,** Plaza del Mercado (✆ 95-633-83-34), Monday-to-Saturday shows begin at 10:30pm and 12:30am. The cover of 18€ includes the first drink, and reservations are suggested. More organized and slightly more upmarket, **Tablao del Bereber,** Calle Cabezas 10 (✆ **95-634-00-16;** www.tablaodelbereber.com) has shows daily except Sundays at 3pm for lunch and at 9pm for dinner, both then followed by performances. Call ahead for the latest prices as they were being changed at the time of writing.

EL PUERTO DE SANTA MARÍA

610km (379 miles) S of Madrid, 22km (14 miles) NE of Cádiz, 12km (7½ miles) S of Jerez de la Frontera, 102km (63 miles) S of Seville.

Part of the "Sherry Triangle," this old, dilapidated port is most easily reached from Cádiz (see Chapter 10), but it's also within easy reach of Jerez de la Frontera (see earlier). A historic port, it opens onto the northern shores of the Bay of Cádiz. Nearby are some choice white-sand beaches of the Costa de la Luz. The Terry and

Osborne sherry and brandy *bodegas* dominate the town. Many summer visitors come just for the seafood bars (see "Where to Dine," below).

Essentials

GETTING THERE   If you're already in Cádiz, the easiest way to get here is to take a boat. **El Vaporcito** (© 62-946-80-14; www.vapordeelpuerto.com), a private **ferry** company, has boats departing from a dock behind Estación Marítima near the Transportes Generalics Comes station at Plaza de la Hispanidad. Five to six ferries leave per day, taking 40 to 45 minutes and costing 3€ one way, 5€ return. Departures from Cádiz are usually 10am, midday, 2pm, 4:30pm, and 6:30pm (and 8:30pm between June and mid-September). A frequent municipal catamaran service (© 90-245-05-50; www.cmtbc.es) runs from Cádiz, with services currently departing about every half-hour and running slightly later than the ferries.

There is also a direct service by **train** from Seville, or suburban trains from Jerez de la Frontera or Cádiz. For information call **RENFE** (© 90-232-03-20; www.renfe.es). There's no service between mid-December and January; it resumes February 1.

If you have a **car** and are in Jerez, just follow the signs south. There are two arteries going into Puerto de Santa María; the N-IV is faster.

VISITOR INFORMATION   The very helpful local **tourist office** is at Luna 22 (© 95-654-24-13; www.turismoelpuerto.com). Just head straight down the street in front of you as you come off the ferry. It's open daily 10am to 2pm and 5:30 to 7:30pm (8:30pm May to September). They have a good map of the town and lists of monuments, hotels, and sherry houses with opening hours and entry fees. At the time of writing there were plans for the office to move to new premises close to the castle in the Aranibar Palace, Plaza del Castillo.

Exploring the Town

El Puerto has had its fair share of illustrious visitors. Columbus once lived in a house at Cristóbal Colón. Look for a marker. Washington Irving spent the fall of 1828 here at Calle Palacios 57. Unfortunately these houses can only be viewed from the outside.

Although Jerez is a far more appealing destination for *bodega* hopping, you can visit **Terry** at Calle Tonelernos 1 (© 95-615-15-00; www.bodegasterry.com). Wine tastings are only on Monday to Friday at 10:30am and 12:30pm and Saturdays at midday. Admission is 8€. No reservations are needed. Another sherry *bodega* of interest is **Osborne-Bodega de Mora,** Calle Los Moros 7 (© 95-686-91-00; www.osborne.es/rrpp). It has English-language tours Monday to Friday at 10:30am (Spanish tours at 11am and midday) and Saturdays at 11am (Spanish tour at midday). Entrance is 7.50€ and you need to book in advance.

Or else combine tasting with a spot of history. On the site of an old mosque, **Castillo de San Marcos,** Plaza de Alfonso s/n (© 95-685-17-51), was built in the 13th century and is now owned by the Caballero sherry house. It was constructed by Alfonso X against future Muslim invasions from North Africa. Later it was the address of the Duke of Medinaceli, who welcomed Columbus here but refused to finance his journey, thinking it impractical. Within these walls Juan de la Cosa drew the first map ever to include the New World. The castle is open for guided tours without tastings by appointment only (© **95-685-17-51**) on Tuesdays. From Wednesday to Saturday, charging 5€ for adults, 2€ for children aged 17 and under, tours in English followed by sherry tastings are at 1:30pm and in Spanish at 10:30am, 11:30am, and 12:30pm. Evening tours and tastings are also available Tuesday to Saturday at 7pm and 8pm but you need to call a different phone number in the morning to reserve a place: (© **62-756-93-35**).

The natural focus of the town is Plaza de España and the main church, the **Iglesia Mayor Prioral** (© **95-685-17-16**), with its fine ornate Baroque entrance, the Puerta del Sol (Sun Gate). This style of highly intricate carving is known as *Plateresque* because it evokes the fine precision of a silversmith's work (*platero* means silversmith). It's open daily from 8:30am to 12:45pm (midday on Saturdays) and 6 to 8:30pm. The port also has a historic bullring, the neo-Mudéjar **Plaza de Toros,** Los Moros (© **95-654-12-50;** www.plazadetoroselpuerto.com), dating from 1880. It was the gift of a local sherry producer, Thomas Osborne, who designed it to seat 12,816 people, the exact population of the town in those days. Unfortunately it's not open for visits outside bullfight days, but if you'd like to watch a bullfight it's one of the best arenas in Andalusia. The main bullfighting season is mid-summer—July and August. Ask at the tourist office or see the website for more information.

Where to Stay

Del Mar   About a 15-minute walk from the center of town, west of the bullring, this hotel is one of the more affordable in a town known for its good value and attractive rooms. Built in 1994, its midsize bedrooms are like those in a simply but comfortably furnished private home, with an adjoining tiled bathroom. The hotel is agreeable and unpretentious, the staff welcoming and helpful.

Av. Marina de Guerra, 11500 El Puerto de Santa María. © **95-687-57-00.** Fax 95-685-87-16. www.delmarhotel.es. 41 units. 65€–115€ double. AE, MC, V. Parking 6€. **Amenities:** Cafeteria; room service; babysitting; rooms for those w/limited mobility; Wi-Fi. *In room:* A/C, TV, minibar.

Duques de Medinaceli ★★★   One of the most pleasant hotels in all Andalusia, this converted 18th-century palace is the epitome of style and luxury. It's elegant, but with just 28 rooms, the atmosphere is warm and inviting. Tastefully renovated, it has retained old features, including the town's most impressive Andalusian courtyard with columns and a fountain. Bedrooms are large and beautifully furnished with antiques or good reproductions. The building's many Mudéjar architectural flourishes are perfectly complemented by beautifully tranquil gardens. There's an attractive pool and the on-site restaurant, Reina Isabel, a favorite of sherry producers, has first-rate meals.

Plaza de los Jazmines 2, 11500 El Puerto de Santa María. © **95-686-07-77.** Fax 95-654-26-87. www.jale.com/dmedinaceli. 28 units. 126€–290€ double; 286€–380€ junior suite; 383€–407€ suite. AE, MC, V. Free parking. **Amenities:** Restaurant; bar; babysitting; outdoor pool; room service; sauna; rooms for those w/limited mobility. *In room:* A/C, TV, hair dryer, minibar.

Los Cántaros   If you're on a budget, try to stay at this modest but appealing choice in the city center near the riverbanks of Guadalete. It's right in the midst of the Ribera del Marisco area—*the* place at night with its busy bars and seafood restaurants. The building was constructed in 1983 on the site of a former women's prison; today the rooms are more comfortable and attractively decorated. A few of the 17th-century urns uncovered here during the conversion (Los Cántaros means

El Puerto de Santa María

"the urns") are on display in the hotel lounge. Midsize bedrooms have tiled bathrooms with tub/shower combos.

Calle Curva 6, 11500 El Puerto de Santa María. ✆ **95-654-02-40.** Fax 95-654-11-21. www.hotellos cantaros.com. 39 units. 78€–136€ double. AE, DC, MC. Parking 10€. **Amenities:** Cafeteria; bar; room service; nonsmoking rooms; Wi-Fi. *In room:* A/C, TV, hair dryer, minibar.

Monasterio de San Miguel ★★ If this hotel had a more tranquil location it would equal Duques de Medinaceli. Regardless, it's a sumptuous place to stay—as the Spanish royal family thought when they visited. Originally an 18th-century Capuchin convent and church, the hotel has been meticulously renovated, with much of the original design left intact. Midsize bedrooms are beautifully and tastefully furnished, with luxuriously tiled bathrooms. They open onto private balconies overlooking a first-class swimming pool. You can wander through the hotel's gardens, stopping for drinks in the Andalusian courtyard with a bubbling fountain. **Restaurant Las Bóvedas** in a large, vaulted hall is one of the best in the area. The chef specializes in local seafood.

Virgen de los Milagros 27, 11500 El Puerto de Santa María. ✆ **95-654-04-40.** Fax 95-654-26-04. www.jale.com/monasterio. 175 units. 105€–200€ double; 150€–250€ junior suite; 275€–375€ suite. AE, MC, V. Parking 13€. **Amenities:** Restaurant; cafeteria; bar; babysitting; outdoor pool; room service; nonsmoking rooms; rooms for those w/limited mobility. *In room:* A/C, TV, hair dryer, minibar.

Where to Dine

Many residents of Cádiz come over just for the evening to sample the *marisco* (seafood) bars along Ribera de Marisco (Shellfish Way). The tourist office (see above) can provide you with six different tapas routes (*rutas de la tapa*), taking in more than three dozen different bars, each with its own specialties. Along Ribera de Marisco, our favorite is **Romerijo** (✆ 95-654-12-54; www.romerijo.com), although many nearby are almost as good, including **Además Tapía, Casa Paco, Paco Ceballos, El Pijota,** and **Bar Jamón.** No phones, no reservations—just show up at night and start eating.

El Faro de El Puerto ★ ANDALUSIAN/SEAFOOD Slightly outside of town, this converted villa is the best restaurant here. In typically Andalusian surroundings, El Faro uses market-fresh ingredients to showcase local food. The sherry producers of the area always take their best clients here. You can order roast suckling pig and tender, garlic-studded baby lamb—another classic. A wide selection of fish based on the catch of the day is featured nightly. Grilled medallions of monkfish are another treat.

Carretera de Fuentebravia Km 0.5. ✆ **95-685-80-03.** www.elfarodelpuerto.com. Reservations recommended. Main courses 8€–28€; *menú degustación* (tasting menus) 59€–62€. AE, DC, MC, V. Daily 1–4pm; Mon–Sat 9–11pm.

Los Portales SEAFOOD/ANDALUSIAN If you fancy something a bit more formal in the Ribera del Marisco area, this is my pick. Since 1978, this friendly, traditional-style eatery has been heavily patronized by *gaditanas* (locals), who swear by its offerings and often take their out-of-town visitors here. With some of the most professional service in the area, it's dedicated to turning out market-fresh cuisine that's hearty and full of flavor. Unsurprisingly, seafood is top quality here. Chef Paco Custodio's cooking is all about the locally caught produce from Cádiz bay. Try the fresh sea bass in lobster sauce or go for the catch of the day. Shellfish is excellent, in particular the house specialty Los Portales clams—cooked in local *fino* sherry with fried garlic, parsley, and Iberian ham. Meat eaters can try the garlic-doused lamb chops grilled with potatoes, tender grilled entrecote, or baby beef in tangy mustard sauce.

Ribera del Río 13. ✆ **95-654-21-16.** www.restaurantelosportales.com. Reservations recommended. Main courses 8€–18€. AE, MC, V. Daily noon–4:30pm and 7:30pm–12:30am.

SANLÚCAR DE BARRAMEDA

24km (15 miles) NW of Jerez de la Frontera

This port, though relatively unimportant today, lives on in nautical history. Columbus sailed from here on his historic third voyage to the New World in 1498. In 1519, Magellan set out from Sanlúcar to launch his circumnavigation of the globe.

At the mouth of the Guadalquivir River, Sanlúcar borders the Cota de Doñana National Park (p. 316) and is a good base from which to explore this wilderness. There's a wide range of sandy beaches around the port, part of the Costa de la Luz, but most visitors come to visit the sherry *bodegas* and to dine in the seafood restaurants. Along with Jerez de la Frontera and El Puerto de Santa María, Sanlúcar is the third corner of the famous "Sherry Triangle."

Essentials

GETTING THERE Regular bus services from Jerez are run by **Linesur** (✆ **95-634-10-63;** www.linesur.com), taking about 30 minutes and costing 1.79€ for one way. **Los Amarillos** (✆ **95-638-50-60;** www.losamarillos.es) runs buses to Sanlúcar from Seville taking between 1½ and 2½ hours and costing 7.54€, and Cádiz taking about an hour and costing 3.21€. The Cádiz service also stops at El Puerto de Santa María. All services run at frequent intervals during the day, usually one an hour.

From Jerez or El Puerto de Santa María, signs point motorists northwest to Sanlúcar. Driving time from either town is about 20 minutes.

VISITOR INFORMATION The helpful local **tourist office** is on Calzada Duquesa Isabel s/n (some maps have this road marked as Calzada del Ejército), several blocks inland from the beach (✆ **95-636-61-10;** www.turismosanlucar. com). It's open Wednesday to Friday 10am to 2pm and 5 to 7pm, and Saturday to Tuesday 10am to 2pm. Here you can pick up a handy map and information about tours of the Cota de Doñana National Park and visits to sherry houses (*bodegas*).

Exploring the Town

Sanlúcar is famous for its distinctive *manzanilla* wine, the driest of all sherries, which acquires a dry, slightly salty tang from the winds blowing across the sea from North Africa. The town is also known for having some of Spain's best seafood. Many Andalusians come here just to dine, particularly for lunch at the weekends.

Whilst the busy waterfront restaurants on Bajo de Guia are often thronged with visitors, the attractive, sleepy **Old Town,** a couple of blocks inland, remains surprisingly tourist-free and well worth a wander for an hour or so. Start your exploration on the landmark **Plaza del Cabildo,** a delightful square ringed with palm trees and a clutch of attractive local tapas bars with terraces, popular with local families on Sunday afternoons. Just to the left as you exit the top of Plaza del Cabildo is **Iglesia** de la Trinidad, which dates from the 15th century. It's open Monday to Saturday from 10am to 1pm. Head up the hill along Calle Bretons past the town's old market which is one of the most attractive in Andalusia. At the top on your right is the town hall (*ayuntamiento*) formally the **Palacio de Orleans y Borbo**.

A left turn along Calle Caballero brings you to **Palacio de Los Duques de Medina Sidonia** (*Ⓒ* 95-638-80-00; www.fcmedinasidonia.com). The *palacio* remains the home of the current Duchess of Medina Sidonia to this day and it's a treasure trove of ornate salons filled with antiques and the works of such Spanish masters as Goya and Morales. You can take a guided tour of the mansion but only on Sundays at 11am and midday. It costs 3.50€. The beautiful gardens and coffee shop and bar are, however, open more frequently, from Monday to Friday 8:30am to 1pm and 3 to 6pm and weekends from 9am to 1pm. If you want to feel like a real duke or duchess, then you can also stay in one of the 11 rooms and suites here. (See "Where to Stay" below.)

The 14th-century **Iglesia de Nuestra Señora de la O,** Plaza de la Paz (*Ⓒ* **95-636-05-55**), is right next to the Palacio de Los Duques de Medina Sidonia and well worth a look inside. Unfortuately it's only open a half-hour before and after each Mass, Monday to Friday at 8pm and Sunday at 9am, 11am, and 8pm. Admission is free. Although much altered over the years, this is Sanlúcar's greatest church. Its impressive interior has a Gothic and Mudéjar portal that depicts lions bearing coats of arms. A short walk farther along this road brings you to Sanlúcar's castle, the **Castillo de Santiago,** Calle Cava del Castillo (*Ⓒ* **95-608-83-26;** www. castillodesantiago.com). Guided tours take place Thursdays to Sundays at 11am, midday, and 1pm and cost 5€ for adults, 3€ for children. There's not a huge amount to see, but the views from the ramparts across the town to the sea are impressive.

Finally, pay a visit to one of Sanlúcar's famous *bodegas* where the delicate *manzanilla* is produced. Unlike Jerez, there are few to choose from. The best is right next to the castle and it's also the home of the largest producer of *manzanilla*: **Antonio Barbadillo,** Calle Sevilla 25 (*Ⓒ* **95-638-55-00;** www.barbadillo.com). You can visit the museum here Tuesday to Saturday 10am to 3pm (open until 6pm Wednesdays) or take a full tour of the *bodega* for 3€. Tours in English run Tuesday to Saturday at 11am, with Spanish tours at midday and 1pm.

Down on the waterfront, the seafood restaurants do a roaring trade, particularly at lunchtimes. See "Where to Eat" below. Here, too, you'll find the **Centro de Visitantes de Doñana,** Fábrica de Hielo, Avenida Bajo de Guía s/n (*Ⓒ* **95-636-38-13;** www.visitasdonana.com) in the attractive old factory where ice was made to keep the port's catches of seafood fresh. There are two floors of exhibits about the National Park and its flora and fauna and you can book tours to explore it. The most straightforward is a boat cruise around the fringes of the park aboard the **Real Fernando ★**, which costs 16.20€ for adults and 8.10€ for children. This is more a cruise for daytrippers than serious naturalists, but it's very pleasant heading up the Guadalquivir River and making a couple of stops in the park. Cruises last 3½ hours and depart April to October daily 10am and 4pm. From November to March at 10am only. Reservations through the visitor center or by phone are essential.

If you want to take a more in-depth tour of the National Park, the staff at the visitor center can make suggestions and bookings for you. **Viajes Doñana**

(**© 95-636-25-40**) does 4WD trips into the park which last 3½ hours, comprising a 60km (37-mile) drive visiting the three key ecosystems. They cost 39€ per person. You can also book by phone on the number above.

Serious bird-watchers and walkers should head north to the park's other entrances at El Rocio and Matalascañas, where the options and facilities are more numerous. See p. 316 for more information.

Where to Stay

Hospederia Duques de Medina Sidonia ★ 🎒
The Palace of the Duchess of Medina Sidonia has remained in the same family for 700 years. But nine rooms and one suite have been opened for guests in a far wing of the palace. Decorated with ancient heirlooms and antique furniture, they are elegant and comfortable. All have large, well-equipped bathrooms and some have a bathtub and shower. The hotel's real delight is that sense of living in someone's very beautiful private home. The common rooms with their Roman pillars, huge oak beams, tapestries, and oil paintings along with the flower-filled garden and patio area are what make a stay here special.

Plaza Condes de Niebla 1, 11540 Sanlúcar de Barrameda. © **95-636-01-61.** Fax 95-636-01-61. www.ruralduquesmedinasidonia.com. 10 units. 75€–120€ double (including breakfast). No Cards Accepted. Free parking. **Amenities:** Tea room; bar/cafeteria; nonsmoking rooms; Wi-Fi. *In room:* A/C, TV.

Hotel Barrameda ✍
Opened in 2008, this new hotel in the center of the Old Town offers a pretty good compromise between price and quality. It's comfortably, but simply, furnished with modern dark wood furniture in bright and airy bedrooms around a central patio with an attractive central fountain. Common areas are similarly bright and modern with dark leather armchairs and Scandinavian-style pine furnishings. There's a large sun-terrace with sun-loungers on the roof and staff members are friendly and helpful too. Ask for one of the larger luxury rooms for a private terrace.

Calle Ancha 10, 11540 Sanlúcar de Barrameda. © **95-638-58-57.** Fax 95-638-58-79. www.hotelbarrameda.com. 30 units. 53€–90€ double. AE, MC, V. Parking 8€. **Amenities:** Bar; cafeteria; room service; solarium; rooms for those w/limited mobility; Wi-Fi. *In room:* A/C, TV, phone.

Hotel Los Helechos ★
This former family villa has been successfully converted into one of the coziest hotels in the area. A large building with a central Andalusian patio with fountain, corridors, and very old tiles, it is inviting and home-like, with some of the most affordable prices in town. The midsize bedrooms have been modernized yet they are traditional in decor, with heavy curtains, tasteful, comfortable furnishings, and tiled bathrooms. The staff can arrange excursions to the Doñana National Park.

Plaza Madre de Dios 9, 11540 Sanlúcar de Barrameda. © **95-636-13-49.** Fax 95-636-96-50. www.hotelloshelechos.com. 54 units. 54€–69€ double; 74€–89€ triple; 94€–110€ quad. AE, MC, V. Free parking. **Amenities:** Bar; room service; babysitting; solarium; rooms for those w/limited mobility. *In room:* A/C, TV.

Posada de Palacio ★ ☺
This attractive small hotel is converted from a 17th-century private family home. Rooms are arranged on two floors around a fern-filled, airy, central Andalusian patio with corridors and the characteristic arches. Under high ceilings, the furniture is a mixture of original antiques and contemporary pieces.

Regional artifacts add to the homely atmosphere. Bedrooms are attractively and comfortably furnished. They vary in size considerably and some have private sitting rooms and balconies. There's also a quadruple room which is handy for families.

Caballeros 9–11, 11540 Sanlúcar de Barrameda. (© **95-636-48-40.** Fax 95-636-50-60. www.posadade palacio.com. 24 units. 88€–157€ double; 141€–179€ quad. AE, DC, MC, V. Free parking. **Amenities:** Breakfast lounge; bar; room service; nonsmoking rooms. *In room:* A/C, TV, hair dryer.

Where to Dine

Bigote ★ SEAFOOD/SPANISH   All of the restaurants along Bajo de Guía serve top quality, sparklingly fresh seafood, but I think this place has the edge. Locals will tell you it does the best shellfish paella at the port. With its maritime decor and wide windows, there's a real *bodega* atmosphere. In summer it's packed, so you must reserve. The crabs you see in the market, with enormous white claws, known locally as *bocas de las islas* (mouths of the islands) are served here, as are clams with fine shells, which are marinated or cooked with paprika, rice, or noodles. Sea snails and razor clams also appear. Signature dishes are baby shark with seafood sauce, red snapper in vinaigrette, and fried fish. Fried *acedias* (a type of delectable small sole) and *langostinos* are other specialties. If you can't get a table here, try nearby Casa Juan.

Bajo de Guía s/n. (© **95-636-26-96.** Reservations recommended. Main courses 8€–25€. AE, DC, MC, V. Mon–Sat 1:30–4pm and 8:30–11:30pm. Closed Oct 20–Nov.

Casa Balbino SPANISH/TAPAS   If you're staying a night or two, make sure to spend a relaxed evening in the convivial ambiance of the lovely old main square in the Old Town's Plaza Cabildo. There's a whole host of tapas bars to tempt you, all with pretty terraces right on the square, perfect for people-watching. My favorite is family-run Casa Balbino, which has been serving its fine food and wine from behind its traditional zinc-topped counter since 1939. Here the tapas board features all manner of interesting things. House specials include *ortiguillas* (sea anemones) and *tortilla de camarones* (deep fried shrimps), but it's all good.

Plaza del Cabildo 14. (© **95-636-26-47.** www.casabalbino.com. Tapas 2€–5€. MC, V. Daily 1:30–11:30pm. Closed Jan.

Los Corrales ★ SEAFOOD/SPANISH   If you want to sample seafood closer to the Old Town or you prefer classically prepared Andalusian meat dishes, then this place, several blocks from the beachfront, is worth a visit. Try the pork tenderloin with three cheeses or the succulent T-bone steak. Good rice dishes include paella with pork, chicken, and shellfish, or a slightly different version—maritime-style rice—with fish and shellfish. Seafood dishes are good too, such as grilled king prawns served simply with garlic butter and parsley or the oven-baked red snapper cooked with shrimp, which is a signature dish. The fruit trees around Sanlúcar are famous, and in summer fresh apricots, pears, plums, and peaches turn up in various desserts. Note that the name of this road has changed; marked on some maps as Calzada Duquesa Isabel.

Av. Calzada del Ejército 44. (© **95-636-49-06.** www.restauranteloscorrales.com. Reservations recommended. Main courses 11€–25€. AE, DC, MC, V. Daily 1:30–5pm and 8–11pm. Closed Nov 2–25.

Venta Antonio ★ SEAFOOD/SPANISH   Outside town, this family business has been luring seafood lovers since it opened in 1966. The ever-changing menu uses the best fish and shellfish caught that day and on sale at local markets. The fish can be cooked more or less to your specifications—that is, grilled, oven-baked, or fried. The list of seafood is impressive, including crabs, sea snails, fresh shrimp, sea-bullock, lobster, and even *percebes* (goose barnacles). Fish platters come with mashed potatoes, special sauces such as tomato or béchamel, and fresh vegetables.

Carretera Jerez-Sanlúcar Km 5. ℂ **95-614-05-35.** www.restauranteventantonio.com. Reservations recommended. Main courses 12€–18€. AE, DC, MC, V. Tues–Sun 1:30–4:30pm; Tues–Sat 8–11pm.

CÁDIZ & THE COSTA DE LA LUZ

Although foreign visitors often overlook the south-western corner of Spain, it is a prime destination for Spanish visitors from other regions of the country.

10

Beaches of all kinds have put this coastal area on the tourist maps. The province of Cádiz alone has 260km (161 miles) of coast and 138km (85 miles) of beaches. The Costa de la Luz has some of the region's most beautifully unspoilt coastline, including coves, inlets, sandy stretches, and isolated strips. It's particularly impressive to the immediate north of Tarifa, where unique off-shore winds have made the beaches a wind- and kitesurfing Mecca. Neighboring Huelva province, associated with Columbus, has lovely beaches that stretch from its eastern border to its frontier with Portugal in the west. Here, too, development along the coastline has been mercifully high-rise free.

The two major cities, each capital to the province of the same name, are Cádiz and Huelva. Huelva can be skipped if you're pressed for time, but Cádiz is one of Andalusia's hidden gems. Long known as a seafaring port, it once dominated trade between Spain and the New World.

Much of modern Cádiz can be passed by, but the seaside promenades and its Old Town can easily take up a day or more of your time. With its sailors' alleyways and high-turreted houses, this is a remnant of the great days of the Spanish empire.

Heading south and east from Cádiz you can visit Europe's southernmost port city, Tarifa, which is quite delightful and well worth an overnight stay. Cádiz is also convenient for visiting El Puerto de Santa María, part of the fabled Sherry Triangle (see Chapter 9).

Even if you don't fall in love with large, sprawling, and industrialized Huelva, you can use it as a base for exploring the province's many riches. In addition to relaxing at the region's first-class coastal resorts, you can explore the Cota de Doñana National Park, sited at the estuary of the Guadalquivir River, and the country's largest wildlife reserve. Visitors often stay 2 days and then wish they'd budgeted more time.

CÁDIZ

122km (76 miles) S of Seville, 625km (388 miles) SW of Madrid, 32km (20 miles) SW of Jerez de la Frontera

At the end of a peninsula, Cádiz separates the Bay of Cádiz from the Atlantic. It was here that Columbus set out on his second and fourth voyages.

Cádiz (pronounced "*Cah*-deeth") was founded, according to legend, by Hercules himself some 3,000 years ago. The seafaring Phoenicians settled here around 1100 B.C. and in 501 the conquering Carthaginians landed. They were followed by the Romans in 206 B.C. Cádiz was to see other conquerors, notably the Visigoths and the Muslims. The rule of the Moors came to an end in 1262 when King Alfonso X brought the port under the yoke of Spanish rule.

In 1587, Sir Francis Drake, whom Spaniards still refer to as a *pirata,* sailed into Cádiz and caused much damage in a raid, delaying the Armada. In 1596 Cádiz suffered its most devastating attack yet when combined Anglo and Dutch ships arrived at the harbor to burn the city to the ground.

Cádiz bounced back and in the 1700s reached the zenith of its power and prestige—attracting Napoleon's greedy eye. French troops invaded and Cádiz became the capital of occupied Spain. In the 19th century, the loss of the American colonies, on which the prosperity of Cádiz depended, plunged the port into a long slumber, from which it only started to recover in the 1970s. Long a bastion of liberal thought and tolerance, Cádiz saw more bloodshed during the Spanish Civil War in the 1930s when its townspeople fought—but lost—in their struggle against Franco's fascists.

Today this modern, bustling Atlantic port is a melting pot of Americans, Africans, and Europeans who are docking or passing through. The old quarter teems with local characters, little dives, and seaport alleys. The narrow cobblestone streets, which open onto charming small plazas, evoke an old city in North Africa. Cádiz is also a big fishing center, and a major departure point for ships sailing to the Canary Islands, a cluster of Spanish territories off the coast of West Africa.

Spanish visitors flock to Cádiz in summer for its beaches and their cool breezes which offer merciful relief from the stifling heat inland, and for the city's famous *Carnaval* in February, one of the most extravagant in Europe. Music from mandolins, tambourines, guitars, and even whistles fills the air. Seemingly everybody in town parades through the streets in costumes. Singing, dancing, and riotous street behavior characterize the event, which lasts all night long, ending when revelers flood the cafes for freshly cooked *churros* (like doughnut sticks), which they dunk into steaming hot cups of chocolate. The Cádiz carnival is usually during the second week of February.

Essentials

GETTING THERE   Twelve daily **trains** arrive from Seville (taking 1 hr, 45 min.), Jerez de la Frontera (45 min.), and Córdoba (3 hr). A one-way fare from Seville costs 13€, from Córdoba 17€ to 34€, and from Jerez 5€. The train station is on Avenida del Puerto, Plaza de Sevilla 1 (© **90-232-03-20;** www.renfe.es), on the southeast border of the main port.

Four daily nonstop **buses** run from Madrid to Cádiz. Trip time is 8 hours and 45 minutes, and it costs 26€ for a one-way ticket. The bus from Madrid is run by **Secorbus** (© **95-625-74-15;** www.socibus.es) at Avenida José León de Carranza

Cádiz

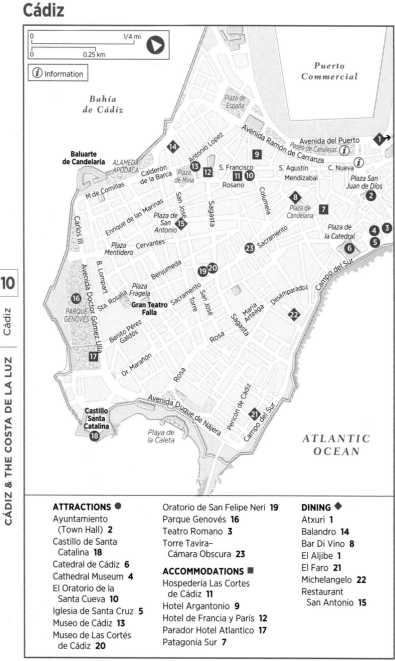

ATTRACTIONS ●

Ayuntamiento
(Town Hall) **2**
Castillo de Santa
Catalina **18**
Catedral de Cádiz **6**
Cathedral Museum **4**
El Oratorio de la
Santa Cueva **10**
Iglesia de Santa Cruz **5**
Museo de Cádiz **13**
Museo de Las Cortés
de Cádiz **20**

Oratorio de San Felipe Neri **19**
Parque Genovés **16**
Teatro Romano **3**
Torre Tavira–
Cámara Obscura **23**

ACCOMMODATIONS ■

Hospedería Las Cortes
de Cádiz **11**
Hotel Argantonio **9**
Hotel de Francia y París **12**
Parador Hotel Atlantico **17**
Patagonia Sur **7**

DINING ◆

Atxuri **1**
Balandro **14**
Bar Di Vino **8**
El Aljibe **1**
El Faro **21**
Michelangelo **22**
Restaurant
San Antonio **15**

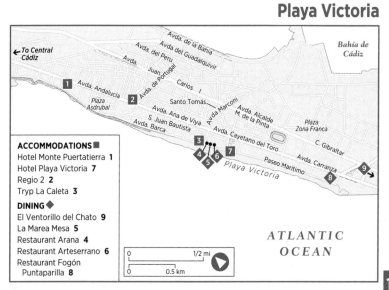

ACCOMMODATIONS ■
Hotel Monte Puertatierra **1**
Hotel Playa Victoria **7**
Regio 2 **2**
Tryp La Caleta **3**

DINING ◆
El Ventorillo del Chato **9**
La Marea Mesa **5**
Restaurant Arana **4**
Restaurant Arteserrano **6**
Restaurant Fogón
   Puntaparilla **8**

10

CÁDIZ & THE COSTA DE LA LUZ

Cádiz

(N-20). However, most people arrive from Seville on a vehicle run by **Transportes Generales Comes** (☎ **90-219-92-08;** www.tgcomes.es). Arrivals number 9 to 11 per day, taking 2 hours and costing 12€ for a one-way ticket. These buses arrive at a temporary terminal just to the side of the rail station a short walk from the Old Town.

Driving from Seville, the AP-4/E-5, a toll road, or N-IV, a toll-free road running beside it, will bring you into Cádiz. For the 5.90€ cost I'd recommend the toll road. The N-IV tends to get clogged with large lorries.

VISITOR INFORMATION   The **Cádiz municipal tourist office** is in a modern octagonal building in the gardens on Paseo de Canalejas (☎ **95-624-10-01;** www.cadiz.es). It's open Monday to Friday 8:30am to 6:30pm and 9am to 5pm at weekends. Helpful staff can provide a free town map featuring four themed walking routes. There's an accompanying leaflet and stops are marked throughout the town with descriptive panels in English—an excellent introduction to the city's unique history. Ironically though, I find the free map provided by the **Andalusia regional tourist office,** Av. Ramón de la Carranza s/n (☎ **95-620-31-91;** www.andalucia. org) easier to read, so step in here as it's just a block away. Staff members are similarly helpful and it's open during the summer, Monday to Friday 9am to 8pm and weekends 10am to 2pm. Winter hours are Monday to Friday 9am to 7:30pm and weekends 10am to 1:30pm.

GETTING AROUND   Cádiz is well served by a network of **buses,** which are the cheapest way to get about. A single ride on any city bus costs 1€. Most residents save money by buying a **Bonobus Pass** for 6.35€, valid for 10 rides. It's sold at news kiosks and tobacco stands. Bus nos. 1 and 7 travel frequently between the New Town and the Old Town, and no. 2 makes frequent runs around the Old Town's sea-fronting periphery. Most of the inland streets of the Old Town are, however, much too narrow for bus access. For more information about routes, call **Tranvia de Cádiz** at ✆ **95-621-21-47.** You can pick up a bus map from either tourist office.

Motorists who arrive in Cádiz have usually rented a **car** in Seville (see Chapter 3) to drive south. Once in Cádiz, you'll have to cope with the parking. Many hotels have parking garages in their basements, charging approximately 9€ to 14€ per day. If you're driving a lot in a rented car, the convenience of parking at your hotel is definitely worth it. As for parking in the Old City, you'll find underground parking garages scattered throughout the Old Town, each of them charging around 1€ per hour with a maximum daily rate of 9.90€. There are metered zones for on-street parking too, but it's hard to find a free space. Unless you're a very experienced driver, don't try and drive around the center of the Old City with your car, since roads are unbelievably narrow—stick to the peripheral avenues flanking the seafronts instead.

Once in Cádiz, you can also rent a car. If you're staying in the Old Town try **ATESA,** Avenida del Puerto 1 (✆ **95-626-66-45;** www.atesa.es), open Monday to Friday 9am to 1:30pm and 4:30 to 7:30pm, Saturday 9am to 1pm. If you're at Playa Victoria try **Avis,** Hotel Tryp Caleta, Avenida Amilcar Barca 47, (✆ 95-625-59-81), open Monday to Friday 9am to 1:30pm and 4:30 to 7:00pm, Saturday 9:30am to 1pm.

You can walk around the Old Town on foot, which is about the only way to see it. To go farther afield, call a **taxi** at ✆ **95-621-21-21.**

[FastFACTS] CÁDIZ

Currency Exchange ATMs are scattered throughout the city with a cluster of banks around Plaza San Juan de Dios in the center and along Avenida Ramón de Carranza facing the port. The most central bank with ATMs is **Banco Santander Central Hispano,** Calle Columela 13 (✆ **90-224-24-24**), open Monday to Friday from 8:30am to 2:30pm.

Dentists If you have a dental emergency, inquire at your hotel or the local tourist office, which has been known to make emergency phone calls around town for visitors in dental pain. Two local dental clinics are **Urgencia**

Dental Avenida, Av. Ana de Viya 32 (✆ 95-620-00-82), and the **Clínica Dental Brasil 8,** Calle Brasil 8, (✆ **95-626-24-69**).

Emergencies To summon the police, dial ✆ **091.** To report a fire or call an ambulance, dial ✆ **085** or ✆ 95-627-00-80.

Hospital The biggest and best equipped of the local hospitals is **Hospital Universitario Puerta del Mar,** Av. Ana de Viya 21 (✆ **95-600-21-00**).

Internet Cafe You'll find a battery of computers at **Novap,** Cuesta de las Calesas 45 (✆ **95-626-44-68**), across from the railway station in Old Cádiz. It charges

1.20€ per hour for access. You'll find a local branch of Western Union and international and national phone cards for sale. Open daily 11am to 11pm.

Newspapers Local Spanish-language dailies include *Diario de Cádiz,* with a relatively right-wing agenda, selling for 1€ each, and the more centrist *Cádiz Información,* also priced at 1€ per copy. For information on cultural and pop events in Andalusia, the tourist office distributes a free monthly tourist magazine called *¿Qué Hacer?*

Pharmacy Each of the many pharmacies scattered throughout the city prominently displays the name, address, and phone number of whatever pharmacy is scheduled to be open overnight. A particularly central pharmacy to the Old City is **Farmacia Colorado,** Calle Cobos 2, on the corner of Calle Cristóbal Colón (📞 **95-628-26-03**).

Post Office The main branch is at Plaza de las Flores (aka Plaza Topete; 📞 **95-621-05-11**). It's open Monday to Friday 8:30am to 8:30pm and Saturday 9:30am to 2pm.

Toilets A few public toilets are scattered throughout various neighborhoods of the New and Old

Towns, most notably a cluster positioned on the Avenida Ramón de Carranza, and one at the Plaza de Mina. If I'm far from either of these points, I usually duck into the nearest bar, often opting to buy something (coffee, mineral water, beer) on the way out.

Exploring Cádiz

A stroll along Cádiz's **seaside promenades** ★★ is reason enough to visit. The port city's *paseo* runs around the Old Town and along the sometimes-turbulent Atlantic Ocean. There's no better way to understand the city and its relationship to the sea than to walk these handsomely landscaped waterfront *paseos* that double as public gardens. The southern and western promenades look out over the ocean; the most scenic is **Parque Genovés ★**, with exotic trees and plants from all over the world, including a palm garden, just like the type enjoyed in the oases of North Africa across the sea. Chattering monkeys are sometimes on hand and summer concerts are presented here.

From the Parque Genovés, if you follow Avenida Duque de Nájera, it will lead you to **Playa de la Caleta,** one of the most popular beaches of Cádiz. At the northern end of this bay stands **Castillo de Santa Catalina** (📞 **95-622-63-33**). It was built in 1598 and for many decades was the port's main citadel. Except for the views, there isn't that much to see here, but it's open to visitors. Admission is free. Winter opening hours are daily 10:30am to 6pm; summer hours are 10am to 8pm.

The promenade stretches all the way to the New Town and can be entered at many places, especially Plaza Argüelles or Calle Fermín Salvochea, off Plaza de España. Along this promenade, some of the most beautiful places or squares in the city look across to the far shore of Bahía de Cádiz.

Catedral de Cádiz This gold-domed Baroque peacock by architect Vicente Acero has a neoclassical interior dominated by an outstanding apse. Construction began in 1720 but the cathedral wasn't completed until 1838. The tomb of Cádiz-born composer Manuel de Falla (1876–1946) is in a splendid crypt. Haydn composed *Seven Last Words* for this cathedral, which was the last great cathedral erected

Inhabitants from 80 Million Years Ago

All of the historic buildings in Cádiz's medieval core are crafted from a sedimentary limestone known locally as "oyster rock." Within many of the stones, you can see the shells of crustaceans that were alive 80 million years ago and whose petrified carcasses (in the form of this rock) were brought to the surface at the point where the tectonic plates of Europe and Africa collided in Cádiz.

in Spain financed by riches from the New World. There's a small **museum** too (© **95-628-66-20**), which is laden with a treasure trove that includes the *Custodia del Millón,* a monstrance set with a million precious stones. Much of the gold, silver, and precious jewels on show here came from the New World. Note Enrique de Arfe's processional cross, which is carried through the streets in the annual Corpus Christi parades. The museum is in a restored 15th-century house called the Casa de la Contaduria in Plaza Fray Félix. To reach it, duck down a small alleyway to the left of the cathedral under an old arch (the Arco de la Rosa) and turn right.

Right next to the cathedral museum is the church, **Iglesia de Santa Cruz,** Plaza Fray Félix (© **95-628-77-04**), which was the original cathedral, built in the 1200s. The invading British destroyed this *catedral vieja* in 1592 but it has been rebuilt. The cathedral is open Mondays 5:30 to 7:45pm, Tuesday to Saturday 10am to 1pm and 5:30 to 7:45pm, Sundays 10am to midday and 6:15 to 7:30pm. Admission is free.

On the seafront to the rear of the Iglesia de Santa Cruz, there are the somewhat unimpressive ruins of what was once a mammoth **Teatro Romano** (© **95-626-47-34**). The visitor entrance is on Campo del Sur. Open daily from 10am to 2:30pm and 5 to 7pm/8 to 10pm in summer (closed all day Tuesday). Admission is free.

Plaza Catedral. © **95-625-98-12.** Combined ticket for cathedral and museum 5€. Mon–Sat 10am–6:30pm. Sun 1:30–6:30pm.

El Oratorio de la Santa Cueva ★ ⛪ Often neglected by visitors, this neoclassical oratory was constructed in 1780 and is attached to a church, Iglesia del Rosario. In the complex there is a Capilla Baja (lower chapel) and a rather lavish, oval Capilla Alta (upper chapel). The upper chapel is the more intriguing of the two. Here, three of the building's eight arches frame **Goya's paintings ★** *The Guest at the Wedding, The Last Supper,* and *The Miracle of the Loaves and the Fishes.* This art is reason enough to visit, but if you also want to see the subterranean chapel, take the steps that lead downstairs. Here you'll find a *Crucifixion* sculpture, an 18th-century work believed to have inspired Joseph Haydn to write the score of *Seven Last Words* for the Catedral de Cádiz (see above).

Constitutional Celebrations in 2012

Cádiz is gearing up for the 200th anniversary of the signing of the first **Spanish constitution** here in 1812. The Spanish were retreating under prolonged attack by the French armies of Napoleon Bonaparte and the tiny peninsula of Cádiz remained their final stronghold. Here the remaining Spanish generals set out to write the first Spanish constitution. This document was the most liberal of its kind at the time, devolving significant powers from the monarchy to the commercial classes. It became the basis for constitutions in many countries including Norway, Portugal, and Mexico. 2012 will be a year of celebrations including film and theater festivals and street parties. In the meantime some of the city's historic attractions are having facelifts and are **closed** to visitors, in particular the Museo de Las Cortés de Cádiz and the Oratorio de San Felipe Neri. If you're interested in Spanish history, pick up an 1812 walking route booklet from the municipal tourist office and visit the 1812 Interpretation Center at Calle Ancha, 19 (© **95-680-72-39**).

Calle Rosario 10A. ✆ **95-622-22-62.** Admission 3€. Tues-Fri 10am-1pm and 4:30-7:30pm (summer 5-8pm); Sat-Sun 10am-1pm.

Museo de Cádiz ★ This museum is housed in two adjacent buildings, one a former Franciscan convent, the other a contemporary structure. It has three sections, one devoted to archaeology, one to fine arts, and one to the ethnological collection and contemporary art collections. Among the ancient relics, the most intriguing collection is a series of two 5th-century-B.C. Phoenician **sarcophagi ★** carved into human likenesses. Depicting both a man and a woman, these tombs were copied by Greek artists after Egyptian models. There is also an intriguing collection of rare Phoenician jewelry and (mostly) headless Roman statues. The Fine Arts Department is rich in 17th-century Spanish painting, and is known especially for its works by **Zurbarán.** Dating from the peak of his mastery between 1630 and 1640, these 21 magnificent **paintings ★★** of angels, saints, and monks were brought here from a Carthusian monastery in Jerez de la Frontera and are today the pride of Cádiz. Zurbarán was at his best when painting his *Quartet of Evangelists.* Murillo and Ribera are among the other old Spanish masters represented. In the ethnological section, the folklore of the province lives again in the Tía Norica puppet theater, with its props and characters that have delighted young and old for years.

Plaza de Mina s/n. ✆ **95-620-33-71.** www.museosdeandalucia.es. Admission 1.50€. Free to E.U. passport holders. Free to all on Sun. Tues 2:30-8:30pm; Wed-Sat 9am-8:30pm; Sun 9am-2:30pm.

Museo de Las Cortés de Cádiz This is the city's history museum, its chief exhibit being a big, detailed model of Cádiz as it looked in the 1700s at the height of its glory. Made in mahogany and marble for King Carlos III, it is so fascinating it makes the museum worth a visit even if you don't look at the other exhibits. The museum also has exhibits relating to the declaration of the Spanish constitution in 1812, including the original documents and a mural of the declaration. At the time of writing the museum was undergoing restoration works scheduled to re-open in time for the Cádiz 2012 constitutional celebrations (see box above).

Calle Santa Inés 9. ✆ **95-622-17-88.**

THE OLD TOWN ★★★

Even if you have to skip all the monuments, take a stroll through the Old Town. Start at **Plaza San Juan de Dios,** one of the busiest squares, directly across from the water-bordering Avenida del Puerto and the wide "green lung" of Paseo de Canalejas. This is an ideal place to sit at a cafe and people-watch. You'll also be in the shadow of the neoclassical Isabelline **Ayuntamiento (Town Hall),** Plaza San Juan de Dios s/n (📞 **95-624-10-00**), open on Saturday only from 11am to 1pm; admission is free. Built in two sections, one in 1799 and the other in 1861, the town hall is dramatically illuminated at night. Inside there's not much to see except an impressive chapter house.

Follow Calle Nueva (which becomes Calle San Francisco and is one of the Old Town's nicest shopping streets along with parallel Calle Rosario) west from Plaza de San Juan de Dios. You arrive at another bustling landmark square, **Plaza de San Francisco.** Enveloped by white and yellow town houses, the square is studded with orange trees and adorned with beautiful streetlamps. It is one of the best places for an evening *paseo* (stroll).

To the immediate west of Plaza de San Francisco is Cádiz's third landmark square, **Plaza de Mina ★**, site of the Museo de Cádiz (see above). This is a big, leafy plaza filled with palm trees. There are plenty of benches about if you'd like to sit awhile and watch the world go by. On the western side of the plaza, you can gaze on the stunning, heavily ornamented facade of the Colegio de Arquitectos (College of Architects).

Oratorio de San Felipe Neri   If you head up Calle San José from Plaza de la Mina, you come to one of the city's finest Baroque churches where the country's first liberal constitution was declared in 1812. The Cortés (Parliament) met here to reform the government, which at the time was under the control of Joseph Bonaparte, stooge of his brother Napoleon. Inside the oval-shaped interior, the main work of art, an *Immaculate Conception* by Murillo, is displayed over the main altar. The church is crowned by a vast cupola. Along with the Museo de Las Cortés de Cádiz, this was undergoing restoration works scheduled to re-open in time for the 2012 celebrations.

Calle Santa Inés 38. 📞**95-621-16-12.**

Torre Tavira–Cámara Obscura   During the 18th- and early-19th-century heyday of Cádiz's monopoly of trade with the New World, wealthy merchants throughout Cádiz competed for the first views of their ships returning home. Many of the city's canny merchants added towers as observation platforms to their homes and businesses, sometimes stationing eagle-eyed employees who constantly scanned the surrounding seas for returning ships as well as for French or English invaders.

One of the tallest of these, Torre Tavira, has installed an industrial-style metal staircase that gets visitors, after a lung-wrenching journey, to the top of one of the original towers. You pay an admission fee at the base. Once on top, you'll be treated to an explanation in English of the Cámara Obscura, formed of a pipe, a magnifying lens, and a concave-shaped drum, about 1.5 to 1.8m (5–6 ft) in diameter, that's covered in nonreflective white canvas. By manipulating the direction of the lens, the operator can give the audience a surprisingly clear view over the top of the city.

After visiting Torre Tavira, head southeast for a couple of blocks and you'll reach **Plaza de Topete ★**. Locals call the square Plaza de las Flores (Plaza of the Flowers) because it's full of flower stalls selling colorful, fragrant blooms. There are some nice cafes here too. Immediately southwest of the plaza you'll find the busy **Mercado Central (Central Market).** Behind its historic facade there's a brand new modern interior packed with well-organized stalls selling all manner of fresh local produce—vibrantly colored vegetables and flappingly fresh seafood.

Marqués del Real Tesoro 10. ☎ **95-621-29-10.** www.torretavira.com. Admission 4€ adults, 3.30€ students and children. June–Sept daily 10am–8pm; Oct–May daily 10am–6pm.

BEACHES

If it's a beach you're after, head for the wide-open and sunny sands of the **Playa Victoria ★**, a quite developed but still appealing beach that's a household name for beach lovers throughout the region. It's probably one of the best beaches in Spain, with wide and Champagne-colored sands and excellent facilities including showers, toilets, and play areas for kids. Arc lights illuminate the beach like a stage every night until around midnight. Dozens of different tapas bars, restaurants, and nightlife options are found at the edge of the beach. **Paseo Marítimo** is the main drag along Playa Victoria and in summer it has the most active *chiringuitos* (beach bars) in the province. It's richly developed and commercial but not at all junky: great fun for a boisterous summer night out that stretches on 'til dawn. On Playa Victoria's outer fringes, there is an isolated and savage section of beach where the waves pound more heavily and the sense of isolated nature increases. This wilder beachfront is more apparent on the causeway linking modern Cádiz to its outlying suburbs and the rest of Spain, but its natural atmosphere is rather tempered by the noise of the road right next to it.

If you're staying in the Old Town, there's a beach here too. **Playa de la Caleta** is relatively narrow and is hemmed in by rocky shoals at low tide. There are no changing booths or public toilets. Known as a "natural beach," it's immediately adjacent to structures and fortifications, the foundations of which, in some cases, are more than 3,000 years old. Set near the extreme western edge of the Old Town, Playa de la Caleta is sometimes known as "Baño de la Viña" after the neighborhood (**Barrio de la Viña**) that abuts it. That same neighborhood—a churning, overcrowded cauldron of local color—is credited with originating the version of *Carnaval* that's now fervently celebrated in Cádiz and in some of Spain's former colonies, notably Cuba. Access to this "City Beach" is free and possible at all hours of the day and night without restriction and without supervision.

Where to Stay

Perhaps because many of the tourists who visit the city arrive (and sleep) aboard huge cruise liners, Cádiz Old Town has a dearth of top-end accommodation. So, if you want modern trappings and luxury (and a very fine stretch of sand and sea too) then you're best off in one of the modern hotels on Playa Victoria. If you prefer to be near the history and local tapas bar action then choose a hotel in the Old Town. Whilst it lacks five-star luxury it does have several nice, atmospheric mid-price options. During the February carnival, rooms are booked months in advance, so reserve early. Be aware that at that time hoteliers charge whatever the market will bear.

EXPENSIVE

Hotel Playa Victoria ★★ At present, this is the best appointed and most comfortable hotel in Cádiz. (I reckon the government-run parador will probably give it a run for its money when it reopens in 2012.) The Playa Victoria's modern, stylish design makes its more conventional and conservative-looking competitors on the beachfront look a bit old fashioned. Its location directly on the sands of one of the best beaches in Andalusia guarantees high room occupancy. Comfortable bedrooms have all the mod-cons you'd expect in a top-end hotel. Each has a mix of polished beige stone and dark tropical hardwood imported from one of Spain's former colonies in the New World, a richly tiled or stone-sheathed bathroom, furnishings including a writing table, and, best of all, a wide, serpentine-shaped balcony, most of which overlook the spectacular beachfront and the sea. The lobby is a postmodern study in dramatic lighting, multilevel tiers, and stone-sided minimalism, around a cozy, big-windowed bar. The in-house restaurant, **Isla de León,** has a sumptuous breakfast buffet.

Glorieta Ingeniero La Cierva 4, 11010 Cádiz. ✆ **95-620-51-00.** Fax 95-626-33-00. www.palafoxhoteles. com. 188 units. 133€–175€ double. AE, DC, MC, V. Parking 16€ per day. **Amenities:** Restaurant; bar; outdoor pool; room service; nonsmoking rooms; rooms for those w/limited mobility. *In room:* A/C, TV, minibar, Wi-Fi.

Parador Hotel Atlantico Previously the most luxurious accommodation in the Old Town, Cádiz's parador is undergoing a complete rebuild and is due to re-open in early 2012. The sneak preview plans I've seen suggest it will be ultra-modern in style, making the most of the sea views with large expanses of glass and state-of-the-art technology as standard. See the website for latest information.

Duque de Nájera 9, 11002 Cádiz. ✆ **95-622-69-05.** Fax 95-621-45-82. www.parador.es.

MODERATE

Hospedería Las Cortes de Cádiz ★ 🛏 One of the nice options in the Old Town, this hotel is situated in a patrician merchant's house originally built in 1859 on profits generated from trade with Spain's New World colonies. The hotel's centerpiece is a graceful three-story courtyard lined with stone columns and capped with a skylight. Each of the bedrooms evokes late-19th-century Cádiz, with a variety of mostly monochromatic color schemes that includes a courageous use of vibrant pinks, blues, and buttercup yellow. Each of the other rooms is named for a historical event or person significant to the history of Cádiz. My favorite is La Caleta, with a mirador-style glassed-in balcony overlooking the busy pedestrian traffic on the street below. This was the Old Town's first hotel to combine a historic core with modern-day conveniences. Unsurprisingly others have followed this successful formula.

Calle San Francisco 9, 11004 Cádiz. ☎ **95-622-04-89.** Fax 95-621-26-68. www.hotellascortes.com. 36 units. 78€–138€ double. Rates include breakfast. AE, MC, V. Parking 18€ per day. **Amenities:** Restaurant; bar; exercise room; limited room service; minispa; rooftop sun terrace; sauna. *In room:* A/C, TV, hair dryer, minibar, Wi-Fi.

Hotel Argantonio ★★   This is probably my favorite hotel in the Old Town at the moment. Set in an attractively restored old town house around a bright patio with a small marble fountain, it's the kind of place you find all over Seville, but in very short supply in Cádiz. Rooms and common areas have a romantic Moorish edge with attractive crenelated archways, colorful geometric tiles and mirrors, vases, and antiques—some available to buy. Rooms are not large, but they are bright and airy with more of those attractive Moorish flourishes, each a little different from the others. They are finished to a high standard, with plasma TVs. The suite is lovely with a four-poster bed and whirlpool bath, but I prefer the 2nd and 3rd floor doubles which have balconies overlooking the street. One of the rooms has disabled access and prices include breakfast and free use of the minibar (truly remarkable!).

Calle Argantonio 3, 11004 Cádiz. ☎ **95-621-16-40.** Fax 95-621-48-02. www.hotelargantonio.com. 15 units. 85€–107€ double; 175€–200€ suite. MC, V. **Amenities:** Bar; rooms for those w/limited mobility. *In room:* A/C, TV, minibar, Wi-Fi.

Hotel Monte Puertatierra ☺   This functional but well-appointed hotel just a short walk from the beach at Playa Victoria is Tryp La Caleta's chief competition, the latter having a slight edge. I've included it here because it has more varied room types than almost any other hotel in town—double or double with lounge, triple, king-size, and family units—handy if you have the kids in tow. Midsize bedrooms are furnished with modern pieces, color-coordinated fabrics, and often painted provincial wooden furniture. Both regional and national dishes are served in the on-site restaurant or the more affordable cafeteria.

Av. de Andalucía 34, 11008 Cádiz. ☎ **95-627-21-11.** Fax 95-625-03-11. www.hotelesmonte.com. 98 units. 115€–155€ double. DC, MC, V. Parking 10€. **Amenities:** Restaurant; cafeteria/bar; babysitting; room service; nonsmoking rooms; rooms for those w/limited mobility. *In room:* A/C, TV, hair dryer, minibar, Wi-Fi.

Tryp La Caleta ★ ☺   Directly across the sea-fronting boulevard of one of the best and most crowded beaches in Andalusia, this hotel is a cheaper, less stylish alternative to the Playa Victoria, which is less than two blocks away. A large, nine-story hotel, it lacks the dramatic and innovative design of the Playa Victoria. Nonetheless, it's extremely comfortable (albeit conservative and a bit staid), well equipped and maintained, and centrally located in the heart of the bar, beach, and nightlife action of new Cádiz. Expect families with children in summer, an ongoing round of conventioneers traipsing in and out, and a winning collection of bars and cafes that cater to guests and nonguests alike. Many rooms have windows that face the sea (but alas, no balconies). There's no swimming pool here, something I find surprising for a hotel of this size and rating, but the beach is a few steps away. The restaurant has children's menus.

Av. Amilcar Barca 47, 11009 Cádiz. ☎ **95-627-94-11.** Fax 95-625-93-22. www.solmelia.com. 143 units. 105€–165€ double; 150€–210€ suite. AE, DC, MC, V. Parking 13€ per day. **Amenities:** Restaurant; bar; cafeteria; room service; rooms for those w/limited mobility. *In room:* A/C, TV, hair dryer, minibar.

INEXPENSIVE

Hotel de Francia y París   If you want to be smack in the heart of old Cádiz, safe and relatively comfortable, this is an unpretentious, viable choice. Originally built in 1902 then garnished with Art Deco and 1950s-era overlays, this five-story, white-fronted structure offers good value, but has little atmosphere; rather surprising as the guest list reads like a who's who of Spanish culture. (Writers and poets Ortega y Gasset and José María Peman both stayed here throughout the post-World War II era.) Simple bedrooms are clean but have rather dowdy angular wooden furniture. Many of the rooms have small balconies opening onto the square.

Plaza de San Francisco 2, 11004 Cádiz. ☏ **95-621-23-19.** www.hotelfrancia.com. 57 units. 80€–90€ double; 131€ suite. AE, DC, MC, V. **Amenities:** Bar. *In room:* A/C, TV.

Patagonia Sur ★   A brand new, well-appointed hotel in the center of the Old Town, the Patagonia is just 100 meters from the cathedral. Its 16 rooms are rather small, but they are equipped to a high standard with modern fittings and extras like bidets, hair dryers, and safes. The two top-floor "attic" rooms are my favorites as both have roof terraces with nice views across the rooftops of the Old Town. Of the two, no 52 is roomier. On the ground floor there's a bright and airy bar where breakfast (8€) is served in the mornings. If you're looking for a good-value budget option right in the heart of the Old Town, this place ticks all the boxes.

Calle Cobos 11, 11005 Cádiz. ☏ **85-617-47-47.** Fax 85-617-43-20. www.hotelpatagoniasur.com. 16 units. 80€–110€ double. MC, V. **Amenities:** Bar; lounge; room service; nonsmoking rooms; rooms for those w/ limited mobility. *In room:* A/C, TV, hair dryer, minibar.

Regio 2   If you're looking for a relatively cheap option near Playa Victoria, Regio 2 is a pretty good choice. It was built in 1981, but was renovated in 2008 and offers bathrooms with tub/shower combos in each of its simple but clean and pleasant rooms. It's a short walk from the beach but it's located on a major road, so rooms at the front of the hotel suffer a little from street noise despite the double glazing.

Av. de Andalucía 79, 11008 Cádiz. ☏ **95-625-30-08.** Fax 95-625-30-09. www.hotelregio2.com. 40 units. 75€–103€ double. MC, V. Parking 10€. **Amenities:** Bar; lounge; room service; nonsmoking rooms. *In room:* A/C, TV.

Where to Dine

EXPENSIVE

El Ventorillo del Chato ★ 🏛ANDALUSIAN   El Chato ("pug nose") is the nickname of the original founder of this inn, built in 1780. While technically under house arrest, the Spanish king, Fernando VII, came here for food, drink, and sex with the local prostitutes. Now it's an enormously charming restaurant, with a wood-burning stove, flowers, and 19th-century antiques. Try the *arroz del señorito* (a paella of shellfish taken from the shells and cleaned before cooking), *arroz negro con chocos* (squid with rice colored by its own ink), or *dorada en berenjena confitada al vino tinto* (gilthead sea bream with eggplant cooked with red wine sauce). There are two floors, including the basement, which has occasional flamenco shows on the original *tablao* (flamenco dance floor). Unexpectedly for such a nice restaurant, it's about 10 minutes out of town on the busy causeway road

Carretera de Cádiz a San Fernando Km 2. ☏ **95-625-00-25.** Reservations recommended. Main courses 14€–30€; tasting menu 45€. AE, DC, MC, V. Mon–Sat 1–4pm and 9pm–midnight.

MODERATE

Atxuri ★ BASQUE/ANDALUSIAN   Atxuri, a block behind the Palace of Congress in the historic district, is one of the best-loved restaurants in this old port city and has been in the same family for half a century. The light interior is in typical Mediterranean port style, with white stucco walls hung with paintings. The menu includes fresh anchovies in virgin olive oil with a green leaf salad, *merluza al achuri* (hake casserole with green asparagus sauce), and *pardo al brandy* (red snapper in brandy sauce). Another excellent dish is *bacalao en rosa verde* (salt cod in tomato-and-vegetable sauce). Desserts include lemon mousse or *tocinillo de cielo* (a hearty regional pudding). (Atxuri is the Basque spelling. You sometimes see the restaurant referred to as Achuri in restaurant guides.)

Calle Plocia 7. ✆ **95-625-36-13.** Reservations recommended. Main courses 12€–20€. AE, MC, V. Daily 1:15–5pm; Thurs–Sat 9–11:30pm. Closed Dec 23–Jan 8.

Balandro ★★ SPANISH/MEDITERRANEAN/MODERN   Run by the Vélez brothers who have a following on the local dining scene, Balandro offers creative, stylish modern cuisine in a refined, but not remotely stuffy, environment. As you'd expect for Cádiz, seafood features prominently. Sea bass rolls with prawns and foie gras are a specialty, but less complex dishes like lobster stew and sole filets offer great flavors too. Meat dishes are equally tempting, with dishes like filet of duck breast on apple compote flavored with a Pedro Ximénez reduction bound to get your mouth watering. If you want something lighter, opt for one of the fresh pasta dishes. In fact—it's probably my favorite restaurant in Cádiz.

Alameda de Apocada 22. ✆ **95-622-09-92.** Reservations recommended. Main courses 9€–18€. AE, MC, V. Tues–Sat 1–4:30pm; 8–11:15pm.

El Aljibe ★★ ANDALUSIAN   Near the train station, this restaurant has interior balconies, wooden ornaments, and antique furnishings. It's run by local chef Pablo Grosso, who's a bit of a legend on the Cádiz dining scene—unsurprisingly it's a local favorite. The restaurant itself is early 19th century but has been restored many times since. It's rustic in decor but refined in its ambiance and the food gets better every time I visit. Highly recommended are the foie gras of duckling with pepper sauce, scallops au gratin with prawns, and the lamb ribs with honey sauce. A signature dish is the duck casserole with wine sauce. Desserts are delicious and made fresh daily.

Calle Plocia 25. ✆ **95-626-66-56.** www.grupogrosso.com. Reservations recommended. Main courses 12€–18€. AE, DC, MC, V. Daily 1–5pm and 8pm–midnight.

El Faro ★★★ SEAFOOD/ANDALUSIAN   Since its opening in 1964, this has been the Old Town's best and most respected restaurant, featuring a busy tapas bar near the Mudéjar entrance. The formal restaurant is popular with the political and media-related communities of Cádiz. Famous faces seen dining here include Pierce Brosnan and Halle Berry. Tempting specialties include fresh fish and shellfish based on the catch of the day. Begin perhaps with the seafood soup and follow with the roulades of sole with fresh spinach, hake with green sauce, or a delectable monkfish with strips of serrano ham. Fish baked in a salt crust, which seals in the aroma and juices, is also particularly good. The waiting staff is one of the most attentive in Cádiz.

Calle San Félix 15. ✆ **95-621-10-68.** Reservations recommended. Main courses 12€–24€; fixed-price menu 40€. AE, DC, MC, V. Daily 1–4:30pm and 8:30pm–midnight.

On a hot summer day, the best place to be in Cádiz is ordering a cone at **Heladería-Café Salón Italiano,** Calle San José 11–13 (📞 **95-622-18-97**). This ice cream emporium has been a local favorite since the 1940s. It serves velvety smooth ice cream concoctions, more than 30 flavors in all. Two specialties are made with Sevillana oranges or prickly pears grown in Cádiz province. The setting is large, sun-flooded, and a bit antiseptic, with a marble bar top where adults order coffee along with ice cream. Open daily from 9am to 11pm; one scoop costs 1.20€.

Restaurant Arteserrano CONTINENTAL/TAPAS   This is one of the largest and most substantial of the tapas bars and restaurants on the main drag at Playa Victoria. Its fast-moving kitchen chugs out vast amounts of food, especially after 10pm when the place can get mobbed. There's a tapas bar near the front entrance trimmed in russet-colored porphyry marble, exposed brick, and wood paneling, and sidewalk tables in front. One dining area is perched on a balcony overlooking the crowded bar. Menu items include long lists of both meat and fish. Signature dishes include baked baby lamb, veal cutlets, and grilled *langostinos*. From a deli-style display case in front, you can take away selections of cheese, sausage, cured meats, and smoked fish. During peak hours (10pm–1am most summer evenings), it's hard to find a place even to stand.

Paseo Marítimo 2. 📞 **95-627-72-58.** Reservations recommended for dinner. Main courses 10€–20€. AE, MC, V. Daily 1–5pm and 8pm–1:30am.

Restaurant San Antonio ★ 🏛 GADITANA   Behind a pale pink facade that overlooks Cádiz's biggest plaza, this stylish and appealing restaurant specializes in local recipes, many at least a century old. Nothing about the place evokes the kind of woodsy-looking taverns of the Old Town—in fact, you'll get the definite sense that you're in an ambitious restaurant here, with uniformed waiters, a small zinc-covered bar near the entrance, and tables that are just a bit too close together. A well-intentioned and hardworking staff will recommend dishes that include a *parrillada* (mixed grill) of fish; house-style codfish; octopus prepared any way you like it (best either stuffed or deep-fried); Cádiz-style fried fish; rice with shellfish; *arroz a la marinera* (rice with lobster, prawns, and shellfish); and a dish that was exported to Cuba and popularized almost instantly: *ropa vieja* (braised skirt steak in brown sauce).

Plaza San Antonio 9. 📞 **95-621-22-39.** Reservations recommended. Main courses 12€–22€. AE, DC, MC, V. Daily 1–4pm and 8:30pm–midnight.

INEXPENSIVE

Bar Di Vino ★ TAPAS   Bar Zapata which used to be located here was a bit of a find, and thankfully its replacement is also well worth a visit. Whilst its predecessor was all about good-value, no-nonsense tapas, Di Vino has taken things up a notch. It serves creative, interesting tapas with a Basque edge. They cost a bit more, but I think they're worth it. Try the vegetable parcels, the *chorizo* and *chistorras* (Basque sausage) brochettes, or the potato and crab parcels. There's a great selection of wines by the glass too. They have several tables on pretty Plaza Candelaría which is a perfect location too.

Plaza de Candelaría 1. **95-690-30-36.** Tapas and platters 3.25€–15€; glasses of wine 1.90€–3.50€. No credit cards. Tues-Sat noon-4pm; Mon-Sat 8pm-midnight.

La Marea Mesa SEAFOOD/TAPAS Come here for beer, cheap seafood, tapas, and lots of bustle and local color, but expect a slightly cynical, overworked staff. La Marea Mesa defines itself as a *cervecería* (beer hall) with a busy kitchen; indeed, the venue is unpretentious and fast-paced, with good, abundant food. The decor is modern, with touches of varnished pine, bright lighting, and lots of bubbling aquariums. It gets busier as the evening progresses (it's jammed after 10:30pm). There are plenty of outdoor tables under a tent facing the beach, but you'll get a closer view of the culinary and social rituals from the back of the stand-up bar. The menu lists at least eight different preparations of rice, including versions with capers and *rondelles* of octopus, with salsa verde, and with cod, plus a salad of fried shrimp, braised codfish, and *revueltos* (scrambled eggs) with shellfish and fresh asparagus.

Paseo Marítimo 1. **95-628-03-47.** *Half-raciones* 4.50€–6.50€; *Raciones* 8.50€–13€; some shellfish *raciones* 35€. AE, DC, MC, V. Daily 1-5pm and 8:30pm-midnight.

Michelangelo ☺ITALIAN/PIZZA If you're looking for no-nonsense pizza and pasta then Michelangelo ticks all the right boxes. It's tucked away in a small modern square between the market and the seafront. Service is friendly and efficient and pizzas are hot, crisp, and generously topped. Wine by the glass is very good. They deliver too.

Calle Abreu 11. **95-621-19-16.** Pizzas 7.50 €–11.50€; main courses 9€ to 16€. MC, V. Daily 1-5pm and 8:30pm-midnight.

Restaurant Arana ☺ANDALUSIAN/GADITANA Unlike the more rustic and woodsy-looking restaurants around it, Arana is directly in front of the beach, midway between Tryp La Caleta and the Hotel Playa Victoria. Menu items include broad beans with ham, platters of cured Iberian meats, diced tuna with roasted peppers, sirloin steak with Roquefort sauce, minted loin of codfish, breast of duck, and a fine version of local anchovies marinated in (what else?) local olive oil. The cooking is precise and reflects the region's high culinary standards. They do a kids' menu too, so it's ideal for family dining.

Paseo Marítimo 1. **95-620-50-90.** Tapas 2€–3.50€; main courses 12€–25€; set-price menu 28€–45€. AE, DC, MC, V. Daily 1-5pm and 8pm-1am.

Restaurant Fogón Puntaparilla GRILLED/ANDALUSIAN Set directly on the narrow one-way street that fronts the beach, at the far end of the Paseo Marítimo, this is a no-nonsense but well-managed grill restaurant. The specialty is meat and, to a lesser extent, fish. It's charming and cozy, with fair prices and generous portions. There's grilled lamb or chicken cutlets; chicken, pork, veal, or beef steaks; a mixed grill with fried potatoes and garlic sauce; and a local roasted veal specialty. If you're a vegetarian who has stumbled into this place by accident, try the platter of grilled vegetables. A small selection of fish includes the ubiquitous local staple: *bacalao* (codfish).

Paseo Marítimo-Cortadura. **95-620-13-32.** Main courses 6€–26€. DC, MC, V. Wed-Mon noon-5pm and 8pm-1am.

Shopping

If you're into arts and crafts, look out for artisan shops displaying the Artesanía de Cádiz logo. They've been vetted by the Town Hall and have gained this mark for

DINING LOCAL style IN OLD CÁDIZ

Thanks to its location on a peninsula jutting toward North Africa and the Americas, the geography of old Cádiz is strictly delineated by constraints of space. Closest to the Malecón, a panoramic, sea-fronting promenade, is the La Viña neighborhood, where everyone seems to know everyone and families go back for generations. Visit the dyed-in-the-wool local haunts here at around 8:30pm to experience them at their most convivial. At that time the **Calle Virgen de la Palma** throws off its daytime slumber and revs into action.

Along the cobblestone street, at least a dozen workaday, unpretentious restaurants are jammed together. A good choice is **Bar La Palma,** Calle Virgen de la Palma 7 (✆ **95-622-85-87**), a hole in the wall whose clients either stand up at the rough-and-tumble bar or sit at a table on the street outside. Choose a variety of tapas and *raciones,* perhaps adding a portion of *papas alinades* (vinegar-soaked potato salad) with grilled peppers and a platter of grilled fish of *herreros, sardinas,* or *zapatillas,* costing from 3.50€ to 9€ each. The house specialty is grilled Spanish mackerel, caught off the coast of Mauretania.

quality. There's a warren of workshops at the **Galería Artesanal "el Pópulo"** at Calle San Antonio Abad, 14. Here you'll find leatherware, ceramics, engravings, and textiles being fashioned by local artisans and available for purchase at reasonable prices. The city tourist office has an **Artesanía de Cádiz** brochure which lists all these places and more and marks them on a map too.

If you're a foodie, hunt down the very lovely **Hecho in Cádiz,** Plaza Candelaría 7 (✆ **95-628-31-97**). On a tucked-away corner of Plaza Candelaría, this little shop has specialized in regional food products since the 1750s. You'll find caches of honey, wines (especially sherries, some fine vintages selling for only around 7€ per bottle), cheeses, olive oils, and processed meats, especially sausages (*chorizos*). Open Monday to Saturday from 10am to 2pm and Monday to Friday from 6 to 9:30pm.

Cádiz After Dark

In Cádiz, the city's role as a beach resort deeply affects the way night owls party after dark. In winter, when cold winds blow in from the Atlantic across the Bahía de Cádiz, nightclubbers find shelter in the Old Town, especially in its northernmost quadrant, the neighborhood radiating out from the **Plaza de San Francisco.** Here, in a labyrinth of impossibly narrow streets, cubbyhole tapas bars get going after around 10pm and roar 'til 4am.

For an early tapas adventure, head for **Casa Manteca,** Corralón de los Carros 66 (✆ **95-621-36-03**), the best-known tavern in the Barrio La Viña. Over the years this was the preferred hangout for local bullfighters and flamenco singers and dancers. Its sherry comes from the vineyards of neighboring Sanlúcar de Barrameda. Dig into the fresh anchovies, regional sausages, caviar, and the best-tasting *chacina* (Iberian ham) in town. Most tapas range from 1.75€ to 3.50€. Hours are Tuesday to Sunday noon to 4pm and 8pm to 1am, except June to September when it is open daily.

After that, beginning around 4am, many locals head to **El Hoyo,** Calle Manuel Rancés (no phone), a short walk north of the Plaza de San Francisco. There's a somewhat arbitrarily imposed cover charge of 5€, which tends to be waived if you're attractive and female, or male and friendly with the doorkeepers, or if you look like a Spanish pop star. There's also a strip of good, modern, late-night music bars and nightclubs on Punta de San Felipe across Plaza de España, close to the old harbor walls. Most don't get going 'til midnight and stay open 'til dawn. Cover charges are usually around 5€ to 12€. My favorite for stylish drinking with funky people is **Le Chic Baroque Lounge,** Punta de San Felipe s/n (no phone; www.clublechic.com), with its silver chandeliers, mirror balls, and black furniture. For live music of all sorts, try **Sala Supersonic,** Punta de San Felipe s/n (no phone; www.myspace.com/salasupersonic).

In summer (late May to late September), nightlife beginning after 10pm and continuing 'til around 4am or later moves to the beachfronts, especially the Playa Victoria. There's a slew of boisterous bars along the Paseo Marítimo that fronts the beach. One of my favorites is the **Woodstock Bar,** in the Edificio Europlaya, Paseo Marítimo 11 (© **95-626-57-74;** daily 4pm–3am). Woodsy and paneled, it has big windows overlooking the beach and attracts a good-looking crowd in their 20s and 30s. There are pool tables out the back and sports games shown on the TVs. Beer costs from 1.50€ to 3€. Or try even noisier **Taberna Hispañiola** at Paseo Marítimo 4, bedecked with pirates and skeletons, and **Radio City** right next door.

Beginning around 2:30am there's a migration to nightclubs that include **Barabass,** Calle Muñoz Arenillas 4–6 (© **95-607-90-26**), very close to Glorieta Ingeniero La Cierva and the Playa Victoria Hotel. It's known for themed parties that vary with the night of the week. This street has several lively lounge bars on it too.

GAY & LESBIAN NIGHTLIFE

There's lots of gay life in Cádiz, but it's not well organized. Gay taverns open and close with the lifespan of sickly butterflies; unfortunately, they don't publish their phone numbers, and hours are unpredictable. Most get going after midnight and remain open 'til just before dawn. They're usually closed on Sunday, Monday, and sometimes Tuesday nights. None of the gay bars serve food. They tend to be close to the seedy areas of the railway station or the cruise-ship terminals, or even at the Plaza de Sevilla or on one of the narrow streets of the Old Town. The current "hot" addresses (all subject to change by the time of your arrival) include **Bar Poniente,** Calle Beato Diego de Cádiz s/n, and **Bar Averno,** Calle San Antonio Abad s/n.

The cultural center of the port is **Gran Teatro Manuel de Falla,** Plaza Fragela (© **95-622-08-34**), where the finest performances are offered during the winter months. The tourist office always keeps an up-to-date program.

TARIFA & SOUTHERN COSTA DE LA LUZ ★

23km (14 miles) W of Algeciras, 713km (443 miles) S of Madrid, 98km (61 miles) SE of Cádiz

The Costa de la Luz (**Coast of Light**) stretches from the Guadiana River and the Portuguese border in the far west of Andalusia right down to Tarifa and the Strait of

Gibraltar in the far south, with Cádiz more or less in the middle. Dotting the coast are long stretches of sand, pine trees, fishing cottages, and sleepy whitewashed villages.

The **Huelva district** forms the northwestern half of the Costa de la Luz and some stretches of this coast have seen fairly low-key development with some nice resort hotels and attractive stretches of sand without the vast numbers of foreign tourists that flock to the Costa del Sol. For more information about this section, see p. 306. The southern half in the Cádiz district stretches from **Tarifa** in the south northwards, past Cádiz to **Sanlúcar de Barrameda,** the spot from which Magellan embarked in 1519 on his voyage around the globe. Columbus also made this the homeport for his third journey to the New World. (See Chapter 9 for more information.)

To travel between the northern and southern portions of the Costa de la Luz, you must go inland via Seville, since no roads go across the Cota Doñana National Park and the marshland near the mouth of the Guadalquivir River.

With a population of some 17,000 people, **Tarifa** is the southernmost city in continental Europe. It's so close to the North African coastline that it's practically in Morocco, to which it was joined in prehistoric times. It's directly across the Strait of Gibraltar from the Moroccan coastal city of Tangier. This is one of the few places in the world where you can view two different continents and two wide-open seas at once, the Mediterranean and the Atlantic Ocean. Named for the Moorish military hero Tarik, the city has kept more of its Arab character than any other town on Andalusia's coastline. Narrow cobblestone streets lead to charming patios filled with flowers.

Two factors have inhibited the development of Tarifa's beautiful 5km (3-mile) long white beach, the **Playa de Lances.** It's still a Spanish military zone in parts, and the wind which blows almost half the time makes sunbathing an unpromising prospect. For windsurfers, though, the strong western breezes are unbeatable. Tarifa is filled with shops that rent windsurfing equipment and give advice about the best locales. The influx of surf dudes and gals has brought renewed vigor to this little town in summer time and there's a buzzing nightlife and a handful of genuinely charming boutique hotels and guesthouses, meaning it's well worth taking time out here for a few days to relax and enjoy the vibe. In winter the town returns to its sleepy old ways and it's very quiet, with many of the hotels and restaurants shutting up shop.

Essentials

GETTING THERE **Transportes Generales Comes,** Calle Batalla del Salado 19 (① **90-219-92-08;** www.tgcomes.es), has good **bus** links from nearby towns and key points in Andalusia. When its office is closed, you can purchase tickets directly from the driver. The most frequented bus route is from Algeciras, 23km (14 miles) to the west. About five buses per day make the run into Tarifa in just 30 minutes (www.tgcomes.es/horarios_14.htm.) Four buses a day from Cádiz take 1½ hours.

Tarifa is the southernmost point on the E-5 (also known as the N-340), a 23km (14-mile) drive southwest from Algeciras. The journey takes around 45 minutes as the road climbs and curves its way along the coastline offering spectacular views of

[FastFACTS] TARIFA

Currency Exchange
For currency exchange head for the **Banco Santander,** Calle Batalla del Salado 17 (📞 **90-224-24-24** or 📞 95-668-49-07), open Monday to Friday from 8:30am to 2pm and Saturday from 8:30am to 1pm. There are several banks with ATMs at the intersection between the main roads into town from Cádiz and Algeciras, Calles Batalla del Salado and Amador de los Ríos.

Emergencies In an emergency, dial 📞 **112.** The police station is at Plaza Santa María 3 (📞 **95-668-41-86**). In a **medical emergency,** call **Cruz Roja Española in Tarifa** at 📞 **95-668-48-96.**

Post Office The **post office**, or *correos*, is at Calle Coronel Moscardó 9 (📞 **95-668-42-37**), off Plaza San Mateo. Hours are Monday to Friday from 8:30am to 2:30pm and Saturday from 9:30am to 1pm.

Gibraltar and across the Strait to Africa. From Cádiz, Tarifa is about a 1½ hour drive, 114km (98 miles) southeast along the A-48/E-5.

VISITOR INFORMATION The **Tarifa Tourist Office** is on Paseo de la Alameda s/n (📞 **95-668-09-93;** www.aytotarifa.com), and it's open June to September, Monday to Friday from 10:30am to 1:30pm and 4:30 to 7:30pm and Saturday and Sunday from 10:30am to 2:30pm. From October to May, hours are Monday to Friday from 10:30am to 1:30pm and 4 to 6pm, Saturday from 10am to 1:30pm.

Tarifa Walking Tour

Ancient Tarifa ★★ was enclosed by town walls and several sections remain today. The main entrance to the Old Town is the **Puerta de Jerez,** which, although it looks Moorish, is actually more recent, constructed by the Catholic monarchs after the 13th–15th-century Reconquista. Once through this ancient archway you find yourself in an attractive warren of tiny streets flanked with whitewashed houses. If you want to, just wander at will and dip into the occasional cafe or boutique. Or take an immediate left down Calle Pes which becomes Calle Colón. On the right you'll find the bustling, attractive covered **Mercado (Central Marketplace)** where you can see all manner of fresh produce on sale. The building, which is Mudéjar in style, is worth a visit in itself.

Take a right turn through a small covered passageway and you reach **Paseo de la Alameda,** the Old Town's principal square. To the right at the top end of the square you'll find the helpful **tourist information office**. (See "Visitor Information" above.) At the bottom of the square you come to the port where fast, frequent ferries depart for the Moroccan town of Tangier, a fascinating, sense-invading day trip.

Right next to the port is the Old Town's most important monument, the **Castillo de Guzmán,** built in 960 on the orders of Abd ar-Rahman III, the Caliph of Córdoba. From 1292 until the mid-1990s this was a garrison for Spanish troops. Since then it has been turned into a town museum. You can walk along its parapets which offer panoramic views out to sea towards Morocco. It's open Tuesday to Sunday from 10am to 2pm and 6 to 8pm, charging an admission of 2€.

From the Castillo you can walk up **Calle Sancho IV El Bravo**—the main street which bisects the Old Town. Here you'll find lots of pleasant, slightly bohemian feeling cafes ideal for a drink and a spot of people-watching. The most intriguing church in Tarifa is **Iglesia de San Mateo** at its eastern end. It's open daily from 8am to 1pm and 5:30 to 9pm; admission is free. Behind a decaying Baroque facade, the church's interior is late Gothic, with elegant rib vaulting in the nave and more modern stained-glass windows above. Reliefs of Christ and his apostles decorate the vaulting, and there is an impressive depiction of the crucified Christ by noted sculptor Pedro de Mena on the right aisle. The church also possesses a tombstone from the 7th century that proves the Christians had settled in Tarifa before the arrival of the conquering Muslims in 711. The streets off Calle Sancho IV El Bravo are perfect for exploring further; their layout hasn't varied since the days of the Moors. These days they are filled with cafes, bars, and interesting boutiques.

Tarifa's sheltered and sandy town beach, **Playa Chica,** is ideal for a spot of sunbathing and a cooling dip in the sea, though it's quite small and can get pretty crowded. See "Beaches & Windsurfing" below for more on the beaches around Tarifa.

A little way out of Tarifa, bird-watchers come to visit the spectacular **Mirador del Estrecho ★★**, a lookout point that's great for watching bird migrations across the Strait of Gibraltar and that incidentally offers panoramic views. The lookout point is 7km (4⅓ miles) east on the E-5.

Another nearby attraction is the Roman ruins at **Baelo Claudia,** 10km (6 miles) to the north. These ruins were from a settlement here from the 2nd century B.C. The hamlet grew rich from a relish known as *garum,* a rotting mass of horror made from fish blood, heads, entrails, and soft roe from tuna and mackerel. Most of what you see today is from the 1st century A.D. when Emperor Claudius made the town a self-governing township. Discovered in 1917, the town was excavated, including ruins of its forum, three temples (Jupiter, Juno, and Minerva), and the remains of a basilica. The ruins of a theater have been restored, and the former main street can be traversed. The ruins of public baths can also be seen, even the fish factory where the highly valued *garum* was produced. The ruins (© **95-668-85-30;** www.museosdeandalucia.es), can be visited June to September, Tuesday to Saturday from 10am to 8pm and Sunday from 10am to 2pm. In other months, hours are Tuesday to Saturday from 10am to 6pm in winter (until 7pm March to May and October and until 8pm June to September) and Sunday from 10am to 2pm all year. Admission is free. In front of Baelo Claudia is possibly the most beautiful beach in Spain, **Bolonia.** Climb the dune to the north and turn round to see spectacular views across to the sea to Morocco.

BEACHES & WINDSURFING

The **beaches** of the Costa de la Luz between Cádiz and Tarifa are some of the most unspoilt in Andalusia and well worth exploring. Expect grand vistas of the coast of Africa and a rolling, treeless, and scrub-covered wild landscape. The terrain is affected by the constant drying winds blowing northward from the Moroccan Sahara.

Tarifa and the villages flanking it form the **kite and windsurfing** capital of Europe. The main beaches are **Playa de Los Lances** immediately north of Tarifa—a wild, wide stretch of sand which is quite windswept and with few facilities. The drawbacks here are high winds and a strong undertow, so it's better left to the experts. **Playa Valdevaqueros** adjoins Playa de Los Lances and has more facilities,

A whale OF A TIME

Thanks to its location where the waters of the Atlantic and the Mediterranean meet, Tarifa is one of the best spots in Europe for **whale watching**. In addition to common whales, pilot whales, sperm whales, and even killer whales are regularly spotted on these trips. You'll quite probably see dolphins too. It's almost guaranteed you will see whales of one species or another quite close up and if you don't, most companies offer another trip for free.

Typical costs for a 2-hour trip are 30€ for adults and 20€ for children. Reputable operators include **Turmares**, Av. Alcalde Juan Nuñez 3 (𝄞 **95-668-07-41** or 𝄞 69-644-83-47; www.turmares.com), **FIRMM España,** Calle Pedro Cortés 4 (𝄞 **95-662-70-08** or 𝄞 61-945-94 41; www.firmm.org), and **Whale Watch España**, Av. de la Constitucion 6 (𝄞 **95-668-22-47**; www.whalewatch tarfifa.net).

with several kitesurfing schools and beach restaurants (*chiringuitos*). On the other side of the huge sand dune at the north end of Valdevaqueros, **Punta Paloma** is also excellent for kite and windsurfing and better protected, so good for beginners.

If you're looking for relaxation rather than action, head for **Playa Bolonia** close to the famous Roman ruins at Baelo Claudia, a lovely curved stretch of sheltered sand backed by wild dunes. A short distance farther north, **Playa de Zahara** near the hamlet of **Zahara de los Atunes,** is also popular with locals. It's an attractive stretch of sand a bit more sheltered from the wind. It also has excellent *chiringuitos* serving some of the best and freshest tuna tapas in all of Spain. **Playa de los Alemanes** in between Bolonia and Zahara is another beautiful, sheltered, quiet cove with crystal clear water.

Surfers should head for **Playa del Palmar,** just north of Zahara, which is nice and sandy with consistent swell offering good long breaks. There's a relaxed, slightly hippy-style vibe here and it's a good place to sip a *mojito* and watch the sunset. There's a similar chilled-out, beach party vibe on the beach at nearby **Los Caños de La Meca.**

If you like your sunbathing clothing-free, Punta Paloma, Bolonia, and the stretch of beach between Palmar and Conil all have **nudist** sections.

To try your hand at kiteboarding or windsurfing, head for the many schools in Tarifa along Calle Batalla del Salado or better still by the beaches at Punta Paloma and Valdevaqueros. Schools should carry a valid city council operators' license which means they are fully qualified and insured. Check for the AEOKT sign (*Associacion de Escuelas Officiales de Kitesurf de Tarifa*). You can also hire gear from many of them. **Tarifa Spin Out Surfbase** (𝄞 **95-623-63-52**; www.tarifaspinout.com) at Playa Valdevaqueros has been operating since 1988 and is one of the best schools in the area. Windsurf rentals cost 27€ per hour or 60€ per day, a basic first lesson at kitesurfing costs 100€, with a maximum of 4 people in a group.

Where to Stay

Hostal Alameda On the busiest square in the Old Town, this hotel occupies an enviable position right in the midst of the restaurants and bars of the Paseo Alameda.

The fascinating city of **Tangier** on the Moroccan coast is just 35 minutes away from Tarifa by fast ferry and a visit makes for a fascinating day trip or short break. Two companies offer ferry services. **FRS Ferries** (📞 **95-668-18-30**; www.frs.es) has up to 8 daily departures at 2-hour intervals between 9am and 11pm. A round-trip passage costs 66.60€ for adults and 40€ for children. **Grupo Comarit** (📞 **95-668-27-68**; www.comarit.es) has a similar number of departures also at 2-hour intervals daily leaving between 8am and 10pm. Prices are virtually the same, at 64.80€ for adults and 37.80€ for children.

Both companies have offices at the port right next to the Castillo de Guzman El Bueno and the Paseo de la Alameda. Just show up and buy tickets for the next available crossing. Both also offer day trip and overnight excursion packages of ferry crossing, bus transfer into Tangier, meals, guided tours, and accommodation.

For these prices, you get clean and comfortable but basic rooms—small but tidy and furnished with mostly pinewood pieces. The place has a certain charm and character. The hospitable staff will serve you a continental breakfast.

Paseo Alameda 4, 11380 Tarifa. 📞 **95-668-11-81.** www.hostalalameda.com. 11 units. 55€–90€ double. MC, V. **Amenities:** Restaurant (for hotel guests only). *In room:* A/C, TV, no phone.

Casa Blan+co ★   Don't be put off by the rather dumb name. This brand new palace house conversion right in the middle of the Old Town is stylish and sophisticated. In fact, some might find the decor a bit too avant-garde with funky round sofas, ladders leading up to mezzanine bed areas, and even futons on glass platforms over the bathrooms. It's a little short on creature comforts, although there's no skimping on high-tech amenities—all the rooms have plasma TVs, and the hotel has its own flotation tanks and solarium which seem to fit Tarifa's laid-back, trendy vibe.

Calle Nostra Señora de la Luz s/n, 11380 Tarifa. 📞 **95-668-15-15.** Fax 95-668-19-90. www.casablan-co.com. 7 units. 90€–133€ double. Rates include breakfast. MC, V. **Amenities:** Breakfast lounge. *In room:* A/C, TV.

Dar Cilla ★★ 📱   This atmospheric and friendly set of apartments has been tastefully renovated by owner Zoë Ouwehand-Reid and makes a great base for staying a few days and exploring the area. All the rooms are self-catering with simple kitchen facilities—ideal for fixing your own breakfasts and simple suppers. Rooms are decorated in attractive Moroccan style, with antique furniture and lots of drapes and carpets. What really makes this place stand out though is its delightful roof terrace. There's nothing nicer than sipping a glass of chilled wine, taking in the lovely views across the Old Town and across the Strait of Gibraltar to Morocco. It's very convivial and you'll probably end up meeting other guests, and chances are Zoë will join you for a chat too. She's a perfect host and can recommend all sorts of day trips and sightseeing ideas. So much so she's written a book: *Tarifa Inside Out And Round About* is a handy guide for the area. A couple of the apartments are singles.

Calle Amador de los Rios 16A, 11380 Tarifa. 📞 **65-346-70-25.** www.darcilla.com. 8 units. 50€–240€ one-, two- and four-person apartments. Minimum stay of 2 or 3 nights depending on the season. MC, V.

Amenities: Terrace; Wi-Fi. *In room:* Kitchen with small cooker, fridge, kettle, toaster, cooking and dining utensils (no A/C).

Escondite del Viento ★ 🏨 This is another contemporary conversion of a town house in the midst of Tarifa's Old Town and I think it's one of the best. Like Casa Blan+co (see above), it's designer and modern in style, but I think the combination of new with old works a little better here. The bedrooms are a seamless blend of smoked glass, steel, and wood with bright splashes of color on the walls and large comfy beds. They're kitted out with all the latest gadgets like plasma TVs and lights that turn on with the wave of a hand. Bathrooms are a good size and fitted with powershowers and glass washbasins. It all adds up to a refined, contemporary, and relaxing experience. The best rooms are those in the attic as they have private terraces.

Calle Comendador 1, 11380 Tarifa. © **95-668-19-01.** Fax 95-668-27-71. www.esconditedelviento.com. 7 units. 90€–140€ double. Rates include breakfast. MC, V. *In room:* TV, DVD, hair dryer, Wi-Fi.

La Calzada 🍴 One of the great bargains of Tarifa, La Calzada attracts those who prefer to stay near the town's main square rather than at one of the surfer places along the beach. Formerly a private home, it was converted in 2000 into this little inn. Bedrooms are small but well maintained and comfortably but basically furnished. Decor relies for the most part on colorful Andalusian tiles. Each room contains a tiny tiled bathroom with shower and not much room to spread out your stuff. You can easily walk to the restaurants, tapas bars, and attractions of town. Don't expect too much and you should be delighted here, at least when it comes time to pay the bill.

Justino Pertínez 7, 11380 Tarifa. © **95-668-14-92.** Fax 95-668-03-66. www.hostallacalzada.com. 8 units. 50€–90€ double. MC, V. **Amenities:** Breakfast lounge. *In room:* A/C, TV, Wi-Fi.

Pensión Correos This basic guesthouse is in front of the post office in the center of town. A former private house converted in 1999, it attracts guests on a budget. Comfortable bedrooms are simply furnished. Surfers pile in here, sleeping three to five a room. Bedrooms on the ground floor don't get enough daylight, but the upper rooms open onto scenic views of the town. There are virtually no amenities, but there is a roof terrace enclosed by low white walls. Many restaurants are just a short walk away.

Calle Coronel Moscardó 8, 11380 Tarifa. © **95-668-02-06.** 9 units. 40€–100€ double. MC, V. Free parking nearby. **Amenities:** Wi-Fi. *In room:* No phone.

Posada La Sacristia ★ 🏨 Bosco Herrero and Miguel Arregui have transformed this 17th-century stable into something quite wonderful. In the historic center of Tarifa, they have restored and converted La Sacristia into a hotel of charm and grace. The rooms are quite small, but attractively furnished—some with canopied beds, Victorian mirrors, antique lamps, and Moroccan-style tiled floors. All have new, well-equipped bathrooms and some of the suites have freestanding bath tubs. There are fully equipped apartments available for rent elsewhere in the Old Town, some with views across the Strait of Gibraltar. There's also an excellent in-house restaurant.

Calle San Donato 8, 11380 Tarifa. © **95-668-17-59.** Fax 95-668-51-82. www.lasacristia.net. 10 units. 115€–135€ double; 250€ suite. Rates include continental breakfast. AE, DC, MC, V. **Amenities:** Restaurant; bar. *In room:* A/C, TV.

Posada Vagamundos ★   This attractive conversion of an 18th-century building, formerly part of the nearby Church of San Francisco, is perfectly located right in the midst of the Old Town. The building has been restored with care and retains original elements like wooden beams while incorporating nice Moorish touches like horse-shoe-shaped arches and lanterns. The 11 rooms are quite small and simply furnished but they're comfortable and atmospheric. There's a nice cafeteria on the ground floor with an open terrace in one of the most picturesque streets of the Old Town.

Calle San Francisco 18, 11380 Tarifa. ✆ **95-668-15-13.** Fax 95-668-15-38. www.posadavagamundos. com. 11 units. 60€–115€ double. Price includes breakfast. MC, V. **Amenities:** Cafeteria/bar. *In room:* No phone.

NEARBY PLACES TO STAY

100% Fun   With a name like this, you won't be surprised to learn that this place is another great favorite with the surf crowd and close to the beaches. Rooms are a good size and simply but attractively furnished with Moroccan flourishes. But it's for the scene and the surfing that people come here. There's a wind and kitesurf school on site and regular party nights. Ideal if you're young and want to have fun, otherwise, possibly not for you.

Carretera de Cádiz Km 76, 11380 Tarifa. ✆ **95-668-03-30.** Fax. 95-668-00-13 www.100x100fun.com. 22 units. 80€–130€ double. Rates include breakfast. MC, V. **Amenities:** Restaurant; bar; outdoor pool. *In room:* A/C, TV, minibar.

Hurricane Hotel   Set up by legendary local hotelier James Whaley long before there were hotels catering for the surfer community, this place is a bit of a legend. Seven kilometers (4⅓ miles) west of Tarifa, it's well located for the beaches and so popular with the windsurfing set that rooms can be booked months in advance. It's charmingly built in Moorish style with arches, balconies, and ivy climbing the walls in subtropical gardens. Ask for a room near the pools as those on the roadside can be a bit noisy. There's a kitesurfing school on site and stables for those who like to ride horses along the beach.

Carretera de Cádiz Km 78, 11380 Tarifa. ✆ **95-668-49-19.** Fax 95-668-03-29. www.hurricanehotel.com. 33 units. 87€–143€ double; 145€–243€ suite. Rates include continental breakfast. AE, MC, V. Free parking. **Amenities:** Restaurant; health club; 2 outdoor pools. *In room:* A/C, TV, hair dryer, minibar, Wi-Fi.

La Codorniz ★   One of the best hotels in the area is outside of town on the road to Cádiz, within walking distance of the beach at La Peña, so ideal if you're here for the wind and waves. It's a typically graceful Andalusian structure of two stories, with whitewashed walls and colored tiles. Bedrooms are a bit small but have balconies, tiled floors, simple but comfortable furnishings (tasteful wooden pieces), and tiled bathrooms. Instead of a double, you can live more privately in one of the bungalows in the landscaped grounds. A very good on-site restaurant serves regional dishes.

Carretera Cádiz Km 79, 11380 Tarifa. ✆ **95-668-47-44.** Fax 95-668-41-01. www.lacodorniz.com. 37 units. 67€–130€ double. AE, DC, MC, V. Free parking. **Amenities:** Restaurant; bar; outdoor pool; Wi-Fi. *In room:* A/C, TV, hair dryer, minibar.

Where to Dine

Mandragora ★★ SPANISH/MOROCCAN   One of the best places to dine in the Old Town at the moment and very popular, Mandragora serves up an interesting blend of local and North African cuisine. As it's tucked away behind the main church in the Old Town, the Iglesia de San Mateo, not too many people stumble upon it by chance. Menu favorites include baked lamb with plums and almonds, monkfish tagine, and honey-basted sirloin. It's simply furnished and not at all pretentious, just good food, great atmosphere, and decent house wine. They don't take reservations here, so show up early to avoid waiting for a table, particularly at weekends.

Calle Independencia 3 © **956 68 12 91.** Reservations not possible. Main courses 9€-19€. MC, V. Tues-Sun 7:30-11:30pm. Closed 2 weeks in Feb.

Morilla ★ ☺ANDALUSIAN   If you're looking for something typically local, this is the place to come to. Family-owned and run, Morilla is the oldest restaurant in Tarifa and is situated in front of the big church in the old center. It serves up great, no-nonsense food with fast and friendly service. The restaurant is split into an area with bar and tapas, an area for the restaurants, and an outdoor terrace with 10 tables. Unlike a lot of restaurants in Tarifa, Morilla is open all year round and serves food all day long. The delicious *gambas pil pil* (prawns in spicy tomato sauce) is a fantastic dish to start with. Follow with steaks either with peppercorn sauce or Roquefort sauce. As it's very Spanish, you can also eat really late here, with orders being taken right up to midnight.

Calle Sancho IV El Bravo 2, 11380 Tarifa. © **95-668-17-57.** Reservations not necessary. Main courses 7€-19€. MC, V. Mon-Sun 10pm-1am.

Posada La Sacristia ★★ INTERNATIONAL/ANDALUSIAN   If you're after a fine dining experience, then this is the place to come to in Tarifa. The Posada La Sacristia's restaurant is the hippest place in town. It's refined and elegant and food is a top quality combination of local and international styles. The sushi is particularly good. Steaks are also melt-in-the-mouth delicious. Set in a glass-roofed courtyard inside a restored old town house, the situation is also pretty hard to beat.

San Donato 8, 11380 Tarifa. © **95-668-17-59.** Reservations recommended. Main courses 11€-25€. AE, MC, V. Tues-Sun 1-4pm and 8-11pm. Closed Jan.

Restaurante Vaca Loca ANDALUSIAN   Meat lovers flock to the "crazy cow" as it's called. Generous portions of big juicy steaks are broiled and basted on the wood chip barbecue .The setting, in a small square right in the middle of the Old Town, is also pretty perfect. Non-meat eaters are well served with tasty vegetable kebabs. They don't take reservations and the place can get very busy, so show up early (before 10pm).

Calle Cervantes 6. No phone. Reservations not possible. Main courses 10€-24€. MC, V. Daily 7pm-midnight.

Restaurante Villanueva ANDALUSIAN   This 1888 *fonda* is still going strong. In the town center near Puerta de Jerez, it was built in the Moorish style with a terrace, plenty of tiles, and wrought-iron furniture. The warm hospitality covers up for the simple, austere decor. The best choice is the fresh fish bought that day at the market and the best preparation is *a la plancha* (grilled), laden with garlic (*al ajillo*), or fried. Or try the fish fry mix with mussels and shrimp, served with a savory tomato sauce.

Av. de Andalucía 11. ☎ **95-668-41-49.** Reservations recommended. Main courses 7€–25€. DC, MC, V. Tues–Sun 1–4pm and 8–11pm. Closed Jan.

Tarifa after Dark

In the summer months, Tarifa's Old Town is great fun at night, with buzzing tapas joints and funky bars aplenty. If you fancy starting your evening with a few tapas, head for Calle Guzman El Bueno next to the castle, which is a bit less touristy and more authentic than other areas. Try the excellent fried anchovies (*boquerones fritos*) and aubergines in honey (*berenjenas con miel*) at busy **La Posada** at no. 3 (☎ **63-692-94-49**), tuna balls in salsa (*albóndigas de atún con salsa de tomate*) at **El Feo** at no. 10 (☎ **63-854-16-47**), and the chicken kebabs with honey (*brochetas de pollo con miel*) at **El Pasillo** at no.14 (☎ **95-668-49-48**). Adjacent Calle Sancho IV El Bravo, the main street through the Old Town, is packed with busy bars and cafes and full of atmosphere. The most famous and best for people-watching is the excellent **Café Central** at no. 10 (☎ **95-668-28-77**) which has a big terrace and airy, dark wood bar. (Breakfasts here are also great for the following morning.)

As the night draws on you can head for the divey cocktail bars in the smaller streets off Sancho IV El Bravo. Calle San Francisco is particularly good. **Moskito** at no. 11 (no phone; www.moskitobar.com) serves up a mean *mojito* and it's open every night from 11pm. Smoother corner bar **Blanco** at no.8 is brighter and more chilled out. And if you really want to club it until the early hours, hop in a cab or walk 20 minutes along Calle Batalla del Salado out of town on the Cádiz road to the Poligono La Vega, a small industrial estate where you'll find several cool nightclubs, in particular the world-famous **Café del Mar** (☎ 69-635-75-46; www.cafedelmartarifa.es) which is open until 6:30am. For something cooler and less noisy, head for the very smooth **Beach Chill Out** bar at Pintor Guillermo Perez Villalta 60 (☎ **95-668-53-61**) on the seafront on the way out of town, which is open 'til 2am every day.

HUELVA

92km (57 miles) W of Seville, 629km (390 miles) SW of Madrid

Huelva, capital of the beautiful province of the same name, is itself rather ugly and industrial. For those heading west into bordering Portugal, the area makes a good stopover. Columbus buffs also come here to visit the bay from which the explorer set sail and to explore the monastery at La Rábida where he spent time praying for success and seeking spiritual guidance before his voyages of discovery.

The Costa de la Luz coastline either side of Huelva is the center of one of the largest concentrations of beaches in Spain, and is visited mainly by Spaniards who don't stay at the port but at the attractive beach resorts along the coast. The city doesn't have much to offer when it comes to tourist attractions, but it's a friendly place nonetheless.

Essentials

GETTING THERE   The port city of Huelva has good rail links with the rest of Spain. RENFE **trains** arrive at Avenida de Italia (☎ **90-232-03-20;** www.renfe.es). Three to four trains run daily from Seville, taking 1½ hours and costing 9.80€ one way.

Huelva

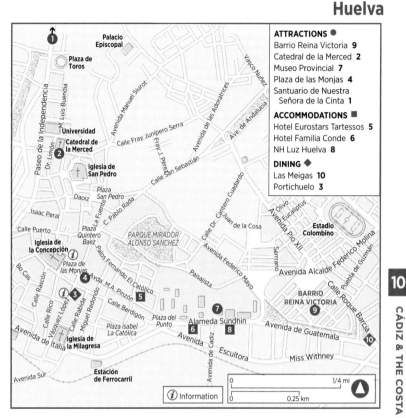

ATTRACTIONS ●
Barrio Reina Victoria **9**
Catedral de la Merced **2**
Museo Provincial **7**
Plaza de las Monjas **4**
Santuario de Nuestra
  Señora de la Cinta **1**

ACCOMMODATIONS ■
Hotel Eurostars Tartessos **5**
Hotel Familia Conde **6**
NH Luz Huelva **8**

DINING ◆
Las Meigas **10**
Portichuelo **3**

Huelva also has **bus** links to Seville. Buses run at least hourly, half-hourly at peak times, and there are around 18 to 30 per day. The journey takes 1¼ hours and costs 8€ for a one-way ticket. The bus station is at Avenida Dr Rubio s/n (✆ **90-211-44-92;** www.damas-sa.es).

Most motorists **drive** from Seville. Follow the E-1/A-49 west from Seville. There is no coastal road linking Cádiz and Huelva. Motorists from Cádiz head north on an express highway, the AP-4/E-5, and then cut west toward Huelva just south of Seville.

VISITOR INFORMATION   The handiest tourist office is the **Huelva City Tourist Office** booth situated on Plaza de las Monjas. Staff members are friendly and helpful. They have free maps showing the main sights, hotels, and various themed walking routes around the town. It's open Monday to Saturday 10am to 2pm and 3:30 to 8:30pm, (Saturday afternoon hours 4:30 to 6:30pm). The regional **Andalucia Tourist Office** is just down from Plaza de las Monjas at Plaza Alcade Cota Mora 2 (✆ **95-965-50-200;** www.andalucia.org). As always, their city map is

[FastFACTS] HUELVA

Currency Exchange
For currency exchange, the most central place with ATMs is **Banco Santander Central Hispano** at Calle Palacios 10 (© **90-224-24-24** or © 95-928-15-35), open Monday to Friday from 8:30am to 2:30pm.

Emergencies The **Huelva police station** is at Paseo de la Glorieta (© **95-924-19-10**). **Cruz Roja (Red Cross)** is at Paseo Buenos Aires s/n (© **95-926-12-11**), fronting the cathedral.

Hospital For other less-pressing ailments, go to the **Hospital General Juan Ramón Jiménez** on Ronda Exterior Norte s/n (© **95-920-10-00**).

Post Office The **Huelva post office** is at Av. de la Ría s/n (© **95-954-05-65**). Hours are Monday to Friday from 8:30am to 8:30pm and Saturday from 9:30am to 2pm.

clearer and easier to use. It's open Monday to Friday 9am to 7:30pm, Saturday and Sunday 9:30am to 3pm.

The **Huelva Province Tourist Office** (Patronato Provincial de Turismo de Huelva) is at Calle Fernando el Catolico 18 (© **95-925-74-03;** www.turismo huelva.org). It's a useful source of information for visiting the rest of the region of Huelva if you want to venture farther afield. It's open Monday to Friday 8am to 2pm.

Exploring Huelva

When Columbus set out from across the Tinto River to chart a new sea passage to India, he brought rugged Huelvan sailors with him. After the sailors stumbled on the Americas, Huelva entered into a grand period of prosperity based on trade with the New World. Eventually Huelva's supremacy was lost to Seville and later to Cádiz, which came to dominate the gold and silver routes from the New World. A final blow was the Lisbon earthquake of 1755 that flattened much of Huelva. This has left the city with far fewer grand historic buildings than, say, Seville or Cádiz, and as a result it feels distinctly more modern (read less historic) as you walk around it.

The **Fiestas Colombinas** ★, which begins on August 3, is a week-long riot of concerts, *corridas* (bullfights), food, processions, and competitive races.

A large statue on the west bank of the river at Punta del Sebo commemorates the departure of Columbus on his third voyage of discovery. About 7km (4½ miles) up on the east bank of the Tinto River, this monument marks the exact spot where Columbus's ships were anchored while being loaded with supplies before departure.

To see other sights of Huelva, begin in the center of town at **Plaza de las Monjas,** a palm-lined square where you can pick up a map from the city tourist booth. From here, you can branch out in several directions to take in the highlights.

About a 10-minute walk northwest along Avenida Martín Alonso Pinzón, takes you to the **Museo Provincial,** Alameda Sundheim 13 (© **95-965-0424;** www. museosdeandalucia.es), open Tuesday 2:30 to 8:30pm, Wednesday to Saturday 9am to 8:30pm, and Sunday 9am to 2:30pm. Admission is free. The archaeology department on the ground floor feels a bit old and dusty. It focuses on the port's illustrious past, with banks of glass cabinets of artifacts that range from the Stone Age to the era of the Moorish takeover and an exhibition about the ancient city of Tartessus.

The first floor displays the recently renovated fine arts section, a modest collection of paintings from the 18th, 19th, and 20th centuries. They're nicely lit and laid out, but don't come close to the far superior collections in Seville, Córdoba, and Granada.

After leaving the museum, you can walk a further 10 minutes and visit **Barrio Reina Victoria,** east of the museum alongside Avenida de Guatemala. Constructed by the Río Tinto Mining Company in the early part of the 20th century, it was designed by British architects to evoke their homeland. Workers lived along the tree-lined streets in bungalows with rose gardens.

Huelva's grandest church is **Catedral de la Merced,** Plaza de la Merced s/n (© **95-924-30-36**). Constructed in 1606, it was not damaged in the earthquake. Its facade, painted a vivid salmon pink, has beautiful belfries. Inside, the decor is white Baroque. The church contains an image of the *Virgen de la Cinta,* patron saint of Huelva. The building is officially open for Mass at 8pm daily and additionally at 11am and 12pm on Sundays. It's also often open during the rest of the day.

For a church with links to Columbus, head for the restored 15th-century **Santuario de Nuestra Señora de la Cinta,** Plaza Conquero (© **95-925-11-22**), 3km (1¾ miles) from the center on the road heading to Portugal. You can catch bus no. 6 from outside the central bus station or, if you're feeling energetic, it's a pleasant walk with great views out across the Odiel River estuary along Avenida Manuel Siurot through the Parque Moret. This was one of the churches where Columbus came to pray for the success of his voyage. Attractions under its Mudéjar ceiling include an impressive altar grille, a fresco of the Madonna from the Middle Ages, and 1920s tiles depicting scenes of the life of Columbus by the artist Daniel Zuloaga. Open Monday to Saturday 9am to 1pm and 4 to 7pm, Sundays 9:30am to 1:30pm and 4 to 7pm. Admission is free.

Where to Stay

Hotel Eurostars Tartessos ★ Currently the best choice in Huelva, the Eurostars Tartessos offers 100 recently refurbished, modern rooms and suites. Bright and functional in style, with parquet wood floors and dark wood headboards, all have a large writing desk, Wi-Fi, and satellite TV. Spacious, well-lit bathrooms have dark marble walls and white suites featuring fittings you'd expect from a quality hotel. There's a good in-hotel restaurant. It's two minutes' walk from Plaza de las Monjas.

Av. Martin Alonso Pinzón 13, 21003 Huelva. © **95-928-27-11.** Fax 95-925-06-17. www.eurostars tartessos.com. 100 units. 53€–79€ double; 109€–139€ junior suite. AE, MC, V. Parking 11€. **Amenities:** Restaurant; bar; gym; room service; rooms for those w/limited mobility. *In room:* A/C, TV, hair dryer, minibar, Wi-Fi.

Hotel Familia Conde 🍴 If you're on a budget, this recently renovated hotel is a good option, nicely located midway between the Museo Provincial and Plaza de las Monjas. It's simply but adequately furnished with wooden bedframes on parquet floors; most bedrooms are small to midsize, each with a tiled bathroom. The better rooms open onto balconies. Top-floor rooms or those overlooking the patio are the best. All are clean, bright, and well maintained. It's on a main road and there's a busy bar immediately opposite the hotel which may disturb light sleepers in the front rooms. The on-site cafeteria is very affordable.

ON THE trail OF CHRISTOPHER COLUMBUS

You can follow the trail of Spain's most famous explorer a little farther out of town. La Rábida, 8km (5 miles) east of Huelva, is home to the monastery where Columbus gained spiritual guidance before his voyages and the wharf from which his ships set sail.

In the chapel at the **Monasterio de la Rábida ★**, Zona de la Rábida s/n (📞 **95-935-04-11;** www.monasterio delarabida.com), Columbus prayed for success on the eve of his voyage with his son, Diego. And it was here he revealed his plans to friars Juan Pérez and Antonio de Marchena. They were so convinced of the brilliance of his scheme for a new route to India that they interceded on his behalf with Queen Isabella, who agreed to finance the expedition. This monastery, which is also called Santa María de La Rábida, is known as "the birthplace of America."

The church's chief treasure is the venerated *Virgen de los Milagros* **(Virgin of the Miracles),** dating from the 1300s. In the cloisters of the first flower-bedecked patio, you'll also find a series of interesting Cubist-style frescoes painted in 1930 by Daniel Vázquez Díaz, a noted artist from Huelva. And of particular charm is a Mudéjar cloister from the 15th century, adjoining the monks' refectory where Columbus and his son dined.

Upstairs you can visit a gallery with an exhibition of all the known pictures of the explorer and many of his crew, along with the **Sala Capitular (Chapter House)** where Columbus made his final plans before embarking and the **Sala de Banderas (Flag Room)** which features flags and caskets of soil from each of the South and Central American countries that were once Spanish territories.

Admission is 3€ and includes a free audio guide. Morning opening hours are 10am to 1pm Tuesday to Saturday and 10:45am to 1pm Sundays. Afternoon hours vary by season: April to July and September 4 to 7pm, August 4:45 to 8pm, rest of the year 4 to 6:15pm. Closed Mondays.

Just below the monastery, set in fir-tree-lined gardens, you can also visit **El Muelle de las Carabelas,** Paraje de la Rábida (📞 **95-953-05-97)** the wharf from which his ships set sail. From this now heavily silted bay, three caravels—the *Pinta,* the *Niña,* and the *Santa María*—set out to explore the Sea of Darkness. The complex contains replicas of the three caravels—shockingly small to house a crew of 90, plus 30 officers, for 2 months and 10 days. Look also for maps tracing Columbus's voyage, and a 20-minute film of the trip, which kids will enjoy. Admission is 3.50€ for adults, 1.50€ for children aged 5 to 18. From June to August hours are Tuesday to Friday 10am to 2pm and 5 to 9pm, weekends 11am to 8pm; September to May, Tuesday to Sunday 10am to 7pm. Closed Mondays.

Alameda Sundheim 14, 21003 Huelva. 📞 **95-928-24-00.** Fax 95-928-50-41. 54 units. 57€–69€ double. Rates include continental breakfast. DC, MC, V. Parking 10€. **Amenities:** Cafeteria; bar; babysitting; room service. *In room:* A/C, TV, hair dryer, minibar, Wi-Fi.

NH Luz Huelva ★   After the Eurostars, this modern chain hotel is as good as it gets in Huelva. Immediately opposite the Museo Provincial, near the Congress Hall and the train station, it opened in 1992, but has been updated. A seven-story building with balconies, it follows the usual NH style, with functional but comfortably modern fixtures and fittings. Bedrooms, including five suites, are furnished with matching blue fabrics and light wooden furniture. Midsize rooms have a well-maintained tiled bathroom with a tub/shower combo. The hotel fills up—mainly with business clients in the cooler months and vacationers in the summer. What I like about NH hotels is the attention to detail—a choice of pillows, a breakfast for early risers, a good toiletries kit, sharp citrusy soap and shower gels. The outdoor cafe and bar are very pleasant in summer. Alameda Sundheim can be a bit noisy, so ask for a room at the rear.

Alameda Sundheim 26, 21003 Huelva. ✆ **95-925-00-11.** Fax 95-925-81-10. www.nh-hoteles.com. 107 units. 55€–98€ double; 145€–175€ suite. AE, DC, MC, V. Parking 13€. **Amenities:** Cafe; bar; room service; babysitting; nonsmoking rooms. *In room:* A/C, TV, hair dryer, minibar, Wi-Fi.

ON THE OUTSKIRTS

Parador de Mazagón ★★   One of the best hotels in the area is 23km (14 miles) west of Huelva and 6km (3½ miles) from the center of Mazagón on a peaceful pine grove cliff overlooking a sandy beach. The rambling, single-story structure is like a *cortijo* (a Spanish farmhouse complex) but it was actually built in the 1960s. Comfortable, spacious rooms have balconies and terraces overlooking an expansive garden with a swimming pool. Pine groves slope down to the white-sand beach at Mazagón, a small village with a number of restaurants. I prefer to stay in this village outside Huelva rather than at one of the more impersonal hotels in the city center. You're within easy distance of the Parque Nacional de Doñana and the associations with Christopher Columbus. Even if you're just driving around the area, consider a lunch stop here. The chef specializes in regional dishes, including stuffed baby squid.

Carretera de San Juan del Puerto a Matalascañas s/n, 21130 Mazagón. ✆ **95-953-63-00.** Fax 95-953-62-28. www.parador.es. 63 units. 148€–171€ double; 221€–255€ suite. AE, DC, MC, V. Free parking. Exit from Mazagón's eastern sector, following the signs to the town of Matalascañas. Take the coast road (Hwy 442) to the parador. **Amenities:** Restaurant; bar; lounge; limited room service; babysitting; gym; Jacuzzi; outdoor pool; indoor pool; outdoor unlit tennis court; sauna; nonsmoking rooms; rooms for those w/limited mobility. *In room:* A/C, TV, dataport, hair dryer, minibar.

Where to Dine

El Paraíso ★ 🍴 ANDALUSIAN   This restaurant on the road from Huelva to El Portil is not easy to find, but it's well worth hunting down as it serves some of the finest meals in the province. The fish dishes are some of the freshest in the area, especially *lubina a la sal*, sea bass cooked in a salt crust (removed before serving) to seal in the juices. Sea bass is also served with a bay leaf-flavored sauce. Several rice dishes are popular with local foodies, including a favorite of fresh crab with vegetables grown in the province. The catch of the day can be ordered grilled (*a la brasa*) or with garlic (*al ajillo*). Meat eaters will enjoy the juicy steaks, and the reliable dessert menu features homemade sweets, including the special pine-nut-and-chocolate cheesecake.

Carretera de Huelva/El Portil, Punta Umbría. ✆ **95-931-27-56.** Reservations recommended. Main courses 18€–24€. AE, DC, MC, V. Daily 12:30–5pm and 8:30pm–midnight. From Huelva, follow the signs to Punta Umbría and cross the bridge over the Odiel River. Continue toward Punta Umbría, passing under 2 bridges. At the 2nd bridge, turn right for 1km (.6 mile) until you come to the restaurant. It's on the other side of the road, but you can double-back using the roundabout just after it.

Las Meigas GALICIAN/BASQUE   This modern restaurant combines two of Spain's best northern cuisines in a far-southern setting—a real change of pace from typical Andalusian fare. In front of Plaza América, it's decorated in a typical rustic-tavern style, with wooden furniture, candles, and glass. In a town not noted for first-class restaurants, Las Meigas's fine food and total lack of pretension stand out. I like the fried sea bass flavored with lots of garlic and parsley, and scampi with local ham and a white sauce. One regional dish on the menu is a platter of small squid flavored with their own *tinta* (ink) and cooked with rice. A Basque classic is the hake (*merluza*) with potatoes, garlic, pepper, and olive oil. Desserts are made fresh daily.

Av. Guatemala 44. ✆ **95-928-48-58.** Reservations recommended. Main courses 12€–18€. AE, DC, MC, V. Daily 1–4pm and 8pm–midnight.

Portichuelo ★ANDALUSIAN   Bright, modern, and busy, this is, in my opinion, the best restaurant in town. Run by the local Gomez family, it's been going for 12 years and has a good local reputation, hosting actors, politicians, and businesspeople. There's a tapas bar at the front and stylish restaurant behind, but on a warm sunny day I prefer to sit at a table in the pretty square outside. Food is no-nonsense stuff, well prepared with fresh local ingredients. Shellfish dishes are always good, particularly the prawns. If you're feeling more experimental, see if they have *navajas* (razorfish) or *carillada* (slow-cooked pig's cheek) on the menu. The tapas bar is great fun in the evenings so come here for a drink and a snack if not for a full meal.

Calle Vazquez Lopez 15. ✆ **95-924-57-68.** Reservations recommended. Main courses 7€–17€. Set menus from 36€ to 58€. MC, V. Daily 10:30am–5:30pm and Mon–Sat 8:30pm–midnight.

10 Huelva after Dark

On a tapas-crawl through the Old Town, stop in at **Taberna El Condado,** Sor Angela de la Cruz 3 (✆ **95-926-11-23**), a rustic tavern beloved by locals, a stone's throw from the Hotel Eurostars Tartessos. Here you can enjoy fried hake, succulent hams, salmon, and various meat dishes, including meatballs. Tapas and *raciónes* range from 3€ to 18€. It's open Tuesday to Sunday 8pm to 1am, closing for 15 days in August (dates vary). Next head for **Portichuelo** (see "Where to Dine" above) which has great tapas as well as being a good restaurant. A 5-minute walk down towards the river brings you to **La Pandorga,** Calle Marina 24 (✆ **95-925-15-69**), a friendly local tapas bar doing modern interpretations of regional favorites like seafood rice cakes and cod-stuffed Spanish tortilla. Tapas cost between 2€ and 3€. It's open Monday to Friday 1:30 to 5:30pm and 8:30 to 11:30pm and Saturdays 1:30 to 7pm.

If you want to mix with young funky people, head for the cool confines of **Casona,** Alameda Sundheim 11 (no phone), a trendy garden lounge bar and club with white leather sofas, plasma screens, and flower murals on the walls. Music tends to be chill-out, electronica in style with a smattering of disco thrown in. It's right opposite the NH Luz hotel and is open Monday to Friday 8pm 'til late. At weekends it opens at 4pm and goes on 'til the last person leaves. No cover charge; beers cost 5€, spirits 8€.

SIDE TRIPS FROM HUELVA

The coastal areas of the Costa de la Luz east and west of Huelva are more intriguing than the industrialized city itself. You can head west toward the Portuguese border and the frontier town of Ayamonte and some of the region's nicest beaches, or east to explore the Cota de Doñana National Park, Spain's largest wildlife reserve.

Ayamonte

Built on the slopes of a hill on which a castle-fortress once stood, Ayamonte is a sleepy little place with an attractive Old Town and a marina, 37km (22 miles) east of Huelva via the A-49/E-1. There's a bit of a British expat vibe to the place and as a result more people speak English in the bars and shops than you'd normally expect in a Spanish town of this size. It also has more of a Portuguese flavor than any other in Andalusia. That's perfectly understandable since Portugal, or more specifically the unremarkable town of Vila Real de Santo Antonio, is only a short ferry ride away. Ferries leave every 30 minutes throughout the day from 9:30am to 8:30pm, charging 1.85€ for a one-way passage and taking just 10 minutes. Ferries depart from the riverside promenade, Muelle de Portugal, in Ayamonte (© **95-947-06-17**). Motorists can drive across the International Bridge over the Guadiana.

If you don't drive from Huelva to Ayamonte, take one of the frequent buses connecting the two. Buses depart the main bus station at Huelva (see Huelva "Getting There") at the rate of about one an hour during the day and arrive in Ayamonte at the station at Avenida Cayetano Feu s/n (© **90-211-44-29**) east of the town center. There are also four buses daily between Ayamonte and Isla Cristina (three at weekends). The **tourist office** at Calle Huelva 27 (© **95-932-07-37;** www.ayto-ayamonte.es) can provide bus timetables, but they aren't particularly helpful for much else. It's open Monday to Friday from 10am to 8pm and Saturday from 10am to 2pm.

There's not much in the way of sightseeing in Ayamonte. You're best off enjoying the atmospheric Old Town with its warren of narrow streets centered around **Paseo de la Ribera,** the principal square, where there are several nice tapas bars for a relaxed drink and a bite. If you want to see some historic sites, try ducking into the **Iglesia de San Francisco** on Calle San Francisco to see its stunning Mudéjar *artesonado* ceiling. The church dates from 1521 and was declared a landmark in 1935. Its chief artistic treasure is an altarpiece from the 16th century. Unfortunately it's only open on Friday afternoons and Sunday mornings. If you continue on the same street up a steep, quite long hill, you reach pretty **Iglesia de San Salvador,** dating from the 15th century. You can climb its tower (if it's open) for a panoramic view of the town, the river, and the Algarve coast of Portugal to the west. Opening hours are pretty erratic here too, but the views from in front of the church out across the estuary make it worth the trek.

Most visitors spend little time in Ayamonte and head instead to its major beach, **Playa Isla Canela** ★, 7km (4⅓ miles) to the south. Buses from Ayamonte run there, departing summers-only from the Paseo de la Ribera. You can pick up timetables from the tourist office. If Isla Canela is too crowded, you can continue eastward to another good beach, **Playa Punta del Moral.** The beaches here open onto calm waters because of sandbars 50 to 100m (164–328 ft) from the shore. These sandbars become virtual islands at low tide.

The tapas bars in the old fishing village of **Punta del Moral,** slightly to the north of Ayamonte, are very popular with locals and rightly so. Fresh fish is the way to go here. You'll also find plenty of places for lunch in Ayamonte, most clustered around Paseo de la Ribera in the heart of town. Go for the *raciones* of Jabugo ham and the fresh fish based on the catch of the day. The best seafood in town is served at **Casa Luciano,** Calle del Condado 1 (© **95-947-10-71;** www.casaluciano.com). It's tucked away on the ground floor of a rather uninspiring apartment block across the harbor from Paseo de la Ribera. The dining here is fairly standard Andalusian fare, with well-prepared classics like oxtail alongside slightly more interesting seafood dishes like shrimp and ham-stuffed squid, but I recommend keeping it simple and going for fresh fish of the day oven-baked or grilled. It's open Monday to Saturday 1 to 4pm and 8 to 11:30pm. An alternative is to head up the hill out of town to the **Parador de Ayamonte** and eat at the restaurant there, where you can enjoy expansive views whilst you dine. Or for something a little more classy, try the **Vincci Seleccion Canela Golf Resort'**s in-house restaurant (see below).

WHERE TO STAY & DINE

Hotel Riavela   This is the oldest and most traditional hotel in Ayamonte, and if you're on a budget it's the one to go for. It's clean, but don't expect too much. These days the place feels a bit rundown and unloved, and it's a good 15-minute walk into the Old Town. The better rooms open onto balconies with town views. Rooms are midsized and furnished simply with handcrafted Andalusian wooden pieces. No meals other than breakfast are served. The parador (see above) is far better if you can afford it.

Calle Canto de la Villa s/n, 21400 Ayamonte. ✆ **95-947-19-19.** Fax 95-947-19-29. www.hotelriavela. com. 25 units. 52€–72€ double. AE, MC, V. **Amenities:** Breakfast room. *In room:* A/C, TV.

Parador de Ayamonte ★★ ✦   Without doubt the best hotel in Ayamonte, this parador opened in 1966 and was built in a modern style typical of the time. It boasts Nordic-inspired furnishings with lots of pinewood paneling. Most rooms are medium in size, comfortably appointed, and include tiled bathrooms. Perched on top of the hill on the outskirts of town, on the site of the old castle of Ayamonte, it has sweeping views of the river, the road suspension bridge into Portugal, and the surrounding towns. A sunset drink by the pool here is hard to beat. The in-house restaurant is quite impressive, serving well-cooked local favorites like squid with broad beans and paprika-spiced ray, so even if you don't stay here, consider it for lunch or dinner. The parador is located on the main road into town from the autoroute.

Av. de la Constitución s/n, 21400 Ayamonte. ✆ **95-932-07-00.** Fax 95-902-20-19. www.parador.es. 54 units. 104€–137€ double; 187€–242€ suite. AE, DC, MC, V. Free parking. **Amenities:** Restaurant; bar; babysitting; outdoor pool; room service; nonsmoking rooms; rooms for those w/limited mobility; Wi-Fi. *In room:* A/C, TV, hair dryer, minibar.

Vincci Seleccion Canela Golf Resort ★★   Forty kilometers (25 miles) west of Huelva, and about a 10-minute drive out of Ayamonte, this is one of the nicest resorts along the Costa de la Luz, featuring an 18-hole golf course set against a backdrop of orange, olive, and eucalyptus trees with sloping sand dunes. Built near an estuary of the Guadiana River, this modern hotel with traditional architectural design was created specifically for golf tourism, but it's quite popular with couples looking for a spot of peace and relaxation away from busy Huelva and Seville. The attractive structure evokes an elegant Portuguese country house, with Andalusian motifs and faux Arab stucco. The course is carefully tended and is more or less flat, with furrowed pathways that wind around the dune-like contours. The lakes and water traps are natural canals and marshes, with the local flora and fauna left intact.

Bedrooms are spacious and luxurious, each with a beautiful tiled bathroom. Beds are really comfortable, and I think the food here is even better than at the parador.

Golf Norte, Carretera de Isla Canela s/n, 21409 Ayamonte. (© **95-947-78-30.** Fax 95-947-78-31. www. vinccihoteles.com. 58 units. 170€–300€ double. AE, DC, MC, V. **Amenities:** Restaurant; bar; coffee shop; beauty salon; fitness center; 18-hole golf course; outdoor pool; sauna; steam bath; room service; non-smoking rooms. *In room:* A/C, TV, hair dryer, minibar, Wi-Fi.

Isla Cristina

As the name suggests, this attractive little holiday town was once an island. Today, however, landfill has linked it to the mainland. It is 8km (5 miles) east of Ayamonte and 55km (34 miles) west of Huelva. Enveloped by tidal estuaries, the beach at Isla Cristina is today flanked with blocks of holiday apartments, many owned by Sevillanos who flock here in July and August. The fishing port—the second most important in Huelva province—supplies fish to Córdoba and Seville, even Madrid.

Development along the coastline here has been low key. Hotels and apartment buildings are set back a short way from the town's main beach (Playa de la Gaviota), which is backed by wild, slightly windswept dunes. There's a pleasant boardwalk starting at the bottom of Calle Arquitecto Aramburu Maqua which you can stroll along through the dunes from one end of the beach to the other. An even better beach, **Playa Central,** is 2km (1¼ miles) east of the center. This whole stretch of coast east from Isla Cristina features some of the region's most attractive and undeveloped beaches, some 29km (18 miles) of golden sands. It's easy to explore them using local bus services (see below).

In the heart of the village itself, life centers on attractive Plaza de las Flores. To the southeast of this square is the helpful **tourist office,** Calle San Francisco 12 (© **95-933-26-94;** www.islacristina.org), open Monday to Friday 10am to 2pm and 5:30 to 7:30pm, Saturday and Sunday 10am to 2pm from March 1 to October 31. Frequent buses from the main bus station in Huelva arrive at the bus terminal along Ronda Norte. Hourly local buses connect from here to the beach and on to some of the other nice stretches of sand farther along the coast. There are also four buses daily between Ayamonte and Isla Cristina (three at weekends).

The town, especially in summer, is filled with little fish eateries and tapas joints, some of which come and go with the seasons. For more substantial dining, sample the menus at the restaurants of the two hotels below.

For tapas before dinner, head to the northwest point of town, a peninsula between the harbor and the Plaza de las Flores. Walk the pretty narrow, cobblestone streets flanked by whitewashed homes of Cristina's fishing colony. You'll find many bars serving freshly made tapas in this area, some with outdoor patios. Flamenco can be heard at some of these taverns in summer, when visitors pile into town.

WHERE TO STAY & DINE

Hotel Barcelo Cristina ★ ☺   Right on the beach, this modern resort hotel offers every amenity and is the best equipped of the accommodation options in Isla Cristina. Rooms are spacious, many with king-size beds and balconies with sea views. Furniture is simple but comfortable. There's a good-sized outdoor pool surrounded by palm trees with a poolside bar and shaded patio areas for relaxing out of the sun. Parents really appreciate the childcare facilities which include Barcy Camp for older kids. They get to camp out for the night in the hotel gardens in a specially constructed kids' camp tent. A range of family apartments and family rooms is available too.

Calle Doctor Delgado Carrasco, s/n. 21410. Isla Cristina. ✆ **95-962-11-00.** Fax 95 933-02-28. 200 units. 72€–170€ double; 86€–190€ apartments. Parking 9.50€. AE, DC, MC, V. **Amenities:** Restaurant; bar; babysitting; gym; kid's club; outdoor pool; room service. *In room:* A/C, TV, hair dryer, minibar, Wi-Fi. Minimum 3-night stay during peak summer season.

Hotel Plata Isla Cristina   Near the beach, this was the first hotel to open at Isla Cristina, and it remains a favorite for regular visitors. For most of its life, it was known as Los Geranios, and it retains its predecessor's physical appearance, with architecture evoking the late 1960s (no great compliment). The midsize rooms are, however, attractively and comfortably furnished, mostly with rustic wooden pieces and flowery fabrics. The restaurant offers an array of tasty regional specialties costing from 35€.

Av. de la Playa, 21410 Isla Cristina. ✆ **95-933-18-00.** Fax 95-933-19-50. 36 units. 50€–80€ double. AE, DC, MC, V. **Amenities:** Restaurant; bar; babysitting; outdoor pool; room service. *In room:* A/C, TV, hair dryer, Wi-Fi.

Paraíso Playa ✔   Opening onto the fishing port, this seaside, two-story house with yellow walls and a stone fence opened in 1972, two years after Los Geranios (Hotel Plata Isla Cristina; see below) launched tourism on the island. I think it's slightly nicer than the Plata, keeping up with the times a little better, each year undergoing minor renovations to keep it in top form. Well run and with a good staff, the hotel offers smallish bedrooms furnished with light wood pieces; each comes with a tiled bathroom. There's a small swimming pool and shady patio too. Book early in July and August. The restaurant serves very good and very fresh fish dishes, usually relying on the catch of the day. Meals begin at 19€.

Av. de la Playa, 21410 Isla Cristina. ✆ **95-933-02-35.** Fax 95-934-37-45. www.hotelparaisoplaya.com. 40 units. 55€–115€ double. AE, DC, MC, V. Closed Dec 15–Jan 15. **Amenities:** Restaurant; bar; outdoor pool. *In room:* A/C, TV.

Coto de Doñana National Park ★★★

Covering some 55,000 hectares (136, 000 acres), the **Coto de Doñana National Park** is one of Spain's largest wildlife reserves and one of the continent's last great wildernesses. At an estuary of the Guadalquivir River, it is also one of the world's greatest wetland sites for migrating birds. Bird-watchers by the thousands flock here in spring when hundreds of flocks of breeding birds fly in to nest in the wetlands. In all, there are over 300 different species of birds, including colonies of storks, buzzards, kites, kestrels, and egrets, plus 33 species of mammals, 12 species of fish, and 18 species of reptiles. There have even been sightings of the Spanish imperial eagle. Mammals on the verge of extinction, including a rare lynx, also live here. Wild boar can be seen in the *marismas* (swamps).

There are five visitor centers around the edge of the park. The best **bird-watching** base is the village of **El Rocío** on the northwestern edge of the marshes. The marshes and pinewoods here teem with honking wild geese and white storks. The closest visitor center to here is at **La Rocina** (✆ **95-944-23-40**), less than 2km (1 mile) west of El Rocío. A 3.5km (2-mile) boardwalk has been built through the wetlands, taking you through thick reed beds and dense scrubland. It also has several hides to look for birds over the final section of the La Rocina stream. Along the way you might encounter such birds as egrets, herons, and ibis. Don't forget to bring some binoculars. The center is open daily from 9am to 2pm and 3 to 9pm. Free maps are provided. Several companies offer 4WD jeep tours from El Rocío which typically last around 4 hours. These need to be booked in advance. The best operator is **Discovering Doñana** (𝄞 **95-944-24-66;** www.discoveringdonana.com). They can also provide guided walking tours and Jose, the director, is a real authority on the birds of the park too.

There's another information center at **El Palacio de Acebrón** (𝄞 **95-950-61-62**), 5km (3 miles) to the west of La Rocina with the same opening hours. This remarkable former hunting lodge has an exhibition tracing the history of the park. Bring a picnic as this is an ideal spot for lunch. From the car park here you can do a short 1.5 km (.9-mile) long circular walking trail that winds its way through an outstanding mosaic of cork oak forests, reed beds, pine forests, and the thickest riverbank forests.

From La Rocina, a drive of 9km (5½ miles) will take you west to the **Centro Recepción del Acebuche** (𝄞 **95-943-04-32**), the park's main interpretive center housed in a lovely old Andalusian hacienda. It's open daily June to September from 8am to 9pm; October to May daily 8am to 7pm. Here you'll find a restaurant, a souvenir shop, a video room, and an exhibition room. This is the best place to get books and other printed material on Doñana. From here you can do a 4.5 km (6-mile) signposted trail path that offers wide views over the lagoons and shady sections through the pine forests. There are longer walking trails through the park for more serious hikers and certain trails that require you to walk with a guide. Ask at the center for more information or contact Discovering Doñana (see above).

Jeep tours, which must be reserved in advance, depart from Acebuche as well, conducted by local cooperative group **Marismas del Rocío** (𝄞 **95-943-04-32;** www.donanavisitas.es). They typically cost 26€ per person and last 4 hours. In winter, tours depart daily (except Mondays) at 8:30am and 3pm and in summer, daily (except Sundays) at 8:30am and 5pm. The tours take you through an area of the park stretching for 70km (43 miles) across scrubland, sand dunes, salt marshes, and beaches. Bring a pair of binoculars. In summer most of the birds disappear when the marshes dry up. In their place you'll see grazing horses and deer.

To reach Acebuche, drive 12km (7½ miles) south on the A-483 from El Rocío, and then go for 1.6km (1 mile) west (it's signposted).

Continue on the same road past Acebuche to reach the **Mundo Marino Eco Museum,** Avenida de las Adelfas s/n (𝄞 **95-944-80-86**) at Matalascañas. A guided tour costing 4€ takes you through five themed rooms showing the different ecosystems and ethnographical features along the coast of Doñana, from shifting dunes to unspoiled beaches with annual whale appearances. Kids will find the full-size whale skeletons particularly exciting. Close by at the eastern end of Matalascañas, behind the Gran Hotel El Coto, there's a car park next to the beach from where you can take a short 1.5 km (.9-mile) boardwalk through the dunes which represent a completely different biosphere. The trail takes you through the whole process of the creation of the marching dunes from the sandy white beaches to the pine forests between dunes. It's also possible to do horse riding excursions along the beach here.

WHERE TO STAY & DINE

El Cortijo de Los Mimbrales ★★ 🎁 Three kilometers (1¾ miles) southwest of Rocío on 1,000 hectares (2,471 acres) of flatlands mostly devoted to farming and the cultivation of citrus crops, this is the best place to stay in the park. It's a sprawling compound of attractive white-walled, tile-roofed cottages along walkways lined with trees. Decor focuses on rustic, historic earthy farm implements and terracotta. Thick masonry walls and ample use of tiles and stone, plus occasional splashes of bright, vibrant color, especially ocher and blue, give a rustic charm and tranquility A few of the cottages and villas on site are privately owned. Those available to guests are clean, functional, and cozy, albeit a bit sunbaked and dusty during the summer months. For those hot sunny days, there's a large outdoor pool, surrounded by leafy gardens, perfect for cooling off. During the Rocío Feria, the area's biggest folkloric and religious event, the hacienda can be crowded and boisterous. Otherwise, it's quiet, restrained, and committed to exposing the natural beauty of the surrounding park. Don't come expecting nightlife or entertainment other than walks and horse-back riding, which can be arranged on the fringes of the park.

The in-house restaurant prepares a hearty mix of regional and international cuisine, specializing in duck prepared with local oranges; at least three kinds of local saltwater fish, either grilled or baked in salt crusts; freshwater crayfish with local wines; and roasted goat in the style of Segovia.

Carretera Rocío a Matalascañas, A-483 Km 30, 21750 Almonte. ✆ **95-944-22-37.** Fax 95-944-24-43. www.cortijomimbrales.com. 41 units. 100€–165€ double; 200€–380€ cottages. Rates include breakfast. Rates are higher during Christmas, Holy Week, and the Rocío Feria. AE, DC, MC, V. **Amenities:** Restaurant; bar; outdoor pool; golfing at a site 11km (6¾ miles) away; horseback riding; mountain bike rentals. *In room:* A/C, TV, hair dryer, minibar.

THE COSTA DEL SOL

The mild winter climate and almost-guaranteed summer sunshine make this stretch of Mediterranean shoreline, known as the **Costa del Sol (Sunshine Coast),** a year-round destination. From the harbor city of Algeciras, it stretches east to the port city of Almería. Sandwiched in between is a steep, rugged coastline set against the Sierra Nevada. You'll find poor-to-fair beaches, sandy coves, whitewashed houses, olive trees, lots of new apartment houses, fishing boats, golf courses, resort hotels, souvenir stands, fast-food outlets, and a wide variety of visitors.

This coastal strip no longer enjoys the chic reputation it had in Franco's day. It's overbuilt and spoiled in some places, though you can still find posh sections like Puerto Banús.

Today, frankly, the coast is better for **golf** than for beaches. The best resorts are **Los Monteros** (② 95-286-11-99) in Marbella, the leading course; **Hotel Atalaya Park** in Estepona (② 95-288-90-00); and **Golf Hotel Guadalmina** in Marbella (② 95-288-22-11). To learn more, pick up a copy of the monthly magazine *Costa Golf* at any newsstand. Many golfers prefer to play a different course at every hotel. Usually, if you notify your hotel reception desk a day in advance, a staff member can arrange a playing time.

Water-skiing and windsurfing are available in many resorts, and all types of boats can be rented from various kiosks at all the main beaches. You don't have to search hard for these outfitters—chances are they'll find you.

From June to October the coast is mobbed, so make your hotel reservations in advance. At other times innkeepers are likely to roll out the red carpet as there's an oversupply of hotel rooms that's been exacerbated by the economic downturn.

Many restaurants close around October 15 for a much-needed vacation. Remember, too, that many supermarkets and other facilities are closed on Sunday.

ALGECIRAS

679km (422 miles) S of Madrid, 132km (82 miles) W of Málaga

Not really a destination in itself, Algeciras is a refueling stop on the way to **Tangier** in Morocco or to chicer oases like **Marbella** to the east. Algeciras can also be a base for day trips to **Gibraltar** (discussed below). If you don't have time to visit "the Rock," you can at least see it from Algeciras—it's only 10km (6 miles) away.

Despite an intriguing history, there is very little of interest here. Near the southern tip of Iberia, Algeciras was once the ancient Roman port of Portus Albo. In 713 it was refounded by the Moorish invaders. In 1344 Alfonso XI of Castile recaptured it in the name of the Christians, but it was destroyed once again by Mohammed V of Granada in 1368.

Today little remains from all these conquerors, and, in fact, Algeciras's architecture is some of the most undistinguished of any port its size along the Costa del Sol. Franco's dream was to turn the dreary port into a commercial hub to dwarf Gibraltar's success. (Of course, his ultimate goal was to force Her Majesty's Army out of Iberia.) He set about building ugly concrete bunker-type architecture and ill-conceived high-rises that remain to this day. As do the British, who still house their troops on Gibraltar.

If you're waiting for a boat and have time to spare, head for **La Plaza Alta,** the orange tree-lined square with a fountain in the center of town. Dating from 1807, the square boasts two churches, **Iglesia de Nuestra Señora de la Palma,** constructed in 1723, and the **Capilla de Nuestra Señora de Europa,** constructed sometime in the 1700s. A short walk along Calle Alfonso XI brings you to the site of some recent excavations of the old town walls and the shady and attractive **Parque Maria Christina**, with palm trees, fountains, and benches.

If you have more time to spare, head for the nearest good beach. The best one is **Playa de Getares,** 5km (3 miles) south of the port. It's unattractively built up, but the sands are golden and stretch for some 3km (2 miles).

Essentials

GETTING THERE & AROUND   The local RENFE office is at the top of Calle Juan de la Cierva (© 90-232-03-20; www.renfe.es). From Madrid, two **trains** daily make the 5½ hour trip; the fare is 64.50€. From Málaga, you have to transfer in Bobadillo or Antequera; typical journey time is 5 hours.

Various independent **bus companies** serve Algeciras, with buses arriving at the main bus station at Calle San Bernardo 1, 1½ blocks to the left when you exit the port complex, right next to the rail station. **Empresa Portillo** (© 90-245-05-50; www.ctsa-portillo.com) runs eight buses a day along the Costa del Sol to Algeciras from Málaga (3 hr). It also sends one bus a day to Córdoba (6 hr) and two buses a day to Granada (5 hr). To make connections to or from Seville and Jerez, use **Linesur,** Calle San Bernardo s/n (© 95-666-76-49; www.linesur.com). Eight buses a day go to Jerez de la Frontera (75 min) and continue on to Seville (2½ hr). **Transportes Generales Comes** (© 95-665-34-56; www.tgcomes.es) sells tickets to **La Línea,** the border station for the approach to Gibraltar.

By **road,** the high-speed toll highway (AP-7/E-15) runs from Málaga west to just past Estepona where you take the A-7 to Algeciras. If you're driving south from

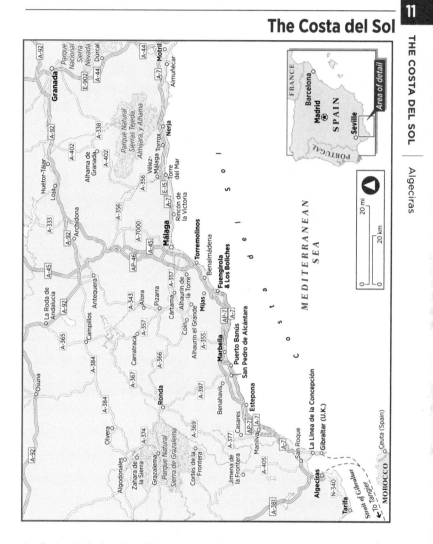

Seville (or Madrid), take toll highway AP-4/E-5 to just before Cádiz and then connect with the A-381 southwest to Algeciras.

Most visitors in Algeciras plan to cross to Tangier, Morocco. Two companies offer **ferry** crossings. **Transmediterranea** (© **90-245-46-45;** www.transmediterranea. es) has six high-speed crossings a day, which take about an hour to do the journey. Typical prices are 50€ return for foot passengers and 200€ return for two passengers and a car. **Comarit Espana,** Estación Marítima (© **95-663-41-49;** www.comarit. es) has 13 daily sailings at 2-hour intervals. Prices are similar at 40€ return for foot passengers and add another 130€ return if you take a car.

TEEING OFF: A golden TRIANGLE OF GOLF

Faced with more than 40 places to take a swing on the Costa del Sol, golfers are often overwhelmed by the choice of courses, many of which are championship venues. Here's a trio of courses that rank among the greatest in Europe—no apologies to Scotland.

o **San Roque Golf & Country Club,** Urbanización San Roque, Carretera A-7 Km 127, Sotogrande-San Roque (© **95-661-30-30;** www. sanroqueclub.com), was created by two Englishmen, former Ryder Cup players Tony Jacklin and Dave Thomas, on the grounds of the summer palace of the Domecq sherry dynasty. The back 9 features two of the finest holes along the coast.

o **Club de Golf Valderrama,** Av. de los Cortijos s/n, Sotogrande-San Roque (© **95-679-12-00;** www. valderrama.com), is currently *número uno* among the golf courses of the Costa del Sol.

Golf World called it "daring, dramatic, demanding". The course was first designed by the grand old man himself, Robert Trent Jones, Sr. Seve Ballesteros (the "Arnold Palmer of Spain") designed the notorious 17th hole, which Ryder Cup players describe as "one of the most strategically challenging holes in the world." Pines and cork trees keep this par-72 course wickedly challenging.

o **Real Club de Golf Sotogrande,** Paseo del Parque, Sotogrande (© **95-277-77-77;** www.golf sotogrande.com), is a par-72 course also laid out originally by Robert Trent Jones, Sr. Its 11th hole is buffeted by two prevailing winds blowing in different directions. Many of the fairways are 40 to 50 yards long, and the course is riddled with shimmering lakes evocative of Florida.

VISITOR INFORMATION The **tourist office**, located just off the port at Juan de la Cierva (© **95-678-41-31;** www.andalusia.org) is, in theory, open Monday and Tuesday 9am to 3:30pm, Wednesday to Thursday 9am to 3:30pm and 4 to 7pm, Saturday and Sunday from 10am to 2pm. However, when I arrived at 5pm on a Wednesday it was shut.

Where to Stay

AC Algeciras ★ ⚭ There are a lot of seedy joints in Algeciras where you can lay your head. This newly constructed hotel isn't one of them. It's the most modern and up to date in town. In front of the Puerto Marítimo, it's only 1km (½ mile) from the city center. Modern rooms are comfortable, and the hotel is well maintained. Most guests are in Algeciras just to wait for the ferry to Tangier. Rooms are midsize to spacious, with large bathrooms, and most of the rooms open onto views of Gibraltar.

Calle Hermanos Portilla s/n, 11204 Algeciras. © **95-663-50-60.** Fax 95-663-30-61. www.achotels.com. 108 units. 60€–112€ double; 78€–126€ suite. AE, DC, MC, V. Parking 11€. **Amenities:** Restaurant; babysitting; fitness center; nonsmoking rooms; room service; solarium; Turkish bath; rooms for those w/limited mobility. *In room:* A/C, TV, hair dryer, minibar, Wi-Fi.

Alborán ★ 👜 One of the best nearby hotels is 4km (2½ miles) east of Algeciras along the A-7 with a good beach a 2-minute walk from the grounds. Dating from 1990, the hotel is attractive architecturally, built in typical Andalusian style with patios and Mozarabic motifs. Rooms are flooded with sunlight and comfortably furnished, each with a modern tiled bathroom. Lots of plants and flowers make for an inviting ambience.

Alamo, 11205 Algeciras. 📞 **95-663-28-70.** Fax 95-663-23-20. www.hotelesalboran.com. 79 units. 64€–126€ double. AE, DC, MC, V. **Amenities:** Restaurant; bar; babysitting; nonsmoking rooms; room service; solarium. *In room:* A/C, TV, hair dryer.

Don Manuel 🍴 Because of its central location, the Don Manuel is ideal for quick getaways if you have to catch an early boat. Built in 1992 in the style of a guesthouse or small inn, its bedrooms are small but comfortably and tastefully furnished, with slightly cramped bathrooms. There's not much in the way of facilities or amenities, but at these prices, no one complains.

Segismundo Moret 4, 11201 Algeciras. 📞 **95-663-46-06.** Fax 95-663-47-16. 15 units. 45€–57€ double. AE, DC, MC, V. *In room:* A/C, TV, hair dryer (in some).

📎 BEACHES: THE good, THE BAD & THE NUDE

It would be good to report that the Costa del Sol is a paradise for swimmers and sunbathers. But actually, it's not really; although it was the allure of beaches that originally put the "sol" in the Costa del Sol in the 1950s.

The worst beaches—mainly pebbles and shingles—are at Nerja, Málaga, and Almuñécar. Moving westward, you encounter the gritty, grayish sands of Torremolinos. The best beaches here are at El Bajondillo and La Carihuela (which borders an old fishing village). Another good stretch of beach is along the meandering strip between Carvajal, Los Boliches, and Fuengirola. In addition, two good beaches—El Faro and La Fontanilla—are on either side of Marbella. However, all these beaches tend to be overcrowded, especially in July and August. Crowding is worst on Sunday from May to October when beaches are overrun with family picnickers and sunbathers.

All public beaches in Spain are free; many have toilets and showers and the more popular ones usually have lifeguards on patrol. You'll often find small fish restaurants (*chiringuitos*) on the beaches too, often serving better, fresher seafood than you'll find in more upmarket restaurants elsewhere.

The Spanish have a pretty relaxed attitude to nudity on beaches. Many women go topless and nudity is quite common on some of the less frequented beaches. Some naturist beaches are officially designated and signposted as such by local councils. However, there are many other "tolerated" beaches, where people traditionally sunbathe nude, and at these you tend a get a total live-and-let-live mix of sunbathers: topless, swimsuited, and nudist. If you want to bare it all, head for the **Costa Natura**, about 3km (2 miles) west of Estepona. This was Spain's first official nudist resort, opening in 1979. Other popular nudist beaches on the Costa del Sol include **Playa de las Dunas**, Cabopino near Marbella a long sandy nudist beach backed by dunes and pine trees, and Benalnatura, a tiny naturist paradise near the casino in **Benalmádena**. There are showers, toilets, a barbecue area, and a great little *chiringuito*.

Hotel Al-Mar ★ The government-rated three-star Al-Mar is one of the best choices in town, with rooms recently renovated. It's very near the port, where the ferries leave for Ceuta and Tangier. This large hotel boasts blue-and-white Sevillian and Moorish decor. The midsize guest rooms are well maintained and furnished in an Andalusian style, with good beds and bathrooms. A fourth-floor drawing room provides a panoramic view of the Rock.

Av. de la Marina 2–3, 11201 Algeciras. ✆ **95-665-46-61.** Fax 95-665-45-01. www.hotelalmar.com. 192 units. 87€–94€ double; 88€–95€ junior suite. Rates include buffet breakfast. AE, DC, MC, V. Parking 7.50€. **Amenities:** Restaurant; bar; rooms for those w/limited mobility. *In room:* A/C, TV.

Hotel Reina Cristina ★ In its own park on the southern outskirts of the city (a 10-minute walk south of the rail and bus stations), this is the town's leading hotel, having hosted over the years everyone from Sir Winston Churchill to Franklin D. Roosevelt, along with World War II spies. It's a Victorian building with turrets, ornate railings, a pastel-painted facade, and a view of the faraway Rock of Gibraltar. There's a small English-language library and a semitropical garden. The comfortable, high-ceilinged rooms have excellent furnishings and comfortable beds and bathrooms.

Paseo de la Conferencia s/n, 11207 Algeciras. ✆ **95-660-26-22.** Fax 95-660-33-23. www.reinacristina. es. 188 units. 93€–107€ double; 175€–259€ suite. Rates include breakfast. AE, DC, MC, V. Free parking. **Amenities:** 2 restaurants; 2 bars; 2 pools; room service; sauna; tennis courts; Internet. *In room:* A/C, TV, hair dryer (in some).

Where to Dine

Because Algeciras is not known for its restaurants, many visitors dine at their hotels instead of taking a chance at the dreary little spots along the waterfront.

Montes SPANISH/ANDALUSIAN This is just a little port-side eatery, but it's the most popular and serviceable place in town. Throughout the afternoon and deep into the night, the casual diner is filled with foreign travelers, most either returning from or going to Morocco on one of the ferries. You can fill up on nearly 30 varieties of freshly made tapas, most of them fish or vegetable based. The fresh catch of the day is always on the menu, fried or stewed. The chef's specialties include paella with shellfish. Of the meat dishes, the baby beef roast is the perennial favorite.

Calle Juan Morrison 27. ✆ **95-665-42-07.** Main courses 12€–18€. MC, V. Daily noon–5pm and 7pm–midnight.

GIBRALTAR

20km (12 miles) E of Algeciras, 77km (48 miles) SW of Marbella

Where else would you find a town that is also a country? The smallest self-governing territory in the world, Gibraltar is only 5.8 sq. km (2¼ sq. miles) in size, but it has its own airport, currency, postage stamps, newspapers, radio, TV, naval and military garrisons, two cathedrals, and a casino. "The Rock" enjoys a pleasant climate and has a recorded history dating from A.D. 711 and traces of cave occupation 40,000 years ago.

The Rock of Gibraltar is a massive limestone rock rising out of the sea to a height of 425m (1,396 ft). It is often referred to as the Gateway to the Mediterranean and was originally a Phoenician trading post called Calpe. In Greek mythology it was the northern bastion of the Pillars of Hercules. Abyla (now Jebel Musa at Ceuta) was

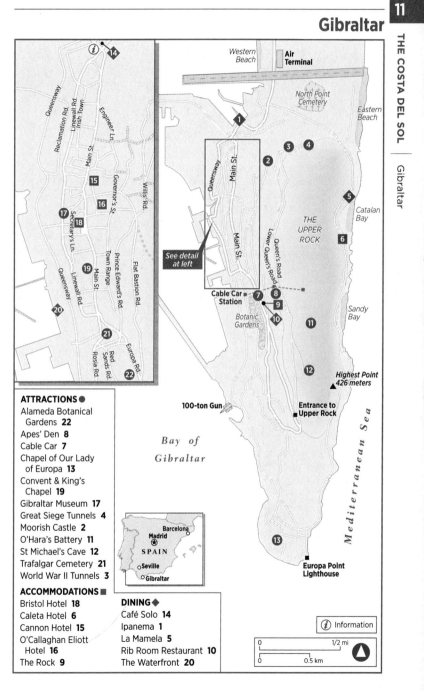

ATTRACTIONS ●
Alameda Botanical
  Gardens **22**
Apes' Den **8**
Cable Car **7**
Chapel of Our Lady
  of Europa **13**
Convent & King's
  Chapel **19**
Gibraltar Museum **17**
Great Siege Tunnels **4**
Moorish Castle **2**
O'Hara's Battery **11**
St Michael's Cave **12**
Trafalgar Cemetery **21**
World War II Tunnels **3**

ACCOMMODATIONS ■
Bristol Hotel **18**
Caleta Hotel **6**
Cannon Hotel **15**
O'Callaghan Eliott
  Hotel **16**
The Rock **9**

DINING ◆
Café Solo **14**
Ipanema **1**
La Mamela **5**
Rib Room Restaurant **10**
The Waterfront **20**

the southern bastion. Hercules is said to have stood with a foot on each "pillar," pushed them apart, and formed a bridge across the straits. When the Phoenicians dominated the Mediterranean, it was recorded that Calpe was the end of the world, the point beyond which no trader should venture.

In 711, a Berber called Tariq ibn-Ziyad landed and named the Rock "Gibel Tarik" (mountain of Tarik), from which the name of Gibraltar is derived. The Rock was captured from the Moors in 1309 by the marauding Guzman El Bueno and then recaptured by the Moors in 1333. In 1462 Spain seized and fortified the Rock against further attack, but in 1704, during the Spanish War of Succession, a joint Anglo-Dutch fleet, under the command of Prince George of Hesse Darnstadt, made a surprise attack, capturing the fortress with little opposition.

The Spanish and the French have since made attempts to conquer the Rock by siege, bombardment, tunneling, and, finally, with specially reinforced ships, which the British set fire to with red-hot cannonballs.

Three treaties have confirmed Gibraltar as a British possession—Utrecht, 1713; Seville, 1727; and Versailles, 1783. In two world wars, the Rock was invaluable in keeping the Mediterranean open in spite of aerial bombardment. Its only land frontier—referred to by many Gibraltarians as the Garlic Wall—was closed by the Spaniards in 1966, in an attempt to enforce Spanish sovereignty on the people. The Spanish finally banned all trade to Gibraltar in 1969 in an attempt to bring further pressure to bear. But the Gibraltarians, in a free vote, decided by 12,138 to 44 to remain under British rule.

The Franco government closed the gate to Gibraltar, creating a blockade and causing hardship for people on both sides of the frontier. The closure lasted from 1969 to 1985. Under King Juan Carlos, the frontier was reopened to visitors entering from Spain. "Gib," its nickname, is today a major offshore financial center.

Three languages are spoken here: English, Spanish, and the local dialect which is a strange combination of the two. The community is made up of Gibraltarians, Britons, Spaniards, and a few Italians and Indians.

The town of Gibraltar is on the west side of the Rock around the harbors. Unlike the rest of the Costa del Sol, which is really only about beaches and golf courses, Gibraltar has historical sites in abundance. Whilst you can visit the top attractions in 3 to 4 hours, many visitors allot a full day or even an overnight stay.

Essentials

GETTING THERE   If you're **driving** to Gibraltar, you arrive first in the Spanish town of La Línea. From the western part of the Costa del Sol, take the A-7/E-15 east toward La Línea, turning south at the signpost into town. If you're in the eastern Costa del Sol, follow the A-7/E-15 southwest to the turnoff for La Línea. Usually it's a quick wave of your passport at the border guards when you reach the border, but avoid rush hour periods when queues can build up on both sides. Most hire companies cover you for taking a car hired in Spain into Gibraltar, but check at the time of hire to be sure. There are no visa requirements for U.S., E.U., or Commonwealth country passport holders.

You can also fly directly from the U.K. to Gibraltar (with no touchdown in Spain). **British Airways** (© **34-90-211-13-33;** www.ba.com) flies daily from London Heathrow, **Monarch Airlines** (© **350-200-411-69;** www.monarch.co.uk) daily from Luton and three times weekly from Manchester, and e**asyJet** (www.easyjet. com) daily from London Gatwick. The flight takes 2½ hours from London. For more information, call **Gibraltar Airport** at ✆ **350-200-730-26.** A brand new airport terminal will be opening in 2012, offering better connections not just for Gibraltar but also the southern part of the Costa del Sol too.

There are no **buses** into Gibraltar from the Costa del Sol. You have to walk across the border and pick up another bus or taxi. However, all the major towns on the coast are linked to La Línea, the Spanish border town. **Empresa Portillo** (✆ **90-245-05-50;** www.ctsa-portillo.com) has regular services to La Línea from points all along the coast including Málaga, Fuengirola, Estepona, and Marbella.

Once across the border, bus no. 9 will take you to the marketplace terminus in the town center or to the base of the funicular station, to be taken "upstairs" to see the major attractions of the "rock nation," all of which tower over Gibraltar (see below).

You can also walk into town from the border, but it takes 15 to 20 minutes.

GETTING AROUND Since driving is difficult, you can explore Gibraltar on foot, by cable car, by bus, or by inexpensive taxi tour. Bus nos. 3, 9, and 10, caught at the border, are used mainly for getting from one point to another in Gibraltar. Once you've reached either the town or the top of the cable-car station, you can explore on foot. If you plan to use the buses frequently, buy an unlimited day pass on the bus for 2€.

One of the most convenient ways to explore the Rock is in a taxi operated by **Gibraltar Taxi Association** (✆ **350-200-700-27;** www.gibtaxi.com). The drivers are all licensed guides so they know the terrain well and can easily navigate the twisting, narrow streets. The standard "Official Rock Tour" visits all the major attractions and lasts between 1½ and 3 hours depending on how long you spend visiting the sites. It typically costs £22 per person, based on 4 people sharing one of the roomy minibus taxis. This price includes entry fees. Of course, if you want to see

CULTURAL conflicts IN A BRITISH COLONY

Gibraltar has a distinctly unique feel to it. It's not quite British, but neither is it Spanish. Gibraltar is actually a self-governing British colony, even though Spain continues to stake a claim to its sovereignty.

Cultural conflicts are an ongoing embarrassment, and the presence of such a strong British military presence right on the doorstep is a direct reminder of humiliation endured by Spain in regimes past. References to Lord Nelson and British colonialism are evident almost everywhere you look,

and the allure of Merrie Olde England can feel a bit out of place in the blazing south Iberian sun.

In 2002 the Gibraltar government held a referendum asking its citizens to decide whether Britain should share sovereignty with Spain. The result was a resounding 'no'. Spain's official long-term goal is for a period of joint sovereignty leading to Gibraltar eventually becoming part of Spain, but the Gibraltarians remain determined to retain their status as British citizens.

more of the Rock, more extensive tours can be arranged. The tours are very popular, particularly in the summer months, so book in advance by phone or e-mail.

Taxi stands are at the Gibraltar/La Línea frontier or in the town at spots like Cathedral Square, Coach Park, Casemates Square, Piazza-Town Centre, and Trafalgar Cemetery.

VISITOR INFORMATION   For tourist information, go to the helpful **Gibraltar Tourist Office,** Watergate House, Casemates Square (📞 **350-200-450-00;** www. gibraltar.gov.uk). Hours are Monday to Friday from 9am to 5:30pm. There's a small information booth at the Spanish border that's open daily from 7am to 10pm.

[FastFACTS] GIBRALTAR

Area Code Dialing codes for Gibraltar have recently changed. To dial Gibraltar from any other country, including Spain, the country code is 📞 **350.** Local five-digit numbers have all had 200 added in front of them.

Bookshop & Newspapers The **Gibraltar Bookshop,** 300 Main St (📞 **350-200-718-94**), is the biggest and best stocked in the colony, with many different English newspapers and the most complete section of books about Gibraltar on display anywhere.

Currency Euros are accepted in most of the shops, but expect a bad exchange rate. In lieu of euros, use British pounds or the Rock's own sterling

government notes, which are not legal tender elsewhere in the U.K.

Dentists If you have a dental emergency, contact the **Dental Care Center,** 216 Main St. (📞 **350-200-788-44**).

Emergencies For an ambulance or in case of fire, dial 📞 **190;** for a police emergency, dial 📞 **112** or 📞 **199.**

Hospital For medical services, including emergencies, go to **St Bernard's Hospital** in the Europort (📞 **350-200-797-00**).

Internet Access The **PC Clinic,** 17 Convent Place (📞 **350-200-499-91;** www.pc-clinic-gib.com), about a block uphill from Main Street, charges £3 per hour with a minimum charge of £1.

Pharmacy Calpe Pharmacy, 232 Main St (📞 **350-200-772-31**), is one of the most visible in the colony. If you have an emergency, the owner publishes his home phone (📞 **350-200-785-07**) for after-hours assistance, and also posts the address and phone of other pharmacies with different opening hours.

Post Office The **Gibraltar post office** is at 104 Main St (📞 **350-200-756-62**) and is open June to mid-September Monday to Friday from 9am to 2:15pm, Saturday from 10am to 1pm. Off-season hours are Monday to Friday from 9am to 4:30pm and Saturday from 10am to 1pm. All charges must be paid in British pounds sterling.

Exploring Gibraltar

If you're pressed for time, I suggest you bypass Gibraltar town and concentrate instead on the **Upper Rock Nature Reserve ★★★**, the area at the top of the Rock accessible from the entrance at Jews' Gate, where you will find St Michael's Cave, the Apes' Den, the Great Siege Tunnels, and the ruins of the old Moorish

Monkey Business

Despite their name, the Barbary Apes aren't really apes but cinnamon-colored tail-less monkeys (macaques). Legend has it that the first monkeys were either brought here by the Moors or that they found their way through a tunnel that linked St Michael's Cave with Africa. The monkeys are carefully protected by the British, who have a saying: "When the apes leave the Rock, so will the British." They're fed daily which has helped keep the monkeys in the Reserve and stop them descending to the town for food. However, there have been recent reports of smaller groups scavenging around hotels for food and even finding their way into bedrooms where doors to balconies have been left open. It's important to remember that whilst they are used to human contact, these are wild animals and they can be unpredictable. Maintain a sensible distance and do not feed them—there's a fine of £500.

Castle. All of these attractions are open daily from 9:30am to 6:30pm. A combination ticket to the attractions costs £10. There are two additional attractions in the Reserve not covered by the combination ticket: the World War II tunnels and O'Hara's Battery.

If you don't opt for a taxi tour, the **cable car** (© 350-200-778-26) is a really scenic way to access the Reserve. Return tickets cost £9 for adults and £4.50 for children. More energetic vistors opt to take the cable car up to the summit and then walk back down, visiting the attractions on the way. This is a great way to experience the Rock, but it takes a good 3 to 4 hours and it's quite a long walk. The cable-car departure point is at the foot of the Alameda Botanical Gardens at the far end of Main Street, which is a 20-minute walk from Casemates Square. If you don't feel like walking, bus no. 3 will take you there. Cable cars depart every 10 minutes from 9:30am to 7:45pm, with the last return at 7:45pm.

The cable car used to stop first at the **Apes' Den,** along Old Queen's Road. At the time of writing, however, this stop had been suspended. If you can't get off here, don't worry, you'll see plenty of these famous Barbary apes cavorting on the sides of rocks all around the Reserve.

If you've taken the cable car, you'll arrive at the top of the Rock to truly spectacular views ★★★ back towards Spain and across the Mediterranean to Morocco, which is usually clearly visible. Vertigo sufferers may want to give this a miss as you can feel pretty exposed up here and the drop off is quite extreme.

A short walk down St Michael's Road brings you to Douglas Lookout with more views and **O'Hara's Battery,** Upper Rock (© 350-200-459-57), site of a huge gun, its barrel measuring 2.8m (9 ft 2 in). The gun had a range of nearly 27½ kilometers (30,000 yards), enough to fire a shell right across the bay into Africa. Entry to visit the gun and the small complex of tunnels and support structures costs £3.50 and it's not included in the combination ticket. Open Monday to Saturday 10:30am to 5:30pm.

St Michael's Cave ★ is the site you reach next if you're walking down from the top. (It's the first site you reach if you've chosen to enter the Reserve through Jews' Gate.) This remarkable complex of caves, a result of millions of years of erosion of the soft limestone by water dripping from above, is stuffed with stalagmites and stalactites. One of the largest caves has been turned into a full-scale subterranean auditorium which is used for concerts and other live performances.

From St Michael's Cave you can walk along Queen's Road through the Reserve to its northern end facing Spain. If you've not seen the apes already, you can make a short detour left down Old Queen's Road where you'll find the Apes' Den. The walk takes about 45 minutes and there are fine observation points along the road with views over the harbor and toward Spain. At the end of the road, you reach the Upper Galleries, now known as the **Great Siege Tunnels**. These are large tunnels and rooms hewn in solid rock that were used as vantage points for guns hauled up to the Rock to protect it from the Spanish mainland. The tunnels were carved out during the Great Siege of 1779 to 1782, an incredible undertaking given that much of it was dug out by hand and most of the population was weak with hunger. Legend has it that Governor Lord Napier entertained Ulysses S. Grant, the former U.S. president, in 1878 with a banquet here in St George's Hall, one of the largest of the rooms carved out inside the rock.

Just below the Great Siege Tunnels, you come to the **World War II Tunnels**, Hays Level, Princess Caroline's Battery (✆ **350-200-459-57**). Tunneling continued after the Great Siege and reached its zenith during World War II when the Allies believed a German invasion attempt was almost certain. There are now 30km (18.6 miles) of tunnels and interconnected rooms criss-crossing the interior of the rock, a greater surface area than the Rock's road network. This guided tour takes you to see where thousands lived and worked during the war, inside the Rock. Entry costs £8 for adults and it's open Monday to Friday 10am to 5:30pm.

Directly south of the tunnels are the ruins of the **Moorish Castle,** which you can skip if you're short of time. It was constructed by the descendants of Tariq who captured the Rock in 711. The nearby 1333 **Tower of Homage** dominates the only land entrance to Gibraltar. Many daytrippers end their sightseeing of Gibraltar at this point. It's a 15-minute walk from here down into the town. If you have time, once you reach the heart of town you can cover the attractions immediately below on foot.

Gibraltar Museum, Bomb House Lane (✆ **350-200-742-89**; www.gibmuseum.gi), is installed in a 14th-century Moorish bathhouse. The museum is just off Main Street, past the Roman Catholic Cathedral of St Mary the Crowned. To anyone intrigued with the history of the Rock, the exhibits are fascinating. There is a large-scale model of the Rock, showing every dwelling existing in 1865, plus much of the land reclamation since then. There's also a reproduction of the famous "Gibraltar woman," the ancient skull discovered in 1848 in Forbes's Quarry. Other exhibits depict the history from prehistoric cave-dwelling days to the present. There's a mass of artifacts, cannonballs, weapons, and military uniforms. Admission is £2. The museum is open Monday to Friday from 10am to 6pm and Saturday 10am to 2pm.

Convent and King's Chapel, Main Street, is the official residence of the governor, Queen Elizabeth's representative on Gibraltar. The convent was named in 1531 when a wealthy Spaniard gave the Franciscan friars land, materials, and money to erect a convent and a chapel for the burial of himself and his family. There is no sign today of their graves. King's Chapel is open to view, but the convent, a private home, is not. There is a 1,000-year-old dragon tree standing on the grounds that you can see if you look down the hill behind the Roman Catholic cathedral.

At the top end of Main Street, just outside the town gate, where there was once a drawbridge and a moat, is the **Trafalgar Cemetery,** a charming garden blazing with geraniums. Tombstones commemorate many who fell in the battles of Algeciras, Trafalgar, Cádiz, and Málaga in the early years of the 19th century. A short walk farther on brings you to the cable car departure point and, just nearby, the **Alameda Botanical Gardens,** Red Sands Road (www.gibraltargardens.gi), a fragrant, shady expanse of trees, shrubs, and walks with a small conservation park at its center.

For a final view from Gibraltar, many visitors like to head out to **Europa Point ★★**, often called "the end of Europe." (The most southerly point in Europe is actually **Tarifa,** p. 297, in Spain which can be seen in the distance.) You can either add a visit to Europa Point to your taxi tour or you can reach it from the center of Gibraltar via bus no. 3 from Line Wall Road, just off Main Street. Departures are every 20 to 30 minutes during the day and cost 60p one way.

At Europa Point is the **lighthouse** built in 1841 by Trinity House, the general lighthouse and pilotage authority for Great Britain, incorporated in 1514 by Henry VIII. It remains the only Trinity House lighthouse outside the United Kingdom. Here, too, is Lloyd's of London's only foreign spotting station, recording every merchant ship entering or leaving the Mediterranean. Gibraltar was one of the two ancient Pillars of Hercules according to Greek mythology. The other so-called pillar is 23km (14 miles) across the Strait of Gibraltar in North Africa. Looking out from the lighthouse at Europa Point, you should be able to see the other Pillar of Hercules across the strait to the west of Ceuta. It's a mountain called Jebel Musa (formerly Mount Abyla).

DOLPHINS, diving, FISHING

The waters around the Rock are teeming with all manner of interesting wildlife and you can get up close and personal to it either on or below the waves.

There are three species of dolphin found in the Bay of Gibraltar: the Common, the Striped, and the large Bottle Nosed dolphin. It's relatively easy to see them if you take a boat trip out into the bay. Three companies run excellent **dolphin-watching trips** that typically last a couple of hours departing at least daily. **Dolphin Adventure,** (✆ 350-200-506-50; info@dolphin.gi) and **Dolphin Safari** (✆ 350-200-719-14; dolphin@gibraltar. gi), both at Marina Bay, and **Dolphin World** (✆ 350-544-810-000; reservations@dolphinworld.gi) at the ferry

terminal. Typical prices are £20–£25 for adults; £10–£15 for children.

Gibraltar offers some of the best diving in the Mediterranean. Heading below the waves on a **dive trip** offers not just a glimpse into a teeming world of colorful fish, but also the chance to dive interesting wrecks for more accomplished divers. Contact **Dive Charters** (✆ 350-200-456-49; www.divegib.gi), the Rock's only 5-Star PADI diving center, for more information.

If you fancy trying your hand at landing a big fish, **Straits Fishing** (✆ 350-572-740-000) offers big game tuna **fishing trips** with a fully rigged 8m (26 ft) boat. Typical cost for a 6-hour trip is £500 for two people.

Just off Europa Road, back toward the town and east of the Rock, is the **Chapel of Our Lady of Europa.** This chapel is much venerated and often saluted by passing vessels. Before the lighthouse was built, the small chapel kept a light burning day and night to warn vessels of the treacherous passage. This small Catholic chapel, converted in 1462, was once a mosque. Today there's a small museum with a 1462 statue of the Madonna and some artifacts. Admission is free and the chapel is open Monday to Friday from 10am to 1pm and 2 to 6pm; it's closed Tuesday afternoons and weekends.

Where to Stay

Accommodation options in Gibraltar are limited and tend to be more expensive than the Costa del Sol. During the summer, you must reserve in advance.

Bristol Hotel   In the center of Gibraltar, this colonial-style hotel has a subtropical garden and a swimming pool. The bright, white-painted building is on a pretty square opposite the Anglican church. Mostly, bedrooms are spacious and comfortable. Prices of guest rooms depend on whether the rooms face outward or to the interior. Most rooms have twin beds, and there are some family rooms (two adults and two children).

10 Cathedral Sq., Gibraltar. ✆ **350-200-76-800.** Fax 350-200-77-613. www.bristolhotel.gi. 60 units. £81–£87 double; £93–£99 triple. DC, MC, V. **Amenities:** Bar; outdoor pool; nonsmoking rooms; rooms for those w/limited mobility. *In room:* A/C, TV, dataport, fridge, hair dryer, Wi-Fi.

Caleta Hotel ★   Right now I think this, Gibraltar's largest hotel, is also its nicest. Unfortunately it's not particularly well located for visiting the sights. It's set on the eastern side of the Rock at the end of La Caleta (Catalan Bay), which is the Rock's prettiest cove, nicely sheltered for swimmers and a 15-minute bus (no. 4) or taxi ride from town. A holiday hotel, it's built on the rocks over the sea with several lovely sun terraces and a swimming pool with steps down to the water. Most bedrooms have balconies overlooking the water and are attractively and comfortably furnished, each with a tiled bathroom. The hotel's small and leafy English garden has nice views. Its Italian dining room is one of the best hotel restaurants on the Rock and the English bar here is a cozy retreat for a pint.

Sir Herbert Miles Rd, Catalan Bay, Gibraltar. ✆ **350-200-765-01.** Fax 350-200-710-50. www.caleta hotel.gi. 160 units. £189 double. Winter reductions. AE, DC, MC, V. **Amenities:** Restaurant; bar; babysitting; gym; outdoor pool; room service; nonsmoking rooms. *In room:* TV, minibar, hair dryer, Wi-Fi.

Cannon Hotel   Owned and operated by Joe Bossano, one of the former chief ministers of Gibraltar, this informal downtown hotel occupies an old-fashioned 19th-century house on a narrow lane a few steps north of Main Street. Don't expect grandeur—everything is very English-pubby-style, with a reception desk a few steps from the bar, a lobby-cum-drinking area where everyone sees and hears everything. The midsize rooms are light and airy with twin beds.

9 Cannon Lane, Gibraltar. ✆ **350-200-517-11.** Fax 350-200-517-89. www.cannonhotel.gi. 18 units. £38 double without bathroom; £46 double with bathroom. Rates include English breakfast. MC, V. **Amenities:** Restaurant; bar; nonsmoking rooms. *In room:* No phone.

O'Callaghan Eliott Hotel ★   This old Holiday Inn has been converted into a winning choice on an attractive tree-lined square in the Old Town and until The Rock (see below) gets its refit, I think this is your best bet for comfort and convenience.

Bedrooms are among Gibraltar's finest, each furnished with contemporary, comfortable pieces. Most rooms have views of the Strait of Gibraltar and beyond to North Africa. The Palm Court and the Victoria Garden restaurant are among the Rock's better dining choices, with international and Mediterranean specialties, plus a *carte* of regional wines. The highlight is its rooftop pool and terrace, with great views.

Governor's Parade, Gibraltar. © **350-200-705-00.** Fax 350-200-702-43. www.ocallaghanhotels.com. 120 units. £90–£185 double; £135–£330 suite. AE, DC, MC, V. **Amenities:** 2 restaurants; 2 bars; gym; sauna; outdoor pool; room service; nonsmoking rooms; rooms for those w/limited mobility. *In room:* A/C, TV, hair dryer, Wi-Fi.

The Rock ★ This is one of the Mediterranean's most famous hotels, frequented by all manner of illustrious people. The setting is impressive, on the Rock's sunny western side with views of the Spanish coastline and North Africa. Originally built by the Marquis of Bute in 1932, it's the place for the British traditionalist dreaming of lost colonial empires with swishing ceiling fans and waiters in tuxedos—service is excellent. There's a 3.6-hectare (9-acre) landscaped garden with an outdoor pool and a wisteria-covered terrace perfect for a sundowner. Bedrooms are spacious and many have delightful views across the sea towards Tarifa. Unfortunately it feels a little jaded in places now; carpets are a bit worn, paintwork a little tired. There are rumors that the hotel is soon to be completely refitted and, that being the case, it will rightly regain its crown as Gibraltar's most sought-after address.

3 Europa Rd, Gibraltar. © **350-200-730-00.** Fax 350-200-735-13. www.rockhotelgibraltar.com. 104 units. £180 double; £195–£295 suite. AE, DC, MC, V. **Amenities:** Restaurant; bar; outdoor pool; room service; nonsmoking rooms; rooms for those w/limited mobility. *In room:* A/C, TV, hair dryer, Wi-Fi.

Where to Dine

Café Solo ENGLISH   None of the dining options on Casemates Square are brilliant, as it's the epicenter of the tourist zone, but this cafe is, for me, the standout option. Pleasant and with a staff that copes well with the crowds, it serves freshly made salads, wraps, pasta dishes and more all day long. Daily specials include more substantial dishes like lamb tagine, and oven-roasted chicken in red wine sauce. The cafe also has a chunk of the terrace space on the square. At night this part of town gets a bit noisier and boozier, but at lunch time and early evening it's pleasant.

Unit 7, ICC, Casemates Sq. © **350-200-481-85.** Main courses £6.95–£15. MC, V. Mon–Sat 9am–11pm; Sun 12pm–11pm.

Ipanema BRAZILIAN   If you like barbecue, this is the place. It's in the glitzy new marina development, Ocean Village, which, a mere two-minute walk from Casemates Square, is now the place to go for more upmarket dining and drinking. Special waiters or "pasadors" pass from table to table with huge chunks of grilled meat on spits which they carve for you: perfectly seasoned beef, lamb, pork, chicken, and Brazilian sausages; you can try whatever takes your fancy. Or go for the huge all-you-can-eat buffet. Service is good and friendly and the atmosphere is fun and relaxed.

Unit 11, Ocean Village Promenade. © **350-216-488-88.** Lunch £9.95; dinner £15.95. MC, V. Mon–Sat 12:30–3.30pm and 7:30–11pm, Sun 1–4pm.

La Mamela ★ ITALIAN   Without doubt, the best Italian restaurant and quite probably the best fish restaurant on the Rock, La Mamela is a small, homely traditional family restaurant on the east side overlooking Caleta Bay, one of Gibraltar's prettiest bays. If you're staying at the Caleta Hotel it's a five-minute walk, otherwise drive or catch a bus or a taxi. Fish dishes depend on the catch of the day, but typically include cod, sea bass, and sole. There are wrigglingly fresh lobsters and they do a great paella. For non fish-eaters, the pepper pork loin is recommended. The lovely views from the restaurant's little terrace overlooking the bay complete the package.

Catalan Bay. ✆ **350-200-723-73.** Reservations required. Main courses £11–£18.25. MC, V. Mon–Sat 12:30–3.30pm and 7:30–11pm; Sun 1–4pm.

Rib Room Restaurant ★ INTERNATIONAL   The Rock Hotel's restaurant remains the single finest dining room on Gibraltar. From your table, you can enjoy views across the bay to the Spanish coastline and Morocco. There's both an a la carte and a daily changing menu. The seafood is fresh, and other top-quality dishes include pan-roasted filet of lamb with a basil salsa, and seared filet of beef with grilled baby leeks and a truffle foie gras. Starters are especially imaginative, like the pumpkin-and-pancetta risotto and the wok-seared black-pepper beef with asparagus and a charred pineapple salad. For dessert, try chocolate souffle pancakes with cold vanilla custard.

In the Rock Hotel, 3 Europa Rd ✆ **350-200-730-00.** Reservations required. Fixed-price menu £32; main courses £22–£28. AE, DC, MC, V. Daily 7–10pm.

The Waterfront ★ INTERNATIONAL   Located on the tranquil harborside at the new Queensway Quay Marina, the Waterfront's setting is perfect for a lazy brunch or romantic evening meal. It's probably my favorite restaurant on the Rock right now. There's a seriously long menu good for every taste, including a good range of vegetarian options and, for Brits missing home, a selection of curries. You might start with sauteed wild field mushrooms with braised Puy lentils on toasted farmhouse bread, then move on to chicken breast stuffed with spicy black pudding, wrapped in pancetta, with hazelnut dressing or pan-roasted filet of sea bass, pappardelle, mussels, crab, and saffron. Finish off with zingy homemade lemon meringue pie. Prices are very reasonable too and there's a good wine list.

4/5 Ragged Staff Wharf, Queensway Quay. ✆ **350-200-456-66**. www.gibwaterfront.com. Main courses £11.50–£24. AE, MC, V. Daily 9am–11pm.

Shopping

Gibraltar Crystal Factory   For a more unusual souvenir, head to this interesting shop and workspace right on busy Grand Casemates. Here you can see master glass blowers crafting molten glass into beautiful crystal items. All products are genuinely handmade, each with their own certificate of authenticity. Prices range from a few pounds to several hundred. Grand Casemates, ✆ **350-200-501-36.** www.gibraltarcrystal.com.

Golden Eagle Liquors   Whilst non-brand spirits in Spain are generally very good value, upmarket non-Spanish wines, and in particular proper Scotch whiskies, tend to be much pricier. There are plenty of places on Main Street taking advantage of Gibraltar's duty free status. This place has a good selection of French, Italian, and Australian wines, and an even better selection of the kinds of rare whiskies that made the British Empire function. 286 Main St ✆ **350-200-759-13.**

Marks & Spencer   In a colony that's as English as Gibraltar, a well-lit branch of Britain's most omnipresent department store chain is no surprise. This one is air-conditioned and loaded with an abbreviated but very British collection of men's and women's clothing. Yes, you can buy umbrellas, raincoats, and English marmalade made with Spanish oranges. This particular store is in two separate branches along the same street, almost immediately adjacent to one another. 235 and 215 Main St ✆ **350-200-758-57.** www.marksandspencer.com.

The Rock after Dark

The bustle on Main Street, with "downtown" Gibraltar's densest concentration of shops, dies down a little when the shops close. After dark much of the action takes place one block south of Main Street's western end on a parallel street known formally as Irish Town and informally as "Back Street." One of the best bars here is the **Clipper,** 78B Irish Town (✆ **350-200-797-91;** www.theclipper.gi), its decor dotted with engravings of clipper ships and memorabilia of the Royal Navy, with foaming pints of beer and shots of whisky the orders of the day. It also serves English breakfasts throughout the day and classic pub grub like jacket potatoes and steak and kidney pie or beef stroganoff in the evenings. Nearby **Corks Wine Bar,** 79 Irish Town (✆ **350-200-755-66**) is a long-standing favorite which has just had a refit, with food, international beers and wines, and DJ sets when things warm up later in the evening.

Other recommended pubs for a taste of Britannia on the Med are **All's Well,** Casemates Square (✆ **350-200-729-87**), known for its Bass beers and steak-and-ale pie; **Star Bar,** Parliament Lane (✆ **350-200-759-24**), said to be the oldest bar in Gib; and **Lord Nelson Bar Brasserie,** 10 Casemates Sq. (✆ **350-200-500-09**), done up to represent Nelson's ship with a beamed cloud-and-sky ceiling and a spacious terrace.

The new **Ocean Village Marina** development just west of Casemates Square is a welcome addition to nightlife on the Rock, with a slew of trendy modern waterfront eateries and bars to choose from including **Savannah Lounge,** 27 Leisure Island, Ocean Village (✆ **350-200-666-66;** www.savannah.gi), which is a cool bar, restaurant, and nightclub, hosting DJ sets on most Friday and Saturday nights. Gamblers can check out **Gala Casino,** Ocean Village. (✆ **350-200-766-66;** www.galacasinogibraltar.com), which requires smart casual dress. There's a cocktail bar and chargrill restaurant and the gaming room is open from 10pm to 4am Monday to Wednesday, 10am to 6am Thursday to Saturday and noon to 5am Sundays. Poker, slots, roulette and more are available along with betting on sports fixtures and bingo.

ESTEPONA

85km (53 miles) W of Málaga, 639km (397 miles) S of Madrid, 46km (29 miles) E of Algeciras

A town of Roman origin and the most westerly of the coast's burgeoning fishing villages, Estepona hasn't been taken over by high-rises. Less developed than Fuengirola or Torremolinos and with a more Spanish feel than expat-heavy Marbella, it's quite a likeable place, if a little small and sleepy. It still has an old quarter of narrow cobblestone streets and dozens of tapas bars. Traces of the past remain: a round tower constructed to protect the villagers from the raids of Barbary pirates, who took not only all valuables, including food, but the most beautiful women as well.

Today Estepona's recreational port is an attraction, as are its beaches: the main town beach, La Rada, 3km (2 miles) long; and the sheltered cove of El Cristo to the east of the port only 550m (1,800 ft) long. Both are good for families: pleasantly quiet, with good facilities and cheap beachbar restaurants (*chiringuitos*). Estepona also has an interesting 18th-century parish church, with a ruined old aqueduct nearby (at Salduba).

Essentials

GETTING THERE   The nearest **rail** links are in Fuenginola. However, Estepona is on the **bus** route from Algeciras to Málaga. If you're driving, head east from Algeciras along the A-7/E-5.

VISITOR INFORMATION   The **tourist office,** Av. San Lorenzo 1 (📞 **95-280-20-02;** www.estepona.es), is open Monday to Friday from 9:30am to 7:30pm and Saturday from 10am to 1:30pm. Pick up a free map with a short walking tour of the Old Town.

A Stroll around the Old Town

There's not a huge amount to see in Estepona and a 20-minute wander will cover most of the sites. From the tourist office walk down to Estepona's town beach, **Playa de la Rada,** and turn left along the attractive garden-fringed promenade (**Paseo Marítimo**), particularly pleasant in the early evening. Head inland at the end of the block up Calle Viento. The ruins of the 16th-century **Castillo de San Luis** are on your left after a couple of blocks as you enter Plaza Canada. Continue across the square and you'll reach Estepona's attractive town hall (**Ayuntamiento**) in a typical Andalusian palace house. Turn right and take the next left and right and you reach Plaza de San Francisco with its attractive church, the **Iglesia de Nostra Señora de los Remedios**. Originally built as a Franciscan Monastery in the 18th century, it has an interesting entrance doorway decorated with Marian, Franciscan, and Pre-Colombine iconography. Retrace your steps to Calle Santa Ana and walk down it towards the sea. A left turn along Calle Carlos Herrera brings you to the town's pretty main square, **Plaza de los Flores ★** which is filled with flowers and has a fountain at its center. There are lots of pleasant terrace bars here, perfect for a cool drink in the afternoon sunshine.

Where to Stay

Close to Estepona you'll find several of the top resorts along the Costa del Sol, the ultimate in luxury living. If you want the most idyllic, the most luxurious, and the grandest, stay at the Kempinski Bahía Estepona, although all of the top hotels are luxe all the way. Don't be afraid to ask for the latest special offers at all of these places; the economic slowdown means rooms can often be had at serious reductions.

What's missing in Estepona are the cheap concrete block bunkers catering to package tours. For most people that's a bonus, but if you're a frugal traveler who really wants "the beach on a budget," you're better off heading for Torremolinos or Fuengirola. It's not as pretty there, but it's a lot easier on your wallet.

EXPENSIVE

Atalaya Park Golf Hotel & Resort ★★ ☺   Midway between Estepona and Marbella, this modern resort complex attracts sports- and nature-lovers. Its tranquil beachside location sits in 8 hectares (20 acres) of subtropical gardens. Spacious rooms furnished in an elegant modern style are well maintained and inviting. Guests have complimentary use of the hotel's extensive sports facilities, including two magnificent golf courses. Many northern Europeans check in and almost never leave the grounds.

Carretera de Cádiz Km 168.5, 29688 Estepona. © **95-288-90-00.** Fax 95-288-90-02. www.atalaya-park.es. 475 units. 140€–240€ double; 285€–320€ suite; 500€ bungalow. AE, DC, MC, V. Free parking. **Amenities:** 5 restaurants; 2 bars; babysitting; health club; kids' club; nightclub (summer only); 6 outdoor pools; 2 18-hole golf courses; 9 outdoor tennis courts (6 lit); nautical sports center; sauna; solarium. *In room:* A/C, TV, hair dryer, minibar, Wi-Fi.

Gran Hotel Elba Estepona ★★   Set just back from Playa de Costa Natura about a 5-minute drive towards Algeciras from Estepona, the Elba is a modern spa hotel. It features an attractive domed reception area opening onto the sea, the Mediterranean sky flooding it with light. There's a lovely outdoor pool with similar sea views. For me it's the spa that really makes the place. It specializes in Thalassotherapy (seawater-based) treatments, with all sorts of plunge pools and treatment rooms. Four restaurants offer a variety of styles and cuisines, with terraces looking on to the sea. Rooms are modern and comfortable—though not particularly stylish. They're equipped with large beds and all modern conveniences and all have balconies or private terraces.

Carretera de Cádiz Km 153, 29680 Estepona. © **95-280-92-00**. Fax 95-280-92-01. www.hoteleselba. com. 231 units. 135€–200€ double; 150€–290€ junior suite. AE, DC, MC, V. Free parking. **Amenities:** 4 restaurants; bar; babysitting; health club; library; outdoor pool; room seervice; sauna; spa; whirlpool. *In room:* A/C, TV, hair dryer, minibar, Wi-Fi.

Kempinski Hotel Bahía Estepona ★★★   One of the most luxurious retreats in this part of the Costa del Sol, this modern resort hotel offers a lush, elegant lifestyle. Between the main coastal route and the beach, the Kempinski borrowed heavily from nearby Morocco to create this oasis, with hanging gardens adding a dramatic touch. The property opens onto beautifully landscaped and luxuriant palm-studded gardens fronting the ocean. Guest rooms are airy and spacious, with balconies or private terraces overlooking the sea. They're all finished to an exceptionally high standard, giving the Kempinski the edge over its nearby competitors. Many expats living in the area flock here for the Sunday afternoon jazz brunch, the most elaborate on the western part of the Costa del Sol. Top European chefs turn out carefully crafted regional specialties and international dishes.

Carretera de Cádiz Km 159, Playa el Padrón, 29680 Estepona. © **95-280-95-00.** Fax 95-280-95-50. www.kempinski-spain.com. 148 units. 190€–390€ double; 465€–700€ junior suite; from 700€ suite. AE, DC, MC, V. Free parking; 12€ garage. **Amenities:** 4 restaurants; 3 bars; babysitting; fitness center; gym; 3 pools (1 indoor); room service; tennis court; sauna; spa; nonsmoking rooms. *In room:* A/C, TV, hair dryer, minibar, Wi-Fi.

MODERATE

El Paraíso Costa del Sol ★   Between Marbella and Estepona in front of Costalita Beach, the impressive El Paraíso Costa del Sol is the leading moderately priced establishment in town. I've seen prices as low as 70€ for a double room on the hotel's special offers web page. This modern building, constructed in the 1980s, is 12km (7½ miles) from the center of Estepona. Bedrooms open onto balconies fronting the Mediterranean. Expect a midsize to fairly spacious room, furnished in a typical resort style—comfortable but not special. The best feature here is the panoramic bar on the seventh floor. The hotel also has a children's play area.

Urbanización El Paraiso, Noreste, Carretera de Cádiz Km 167, 29680 Estepona. © **95-288-30-00.** Fax 95-288-20-19. www.hoteltrhparaisocostadelsol.com. 176 units. 134€–193€ double; 252€–317€ suite. AE, DC, MC, V. Free parking. **Amenities:** 2 restaurants; 4 bars; babysitting; 2 pools (1 indoor); children's pool; room service; sauna. *In room:* A/C, TV, hair dryer, minibar, Wi-Fi.

INEXPENSIVE

Buenavista   This comfortable if modest little *residencia* beside the coastal road opened in the 1970s and it's the only place I can recommend that's actually in the town itself. (All the higher-class accommodation is resort-based.) Twenty of the small, but clean rooms have terraces overlooking the beach, but they can be a bit noisy in summer from the seafront traffic. The 18 rooms at the back of the hotel don't have views, but are quieter. Beds are comfortable, and the little bathrooms have shower stalls. All in all, a perfectly adequate option if you're on a budget.

Av. de España 180, 29680 Estepona. © **95-280-01-37.** Fax 95-280-55-93. www.buenavistaestepona. com. 38 units. 45€–65€ double. MC, V. *In room:* TV.

Where to Dine

In summer, the cheapest places to eat in Estepona are the **chiringuitos,** little dining areas set up by local fishermen and their families right on the beach and often excellent. Naturally they feature seafood, like sole and sardine kabobs grilled over an open fire. You can usually order a fresh salad and fried potatoes; desserts are simple.

El Pescador ★ SEAFOOD/SPANISH   Most of the dining options in the Old Town are cheap and cheerful, but this place is a real notch up on the quality scale. Without doubt the best fish restaurant in town with a very pleasant location right on the beach front, it's very Spanish and local. Choose from freshly cooked lobster, oven-baked bream in garlic and butter sauce, and all manner of freshly grilled fish. Or go for the catch of the day and keep it simple. Clams, prawns, and scallops also feature on the menu, as do rice dishes. Service can be a bit brusque, but persevere, it's worth it!

Edificio Madrid 51, Paseo Maritimo, 29680 Estepona. © **95-280-43-93.** Main courses 12€–30€. MC, V. Daily 1–5pm and 8pm–midnight. Closed mid-Jan to mid-Feb.

La Alcaría de Ramos ★ 🍴 SPANISH   This country retreat, a short distance from the Paraíso and Atalaya hotels, is decorated like an old summerhouse, with a beautiful terrace garden. The chef and owner, José Ramos, has won many national gastronomic competitions and has been creating intriguing variations on traditional recipes since the early 1990s. He'll cook you such dishes as *tortas de patatas* (superb potato cakes!). Try *crepes de aguacate con gambas* (avocado crepes with shrimp) and *pato asado con puré de manzana y col roja* (grilled duck with apple puree and red cabbage) or the *parrillada de pescado y mariscos* (assorted grilled fish and shellfish). For dessert, go for *helado frito con frambuesa* (fried ice cream with raspberry sauce).

Urbanización El Paraíso Vista al Mar 1, N-340 Km 167. © **95-288-61-78.** Reservations recommended. Main courses 15€–22€. MC, V. Mon–Sat 7:30pm–midnight.

Estepona after Dark

The resort hotels often bring in flamenco dancers and musicians to entertain in the summer months. Otherwise, after-dark diversions in Estepona town consist mostly of hitting the tapas bars. There are two spots to choose from. For relaxed terraces and romantic squares, head for pretty **Plaza de Los Flores** and adjoining **Plaza Dr Acre** right in the center of the Old Town. There are plenty of cheap and friendly tapas joints here. If you're tired of the old Spanish tapas regulars, make for **Madu-Bar,** Plaza Dr Acre 23 (✆ **95-280-62-31**), which is just a bit more young and funky and serves wraps, steaks, and salads from around 5€. For the seriously traditional tapas jaunts where you stand up at the bar, head for Calle Caridad—a long street lined with little neighborhood bars that starts just east of Plaza Dr Acre. One of the best is tiny **Bodega Sabor Andaluz,** Caridad 4 (✆ **95-279-10-30**), which has especially good seafood, but it's a good 30-minute walk along the street from the plaza end.

PUERTO BANÚS

8km (5 miles) E of Marbella, 782km (486 miles) S of Madrid

A favorite resort for international celebrities, the coastal village and marina of **Puerto Banús** was created almost overnight just for tourists. If you associate Marbella with images of luxury yachts and supercars, think again. It's actually Puerto Banús that's the real epicenter of the high-rolling holiday zone on the Costa del Sol. In the exclusive marina you'll see huge yachts moored in front of expensive restaurants and luxury boutiques. That's not to say it's totally out of reach of normal people. It's not stupidly expensive, and it makes an interesting lunch stop or evening out—relaxed, refined, and good fun. The decent beach here tends to be less crowded than those at Marbella.

Essentials

GETTING THERE   To reach the town, take one of 15 **buses** that run daily from Marbella or drive east from Marbella along the E-15 or the old N-340 Cádiz road. If you're staying in Marbella, there's an hourly ferry service to the marina at Puerto Banús, operated by **Fly Blue** (✆ **66-382-79-86**). Boats leave the Puerto Deportivo in Marbella from 11am to 6:30pm. The cost is 15€ for adults; 8€ for children.

VISITOR INFORMATION   The **tourist office** (✆ **95-281-85-70**) has a small kiosk on the main Plaza Antonio Banderas just a block back from the marina. It's open Monday to Friday 9am to 8:30pm and 10am to 2pm at weekends.

Where to Stay

Golf Hotel Guadalmina ★ ☺   In the residential area of Guadalmina, around 5km (3 miles) west of Puerto Banús, this resort hotel, a landmark on the coast since 1959, is surrounded by two scenic golf courses and the Mediterranean. All the rooms, both in the original building and in a new 91-room wing, are midsize to spacious. Bedrooms are comfortable and well furnished, and the decor is typical Andalusian. Most desirable rooms open onto the sea, one of the golf courses, or the hotel's gardens. Spanish and international cuisine is served at the first-class **Cocoa.** Golfers check in here in droves, and families with kids love the impressively large pool and the shallow kiddie pool. There's a really good spa here too.

Urbanización Guadalmina Baja, 29678 Marbella. ✆ **95-288-22-11.** Fax 95-288-22-91. www.hotel guadalmina.com. 178 units. 108€–320€ double; 140€–520€ junior suite; 240€–800€ suite. Rates include breakfast. AE, DC, MC, V. **Amenities:** 2 restaurants; bar; babysitting; fitness center; 2 nearby golf courses; outdoor pool; room service; spa; rooms for those w/limited mobility. *In room:* A/C, TV, hair dryer, minibar, Wi-Fi.

Park Plaza Suites Hotel   Although Puerto Banús is usually visited on a day trip, it does have a hotel. Often yachties stay here when they need a break from their pleasure boats. This sleekly modern hotel near the harbor offers elegant, spacious double rooms or glamorous but expensive suites. The rooms are attractively and comfortably furnished, and many restaurants and nightclubs are easily accessible from here.

Paseo Marítimo de Benabola, 29660 Puerto Banús. ✆ **95-290-90-00.** Fax 95-281-28-46. www.park plazasuiteshotel.com. 50 units. 167€–256€ double; 384€ suite. DC, MC, V. Parking 15€. **Amenities:** Restaurant; bar; gym; Jacuzzi; room service. *In room:* A/C, TV, minibar, hair dryer.

Where to Dine

Antonio ★ SEAFOOD/INTERNATIONAL   This long-time favorite is the best place to watch Puerto Banús's chic port life. Opt for a table on the terrace and watch the beautiful people. The first-class cuisine lives up to the setting, which has modern paintings on the wall, lots of greenery, and a black-and-white color scheme. The chef, Juan Trujillo, knows how to balance colors, textures, and flavors, creating such dishes as the best filet mignon in the area, well-flavored pork chops, and a tender, moist loin of veal. An all-time favorite is sea bass baked in salt to keep its moisture and aroma.

Muelle de Ribera. ✆ **95-281-35-36.** Reservations required. Main courses 25€–32€. AE, DC, MC, V. Daily 1–4pm and 7:30–11pm (until 12:30am Aug–Sept).

Cipriano ★★ SEAFOOD/MEDITERRANEAN   Serving some of the finest food at the port, this deluxe restaurant is the number-one choice of the rich and sometimes famous who arrive in Puerto Banús on their multimillion-dollar yachts. It's set a couple of blocks back from the marina. Cipriano is divided into several sections for maximum privacy, each luxuriously decorated in Andalusian style, with elegant fabrics and many colors. There's a casual, semiformal atmosphere among the well-heeled guests. Lobster is always excellent, as is the paella Cipriano. Or order a perfectly grilled entrecote in a pepper sauce, followed by one of the freshly made desserts, like baked apple with cinnamon ice cream.

Edificio de Sevilla, Av. Playas del Duque. ✆ **95-281-10-77.** Reservations required. Main courses 20€–50€; fixed-price menus 45€–109€. AE, DC, MC, V. June–Sept daily 1–4pm and 8pm–midnight; off season Mon–Sat 1–4pm and 7:30pm–midnight.

Dalli's Pasta Factory ✒ PASTA   The meals here, of pasta, pasta, and more pasta served with garlic bread and a carafe of house wine, are a great bargain in pricey Puerto Banús. In a setting that's a cross between high-tech and Art Deco, you can order nutmeg-flavored ravioli with spinach filling, *penne all'arrabbiata*, lasagna, and several kinds of spaghetti.

Muelle de Rivera. ✆ **95-281-86-23.** Pastas 10€–16€; meat platters 16€–22€. AE, MC, V. Daily 1:30–4pm and 7pm–midnight.

Don Leone INTERNATIONAL   Many residents in villas around Marbella drive to this luxuriously decorated marina-side restaurant for dinner, and it can get crowded. Begin with the house minestrone and then follow with pasta in clam sauce; lasagna is also a regular treat. Meat specialties include veal parmigiana and roast baby lamb, and the fish dishes are also worth a try, especially the *frita mixta de pescados* (mixed fish fry). They do pizzas and wraps, and vegetarians are well catered for. The wine list is one of the best along the coast.

Muelle de Rivera 44. (𝒞 **95-281-17-16.** Reservations recommended. Main courses 16€–22€. AE, MC, V. Daily 1–11:30pm.

Shopping

There's a scattering of very upmarket boutiques in the marina selling designer gear for the well-financed. You'll find Burberry, Dolce & Gabbana, Armani, and Dior along the waterfront on Muelle Ribera. Of particular note are the gorgeous creations of American designer **Tom Ford,** Muelle Ribera, Casa F (𝒞 **95-281-70-44;** www. tomford.com). Formerly designer for Gucci, he's based in Italy and this is his only outlet in Spain. Tom's fabulously cut suits, shirts, and ties are only for those with serious cash to burn. An off-the-peg jacket I rather liked the look of was 2,500€.

MARBELLA ★

60km (37 miles) W of Málaga, 45km (28 miles) W of Torremolinos, 80km (50 miles) E of Gibraltar, 76km (47 miles) E of Algeciras, 600km (373 miles) S of Madrid

Although packed with visitors and only slightly less popular than Torremolinos, **Marbella** is still the chicest resort along the Costa del Sol, with some of the region's best upscale resorts coexisting with more affordable hotels. An Andalusian port at the foot of the Sierra Blanca, Marbella displays traces of its past in its palatial town hall, medieval ruins, and ancient Moorish walls. The biggest attractions in Marbella, however, are **El Faro, La Fontanilla,** and **La Venus,** the three main beaches. There are other, more secluded, beaches, but you need your own transportation to get there.

Marbella's chic reputation dates from the beginning of the Eisenhower era. The Marquis don Ricardo Soriano and his nephew, Prince Alfonso Hohenlohe, started spreading the word in 1953. Soon the Duke and Duchess of Windsor and lesser mortals came to see what this sleepy coastal town was all about. The Rothschilds heard about it, as did Saudi emirs. Marbella was on its way; its discovery by jet-setters brought long-overdue prosperity. Many resorts have better beaches and more attractions than Marbella, so: "Why do such chic people still flock here, people who could vacation anywhere?" A local resident, Rafael Trujillo, said, "Rich people come here because other rich people come here."

One can only regret not having seen Marbella in the 1960s and 1970s, even though Franco was in power. Those were the days before concrete tower blocks grew up around its old quarter and fishing port. Fortunately, old Marbella, with its flower-filled balconies and whitewashed houses, remains delightful, and a complete surprise after the brash resorts farther up the coastline like Torremolinos and Fuengirola. Make the **Patio de los Naranjos (The Orange Tree Patio) ★★★** your focal point for a night wandering the cobblestone streets of the Old Town. Here you can enjoy the fountains and cafes with sidewalk tables where you can sit back and watch the world go by.

Essentials

GETTING THERE   The main **bus link** is between Málaga and Marbella, with **Empresa Portillo** (☎ 90-245-05-50; www.ctsa-portillo.com) running 17 buses a day, the trip taking 1 hour and 25 minutes. There are also regular departures from Estepona, Algeciras, and Torremolinos. Three buses each come from Madrid and Barcelona. The bus station is on the outskirts of Marbella on Avenida Trapiche, a 5-minute ride from the center of town.

If you're **driving,** Marbella is the first major resort as you head east on the A-7/E-15 from Algeciras. You can also take the high-speed toll road, the AP-15. Be warned that parking is completely nightmarish.

VISITOR INFORMATION   The main **tourist office,** Glorieta de la Fontanilla s/n (☎ 95-277-14-42), is open Monday to Friday from 9am to 9pm and Saturday from 10am to 2pm. However, if you're staying in or near the Old Town, the smaller branch right in the center, Plaza de los Naranjos (☎ 95-282-35-50) is far more convenient and has the same opening hours. The tourist board's excellent website **www.marbellaexclusive.com** is well worth a look too.

Exploring the Beaches

From Guadalamina to Cabopino, the Marbella coastline stretches for 26km (16 miles) of sunny, sandy beaches. Since 2000, Marbella's beaches have been cleaned up and landscaped with oases of palms. In some places traditional showers have been replaced with giant elephant statues spraying water from their trunks. The season extends from May to October, as the shores are protected by the Sierra Blanca mountains. Many of the beaches have pedestrian promenades beside them, lifeguards, public toilets, and places to rent equipment like sunbeds, water bikes, jet skis, and canoes.

Within the limits of Marbella and bordering it on either side are three equally good beaches, **La Fontanilla** and **El Faro,** to the west side of the Puerto Deportivo (leisure port), and **Playa de Venus** to the east, directly below the Old Town. These beaches of fine dark golden sand are filled with hammocks, parasols, seaside taverns, bars, and even modest shops. Unfortunately, being so close to the city center, they get pretty overcrowded in summer.

Other good beaches west of Marbella include **Playa Casablanca,** connecting with La Fontanilla. Immediately west of here the well-maintained **Playa Nagueles** is used by guests of the exclusive Marbella Club and Puente Romano among others. On the so-called "Golden Mile" of Marbella, this beach has mostly gray sand. It's often very crowded, and its watersports include windsurfing, kayaking, jet-skiing, and more.

East of Málaga's Old Town you find **Playa de la Bajadilla,** which you reach before arriving at the fishing port. The beach has grayish sand and calm waters and beach-fronting restaurants.

Other quieter beaches include **Playa El Cable,** a small, dune-backed city beach with gray sand close to the fishing port, where football matches are played on weekends. Also less crowded in summer is the adjoining 3km- (1¼ mile-) long **Playa El Pinillo,** though noise from the main road and the go-kart track complex behind the beach can take the edge off the beach's charm.

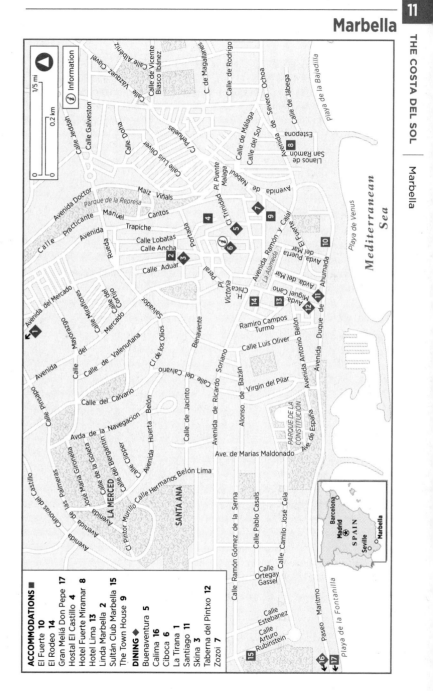

Mediterranean Sea

Playa de Venus

playa de la Bajadilla

Playa de la Fontanilla

ACCOMMODATIONS ■
El Fuerte **10**
El Rodeo **14**
Gran Meliá Don Pepe **17**
Hostal El Castillo **4**
Hotel Fuerte Miramar **8**
Hotel Lima **13**
Linda Marbella **2**
Sultán Club Marbella **15**
The Town House **9**

DINING ◆
Buenaventura **5**
Calima **16**
Ciboca **6**
La Tirana **1**
Santiago **11**
Skina **3**
Taberna del Pintxo **12**
Zozoi **7**

(i) Information

1/5 mi
0.2 km

If you want to hang out with the young and beautiful set during the day, you won't find many of them on the beaches. Marbella is one of *the* places for achingly trendy beach clubs, where modelesque boys and girls in designer swimsuits and shades loll around azure pools on bright white sunbeds-for-two looking lovely. As evening draws on, many of the clubs turn into über-trendy nightclubs, with live music and events taking place throughout the summer. The current favorites are **Nikki Beach** in the Hotel Don Carlos, Ctra de Cádiz Km 192 (✆ **95-283-62-39; www.nikkibeach. com**), which has spawned similar clubs all over the world and even has its own clothing range, and **Ocean Club**, Av. Lola Flores (✆ **95-290-81-37; www. Oceanclub.es**), in Puerto Banús.

Playa Los Monteros, near El Pinillo, is part of the urban development complex of Los Monteros. Its rock-free beach of gray sand is separated from the development by sand dunes.

Also explore the gray sands of **Playa Alicante** at Urbanización Sea and **Playa Real de Zaragoza,** also connected with an urban development. **Playa Vibora** is linked to the Urbanización Elvia. This calm, less well-known beach is set against a backdrop of some ugly buildings. Finally, there's tiny **Playa Las Cañas,** connected with the urban development of Artola.

Where to Stay

Marbella's beautiful setting attracts some of the best hotels along the Costa del Sol.

VERY EXPENSIVE

Marbella Club ★★★   This is perhaps the finest of all Costa del Sol resorts. Until a few equally chic hotels were built along the Costa del Sol, the snobbish Marbella Club reigned as the exclusive hangout of aristocrats and tycoons. Established in 1954, the resort sprawls over a landscaped property that slopes down to its private beach. Small, ecologically conscious clusters of garden pavilions, bungalows, and small-scale annexes are set in some of the loveliest gardens along the coast. Hotel rooms along the Costa del Sol don't come much better than these varied and spacious choices, often with canopy beds, private balconies, or terraces. Roomy bathrooms have dual basins and tub/shower combos. The clientele is international, elegant, and appreciates the resort's small scale and superb service. The spa, one of the best on the Costa del Sol, offers a full range of thalassotherapy and beauty treatments.

Bulevar Príncipe Alfonso von Hohenlohe, 29600 Marbella. ✆ **95-282-22-11**. Fax 95-282-98-84. www. marbellaclub.com. 121 units. 250€–370€ double; from 500€ suite. AE, DC, MC, V. Free parking. **Amenities:** 2 restaurants; bar; babysitting; health club; 3 pools (1 indoor); room service; sauna; spa; Turkish bath. *In room:* A/C, TV, hair dryer, minibar.

Puente Romano ★★★   Devotees rank this resort right up there with the Marbella Club, but I'll give it the runner-up prize. The hotel was originally built as a cluster of vacation apartments. In the early 1970s, a group of entrepreneurs transformed it into one of the most unusual hotels in the south of Spain. Although it sits close to the frenetic coastal highway midway between Marbella and Puerto Banús, and some have dismissed it as "more flash than class," it still enjoys a loyal following. Inside the complex, there are arbor-covered walkways, cascading water, masses of vines, and a subtropical garden. The spacious Andalusian-Mediterranean-style rooms have semi-sheltered balconies. Bathrooms have tub/shower combos.

Carretera de Cádiz, Km 177, 29600 Marbella. ✆ **95-282-09-00.** Fax 95-277-57-66. www.puente romano.com. 285 units. 220€–419€ double; from 406€ suite. AE, DC, MC, V. Limited free parking. **Amenities:** 3 restaurants; 2 bars; babysitting; golf nearby; health club; 3 outdoor pools; room service; sauna; steam room; 10 tennis courts; watersports equipment; rooms for those w/limited mobility. *In room:* A/C, TV, hair dryer, minibar, Wi-Fi.

EXPENSIVE

Don Carlos Beach & Golf Resort ★★★ One of the most dramatic hotels on the coast, the Don Carlos rises on a set of angled stilts above a pine forest. Between the hotel and its manicured beach, the best in Marbella, are 4 hectares (9¾ acres) of award-winning gardens. The hotel's low-lying terraces attract high-powered conferences from throughout Europe. Each of the spacious rooms has lacquered furniture and a bathroom with a tub/shower combo. This hotel is also home to the ultra cool Nikki Beach beach club (see box "Beach Babes and Beaus" above.)

Carretera de Cádiz Km 192, 29604 Marbella. ✆ **95-276-88-00.** Fax 95-283-34-29. www.hoteldon carlos.com. 243 units. 184€–304€ double; 282€–1,106€ suite. Rates include buffet breakfast. AE, DC, MC, V. Free parking. **Amenities:** 2 restaurants; 2 bars; babysitting; health club; 2 outdoor pools; sauna; room service; 12 tennis courts; rooms for those w/limited mobility. *In room:* A/C, TV, hair dryer, minibar, Wi-Fi.

El Fuerte ★★ ☺ I'd give the edge to Gran Meliá Don Pepe, but of the hotels in Marbella proper, this resort is in a neck-and-neck race with the Fuerte Miramar. Opening onto a good sandy beach, the hotel opened back in Marbella's jet-setting heyday, but has since been completely overhauled. It's surrounded by attractive and well-maintained gardens. Inside, decorators have been busy, matching the draperies and adding splashes of color in the various wallpapers. A beach restaurant specializes in grilled daily caught fish. The staff here is helpful, and the amenities are excellent.

Av. del Fuerte, 29600 Marbella. ✆ **95-286-15-00.** Fax 95-282-44-11. www.fuertehoteles.com. 263 units. 135€–289€ double; from 293€ suite. AE, DC, MC, V. Parking 6€. **Amenities:** Restaurant; cafe; fitness center; covered pool; outdoor pool; golf nearby; room service; sauna; lit outdoor tennis court; Turkish bath; nonsmoking rooms. *In room:* A/C, TV, hair dryer, minibar, Wi-Fi (in some).

Gran Meliá Don Pepe ★ Just on the western edge of Marbella itself, a 20-minute walk along the beachfront from the city's historic core and right next to a good beach, Meliá is a popular upmarket chain in Spain, and this is one of its finest showcases. It's housed in a standard-looking hotel block, but the interior decor is top quality and luxurious. Most of the midsize to spacious bedrooms open onto views of the Mediterranean and well-landscaped tropical gardens. Expect tasteful fabrics, creamy colors, rich classically styled decorations, and a vaguely Moorish motif.

José Meliá, 29602 Marbella. ✆ **90-214-44-40.** Fax 95-277-99-54. www.gran-melia-don-pepe.com. 201 units. 177€–456€ double; 569€–2,500€ suite. AE, DC, MC, V. Parking 20€. **Amenities:** 4 restaurants; 2 bars; babysitting; gym; Jacuzzi; 3 pools (1 heated indoor); room service; sauna; Turkish bath; nonsmoking rooms; rooms for those w/limited mobility. *In room:* A/C, TV, kitchenette (in some), hair dryer, minibar.

Hotel Fuerte Miramar ★★ This hotel is more modern than its sibling, El Fuerte, having opened on the Marbella beachfront in 2001. Its main claim to fame

345

is its complete hydrotherapy and spa center, offering a wide range of treatments. The hotel is very comfortable; its midsize to spacious bedrooms have tiled bathrooms and balconies opening onto Mediterranean vistas. There's a bright, airy feel to the rooms, lots of carpeting and minor decoration, but the net result is more functional than stylish. The heated outdoor pool is in use early in the spring and late into the autumn.

Plaza José Luque Manzano, 29600 Marbella. ✆ **95-276-84-00.** Fax 95-276-84-14. www.fuertehoteles. com. 226 units. 99€–268€ double. AE, DC, MC, V. Free parking outdoors; 7€ indoors. **Amenities:** 2 restaurants; 2 bars; outdoor pool; room service; spa/hydrotherapy center. *In room:* A/C, TV, hair dryer, minibar, Wi-Fi.

Los Monteros ★★★ Around 7km (5 miles) east of Marbella, this swanky government-rated five-star establishment has been catering to the rich and famous for nearly half a century. It's right in the heart of the so-called "Golf Mile" along the coast and is increasingly popular with mega-rich Russians. Spacious bedrooms are tastefully and elegantly furnished in warm hues and imported fabrics. Bathrooms are well accessorized and come with tub/shower combos. All feature private balconies and views to the gardens. El Corzo serves first-rate fusion food (Andalusian and international). Spanish classic dishes are given a modern twist in the Flamingo Restaurant. The beach club, La Cabane, is one of the best along the coast.

Urbanización Los Monteros, Carretera de Cádiz, Km 187, 29600 Marbella. ✆ **95-277-17-00.** Fax 95-282-58-46. www.monteros.com. 170 units. 220€–590€ double; from 700€ suite. AE, DC, MC, V. **Amenities:** 2 restaurants; bar; babysitting; gym; 2 outdoor pools; room service; sauna; nonsmoking rooms; rooms for those w/limited mobility. *In room:* A/C, TV, hair dryer, minibar, Wi-Fi.

Sultán Club Marbella On the outskirts of Marbella, a 10-minute drive from the center, this apartment hotel is in the residential district of Milla de Oro, just a short walk to the beach. Opened in 1997, it's designed to evoke luxury living enjoyed by the sultans of old. The interior brims with tropical plants and fountains. One- or two-bedded apartments have a large balcony, dining room, and fully equipped kitchen.

Calle Arturo Rubinstein, 29600 Marbella. ✆ **95-277-15-62.** Fax 95-277-55-58. www.monarquehoteles. es. 76 units. 103€–250€ 1-bedroom apt; 130€–312€ 2-bedroom apt. AE, DC, MC, V. Parking 10€. **Amenities:** Restaurant; bar; babysitting; health club; massage; 2 pools (1 heated indoor); room service; sauna; spa. *In room:* A/C, TV, hair dryer.

MODERATE

El Rodeo 🏆 Even though this modern hotel is just off Marbella's main coastal road, it's quiet and secluded. It's certainly not the most attractive of hotels in the area, situated in a large apartment block, but it's clean and good value for money given its location, a moment's walk from both the beach and the Old Town. Guests and locals gather in the newly renovated bar. The midsize rooms are functional; all bathrooms have tub/shower combos. The hotel is open year-round; peak season runs June to October.

Víctor de la Serna s/n, 29600 Marbella. ✆ **95-277-51-00.** Fax 95-282-33-20. www.monarquehoteles.es. 100 units. 65€–140€ double. AE, DC, MC, V. **Amenities:** Restaurant; bar; outdoor pool. *In room:* A/C, TV.

Hotel Rincón Andaluz ★ ☺ In a stylish area of Marbella 1km (⅔ mile) from Puerto Banús, this government-rated four-star hotel in a park is meant to evoke a *pueblo andaluz* (Andalusian village). The resort is only 500m (1,640 ft) from a good beach. Large rooms are tastefully decorated and fully equipped; all with at least a small living room (those in the suites are larger). Ground-floor rooms have direct access to the gardens; others open onto balconies. Minimum 5-night stay in peak season.

Carretera de Cádiz Km 173, 29660 Marbella. © **95-281-15-17.** Fax 95-281-41-80. www.hotelrincon andaluz.com. 315 units. 80€–140€ double; 220€ suite. Rates include breakfast. AE, DC, MC, V. Free parking. **Amenities:** Restaurant; 2 bars; children's playground; 2 outdoor pools; 1 pool for kids; room service; nonsmoking rooms. *In room:* A/C, TV, hair dryer, minibar.

The Town House ★★★ 🎁 Deep in the heart of the Old Town, this former private home is now the town's most romantic boutique hotel, an oasis of relaxed tranquility. It's my personal favorite. Most guests' days begin with morning coffee and breakfast in the cool ground-floor bar and end with a cold drink on the roof terrace as the sun sets. The house is set on a corner in a quiet square in the Old Town, a 5-minute walk to the beach. Midsize bedrooms were designed with exquisite care, with antique objects combined with contemporary design and modern comforts. Some rooms have bath and shower, others just showers. My favorite is no. 9 with its small private east-facing roof terrace. Or go for room no. 6 with its four-poster bed. The staff here is really helpful too. It feels like you're staying with friends.

Plaza Tetuán, Calle Alderete 7, 29600 Marbella. © **95-290-17-91.** www.townhouse.nu. 9 units. 125€–145€ double. MC, V. **Amenities:** Bar; rooftop terrace; room service. *In room:* A/C, TV, DVD, Wi-Fi.

INEXPENSIVE

Hotel Artola Golf ★ Between Fuengirola and Marbella, close to Cabopino marina and a short walk from Artola beach, this charming place was originally an old staging post for travelers en route to Gibraltar. Converted into an inn in the 1970s, the architecture is typically Andalusian, with a stucco-and-wood facade and terracotta roof surrounded by a garden and patio. Inside it still looks old and has colorful tiles and decorative wooden wall panels and beams. Midsize rooms are comfortable and have Moorish details. There's a nine-hole golf course in the grounds too.

Carretera de Cádiz Km 194, 29600 Marbella. © **95-283-13-90.** Fax 95-283-04-50. www.hotelartola. com. 31 units. 88€–112€ double; 136€–162€ suite. AE, MC, V. Free parking. **Amenities:** Restaurant; bar; babysitting; golf course; outdoor pool; room service. *In room:* A/C, TV, Wi-Fi.

Hostal El Castillo At the foot of the castle in the narrow streets of the Old Town, this small hotel opens onto a minuscule square used by the adjoining convent and school as a playground. There's a small, covered courtyard. The spartan rooms are scrubbed clean and have bathrooms with tub/shower combos. No breakfast is served, and the staff speaks only a little English.

Plaza San Bernabé 2, 29601 Marbella. © **95-277-17-39.** Fax 95-282-11-98. www.hotelelcastillo.com. 26 units. 38€–52€ double. MC, V. *In room:* A/C, TV.

Hotel Lima 🍴 Tucked in a residential area between the Old Town and the beach, the Lima is more secluded than other hotels nearby. The modern structure has plain rooms with Spanish provincial furnishings and private balconies. It's clean, friendly, well looked after and a good budget choice. There are triple rooms as well.

Av. Antonio Belón, 29600 Marbella. © **95-277-05-00.** Fax 95-286-30-91. www.hotellimamarbella. com. 64 units. 62€–96€ double; 80€–123€ triple. AE, DC, MC, V. Parking 13€. **Amenities:** Restaurant; babysitting; massage; room service. *In room:* A/C, TV, hair dryer, minibar.

Linda Marbella 🎁   Bargains are hard to come by in the center of Marbella, but this is your best bet if you like more of a bed-and-breakfast-style room. Right in the heart of the Old Town, the little inn opened in 2002 and became deservedly popular almost overnight. Don't expect grand living, but the small rooms are well maintained and comfortable. Bathrooms are a bit cramped but serviceable, each with a shower stall.

Ancha 21, 29600 Marbella. ✆ **95-285-71-71.** Fax 95-276-61-61. www.hotel-lindamarbella.com. 15 units. 50€–80€ double. MC, V. *In room:* A/C, TV.

NEARBY PLACES TO STAY

Castillo de Monda ★★ 🏠   In 1996, a group of entrepreneurs transformed the crumbling ruins of an 8th-century Moorish fortress into this showplace, in a sleepy White Village 12km (7½ miles) north of Marbella. El Castillo de Monda is a calm oasis in a region that grows glitzier by the year, and its location is stunning, high on a ridge with sweeping views across the hill. Spacious rooms are beautifully maintained and traditionally furnished. There's a lovely outdoor pool and terrace.

El Castillo s/n, 29110 Nonda (Málaga). ✆ **95-245-71-42.** Fax 95-245-73-36. www.castillodemonda.es. 28 units. 113€–136€ double; 194€–224€ suite. MC, V. Free parking. **Amenities:** Restaurant; bar; babysitting; outdoor pool; room service; nonsmoking rooms. *In room:* A/C, TV, hair dryer.

Refugio del Juanar ★ 🏠   The former hunting lodge of King Alfonso XIII has been turned into this hotel and restaurant, an ideal retreat from Marbella and a favorite with aristocrats and politicians, including Charles de Gaulle. In the heart of the Sierra Blanca, 4km (2½ miles) from the town of Ojén, which is 10km (6 miles) north of Marbella, the inn is at the southern edge of a mountainous wilderness, Serranía de Ronda, inhabited by wild ibex. The forests surrounding the inn have well-marked paths for those who want to go trekking. Midsize bedrooms, in old-fashioned Spanish hacienca style, are comfortable; each bathroom has a tub or shower. A log fire roars downstairs in winter, and six rooms have their own fireplaces. The on-site rustic-looking restaurant serves excellent Spanish cuisine. If you're dropping by for lunch while in the area, meals start from 36€. including 2-hour use of a room for a siesta!

Sierra Blanca s/n, 29610 Ojén. ✆ **95-288-10-00.** Fax 95-288-10-01. www.juanar.com. 26 units. 80€–135€ double; 150€–200€ suite. Free parking. AE, DC, MC, V. **Amenities:** Restaurant; bar; outdoor pool; room service (8am–midnight), tennis court. *In room:* TV, hair dryer, minibar.

Where to Dine

EXPENSIVE

Buenaventura ★ ANDALUSIAN/SPANISH   Other restaurants in Marbella, including La Hacienda, are more glamorous, but Buenaventura holds its own with solidly reliable food at reasonably affordable prices. In the oldest quarter of Marbella, it is full of charm. The 1937 building was constructed in typical Andalusian style with an internal patio, hanging flowerpots, and wooden columns. The restaurant is well known for excellent red wines, including the best vintages from Andalusian vineyards. The chef, Alexis Gonzalez, dazzles with his savory creations. He's known for his roast pork, perfectly flavored with cumin and the freshest, daily caught grilled fish.

Plaza de la Iglesia de la Encarnación 5. ✆ **95-285-80-69.** Reservations recommended. Main courses 16€–33€; *menú degustación* 70€ including wine. MC, V. July–Aug daily 7pm–1am; Sept–June daily 1–11:30pm.

Calima ★★★ ANDALUSIAN/INTERNATIONAL   Dani García made his name as the most exciting and innovative chef in Marbella and he's now opening restaurants elsewhere in Andalusia too. This thoroughly inventive chef injects liquid nitrogen into olives. When one explodes, he serves the popcorn-like morsels with fresh lobster salad. Or he'll take wild baby shrimp and arrange them on a slate heated to 300°F, which he garnishes with an olive-oil emulsion and fennel dust. But, for the most part, he keeps his menu local, using the famous local ingredients: olive oil, *jamón* (Andalusian ham), and sherry. Dine on a large terrace overlooking the ocean. The fresh Mediterranean and Atlantic seafood is some of the best along the coast. The wine list is impressive. After dinner head for the piano bar, **El Almirante,** for live music and shows in season.

In the Gran Meliá Don Pepe. Calle José Meliá. ☏ **95-276-42-52.** Reservations required. Main courses 22€–38€. AE, DC, MC, V. Tues-Sat 1:30-3:30pm and 8:30-10:30pm.

El Portalón ★ SPANISH/INTERNATIONAL   This is one of Marbella's most stylish dining enclaves with an urbane staff. Menu selections include time-honored Iberian dishes such as suckling lamb and pig slowly roasted in a wood-burning oven, grilled meats, and fish that's bought fresh daily. Try grilled sea bass with a julienne of fresh vegetables, or entrecote of beef with fresh vegetables and red wine sauce. Sample the excellent selection of Spanish wines in the Art Deco-style pavilion called the "vinoteca". The restaurant is about a mile west of town on the road to Puerto Banús.

Carretera de Cádiz Km 178. ☏ **95-282-78-80.** Reservations recommended. Main courses 29€–38€. AE, DC, MC, V. Mon-Sat 1-4pm and 8-11:30pm.

La Hacienda ★★★ INTERNATIONAL   La Hacienda, a quiet place 13km (8 miles) east of Marbella, serves some of the best food on the Costa del Sol. In cooler months you can dine in the rustic tavern in front of an open fireplace. In fair weather, meals are served on a patio partially encircled by Romanesque arches. Appetizers often include foie gras with lentils and lobster croquettes. For a main dish, try roast guinea hen with cream, minced raisins, and port. An iced soufflé finishes the meal nicely.

Urbanización Hacienda Las Chapas, Carretera de Cádiz Km 193. ☏ **95-283-12-67.** www.restaurantela hacienda.com. Reservations recommended. Main courses 20€–30€; fixed-price menu 45€. AE, DC, MC, V. July/Aug daily 8:30pm-midnight (closed Mon in July); Sept-June Wed-Sat 7:30-11:00pm; Sun 1:30-3:30pm and 7:30-11:00pm. Closed Nov.

La Meridiana ★★★ ITALIAN/INTERNATIONAL   A short distance outside old Marbella, opposite the exclusive Puente Romano hotel, this may not be the most sophisticated restaurant on the Costa del Sol, but its garden terrace makes it the most romantic. And it serves some of the best cuisine as well. The menu of Italian and Andalusian specialties changes four times yearly. Some of the most tantalizing items on the menu include wild sea bass seasoned with thyme and served with a prawn sauce, or roast monkfish with a red pepper preserve on a bed of onion puree. Or order the house specialty: roast duck flambé in Calvados with truffles, fried onions, dates, and dried figs. The nightclub, La Notte, is a hot spot for late-night revelers.

Camino de la Cruz s/n. ☏ **95-277-61-90.** www.lameridiana.es. Reservations required. Main courses 16€–25€. AE, DC, MC, V. Mon-Fri 1:30-6:30pm and 8:30-11:30pm, Weekends 8:30-11:30pm.

Marbella Club Restaurant ★★ INTERNATIONAL   Perhaps the nicest meals here are those served on the terrace in good weather. Lunch is traditionally an overflowing buffet served in the beach club. You dine amid blooming flowers, flickering candles, and strains of live music—a Spanish classical guitarist, a small chamber orchestra playing 19th-century classics, or a South American vocalist. Menu items, inspired by European cuisines, change with the season. You might begin with beef carpaccio or lobster salad delicately flavored with olive oil. Specialties include one of the coast's most savory paellas, and tender veal cutlets from Avila.

In the Marbella Club, Bulevar Príncipe Alfonso von Hohenlohe s/n. ⓒ **95-282-22-11.** Reservations recommended. Lunch buffet 70€; dinner main courses 12€–35€. AE, DC, MC, V. Summer daily 1:30–4pm and 9pm–12:30am; winter daily 1:30–4pm and 8:30–11:30pm.

Skina ★★★ ANDALUSIAN/MEDITERRANEAN   In the middle of the Old Town, this stylish new eaterie is a cut above the rest and without doubt the best dining option in this area of Marbella. It's intimate and comfortable, a world away from the showier places farther out of town. The dishes served up by chef Jacobo Vazquez and his team are innovative and delicious. Start with oxtail croquettes with seasonal mushrooms, then try baby lamb shoulder with apricots, venison with red fruit infusion, or sea bass with eel risotto and goji berries as a main. Finish off with the zen chocolate dessert which has to be tried to be believed. The wine list is excellent, particularly good for Málaga region wines. For a serious meal, try the tasting menu (*menú de degustación*).

Calle Aduar 12. ⓒ **95-276-52-77.** www.restauranteskina.com. Reservations required. Main courses 22€–30€; tasting menu 74.90€. AE, MC, V. Mon–Sat 7:30–11:30pm.

Villa Tiberio ★ ITALIAN/INTERNATIONAL   Villa Tiberio's proximity to the upscale Marbella Club ensures a flow of visitors from that elite hotel. In what was originally a private villa during the 1960s, it serves the most innovative Italian food in the region, and attracts many northern European expatriates living nearby. Appetizers include thinly sliced smoked beef with fresh avocados and oil-and-lemon dressing, and *fungi fantasía* (a large wild mushroom stuffed with seafood and lobster sauce). Especially tempting is the *pappardelle alla Sandro*—named after the restaurant's flamboyant owner Sandro Morelli—large flat noodles studded with chunks of lobster, tomato, and garlic. Main dishes include sea bass with cherry tomatoes, basil, and black truffle oil; duck baked with orange and Curaçao liqueur; and *osso buco* (veal shanks).

Carretera de Cádiz Km 178.5. ⓒ **95-277-17-99.** www.villatiberio.com. Reservations recommended. Main courses 17€–24€; fixed-price menus 50€–55€. AE, DC, MC, V. Mon–Sat 7:30pm–12:30am.

MODERATE
Casa de la Era ★ 📷ANDALUSIAN   This little discovery outside Marbella is in a rustic hacienda-like house, its internal patios full of plants, trees, and flowers. Hanging hams and ceramics add to the old-fashioned look. Charming waiters help you choose the chef's specialties: noodles with angler fish and baby clams, baby goat from the mountains above Málaga, and savory codfish in a spicy fresh tomato sauce. For beef eaters, the sirloin *a la ibérica* comes with a tangy sauce of fresh bay leaf and cloves. More enjoyable still, the restaurant has a beautiful terrace to dine on.

Finca El Chorraero-Carretera de Ojén. ⓒ **95-277-06-25.** www.casadelaera.com. Reservations recommended. Main courses 10€–19€. AE, DC, MC, V. Mon–Sat 1–11pm. July and Aug 8pm–midnight.

Ciboca SPANISH   In the heart of Marbella's historic medieval core, the attractive Ciboca occupies a 500-year-old building surrounded with vines and flowers. Tables are moved onto the historic square outside in good weather. A full roster of Spanish wines accompanies dishes that include virtually every kind of fish. I particularly like the sea bass baked in a salt crust. Also appealing is roasted lamb scented with Andalusian herbs, and tournedos served with a perfectly made béarnaise sauce.

Calle Valdes 3 (just off Plaza de las Naranjos). *(C)* **95-277-37-43.** Reservations recommended. Main courses 13€-28€. MC, V. Mon-Sat noon-11pm.

La Tirana ★ ANDALUSIAN/SPANISH   Close to the Gran Melia Don Pepe hotel, about a 20-minute walk from the Old Town, this charming restaurant is in a 1940 Andalusian house with a Moorish-style garden. The pretty decor is rather like a country restaurant in North Africa, opening onto a beautiful courtyard. The skillful cooking is very up to date, with inventive flavor combinations. Perhaps begin with a classic bowl of *salmorejo* with avocado or *ajo blanco a la malagueña* (almond soup). For main courses, order the savory oven-baked lamb with Moroccan-style couscous and mint sauce. Also good is fresh tuna sautéed with spices and served in a tangy tomato sauce.

La Merced Chica, Huerta Márquez. *(C)* **95-286-34-24.** www.restaurantelatirana.es. Reservations recommended. Main courses 22€-28€. AE, MC, V. Daily 8:30pm-midnight. Closed Sun and Mon in winter.

Santiago ★ SEAFOOD/INTERNATIONAL   This nice seafood restaurant is right on the Playa de la Venus seafront, just down from the Old Town. The decor, the tapas bar, the summertime patio, and fresh fish dishes make this one of the most popular places in town. Savory fish soup is well prepared and well spiced. Follow with a generous serving of sole in Champagne or grilled or sautéed turbot. The menu also offers many meat dishes. For dessert, try a serving of manchego cheese.

Paseo Marítimo 5. *(C)* **95-277-00-78.** Reservations required. Main courses 22€-30€. AE, DC, MC, V. Daily 1-5pm and 9pm-1am.

Taberna del Pintxo ★★ BASQUE/ANDALUSIAN   A *pintxo* is a Basque-style tapas. (Pintxo means 'spike' and refers to the small wooden skewer pushed through the tapa so you can pick it up and eat it easily.) On busy Calle Miguel Cano, this little tavern has taken tapas to the next level, serving up delicious bites like chicken with ginger, coriander, garlic, and white onion; duck magret with balsamic sauce and sesame; squid with coriander, lemon, and garlic; and tuna with cardamom and juniper. Sometimes it can be difficult to get served in the busy neighborhood tapas bars. Here they've solved the problem: tapas are paraded past you by waiting staff and you can take your pick of whatever takes your fancy. They are all delicious, so take your time and choose wisely! Accompany them with a glass of local red wine or an ice-cold beer.

Av. Miguel Cano, 7. *(C)* **95-282-93-21.** www.latabernadelpintxo.com. Tapas 2€-3.50€. MC, V. Daily noon-midnight.

Zozoi ★ INTERNATIONAL   Rightly popular with a hip young local crowd, this friendly little place on a bustling square in the Old Town serves great quality, interesting dishes at very reasonable prices. Dishes are simple, fresh, and attractively presented. Starters include warm goat's cheese marinated with honey and thyme, whilst mains include roasted skate wing with lemon and ginger pickle and Parmesan-crusted veal escalope. For dessert try the light bourbon vanilla ice cream coated with roasted sugar. Or just go for one of the pizzas.

Plaza Altamirano 1. ✆ **95-285-88-68.** www.zozoi.com. Reservations required. Main courses 14€–25€. AE, MC, V. Mon–Sat 7:30pm–1am.

Shopping

While other Andalusian villages may inspire you to buy handicrafts, Marbella's international glamour might just incite so much insecurity you'll want to rush out to accessorize. Should you feel seriously underdressed, head for the designer shopping offered in nearby Puerto Banús (see "Shopping" section in Puerto Banús).

A MARBELLA tapas-CRAWL

To rub shoulders with the locals and experience a taste of Spain, eat in the tapas bars. Marbella boasts more hole-in-the-wall tapas bars than virtually any other resort town on the Costa del Sol.

Prices and hours are remarkably consistent. The coffeehouse that opens at 7am will switch to wine and tapas when the first patron asks for them (sometimes shortly after breakfast), then continue through the day dispensing wine, sherry, and, more recently, bottles of beer. On average, tapas cost 2.50€ to 5€; locals tend to order them one at a time, but some foreign visitors configure them into *platos combinados.*

Tapas served along the Costa del Sol are principally Andalusian in origin, with an emphasis on seafood. One of the most popular plates, *fritura malagueña,* consists of fried fish based on the catch of the day. Sometimes *ajo blanco,* a garlicky local version of gazpacho made with almonds, is served, especially in summer. Fried squid or octopus is another favorite, as are little Spanish-style herb-flavored meatballs (*albondigas*). Other well-known tapas include *tortilla* (a thick omelet made with layered slices of potato), *gambas a la plancha* (grilled shrimp), *piquillos rellenos* (red peppers stuffed with fish), *bacalao* (salt cod), and mushrooms sautéed in olive oil and garlic.

Tapas bars line several of the narrow streets of Marbella's Old Town. My favorite for totally authentic neighborhood tapas bars is tiny **Calle San Lázaro** off Plaza de la Victoria. Close by, **Bar Altamirano,** Plaza Altamirano 4, (✆ **95-282-49-32**), does some of the freshest fried seafood in town; absolutely delicious and huge portions. Towards the seafront, **Calle Miguel Cano** has several really nice, slightly more upmarket tapas bars, in particular the excellent **Taberna del Pintxo,** Av. Miguel Cano 7 (✆ **95-282-93-21**) (see p. 351) and **Bodega La Venensia,** Av. Miguel Cano 15 (✆ **95-285-79-13**).

In August especially, when you want to escape wall-to-wall people and the heat and noise of the Old Town, head for one of the shoreline restaurants and tapas bars called *chiringuitos.* All serve local specialties, and you can order a full meal, a snack, tapas, or a drink. **Pepe's Bar,** Av.del Mar s/n (✆ **95-282-24-75**), right on Playa de la Venus, is one of the most convenient for the Old Town, as is **Chiringuito El Faro,** Playa El Faro s/n, (✆ **95-276-50-57**). Around 8km (5 miles) east of the Old Town, close to Los Monteros hotel, another favorite is **Los Sardinales,** Playa del Alicate (✆ **95-283-70-12**), which serves some of the best sangria in the area.

For more Andalusian-style fashion, head for Sevillian design shop **El Caballo**, Calle Huerta Chica 14 (© 95-277-10-26; www.elcaballo.es), with its stylish leatherware and womenswear. If art is your passion, one of Marbella's most appealing galleries is also in the Old Town: the **Galleria d'Arte Van Gestel,** Plaza de los Naranjos 11 (© 95-277-48-19). For purchasing Andalusia's regional ceramics, your best bet is **Cerámica San Nicolás,** Plaza de la Iglesia 1 (© 95-277-05-46).

And if your search for fine art carries over to **Puerto Banús,** consider an overview of the contemporary artwork displayed at the **Sammer Gallery,** Av. de Julio Iglesias 3, Las Terrazas de Banús, Local 10–16 (© 95-281-29-95).

Marbella after Dark

There's more international wealth hanging out in the watering holes of Marbella, and a wider choice of glam (or pseudoglam) discos, than virtually anywhere else in the south of Spain. None of these get going until midnight or later and to get into most you need to dress smart and sophisticated. Most are situated towards Puerto Banús. Foremost among these is the ultra-chic **Olivia Valere,** Carretera Istan, N-340 Km 0.8 (© 95-282-88-61). Housed in a Moorish-style replica of the Alhambra and the Mezquita, it has to be seen to be believed. It's usually open Friday and Saturday from midnight to 7am, with a cover of 30€. The likes of Bruce Willis, Mariah Carey, and Kate Moss have all enjoyed late nights out here. Another fashionable place to rendezvous at night is **Vanity** (no cover), Camino de la Cruz s/n (© 95-277-76-25), next to the swanky La Meridiana restaurant (p. 349). It too has a Moorish edge to its decor and offers a terrace and an elegant atmosphere with rich decoration. Live music and shows are presented here during its nightly hours from 12:30 until 4am. For full-on nightclub action, head for **Dreamers**, Carretera de Cádiz Km 175 (© 95-281-20-80; www.dreamers-disco.com). This 1,400 capacity super-club hosts all the big names on the house music circuit, with go-go dancers and live acts in between. If you fancy a night out at any of these venues, call ahead and try and get on a guest list or book a VIP table. Expect to spend plenty of money on drinks, which are seriously pricey.

If you're in the heart of historic Marbella, enjoy a night in the bars and *bodegas* of the Old Town. Start your evening along Calle Peral for a few quiet drinks in the funky bars here. The top **La Cuisine,** Plaza Puente Ronda 2 (© 95-282-56-88), does a seriously sharp *mojito*. Hidden away behind Plaza de Los Naranjos, **Town House,** Calle Alamo 1 (no phone), is a tiny, smokey little dive in an old patio house serving beer and mayhem from 10pm until very late. Busy and very atmospheric, with a touch of old British colonial pub to it, **Mombasa Marbella,** Av. Miguel Cano 1 (© 95-277-96-35) will take things up a notch on the volume and drinking scale for you. And if you want to dance 'til dawn in the Old Town, **Buddha Marbella,** Av. del Mar 3 (© 95-277-2891; www.buddhamarbella.com), plays young trendy house music, but is actually very friendly and patronized by locals.

For entertainment of a more traditionally Andalusian variety, the best flamenco club in town is **Tablao Flamenco Ana María,** Plaza del Santo Cristo 5/4, (© 95-282-31-07). I think it's the most authentic place for foreign visitors with a limited knowledge of Spanish. The long, often-crowded bar area sells tapas, wine, sherry, and a selection of more international drinks. On the stage, singers, dancers, and musicians perform flamenco and popular songs. Performances are Tuesday to

Saturday from 10:30pm. Another nice flamenco option if you fancy dinner too is **Restaurante Patio de los Perfumes,** Calle Aduar 1 (© **95-282-86-50**), which has shows on Tuesdays and Thursdays at 10pm from May to September. Bookings are essential.

Seven kilometers (4½ miles) west of Marbella, near Puerto Banús, **Casino Marbella,** Hotel H10, Andalucía Plaza, (© **95-281-40-00;** www.casinomarbella.com), is on the lobby level of the H10 Hotel resort complex. The focus is on gambling, and mobs of visitors from northern Europe flock here. Individual games include French and American roulette, blackjack, punto y banco, craps, and chemin de fer. You can dine before or after gambling in the **Casino Restaurant,** a few steps above the gaming floor. The tasting menu is 50€ per person including wine. Jackets are not required for men, but shorts and T-shirts are not allowed. The casino is open daily from 7pm to 4am. A passport or ID card is required for admission.

FUENGIROLA & LOS BOLICHES

32km (20 miles) W of Málaga, 104km (64 miles) E of Algeciras, 574km (356 miles) S of Madrid

The fishing towns of **Fuengirola** and **Los Boliches** are halfway between Marbella and Torremolinos. A promenade along the water stretches 4km (2½ miles). Fuengirola and quieter Los Boliches are 0.8km (½ mile) apart.

These towns don't have the facilities or drama of Torremolinos and Marbella, but this has attracted hordes of budget-conscious European tourists. Accommodation here is aimed firmly at the mid-market package tourist trade, a little better in quality and more family-orientated than Torremolinos, but not in the same league as Marbella.

Essentials

GETTING THERE Fuengirola is on the coastal **metro** route (*cercanias*) with regular trains from Málaga and Torremolinos. Trains depart every 30 minutes, taking 20 minutes from Torremolinos and 50 minutes from Málaga. They arrive at the underground station at Av. Juan Gómez Juanito, close to Fuengirola town center. Call **RENFE** (© **90-232-03-20;** www.renfe.es) for more information.

Fuengirola is also on the main Costa del Sol **bus** route from Algeciras (2 hr) and Marbella (45 min.) in the west, or Málaga (45 min.) in the east. Buses arrive at the small bus terminal close to the town center at Av. Matías Sáenz de Tejada and are operated by **Empresa Portillo** (© **90-245-05-50;** www.ctsa-portillo.com). If you're driving, Fuengirola is easily accessible from the main A-7 coast road and the AP-7/E-15 high-speed toll road.

VISITOR INFORMATION The **tourist office,** Paseo Jesús Santos Rein 6 (© **95-246-74-57;** www.visitafuengirola.com), is open Monday to Friday from 9:30am to 2pm and 5 to 7pm, and Saturday from 9:30am to 1:30pm.

Exploring Fuengirola

Don't—I repeat, don't—come here for the attractions. There aren't many, and you can skip them all without suffering cultural deprivation. Frankly, if you have a day for sightseeing, I recommend that you don't spend it in Fuengirola but head for the hill town of **Mijas,** one of the Pueblos Blancos of Andalusia. See Chapter 9.

HIGHWAY OF death

The N-340—known variously as the **Carretera Nacional** and the **Carretera Cádiz** (the road to Cádiz)—is one of the most dangerous in all of Europe. More like a city street than a highway, it stretches for 100km (62 miles) right through the town centers, where there are a lot of drunken revelers, particularly later at night, and divides *urbanizaciones* (overcrowded urban developments).

Even so, motorists—both Costa del Sol natives and visiting foreigners—treat it like a raceway. There are some 100 fatalities a year. A lot of accidents are caused by Brits unfamiliar with driving on the right-hand side. Two particularly horrendous areas are the stretch of highway between Málaga airport and the resort of Torremolinos to the west, and the stretch of road west from Marbella along the highway to the port of Algeciras.

For tourists, the opening of **Autopista del Sol (A-7),** a four-lane motorway, has somewhat alleviated the dangers. This new expressway links Estepona in the west to Nerja (via Málaga) in the east. The brand new **toll** section from Málaga to Estepona (the AP-7) has made driving along the coast even faster and much safer. It's well worth the cost of around 13€ for the whole stretch.

Fuengirola is known for its 8km (5 miles) of good quality sandy **beaches** which are some of the best on the Costa del Sol. They're fronted by rather ugly high-rise hotels and residential blocks where many Spanish own summer apartments. There's a promenade flanked by palm trees. The main town beach, **Playa de Fuengirola,** is the easiest to access and has fine dark gold sand with plenty of facilities including showers, beach bars, toilets, and lifeguards. Immediately west is **Playa Santa Amalia,** one of the best-equipped beaches in the area. It's very much a family beach and is flanked by seafood restaurants, shops, and hotels. Fishing, windsurfing, and sailing are popular pastimes. **Playa El Ejido** follows this, right before you cross the Fuengirola River on the N-340, adjoining **Playa Santa Amalia.** This small lake, formed before the river joins the sea, attracts families with children to its safe waters.

Immediately east of Playa de Fuengirola is **Playa San Francisco,** a smaller beach of dark gold sand which curves around to form a marina. You can fish from here and enjoy dolphin safaris and diving. There's a decent swell sometimes, which makes it popular with windsurfers and bodyboarders. Immediately after this come the beaches of Los Boliches, which I prefer to those of Fuengirola. **Playa Los Boliches** and adjoining **Playa Las Gaviotas** are the best equipped, with access for wheelchairs and seafood restaurants, hotels, and shops along the seafront. Slightly quieter **Playa Torreblanca** is one of the most popular beaches, a stretch of fine dark gold sand with tranquil waters safe for children and magnificent views of the Fuengirola bay. Finally, **Playa Carvajal** is quieter still; it offers showers and a beach bar but no public toilets.

Where to Stay

Hotel Yaramar   One of the better high-rise hotels aimed predominantly at British package tourists, the Yaramar has been recently refurbished and many of its rooms have sweeping views out to sea. There's a good-sized outdoor pool on the large first-floor terrace. Rooms are simply furnished, but well equipped and quite spacious. The hotel also has a small shopping arcade. Be aware that it does get very full with British families and older couples on package breaks in the busy summer months though.

Paseo Marítimo Rey de España 64, 29640 Fuengirola. © **95-292-11-00.** Fax 95-247-30-10. www.hotelyaramar.es. 242 units. 100€–150€ double. Prices include buffet breakfast. AE, MC, V. **Amenities:** Restaurant; bar; outdoor pool; room service; nonsmoking rooms. *In room:* A/C, TV, hair dryer, minibar.

Villa de Laredo 🏄 With a panoramic site on the waterfront promenade, this good-value inn is a block east of the main port. One of the more modern hotels in town, it doesn't attempt to equal the luxury larger resort hotels on the periphery. Bedrooms are newly styled and comfortable; small bathrooms have tub and shower. Try for one of the rooms with a small terrace onto the seafront promenade. The featured attraction of the villa is its small rooftop pool, with views of the Paseo Marítimo. It's popular with Spanish couples and families, with some triple rooms.

Paseo Marítimo Rey de España 42, 29640 Fuengirola. © **95-247-76-89.** Fax 95-247-79-50. 74 units. 62€–160€ double. AE, MC, V. **Amenities:** Restaurant; bar; outdoor pool; room service; nonsmoking rooms. *In room:* A/C, TV, hair dryer, minibar.

NEARBY PLACES TO STAY

The Beach House ★★ 🏨 Why recommend a hotel that currently isn't open? Well, hopefully it will be by the time you are reading this. Owned and created by the same Swedish couple behind the delightful Town House in Marbella, the Beach House is an oasis of calm and tranquility on a coastline that's usually more about cheap beer and noisy nightclubs. It's on the ocean's edge with a lovely pool overlooking the beach. The hotel has just 10 rooms and one suite, all in Scandinavian style with minimal fuss and genuine asthetic appeal. Think dark wood, modern furniture, and white marble floors and furnishings. Service here is friendly and genuinely helpful. I hope they'll be open again for business in 2011.

Urbanismo El Chaparral, Ctra de Cádiz N-340 Km 203, 29649, Mijas Costa. © **95-249-45-40.** Fax 95-249-45-40. www.beachhouse.nu. 11 units. 125€–140€ double. Rates include breakfast. AE, MC, V. **Amenities:** Outdoor pool; room service; nonsmoking rooms. *In room:* A/C, TV, DVD player.

Hotel Las Islas ★★ 🏨 Another hidden gem surrounded by package tourism high rises, Las Islas is a charming boutique hotel. The pool is surrounded by palms, banana trees, and jacaranda trees, perfect for relaxing and unwinding. There's a touch of Morocco about the decor of the 12 garden-facing rooms, with richly colored bedspreads and Moorish-style lamps and cushions. All rooms have balconies. Fairuz is one of the top Lebanese restaurants on the Costa, serving succulent meats and delicious veggie dishes. The *kofte* (minced lamb kebabs) is particularly tasty.

Calle Canela 12, Torreblanca del Sol, 29640, Fuengirola. © **95-247-55-98.** Fax 95-266-15-08 www.lasislas.info. 12 units. 95€ double. Rate includes breakfast. AE, MC, V. **Amenities:** Outdoor pool; nonsmoking rooms; Wi-Fi. *In room:* A/C, TV.

Where to Dine

Don Pé CONTINENTAL In hot weather, Don Pé patrons dine in a courtyard where the roof can be adjusted to allow in light and air. In cold weather, a fire on the hearth lights up the heavy ceiling beams and rustic accessories. The menu features a selection of game dishes, like medallions of venison, roast filet of wild boar, and duck with orange sauce. The ingredients come from the forests and plains of Andalusia.

Calle de la Cruz 17 (off the Av. Ramón y Cajal), Fuengirola. ✆ **95-247-83-51.** Reservations recommended. Main courses 7€–21€. MC, V. Mon-Sat 7pm-midnight.

La Langosta ★ ☺ INTERNATIONAL/SEAFOOD   A stone's throw from Fuengirola and two blocks from the beach, La Langosta is one of the best restaurants in the area. The Art Deco dining room is a welcome relief from the ever-present Iberian rustic style elsewhere. The menu features a variety of seafood, as well as Spanish dishes like *gazpacho andaluz* and prawns *al ajillo* (in olive oil and garlic). Lobster is prepared thermidor-style or however you want; among the beef offerings is an especially succulent version of chateaubriand. The staff is particularly well trained and helpful. Kids will be happy too as there's a children's menu available for 7.50€.

Calle Francisco Cano 1, Los Boliches. ✆ **95-247-50-49.** Main courses 15€–29€; tasting menu 35€. AE, DC, MC, V. Mon-Sat 7-11:30pm. Closed Dec-Jan.

Monopol ★★ ☺ SEAFOOD   This popular dining spot is in a neck-and-neck race with Patrick Bousier for the title of best restaurant in Fuengirola. With its nautical decor and blue-and-white Mediterranean colors, it's popular with the boating and yachting set. A bright, cheery place with a friendly waitstaff, its chefs prepare some of the best and freshest-tasting seafood in the area. Lobster can be prepared several ways, and a kettle of well-flavored mussels is always a delight. Ask for the kids' menu.

Palangreros 7. ✆ **95-247-44-48.** Reservations recommended. Main courses 13€–24€. AE, DC, MC, V. Mon-Sat 8-11:30pm. Closed July 15-Sept 1.

Moochers Jazz Café & Restaurant INTERNATIONAL   View this popular spot near the beach as your dining and entertainment option as there's live music nightly in summer. You may not necessarily hear the sounds of New Orleans, but expect blues and perhaps some rock. London expats Yvonne and Andy have a menu different from any other in town—huge crepes filled with seafood, chicken, vegetables, and more and delicious vegetarian food. There's a 10% discount on offer if you arrive before 7:30pm.

Calle La Cruz 17. ✆ **95-247-71-54.** Reservations recommended. Main courses 7.50€–20€. AE, MC, V. Daily 6pm-1am.

Portofino ANDALUSIAN/INTERNATIONAL   In front of the Paseo Marítimo promenade, this popular rustic-style tavern with lots of hanging plants and regional artifacts draws an international crowd, and the kitchen uses fresh ingredients for dishes ranging from a creamy lasagna with meat to a tender grilled pork with port wine sauce and fresh herbs. Most popular are the fresh fish dishes of the day, like filet of sole with fresh vegetables. Desserts are fairly standard.

Rey de España 29, Paseo Marítimo. ✆ **95-247-06-43.** Reservations recommended. Main courses 12€–24€. AE, MC, V. Tues-Sun 1-3:30pm and 6:30-11:30pm. Closed first 3 weeks July.

Fuengirola after Dark

Standard nightlife for the many British package tourists that stay here in the summer involves imbibing large quantities of beer in the pubs on or close to the Paseo Marítimo and watching live football (soccer) on the TV. Calle de la Cruz is the place to head for if this is your idea of a good night out. If you want to keep going later and

THE COSTA: AN ode TO LOST VIRGINITY

Once the Costa del Sol was a paradise, a retreat of the rich and famous, and in the words of British author Laurie Lee, "beautiful but exhausting and seemingly forgotten by the world." The world has now discovered this Mediterranean coastline with a vengeance.

Some social historians claim that the Costa del Sol—no one knows when or how that touristy moniker debuted—had its roots in 1932 when Carlotta Alessandri arrived, buying property west of the village of Torremolinos and announcing that she was going to launch "a Spanish Riviera to equal the French Riviera." Before she could achieve her dream, the Spanish Civil War intervened.

The Marquis of Najera arrived in Torremolinos after World War II, bringing his fellow blue bloods. In time, Spanish noble families, along with a collection of more questionable royals and aristocrats, arrived to bask in the sun. Artists, writers like Ernest Hemingway and James Michener, even movie stars, followed.

In the 1960s, hippies arrived in Torremolinos and brought their drugs with them. You would never have known a right-wing dictator was in power: flower power and the wafting smell of pot filled the streets.

Turmoil in the Middle East and the 1973 oil crisis drove thousands of Arabs to the coast, seeking safer havens. The fall of the Shah of Iran drove many other rich Iranians here. Their presence is still felt in large measure today.

In the 1970s, the London tabloids dubbed Costa the "Costa del Crime." A lack of extradition laws between Spain and Britain—a situation that's since been remedied—encouraged the arrival in Spain of dozens of "British jack-the-lad crooks." These embezzlers and con artists fled justice in England and headed for the coast, where they partied extravagantly and uninhibitedly.

By the time the 1980s arrived, the reputation of the coast had largely shifted from caviar and Champagne to burgers and beer. Despite that, many big names continued to visit. Sean Connery, for example, was an annual visitor until 1998, and Antonio Banderas and Melanie Griffith own a second home in Los Monteros on the outskirts of Marbella. Julio Iglesias has a villa near Coín, and Bruce Willis owns a retreat outside Estepona.

Today Torremolinos is a place where everyone and anyone can let loose. Lager louts parade through the narrow streets at night pursuing wine, women, and song. Religious cultists, real-estate hawkers, Las Vegas-style showgirls, and male hustlers in well-filled bikinis—all feel at home here. Even young Middle Eastern women, minus their burkas, can be seen on the beach in bikinis.

dance off some of the booze, head for the tackiest disco in town, **Mai Tai,** Edificio El Puerto, Paseo Marítimo (© **69-663-96-17**) Don't expect glamour or class, but you'll have a good time if you're in the right mood.

For something more Spanish, head for the tapas bars. Much of the Spanish nightlife centers on **Plaza Constitución** and also along the **Paseo Marítimo,** but to find something altogether more authentic, head for **Plaza Yates,** an enclosed square that's the most charming in town. On the square itself and on streets branching off it are several little tapas bars. Poke your nose in and check them out. If one appeals, head inside. For something a bit more upscale, head over to **El Tostón** ★ San

Pancracio, Alfonso XIII (☎ **95-247-56-32**), which is also a regular restaurant—and a good one at that. Inside a traditional tapas bar has wine barrels lining the walls and six or so tables for more serious dining. The *jamón ibérico* is reason enough to trek over and the excellent wine and air-conditioning complete the package. Open daily 1 to 11:45pm.

Plays, concerts, English-language musicals, and performances by amateur local troupes are all regularly staged at the **Salón de Varie Variétés Theater,** Emancipación 30 (☎ **95-247-45-42;** www.salonvarietestheatre.com). This is the only English-language theater on the Costa del Sol and its season runs from October to May. Tickets typically cost 18€ for adults, half price for children. The box office is open Monday to Friday from 10:30am to 1:30pm and 7 to 8pm. Concerts are also presented at the **Palacio de la Paz,** Recinto Ferial, Av. Jesús Santos Rein (☎ **95-258-93-49** or ☎ 266-38-00). This modern theater is between Los Boliches and Fuengirola's center.

TORREMOLINOS

15km (9 miles) W of Málaga, 122km (76 miles) E of Algeciras, 568km (353 miles) S of Madrid

This Mediterranean beach resort, Spain's biggest, is known as a melting pot of visitors, most of them European and American. The Americans come here to relax after a whirlwind tour of Europe, the Europeans for a package holiday week in the sun— the living is easy, the people are fun, and there are no historical monuments to visit. Once a sleepy fishing village, Torremolinos has been engulfed in a cluster of cement-walled resort hotels. Prices are on the rise, but it remains one of Europe's vacation bargains.

Just because Torremolinos is one of the oldest and most famous resorts along the Costa del Sol doesn't mean it's the best: Marbella in particular is far classier. Because of its ghastly concrete-block architecture, filled with cheap rooms for package tours, Torremolinos has been called a holiday inferno by some, and it's fashionable for travel writers to mock it. One Spanish-language guide, written for nationals, recommends that Spanish visitors give Torremolinos a "wide berth." Yet for all its detractors, this resort is a kitschy hit, with crowds of northern Europeans coming year after year for the sheer offbeat fun. Come with the right attitude and you'll have a good time.

Essentials

GETTING THERE Málaga airport is just a 15-minute drive up the road and frequent local **trains** (*cercanias*) run at half-hourly intervals throughout the day from the terminal at Málaga, taking just 10 minutes. For train information call **RENFE** ☎ **90-232-03-20** or visit www.renfe.es.

Buses operated by **Empresa Portillo** (☎ **90-245-05-50;** www.ctsa-portillo. com) run every 15 minutes between Málaga and Torremolinos, leaving from Málaga's Muelle Heredia station rather than the main bus station and arriving at the bus station in Torremolinos on Calle Hoyo. There are onward bus connections right down the Costa del Sol from here, also operated by Empresa Portillo.

If you're driving, take the A-7/E-15 west from Málaga or the A-7/E-15 east from Marbella. You can also use the high-speed toll road (AP-7).

GETTING AROUND   Driving around Torremolinos in a car is no way to spend a relaxing holiday. Parking and the one-way system are both pretty nightmarish. However, the local bus no. 2 is a handy service, making a frequent circuit from the bus station along the main beachfront (Paseo Marítimo) and back up into the town, stopping at or near many of the main hotels. Buses run about every 40 minutes during the day.

VISITOR INFORMATION   The **tourist information office,** Plaza de las Comunidades Autonomas (© **95-237-19-09;** www.visitetorremolinos.com), is open daily 10am to 2pm and 6 to 8pm (Mon–Fri 9:30am–2:30pm in winter).

Exploring Torremolinos & Benalmádena

The things you won't find here are the towers (*torres*) and windmills (*molinos*) that originally gave the little fishing village its name. They've been bulldozed and replaced with garish concrete towerblocks. Today Torremolinos has been rechristened "Torrie" by its hordes of package-tour devotees.

Most visitors are here for the beaches, not the architecture. There are three: **El Bajondillo** (aka Playa de Bajondill), Playa de Playamar, and **La Carihuela,** the latter bordering the old fishing village now engulfed by development. The sands are dark brown and somewhat grainy. These beaches are packed in July and August, when you'll find yourself lying next to a dishwasher from Hamburg, a telemarketer from Leicester, and a janitor of an office building in Stockholm. Let the rich and famous enjoy Marbella. Torremolinos is blue collar—and proud of it. It's not actually that hard to escape the crowds. If you head farther west along the seafront past Playa de Playamar, you reach **Playa de Los Alamos,** which is far less developed, with some nice beach bars. It's popular with locals from Málaga.

Unless Torremolinos is leveled to the ground and rebuilt, it will always be a tacky parody of a Spanish seaside resort. Even so, there have been signs of improvement, especially in the recently finished promenade along the seafront that runs all the way to the old fishing village of La Carihuela. It's quite panoramic for the most part. Some of the most offensive stores in the old quarter of Torremolinos—those hawking dildos, for example—are gone, and it's quite pleasant to wander the narrow streets and maze of old alleys. You certainly never have to worry about getting a drink, as the bar-per-block ratio is about three to one.

City officials try to amuse their summer visitors with free events, including music and dance festivals, and even jazz concerts and sporting competitions.

TORRIE'S HEARTLAND & LA CARIHUELA

The resort is divided into two parts, the main town and the fishing village below. Locals, especially British expats, call the main square **"Central T-town."** It centers on traffic-clogged Plaza Costa del Sol, where you'll see an international parade of passersby. The main shopping street leading from the plaza down towards the seafront is **Calle San Miguel,** hawking some of the junkiest souvenirs in Andalusia. But, surprise, surprise, some excellent Spanish goods will often appear in a shop selling otherwise tawdry crafts, particularly in the small arcades leading off left and right.

Brash, bold **Plaza Nogalera** in the heart of Torremolinos is active day and night. Expect sangria bars, gay hangouts, dance clubs, tapas bars—and inflated prices. Pick and choose carefully here.

Torremolinos

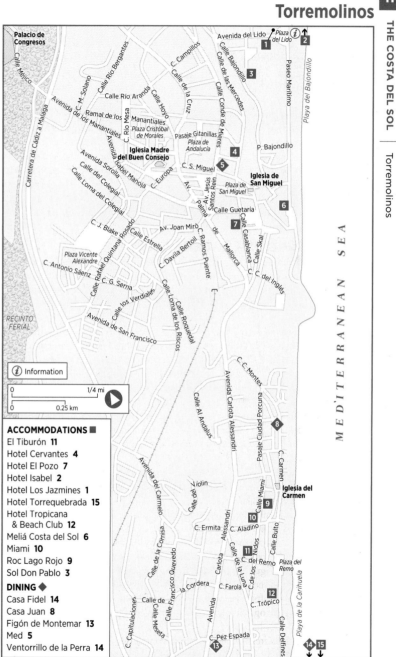

Palacio de Congresos

Avenida del Lido

Plaza del Lido

Calle Métito

Calle Río Bergantes

C. Campillos

Calle Bajondillo

Calle de las Mercedes

Calle Conde de Mieres

Paseo Marítimo

Playa del Bajondillo

Calle Río Aranda

Calle Hoyo

Calle de la Cruz

Avenida de los Manantiales

Ramal de los Manantiales

C. M. Solano

C. Río Mesa

Manantiales

Plaza Cristóbal de Morales

Pasaje Gitanillas

Plaza de Andalucía

P. Bajondillo

Carretera de Cádiz a Málaga

Avenida Sorolla

Avenida Isabel Manoja

Iglesia Madre del Buen Consejo

C. Europa

C. S. Miguel

Iglesia de San Miguel

Calle del Colegial

Calle Loma del Colegial

Av. Jesús Santos Rein

Palma

Plaza de San Miguel

Av. de Mallorca

Calle Guetaría

Calle Casablanca

Calle Skal

C. J. Blake

Calle Rosado

Calle Estrella

Av. Joan Miró

C. Ramos Puente

Calle Dávila Bertoil

C. C. del Inglés

Plaza Vicente Alexandre

C. Antonio Sáenz

Calle Rafael Quintana

C. C. G. Serna

Calle los Verdiales

Calle Loma de los Riscos

Calle Roquedal

RECINTO FERIAL

Avenida de San Francisco

MEDITERRANEAN SEA

Information

0   1/4 mi
0   0.25 km

C. C. Montes

Avenida Carlota Alessandri

Pasaje Ciudad Porcuna

Calle Al Andalus

C. Carmen

Iglesia del Carmen

Avenida del Carmelo

Calle del Violín

Calle Miami

Calle Bulto

C. Ermita

C. Aladino

Avenida Carlota Alessandri

Calle de los Nidos

C. del Remo

Plaza del Remo

C. de la Comisa

Calle Francisco Quevedo

Calle Meseta

la Cordera

C. Farola

C. de la Luna

Calle Delfines

Playa de la Carihuela

C. Capitulaciones

C. Pez Espada

C. Trópico

Plaza del Remo

ACCOMMODATIONS ■

El Tiburón **11**
Hotel Cervantes **4**
Hotel El Pozo **7**
Hotel Isabel **2**
Hotel Los Jazmines **1**
Hotel Torrequebrada **15**
Hotel Tropicana
  & Beach Club **12**
Meliá Costa del Sol **6**
Miami **10**
Roc Lago Rojo **9**
Sol Don Pablo **3**

DINING ◆

Casa Fidel **14**
Casa Juan **8**
Figón de Montemar **13**
Med **5**
Ventorrillo de la Perra **14**

La Carihuela ★ is west of Torrie's center and is most often approached via Avenida Carlotta Alessandri. It has far more Spanish flavor than the town itself, and many old fishermen's cottages, but that's not a compelling reason to visit.

Most people visit Carihuela for its excellent fish restaurants, many of which are found along Paseo Marítimo. On a summer evening when the center of Torremolinos is blistering hot, a summer promenade in Carihuela, enjoying the fresh sea breezes, is the way to go. Andalusian families, who throng here by the thousands, seem to agree.

If you have children in tow, you can take them to **Aquapark** at Calle Cuba, (© **95-238-88-88;** www.aqualand.es), just off the bypass in the vicinity of the Palacio de Congresos (a convention center). This water park is filled with the usual attractions, including "water mountains," pools, artificial waves, and water chutes. Other attractions include "kamikaze," the highest water toboggan on the Continent, and a "black hole" of tubes with sharp drops and turns. At least it's a great way to cool off in summer. Admission is 22.50€ adults, 16.50€ kids, and it's open May, June, and September daily from 11am to 6pm and in July and August daily from 10am to 7pm.

MORE FUN IN BENALMÁDENA [KDS]

Nine kilometers (5½ miles) west of Torremolinos, Benalmádena (also called Benalmádena-Costa) is a virtual suburb of Torremolinos, but I think it's rather nicer.

Package-tour operators fill up most of the hotels here and it's not the kind of place you should expect to pay full price. **Puerto Marina Benalmádena,** its yachting haven, is its smartest part and is a popular rendezvous on a hot summer night, especially with young *Málaguenos.* Also intriguing is the village proper, **Benalmádena-Pueblo,** the center of the Old Town or what's left of it. It's set a little way inland and unlike the heart of old Torremolinos, this pueblo hasn't been completely spoiled. It'll give you a preview of what a small Andalusian town looks like, provided you decide to venture no farther inland. The area is bounded by shops, bars, and other services.

One of the best aquariums in Andalusia is **Sea Life Benalmádena,** at Puerto Marina Benalmádena (© **95-256-01-50;** www.sealife.es). In summer it is open daily from 10am to midnight (closes at 6pm in the off season), charging an admission of 13.95€ for adults, 10.95€ children aged 3 to 11, those aged 2 and under free. (If you buy tickets from the website you can get discounted rates.) Most of the fish come from local waters, including some fierce sharks, sunfish, and rays swimming around the walk-through glass tunnel.

Tivoli World is the largest amusement park along the coast. In Arroyo de la Miel, at Avenida Tivoli s/n (© **95-257-70-16;** www.tivoli.es), its chief attraction is a 4,000-seat open-air auditorium. Sometimes world-class artists perform here; check when you visit. Expect anything from Spanish ballet to flamenco to corny French cancans. There are at least three dozen restaurants, snack bars, a Ferris wheel and roller coasters. Naturally, there are so-called Wild West shows of the Buffalo Bill and Calamity Jane variety. Open Tuesday to Sunday May and June from midday to 7pm (10pm on some weekends), July to mid-September daily from 6pm to 1am. Regular admission is 7€.

To cap off your visit, board the *teléferico* or cable car (© **91-541-11-18;** www.teleferico.com), close to Tivoli World. For 13€, you can ascend to the top of Monte

Calamorro for a panoramic sweep of the Costa del Sol and then return. Also rewarding is a 13€ boat cruise linking Benalmádena with Fuengirola. In the peak season, there are about four sailings per day depending on demand. Boats depart from **Costasol Cruceros** at the harbor at Benalmádena. For more information or reservations, call ℂ **95-244-48-81** (www.costasolcruceros.com). The same company also offers dolphin-watching trips costing 15€ per person.

Where to Stay
MODERATE

Hotel Cervantes ★   The government-rated four-star Cervantes is in a shopping center, beside a maze of patios and narrow streets of boutiques and open-air cafes, and a 7-minute walk to the beach. Rooms have modern furniture and spacious terraces; many have balconies with sea views and there's a garden. Bathrooms have tub/shower combos. In midsummer this hotel is likely to be booked up with tour groups from northern Europe. A summer feature is the lunch buffet and barbecue by the pool.

Calle las Mercedes s/n, 29620 Torremolinos. ℂ **95-238-40-33.** Fax 95-238-48-57. www.hotasa cervantes.com. 397 units. 84€–169€ double. AE, DC, MC, V. **Amenities:** Restaurant/cafeteria; 2 bars; babysitting; health club; 2 pools (1 heated indoor); room service; sauna; rooms for those w/limited mobility. *In room:* A/C, TV, hair dryer.

Hotel Isabel 🍴   One of the best bargains in Torremolinos itself, as opposed to on the outskirts, is this hotel on the beach with a series of balconied terraces for those who demand a sea view. Thirty-six of its rooms offer sea views, and naturally they are rented first. Units for the most part are midsize and furnished comfortably, with matching spreads and curtains and bland art. Tiled floors are soothing in the heat. There is no restaurant, but literally dozens are within a 5-minute walk from your door.

Paseo Marítimo 97, 29620 Torremolinos. ℂ **95-238-17-44.** Fax 95-238-11-98. www.hotelisabel.net. 70 units. 90€–158€ double. AE, DC, MC, V. **Amenities:** 2 bars; babysitting; outdoor pool; room service; rooms for those w/limited mobility. *In room:* A/C, TV, hair dryer.

Hotel Tropicana & Beach Club ★   This government-rated four-star hotel is right on a beach at the beginning of the La Carihuela coastal strip. With its own beach club, Tropicana is attractive mainly because it's removed from the summer hysteria in the heart of Torremolinos. As you'd expect, there's a tropical theme to the decor. Bedrooms are comfortably furnished and midsize and most rooms open onto private balconies with sea views. Try the seafood restaurants a 5-minute stroll from the hotel, or eat at the Tropicana's Restaurante Mango, on its sea-facing terrace.

Trópico 6, 29620 Torremolinos. ℂ **95-238-66-00.** Fax 95-238-05-68. www.hotel-tropicana.net. 84 units. 98€–155€ double. Rates include continental breakfast. AE, DC, MC, V. Free parking. **Amenities:** Restaurant; bar; babysitting; beach club; game room; outdoor pool; room service. *In room:* A/C, TV, hair dryer, minibar.

Meliá Costa del Sol ★   This hotel is centrally located on the seafront along Playa de Bajondillo, a 10-minute walk from the shopping area of Torremolinos. The midsize rooms are modern and well maintained, and each has a well-kept bathroom with a tub/shower combo. However, the hotel is popular with package tour groups.

Paseo Marítimo 11, 29620 Torremolinos. ℂ **95-238-66-77.** Fax 95-238-64-17. www.meliacostadelsol. solmelia.com. 540 units. 95€–202€ double. Rates include buffet breakfast. AE, MC, V. Free parking.

Amenities: 2 restaurants; 2 bars; babysitting; health club and spa; outdoor pool; room service; non-smoking rooms; rooms for those w/limited mobility. *In room:* A/C, TV, hair dryer, minibar, Wi-Fi.

Roc Lago Rojo ★ 🎁   In the heart of the fishing village of La Carihuela, Roc Lago Rojo is the area's nicest place to stay. It's only 45m (148 ft) from the beach and has its own gardens and sunbathing terraces. Studio-style rooms, all with terraces with views, are tastefully furnished. Bathrooms have showers. In the late evening there is disco dancing on offer.

Miami 5, 29620 Torremolinos. ✆ **95-238-76-66.** Fax 95-238-08-91. www.roc-hotels.com. 144 units. 50€–140€ double. Children aged 2–12 50% discount. Rates include breakfast. AE, DC, MC, V. **Amenities:** Restaurant; bar; babysitting; outdoor pool. *In room:* A/C, TV.

Sol Don Pablo ★   One of the better hotels in the center of Torremolinos, Don Pablo is in a modern building a minute from Playa de Bajondillo, with its own garden and playground areas. The surprise is the glamorous interior, which borrows heavily from Moorish palaces and medieval castle themes. Arched-tile arcades have splashing fountains, and the grand staircase features niches with life-size stone nudes. The comfortably furnished rooms have sea-view terraces.

Calle Bajondillo 36, 29620 Torremolinos. ✆ **95-238-38-88.** Fax 95-238-37-83. www.soldonpablo.sol melia.com. 443 units. 75€–185€ double. Rates include buffet breakfast. AE, DC, MC, V. **Amenities:** Restaurant; 2 bars; babysitting; 2 pools (1 indoor); limited room service. *In room:* A/C, TV, hair dryer, minibar.

INEXPENSIVE

El Tiburón 🏊   Just 60m (196 ft) from La Carihuela beach, this medium-size hotel is one of the most affordable in the area to the immediate west of Torremolinos, and many devotees book rooms here every year. It looks like an inviting, overgrown Mediterranean seaside house, with a beautiful terrace overlooking the water and shady palm trees. Life revolves around a central patio in the classic Andalusian style. Small to midsize bedrooms are traditionally and comfortably furnished. Thirty-two of the bedrooms have private terraces, and some of the rooms are suitable for triple use. There is no restaurant, but some excellent seafood eateries are only minutes from your doorstep.

Los Nidos 7, 29620 Torremolinos. ✆ **95-238-13-11.** Fax 95-238-22-44. 40 units. 46€–78€ double. AE, DC, MC, V. **Amenities:** Bar; outdoor pool. *In room:* TV.

Hotel El Pozo 🏊   In one of the liveliest sections of town, a short walk from the train station, this hotel isn't for light sleepers. It's usually filled with budget travelers, including students from northern Europe. The lobby level has professional French billiards and heavy Spanish furniture. Small rooms with tub/shower combos are furnished in a simple, functional style. Nothing special, but the price is right.

Casablanca 2, 29620 Torremolinos. ✆ **95-238-06-22.** Fax 95-238-71-17. 28 units. 45€–70€ double. DC, MC, V. **Amenities:** Bar. *In room:* A/C, TV.

Hotel Los Jazmines   Close to Bajondillo beach, Los Jazmines faces a plaza at the foot of the shady Avenida del Lido. Sun seekers will love its terraces, lawns, and an irregularly shaped swimming pool. The small rooms (all doubles) seem a bit impersonal, but have little balconies and compact bathrooms with tub/shower combos. It's a good hike up the hill to the town center from here.

Av. de Lido 6, 29620 Torremolinos. ☏ **95-238-50-33.** Fax 95-237-27-02. www.hotellosjazmines.com. 100 units. 55€–95€ double. AE, DC, MC, V. **Amenities:** Restaurant; bar; pool. *In room:* A/C, TV.

Miami ⚑ The Miami, near the Carihuela section, might remind you of a 1920s Hollywood movie star's home, and it offers good value for money. High walls and private gardens surround the property; fuchsia and bougainvillea climb over the rear patio's arches, and a tiled terrace is used for sunbathing and refreshments. The country-style living room has a walk-in fireplace; compact bedrooms are furnished in a traditional, comfortable style and bathrooms have tub/shower combos. Each has a balcony. Breakfast is the only meal served.

Calle Aladino 14, 29620 Torremolinos. ☏ **95-238-52-55.** www.residencia-miami.com. 26 units. 40€– 64€ double. Rates include continental breakfast. No credit cards. Free parking. **Amenities:** Bar; outdoor pool. *In room:* A/C.

A NEARBY HOTEL

Where Torremolinos ends and Benalmádena-Costa to the west begins is hard to say. Benalmádena is packed with hotels, restaurants, and tourist facilities.

Hotel Torrequebrada ★★ In the late 1980s this became one of the largest government-rated five-star luxury hotels on the Costa del Sol, and it is without a doubt the most luxurious place to stay in the greater Torremolinos area. Five kilometers (3 miles) west of Torremolinos, it opens onto its own beach and has a wide range of facilities and attractions. The casino attracts gamblers. Spacious, handsomely furnished rooms have large terraces with sea views.

Av. del Sol s/n, 29630 Benalmádena. ☏ **95-244-60-00.** Fax 95-244-57-02. www.torrequebrada.com. 350 units. 115€–285€ double; 250€ suite. AE, MC, V. Parking 12€. **Amenities:** 2 restaurants; 2 bars; babysitting; casino; health club; 3 pools (1 indoor); room service; saunas; tennis court; nonsmoking rooms; rooms for those w/limited mobility. *In room:* A/C, TV, hair dryer, minibar, Wi-Fi.

Where to Dine

The cuisine in Torremolinos is more American and Continental than Andalusian. The hotels often serve elaborate four-course meals, but you might want to sample more casual local offerings. A good spot to try is the food court **La Nogalera,** the major gathering place between the coast road and the beach. Open to pedestrians only, it's a maze of passageways, courtyards, and patios for eating and drinking. You can find anything from sandwiches and pizza to Belgian waffles and scrambled eggs.

AT TORREMOLINOS

Med ★★ INTERNATIONAL With all the cheap English pub food and booze around, who'd have imagined this gem of a restaurant right in the heart of Torremolinos? It's not the easiest of places to find. Take the elevator at beach level up to Calle San Miguel. Then hop in another elevator to penthouse level for expansive views. Local chef Richard Alcayde is cooking up a storm with his creative dishes using only the best, freshest Andalusian ingredients. Standout dishes include starters of garlic and almond soup with apple puree, a main dish of scallops with Iberian pork, artichokes, and cream, and cream of passion fruit with cocoa beans for dessert. It's served with a flourish in convivial surroundings. A real find.

Calle de las Mercedes 12. ☏ **95-205-88-30** www.restaurantemed.es. Reservations recommended. Main courses 16€–27€. AE, MC, V. Tues–Thurs 8pm–midnight, Fri–Sun 1–4pm and 8pm–midnight.

AT LA CARIHUELA

To get away from the high-rises, head to nearby La Carihuela. In the old fishing village on the western outskirts of Torremolinos, you'll find some of the best bargain restaurants. Walk down the hill toward the sea to reach the village.

Casa Juan ★ SEAFOOD   In a modern-looking building in La Carihuela, this seafood restaurant is about 1.6km (1 mile) west of Torremolinos's center. There's a lavish display of fish and shellfish near the entrance. You might try *mariscada de mariscos* (shellfish), a fried platter of mixed fish, cod, kebabs of meat or fish, or paella. Of special note is *lubina a la sal*—sea bass packed in layers of roughly textured salt, broken open at your table and deboned in front of you. It's very busy later on.

Calle San Gines 18-20, La Carihuela. ✆ **95-237-35-12.** Reservations recommended. Main courses 10€-42€. AE, DC, MC, V. Tues-Sun 12:30-4:30pm and 7:30-11:30pm. Closed Dec.

Figón de Montemar ★ SPANISH/ANDALUSIAN   One of the better restaurants of Torremolinos, Figón de Montemar is near the beach, and is decorated with glass, tiles, and nautical paraphernalia. Its chefs call the cuisine *cocina de mercado,* meaning menus based on what was good and fresh at the market that day. From the distant mountains comes lamb that is perfectly roasted, seasoned with garlic and spices, and served with a mint sauce. *Merluza* (hake) is baked with fresh spices, and fresh codfish is prepared in a red sauce. For something more adventurous, order oxtail.

Av. Espada 101. ✆ **95-237-26-88.** www.elfigondemontemar.com. Reservations recommended. Main courses 14€-22€. AE, DC, MC, V. Mon noon-1:30pm; Tues-Sat noon-1:30pm and 5:30-8pm. Closed Jan 15-Feb 15.

AT BENALMÁDENA

Casa Fidel SPANISH/ANDALUSIAN   This rustic restaurant makes a good lunch stop when you're exploring Benalmádena-Pueblo (the Old Town of Benalmádena-Costa). If you're staying in the area, try it for dinner. In the cooler months a big roaring fireplace greets you, but in summer the shaded courtyard is the focus. Unlike Ventorrillo de la Perra (see below), the menu here is up to date. Chefs use market-fresh ingredients for dishes such as zucchini stuffed with goat's cheese, or red pepper soup laced with fresh cream and spring onions. In the off season, the hearty T-bone steak for two is perfect. Desserts are standard, although the cooks make a perfect flan.

Maestra Ayala 1. ✆ **95-244-91-65.** Reservations recommended. Main courses 14€-28€. MC, V. Wed-Mon 7:30-10pm. Closed Aug.

Ventorrillo de la Perra ★ 🍴 ANDALUSIAN/SPANISH   If you want a good restaurant at Tivoli World, try this old inn from 1785, one of the oldest restaurants along the Costa del Sol. In this theme park where everything looks as if it were built in 1972 out of concrete, this is a nostalgic journey back to 1800s Andalusia—the Costa del Sol before the invading hordes. Eat on a shaded patio or in the intimate dining room where Andalusian cured hams hang from the ceiling. Order *gazpacuelo malagueño,* which is served warm. It's a combination of rice and potatoes with fresh shrimp. Lamb appears frequently on the menu, as does fresh fish from the day's catch.

Av. Constitución 87, Arroyo de la Miel. ✆ **95-244-19-66.** Reservations recommended. Main courses 12€-28€. AE, DC, MC, V. Tues-Sun 1-4pm and 8pm-midnight.

Torremolinos after Dark

Torremolinos is the most happening spot on the Costa del Sol. The earliest action is always at the bars, which often are open during the day and stay lively most of the night, serving drinks and tapas.

Calle San Miguel is right at the heart of the action and **La Bodega,** San Miguel 40 (© **95-238-73-37**), has a surprisingly authentic atmosphere with colorful clientele and good quality tapas in the midst of touristland. You'll be lucky to find space at one of the small tables, but once you begin to order—platters of fried squid, pungent tuna, grilled shrimp, tiny brochettes of sole—you might not be able to stop. La Bodega is open daily from 12:30 to 5pm and 7:30pm to midnight. Just off the bottom of Plaza San Miguel, another authentic tapas joint that's always busy is **Bodega Quitpenas,** Cuesta del Tajo 3 (© **95-238-62-33**) serving ice cold beer and sherries and the usual tapas favorites daily at lunch and long into the evening. For something a little more stylish try **Matahambre** just off Calle San Miguel at Las Mercedes 14 (© **95-238-12-42**), a modern stylish air-conditioned venue where sophisticated locals mix with the visitors. Tapas are more contemporary and it's open daily from midday to midnight.

If you're rather more chilled out in outlook, head for the far eastern end of the beach at Torremolinos and the cool beach bars on **Playa Alamos** where trendy Malagueños come to have fun at weekends. **Café Del Sol,** Playa Alamos (no phone; www.grupomoliere.com), has a funky open-air beach bar vibe with people dancing and drinking long into the night. **Maracas,** Playa Alamos (no phone; www.maracas bar.es), close by is similar in style and vibe.

For louder dancebar drinks, head for the new stretch of bars on Costa Lago just off Paseo Marítimo. There's a slew of funky joints here where the music is often live and the cocktails are strong. **Jammin Bar** (© **95-238-07-75**; www.jamminbar. com) is one of my favorites, open daily 4pm to very late. **Lombok** right next door is more house-music in style and full of cool people, with similar opening hours.

Torremolinos is the Costa del Sol's biggest gay nightspot and the bars and clubs around Plaza La Nogalera are the places to head for. **El Palladium,** Palma de Mallorca (© **95-238-42-89**), a well-designed nightclub in the town center, is one of the most convivial in Torremolinos with all the usual attractions and a fun, up-for-it mixed crowd. Strobes, spotlights, and a swimming pool set the scene. **La Passion,** Palma de Mallorca 18 (© **60-766-66-63**; www.passiondisco.com) is a newer arrival on the scene and packed to the rafters with people having a good time.

For flamenco, albeit of a touristy kind, head for **Taberna Flamenca Pepe López,** Plaza de la Gamba Alegre (© **95-238-12-84**), in the center of Torremolinos. In an old house (at least old in the Torremolinos sense), this is a tavern-style joint with darkened wooden furnishings. Many of the artists come from the *boîtes* of Seville and Granada, and they perform nightly at 10pm April to October. Shows are substantially reduced during the cooler months, and confined mainly to the weekends—call to confirm first. A 28€ cover includes your first drink and the show.

One of the Costa del Sol's major casinos, **Casino Torrequebrada,** Av. del Sol, Benalmádena-Costa (© **95-244-60-00**; www.casinotorrequebrada.net), is on the lobby level of the Hotel Torrequebrada. It has tables devoted to blackjack, chemin de fer, punto y banco, and two kinds of roulette. The casino is open daily from 3pm to 4am. The restaurant is open nightly 9pm to 2am. Casino admission is 3€. Bring your passport to be admitted. Sensible attire is required to get in, but ties are not necessary.

MÁLAGA ★

548km (340 miles) S of Madrid, 132km (82 miles) E of Algeciras

The capital of the Costa del Sol and Andalusia's largest coastal city, Málaga is a bustling commercial and residential center with an economy that doesn't depend exclusively on tourism. For many rail and air passengers, Málaga is the gateway to the Costa del Sol and visitors often move on to other resorts in the east or west without stopping. I think they're missing out. Málaga is the cultural capital of the coast, with more museums and historic monuments than any other resort in this chapter.

The main arteries of the town span out conveniently from the tourist office at Plaza de la Marina. Paseo del Parque is a palm-lined pedestrian promenade filled with banana trees and fountains, following the boundary of the port. At almost right angles to this is the most famous street in the city, Calle Marques de Larios (often shortened to Calle Larios), from which the winding streets of the historic Old Town span out.

There's beach here too. Paseo Marítimo runs along La Malagueta Beach, but even better are the beaches to the east of Baños de Carmen and El Palo.

The most important art museum in Andalusia, the Picasso museum, is located in Málaga and the soon-to-open Carmen Thyssen-Bornemisza Museum will really put the city on the art world map. Unlike much of the Costa del Sol, Málaga retains its Andalusian identity with plenty of attractive historic buildings, an atmospheric Old Town with tapas bars aplenty, good shopping, and interesting cultural attractions. I think it's a bit of an unexplored gem and deserves at least a couple of days of your time.

Essentials

GETTING THERE Málaga is the best-connected city in Andalusia and the only city with direct connections to North America. Travelers from the U.S.A. can fly direct with **Delta Airlines** (② **800-241-41-41** within the U.S., ② **90-080-07-43** in Spain; www.delta.com) from JFK 4 times weekly June to September. Travelers from Canada have a weekly direct flight from **Transat** (② **1-888-TRANSAT** within Canada; www.airtransat.ca) year-round from Montreal with easy connections to Toronto.

From the U.K. there are upwards of 10 flights a day arriving at Málaga from airports across the country including Gatwick, Stansted, Heathrow, Manchester, Nottingham East Midlands and Birmingham, Edinburgh, and Glasgow. The best value deals are often from **Monarch Airlines** (② **08719-40-50-40** in the U.K., ② **800-09-92-60** in Spain; www.monarch.co.uk) from Gatwick, Manchester, and Luton. Other low-cost operators include **easyJet** (② **90-229-99-92;** www.easyjet.com) from Gatwick, Stansted, Bristol, and Liverpool; and **Ryanair** (② **08712-46-00-00** in the U.K., ② **807-11-01-62** in Spain; www.ryanair.com) from Stansted. Also check **British Airways** (② **08444-93-07-87** in the U.K., ② **902-11-13-33** in Spain; www.britishairways.com) from London Heathrow, though they're usually pricier.

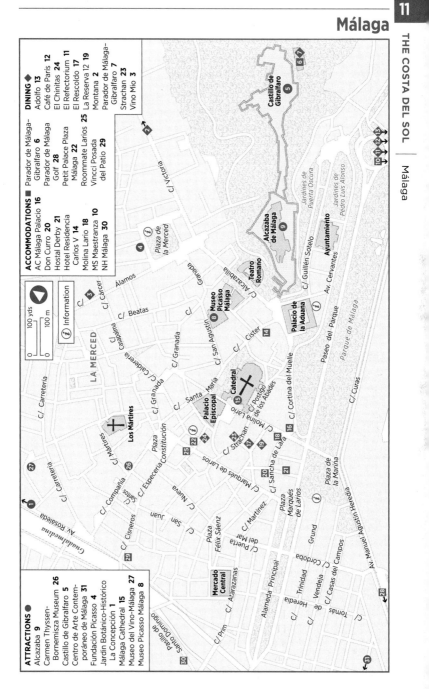

ATTRACTIONS ●
Alcazaba 9
Carmen Thyssen-Bornemisza Museum 26
Castillo de Gibralfaro 5
Centro de Arte Contemporáneo de Málaga 31
Fundación Picasso 4
Jardín Botánico-Histórico La Concepción 1
Málaga Cathedral 15
Museo del Vino-Málaga 27
Museo Picasso Málaga 8

ACCOMMODATIONS ■
AC Málaga Palacio 16
Don Curro 20
Hostal Derby 21
Hotel Residencia Carlos V 14
Molina Lario 18
MS Maestranza 10
NH Málaga 30
Parador de Málaga-Gibralfaro 6
Parador de Málaga Golf 28
Petit Palace Plaza Málaga 22
Roommate Larios 25
Vincci Posada del Patio 29

DINING ◆
Adolfo 13
Café de París 12
El Chinitas 24
El Refectorium 11
El Rescoldo 17
La Reserva 12 19
Montana 2
Parador de Málaga-Gibralfaro 7
Strachan 23
Vino Mio 3

(i) Information

0 100 yds
0 100 m

Airport buses connect to the city center around every 30 minutes from 7am until midnight. Or catch the **train** from the airport. If you're staying in the center, don't get out at the main station—continue one more stop to better located Centro Alameda.

Málaga's main rail station (Estación Maria Zambrano) is now on the AVE high-speed train network, cutting the journey time from Madrid from 4 to just over 2½ hours, with departures often hourly during the day. Five express trains a day connect Seville and Málaga (2 hr). A further six slower services take 2½ hours. For ticket prices and rail information in Málaga, call **RENFE** (© 90-232-03-20; www.renfe.es).

Buses from all over Spain arrive at the main bus station (© **952 350 061;** www.estabus.emtsam.es), on the Paseo de los Tilos, behind the RENFE offices. Buses run to all the major Spanish cities. **Empresa Portillo** (© 90-245-05-50; www.ctsa-portillo.com) runs services to many locations along the Costa del Sol, including Estepona (2 hr), Marbella (1½ hr), Algeciras (3 hr) as well as Cádiz (4 hr) and Ronda (2¾ hr). There are eight buses per day from Madrid (7 hr) operated by **Daibus** (© **95-204-26-17;** www.daibus.es), four per day from Córdoba (3 hr), and seven per day from Seville (3 hr), both operated by **Alsina Graells** (© 91 327-05-40; www.alsa.es).

From resorts in the west (such as Torremolinos and Marbella), you can **drive** east along the new AP-7/E-15 high-speed toll road to Málaga. If you're in the east at the end of the Costa del Sol (Almería), take the A-7/E-15 west to Málaga, with a stop at Nerja.

VISITOR INFORMATION The main **tourist office,** Plaza de la Marina (© **95-212-20-20;** www.Málagaturismo.com), is open Monday to Friday 9am to 6pm and Saturday and Sunday 10am to 6pm (7pm in summer months). There are also tourist information booths with helpful staff at Plaza de la Merced and the post office, Av. Andalucia 1, usually open from 10am to 2pm.

SPECIAL EVENTS The most festive time in Málaga is the first week in August, when the city celebrates its Reconquest by Ferdinand and Isabella in 1487. The big *feria* (**fair**) is an occasion for parades and bullfights. A major tree-shaded boulevard, the Paseo del Parque, is transformed into a fairground with amusements and restaurants.

Exploring Málaga

Alcazaba ★ The remains of this ancient Moorish palace are within easy walking distance of the city center, off the Paseo del Parque. Plenty of signs point the way up the hill. The fortress was erected in the 9th or 10th century, but unlike the better-preserved palace at Granada, this one was constructed with cheaper, softer sandstone as the Moors began to lose their grip on Andalusia. As a result, most of the original structure was destroyed by the elements and much of what you see today is reconstructed. Ferdinand and Isabella stayed here when they reconquered the city. It's a very pleasant walk up the hill along narrow passageways and through dog-legged gateways, with orange trees, fountains, and purple bougainvillea making the grounds even more beautiful. The views overlooking the city and the bay are among the most stunning on the Costa del Sol. If you don't fancy the quite steep walk up, there's a separate entrance on Calle Guillén Sotelo a few minutes' walk round to the right, which has a lift. It's fine for wheelchair access too.

Plaza de la Aduana, Alcazabilla 2. © **95-221-76-46.** Admission 2.10€. Free Sun from 2pm. Combined ticket with the Castillo de Gibralfaro 3.45€. Apr-Oct Tues-Sun 9:30am-8:30pm; Nov-Mar Tues-Sun 8:30am-7pm.

Art's Content

The Picasso Museum has really put Málaga on the art world map and a number of other prestigious galleries are now arriving to join it. Chief among them will be the new **Carmen Thyssen-Bornemisza Museum**. Following the success of the Thyssen-Bornemisza Museum in Madrid, this vastly wealthy European aristocratic family has now paid for the restoration of the 16th-century Villalón Palace on Calle de la Compañía just off Plaza de la Constitución to house more of the family's remarkable art collection. Among the 200 exhibits by Spanish artists of the 19th and early 20th centuries that will be displayed are works by Zurbarán, Zuloaga, Sorolla, and Regoyos. The museum will also host temporary exhibitions of work by French impressionists such as Degas and Gauguin. It is set to open in 2011 and will, without doubt, become one of the city's most impressive cultural sights.

Castillo de Gibralfaro   On a hill overlooking Málaga and the Mediterranean are the ruins of this ancient Moorish castle-fortress, built to protect the Alcazaba palace in the 18th century. There's a small museum containing displays of military uniforms and equipment through the ages, but the main attraction is the views. Close by is the government-run parador which has a good restaurant, so handy for a lunch stop. Be warned that, whilst it looks as if the Alcazaba and the Castillo de Gibralfaro are linked by a pathway, it's not possible to walk from one to the other. To reach the Castillo take a town bus, the Málaga Tour bus, or a taxi. Don't consider walking as it's a long way.

Cerro de Gibralfaro. © **95-212-20-20**. Admission 2.10€. Combined ticket with the Alcazaba 3.45€. Summer months 9am-8pm; winter months 9am-6pm. Microbus: 35, leaving hourly from Alameda Principal and Paseo del Parque.

Contemporáneo de Málaga ★   This contemporary arts center is in a renovated old wholesalers' market and stages the best array of temporary art exhibitions in town, many showcasing the works of international artists such as Alex Katz and Louise Bourgeois. The museum's permanent collection numbers around 400 works and is particularly notable for its works created between the 1950s and the present day, with an emphasis on North American artists of the 1960s such as Lichtenstein and Stella. The museum also focuses some of its exhibitions on up-and-coming Spanish artists, and it also displays photographic studies in its vast exhibition space.

Alemania s/n. © **95-212-00-55.** Free admission. Mid-June to mid-Sept Tues-Sun 10am-2pm and 5-9pm; off season Tues-Sun 10am-8pm.

Fundación Picasso   A well-told tale concerns the birth of Picasso: in October 1891, when the artist was born, he was unable to draw breath until his uncle blew cigar smoke into his lungs. Whether this rather harsh entry into the world had any effect on his work is mere speculation. What cannot be denied is the effect he was to have on the world. He was born and spent the first 17 months of his life in a five-story building in the heart of Málaga's historic quarter. Today the house is the headquarters of the Picasso Foundation and a library for art historians. The Picasso family lived on the second floor. Regrettably, the original furnishings are long gone, but they've been replaced by antiques and furniture from that era. There's also a small permanent exhibition of Picasso ceramics, sculpture, and engravings. The museum also mounts temporary exhibitions featuring avant-garde works from Picasso's time.

Plaza de la Merced 15. ✆ **95-206-02-15.** www.fundacionpicasso.es. Admission 1€. Daily 9:30am-8pm.

Jardin Botánico-Histórico La Concepción ☺   Málaga city has its fair share of green spaces, but if you fancy something altogether more expansive, this huge tropical garden will keep you occupied. There's plenty of space here for kids to let off steam and a picnic area too. The gardens were created around 1855 by the Marquis and Marchioness of Loring and subsequently extended by the Echevarria-Echevarrieta family. They comprise an extensive collection of tropical and subtropical flora arranged in several different climatic zones. Of particular note among the 1,000-plus species are the trees in the enormous wood, where ficuses, araucarias, casuarinas, magnolias, pines, cypresses, and cedars, some over 100 years old, create a remarkable arboretum. The only downside is access. The gardens are about 5km (3 miles) north of the city. Bus no. 2 goes most of the way, but you have to walk for about 15 minutes from the final stop. Some of the Málaga Tour sightseeing buses include it on their itineraries too.

Camino del Jardin Botanico 3. ✆ **95-225-21-48.** www.laconcepcion.ayto-Málaga.es. Admission 1€. Tues to Sun 9:30am-8:30pm (5:30pm Oct to Mar). Bus: 2 (get off at the last stop and walk 15 minutes following the signs).

Málaga Cathedral   This 16th-century Renaissance cathedral in Málaga's center, built on the site of a great mosque, suffered damage during the Spanish Civil War. Locals call it *La Manquita* or "the lady with one arm", because the cathedral's second tower was never completed. However, it remains vast and impressive, reflecting changing styles of interior architecture, and is a national monument. Its most notable attributes are the richly ornamented choir stalls by Ortiz, Pedro de Mena, and Michael. There's also a small museum in two side rooms as you exit the cathedral with displays of some of the cathedral's treasures and ornaments.

Plaza Obispo. ✆ **95-221-59-17.** Admission 3.50€. Mon-Fri 10am-6pm; Sat 10am-7pm; closed Sun and hols. Bus: 14, 18, 19, or 24.

Museo del Vino-Málaga ★   Whilst it doesn't have the cachet of sherry, Málaga's wine industry, once decimated by the arrival of a bug which killed many of the vines, is making a bit of a comeback. You can learn about the province's wine production, which includes fortified wines like sherries and table wines, at this interesting new museum. It's housed in a restored 18th-century palace house and, along with descriptions of how the wine is produced, it contains a collection of more than 400 exhibits including bottle labels, advertising posters for wine and grapes, barrel labels, handpainted sketches, and wooden grape boxes. And, of course, you get to sample some of the wine. If you're a real wine buff you can organize special bespoke tastings.

Plaza de los Viñeros 1. ✆ **95-222-84-93.** www.museovinomalaga.com. Admission 5€ includes two tastings. Mon-Sat noon-2:30pm, 4:30-7:30pm.

Museo Picasso Málaga ★★★   In the old quarter of the city, a short walk from Picasso's birthplace, this landmark museum is the city's main attraction. It's set in a delightful, restored 16th-century Mudéjar palace, Palacio de Buenavista, with a

TOUR DE force

If you want more structure to your Málaga sightseeing, there are plenty of ways to see the city in a more organized fashion.

On foot: The city tourist office (Plaza de la Marina, ☎ 95-212-20-20; www.malagaturismo.com) has eight free maps with different themed walking routes marked on them, each accompanied by a free audio guide. Themes include Romantic Málaga, Religious Málaga, and Picasso's Málaga.

By bus: Málaga Tour (☎ 95-236-31-33; www.malaga-tour.com) has red double decker buses doing a 14-stop circuit of most of the cultural sights. Tickets, valid 24 hours, include an audio guide. It's 15€ for adults and 7€ for children.

By bicycle: Málaga Bike Tours (☎ 60-697-85-13; www.malagabiketours.eu) offers 4-hour guided bicycle tours of the city taking in some of the less-visited areas like the marina and the beach. The tours run daily at 10am from the tourist office and cost 23€. Bike and helmet are provided, reservations at least 24 hours in advance are recommended.

By horse and buggy: Hop aboard one of these and clip clop around the city. The standard tour lasts about an hour and costs 25€ to 30€ per person. The main pick-up points are in Postigo de los Abades behind the cathedral and near the entrance to the Alcazaba in Plaza de la Aduana.

series of contrasting modernist buildings alongside. It was always Picasso's desire that there should be a place for his works in the town of his birth, but the Spanish dictator Franco detested Picasso's politics, and his "degenerate art," and refused the artist's offer to send paintings from France to Málaga in the 1950s. Ultimately, the collection here was made possible by two of Picasso's heirs: his son Paulo's wife, Christine Ruiz-Picasso, and Bernard, Christine's son. The result is a truly astounding collection, which, along with showcasing some of his most famous works, demonstrates the sheer breadth of Picasso's talent—there are sketches, sculpture, and ceramics as well as paintings. Many of the artworks are virtual family heirlooms, including paintings depicting one of the artist's wives, such as *Olga Kokhlova with Mantilla,* or one of his lovers, *Jacqueline Seated.* Basically this is the art Picasso gave to his family or the art he wanted to keep for himself—in all, more than 200 paintings, drawings, sculpture, ceramics, and graphics. Other notable works on display—many of them never on public view before—include *Bust of a Woman with Arms Crossed Behind Her Head, Woman in an Armchair,* and *The Eyes of the Artist.* There is also a memorable painting of Picasso's son, done in 1923. The museum is carefully curated with artworks displayed by theme as well as by chronological order, so you can trace the development of Picasso's different styles from classical sketches to Cubism and beyond. During the restoration work, the Roman and Moorish remains that were discovered are now on display in the basement of the museum.

San Agustín 8. ☎ 90-244-33-77. www.museopicassomalaga.org. Combined permanent collection and exhibitions 8€; half price for seniors, students, and children aged 11–16; free for children aged 10 and under. Free to all last Sun of the month from 3pm. Tues–Thurs 10am–8pm; Fri–Sat 10am–9pm.

Where to Stay

EXPENSIVE

AC Málaga Palacio ★ The leading hotel in the town center, the Palacio opens onto a tree-lined esplanade near the cathedral and the harbor. Most balconies offer views of the port, and horses pulling century-old carriages in the streets below. Mid-size rooms are furnished in modern style with dark wood paneling and steel fixtures and fittings. They have large, firm beds and well-equipped bathrooms with tub/shower combos. The suites here are among the most spacious in the city. Street-floor lounges mix antiques with more-modern furnishings. The Atico bar and restaurant on the top floor offers some of the best views in the city. There's also a rooftop swimming pool.

Cortina del Muelle 1, 29015 Málaga. ☏ **95-221-51-85.** Fax 95-222-51-00. www.ac-hoteles.com. 214 units. 100€–186€ double; 146€–375€ suite. AE, DC, MC, V. Parking 25€ nearby. Bus: 4, 18, 19, or 24. **Amenities:** Restaurant; bar; babysitting; fitness center; outdoor pool; room service; sauna; nonsmoking rooms; rooms for those w/limited mobility. *In room:* A/C, TV, hair dryer, minibar.

Parador de Málaga-Gibralfaro ★ Restored in 1994, this is one of Spain's oldest, most tradition-heavy *paradores*. It enjoys a scenic location high on a plateau near an old fortified castle. Overlooking the city and the Mediterranean, it has views of the bullring, mountains, and beaches. Rooms have private entrances, living-room areas, and wide glass doors opening onto private sun terraces. It's not well located for sightseeing however, requiring a bus or taxi journey to reach the historic center.

Castillo de Gibralfaro s/n, 29016 Málaga. ☏ **95-222-19-02.** Fax 95-222-19-04. www.parador.es. 38 units. 159€–221€ double. AE, DC, MC, V. Free parking. Take the coastal road, Paseo de Reding, which becomes Av. de Pries and then Paseo de Sancha. Turn left onto Camino Nuevo and follow the small signs. **Amenities:** Restaurant (p. 379); bar; outdoor pool; room service; Wi-Fi. *In room:* A/C, TV, hair dryer, minibar.

Parador de Málaga Golf ★★ A tasteful resort hotel created by the Spanish government, this hacienda-style parador is flanked by a golf course on one side and the Mediterranean on another. It's less than 3km (2 miles) from the airport, 11km (6½ miles) from Málaga, and 4km (2½ miles) from Torremolinos. Rooms have private balconies with water views. Some units have whirlpool tubs, others just tiled showers. The furnishings are attractive, and the beds excellent. This restaurant has an indoor/outdoor dining room and a refined country-club atmosphere.

Carretera de Málaga, Torremolinos, 29080 Apartado 324, Málaga. ☏ **95-238-12-55.** Fax 95-238-89-63. www.parador.es. 60 units. 159€–209€ double; 239€–272€ suite. AE, DC, MC, V. Free parking. **Amenities:** Restaurant; bar; babysitting; golf course; room service; outdoor pool; spa; tennis court; Wi-Fi. *In room:* A/C, TV, hair dryer, minibar.

Vincci Posada del Patio ★★★ Currently the best address in town, this brand new, ultra luxurious hotel is housed in two beautifully renovated 16th-century town houses in the historic center. It's Málaga town's only five-star hotel and a serious cut above the competition. Hues of brown, gray, and lime give the spacious contemporary bedrooms a sense of serenity and comfort. Solid wood floors and huge beds come as standard and dark tiles complement the white porcelain in the bathrooms, which have separate shower and bath tub and two basins. If you've got the cash, the two-story suites are remarkable, some with bed decks right up under the eaves, all with lovely chill-out sofa spaces. There's a good-sized sun terrace and a lovely outdoor pool along with a funky bar and restaurant space. Much of the bar's floor is glass and below you can see the remains of Roman and Moorish ruins discovered during the restoration works.

Pasillo Santa Isabel s/n, 29005 Málaga. ✆ **91-490-26-50.** Fax 91-662-67-57. www.vinccihoteles.com. 109 units. 100€–299€ double; 175€–375€ junior suite; 250€–450€ suite. AE, DC, MC, V. Parking 17€. **Amenities:** Restaurant; bars; 2 pools, room service; Wi-Fi. *In room:* A/C, LCD TV, hair dryer, minibar.

MODERATE

Don Curro ✔ Right in the center of old Málaga, just around the corner from the cathedral, this government-rated three-star hotel 100m (328 ft) from the beach is clean, welcoming, and offers great value for money. Traditional in style, and 50 years old, it has been regularly renovated. Most midsize rooms mix classical and modern decor, with lots of wooden furniture. The best rooms are in the more modern wing at the rear of the building. The hotel is family run; public rooms are woodpaneled, and there's a cozy fireplace lounge. There are also 12 single rooms, ideal for solo travelers.

Sancha de Lara 7, 29015 Málaga. ✆ **95-222-72-00.** Fax 95-221-59-46. www.hoteldoncurro.com. 118 units. 97€–115€ double; 110€–155€ suite. Children aged 11 and under stay free in parents' room. AE, DC, MC, V. Parking 13€. **Amenities:** Restaurant; bar; room service. *In room:* A/C, TV, hair dryer, minibar, Wi-Fi.

Molina Lario ★★ Sleek, sophisticated, and comfortable, this is one of the best options in the historic center right now. In a six-story town house that has been cleverly renovated with a bright, glass-bedecked atrium at its core, the hotel blends the historic and the cutting edge with real style. Rooms are a good size and furnished in contemporary manner with contrasting dark wood paneling and bright white walls, white leather armchairs, and white cotton curtains. Beds are big and comfy and the bathrooms well equipped. Wi-Fi and iPod docks are part of the equipment. There's a cool multi-level roof terrace with pool. The hotel's trendy bar/restaurant is reason enough to visit, with regular jazz sessions, wine tastings, and even poetry readings.

Calle Molina Lario 22, 29015 Málaga. ✆ **95-206-20-02.** Fax 95-206-20-01. www.hotelmolinolario.com. 103 units. 90€–190€ double; 200€–250€ junior suite. AE, DC, MC, V. **Amenities:** Restaurant; outdoor pool; room service; rooms for those w/limited mobility. *In room:* A/C, TV, minibar, Wi-Fi.

MS Maestranza Right next to the bullring, about a 10-minute walk from the historic center, this recently renovated hotel offers good-value, mid-range accommodation. Small rooms are simply furnished with bright, airy decor and large beds. Bathrooms are well fitted out, but again small. Rooms at the back of the hotel are quieter and upper floors offer views right into the bullring. The top floor has a small spa with Jacuzzi pool and sun terrace offering sweeping views. The hotel is just a five-minute walk from the town's main beaches, so a good location for sunworshippers.

Av. Cánovas de Castillo 1, 29016 Málaga. ✆ **95-221-36-10.** Fax 95-221-36-19. www.mshoteles.com. 90 units. 95€–280€ double; 125€–300€ junior suite. AE, DC, MC, V. **Amenities:** Restaurant; gym; room service; sauna; rooms for those w/limited mobility. *In room:* A/C, TV, hair dryer, minibar, Wi-Fi.

NH Málaga ★ ✔ In the commercial and historic center, this modern, good- value hotel is well located for sightseeing and shopping. Next to the Puente (bridge) de la Esperanza, it's a well-managed choice with soundproof windows cutting down traffic noise. Bright, modern, functional bedrooms have wooden floors and contemporary furnishings. For such a standard chain format, there are nice extras like a choice of pillows (firm, soft) and deluxe toiletries. Friendly and efficient service too.

Av. Río Guadalmedina s/n, 29007 Málaga. ✆ **95-207-13-23.** Fax 95-239-38-62. www.nh-hoteles.com. 133 units. 75€–195€ double. Rates include continental breakfast. AE, DC, MC, V. Free parking. **Amenities:** Restaurant; 2 bars; babysitting; gym; room service; sauna; rooms for those w/limited mobility. *In room:* A/C, TV, hair dryer, minibar, Wi-Fi.

Petit Palace Plaza Málaga ☺   One of the quirky but cool Hi-tech hotel chain, the Petit Palace is right in the historic center, just off the main shopping street, Calle Larios. The setting is similar to other hotels here: a renovated town house with central patio. But the decor sure isn't. Bright orange and black and white are the hues of choice, contrasting hyper-modern with historic. You'll either love it or hate it. Rooms are similarly bold with modern, but rather flimsy feeling, fixtures and fittings. Hi-tech rooms come with laptop PC, exercise bike, valet press, hydromassage shower, and king-size bed. Family rooms have a king-size bed or twins, plus two bunk beds, so a good-value option for families. Some bathrooms have shower cubicles only. Families also appreciate free baby cots and free use of pushchairs and bikes.

Calle Nicasio Calle 3 (corner of Calle Larios) 29015 Málaga. ✆ **95-222-21-32.** Fax 952 608 646. www. hthoteles.com. 66 units. 70€–90€ double; 90€–130€ family. Rates include continental breakfast. AE, DC, MC, V. Parking 23€. **Amenities:** Restaurant; cafe; rooms for those w/limited mobility. *In room:* A/C, TV, hair dryer, PC (in some), Wi-Fi.

Roommate Larios ★   Vying with the Petit Palace (see above) for funkiest hotel in town, the Larios follows the usual Roommate theme with bold colors and designer-style furniture. The rooms are hyper-modern, with a vaguely Art Deco edge to them and they feel a bit more solid and sophisticated than those of the Petit Palace. They're well appointed and comfortable and bathrooms have shower/tub combos. Junior suites are genuinely spacious with big bathrooms and whirlpool tubs. The sister Roommate Lola, Calle Casas de Campos 17, near the port, offers a very similar package.

Calle Marqués de Larios 2, 29005 Málaga. ✆ **95-222-22-00.** Fax 95-222-24-07. www.hotel-larios.com. 41 units. 120€–170€ double; 150€–230€ suite. AE, DC, MC, V. **Amenities:** Restaurant; bar; babysitting; room service; nonsmoking rooms. *In room:* A/C, TV, hair dryer, minibar, Wi-Fi.

INEXPENSIVE

Hostal Derby ★ 🍴   This is an amazing discovery, not because it's an exceptional place to stay—it's not—but because it charges prices the town hasn't seen since the Franco era. A fourth-floor boardinghouse, it's in the heart of town, on a main square directly north of the train station. Some of the rather basic, cramped rooms have excellent views of the Mediterranean and the port of Málaga. Most units have a shower only. No breakfast is served, and the hotel is very light on extras.

San Juan de Dios 1, 29015 Málaga. ✆ **95-222-13-01.** 16 units, 12 with bathroom. 35€ double with sink; 38€–48€ double with bathroom. No credit cards. **Amenities:** Lounge.

Hotel Residencia Carlos V   This hotel, centrally located near the cathedral, has an interesting facade decorated with wrought-iron balconies and *miradores* (viewing stations). It's a reliable, conservative, good-value choice. Small rooms are furnished in a no-frills style but are well maintained, and bathrooms have tub/shower combos.

Cister 10, 29015 Málaga. ✆ **95-221-51-20.** Fax 95-221-51-29. 50 units. 60€–71€ double. AE, DC, MC, V. Parking 10€. **Amenities:** Breakfast room. *In room:* A/C, TV.

LUXURIOUS PLACES TO STAY NEARBY

Hotel La Bobadilla ★★★ ☺   An hour's drive northeast of Málaga, La Bobadilla is one of the most luxurious retreats in southern Spain. It's a secluded oasis in the foothills of the Sierra Nevada, a 21km (13-mile) drive from Loja, which is 71km (44 miles) north of Málaga. The hotel complex is built like an Andalusian village, a cluster of whitewashed *casas* constructed around a tower and a white church. Every *casa* has a roof terrace and a balcony overlooking the olive grove-studded district. Each is sumptuous and individually designed. The hotel village is on a hillside, on 404 hectares (998 acres) of private, unspoiled grounds.

Finca La Bobadilla, Apartado 144E, 18300 Loja (Granada). ✆ **95-832-18-61.** Fax 95-832-18-10. www. barcelolabobadilla.com. 70 units. 295€–310€ double; 350€–620€ suite. Rates include breakfast. AE, DC, MC, V. Free parking. From Málaga airport, follow signs toward Granada, but at Km 175 continue through the village of Salinas. Take road marked SALINAS/RUTE; after 3km (2 miles) follow signposts for hotel to the entrance. **Amenities:** 2 restaurants; bar; babysitting; fitness center; horseback riding; kids' playground; 2 pools (1 heated indoor); room service; sauna; spa; 2 outdoor unlit tennis courts; whirlpool; rooms for those w/limited mobility. *In room:* A/C, TV, hair dryer, minibar, Wi-Fi.

Villa Padierna/Thermas de Carratraca Hotel & Spa ★★★   Throughout the Franco era and for a few years into the new millennium, this once-imperial villa was a low-rent inn, with an impeccable historic pedigree but no pretensions of glamour. (It had originally been built in 1830 by Ferdinand VII to entertain his guests who included, among others, the Empress Eugénie.) All of that changed in 2007 when it reopened as a government-rated five-star deluxe enclave. In the center of this small spa town (pop. 1,000), with direct access to the healing waters of the source favored by the ancient Romans and then the Arab caliphs, it retains many of the architectural grace notes of its original construction. The posh boutique hotel is now outfitted with plush furniture inspired by late 19th-century French style. Many guests opt for at least some of the spa treatments with waters from the springs.

Calle Antonio Riobbo 11, 29551 Málaga. ✆ **95-248-95-42.** Fax 95-248-95-44. www.termasde carratraca.com. 43 units. 200€–240€ double; 250€–360€ junior suites and suites. Spa packages available. AE, DC, MC, V. 30km (18 miles) north of Málaga. **Amenities:** Restaurant; bar; exercise facilities; room service; spa. *In room:* A/C, TV, hair dryer, Wi-Fi.

Where to Dine

EXPENSIVE

Café de París ★★ FRENCH/SPANISH   Café de París, Málaga's best restaurant, is in La Malagueta, the district surrounding the Plaza de Toros (bullring). Proprietor José García Cortés worked in many top dining rooms before carving out his own niche. His son, José Carlos García, is the chef. Much of Cortés's cuisine has been adapted from classic French dishes, so you might be served crêpes gratinées filled with baby eels or local whitefish baked in a salt crust. Stroganoff is given a Spanish twist with the use of ox meat. Save room for the creative desserts, such as citrus-flavored sorbet made with Champagne or custard-apple mousse.

Vélez Málaga 8. ✆ **95-222-50-43.** Reservations required. Main courses 18€–26€; *menú del día* 40€. AE, DC, MC, V. Tues–Sat 1:30–3:30pm and 8:30–11pm. Closed July 1–15.

Escuela de Hostelería ★ 🍴 MEDITERRANEAN   This impressive restaurant is part of a hotel and catering school housed in a villa from the 1800s. It's 8km (5 miles) outside Málaga and 3km (1¼ miles) from the international airport. In business since the early 1990s, it's mainly patronized by discerning locals with a taste for good food. The monthly changing menu might include freshly caught *merluza* with zesty mussels and mushrooms in a parsley-laced sauce. In autumn, loin of deer with a chestnut purée might appear. The villa is old but the dining room adjoining it is modern, opening onto a garden.

Finca La Cónsula, Churriana. ✆ **95-243-60-26.** Reservations required. Main courses 16€–20€; fixed-price lunch 35€. AE, DC, MC, V. Mon–Fri 1–4pm. Closed Aug.

La Reserva 12 ★ SPANISH/ANDALUSIAN   If you're a wine buff, this place will keep you happily quaffing all evening. Food here is all about the freshest ingredients simply cooked. The finest cuts of meat are grilled as you want; super-fresh fish is baked, grilled, or fried, and there's a great selection of seafood, particularly prawns. More traditional Andalusian dishes include Russian salad, sardines, cod with scrambled egg, and aged hams. And then there's the wine. The cellar here contains many interesting vintages, specializing in the local Málaga wines, but offering quality wines from across Spain. The list from Rioja and Ribera del Duero is exceptional.

Calle Bolsa 12. ✆ **95-260-82-18.** Reservations recommended. Main courses 14€–24€. AE, MC, V. Tues–Sun 1:30–4pm and 8:30–11pm.

Montana ★★ 🍴 MEDITERRANEAN   Behind the facade of this restored 19th-century town house, the owners have created a modern dining space with an attractive cactus- and palm-filled patio—romantic at night. Several of my expat friends reckon this is the finest dining in the city at the moment and I'm inclined to agree. You might start with homemade pate steeped in sherry brandy, and move on to slow roasted pigs' cheeks stuffed with marinated mushrooms, or fried fresh fish of the day with baked clams. Leave room for delectable desserts like pannacota with orange water and red fruit sorbet. Service is attentive and warm. Top quality tapas offer lighter bites.

Calle Compás de la Victoria 5. ✆ **95-265-12-44.** Reservations required. Main courses 14€–24€; set menus at 45€, 50€, and 60€. AE, MC, V. Tues–Sun 1:30–4pm and 8:30–11pm.

Strachan ★ SPANISH/ANDALUSIAN   This traditional Andalusian dining room serves some of the best, traditionally cooked cuisine in town. High quality food and friendly efficient staff have made it a long-term favorite with locals. Dishes to try include monkfish with mussels and prawns in Málaga wine and chicken breast stuffed with camembert, spinach, and ham. Or go for the paella, a huge pan of rice and seafood.

Calle Strachan 5. ✆ **95-222-75-73.** Reservations recommended. Main courses 14€–24€. AE, MC, V. Tues–Sun 1:30–4pm and 8:30–11pm.

MODERATE

Adolfo ★ INTERNATIONAL/ANDALUSIAN   Along the ocean-bordering Paseo Marítimo, this restaurant has been one of the best in Málaga since opening to instant success in the mid-1990s. The decor is hardwood floors and exposed brick walls. Well worth ordering are such daily specials as hake in a green sauce and duck glazed with a sweet wine. The big favorite here, often ordered on special occasions, is roast suckling pig flavored with garden herbs. There's an excellent wine list strong on Andalusian vintages, and friendly, helpful staff.

Ten Types of Coffee

Long before your local *barista* was learning how to make a cappuccino, Malagueños were demanding their morning coffee in all manner of styles. Elsewhere in Andalusia you won't find many more options than with or without milk (*café con leche* or *café solo*), but at Málaga's most famous cafe you can have your coffee hit ten different ways. Located on one of the city's most famous squares, **Café Central,** Plaza de la Constitución 11 (📞 **95-222-49-72**) is a bit of an institution. Legend has it that it was here that all ten types were first created. From a mere hint of coffee in a glass of milk (*nube*—a cloud) to *mitad* (half-and-half) up to *solo* with no milk at all. Take a peak inside to see decorated tiles depicting all ten types on the back wall.

Paseo Marítimo Pablo Ruiz Picasso 12. 📞 **95-260-19-14.** Reservations recommended. Main courses 9€–24€; fixed-price menu 45€. AE, DC, MC, V. Mon-Sat 1:30-4pm and 8:30-11pm. Closed June.

El Chinitas ★ SPANISH/MEDITERRANEAN   In the heart of Málaga, a short walk from the tourist office, is this well-established restaurant. Regular patrons consume a round of tapas and drinks at the associated Bar Orellana next door (which maintains the same hours, minus the mid-afternoon closing), then head to Chinitas for a meal. The place is often filled with locals—always a good sign. The changing menu might include a mixed fish fry, grilled red mullet, shrimp cocktail, grilled sirloin, or shellfish soup. The service is both fast and attentive.

Moreno Monroy 4. 📞 **95-221-09-72.** Reservations recommended. Main courses 10€–18€; fixed-price menu 38€ . DC, MC, V. Daily 1-4pm and 8pm–midnight.

El Rescoldo SPANISH   Calle Bolsa is a good bet for dining in Málaga with a brace of quality dining establishments. This is one of the best, serving good quality traditional Spanish food with a modern flourish. Try the excellent paella, cod with sugar honey glaze, or peppered hake, and interesting starters like liver and monkfish vol-au-vent. Service is friendly and attentive and the terrace tables out on the street offer a romantic option in the cool of the late evening.

Calle Bolsa 7. 📞 **95-222-69-19**. Main courses 11€–22€. AE, MC, V. Daily 12:30-4pm and 5-11:30pm.

Parador de Málaga-Gibralfaro SPANISH   This government-owned restaurant, on a mountainside high above the city, reached on Microbus 35, is especially notable for its view down into the heart of the Málaga bullring. Meals are served in the attractive dining room or under the arches of two wide terraces with sea views. Best bets for dishes are *hors d'oeuvres parador*—your entire table covered with tiny dishes full of tasty tidbits. Two other specialties are an omelet of *chanquetes,* tiny whitefish popular in this part of the country, and chicken Villaroi.

Castillo de Gibralfaro. 📞 **95-222-19-02.** Main courses 11€–23€; fixed-price menu 31€. AE, DC, MC, V. Daily 1-4pm and 8:30-11pm.

Vino Mio INTERNATIONAL/SPANISH ★   This funky bistro, run by charming Dutch proprietor Hélène, has been cooking up inventive tasty dishes since 2003 and has a serious following among savier locals and expats. Breast of duck with teriyaki salsa, Morrocan-style couscous salad, and lamb chops with aromatic herbs are on the menu. Or how about kangaroo? There's a good selection of vegetarian dishes and an extensive, good-value wine list. The good tapas menu offers lighter dining. There's a real buzz about the place, and, to add to the fun, free flamenco shows Sunday to Friday.

Calle Alamos 11. ✆ **95-260-90-93.** www.restaurantevinomio.com. Main courses 11€–19€; tapas 2€–4€. MC, V. Daily 1:30pm–1am.

INEXPENSIVE

For more inexpensive dining options, see "Málaga after Dark," below.

El Refectorium SPANISH   Behind the Málaga bullring, this place becomes hectic during any bullfight with fans and often, after the fight, with the matadors. The cuisine has an old-fashioned flair, and servings are generous. Try a typical Málaga soup, *ajo blanco con uvas* (cold almond soup with garlic and garnished with big muscatel grapes). The fresh seafood is a delight; lamb might be served with a saffron-flavored tomato sauce. Desserts are like the ones Mama made, including rice pudding.

Calle Cervantes 8. ✆ **95-221-89-90.** Reservations recommended on weekends and during bullfights. Main courses 15€–35€. AE, DC, MC, V. Tues–Sat 1:30–5pm and 8pm–midnight.

Shopping

Málaga offers sophisticated, stylish shopping along smart Calle Larios. You'll find cool Spanish boutique chains like lovely womenswear emporium **Bimba Y Lola,** Calle Larios 4 (✆ **95-221-83/43**), along with cool mid-market clothes stores like the ever-popular **Mango,** Calle Larios 1 (✆ **95-222-31-02**) for ladies and **Nicolas** for footwear, Calle Larios 3 (✆ **95-222-84-90**). **El Caballo,** Calle Strachan 4 (✆ **95-222-21-11**), is a must for stylish, very Andalusian clothes for men and women.

For a more unusual souvenir or present, the lovely modern Andalusian ceramics at **Alfajar,** Calle Cister 13 (✆ **95-221-12-72**), are quite special. There are beautifully curvaceous pots, ornaments, table lamps and more. Cerámica Fina, Calle Coronel 5 (✆ **95-222-46-06**), also has a vast showroom full of lovely ceramics from hand-painted thimbles to decorative plates and wall lamps. For something less fragile to pack, Málaga has several shops that sell beautiful hand-painted fans. At Ceylan, Calle Nueva 2 (✆ **95-222-98-91**), they also sell exquisite *mantons* (shawls), stitched by hand in pure silk. And for something totally unexpected and eclectic, you can visit the weekly **flea market** held on Sunday mornings at Paseo de los Martricios.

Málaga's central **food market** is also well worth a browse, if not to buy the fantastically fresh produce, then to admire the historic facade of the building where it's situated at Calle de las Atarazanas 10.

Málaga after Dark

The fun of nightlife in Málaga is just wandering, although there are a few standout destinations. More than just about any other city in the region, Málaga offers night owls the chance to stroll a labyrinth of inner-city streets, drinking wine at any convenient *tasca* and talking with friends and new acquaintances.

Start out along the town's main thoroughfare, **Calle Larios,** adjacent to the city's port. At the top of Calle Larios from Plaza del Siglo, you can gravitate to any of the bars and pubs lining the edges of the **Calle Granada.** If you want to eat well and cheaply, do as the locals do and head for the tapas bars. There are plenty to choose from. Don't expect a refined experience, but the food is some of the most enjoyable and least expensive in Málaga. You can easily fill up on two or three orders of tapas because portions are extremely generous. Most famous of the bunch is the excellent **El Pimpi,** Calle Granada 62 (© **95-222-89-90**), with its ancient walls lined with sweet-smelling Málaga wine barrels and decorated with photos of previous famous visitors including Antonio Banderas, Melanie Griffith, and Tony Blair. Others I like include **La Campana,** Calle Granada 35 (© **95-222-75-66**) and **El Piyayo,** Calle Granada 36 (© **95-222-00-96**). At the far end of Calle Granada the bars become more modern and younger, with sofas and easy chairs on their terraces in the hot summer months. There are several interesting little bars in Plaza Merced just nearby, including buzzing **Calle de Bruselas,** Plaza de la Merced 16 (© **95-260-39-48**).

Other good tapas and bar-sampling areas are the all-pedestrian street, **Calle Compagnía** and nearby **Plaza Uncibaj.** Here you'll find lots of places. Completely unpretentious (and in some cases without any discernible name), they serve glasses of wine and tapas similar to those available from their neighbors.

Two other favorites are **Bar Logüeno,** Marín García 9 (© **95-222-30-48**), just off the other side of Calle Larios. Behind its wrought-iron-and-glass door you find a stucco-lined room with enough hams, bouquets of garlic, beer kegs, and sausages to feed a village for a week. And **La Casa Guardia,** Alameda Principal 18 (© **95-221-46-80**), which many locals say is the oldest tavern in town, serves sherries and Málaga wines straight from the barrel along with fresh seafood tapas.

The best venue for rock and indie music is **Road House,** Calle Alamos 45 (© **95-222-98-50**), with some of the hottest bands in the area. Other rock venues guaranteed to be loud and good are **ZZ Pub,** Tejon y Rodríguez 6 (© **95-244-15-95**), a favorite hangout for university students, and **Zeppelin,** Calle Beatas 3 (© **95-221-59-08**).

If you're after funky nightlife of a more sophisticated variety, the new place to head for is **Arte Lounge Bar,** Calle Convalecientes 5 (no phone). Decorated in almost Dali-esque style with crazy swirls of color, mirrors all over the place, and pink sofas, this is about as cool as it gets. The music varies from full-on disco to funk and hip-hop. It's open Wednesday to Saturday usually 'til very late and Sundays until 10pm. Similarly cool and very popular with trendy young Malagueños is **Sala Gold,** Calle Luis de Velázquez 5 (© **67-009-8-7-49**), open daily until at least 6am. You need to dress to impress to get in here.

The main theater in the province is **Teatro Cervantes,** Ramos Marin s/n (© **95-222-41-00;** www.teatrocervantes.es), which opened its doors in the second half of the 19th century. Reopened in 1987 by Queen Sofia after a long closure, this elegant yet austere building puts on plays in Spanish, as well as concerts and flamenco entertainment of interest to all. The major performances of the Málaga Symphony Orchestra are staged here in winter. The theater is open from mid-September until the end of June; its box office is open Monday to Saturday 11am to 2pm and 6 to 8pm.

NERJA ★★

52km (32 miles) E of Málaga, 168km (104 miles) W of Almería, 548km (340 miles) S of Madrid

Nerja is known for its good beaches and small coves, its seclusion, its narrow streets and courtyards, and its whitewashed flat-roofed houses. Nearby is one of Spain's greatest attractions, the **Cave of Nerja.**

At the mouth of the Chillar River, Nerja gets its name from the Arabic word *narixa,* meaning "bountiful spring." Its most dramatic spot is the **Balcón de Europa (Balcony of Europe)** ★★, a palm-shaded promenade jutting out into the Mediterranean. The walkway was built in 1885 in honor of a visit from the Spanish king Alfonso XIII in the wake of an earthquake that had shattered part of nearby Málaga. There are good beaches either side of the Balcón, mainly small sheltered coves. **Playa Carabeo** to the east is particularly nice. For wider stretches of sand and more facilities, try **Playa Torrecilla** to the west.

Essentials

GETTING THERE   At least 19 **buses** per day make the 1-hour trip from Málaga to Nerja, costing 3.80€ one way. Service is provided by **Alsina Graells** (© **91-327-05-40;** www.alsa.es). Call the bus station, Av. Pescia s/n (© **95-252-15-04**), for information and schedules.

If you're **driving,** head along the A-7/E-15 east from Málaga or take the A-7/E-15 west from Almería.

VISITOR INFORMATION   The **tourist office** at Calle Carmen 1 (© **95-252-15-31;** www.nerja.org) is open Monday to Saturday 10am to 2pm and 6 to 10pm, Saturday 6 to 10pm. It's on the ground floor of the white Town Hall complex.

SPECIAL EVENTS   A **cultural festival** takes place here in July featuring artists, musicians, and dancers from around the world.

Exploring Cueva de Nerja

The most popular outing from Málaga and Nerja is to the **Cueva de Nerja (Cave of Nerja)** ★, Carretera de Maro s/n (© **95-252-95-20;** www.cuevadenerja.es). Scientists believe this prehistoric stalactite and stalagmite cave was inhabited from 25,000 to 2000 B.C. It was undiscovered until 1959, when a handful of boys found it by chance. When it was fully opened, it revealed a wealth of treasures from the days of the cave dwellers, including Paleolithic paintings. They depict horses and deer, but most of these more remarkable paintings aren't open to the public. You can walk through stupendous galleries where ceilings soar to a height of 60m (200 ft). If you've not seen limestone galleries before it's a very impressive site; if you have, you may feel the whole set up is rather touristy. I was particularly unimpressed by the 1€ charge to use the car park on top of the cost of the entry ticket.

The cave is in the hills near Nerja. From here you get panoramic views of the countryside and sea. It's open daily 10am to 2pm and 4 to 6:30pm (all day from 10am until 7:30pm July–August). Admission is 8.50€ adults, 4.50€ children aged 6 to 12, free for children aged 5 and under. Buses to the cave leave from Muelle de Heredia in Málaga hourly from 7am to 8:15pm. Return buses run every 2 hours until 8:15pm. The journey takes about 1 hour and 40 minutes. Buses from Nerja bus station to the caves leave hourly from 8:30am to 9:40pm, the journey takes just 15 minutes.

Where to Stay
EXPENSIVE
Hotel Riu Mónica ★ ☺   This government-rated four-star hotel is in a quite secluded beachfront location about a 10-minute walk from the Balcón de Europa.

In a seven-story building, the comfortable, good-size rooms were recently renovated and have private balconies and midsize bathrooms with tub/shower combos.

Playa de la Torrecilla s/n, 29780 Nerja. ☎ **95-252-11-00.** Fax 95-252-11-62. www.riu.com. 257 units. 120€–195€ double. AE, DC, MC, V. Free parking. **Amenities:** Restaurant; bar; babysitting; kids' playground and pool; outdoor pool; Internet; limited room service; nonsmoking rooms; nightclub; tennis court; rooms for those w/limited mobility. *In room:* A/C, TV, hair dryer, minibar.

Parador de Nerja ★★ This government-owned and -rated four-star hotel is on the outskirts of town, a five-minute walk from the center. On the edge of a cliff, next to the sea, the hotel centers on a flower-filled courtyard with splashing fountain. The spacious rooms are furnished in understated but tasteful style, and midsize bathrooms have tub/shower combos.

Calle Almuñécar 8, 29780 Nerja. ☎ **95-252-00-50.** Fax 95-252-19-97. www.parador.es. 98 units. 148€–171€ double; 295€–340€ suite. AE, DC, MC, V. Free parking. **Amenities:** Restaurant; bar; babysitting; outdoor pool; room service; tennis court; nonsmoking rooms; rooms for those w/limited mobility; Wi-Fi. *In room:* A/C, TV, hair dryer, minibar.

MODERATE

Carabeo ★ 🏠 There is no more tranquil oasis in Nerja than this little inn—one of our favorite stopovers along the coast and very affordable as well. A boutique hotel of charm and sophistication in a typical Andalusian house, Carabeo is in the old sector of town, but an easy walk to the center and just 5 minutes to a good beach. Taste and care have gone into the comfortable furnishings, and the place is filled with antiques and original art. Bedrooms are generally spacious, individually furnished, and with well-chosen fabrics—the British owners have created a homely feel. Each has a small bathroom with a tub/shower combo. The five best rooms open onto sea views and a terrace large enough for sunbeds and a small table for breakfast.

Hernando de Carabeo 34, 29780 Nerja. ☎ **95-252-54-44.** Fax 95-252-17-34. www.hotelcarabeo.com. 12 units. 80€–95€ double; 100€–135€ junior suite; 130€–170€ suite. Rates include continental breakfast. AE, DC, MC, V. Children aged 11 and under not accepted. **Amenities:** Restaurant; bar; exercise room; outdoor pool; sauna; room service. *In room:* A/C, TV, hair dryer, minibar.

Hotel Balcón de Europa Enviably positioned at the edge of the Balcón de Europa, this 1970s hotel offers guest rooms with private balconies overlooking the water and the rocks. At a private beach nearby, parasol-shielded tables are a peaceful place to enjoy the vista. The comfortable, midsize rooms have modern furniture and firm beds. Bathrooms have tub/shower combos.

Paseo Balcón de Europa 1, 29780 Nerja. ☎ **95-252-08-00.** Fax 95-252-44-90. www.hotelbalconeuropa.com. 110 units. 106€–150€ double; 178€–229€ suite. AE, DC, MC, V. Parking 10€. **Amenities:** 2 restaurants; bar; babysitting; massage; outdoor heated pool; room service; sauna. *In room:* A/C, TV, hair dryer, minibar.

Hotel Perla Marina Next to a good beach, Torrenueve, and within walking distance of the center of town, this well-run hotel was built in 1990 but has frequently been renovated. With its whitewashed walls and balconies in some bedrooms, it's a light, airy choice and very Mediterranean in style. An attractive landscaped area looks out to the sea. During the high season, there are flamenco shows and live music. Bedrooms are on the small side but well furnished, often with dark wood pieces.

Mérida 7, 29780 Nerja. © **95-252-33-50.** Fax 95-252-40-83. www.hotelperlamarina.com. 197 units. 99€–157€ double; 145€–185€ suite. AE, DC, MC, V. **Amenities:** Restaurant; bar; outdoor pool; rooms for those w/limited mobility; Wi-Fi. *In room:* A/C, TV, hair dryer, minibar on request.

Plaza Cavana ★ ▮▮   In the center of town, just behind the Balcón de Europa and a short walk from the beach, this two-story hotel has real old-fashioned Andalusian charm. It is behind a typical white facade with wooden balconies. The lobby has a classic decor with marble floors, and guests can relax on a garden patio. Rooms are elegant, spacious, and comfortable, and open onto balconies with either sea or mountain views. The neatly kept bathrooms have tub/shower combos.

Plaza Cavana 10, 29780 Nerja. © **95-252-40-00.** Fax 95-252-40-08. www.hotelplazacavana.com. 39 units. 75€–145€ double. AE, DC, MC, V. Parking 10€. **Amenities:** Restaurant; bar; fitness room; Jacuzzi; 2 pools (1 heated indoor); sauna; Wi-Fi. *In room:* A/C, TV, hair dryer, minibar.

INEXPENSIVE

Hostal Ana ✿   This simple inn is more B&B than *hostal,* and it's one of the best bargains in a town where prices continue to rise dramatically. One of Nerja's more modern structures, it was built in the old style. Only 100m (328 ft) from the landmark Balcón de Europa, Hostal Ana is run by a friendly welcoming couple. Bedrooms are simply furnished yet comfortable; the best unit has a big bathroom with Jacuzzi.

Calle La Cruz, 29780 Nerja. © **95-252-24-22.** www.guideofnerja.com. 17 units. 32€–52€ double. MC, V. *In room:* A/C, TV.

Hostal Miguel   The family-run Miguel is a pleasant, unpretentious inn on a quiet back street about a 3-minute walk from the Balcón de Europa, across from the well-known Pepe Rico restaurant (p. 385). The simply furnished, rather small rooms have been renovated to add more Andalusian flavor. Bathrooms have shower stalls. Breakfast is the only meal served, often on a lovely roof terrace with a view of the mountains and sea. *Note:* Minimum stay of two nights from July 15 to September 15.

Almirante Ferrándiz 31, 29780 Nerja. © **95-252-15-23.** www.hostalmiguel.com. 9 units. 35€–52€ double. MC, V. **Amenities:** Breakfast room. *In room:* ceiling fan, fridge, no phone.

Paraíso del Mar ★ ▮▮   Next door to the more upmarket Parador de Nerja, this little hacienda also offers a panoramic view of the coastline. The former home of a wealthy expatriate has been turned into a comfortable villa near the edge of a cliff opening onto the fabled Balcón de Europa. Bedrooms are tastefully furnished but not luxurious; four come with bathtubs, others have showers. Request a sea-view room; the rooms in the rear make up for the lack of views by being larger or including a Jacuzzi. You can also absorb that view from one of the hotel's public terraces.

Prolongación del Carabeo 22, 29780 Nerja. © **95-252-16-21.** Fax 95-252-23-09. www.jpmoser.com/paraisodelmar.html. 16 units. 90€–130€ double; 125€–165€ suite. AE, DC, MC, V. Parking 10€. **Amenities:** Breakfast room; bar; outdoor pool; sauna. *In room:* A/C, TV, hair dryer, minibar.

Where to Dine

Casa Luque ✿ INTERNATIONAL   With its impressive canopied and balconied facade near the heart of town, Casa Luque looks like a dignified private villa. The interior has an Andalusian courtyard, and in summer a sea-view terrace. Dishes are tasty and portions are generous. Meals change seasonally and might include Andalusian gazpacho, pork filet, or grilled meats. The limited selection of fish includes grilled Mediterranean grouper and freshly caught tuna.

Plaza Cavana 2. ✆**95-252-10-04.** Reservations recommended. Main courses 10€–17€. DC, MC, V. Daily 1:30–3:30pm and 7:30–11pm.

Pepe Rico Restaurant ★ INTERNATIONAL   On the main restaurant and bar strip of the Old Town, Pepe Rico is one of Nerja's finest restaurants. Dine in a tavern room or alfresco on the patio. The specialty of the day—a Spanish, German, Swedish, or French dish—ranges from almond-and-garlic soup to duck in wine. The impressive list of hors d'oeuvres includes smoked swordfish, salmon mousse, and prawns *pil-pil* (with hot chili peppers). Main dishes include filet of sole, roast leg of lamb, prawns Café de Paris, and steak. Considering the quality of the food, the prices are reasonable.

Almirante Ferrándiz 28. ✆**95-252-02-47.** Reservations recommended. Main courses 14€–20€; fixed-price menu 11€–25€ at lunch, 25€ at dinner. MC, V. Mon–Sat 12:30–3pm and 7–11pm. Closed 2 weeks in Dec and 1 week in Jan.

Restaurante Rey Alfonso ★SPANISH/INTERNATIONAL   Few visitors to the Balcón de Europa realize they're standing directly above one of the most unusual restaurants in town. The menu and decor don't hold many surprises, but the close-up view of the crashing waves makes dining here worthwhile. Have a drink at the bar if you don't want a full meal. Specialties include a well-prepared *paella pescado,* Cuban-style rice, five preparations of sole (from grilled to meunière), several versions of tournedos and entrecôte, crayfish in whisky sauce, and crêpes suzette for dessert.

Paseo Balcón de Europa s/n. ✆**95-252-09-58.** Reservations recommended. Main courses 9€–18€. MC, V. Mon–Sat noon–3pm and 7–11pm. Closed 4 weeks Jan–Feb.

Udo Heimer ★ SPANISH/PORTUGUESE   A German, who named the restaurant after himself, welcomes you to his friendly stylish Art Deco villa in a modern development east of the center. His top quality signature dishes, such as young pigeon in a port wine sauce served with fresh vegetables, are particularly good. You might also opt for *tartar de lubina,* thin sliced, raw sea bass seasoned with bay leaf. From the hills comes a tender lamb, roasted perfectly and seasoned with rosemary and thyme. The dessert specialty is memorable, a mango ravioli with a mousse-like texture.

Calle Andalucia 27. ✆**95-252-00-32.** www.udoheimer.net. Reservations recommended. Main courses 20€–25€. MC, V. Daily 7:30–11:30pm. Closed Wed and all of Jan.

FAST FACTS, TOLL-FREE NUMBERS & WEBSITES

12

FAST FACTS: SOUTHERN SPAIN

American Express   The number in Spain is ✆ **90-237-56-37.**

Area Codes   Dial ✆ **011** from the US, ✆ **00** from the UK, then the country code for Spain ✆ **34**.

ATM Networks   Maestro, Cirrus, and Visa cards are readily accepted at all ATMs. See also "Money & Costs" in Chapter 3, "Planning Your Trip to Andalusia," p. 40.

Babysitters   Most major hotels can arrange for babysitters, called *canguros* (literally, kangaroos) or *niñeras*. Rates vary but are usually reasonable.

Business Hours   Banks are open Monday through Friday from 8:30am to 2pm. Most offices are open Monday through Friday from 9am to 6 or 7pm. In July this changes from 8pm to 3pm for many businesses, especially those in the public sector. In August, businesses are on skeleton staff or closed altogether. In restaurants, lunch is usually from 1 to 4pm and dinner from 9 to 11:30pm or midnight. Bars and taverns have no set opening hours. Many open at 8am, others at noon, and most stay open until midnight or later. Major stores are open Monday through Saturday from 9:30 or 10am to 8pm; smaller establishments, however, often take a siesta, doing business from 9:30am to 2pm and 4:30 to 8 or 8:30pm. Hours can vary from store to store.

Car Rentals   See "Toll-Free Numbers & Websites," p. 391.

Drinking Laws   The legal age for drinking is 18. Alcoholic drinks are available in practically every bar, hotel, and restaurant in the city, and by law cannot be served to minors under 18. Bars and establishments selling liquor can open as early as 6am and close as late as 2am. Nightclubs, late-night bars, and after-hours establishments stay open to and after dawn. Generally, you can buy alcoholic beverages in almost any shop; supermarkets sell alcoholic drinks from 9 or 10am until closing time around 9 or 10pm.

   Breathalyzers are used more frequently than in the past and drivers may be subjected to spot checks whether or not they've just had an accident or broken the law. The official permitted limit for drinking is the equivalent to two glasses of wine, two *cañas* (small glasses) of beer, or two glasses of spirits (given the size of Spanish measures, one glass here would suffice if you're thinking of driving).

Driving Rules   See "Getting There & Around," in Chapter 3, "Planning Your Trip to Andalusia."

Electricity   Spain operates on 220 volts AC (50 cycles) using plugs with two round pins.

Embassies & Consulates   If you lose your passport, fall seriously ill, get into legal trouble, or have some other serious problem, your embassy or consulate can help. Regrettably, most of these offices are in Madrid. However, there is a U.S. Consulate in Seville and a British Consulate in Málaga (see "Fast Facts   Seville" in Chapter 5). These are the Madrid addresses and hours: The **United States Embassy,** Calle Serrano 75 (© **91-587-22-00;** Metro: Núñez de Balboa), open Monday to Friday 9am to 6pm. The **Canadian Embassy,** Núñez de Balboa 35 (© **91-423-32-50;** Metro: Velázquez), open Monday to Thursday 8:30am to 5:30pm, and Friday 8:30am to 2:30pm. The **British Embassy,** Calle Fernando el Santo 16 (© **91-700-82-00;** Metro: Colón), Monday to Friday 9am to 1:30pm and 3 to 6pm. The **Republic of Ireland,** Paseo Castellana 46 (© **91-436-40-93;** Metro: Serrano), open Monday to Friday 9am to 2pm. The **Australian Embassy,** Plaza Diego de Ordas 3, Edificio Santa Engracia 120 (© **91-353-66-00;** Metro: Ríos Rosas), open Monday to Thursday 8:30am to 5pm and Friday 8:30am to 2:15pm. **New Zealand,** Plaza de la Lealtad 2 (© **91-523-02-26;** Metro: Banco de España); open Monday to Friday 9am to 2pm and 3 to 5:30pm.

Emergencies   For an ambulance © **061;** or fire © **080.**

Gasoline/Petrol   Cars in Europe run on unleaded petrol (*Sin Plomo*) or diesel (*Gasoleo*). The price of gasoline in Europe is significantly higher than in the U.S. You will often find that service stations have pump attendants rather than being self-service.

Holidays   Holidays include January 1 (New Year's Day), January 6 (Feast of the Epiphany), March 19 (Feast of St Joseph), Good Friday, Easter Monday, May 1 (May Day), June 10 (Corpus Christi), June 29 (Feast of St Peter and St Paul), July 25 (Feast of St James), August 15 (Feast of the Assumption), October 12 (Spain's National Day), November 1 (All Saints' Day), December 8 (Immaculate Conception), and December 25 (Christmas).

No matter how large or small, every city or town in Spain celebrates its local saint's day but you'll rarely know what the local holidays are. Keep money on hand, because you may arrive in town only to find banks and stores closed. In some cases, intercity bus services are suspended on holidays.

Insurance   Insurance to cover you in the event of an emergency is strongly recommended for your trip to Spain.

For travel overseas, most U.S. health plans (including Medicare and Medicaid) do not provide coverage, and the ones that do often require you to pay for services upfront and reimburse you only after you return home.

U.S. citizens requiring additional medical insurance can try **MEDEX Assistance** (© **410/453-6300;** www.medexassist.com) or **Travel Assistance International** (© **800/821-2828;** www.travelassistance.com—for general information on services, call the company's **Worldwide Assistance Services, Inc.** at © **800/777-8710**).

Canadians should check with their provincial health plan offices or call **Health Canada** (© **866/225-0709;** www.hc-sc.gc.ca) to find out the extent of their coverage and what documentation and receipts they must take home if treated overseas.

Travelers from the U.K. should carry their European Health Insurance Card (EHIC), as proof of entitlement to free/reduced-cost medical treatment abroad (☎ **0845/606-2030;** www.ehic.org.uk). Note, however, that the EHIC only covers "necessary medical treatment," and for repatriation costs, lost money, baggage, or cancellation, travel insurance from a reputable company is needed.

Travel Insurance The cost of travel insurance varies widely, depending on destination, cost and length of your trip, your age and health, and the type of trip you're taking, but expect to pay between 5% and 8% of the vacation itself. Get estimates from various providers through **InsureMyTrip.com.**

U.K. citizens and their families who make more than one trip abroad per year may find an annual travel insurance policy is cheaper. Check **www.moneysupermarket.com** to compare prices from a wide range of providers for policies.

Most big travel agents offer their own insurance and will probably try to sell you their package when you book a holiday but you can usually find cheaper elsewhere. The **Association of British Insurers** (☎ 020/7600-3333; www.abi.org.uk) gives advice by phone and publishes *Holiday Insurance*, a free guide to policy provisions and prices. But shop around for better deals: Try **Columbus Direct** (☎ 0870/033-9988; www.columbusdirect.net) or Insure and Go (☎ **0844-888-2787;** www.insureandgo.com).

Trip Cancellation Insurance Trip-cancellation insurance will help retrieve your money if you have to back out of a trip or depart early, or if your travel supplier goes bankrupt. Trip cancellation traditionally covers such events as sickness, natural disasters, and State Department advisories. No trip-cancellation insurance can cover **expanded hurricane coverage** and the **"any-reason"** cancellation coverage—which costs more but covers cancellations made for any reason. You won't get back 100% of your prepaid trip cost, but you'll be refunded a substantial portion. **TravelSafe** (☎ **888/885-7233;** www.travelsafe.com) offers both types of coverage. Expedia also offers any-reason cancellation coverage for its air–hotel packages. For details, contact one of the following recommended insurers: **Access America** (☎ 866/807-3982; www.accessamerica.com), **Travel Guard International** (☎ 800/826-4919; www.travelguard.com), **Travel Insured International** (☎ 800/243-3174; www.travelinsured.com), and **Travelex Insurance Services** (☎ 888/457-4602; www.travelex-insurance.com).

Internet Access Internet access is plentiful, both in cybercafes and in hotels, many of which offer Wi-Fi access these days, which is often free.

Language The official language in Spain is Castilian Spanish (or *Castellano*). Andalusians speak it with a southern accent. In shops, restaurants, hotels, and nightclubs catering to visitors, English is commonly spoken, but elsewhere you will need some basic Spanish and a phrasebook to get by.

Lost & Found Tell all your credit card companies the minute you discover your wallet has been lost or stolen and file a report at the nearest police precinct. Your credit card company or insurer may require a police report number or record of the loss. Most credit card companies have an emergency toll-free number to call if your card is lost or stolen; they may be able to wire you a cash advance immediately or deliver an emergency credit card in a day or two.

Emergency numbers in Spain are: Visa ☎ **90-099-11-24;** American Express ☎ **90-237-56-37** in Spain; MasterCard ☎ **90-097-12-31**.

If you need emergency cash over the weekend when all banks and American Express offices are closed, you can have money wired to you via **Western Union** (☎ **800/325-6000;** www.westernunion.com).

Mail The local postage system is both reliable and efficient, though services such as FedEx are also available. To send an airmail letter or postcard to the United States costs .78€ for up to 20 grams. Airmail letters to Britain or other E.U. countries cost .60€ up to 20 grams; letters within Spain cost .39€.

Post your letters in the post office or in yellow post boxes called *buzones.* Buy stamps in an **Oficina de Correos** (post office) or in an *estanco* (a government-licensed tobacconist easily recognized by its brown and yellow logo). For further information, check the Spanish post office website, www.correos.es.

Allow about 8 days for delivery to North America, generally less to the United Kingdom; but letters can take 2 weeks to reach North America. Rates change frequently, so check at your hotel before mailing anything.

Maps See Chapter 3, "Planning Your Trip to Andalusia " for information on which maps to buy for visiting Andalusia.

Passports The websites listed provide downloadable passport applications as well as the current fees for processing applications. For an up-to-date, country-by-country listing of passport requirements around the world, go to the "International Travel" tab of the U.S. State Department at **http://travel.state.gov**.

Australia Pick up an application from your local post office or any branch of Passports Australia, then schedule an interview at the passport office to present your application materials. Call the **Australian Passport Information Service** at ✆ **131-232,** or visit the government website, www.passports.gov.au.

Canada Passport applications are available at travel agencies throughout Canada or from the central **Passport Office,** Department of Foreign Affairs and International Trade, Ottawa, ON K1A 0G3 (✆ **800/567-6868;** www.ppt.gc.ca). *Note:* Canadian children who travel must have their own passport. However, if you hold a valid Canadian passport issued before December 11, 2001 that bears the name of your child, the passport remains valid for you and your child until it expires.

Ireland You can apply for a 10-year passport at the **Passport Office,** Setanta Centre, Molesworth St, Dublin 2 (✆ **01/671-1633;** www.irlgov.ie/iveagh). Those under the age of 18 and over 65 must apply for a 3-year passport. You can also apply at 1A South Mall, Cork (✆ **21/494-4700**) or main post offices.

New Zealand Pick up a passport application at any New Zealand Passports Office or download it from their website. Contact the **Passports Office** at ✆ **0800/225-050** in New Zealand or ✆ **04/474-8100**, or log on to www.passports.govt.nz.

United Kingdom To pick up an application for a standard 10-year passport (5-yr passport for children under 16), visit your nearest passport office, major post office, or travel agency or contact the **United Kingdom Passport Service** at ✆ **0870/521-0410;** www.ukpa.gov.uk.

United States Download passport applications from the U.S. State Department website, **http://travel.state.gov**. To find your regional passport office, either check on that or call the **National Passport Information Center** toll-free number (✆ **877/487-2778**) for automated information.

Police In an emergency, dial ✆ **112.**

Smoking Smoking restrictions currently apply to all working and most public places, though most bars and cafes still allow smoking except in certain categorized "nonsmoking zones".

However, the first stage of a new bill proposing to ban smoking in all public places (especially restaurants and hotels) was approved by a vast majority in Madrid's

Congreso de Diputados (Parliament) on June 23, 2010. The aim is for a law to be finally passed to this effect by January 1, 2011, following Italy, France, Ireland, and the U.K.

Taxes The internal sales tax (known in Spain as IVA) ranges between 7% and 33%, depending on the commodity. Food, wine, and basic necessities are taxed at 7%; most goods and services (including car rentals) at 13%; luxury items (jewelry, all tobacco, imported liquors) at 33%; and hotels at 7%.

If you are not a European Union resident and make purchases in Spain worth more than 90€, you can get a tax refund. You must complete three copies of a form that the store will give you, detailing the nature of your purchase and its value. Citizens of non-E.U. countries show the purchase and form to the Spanish Customs Office. The shop is supposed to refund the amount due you. Ask at the time of purchase how they will do so and discuss the currency you want.

Telephones See "Staying Connected" in Chapter 3.

Time Spain is 6 hours ahead of Eastern Standard Time in the United States. **Daylight saving time** is in effect from the last Sunday in March to the last Sunday in October. Spain is 1 hour ahead of GMT.

Tipping More expensive restaurants add a 7% tax to the bill and cheaper ones incorporate it into their prices. This is *not* a service charge, and a tip of 5% to 10% is also expected. For coffees and snacks most people just leave a few coins or round up to the nearest euro.

Don't over-tip. The government requires restaurants and hotels to include their service charges—usually 15% of the bill. However, that doesn't mean you should skip out of a place without leaving an extra euro or two. Although tipping is not mandatory for hotel staff, wages in the hospitality industry are extremely low, so any supplement will be more than welcome.

Your hotel porter should get 1€ per bag. Maids should be given 1€ per day, more if you're generous. Tip doormen 1€ for helping with baggage and 1€ for calling a cab. In top-ranking hotels the concierge will often submit a separate bill, showing charges for newspapers and other services; if he or she has been particularly helpful, tip extra. For cab drivers, add about 10% to the fare on the meter. At airports, the porter who handles your luggage will present you with a fixed-charge bill.

In restaurants and nightclubs, a 15% service charge is added to the bill. To that, add another 3% to 5% tip, depending on the quality of the service. Waiters in deluxe restaurants and nightclubs are accustomed to the extra 5%, which means you'll end up tipping 20%. If that seems excessive, remember that the initial service charge in the fixed price is distributed among all the help.

Barbers and hairdressers expect a 10% to 15% tip. Tour guides expect 2€, although a tip is not mandatory. Theater and bullfight ushers get .50€.

Toilets Public toilets (*los servicios*) were once a rarity, but modern, generally well serviced cubicles (*Aseos*) have appeared in most major towns and cost .30€ to use. Bars are legally obliged to let you use their toilets and locals think nothing of just walking in and asking to use them. D (*damas*) or S (*señoritas*) stand for ladies and C (*caballeros*) for men.

Useful Phone Numbers U.S. Department of State Travel Advisory, ✆ **202/647-5225** (manned 24 hr); U.S. Passport Agency, ✆ **202/647-0518**; U.S. Centers for Disease Control International Traveler's Hot Line, ✆ **404/332-4559**; European Health Insurance Card (EHIC) line, ✆ **0845 606 2030**

Visas   These are not required by American, British, Canadian, and New Zealand visitors. Australians need a visa which can be issued on arrival. (See "Entry Requirements" in Chapter 3.)

Water   Although the tap water in Andalusia is safe to drink, most visitors stick to bottled water which is widely available and inexpensive.

TOLL-FREE NUMBERS & WEBSITES

MAJOR INTERNATIONAL AIRLINES

Air France
✆ **800/237-2747** (in U.S.)
✆ **800/375-8723** (in U.S. and Canada)
✆ **087/0142-4343** (in U.K.)
www.airfrance.com

Alitalia
✆ **800/223-5730** (in U.S.)
✆ **800/361-8336** (in Canada)
✆ **087/0608-6003** (in U.K.)
www.alitalia.com

British Airways
✆ **800/247-9297** (in U.S. and Canada)
✆ **087/0850-9850** (in U.K.)
www.british-airways.com

Continental Airlines
✆ **800/523-3273** (in U.S. and Canada)
✆ **084/5607-6760** (in U.K.)
www.continental.com

Delta Air Lines
✆ **800/221-1212** (in U.S. and Canada)
✆ **084/5600-0950** (in U.K.)
www.delta.com

Iberia Airlines
✆ **800/722-4642** (in U.S. and Canada)
✆ **087/0609-0500** (in U.K.)
www.iberia.com

Lufthansa
✆ **800/399-5838** (in U.S.)
✆ **800/563-5954** (in Canada)
✆ **087/0837-7747** (in U.K.)
www.lufthansa.com

Olympic Airlines
✆ **800/223-1226** (in U.S.)
✆ **514/878-9691** (in Canada)
✆ **087/0606-0460** (in U.K.)
www.olympicairlines.com

Qantas Airways
✆ **800/227-4500** (in U.S.)
✆ **084/5774-7767** (in U.K. and Canada)
✆ **13 13 13** (in Australia)
www.qantas.com

Swiss International Air Lines
✆ **877/359-7947** (in U.S. and Canada)
✆ **084/5601-0956** (in U.K.)
www.swiss.com

United Airlines
✆ **800/864-8331** (in U.S. and Canada)
✆ **084/5844-4777** (in U.K.)
www.united.com

US Airways
✆ **800/428-4322** (in U.S. and Canada)
✆ **084/5600-3300** (in U.K.)
www.usairways.com

Virgin Atlantic Airways
✆ **800/821-5438** (in U.S. and Canada)
✆ **087/0574-7747** (in U.K.)
www.virgin-atlantic.com

BUDGET AIRLINES

Aer Lingus
✆ **800/474-7424** (in U.S. and Canada)
✆ **087/0876-5000** (in U.K.)
www.aerlingus.com

Air Berlin
✆ **087/1500-0737** (in U.K.)
✆ **018/0573-7800** (in Germany)
✆ **180/573-7800** (all others)
www.airberlin.com

BMI Baby
✆ **870/126-6726** (in U.S.)
✆ **087/1224-0224** (in U.K.)
www.bmibaby.com

easyJet
℗ **870/600-0000** (in U.S.)
℗ **090/5560-7777** (in U.K.)
www.easyjet.com

Ryanair
℗ **081/830-3030** (in Ireland)
℗ **087/1246-0000** (in U.K.)
www.ryanair.com

Vueling
℗ **001-34-93-151-81-58** (in U.S.)
℗ **091/1263-2632** (in U.K.)
www.vueling.com

CAR RENTAL AGENCIES

Advantage
℗ **866/661-2722** (in U.S.)
℗ 021/0344-4712 (outside of U.S.)
www.advantage.com

AurigaCrown
℗ **95-204-84-90** (Spanish number only)
www.aurigacrown.com

Auto Europe
℗ **888/223-5555** (in U.S. and Canada)
℗ **0800/2235-5555** (in U.K.)
www.autoeurope.com

Avis
℗ **800/331-1212** (in U.S. and Canada)
℗ **084/4581-8181** (in U.K.)
www.avis.com

Budget
℗ **800/527-0700** (in U.S.)
℗ **800/268-8900** (in Canada)
℗ **087/0156-5656** (in U.K.)
www.budget.com

Enterprise
℗ **800/261-7331** (in U.S.)
℗ **514/355-4028** (in Canada)
℗ **012/9360-9090** (in U.K.)
www.enterprise.com

Hertz
℗ **800/645-3131** (for reservations in U.S. and Canada)
℗ **800/654-3001** (for international reservations)
www.hertz.com

National
℗ **800/CAR-RENT** (227-7368; for reservations in U.S. and Canada)
℗ **800/CAR-EUROPE** (227-3876; for reservations in Europe)
www.nationalcar.com

Thrifty
℗ **800/367-2277** (in U.S. and Canada)
℗ **918/669-2168** (international)
www.thrifty.com

MAJOR INTERNATIONAL HOTEL & MOTEL CHAINS

Best Western International
℗ **800/780-7234** (in U.S. and Canada)
℗ **0800/393-130** (in U.K.)
www.bestwestern.com

Four Seasons
℗ **800/819-5053** (in U.S. and Canada)
℗ **0800/6488-6488** (in U.K.)
www.fourseasons.com

Hilton Hotels
℗ **800/HILTONS** (445-8667; in U.S. and Canada)
℗ **087/0590-9090** (in U.K.)
www.hilton.com

Holiday Inn
℗ **800/315-2621** (in U.S. and Canada)
℗ **0800/405-060** (in U.K.)
www.holidayinn.com

Hyatt
℗ **888/591-1234** (in U.S. and Canada)
℗ **084/5888-1234** (in U.K.)
www.hyatt.com

InterContinental Hotels & Resorts
℗ **800/424-6835** (in U.S. and Canada)
℗ **0800/1800-1800** (in U.K.)
www.ichotelsgroup.com

Marriott
℗ **877/236-2427** (in U.S. and Canada)
℗ **0800/221-222** (in U.K.)
www.marriott.com

Radisson Hotels & Resorts
℗ **888/201-1718** (in U.S. and Canada)
℗ **0800/374-411** (in U.K.)
www.radisson.com

Ramada Worldwide
℗ **888/2-RAMADA** (272-6232; in U.S. and Canada)
℗ **080/8100-0783** (in U.K.)
www.ramada.com

Renaissance

☎ **888/236-2427**

www.marriott.com

Sheraton Hotels & Resorts

☎ **800/325-3535** (in U.S.)

☎ **800/543-4300** (in Canada)

☎ **0800/3253-5353** (in U.K.)

www.starwoodhotels.com/sheraton

Westin Hotels & Resorts

☎ **800-937-8461** (in U.S. and Canada)

☎ **0800/3259-5959** (in U.K.)

www.starwoodhotels.com/westin

USEFUL TERMS & PHRASES

Most Spaniards are very patient with foreigners who try to speak their language. Although you might encounter several regional languages and dialects in Spain, Castilian Spanish (*castellano* or simply *español*) is understood everywhere. In Catalonia, they speak *catalán* (the most widely spoken non-national language in Europe); in the Basque country, they speak *euskera;* in Galicia, you'll hear *gallego.* Still, a few words in Castilian will usually get your message across with no problem. In Andalusia you may find the local accent makes it difficult to understand people, as they frequently drop consonants and roll words together. If you explain that you only speak a little Spanish (see below), they'll usually repeat it more slowly for you.

When traveling in Spain, it helps a lot to know a few basic phrases, so I've included a list of simple phrases in Castilian Spanish with which to express basic needs.

ENGLISH & CASTILIAN SPANISH PHRASES

English	Spanish	Pronunciation
Good day	**Buenos días**	*bweh*-nohs *dee*-ahs
How are you?	**¿Cómo está?**	*koh*-moh es-*tah*
Very well	**Muy bien**	mwee byehn
Thank you	**Gracias**	*grah*-syahs
You're welcome	**De nada**	deh *nah*-dah
Goodbye	**Adiós**	ah-*dyohs*
Please	**Por favor**	pohr fah-*vohr*
Yes	**Sí**	see
No	**No**	noh
Excuse me	**Perdóneme**	pehr-*doh*-neh-meh
Give me	**Déme**	*deh*-meh

English	Spanish	Pronunciation
Where is . . . ?	¿Dónde está . . . ?	*dohn*-deh es-*tah*
the station	la estación	lah es-tah-*syohn*
a hotel	un hotel	oon oh-*tel*
a gas station	una gasolinera	*oo*-nah gah-so-lee-*neh*-rah
a restaurant	un restaurante	oon res-tow-*rahn*-teh
the toilet	el baño	el *bah*-nyoh
a good doctor	un buen médico	oon bwehn *meh*-dee-coh
the road to . . .	el camino a/hacia . . .	el cah-*mee*-noh ah/*ah*-syah
To the right	A la derecha	ah lah deh-*reh*-chah
To the left	A la izquierda	ah lah ees-*kyehr*-dah
Straight ahead	Derecho	deh-*reh*-choh
I would like	Quisiera	kee-*syeh*-rah
I want . . .	Quiero . . .	*kyeh*-roh
to eat	comer	ko-*mehr*
a room	una habitación	*oo*-nah ah-bee-tah-*syohn*
Do you have . . . ?	¿Tiene usted . . . ?	*tyeh*-neh oo-*sted*
a book	un libro	oon *lee*-broh
a dictionary	un diccionario	oon deek-syoh-*na*-ryo
How much is it?	¿Cuánto cuesta?	*kwahn*-toh *kwehs*-tah
When?	¿Cuándo?	*kwahn*-doh
What?	¿Qué?	keh
There is (Is there . . . ?)	(¿)Hay (. . . ?)	aye
What is there?	¿Qué hay?	keh aye
Yesterday	Ayer	ah-*yehr*
Today	Hoy	oy
Tomorrow	Mañana	mah-*nyah*-nah
Good	Bueno	*bweh*-noh
Bad	Malo	*mah*-loh
Better (Best)	(Lo) Mejor	(loh) meh-*hor*
More	Más	mahs
Less	Menos	*meh*-nohs
No smoking	Se prohibe fumar	seh proh-*ee*-beh foo-*mahr*
Postcard	Tarjeta postal	tar-*heh*-tah pohs-*tahl*
Insect repellent	Repelente contra insectos	reh-peh-*lehn*-teh *cohn*-trah een-*sehk*-tohs

MORE USEFUL PHRASES

English	Spanish	Pronunciation
Do you speak English?	¿Habla usted inglés?	ah-blah oo-sted een-glehs
Is there anyone here who speaks English?	Hay alguien aquí que hable inglés?	¿eye ahl-gyehn ah-kee keh ah-bleh een-glehs
I speak a little Spanish.	Hablo un poco de español.	ah-bloh oon poh-koh deh es-pah-nyol
I don't understand Spanish very well.	No (lo) entiendo muy bien el español. noh (loh)	ehn-tyehn-doh mwee byehn el es-pah-nyol
The meal is good.	Me gusta la comida.	meh goo-stah lah koh-mee-dah
What time is it?	¿Qué hora es?	keh oh-rah es
May I see your menu?	¿Puedo ver el menú (la carta)?	pweh-do vehr el meh-noo (lah car-tah)
The check (bill) please.	La cuenta por favor.	lah kwehn-tah pohr fah-vohr
What do I owe you?	¿Cuánto le debo?	kwahn-toh leh deh-boh
What did you say?	¿Mande?	(colloquial expression for American "Eh?") mahn-deh
What did you say? (more formal)	¿Cómo?	koh-moh
I want (to see) a room . . .	Quiero (ver) un cuarto . . . or una habitación.	kyeh-roh (vehr) oon kwahr-toh, oo-nah ah-bee-tah-syohn
for two people	para dos personas	pah-rah dohs pehrr-soh-nas
with (without) bathroom	con (sin) baño	kohn (seen) bah-nyoh
We are staying here only . . .	Nos quedamos aquí solamente . . .	nohs keh-dah-mohs ah-kee soh-lah-mehn-teh
1 night	una noche	oo-nah noh-cheh
1 week	una semana	oo-nah seh-mah-nah
We are leaving . . .	Partimos (Salimos) . . .	pahr-tee-mohs (sah-lee-mohs)
tomorrow	mañana.	mah-nya-nah
Do you accept traveler's checks?	¿Acepta usted cheques de viajero?	ah-sehp-tah oo-sted cheh-kehs deh byah-heh-roh
Is there a Laundromat near here?	¿Hay una lavandería cerca de aquí?	eye oo-nah lah-vahn-deh-ree-ah sehr-kah deh ah-kee
Please send these clothes to the laundry	Hágame el favor de mandar esta ropa a la lavandería.	ah-gah-meh el fah-vohr deh mahn-dahr ehs-tah roh-pah a lah lah-vahn-deh-ree-ah

NUMBERS

English	Spanish	Pronunciation
1	uno	(*oo*-noh)
2	dos	(dohs)
3	tres	(trehs)
4	cuatro	(*kwah*-troh)
5	cinco	(*seen*-koh)
6	seis	(says)
7	siete	(*syeh*-teh)
8	ocho	(*oh*-choh)
9	nueve	(*nweh*-beh)
10	diez	(dyehs)
11	once	(*ohn*-seh)
12	doce	(*doh*-seh)
13	trece	(*treh*-seh)
14	catorce	(kah-*tohr*-seh)
15	quince	(*keen*-seh)
16	dieciséis	(dyeh-see-*says*)
17	diecisiete	(dyeh-see-*syeh*-teh)
18	dieciocho	(dyeh-see-*oh*-choh)
19	diecinueve	(dyeh-see-*nweh*-beh)
20	veinte	(*bayn*-teh)
30	treinta	(*trayn*-tah)
40	cuarenta	(kwah-*rehn*-tah)
50	cincuenta	(seen-*kwehn*-tah)
60	sesenta	(seh-*sehn*-tah)
70	setenta	(seh-*tehn*-tah)
80	ochenta	(oh-*chehn*-tah)
90	noventa	(noh-*behn*-tah)
100	cien	(*syehn*)
200	doscientos	(doh-*syehn*-tohs)
500	quinientos	(kee-*nyehn*-tos)
1,000	mil	(meel)

Index

See also Accommodations and Restaurant indexes, below.

General Index

Accommodations

Restaurants